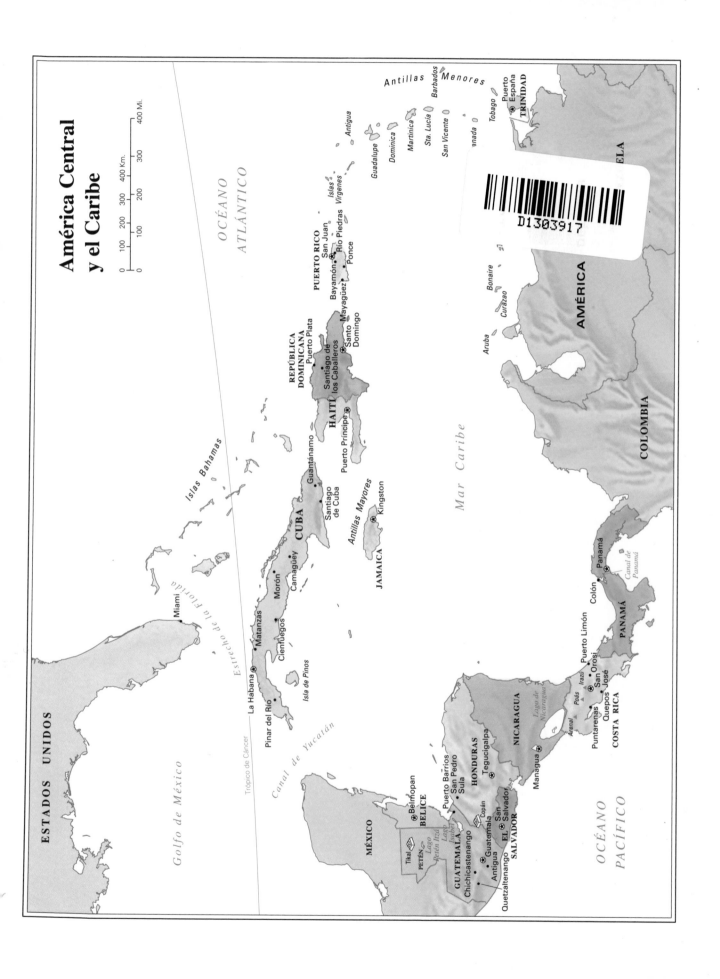

América Central y el Caribe

400 Mi.

| 0 | 100 | 200 | 300 | 400 Km. |
| 0 | 100 | 200 | 300 | 400 Mi. |

ESTADOS UNIDOS

Golfo de México

Miami

Trópico de Cáncer

Estrecho de la Florida

OCÉANO ATLÁNTICO

Islas Bahamas

La Habana
Pinar del Río
Isla de Pinos
Matanzas
Cienfuegos
Morón
Camagüey
CUBA
Santiago de Cuba
Guantánamo

Canal de Yucatán

MÉXICO

Tikal
PETÉN
Lago Petén Itzá
Lago Izabal
Belmopan
BELICE
Puerto Barrios
San Pedro Sula
Copán
Guatemala
GUATEMALA
Antigua
Quetzaltenango
Chichicastenango
EL SALVADOR
San Salvador
HONDURAS
Tegucigalpa

NICARAGUA
Managua
Lago de Nicaragua

Puntarenas
Arenal
Poás
Quepos
Irazú
San José
San Orosi
COSTA RICA
Puerto Limón
Colón
PANAMÁ
Panamá
Canal de Panamá

OCÉANO PACÍFICO

JAMAICA
Kingston

Antillas Mayores

Mar Caribe

HAITÍ
Puerto Príncipe

REPÚBLICA DOMINICANA
Puerto Plata
Santiago de los Caballeros
Santo Domingo

PUERTO RICO
San Juan
Bayamón
Mayagüez
Río Piedras
Ponce

Islas Vírgenes

Antigua

Guadalupe
Dominica
Martinica
Sta. Lucía
San Vicente
Barbados
Granada

Antillas Menores

Tobago
Puerto España
TRINIDAD

Aruba
Curazao
Bonaire

AMÉRICA

COLOMBIA

VENEZUELA

D1303917

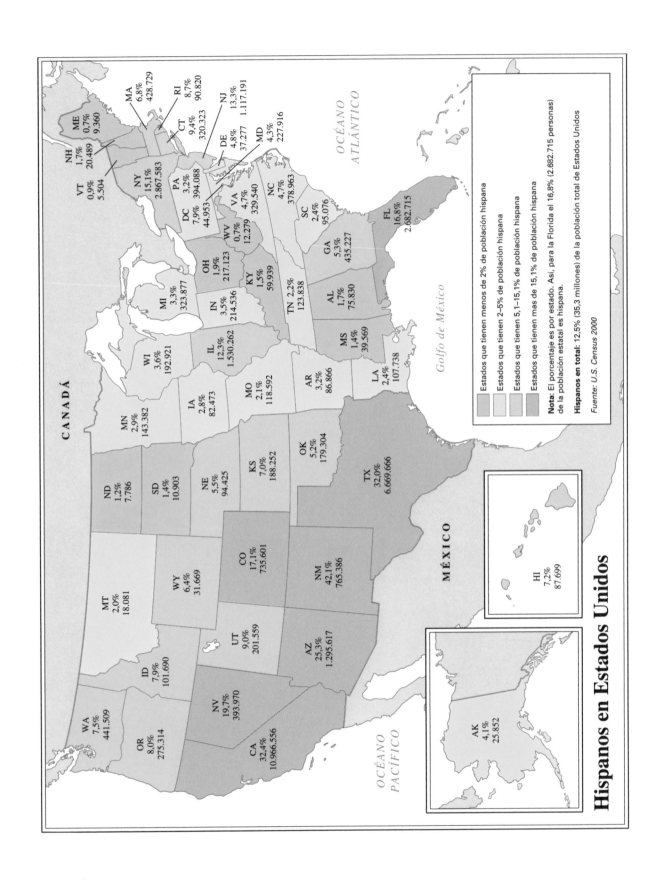

Hispanos en Estados Unidos

OCÉANO ATLÁNTICO

OCÉANO PACÍFICO

Golfo de México

CANADÁ

MÉXICO

Estados que tienen menos de 2% de población hispana

Estados que tienen 2–5% de población hispana

Estados que tienen 5,1–15,1% de población hispana

Estados que tienen mas de 15,1% de población hispana

Nota: El porcentaje es por estado. Así, para la Florida el 16,8% (2.682.715 personas) de la población estatal es hispana.

Hispanos en total: 12,5% (35,3 millones) de la población total de Estados Unidos

Fuente: U.S. Census 2000

ME
0,7%
9.360

MA
6,8%
428.729

RI
8,7%
90.820

NH
1,7%
20.489

NJ
13,3%
1.117.191

CT
9,4%
320.323

VT
0,9%
5.504

NY
15,1%
2.867.583

PA
3,2%
394.088

DE
4,8%
37.277

MD
4,3%
227.916

DC
7,9%
44.953

VA
4,7%
329.540

NC
4,7%
378.963

WV
0,7%
12.279

OH
1,9%
217.123

KY
1,5%
59.939

SC
2,4%
95.076

GA
5,3%
435.227

MI
3,3%
323.877

IN
3,5%
214.536

TN
2,2%
123.838

AL
1,7%
75.830

FL
16,8%
2.682.715

WI
3,6%
192.921

IL
12,3%
1.530.262

MS
1,4%
39.569

MN
2,9%
143.382

IA
2,8%
82.473

MO
2,1%
118.592

AR
3,2%
86.866

LA
2,4%
107.738

ND
1,2%
7.786

SD
1,4%
10.903

NE
5,5%
94.425

KS
7,0%
188.252

OK
5,2%
179.304

TX
32,0%
6.669.666

MT
2,0%
18.081

WY
6,4%
31.669

CO
17,1%
735.601

NM
42,1%
765.386

ID
7,9%
101.690

UT
9,0%
201.559

AZ
25,3%
1.295.617

WA
7,5%
441.509

OR
8,0%
275.314

NV
19,7%
393.970

CA
32,4%
10.966.556

HI
7,2%
87.699

AK
4,1%
25.852

¿Cómo se dice ... ?

Custom Edition with Student Activities Manual

Ninth Edition

Ana Jarvis I Raquel Lebredo I Francisco Mena-Ayllón

CENGAGE
Learning™

Australia • Brazil • Japan • Korea • Mexico • Singapore • Spain • United Kingdom • United States

CENGAGE
Learning™

¿Cómo se dice ... ?
Custom Edition with Student Activities Manual

Ana Jarvis | Raquel Lebredo |
Francisco Mena-Ayllón

Executive Editor:
Maureen Staudt
Michael Stranz

Senior Project Development Manager:
Linda de Stefano

Marketing Specialist:
Sara Mercurio

Senior Production/Manufacturing Manager:
Donna M. Brown

PreMedia Supervisor:
Joel Brennecke

Rights & Permissions Specialist:
Kalina Hintz
Todd Osborne

Cover Image:

For product information and technology assistance, contact us at
Cengage Learning Customer & Sales Support, 1-800-354-9706

For permission to use material from this text or product,
submit all requests online at **cengage.com/permissions**
Further permissions questions can be emailed to
permissionrequest@cengage.com

This book contains select works from existing Cengage Learning resources and was produced by Cengage Custom Solutions for collegiate use. As such, those adopting and/or contributing to this work are responsible for editorial content, accuracy, continuity and completeness.

Compilation Copyright © 2009 Cengage Learning

ISBN-13: 978-1-111-00486-6

ISBN-10: 1-111-00486-2

Cengage Learning
5191 Natorp Boulevard
Mason, Ohio 45040
USA

Cengage Learning is a leading provider of customized learning solutions with office locations around the globe, including Singapore, the United Kingdom, Australia, Mexico, Brazil, and Japan. Locate your local office at: **international.cengage.com/region**

Cengage Learning products are represented in Canada by Nelson Education, Ltd.

For your lifelong learning solutions, visit **www.cengage.com/custom**

Visit our corporate website at **www.cengage.com**

Printed in the United States of America

Dear Students,

¿Cómo se dice…?, Enhanced Ninth Edition, is designed to present the fundamentals of Spanish in order to achieve its goal of helping you attain linguistic proficiency. The Enhanced Ninth Edition involves you in activities that require the communicative use of all four language skills (listening, speaking, reading, and writing). Special care has been devoted to providing practical insights into the cultural diversity of the Spanish-speaking world, because it is as essential to successful communication as linguistic competence.

As you embark on your journey to discovering the Spanish language, allow us to be your guides, together with your instructor, in offering you these tips to make the journey more productive, more interesting, and more enjoyable.

- Take every opportunity to hear, speak, read, and write Spanish.

- Try to relate everything you learn to your own experience, thinking of what you might say in different situations to express your ideas and opinions.

- Try to be aware of the Spanish-speaking community around you.

- Create mental images of what you hear and read, always going from concept to Spanish and vice versa.

- Watch Spanish programs on TV, including the news, and yes, soap operas, or learn some songs in Spanish, because exposure to spoken Spanish will help you internalize the language.

- Remember that learning is not a passive pursuit, but an active one. It is the practice that will help you learn.

Lastly, don't forget, learning Spanish takes time, but with commitment, enthusiasm, and dedication you will achieve your goal.

Un cordial saludo,

Ana C. Jarvis   Raquel Lebredo   Francisco Mena-Ayllón

An Overview of Your Textbook's

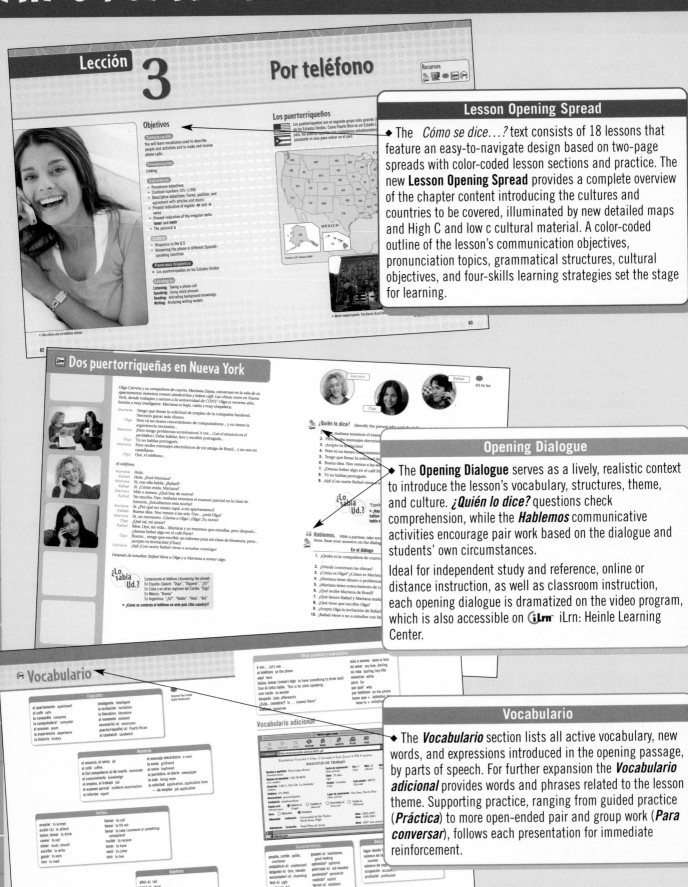

Lesson Opening Spread

◆ The *Cómo se dice...?* text consists of 18 lessons that feature an easy-to-navigate design based on two-page spreads with color-coded lesson sections and practice. The new **Lesson Opening Spread** provides a complete overview of the chapter content introducing the cultures and countries to be covered, illuminated by new detailed maps and High C and low c cultural material. A color-coded outline of the lesson's communication objectives, pronunciation topics, grammatical structures, cultural objectives, and four-skills learning strategies set the stage for learning.

Opening Dialogue

◆ The **Opening Dialogue** serves as a lively, realistic context to introduce the lesson's vocabulary, structures, theme, and culture. *¿Quién lo dice?* questions check comprehension, while the *Hablemos* communicative activities encourage pair work based on the dialogue and students' own circumstances.

Ideal for independent study and reference, online or distance instruction, as well as classroom instruction, each opening dialogue is dramatized on the video program, which is also accessible on **iLrn** iLrn: Heinle Learning Center.

Vocabulario

◆ The *Vocabulario* section lists all active vocabulary, new words, and expressions introduced in the opening passage, by parts of speech. For further expansion the *Vocabulario adicional* provides words and phrases related to the lesson theme. Supporting practice, ranging from guided practice (*Práctica*) to more open-ended pair and group work (*Para conversar*), follows each presentation for immediate reinforcement.

Main Features

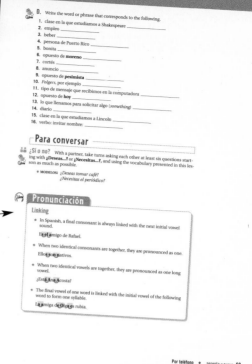

D. Write the word or phrase that corresponds to the following.

1. clase en la que estudiamos a Shakespeare _____
2. empleo _____
3. beber _____
4. persona de Puerto Rico _____
5. bonita _____
6. opuesto de **moreno** _____
7. cortés _____
8. anuncio _____
9. opuesto de **pesimista** _____
10. *Folgers*, por ejemplo _____
11. tipo de mensaje que recibimos en la computadora _____
12. opuesto de **hoy** _____
13. lo que llenamos para solicitar algo (*something*) _____
14. diario _____
15. clase en la que estudiamos a Lincoln _____
16. verbo: invitar nombre: _____

Para conversar

¿Sí o no? With a partner, take turns asking each other at least six questions starting with **¿Deseas...?** or **¿Necesitas...?**, and using the vocabulary presented in this lesson as much as possible.

* MODELOS ¿Deseas tomar café?
          ¿Necesitas el periódico?

Pronunciación

Linking

* In Spanish, a final consonant is always linked with the next initial vowel sound.
  Es el amigo de Rafael.

* When two identical consonants are together, they are pronounced as one.
  Ellos son nativos.

* When two identical vowels are together, they are pronounced as one long vowel.
  ¿Está Ana Acosta?

* The final vowel of one word is linked with the initial vowel of the following word to form one syllable.
  La amiga de Olga es rubia.

Por teléfono • sesenta y nueve 69

Pronunciación

Appearing in *Lecciones 1–18*, the **Pronunciación** section contains pronunciation, linking, and intonation exercises designed to acquaint students with the basic Spanish sounds and with natural speech. Special in-context coverage in *Lecciones 9–18* includes words and expressions from the lesson dialogues that are challenging for English speakers. ◆

Aspectos culturales

En imágenes (*Las telecomunicaciones*)

» Teléfonos públicos en una ciudad hispana

» Una estudiante del Miami Community College habla por teléfono al terminar sus clases.

» Un joven usa un teléfono de Internet (Skype) y sus microcomputadoras.

» Una estudiante usa una microcomputadora de Nueva York.

» Una estudiante universitaria usa una computadora portátil en un café de Internet.

Aspectos culturales

◆ The **Aspectos culturales** section expands on the cultural practices, products, or themes introduced in the lesson's opening dialogue by way of vivid images. The *Ubíquese…y búsquelo* section encourages students to explore the Internet and report their findings to the class.

Ubíquese… y búsquelo
Improve Your Grade
Web Search

As part of an assignment for her Latin American history class, Olga has to go to the Museo del Barrio, and she has asked Mariana to accompany her. Go to **www.cengage.com/highered** to find out more about the Museo del Barrio. What kind of information or exhibits will Olga and Mariana find there? In the next class, team up with two classmates to discuss your findings.

Por teléfono • setenta y uno 71

Estructuras

1. Possessive adjectives (*Los adjetivos posesivos*)

Forms of the Possessive Adjectives

Singular	Plural	
mi	mis	*my*
tu	tus	*your* (fam.)
		your (form.)
su	sus	*his*
		her
		its
		their
nuestro(-a)	nuestros(-as)	*our*
vuestro(-a)	vuestros(-as)	*your* (fam.)

* Possessive adjectives always precede the nouns they introduce. They agree in number with the nouns they modify.

  Yo   necesito   mi   libro.
                                pluma.

  Yo   necesito   mis   libros.
                                plumas.

* **Nuestro** and **vuestro** are the only possessive adjectives that have the feminine endings **-a** and **-as**. The others take the same endings for both genders.

  Nosotros   necesitamos   nuestro   libro.
                                 nuestra   pluma.

  Nosotros   necesitamos   nuestros   libros.
                                 nuestras   plumas.

* Possessive adjectives agree in gender with the thing possessed and not with the possessor. For example, two male students referring to their female professor will say **nuestra profesora**.

* Because **su** and **sus** can have several possible meanings, the form **de él** (or **de ella, de ellos, de ellas, de Ud.**, or **de Uds.**) can be substituted to avoid confusion. The "formula" is: *article + noun + de + pronoun.*

  sus plumas ⟶ las plumas **de él** (**de ella, de Ud.**, etc.)
  su libro ⟶ el libro **de él** (**de ella, de Ud.**, etc.)

  —¿De dónde son **tus** amigos?   *"Where are your friends from?"*
  —**Mis** amigos son de Puerto Rico.   *"My friends are from Puerto Rico."*

  —¿Quién es la profesora de Uds.?   *"Who is your professor?"*
  —**Nuestra** profesora es la doctora Paz.   *"Our professor is Dr. Paz."*

Un
dicho   *Mi casa es su casa.*

72 setenta y dos • Lección 3

Práctica
ACE the Test

A. Complete the following exchanges, using the corresponding possessive adjectives. Then act them out with a partner.

1. Raquel, ¿de dónde es _____ novio?
   _____ novio es de Caracas.
   ¿Y el novio de Marta?
   El novio _____ es de San Salvador.
2. ¿De dónde es el profesor de Uds.?
   _____ profesor es de la República Dominicana.
   ¿Y de dónde es la profesora de Uds.?
3. Sr. Álvarez, ¿_____ hijos (*children*) hablan francés?
   Sí, _____ hijos hablan francés y alemán.
4. ¿Los estudiantes de Uds. estudian por la noche?
   No, _____ estudiantes estudian por la mañana.
5. ¿De dónde es _____ amiga, Srta. Burgos?
   Rosita?
   _____ amigas son de Cádiz.
6. ¿Las hijas (*daughters*) de Uds. trabajan?
   No, _____ hijas no trabajan.

B. Answer the following questions in *the negative,* using the appropriate possessive adjectives.

1. ¿Lorena es la novia de Alberto?
2. ¿Necesitas tu libro de español?
3. ¿La profesora de Uds. es de México?
4. ¿Carlos y Daniel son tus amigos?
5. ¿El Dr. Paz y la Dra. Ruiz son profesores de Uds.?
6. ¿Tú necesitas mis cuadernos?
7. ¿Tú necesitas la dirección de los chicos?
8. ¿Marisa y Olga son las amigas de Claudia?

Para conversar

Deseamos saber... (*We want to know...*) With a classmate, prepare questions you want to ask Olga and Mariana about their apartment, their classes, etc. Some of the questions should be addressed to both of them and some to one of them. Make sure you use the appropriate possessive adjectives.

2. Cardinal numbers 101–1,000 (*Los números...*)

101	ciento uno (and so on)	600	seiscientos
200	doscientos	700	setecientos
300	trescientos	800	ochocientos
400	cuatrocientos	900	novecientos
500	quinientos	1.000	mil

Estructuras

◆ The **Estructuras** section presents an average of four to five clear and succinct grammar points in English with practical examples and contextualized language models. Each presentation is immediately followed by **Práctica** exercises and **Para conversar** activities that range from controlled drills to open-ended activities, including illustration-based activities and pair and group work. Ideal for independent study and reference, as well as online or distance instruction, video tutorials are provided for each grammar topic covered in the program. These tutorials are also available for viewing on **iLrn** iLrn: Heinle Learning Center.

Por teléfono • setenta y tres 73

Así somos

Al escuchar...

Estrategia **Taking a phone call** In a very broad sense, most listening has a purpose, whether to get specific information such as movie times or store hours, follow a lecture for the important points, or simply to provide an ear to a friend. When you get a phone call, you generally expect the caller to let you know the reason for the call, which then tells you how to respond and what specific information to listen for or ask about as the conversation continues.

Hola Javier calls his friend Marta. Listen to their conversation and answer the first question to identify the reason for his call. Then listen a second time for the specifics and answer the remaining questions.

1. ¿Por qué llama a Marta?
2. ¿Qué hay mañana?
3. ¿Dónde estudian Javier y Marta? ¿A qué hora?
4. ¿Para qué clase tiene que escribir un informe Marta?

Al conversar...

Estrategia **Using stock phrases** Having a repertoire of phrases that you can use in particular situations can help take the pressure off speaking, especially when you are beginning to learn a language. It also lets you concentrate on listening and understanding. Here are some phrases you can use.

To show agreement:
Buena idea. (*Good idea.*) **Es verdad.** (*It's true.*)
Por supuesto. (*Of course.*) **Está bien.** (*That's fine/good.*)

To apologize:
Lo siento. (*I'm sorry.*)

To decline or make an excuse:
No puedo. (*I can't.*) **Tengo que...**

¿Estudiamos el lunes? With a partner, agree on a day, time, and place to study Spanish together. Use some of the preceding phrases in your conversation as you try to find a day and time that's convenient for both of you.

¿Qué dice Ud.? What would you say in the following situations? What might the other person say? Act out the scenes with a partner. Take turns playing each role.

1. Describe your best (**mejor**) friend as completely as possible. Add any pertinent information about him/her you deem important.
2. You have agreed to pick up a classmate on your way to school. Inform him/her at what time you come to class in the morning and get the following information:
   a. where he/she lives
   b. at what time he/she returns home in the evening.
3. Your phone rings and you answer it. The call is for you. You and the caller, a friend, make plans for him/her to come to your house to study.
4. You tell a friend three things you have to do tomorrow afternoon.
5. Ask your friend if he/she wants to have something to drink after studying.

Para conocernos mejor To... would like to get to know. Take tu...

1. ¿Vives con tus padres? ¿Dónd...
2. ¿Tú vienes a la universidad l... mañana o por la tarde?
3. ¿Tienes conocimiento de co... electrónicos? ¿De quiénes?
4. ¿Tienes que estudiar mañan...
5. ¿Tienes exámenes parciales ...
6. ¿Deseas comer o beber algo ...

Una encuesta Interview your classmates to identify who fits the following descriptions. Include your instructor, but remember to use the **Ud.** form when addressing him/her. After finishing the survey, get together with two or three classmates and discuss the results.

Nombre

1. Vive en un apartamento.
2. Tiene un compañero (una compañera) de cuarto.
3. Tiene un novio muy guapo (una novia muy bonita).
4. Es un poco terco(-a).
5. Es un poco impaciente.
6. Lee el periódico los domingos.
7. Bebe café por la mañana.
8. Corre todos los días.

Para crear Get together in groups of three and "create" the scenario for this photo. Who are the people? Give them names. What is the relationship they have with each other? Where are they from? What might they say to each other? What plans might they make?

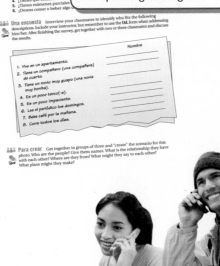

Así somos
◆ The *Así somos* section consists of a series of open-ended activities that synthesize what was learned in order to communicate in real-life situations, including personalized pair- and small-group activities, and training on listening and speaking strategies.

¡Vamos a leer!

Antes de leer

Estrategia **Activating background knowledge** Bringing your own experi... reading helps prepare you for the kinds of information you may encount... about what you know of a topic before reading, you will be better able to ... content of a text and understand more of what you read.

Un mensaje electrónico Aurora Paz and Sergio Guzmán have ... chat room. Before reading an e-mail from Aurora to Sergio, discuss w... what information you would give about yourself to a new cyberfrien... questions you would ask to get to know someone.

A leer

Comprensión As you read the e-mail, find the answers to the following questions.

1. ¿Qué desea Sergio?
2. ¿Aurora es rubia?
3. ¿Qué características positivas tiene?
4. ¿Qué dice la mamá de Aurora?
5. ¿Qué actividades tiene Aurora todos los días?
6. Los sábados, ¿trabaja o sale con sus amigos?
7. ¿Qué ciudades puertorriqueñas menciona Aurora?

El mensaje de Aurora

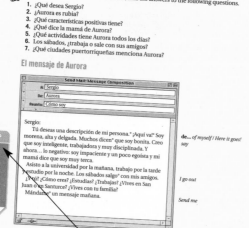

Send Mail: Message Composition
A: Sergio
De: Aurora
Asunto: Cómo soy

Sergio:
    Tú deseas una descripción de mi persona.° ¡Aquí va!° Soy morena, alta y delgada. Muchos dicen° que soy bonita. Creo que soy inteligente, trabajadora y muy disciplinada. Y ahora... lo negativo: soy impaciente y un poco egoísta y mi mamá dice que soy muy terca.
    Asisto a la universidad por la mañana, trabajo por la tarde y estudio por la noche. Los sábados salgo° con mis amigos. ¿Y tú? ¿Cómo eres? ¿Estudias? ¿Trabajas? ¿Vives en San Juan o en Santurce? ¿Vives con tu familia?
    Mándame° un mensaje mañana.

de... of myself / Here it goes!
say

I go out

Send me

LEARNING TIP

As with speaking and pronunciation, paying attention to the words and structures used by the writer of a Spanish text will help you to improve your ability to communicate when you speak or write in Spanish.

¡Vamos a leer!
◆ Appearing in each lesson, the *¡Vamos a leer!* section presents and practices specific techniques and strategies designed to help students become more proficient readers. Reading selections—thematic texts about the Spanish-speaking world as well as authentic magazine and literary selections—reinforce lesson grammar and vocabulary as well as broaden students' cultural knowledge.

Learning Tips
◆ Appearing throughout each lesson, helpful **Learning Tips** offer strategies, relevant cultural information, and study tips to support acquisition.

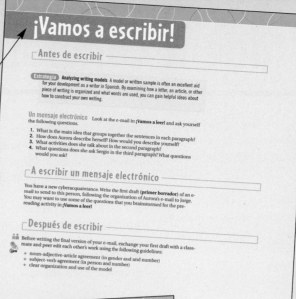

¡Vamos a escribir!

Antes de escribir

Estrategia **Analyzing writing models** A model or written sample is often an excellent aid for your development as a writer in Spanish. By examining how a letter, an article, or other piece of writing is organized and what words are used, you can gain helpful ideas about how to construct your own writing.

Un mensaje electrónico Look at the e-mail in **¡Vamos a leer!** and ask yourself the following questions.

1. What is the main idea that groups together the sentences in each paragraph?
2. How does Aurora describe herself? How would you describe yourself?
3. What activities does she talk about in the second paragraph?
4. What questions does she ask Sergio in the third paragraph? What questions would you ask?

A escribir un mensaje electrónico

You have a new cyberacquaintance. Write the first draft (**primer borrador**) of an e-mail to send to this person, following the organization of Aurora's e-mail to Jorge. You may want to use some of the questions that you brainstormed for the pre-reading activity in **¡Vamos a leer!**

Después de escribir

Before writing the final version of your e-mail, exchange your first draft with a class-mate and peer edit each other's work using the following guidelines:

* noun-adjective-article agreement (in gender and and number)
* subject-verb agreement (in person and number)
* clear organization and use of the model

¡Vamos a escribir!

Correlated to the lesson grammar and vocabulary, *¡Vamos a escribir!* offers clearly articulated process-based writing strategies with specific exercises that guide students in applying those strategies in order to develop their writing skills. ◆

Por teléfono ◆ ochenta y siete **87**

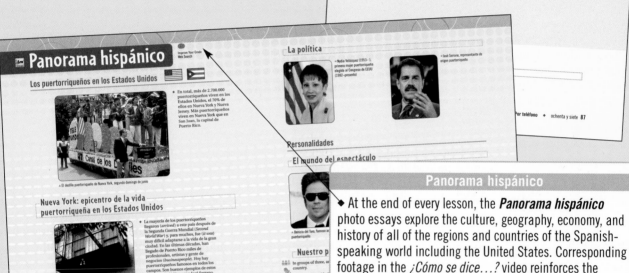

Panorama hispánico

Los puertorriqueños en los Estados Unidos

▲ El desfile puertorriqueño de Nueva York, segundo domingo de junio

* En total, más de 2.700.000 puertorriqueños viven en los Estados Unidos, el 70% de ellos en Nueva York y Nueva Jersey. Más puertorriqueños viven en Nueva York que en San Juan, la capital de Puerto Rico.

Nueva York: epicentro de la vida puertorriqueña en los Estados Unidos

▲ El Nuyorican Poets Café, una de varias (*several*) instituciones neoyorriqueñas

* La mayoría de los puertorriqueños llegaron (*arrived*) a este país después de la Segunda Guerra Mundial (*Second World War*) y para muchos, fue (*it was*) muy difícil adaptarse a la vida de la gran ciudad. En las últimas décadas, han llegado de Puerto Rico miles de profesionales, artistas y gente de negocios (*businesspeople*). Hoy hay puertorriqueños famosos en todos los campos. Son buenos ejemplos de estos éxitos Nydia Velázquez y José Serrano, congresistas; la familia Unanue, dueños de los famosos productos Goya; Ricky Martin y Chayanne, cantantes; Rosalyn Sánchez, Benicio del Toro y muchos más, artistas de Hollywood; Félix (Tito) Trinidad, ex triple campeón de boxeo, etc.

La política

◀ Nydia Velázquez (1953–), primera mujer puertorriqueña elegida al Congreso de EEUU (1992–presente)

◀ José Serrano, representante de origen puertorriqueño

Personalidades

El mundo del espectáculo

▲ Benicio del Toro, famoso actor puertorriqueño

Nuestro p[...]

In groups of three, a[...] country.

1. ¿Hay diversidad[...] ¿Qué nacionali[...]
2. Un norteameri[...]
3. ¿Hay muchos p[...]
4. En su ciudad, p[...]
5. ¿Cuál es la música[...]
6. Además (*Besides*) de las personal[...] nombrar otros artistas puertorriqueños?
7. ¿Qué familias norteamericanas son importantes en el mundo de los negocios?

For the next class: Go to the World Wide Web and find photos from your hometown, state, region, or country. Use the questions from **Nuestro panorama cultural** above as guidelines for choosing them. Be ready to p[...] classmates.

88 ochenta y ocho ◆ **Lección 3**

Panorama hispánico

◆ At the end of every lesson, the *Panorama hispánico* photo essays explore the culture, geography, economy, and history of all of the regions and countries of the Spanish-speaking world including the United States. Corresponding footage in the *¿Cómo se dice...?* video reinforces the content of each *Panorama hispánico* photo essay.

Review

◆ **Self-tests** following *Lecciones 3, 6, 9, 12, 15,* and *18* contain exercises designed to review the vocabulary, structures, and cultural coverage in the three preceding lessons.

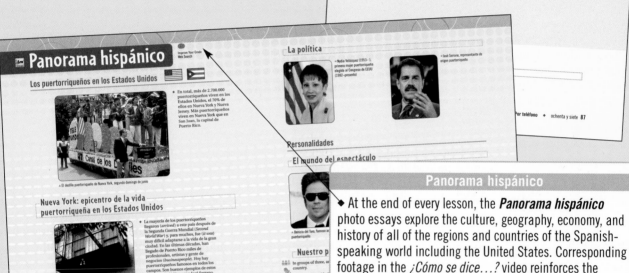

Self-Test

Take this test. When you have finished, check your answers in the answer key pro-vided in Appendix D. Then use a red pen to correct any mistakes you may have made. Are you ready?

Lección 1

A. The alphabet Spell the following last names in Spanish.

1. Vargas
2. Mena
3. Botero
4. Peña
5. Juárez
6. Chávez
7. Dávila
8. Félix
9. Quiroz

B. Cardinal numbers (0–30) Write the following numbers in Spanish.

1. 11
2. 17
3. 30
4. 15
5. 13
6. 28
7. 19
8. 12
9. 14
10. 16
11. 22

C. Colors What colors come to mind when you think of the following?

1. grass
2. a pumpkin
3. a banana
4. rosy cheeks
5. coal
6. a plum
7. a tree trunk
8. the American flag

D. Days of the week Give the days of the week that come *before* the ones men-tioned here.

1. lunes
2. jueves
3. sábado
4. miércoles
5. domingo
6. viernes
7. martes

90 noventa ◆ **Self-Test** [...]

Self-Test Lecciones 1–3

Student Components

Student Textbook

Each of the eighteen lessons in your textbook presents and practices vocabulary, grammar, pronunciation, cultural information, reading, listening, speaking, and writing. Self-tests appear after every three lessons.

Text Audio Program

The *Text Audio Program* contains recordings of the *Vocabulario* and *Pronunciación* sections, *dichos*, sample verb conjugations, and the readings in the *Rincón literario* sections. It also includes the recordings to accompany the *Al escuchar...* and *Al conversar...* activities.

Student Activities Manual (SAM)

The *Student Activities Manual* practices the material presented in your textbook. It is divided into a Workbook section, which focuses on vocabulary, grammar, reading, and writing practice; and a Laboratory Manual section, which focuses on pronunciation and listening comprehension.

SAM Audio Program

The *SAM Audio Program* reinforces your pronunciation and listening skills. It contains recorded material that corresponds to the Laboratory Manual section of the *¿Cómo se dice...? Student Activities Manual.*

NEW! iLrn: Heinle Learning Center

From a single site, you'll access all learning components, including an **eBook** with integrated activities, companion **videos,** a **voiceboard,** an online **Student Activities Manual** (with audio), **online tutoring** options, and more. For more information, turn to the front of the text or visit **ilrn.heinle.com.**

Quia eSAM

This online version of the *Student Activities Manual* contains the adapted content of the printed *SAM* plus the recorded material from the *SAM Audio Program* in an interactive environment that provides immediate feedback so you can monitor your progress. In addition, you can link to the textbook website for additional practice.

Personal Tutor

This valuable online resource gives you access to experienced tutors with degrees in this subject area. You can receive one-on-one tutoring and on-demand help with assignments.

Revised! *¿Cómo se dice...?*, Video Program

This three-tier video program features dramatized versions of the lesson-opening dialogues, geographic footage accompanied by descriptive narratives in Spanish, and sixty-seven grammar presentations, one for each grammar topic covered in the textbook. The video program is designed to help you learn about Spanish-speaking cultures, to practice your listening skills, and to reinforce lesson vocabulary and grammar.

Online Study Center

The *Online Study Center* website includes a variety of resources and practice to be used as you study each lesson or as you review for quizzes and exams. Each section of the website provides valuable resources:

◆ *ACE the Test* includes vocabulary and grammar practice tests, with automatic feedback that helps you understand errors and pinpoint areas you may need to review. *ACE Video Activities* include practice based on short clips from the *¿Cómo se dice...?* video program. Completed activities can be printed or e-mailed directly to your instructor.

◆ *Improve Your Grade* features audio flashcards for additional practice of vocabulary, pronunciation, and verb conjugations; .mp3 files of the *Text Audio Program;* and web search activities that provide practice with lesson vocabulary and grammar while exploring authentic Spanish-language websites. In addition, you'll find weblinks that help you explore concepts presented in the *Ubíquese... y búsquelo* feature of the textbook.

◆ Passkey-protected premium content consists of the *SAM Audio Program* in .mp3 format, the complete three-tier video, and interactive multimedia activities.

Online Study Center is accessible at **www.cengage.com/spanish/comosedice**

Scope and Sequence

Acknowledgments

We wish to express our appreciation to the following colleagues for the many valuable suggestions they have offered in reviews of several editions of ¿Cómo se dice...?

Robert L. Adler, *University of Alabama, Birmingham*
Iris Allocati, *Citrus College*
Jon Amastae, *University of Texas, El Paso*
Richard Auletta, *Long Island University, Brookville, NY*
Ann Bachman, *Seminole Community College*
Ann Baker, *University of Evansville*
Clayton Baker, *Indiana University, Indianapolis*
Deborah Baldini, *University of Missouri, Saint Louis*
Alejandra Balestra, *University of New Mexico*
Thomas Bente, *Temple University*
Mayra E. Bonet, *Lehman College, CUNY*
Paul Budofsky, *New York University*
Renatta Buscaglia, *East Los Angeles College*
Graciela Buschardt, *St. Louis Community College, Meramec*
Ezequiel Cardenas, *Cuyamaca College*
Malcolm Compitello, *Michigan State University*
Humberto Delgado-Jenkins, *DeKalb College*
Diana Diehl, *University of Delaware*
Mario L. D'Onofrio, *Cuyahoga Community College*
Martin H. Durrant, *Mesa Community College*
Deborah Edson, *Tidewater Community College*
Kenneth Eller, *University of Nebraska, Omaha*
María Enrico, *Mercy College*
Barbara P. Esquival-Heinemann, *Winthrop University*
Robert Fedorchek, *Fairfield University*
Ronna Feit, *Nassau Community College*
José Feliciano, *University of South Florida*
Roger Fernández, *Los Angeles City College*
Rosa Fernández, *University of New Mexico*
Rachel Finney, *Richard Bland College*
Carmen Forner, *College of Southern Nevada, Las Vegas*
Mark Forrester, *Burlington County College*
Walter Fuentes, *College of Charleston*
Brian Gilles, *Pasadena College*
John W. Griggs, *Glendale Community College*
Yolanda Guerrero, *Grossmont College*
Peg Haas, *Kent State University*
Janet J. Hampton, *University of the District of Columbia*
Paul Jacques, *Grossmont College*
Mercedes Jiménez, *University of California, Riverside*
Larry King, *University of North Carolina*
Lincoln Lambeth, *College of the Ozarks*
Fidel de León, *El Paso Community College*
Roxana Levin, *St. Petersburg Junior College*
Mark Littlefield, *Buffalo State College*
Christopher Maurer, *Harvard University*
Li McCleod, *University of Saskatchewan*
Kathy McConnell, *Point Loma Nazarene University*
Virginia M. McCready, *Pasadena City College*
Ornella Mazzuca, *Dutchess Community College*

Lección 1

▲ ¿Hola o adiós?

Objetivos

Comunicación
You will learn some greetings and farewells, how to introduce yourself and say where you are from, how to get and give phone numbers, and how to talk about days of the week and dates.

Pronunciación
The Spanish **a** and **e**

Estructuras
- The alphabet
- Cardinal numbers 0–30
- Colors
- Days of the week
- Months and seasons of the year
- Subject pronouns
- Present indicative of **ser**

Cultura
- Names and nicknames in the Hispanic world
- Body language when greeting and bidding farewell in Spanish-speaking societies
- Ways of addressing people in Spanish cultures
- Spanish origins of certain regional and city names in the U.S. and Canada

Panorama hispánico
- Los mexicoamericanos
- Los Estados Unidos hispánicos y el español en el mundo

Estrategias
Listening: Listening for the main idea
Speaking: Speaking for basic communication vs. highly accurate speech
Reading: Recognizing cognates
Writing: Generating ideas by brainstorming

Saludos y despedidas

Los mexicoamericanos

En los Estados Unidos (*United States*) hay unos 40 millones de hispanos. El 60 por ciento (*percent*) son de origen mexicano. La mayoría de ellos están (*are*) concentrados principalmente en Arizona, California, Tejas, Colorado, Nevada y Nuevo México.

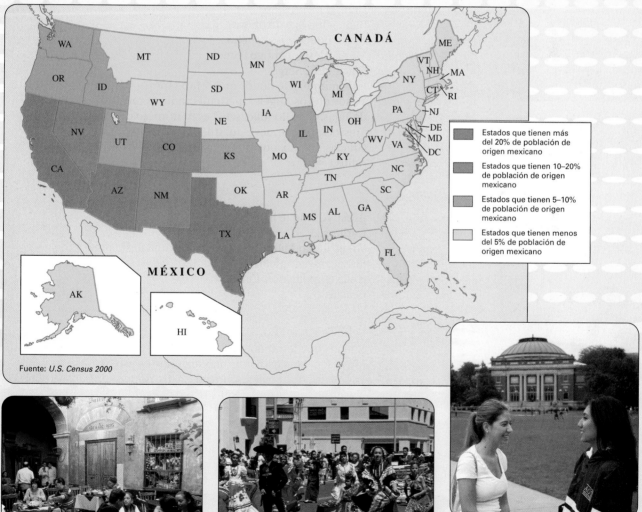

Estados que tienen más del 20% de población de origen mexicano

Estados que tienen 10–20% de población de origen mexicano

Estados que tienen 5–10% de población de origen mexicano

Estados que tienen menos del 5% de población de origen mexicano

Fuente: *U.S. Census 2000*

▲ Dos estudiantes conversan en la Universidad de Illinois.

▲ Café Barrio en Phoenix, Arizona

▲ Desfile folclórico durante la celebración de la Conferencia Internacional de Mariachis en Tucson, Arizona

En la clase

María Inés	Buenos días. Usted es el doctor Trujillo, ¿verdad?
Dr. Trujillo	Sí, señorita. ¿Y usted? ¿Cómo se llama?
María Inés	Me llamo María Inés Hidalgo.
Dr. Trujillo	Mucho gusto, señorita Hidalgo.
María Inés	El gusto es mío, profesor.
Dr. Trujillo	Tome asiento, por favor.
María Inés	Gracias.

En la cafetería

María Inés	Buenas tardes, señora. ¿Cómo está usted?
Señora	Muy bien, gracias. ¿Y tú, María Inés?
María Inés	Bien, gracias. Bueno, hasta mañana.
Señora	Hasta mañana. Saludos a Teresa.
María Inés	Gracias.

María Inés	Hola. ¿Cómo están?
Rodolfo	Bien. ¿Qué hay de nuevo?
María Inés	Nada. Bueno... no mucho...
Rodolfo	María Inés: mi amigo Sergio.
María Inés	Encantada, Sergio.
Sergio	Igualmente. ¿De dónde eres, María Inés?
María Inés	Yo soy de Los Ángeles, pero mi mamá es mexicana y mi papá es de Tejas. Oye, Rodolfo, ¿cuál es tu número de teléfono?
Rodolfo	Tres-ocho-seis-nueve-cuatro-siete-dos.
María Inés	Gracias. Bueno, nos vemos el lunes, Rodolfo. Adiós, Sergio.
Rodolfo y Sergio	Adiós.

En el parque

María Inés	¡Hola! ¿Cómo te llamas?
Carlitos	Carlitos...
María Inés	Yo me llamo María Inés. Oye... ¿hay una fiesta hoy?
Carlitos	Sí... es mi cumpleaños...
María Inés	¡Feliz cumpleaños, Carlitos!
Carlitos	Gracias.

En una fiesta

María Inés	Buenas noches, señor Paz. ¿Cómo le va?
Sr. Paz	Muy bien, gracias. Señorita, ¿de dónde es usted?
María Inés	Yo soy de Los Ángeles. ¿Y ustedes? ¿De dónde son?
Sr. Paz	Nosotros somos de Arizona. Usted es estudiante, ¿verdad?
María Inés	Sí, soy estudiante de la Universidad de California.

María Inés

el Dr. Trujillo

la señora

ACE the Test

Carlitos

Rodolfo

el Sr. Paz

 ¿Quién lo dice? (*Who says it?*) Identify the person who said the following in the dialogues.

1. Sí... es mi cumpleaños. _____
2. Oye... ¿hay una fiesta hoy? _____
3. Tres-ocho-seis-nueve-cuatro-siete-dos. _____
4. Nosotros somos de Arizona. Usted es estudiante, ¿verdad? _____
5. Hasta mañana. Saludos a Teresa. _____
6. Tome asiento, por favor. _____

Hablemos. With a partner, take turns asking and answering the following questions. Base your answers on the dialogue and on your own circumstances.

En el diálogo	¿Y tú?
1. ¿El doctor Trujillo es profesor o estudiante?	¿Tú eres profesor(-a) o estudiante?
2. ¿De dónde es María Inés?	¿De dónde eres tú?
3. ¿De dónde es el papá de María Inés?	¿De dónde es tu papá?
4. ¿De dónde son el señor Paz y sus (*his*) amigos?	¿De dónde son tú y tus amigos?
5. ¿La mamá de María Inés es mexicana o norteamericana?	¿Tu mamá es mexicana o norteamericana?

¿Lo sabía Ud.?

María es un nombre (*name*) muy popular en España y en Latinoamérica. Frecuentemente se usa con otros nombres: Ana María, María Teresa, etc. Se usa también como segundo nombre (*middle name*) para hombres: José María, etc.

◆ **¿Mary es un nombre muy popular en este país? ¿Se usa con otros nombres?**

¿Lo sabía Ud.?
Did you know?

LEARNING TIP

Many social variables are at play when deciding whether to address people formally (**Ud.**) or informally (**tú**). At work, a superior is addressed as **Ud.**, whereas peers are addressed as **tú**. In social situations, consider the speakers' relative ages, their level of acquaintance, and shared commonalities. When in doubt, use **Ud.**

(iLrn) Vocabulario

Cognados (*Cognates*)[1]

la cafetería cafeteria
la clase class
el (la) estudiante student
mexicano(-a)[2] Mexican
mexicoamericano(-a) Mexican-American

mucho(-a) much
no not
el teléfono telephone
la universidad university

Improve Your Grade
Audio Flashcards

Nombres (*Nouns*)

el (la) amigo(-a) friend
el cumpleaños[3] birthday
la despedida farewell
el día day
la fiesta party
el lunes[4] Monday

la mamá, la madre mom, mother
el número number
— de teléfono[5] phone number
el papá, el padre dad, father
el saludo greeting

Verbo (*Verb*)

ser to be

Adjetivos (*Adjectives*)

bueno(-a) good
feliz happy
mi my
nuevo(-a) new

Títulos (*Titles*)

doctor, doctora[6] (Dr.) doctor
profesor, profesora professor
señor (Sr.) mister (Mr.), sir, gentleman

señora (Sra.) madam, Mrs., lady
señorita (Srta.) Miss, young lady

---

[1]words that are very similar in both languages
[2]Names of nationalities are not capitalized in Spanish.
[3]The word **cumpleaños** is always used in the plural form.
[4]The days of the week are not capitalized in Spanish.
[5]English uses a noun with the function of an adjective: phone number. Spanish uses the **de** phrase: **número de teléfono.**
[6]In most Spanish-speaking countries, lawyers and members of many other professions who hold the equivalent of a Ph.D. are addressed as **doctor** or **doctora.**

Saludos y despedidas (*Greetings and farewells*)

adiós good-bye

buenas noches good evening, good night

buenas tardes good afternoon

buenos días good morning

hasta mañana see you tomorrow

hola hello

Nos vemos. See you.

Preguntas y respuestas (*Questions and answers*)

¿Cómo se llama usted? What is your name? (*formal*)

¿Cómo te llamas? What is your name? (*familiar*)

Me llamo... My name is . . .

¿Cómo está usted?[1] How are you? (*formal*)

¿Cómo están ustedes? How are you (all)? (*when speaking to more than one person*)

¿Cómo le va?[2] How is it going (for you)? (*formal*)

Bien. Fine.

Muy bien. Very well.

Otras palabras y expresiones (*Other words and expressions*)

bien well

bueno... well . . . , okay

¿cómo? how?

con with

¿cuál? what?, which?

¿— es tu número de teléfono? What is your phone number?

de from, of

¿dónde? where?

El gusto es mío. The pleasure is mine.

en in, at

encantado(-a) charmed

gracias thanks, thank you

hay there is, there are

hoy today

igualmente likewise

Mucho gusto. How do you do? Nice to meet you. (*Literally*, Much pleasure.)

muy very

nada nothing

¡oye! listen!

pero but

por favor please

¿qué? what?

¿Qué hay de nuevo? What's new?

Saludos a... Say hello to . . .

sí yes

Tome asiento. Have a seat.

tú you (*familiar*)

un, una a, an

usted (Ud.) you (*formal*)

¿verdad? right?

y and

¿Lo sabía Ud.? Se usa **hola** con personas conocidas (*known*), no con extraños (*strangers*).

◆ **¿Cómo saludan ustedes (*do you greet*) al profesor (a la profesora)?**

---

[1]**¿Cómo estás?** How are you? (*familiar*)

[2]**¿Cómo te va?** How is it going (for you)? (*familiar*)

Vocabulario adicional (*Additional vocabulary*)

Expresiones de cortesía
(*Polite expressions*)

Perdón. Pardon me.
Con permiso. Excuse me.

1. Very kind (of you).
2. How is it going?
3. See you around.
4. Bye.

Práctica

A. Match the questions or statements in column A with the responses in column B.

A		B
1. Mucho gusto, profesor. ____		**a.** De nada.
2. Pase y tome asiento, por favor. ____		**b.** Sí, es mi cumpleaños.
3. Muchas gracias. ____		**c.** De Colorado.
4. ¿Cómo está usted? ____		**d.** Igualmente.
5. Hasta mañana. ____		**e.** Sí. ¿Y tú? ¿De dónde eres?
6. ¿De dónde es tu papá? ____		**f.** Gracias.
7. ¿Hay una fiesta hoy? ____		**g.** Roberto Campos.
8. Tú eres de México, ¿verdad? ____		**h.** El gusto es mío.
9. Encantada. ____		**i.** Chau. Saludos a José Luis.
10. ¿Cómo te llamas? ____		**j.** Muy bien, gracias.

B. Complete the following exchanges, using appropriate vocabulary.

1. _____ días, señora. ¿Cómo _____ va?
   Muy bien, Amelia. ¿Qué _____ de nuevo?
   No _____. Bueno... ¡ _____!

2. ¿Cómo se _____ usted, señorita?
   Me _____ Gloria Estévez.
   ¿De _____ es usted?
   De Los Ángeles, _____ mi mamá es mexicana.

3. ¿Es usted _____ de la _____ de California?
   Sí, señor.

4. Hasta la _____, Gabriela.
   Adiós.

5. ¿Cuál es tu _____ de _____?
   Siete-tres-dos-nueve-cinco-seis-cero.

Para conversar

 ¿Qué dicen estas personas? (*What are these people saying?*) With a partner, take turns creating exchanges between the people in the illustrations. Then join another group and compare your ideas with theirs.

Pronunciación

A. The Spanish *a*

The Spanish **a** is pronounced like the *a* in the English word *father.* Listen to your teacher and repeat the following sentences.

Hola, Amanda.

Encantada, señora Paz.

Hasta mañana, mamá.

Hasta la vista, Marta.

Hasta la vista, Ana.

B. The Spanish *e*

The Spanish **e** is pronounced like the *e* in the English word *eight.* Listen to your teacher and repeat the following sentences.

Buenas noches, Teresa.

¿De dónde eres?

¿Es el señor Pérez?

¿Es de Los Ángeles?

Aspectos culturales

En imágenes (*Saludos y despedidas*)

▲ Un hombre y una mujer de negocios se saludan.

▲ Una chica y un chico se saludan con un beso en la mejilla (*cheek*).

▲ Dos amigas se besan en la mejilla (*kiss each other on the cheek*).

Ubíquese... y búsquelo

 Improve Your Grade
Web Search

You are meeting María Inés at calle Olvera and then you are inviting her for coffee, sightseeing, or to eat. Go to **www.cengage.com/highered** to decide where you are taking María Inés. In the next class, team up with two classmates to discuss your findings.

Note: **Ubíquese... y búsquelo** = *Locate yourself and find it.*

▲ En México, dos mujeres profesionales se saludan con el tradicional beso en la mejilla.

▲ Dos amigos se saludan con un abrazo (*hug*).

▲ Dos hermanas (*sisters*) le dan un beso a su mamá.

Estructuras

1. The alphabet (*El alfabeto*)

Letter	Name	Letter	Name	Letter	Name
a	a	k	ka	s	ese
b	be[1]	l	ele	t	te
c	ce	m	eme	u	u
d	de	n	ene	v	ve[2]
e	e	ñ	eñe	w	doble ve
f	efe	o	o	x	equis
g	ge	p	pe	y	i griega
h	hache	q	cu	z	zeta
i	i	r	ere		
j	jota	rr	erre		

ACE the Test

Práctica

A. Spell these well-known acronyms in Spanish.

    FBI   IBM   PTA   NBA   NAACP

Now you and your partner will give each other one acronym to spell.

¡Atención!   Some acronyms are given as one word: **la CIA.**

B. Here are some English last names (*apellidos*) that you are spelling out for your Spanish-speaking friend. Complete each one, adding the missing consonants.

   ◆ **MODELO:**   Lane: <u>ele</u>–a–<u>ene</u>–e

  1. Smith: _____ – _____ – i – _____ – _____
  2. Carey: _____ – a – _____ – e – _____
  3. Budge: _____ – u – _____ – _____ – e
  4. Hewes: _____ – e – _____ – e – _____
  5. Jackson: _____ – a – _____ – _____ – _____ – o – _____

Para conversar

 ¿Cómo se escribe?   A Spanish-speaking person may not know how to spell your name. If that person wants to write it, he or she might ask, **¿Cómo se escribe?**[3] (*How do you write it?*). Learn how to spell your name in Spanish and ask five classmates what their last name is, and how to spell it.

---

[1]be larga
[2]ve corta
[3]Also **¿Cómo se deletrea?** (*How do you spell it?*)

2. Cardinal numbers 0–30 (*Los números cardinales 0–30*)

0 **cero**	7 **siete**	14 **catorce**	21 **veintiuno** (*and so on*)
1 **uno**	8 **ocho**	15 **quince**	30 **treinta**
2 **dos**	9 **nueve**	16 **dieciséis**[1]	
3 **tres**	10 **diez**	17 **diecisiete**	
4 **cuatro**	11 **once**	18 **dieciocho**	
5 **cinco**	12 **doce**	19 **diecinueve**	
6 **seis**	13 **trece**	20 **veinte**	

¡Atención! **Uno** changes to **un** before a masculine singular noun: **un profesor** (*one professor*). **Uno** changes to **una** before a feminine singular noun: **una profesora** (*one professor*).

Práctica

ACE the Test

A. In Los Angeles there are many businesses that are owned by Mexican-Americans. Take turns with your partner reading the telephone numbers that a Spanish-speaking person would call, according to his/her needs.

1. Carlos wants to have his picture taken.
2. Sergio wants to send flowers to his wife.
3. Elena is having car trouble.
4. Lupe needs to have a prescription filled.
5. Fernando needs to make a dinner reservation.
6. Silvia wants to know what time the jewelry store closes.
7. Eva and Luis need an apartment.
8. Antonio wants to know if a bookstore is open on Sundays.

---

[1]The numbers 16 to 29 may also be spelled as separate words: **diez y seis... veinte y uno...**, and so on.

B. Count along in Spanish! Listen to the song, then try to sing it by heart.

Canción infantil (*Children's song*)

Dos y dos son cuatro,
cuatro y dos son seis;
seis y dos son ocho
y ocho dieciséis.

C. Complete the following series of numbers.

1. treinta, veintiocho, veintiséis, ...diez
2. cero, tres, seis, ...treinta
3. treinta y cinco, treinta, ...cinco
4. uno, tres, ...veintinueve

Para conversar

 A. **¿Cuál es tu número de teléfono?**[1]   Ask four members of the class what their name and phone number is and write down the information.

 B. **Una clase de aritmética**   You and your partner are tutoring some Spanish-speaking children. Prepare addition and subtraction problems and have an answer key. The children only deal with numbers up to thirty.

$+$: **más**

$-$: **menos**

$=$: **son**

$16 + 8 =$

$25 - 12 =$

3. Colors (*Los colores*)

Everywhere you go, there are colors! Learn to say them in Spanish.

---

[1]Say "**¿Cuál es su número de teléfono?**" when addressing someone as **usted.**

Práctica

ACE the Test

A. With a partner, take turns naming the colors of the following items.

1. an elephant
2. a banana
3. an orange
4. a leaf
5. rosy cheeks
6. a dark night
7. coffee
8. the American flag

> **LEARNING TIP**
>
> As you look at the world around you, try to name in Spanish the colors you see. Remember that it is always best to go from the concept to the target language (Spanish) and vice versa.

B. With a partner, take turns naming the colors that each student is wearing.

C. This is a painting (**una pintura**) by a Mexican-American painter. With a partner, take turns naming the colors that you see, in Spanish. You can include:

claro *light*   **oscuro** *dark*
(e.g.: **azul claro** or **azul oscuro**)

◆ **MODELOS:** Esto es (*This is*) de color azul claro.
Mira (*Look*), morado oscuro.
Y mira, aquí hay algo (*something*) amarillo.

Para conversar

A. **¿Qué color te gusta?** (*What color do you like?*) Conduct a survey of your classmates, to find out which color is the most popular.

El color más popular es el _____.

B. **¡Somos pintores!** (*We are painters!*) See if everyone knows what colors can be formed by mixing the primary colors.

¿Qué color forman el _____ y el _____?
Forman el color _____.

4. Days of the week (*Los días de la semana*)

~ agosto ~						
lunes	**martes**	**miércoles**	**jueves**	**viernes**	**sábado**	**domingo**
	1	2	3	4	5	6
7	8	9	10	11	12	13
14	15	16	17	18	19	20
21	22	23	24	25	26	27
28	29	30	31			

—¿Qué día es hoy? **¿Sábado?**   *"What day is today? Saturday?"*
—No, hoy es **viernes.**   *"No, today is Friday."*

- In Spanish-speaking countries, the week starts on Monday.
- The days of the week are not capitalized in Spanish.
- The days of the week are masculine in Spanish. The masculine definite articles **el** and **los** are often used with them to express *on*.
- All the days of the week use the same form for the singular and plural (**el lunes – los lunes**). The only exceptions are **sábado** and **domingo** (**el sábado – los sábados**).

ACE the Test

┌ Práctica

A. Knowing that **mañana** means *tomorrow* and **pasado mañana** means *the day after tomorrow,* give information following the model.

◆ **MODELO:** Hoy es lunes.
   Mañana es martes y pasado mañana es miércoles.

1. Hoy es sábado.
2. Hoy es miércoles.
3. Hoy es viernes.
4. Hoy es domingo.
5. Hoy es jueves.
6. Hoy es martes.

B. Using the calendar on the next page, take turns asking a classmate what day a certain date falls on.

◆ **MODELO:** —¿Qué día es el dos de agosto?
   —Es miércoles.

Para conversar

Tu programa favorito In groups of three, ask each other what program from **el canal 27** you like each day.

◆ **MODELO:** —¿Qué programa te gusta los lunes?
—Los lunes me gusta el programa...

CANAL 27
Su canal hispano
Programación 9:00-12:00

	9:00–10:00	10:00–11:00	11:00–12:00
LUNES	Buenos días, Los Ángeles	Programa educativo	Telenovela *María*
MARTES	Hospital General	Música clásica	Tenis
MIÉRCOLES	Música y arte	Ciudades latinoamericanas	Programa político
JUEVES	Una clase de ejercicio	Los jueves con Marisol	Noticias internacionales
VIERNES	Las aventuras de un tigre	Problemas sociales	Telenovela *Tú y yo*
SÁBADO	Programa infantil	Música de México	¡Fútbol!
DOMINGO	Religión	Gimnasia	¡Béisbol!

5. Months and seasons of the year (*Los meses y las estaciones del año*)

A. Los meses

ENERO

L	M	M	J	V	S	D
	1	2	3	4	5	⑥
7	8	9	10	11	12	13
14	15	⑯	17	18	19	20
21	22	23	24	25	26	27
28	29	30	31			

FEBRERO

L	M	M	J	V	S	D
				①	2	3
4	5	6	7	8	9	10
11	12	13	⑭	15	16	17
18	19	20	21	22	23	24
25	26	27	28			

MARZO

L	M	M	J	V	S	D
				1	2	3
4	5	6	7	8	⑨	10
11	12	13	14	15	16	17
18	19	20	㉑	22	23	24
25	26	27	28	29	30	31

ABRIL

L	M	M	J	V	S	D
1	2	3	④	5	6	7
8	9	10	11	12	13	14
15	16	17	18	19	20	21
22	23	24	25	26	27	28
29	㉚					

MAYO

L	M	M	J	V	S	D
	1	2	3	4	⑤	
6	7	8	9	10	11	12
13	⑭	15	16	17	18	19
20	21	22	23	24	25	26
27	28	29	30	31		

JUNIO

L	M	M	J	V	S	D
					1	②
3	4	5	6	7	8	9
10	11	12	⑬	14	15	16
17	18	19	20	21	22	23
24	25	26	27	28	29	30

JULIO

L	M	M	J	V	S	D
1	2	3	④	5	6	7
8	9	10	11	12	13	14
15	16	⑰	18	19	20	21
22	23	24	25	26	27	28
29	30	31				

AGOSTO

L	M	M	J	V	S	D
				1	2	③	4
5	6	7	8	9	10	11
12	⑬	14	15	16	17	18
19	20	21	22	23	24	25
26	27	28	29	30	31	

SEPTIEMBRE

L	M	M	J	V	S	D
						1
②	3	4	5	6	⑦	8
9	10	11	12	13	14	15
16	17	18	19	20	21	22
23/30	24	25	26	27	28	29

OCTUBRE

L	M	M	J	V	S	D
	1	2	3	4	5	6
7	8	9	10	11	⑫	13
14	⑮	16	17	18	19	20
21	22	23	24	25	26	27
28	29	30	31			

NOVIEMBRE

L	M	M	J	V	S	D
				1	2	3
4	5	6	7	⑧	9	10
⑪	12	13	14	15	16	17
18	19	20	21	22	23	24
25	26	27	28	29	30	

DICIEMBRE

L	M	M	J	V	S	D
						1
2	3	4	5	6	⑦	8
9	⑩	11	12	13	14	15
16	17	18	19	20	21	22
23/30	24/31	25	26	27	28	29

◆ To ask for the date say:

—¿Qué fecha es hoy?   *What's the date today?*

◆ When giving the date, always begin with the phrase **"hoy es el..."**

—Hoy es el cuatro de julio.   *Today is the fourth of July.*

◆ Begin with the number, followed by the preposition **de** (*of*), and then the month.

el seis de agosto   *August sixth*

—¿Qué fecha es hoy? **¿El treinta**   *"What's the date today?*
de abril?   *April thirtieth?"*
—No, hoy es **el primero de mayo.**   *"No, today is May first."*

◆ The article **el** is omitted when the day of the week is expressed.

—Hoy es jueves, 20 de abril.   *Today is Thursday, April 20.*

¡Atención!   **Primero** (*First*) is the only ordinal number used with dates. Also, the months are not capitalized in Spanish.

B. Las estaciones del año

▲ la primavera

▲ el verano

▲ el otoño

▲ el invierno

 Un poema

Treinta días trae° noviembre,   *brings*
con abril, junio y septiembre.
De veintiocho sólo° hay uno,   *only*
y los demás,° de treinta y uno.   **los...** *the others*

A. With your partner, look at the dates circled on the calendar on page 17 and take turns saying them in Spanish.

B. Indicate in which season the following months fall in the northern hemisphere.

1. enero
2. octubre
3. julio
4. febrero
5. agosto
6. mayo
7. noviembre
8. abril

C. Knowing that the seasons are reversed in the southern hemisphere, you and your partner take turns indicating in which season the same months fall there.

1. enero
2. octubre
3. julio
4. febrero
5. agosto
6. mayo
7. noviembre
8. abril

D. Listen to a folk song you would hear during the Feast of San Fermín in northern Spain. This feast is famous for bulls being let loose to chase the people through the narrow streets of the old city of Pamplona. After listening to the song several times, try to sing it.

Uno de enero,
dos de febrero,
tres de marzo,
cuatro de abril,
cinco de mayo,
seis de junio,
siete de julio,
San Fermín.

Para conversar

Oye, ¿cuál es tu signo? (*Listen, what's your sign?*) Survey your classmates to find out when everybody's birthday is and what sign everyone belongs to.

♦ MODELO: —*¿Cuándo es tu cumpleaños?*
—*Es el dos de abril.*
—*Oye, ¿cuál es tu signo?*
—*Mi signo es Leo.*

Los signos del Zodíaco

Aries	Tauro	Géminis	Cáncer	Leo	Virgo
(*21 de marzo a 19 de abril*)	(*20 de abril a 20 de mayo*)	(*21 de mayo a 21 de junio*)	(*22 de junio a 22 de julio*)	(*23 de julio a 22 de agosto*)	(*23 de agosto a 21 de septiembre*)

Libra	Escorpión	Sagitario	Capricornio	Acuario	Piscis
(*22 de septiembre a 22 de octubre*)	(*23 de octubre a 21 de noviembre*)	(*22 de noviembre a 21 de diciembre*)	(*22 de diciembre a 19 de enero*)	(*20 de enero a 19 de febrero*)	(*20 de febrero a 20 de marzo*)

6. Subject pronouns (*Pronombres personales usados como sujetos*)

Singular		Plural	
yo	*I*	**nosotros**	*we* (masc.)
		nosotras	*we* (fem.)
tú	*you* (familiar)	**vosotros**	*you* (masc., familiar)
		vosotras	*you* (fem., familiar)
usted	*you* (formal)	**ustedes**	*you* (formal)
él	*he*	**ellos**	*they* (masc.)
ella	*she*	**ellas**	*they* (fem.)

♦ The **tú** form is used as the equivalent of *you* to address a friend, a coworker, a relative, or a child. The **usted** form is used in general to express deference or respect. In most Spanish-speaking countries today, young people tend to call each other **tú** even if they have just met. If in doubt, use **usted**.

♦ The plural form of **tú** is **vosotros(-as)**, which is used only in Spain. In Latin America, the plural form **ustedes** (abbreviated **Uds.**) is used as the plural form of both **usted** (abbreviated **Ud.**) and **tú**.

♦ The masculine plural forms can refer to the masculine gender alone or to both genders together.

—¿De dónde son el Sr. Paz y sus amigos? *"Where are Mr. Paz and his friends from?"*
—**Ellos** son de Arizona. *"They are from Arizona."*

—¿María Inés es mexicoamericana?   *"Is María Inés Mexican-American?"*
—Sí, **ella** es mexicoamericana.   *"Yes, she is Mexican-American."*

—¿De dónde son **ustedes**?   *"Where are you from?"*
—**Nosotros** somos de Tejas.   *"We are from Texas."*

—¿**Tú** eres estudiante?   *"Are you a student?"*
—Sí, **yo** soy estudiante de la   *"Yes, I am a student at the*
    Universidad de California.   *University of California."*

ACE the Test

Práctica

 A. Identify the personal pronoun that corresponds to each picture below.

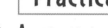 **B.** What pronouns would be used to refer to the following people?

1. el doctor Trujillo
2. María Inés y yo (*fem.*)
3. Rodolfo y Sergio
4. usted y Patricia
5. el señor Paz y sus amigos
6. Enrique y yo

 C. With your partner, take turns saying whether you would use **tú, usted,** or **ustedes** to address the following people.

1. Carlitos
2. your parents' elderly friend
3. two strangers
4. your instructor
5. your best friend
6. an older lady you just met
7. a twelve-year old girl
8. three gentlemen you just met

7. Present indicative of *ser* (*Presente de indicativo del verbo* **ser**)

ser *to be*		
Singular		
yo	**soy**	*I am*
tú	**eres**	*you are* (fam.)
Ud.	**es**	*you are* (form.)
él		*he is*
ella		*she is*
Plural		
nosotros(-as)	**somos**	*we are*
vosotros(-as)	**sois**	*you are* (fam.)
Uds.	**son**	*you are* (form.)
ellos		*they are* (masc.)
ellas		*they are* (fem.)

◆ The verb **ser,** *to be,* is irregular. Its forms, like the forms of other irregular verbs, must be memorized.

◆ The verb **ser** is commonly used to express identity, place of origin, occupation, characteristic, and nationality.

—¿De dónde **son** ustedes?   *"Where are you from?"*
—Nosotros **somos** de México.   *"We are from Mexico."*

—¿Ud. **es** estudiante?   *"Are you a student?"*
—No, yo **soy** profesora.   *"No, I am a professor."*

LEARNING TIP

Say where several people that you know are from, including yourself and your family. Think of people individually and in pairs.

¡Atención!   The indefinite article **(un, una)** is not used after the verb **ser** when describing profession, nationality, religion, or party affiliation unless an adjective follows the noun.

El doctor Trujillo **es profesor.**
But: El doctor Trujillo **es un profesor excelente.**

Un dicho *A saying*

El tiempo es oro[1].

Equivalent: Time is money.

ACE the Test

Práctica

 A. Complete this conversation between two students, using the present indicative of the verb **ser.**

¿De dónde _____ ustedes?
Nosotros _____ de Arizona. ¿De dónde _____ tú?
Yo _____ de Tejas.
¿Y María Inés?
Ella _____ de California.
¿Raquel y Luis _____ de Colorado?
No, de Chicago.

---

[1]gold

B. Say where these people are from, using the information in the illustration.

1. ellos
2. tú
3. Juan, Mario y José
4. Carlos y yo

5. yo
6. nosotras
7. Teresa
8. ustedes

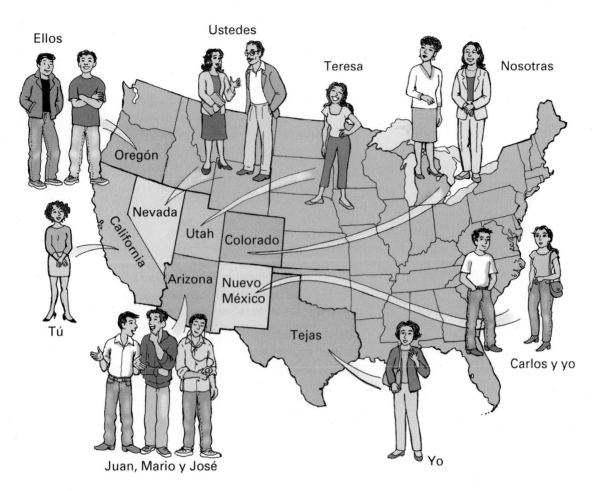

Ellos

Ustedes

Teresa

Nosotras

Oregón

Nevada

California

Utah Colorado

Arizona

Nuevo México

Tejas

Carlos y yo

Tú

Yo

Juan, Mario y José

Para conversar

¡Habla con tu compañero! (*Speak with your partner!*) Ask each other the following questions.

1. ¿Quién (*Who*) eres?
2. ¿De dónde eres?
3. ¿De dónde es tu mamá? ¿De dónde es tu papá?
4. ¿De dónde son tus amigos?
5. ¿Tú y tu familia son norteamericanos?

Now join another pair of students and tell them about yourselves.

Así somos

Al escuchar...

Estrategia **Listening for the main idea** Learning to listen in a foreign language takes practice. Throughout the course, you will practice a variety of techniques to help make the process easier. When you listen for the main idea, focus on getting the general idea of what you hear. Don't worry about understanding every word; just try to grasp what a conversation or passage is about.

 Una llamada de teléfono Rosalía calls Jorge to check on some information. Listen to their phone call and, in one or two words, jot down what the subject of the conversation is.

Al conversar...

Estrategia **Speaking for basic communication** Throughout your study of Spanish, you will be learning to express yourself orally, first with very basic ideas and gradually with greater sophistication. As you start to speak Spanish, remember the following tips.

◆ Keep it simple. Use the vocabulary and structures you already know.
◆ Try to speak clearly and accurately, but don't be afraid to make mistakes.
◆ Use short sentences or phrases to convey what you want to say until you feel more comfortable using Spanish.
◆ Talk to yourself and others whenever you can, using the Spanish you learn in each class.

 Hola, ¿qué tal? Greet a classmate you don't know well and use the following questions to get to know him or her. Then answer your classmate's questions.

¿Cómo estás?	¿Cuál es tu número de teléfono?
¿De dónde eres?	¿Cuándo es tu cumpleaños?

 ¿Cómo somos? Using the appropriate forms of the verb **ser,** describe the following people, using the characteristics below. Then, with a partner, talk about yourselves and your loved ones.

yo	**mi mamá**	**mi papá**	**mis amigos**	**mis amigos y yo**

cómico(-a), realista, optimista, pesimista, estudioso(-a), paciente (impaciente), atlético(-a), inteligente, conservador(-a), liberal, romántico(-a), tímido(-a)

HINT: If the subject is plural, add an **-s** to the adjective if it ends in a vowel. Add **-es** if it ends in a consonant.

 ¿Qué dice Ud.? (*What do you say?*) What would you say in the following situations? What might the other person say? Act out scenes with a partner. Take turns playing each role.

1. You greet your instructor in the morning and ask how he/she is.
2. Someone comes to see you. You tell this person to come in and offer him/her a seat.
3. You ask a lady what her name is and then you ask her ten-year-old daughter what her name is.

Note: Así somos. = *This is the way we are.*

4. Someone is introduced to you.
5. You greet a couple of friends and ask them how they are and what's new.
6. You ask some new acquaintances where they are from and tell them where you are from.
7. You ask a classmate what his/her phone number is, and tell him/her what your phone number is.
8. You are not sure what day today is. You also ask the date.
9. You tell a new friend when your birthday is and what your sign is. You find out that his/her birthday is today!
10. You are going to buy a present for a friend. Ask him/her whether he/she likes (name several colors that come to mind).

 Para conocernos mejor (*To get to know each other better*) Work with a classmate whom you would like to get to know. Take turns asking each other these questions.

1. Hola, ¿cómo estás?
2. ¿Cómo te llamas?
3. ¿De dónde eres?
4. ¿Eres optimista, pesimista o realista?
5. ¿Cuál es tu número de teléfono?
6. ¿Cuándo es tu cumpleaños?
7. ¿Cuál es tu signo?
8. ¿Qué color te gusta?
9. ¿Cuál es tu estación favorita?
10. ¿De dónde es tu mamá? ¿Y tu papá?

Una encuesta (*A survey*) Interview your classmates to identify who fits the following descriptions. Include your instructor, but remember to use the **Ud.** form when addressing him/her. After finishing the survey, get together with two or three classmates and discuss the results.

Nombre

1. Es de otro estado (another state). _____
2. Es tímido(-a). _____
3. Es muy optimista. _____
4. Es impaciente. _____
5. Es muy inteligente. _____
6. Es liberal. _____
7. Es conservador(-a). _____
8. Es del signo de Leo. _____

 Para crear In groups of three, look at this photo and use your imagination to create a story about the people in the picture. Who are they? Give them names. Are they students? Where are they from? What might they say to each other? In general, what's the story behind the photo?

¡Vamos a leer!

Antes de leer (*Before reading*)

> **Estrategia** **Recognizing cognates** Many times Spanish words that look like English ones also have the same or very similar meanings. These words are cognates (**cognados**). You have seen numerous cognates in this lesson; for example, **color, programa, alfabeto,** and the months of the year. **Atención:** Although Spanish-English cognates look alike, they are pronounced differently.

Cognados Look over the following reading and make a list of all the cognates you find. Use your knowledge of common academic subjects in English to help you.

A leer

 ORGANIZACIÓN DE ESTUDIANTES HISPANOS

Nuevos miembros

Sandra Guadalupe Acosta
De: San Diego, California
Especialización: Español

Luis Rodríguez
De: Santa Fe, Nuevo México
Especialización:
Administración de empresas

María Ester Villalobos
De: El Paso, Tejas
Especialización: Educación

Susana Barrios
De: Sacramento, California
Especialización: Biología

Fernando Padilla
De: Phoenix, Arizona
Especialización: Sociología

 Comprensión As you read the information about the five students, find the answers to the following questions.

1. ¿De dónde es la señorita Acosta? ¿Cuál es su especialización (*major*)?
2. ¿De qué estado son Sandra y Susana?
3. ¿De qué ciudad (*city*) es Luis Rodríguez?
4. ¿Cuál es la especialización de María Ester? ¿Y la de Fernando?
5. ¿Quién es de Tejas? ¿Fernando y Luis son de California?

Note: **¡Vamos a leer!** = *Let's read!*

¡Vamos a escribir!

Antes de escribir (*Before writing*)

> **Estrategia** **Generating ideas by brainstorming** Before beginning to write, you need to generate ideas about a topic. Brainstorming is like thinking aloud. Allow your mind to wander and write down all of your thoughts and ideas about your topic. When brainstorming, avoid censoring your ideas. You can discard the least useful or uninteresting ideas later before you actually write.

Un mensaje electrónico (*An e-mail*) You will be exchanging e-mails with a Spanish-speaking student from another state. Before writing your e-mail, brainstorm the type of information and questions you can include.

1. Jot down information that you can provide about yourself. This will include name, origin, nationality, where you are a student, characteristics, etc.
2. Write the questions you want to ask him or her.

A escribir el mensaje electrónico

Now organize your thoughts and the ideas from your brainstorming and write a draft (**borrador**) of the e-mail. Begin your e-mail with **Hola** and close with a farewell phrase.

Después de escribir

 Before writing the final version of your e-mail, your instructor might want you to exchange your first draft with a classmate and peer edit each other's work. Use the following two guidelines.

- ◆ correct use of subject pronouns
- ◆ formation and agreement (with subject) of the verb **ser**

Después de leer... desde su mundo (*from your world*)

 Give some information about yourself.

Nombre y apellido: _____

De: _____

Especialización: _____

As a class, create your own class directory, including this and any other useful information you wish to include.

_____

Note: **¡Vamos a escribir!** = *Let's write!*

Panorama hispánico

Improve Your Grade
Web Search

Los mexicoamericanos

◆ El grado (*degree*) de asimilación a la cultura norteamericana de los mexicoamericanos es muy diverso. Unos se adaptan fácilmente (*easily*) y otros no. La mayoría conserva su lengua y su unidad familiar.

◆ Muchos mexicoamericanos se destacan (*stand out*) en la política, la educación, las artes y la literatura. Muchos han ganado (*have earned*) honores en las fuerzas armadas de este país.

Política y activismo social

◀ Antonio Villaraigosa, Alcalde (Mayor) de Los Ángeles, California

◀ Bill Richardson, Gobernador hispano de Nuevo México

Artes plásticas

Del muralismo mexicano al muralismo mexicoamericano.

▲ *La gran Tenochtitlán* (fragmento), Diego Rivera

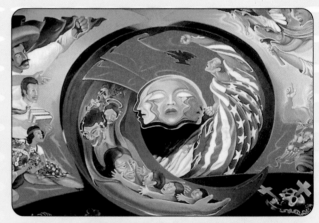

▲ *La antorcha de Quetzalcoatl* (*The Torch of Quetzalcoatl*), mural de Leo Tanguma

Pensamiento[1] y literatura

De la escuela de pensamiento mexicana a la imaginación literaria mexicoamericana.

▲ Sandra Cisneros, escritora mexicoamericana

[1]**Pensamiento** = *Thought*

▲ Artefactos de la exposición permanente de El Museo Mexicano, San Francisco, California

▲ Paseo del Río, San Antonio, Tejas

Los Estados Unidos hispánicos y el español en el mundo

Más (*More*) del 5% de los habitantes del mundo (*world*) hablan (*speak*) español. En los Estados Unidos, unos 39,000,000 de personas hablan este idioma (*language*) como primera (*first*) lengua.

La influencia hispana se nota también (*also*) en otros aspectos de la vida (*life*) como en la comida (*food*), la arquitectura y la música.

En las universidades y en las escuelas (*schools*) secundarias de este país (*country*), miles (*thousands*) de estudiantes toman clases de español.

World Languages
Primary language spoken by the 6 billion people in the world

One quarter of the world's population speak one of three languages.

5% of the world's population speak one of 5,900 languages; 2,400 of which are endangered.

Mandarin Chinese **14.8%**

Spanish **5.5%**

English **5.4%**

85 languages

95% of the world's population speak one of 100 languages.

Bengali	3.2%
Hindi	3.0
Arabic	2.9
Portuguese	2.8
Russian	2.8
Japanese	2.1
German	1.6
Wu Chinese	1.3
Javanese	1.3
Korean	1.3
French	1.2
Vietnamese	1.1

Half of the world's population speak one of 15 languages.

Adapted from *The Boston Globe*. Data from SIL Ethnologue.

Nuestro[1] panorama cultural

In groups of three, answer the following questions about your home state, region, or country.

1. ¿Quién es el gobernador de su estado? ¿Y el vice gobernador?
2. ¿Cuáles son algunos (*some*) pintores (*painters*) y artistas famosos de su región o de su país (*country*)?
3. ¿Cuáles son otros escritores famosos de su país?
4. ¿Hay muchas personas de habla hispana en su ciudad?

---

[1]**Nuestro** = *Our*

▲ Unos estudiantes conversan después de (*after*) las clases.

Objetivos

Comunicación

You will learn vocabulary related to the classroom, useful questions and answers, and some polite expressions.

Pronunciación

The Spanish **i**, **o**, and **u**

Estructuras

◆ Gender and number
◆ Definite and indefinite articles
◆ Cardinal numbers 31–100
◆ Telling time
◆ Present indicative of regular **-ar** verbs
◆ Negative and interrogative sentences
◆ Possession with **de**

Cultura

◆ The 24-hour time system
◆ Study habits

Panorama hispánico

◆ Los cubanoamericanos

Estrategias

Listening: Listening for specifics and guessing intelligently
Speaking: Asking for repetition
Reading: Guessing the meaning of unknown words
Writing: Conducting and reporting an interview

En la universidad

Los cubanoamericanos

Más de medio (*a half*) millón de cubanos viven en Miami, donde ejercen una gran influencia cultural y económica. Antes de la llegada (*arrival*) de los cubanos en 1959, Miami era (*was*) fundamentalmente un centro turístico. Hoy es un centro industrial y comercial de primer orden (*first-class*) y el puente (*bridge*) que une la economía de los Estados Unidos con la de América Latina y con la de España (*Spain*).

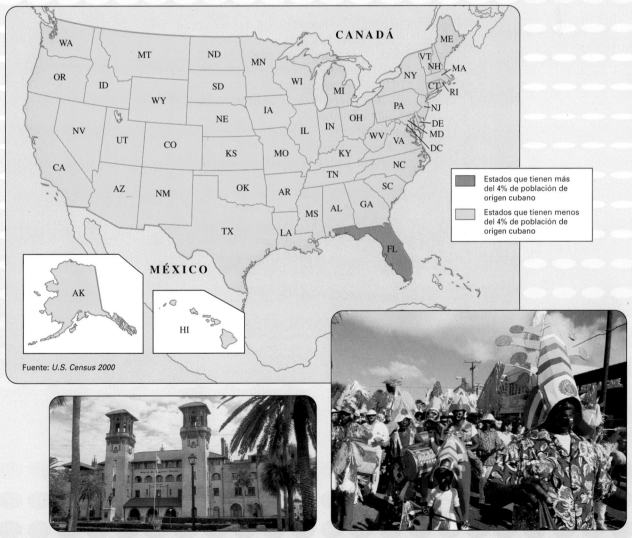

Estados que tienen más del 4% de población de origen cubano

Estados que tienen menos del 4% de población de origen cubano

Fuente: *U.S. Census 2000*

▲ Muestra (*Sample*) de la arquitectura hispánica de la ciudad de San Agustín, Florida, la ciudad europea más antigua (*oldest*) de los Estados Unidos, fundada (*founded*) en 1565

▲ Desfile de comparsas (*costume dancers parade*) durante el Carnaval de la Calle Ocho, en Miami

Gloria, una chica cubanoamericana, habla con un muchacho de El Salvador.

Gloria	¿Qué hora es?
Julio	Son las diez y cuarto. ¿A qué hora es la clase de inglés?
Gloria	A las diez y media. ¡Caramba! ¡Es tarde! Oye, Julio, ¿Olga y tú estudian en la biblioteca esta noche?
Julio	No, yo trabajo en el hospital por la noche. Olga estudia con José Luis.
Gloria	¡Pero chico! Tú trabajas por la tarde también. ¡Y tomas cinco clases! ¿Cuándo estudias?
Julio	Los sábados y los domingos.
Gloria	¡Necesitas más tiempo para estudiar!
Julio	Sí, y también necesito más dinero. Oye, ¿deseas estudiar conmigo el sábado por la mañana?
Gloria	¡Sí! ¿Estudiamos en mi casa? Y por la tarde vamos a la Calle Ocho.
Julio	Buena idea. ¿Cuál es tu dirección?
Gloria	Calle Quinta, número 120. Y mi número de teléfono es 3-54-67-98.
Julio	*(Anota la dirección y el número de teléfono de Gloria.)* ¡Perfecto! Nos vemos el sábado.

Por la tarde, Gloria conversa con una chica norteamericana.

Sandra	Oye, Gloria, ¿cómo se dice *backpack* en español?
Gloria	Se dice "mochila".
Sandra	Gracias. El español es un idioma difícil...
Gloria	No, Sandra. ¡Es fácil! Pero necesitas practicar todos los días.
Sandra	¿Tú hablas otros idiomas?
Gloria	Sí, hablo francés y un poco de portugués. ¿Y tú?
Sandra	Yo hablo italiano.
Gloria	¿En serio?
Sandra	¡Sí! Pizza... ravioles...
Gloria	¡Ay, chica! ¡En ese caso yo hablo chino!

¿Lo sabía Ud.?

Una expresión muy común entre (*among*) cubanos es **chico(-a)** (*young man/girl*), equivalente a las expresiones "*dude*" and "*girl*".

◆ **¿Son muy populares estas expresiones en este país?**

Gloria

Julio

Sandra

ACE the Test

 ¿Quién lo dice? Identify the person who said the following in the dialogues.

1. Yo trabajo en el hospital por la noche. _____
2. ¡Necesitas más tiempo para estudiar! _____
3. ¡Ay, chica! ¡En ese caso yo hablo chino! _____
4. Oye, ¿deseas estudiar conmigo el sábado por la mañana? _____
5. Yo hablo italiano. _____
6. ¿Cómo se dice *backpack* en español? _____
7. ¡Sí! ¿Estudiamos en mi casa? Y por la tarde vamos a la Calle Ocho. _____
8. El español es un idioma difícil. _____
9. ¡Perfecto! Nos vemos el sábado. _____

¿Lo sabía Ud.?

Cuando los hispanos dan (*give*) una dirección, usan primero la palabra **calle** o **avenida,** luego (*then*) dan el nombre de la calle o avenida y luego el número: Calle Quinta # 120.

◆ Además (*Besides*) de la palabra "*street*", ¿qué otras palabras usan en este país cuando dan una dirección?

 Hablemos. With a partner, take turns asking and answering the following questions. Base your answers on the dialogues and on your own circumstances.

En el diálogo	¿Y tú?
1. ¿Gloria es cubanoamericana?	¿Tú eres norteamericano(a)?
2. ¿A qué hora es la clase de inglés?	¿A qué hora es la clase de español?
3. ¿Julio y Olga estudian esta noche?	¿Dónde estudias tú?
4. ¿Julio trabaja en el hospital por la mañana o por la noche?	¿Cuándo trabajas tú?
5. ¿Cuántas clases toma Julio?	¿Cuántas clases tomas tú?
6. ¿Qué necesita Julio?	¿Tú necesitas más tiempo o más dinero?
7. ¿Cuál es la dirección de Gloria?	¿Cuál es tu dirección?
8. ¿Gloria habla otros idiomas?	¿Tú hablas otros idiomas o solamente (*only*) inglés?

Vocabulario

Improve Your Grade
Audio Flashcards

Cognados

americano(-a), norteamericano(-a)
American, North American
cubano(-a) Cuban
el hospital hospital

la idea idea
el italiano Italian (*language*)
perfecto(-a) perfect
el portugués Portuguese (*language*)

Nombres

la biblioteca library
la calle street
la casa house
la chica, la muchacha young woman, girl
el chico, el muchacho young man, boy
el chino Chinese (*language*)
el dinero money
la dirección, el domicilio address
el español Spanish (*language*)

el francés French (*language*)
la hora time (*of day*)
el idioma, la lengua language
el inglés English (*language*)
la mochila backpack
la noche evening, night
la tarde afternoon
el tiempo time

Verbos

anotar to write down
conversar, platicar to talk, to converse
estudiar to study
hablar to speak

necesitar to need
practicar to practice
tomar to take (*e.g., classes*)
trabajar to work

Adjetivos

difícil difficult
fácil easy
otro(-a) other, another
primero(-a) first

a at	**por la noche** in the evening, at night
¡caramba! gee!	**por la tarde** in the afternoon
¿Cómo se dice...?[1] How does one say . . . ?	**¿Qué hora es?** What time is it?
conmigo with me	**Se dice...** One says . . .
¿cuándo? when?	**también** also, too
en ese caso in that case	**tarde** late
¿en serio? seriously?	**todos los días** every day
esta noche tonight	**un poco (de)** a little
más more	**Vamos.** Let's go.
para in order to	
por la mañana in the morning	

Vocabulario adicional

Vocabulario para la clase

LEARNING TIP

You may want to rewrite the words that you're learning in a way that they appear grouped or rearranged under specific categories or themes. For instance, words about the classroom (**la mochila, la ventana, el escritorio, la computadora**, etc.), parts of the day (**la tarde, la noche**), languages (**el español, el francés, el chino**), adjectives of nationality [**español(-a), francés(-esa), chino(-a)**], etc. Write down all thematically related words under the specific core theme or category of meaning (semantic field).

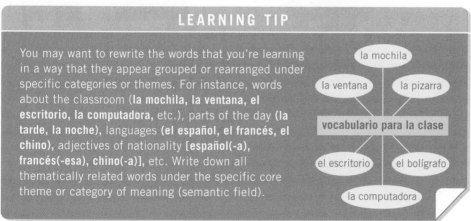

---

[1]**¿Qué quiere decir __?** *What does __ mean?*

Práctica

A. Match the questions in column A with the responses in column B.

A		B
1. ¿Qué hora es? _____		**a.** En la biblioteca o en mi casa.
2. ¿A qué hora es la clase de español? _____		**b.** No, ¡es fácil!
3. ¿Dónde estudiamos esta noche? _____		**c.** No, cubana.
4. ¿Trabajan por la mañana? _____		**d.** Inglés, francés y un poco de portugués.
5. ¿Es norteamericana? _____		**e.** La dirección de Marcelo.
6. ¿El italiano es difícil? _____		**f.** Son las dos y cuarto.
7. ¿Qué idiomas hablan? _____		**g.** ¡Sí, todos los días!
8. ¿Qué anotas? _____		**h.** El sábado.
9. ¿Practicas el español? _____		**i.** A las tres.
10. ¿Cuándo nos vemos? _____		**j.** No, por la noche.

B. Review the words referring to people and objects you see in the classroom, then name the numbered items below.

C. Complete the following sentences, using appropriate vocabulary.

1. Mi domicilio es: _____ Ocho, número 98.
2. Sandra es una _____ americana y Julio es un _____ de El Salvador.
3. El chino es un _____ muy difícil.
4. ¿Cómo se _____ *backpack* en español?
5. ¿Tú necesitas _____ tiempo para _____? ¡Yo también!
6. Sandra y Gloria _____ en la clase.
7. Julio _____ cinco clases.
8. ¿Tú hablas cinco idiomas? ¡Caramba! ¿En _____?

Para conversar

A. Para conocernos mejor You need to complete the following card with information about a classmate. First write the questions that would elicit the appropriate information. Then interview someone in your class and fill out the card. You may also ask additional questions.

> *Mi compañero se llama* _____
>
> *Es de* _____
>
> *Dirección:* _____
>
> *Número de teléfono:* _____
>
> *Trabaja en* _____

B. Una escuelita (*A little school*) With a partner, play the roles of two people who are in charge of opening a small school for about 50 children. Take turns saying what you need for two classrooms (**Necesitamos...**).

Pronunciación

A. The Spanish *i*

The Spanish **i** is pronounced like the double *e* in the English word *see*. Listen to your teacher and repeat the following sentences.

> El chino es difícil.
>
> El inglés es fácil.
>
> Es el domicilio de Mimí.

B. The Spanish *o*

The Spanish **o** is a short, pure vowel. It corresponds to the *o* in the English word *no*, but without the glide. Listen to your teacher and repeat the following sentences.

> Yo no tomo.
>
> Trabajo con Rodolfo.
>
> Hablo un poco de chino.

C. The Spanish *u*

The Spanish **u** is shorter in length than the English *u*. It corresponds to the *ue* sound in the English word *Sue*. Listen to your teacher and repeat the following sentences.

> Mucho gusto, Julio.
>
> Laura usa uniforme.
>
> Estudia en la universidad.

Aspectos culturales

En imágenes (*Estudios superiores[1] en diversas partes del mundo hispano*)

▲ Oaxaca, México

▲ Lima, Perú

Although Spanish is not recognized as an official language in the United States, there is a very large number of Spanish-speaking Americans. For that reason, we include **Estados Unidos** on our map.

Ubíquese... y búsquelo

Improve Your Grade
Web Search

Gloria and Julio are going to Calle Ocho after their study date. You have some extra time to stroll around. Go to **www.cengage.com/highered** to familiarize yourself with this area. What section of Miami are you exploring? What are some of the sights or landmarks that you pass? What would you like to do or see with Gloria and Julio while you are there? In the next class, team up with two classmates to discuss your findings.

---

[1]**superiores** = *higher*

▲ Sevilla, España

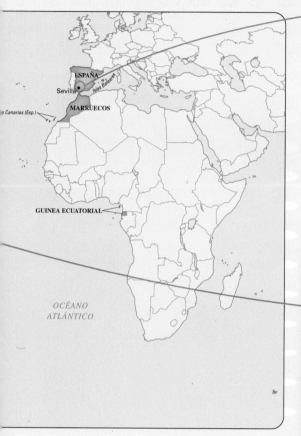

▲ Río Piedras, Puerto Rico

Welcome to:
calle ocho
Kiwanis of Little Havana

Estructuras

1. Gender and number (*Género y número*)

A. Gender

- In Spanish, all nouns—including those denoting non-living things—are either masculine or feminine.
- Most nouns that end in **-o** are masculine, while most nouns that end in **-a** are feminine.

▲ el escritorio

▲ la silla

▲ el libro

▲ la ventana

- Nouns that denote males are masculine and nouns that denote females are feminine.

▲ el hombre

▲ la mujer

> **¡Atención!** Some common exceptions include the words **el día** (*day*) and **el mapa** (*map*), which end in **-a** but are masculine, and the word **la mano** (*hand*), which ends in **-o** but is feminine.

Here are some helpful rules to remember about gender.

- Some masculine names ending in **-o** have a corresponding feminine form ending in **-a: el secretario/la secretaria.**

- When a masculine noun ends in a consonant, the corresponding feminine noun is often formed by adding **-a: el profesor/la profesora.**

- Many nouns that refer to people use the same form for both genders; **el estudiante/la estudiante.** In such cases, gender is indicated by the article **el** (masculine) or **la** (feminine).

- Nouns ending in **-sión, -ción, -tad, -dad,** and **-umbre** are feminine.

la televisión *television*	**la conversación** *conversation*
la libertad *liberty, freedom*	**la universidad** *university*
la muchedumbre *crowd*	

◆ Many words that end in **-ma** are masculine.[1]

el poema *poem*
el programa *program*
el sistema *system*
el idioma *language*
el problema *problem*
el tema *subject, theme*

◆ You must learn the gender of nouns that have other endings and that do not refer to male or female beings.

la pared *wall*
el lápiz *pencil*
el borrador *eraser*
el reloj *clock, watch*
la luz *light*

Práctica

ACE the Test

Place **el**[2] or **la**[2] before each noun.

____ mapa	____ lección	____ sociedad	____ mano
____ ciudad	____ pizarra	____ idioma	____ luz
____ poema	____ marcador	____ hombre	____ libro
____ señor	____ mujer	____ día	____ papel
____ doctora	____ libertad	____ secretario	____ pared
____ papel	____ silla	____ profesor	____ certidumbre (*certainty*)
____ dirección	____ calle	____ español	____ tarde

B. Plural forms

◆ The plural of nouns is formed by adding **-s** to words ending in a vowel and **-es** to words ending in a consonant.

señor**a** → señora**s**   relo**j** → reloj**es**
sill**a** → silla**s**   borrado**r** → borrador**es**
libr**o** → libro**s**   lecció**n** → leccion**es**

¡Atención!   Note that the plural form of **lección** does not have a written accent. See Appendix A.

◆ When a noun ends in **-z,** change the **-z** to **c** and add **-es.**

lápi**z** → lápi**ces**
lu**z** → lu**ces**

◆ When the plural is used to refer to two or more nouns of different genders, the masculine form is used.

dos secretari**as** y un secretari**o** → tres secretari**os**

---

[1]Some feminine words end in **-ma,** such as **la cama** (*bed*) and **la rama** (*branch*).
[2]**el** = *the* (*masc.*); **la** = the (*fem.*)

ACE the Test

Práctica

Write how many items there are in each picture.

1. _____   2. _____   3. _____

4. _____   5. _____   6. _____

2. Definite and indefinite articles (*Artículos determinados e indeterminados*)

A. The definite article

◆ Spanish has four forms that are equivalent to the English definite article *the*.

	Masculine	Feminine	English
Singular	el	la	*the*
Plural	los	las	

el profesor   **los** profesores
la profesora   **las** profesoras
el lápiz   **los** lápices

B. The indefinite article

◆ The Spanish equivalents of *a (an)* and *some* are as follows.

	Masculine	Feminine	English
Singular	un	una	*a (an)*
Plural	unos	unas	*some*

un libro   **unos** libros
una silla   **unas** sillas
un profesor   **unos** profesores

Práctica

A. **¿Qué es?** Identify the following objects or people using the appropriate definite article.

ACE the Test

1. _____

2. _____

3. _____

cos x dx=sinx+C

4. _____

La Habana
N
O   E
S
CUBA
Cuba   Santiago

5. _____

6. _____

◆ MODELO: —¿Hay un cuaderno?
—No, pero hay un libro.

1.　　　　　　　　2.　　　　　　　　3.

4.　　　　　　　　5.　　　　　　　　6.　　　　　　　　7.

 C. With a partner, take turns saying what you need and what you do not need. Use the appropriate indefinite article.

◆ MODELO: *Yo necesito un lápiz.* or
Yo no necesito un libro.

┌ Para conversar ─────────────────

 ¿Qué hay en tu mochila? Identify six or seven students who have backpacks, and have three or four students join each one. These people will take turns asking the student with the backpack whether or not there are certain items in it. For each item mentioned, he/she will say **"sí"**, and show it or simply say **"no"**.

◆ MODELO: *¿Hay una pluma en tu mochila?*

3. Cardinal numbers 31–100 (*Números cardinales 31–100*)

31 **treinta y uno**	53 **cincuenta y tres**	80 **ochenta**
32 **treinta y dos** (*and so on*)	60 **sesenta**	84 **ochenta y cuatro**
40 **cuarenta**	68 **sesenta y ocho**	90 **noventa**
41 **cuarenta y uno** (*and so on*)	70 **setenta**	95 **noventa y cinco**
50 **cincuenta**	77 **setenta y siete**	100 **cien (ciento)**

◆ Note that **y** appears only in numbers between 16 and 99.

 Un dicho

Más vale pájaro en mano que cien volando.

Equivalent: A bird in the hand is worth two in the bush.

LEARNING TIP

Count from 30 to 100 first by twos, then by fives, and by tens.

Práctica

ACE the Test

 When saying phone numbers, people in many Spanish-speaking countries tend to say the first number alone and the rest of the numbers in pairs. Using this system, give the names and phone numbers of the specialists the following people would call for each situation.

1. Your nephew has a bad case of acne.
2. Mrs. Vega thinks she is pregnant.
3. Your grandmother has blurred vision.
4. Your friend's child is sick.
5. Your neighbor has frequent chest pains.

ESPECIALISTAS

Cardiólogos	342-7859
Barrios, Gustavo	561-6294
Martínez, Cristina	
Dermatólogos	402-4180
Carreras, José	829-3785
Rivas, Francisco	
Ginecólogos	607-5391
García, Rosaura M.	243-7160
Torres, Marcelo	
Oftalmólogos	750-4538
López, Arnaldo	962-6875
Ugarte, Eloísa	
Pediatras	806-9952
Méndez, Carolina	693-4931
Rodríguez, Estela	

Para conversar

 ¿Cuánto necesitamos? (*How much do we need?*) You and your partner are in charge of buying school supplies. See what items you need and how much each item costs. First give the price of each item and then take turns indicating how much money you need to buy the items.

◆ **MODELO:** —¿Cuánto necesitamos?
—Necesitamos 75 *dólares para comprar tres mapas.*

Artículos	Precio	Total
3 mapas	$25,00	
40 bolígrafos	$1,50	
200 (doscientos) marcadores	$0,50	
45 borradores	$2,00	
2 tablillas de anuncios	$34,00	
10 cestos de papeles	$3,50	
4 relojes	$10,00	
83 cuadernos	$1,00	

4. Telling time (*La hora*)

◆ To ask what time it is, say, **"¿Qué hora es?"** To tell the time in Spanish, the following word order is used.

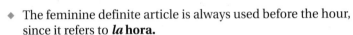

| **Es la** or **Son las** | + | *hour* | + | **y** or **menos** | + | *minutes* |

◆ **Es** is used with **una.**
   Es la una.

◆ **Son** is used with all the other hours.
   Son las cuatro.

◆ The feminine definite article is always used before the hour, since it refers to *la* **hora.**
   Es **la** una y media.
   Son **las** diez y cuarto.

◆ The hour is given first, then the minutes.
   Son las **once** menos **veinte.**

◆ The equivalent of *past* or *after* is **y.**
   Es la una **y** veinticinco.

◆ The equivalent of *to* or *till* is **menos.** It is used with fractions of time up to a half hour.[1]
   Son las ocho **menos** cinco.

¡Atención!   The equivalent of *at* + *time* is **a** + **la(s)** + *time.*

—¿Qué hora es?   *"What time is it?"*
—Son las dos y cuarto.   *"It's a quarter past two."*
—¿A qué hora es la clase?   *"What time is the class?"*
—La clase es a las dos y media. *"The class is at two-thirty."*

◆ To specify whether the time is A.M. or P.M., use **de la mañana, de la tarde,** or **de la noche,** respectively.

—¿La clase es a las 8 **de la mañana?**   *"Is the class at 8 A.M.?"*
—No, ¡es a las 8 **de la noche!**   *"No, it's at 8 P.M.!"*

◆ To indicate that an activity takes place at an undefined time in the morning or in the afternoon, use **por la mañana, por la tarde,** or **por la noche,** respectively.

—¿Estudiamos **por la mañana?**   *"Shall we study in the morning?"*
—No, **por la tarde.**   *"No, in the afternoon."*

---

[1]It is becoming increasingly popular to substitute **y quince** for **y cuarto, y treinta** for **y media,** and **y treinta y cinco, y cuarenta,** etc., for **menos veinticinco, menos veinte,** and so on.

A. With a partner, take turns giving the time indicated on the clocks in the illustration. Start with clock number one.

¿Lo sabía Ud.? Para los horarios (*schedules*) de aviones (*planes*), autobuses, trenes, televisión y algunas (*some*) invitaciones, se usa el sistema de 24 horas. Por ejemplo, las cuatro de la tarde son las dieciséis horas.

◆ **¿Se usa el sistema de 24 horas en este país?**

B. Un mensaje telefónico Based on the information provided in the phone message, complete the statements next to it.

1. El mensaje es para _____.
2. El Sr. Vega trabaja en el _____.
3. El mensaje es de parte de[1] _____.
4. El Sr. Ibarra trabaja para el _____.
5. El número de teléfono del hotel es el _____.
6. El mensaje es: _____.
7. El Sr. Ibarra llamó (*called*) a las _____ de la _____ del _____, 24.
8. En el hotel hay problemas con _____.

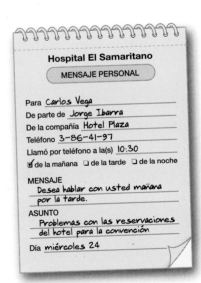

Hospital El Samaritano

MENSAJE PERSONAL

Para Carlos Vega
De parte de Jorge Ibarra
De la compañía Hotel Plaza
Teléfono 3-86-41-97
Llamó por teléfono a la(s) 10:30
☑ de la mañana ☐ de la tarde ☐ de la noche

MENSAJE
Desea hablar con usted mañana por la tarde.

ASUNTO
Problemas con las reservaciones del hotel para la convención

Día miércoles 24

---

[1]**de parte de** = *person who is calling*

C. With a partner, take turns asking each other what time the programs in the listing are on and what programs are on at different times.

◆ **MODELO:** —¿*A qué hora es "Telediario"?*
    —*Es a las seis.*

    —¿*Qué hay a las seis?*
    —*"Telediario."*

Programación del Canal 36

Viernes _____

6:00	Telediario	**9:00**	Noticiero Televisa
6:50	Noticias Internacionales	**9:30**	Música
7:00	Religión	**10:00**	Fútbol
7:30	Música Latina	**11:00**	Noticias de última hora
8:00	"María" (Telenovela)		

┌Para conversar

A. **Horario de clases** This is María Elena's schedule. With a classmate, try to figure out when her classes are.

◆ **MODELO:** —¿*Cuándo es la clase de tenis?*
    —*La clase de tenis es los sábados.*
    —¿*A qué hora?*
    —*A las nueve.*

HORA	LUNES	MARTES	MIÉRCOLES	JUEVES	VIERNES	SÁBADO
8:00–9:00	Psicología		Psicología		Psicología	
9:00–10:00	Biología		Biología		Biología	Tenis
10:00–11:30		Historia		Historia		
12:15–1:00			ALMUERZO²			
1:00–2:00	Literatura		Literatura		Literatura	Laboratorio de Biología
5:00–6:30		Educación Física		Educación Física		
7:00–8:30	Arte		Arte			

B. **Mi horario** With the help of a dictionary and/or your instructor, work with a classmate to make up each other's schedules.

---

²**almuerzo** = *lunch*

5. Present indicative of regular -ar verbs (*Presente de indicativo de los verbos regulares terminados en -ar*)

- Spanish verbs are classified in three main patterns of conjugation, according to the infinitive ending. The three infinitive endings are **-ar, -er,** and **-ir.**

hablar *to speak*

Singular

yo	habl**o**	Yo **hablo** español.	*I speak Spanish.*
tú	habl**as**	Tú **hablas** francés.	*You (inf.) speak French.*
Ud.	habl**a**	Ud. **habla** alemán.	*You (form.) speak German.*
él	habl**a**	Él **habla** italiano.	*He speaks Italian.*
ella	habl**a**	Ella **habla** portugués.	*She speaks Portuguese.*

Plural

nosotros(-as)	habl**amos**	Nosotros **hablamos** español.	*We speak Spanish.*
vosotros(-as)	habl**áis**	Vosotros **habláis** francés.	*You (inf.) speak French.*
Uds.	habl**an**	Uds. **hablan** alemán.	*You (form.) speak German.*
ellos	habl**an**	Ellos **hablan** italiano.	*They (masc.) speak Italian.*
ellas	habl**an**	Ellas **hablan** portugués.	*They (fem.) speak Portuguese.*

—¿Qué idiomas **hablas?**   *"What languages do you speak?"*
—Yo **hablo** inglés y español.   *"I speak English and Spanish."*
—¿Y Pierre?   *"And Pierre?"*
—Él **habla** francés.   *"He speaks French."*

- Regular verbs ending in **-ar** are all conjugated as **hablar** in the chart. Some other common **-ar** verbs are:

desear *to want, wish*
estudiar *to study*
tomar *to take*
necesitar *to need*
regresar *to return*
trabajar *to work*

—¿Uds. **estudian** por la noche?   *"Do you study in the evening?"*
—No, nosotros **estudiamos** por la tarde.   *"No, we study in the afternoon."*

—¿Qué **necesitas** tú?   *"What do you need?"*
—Yo **necesito** un libro.   *"I need a book."*

¡Atención! Notice that the verb forms for **Ud., él,** and **ella** are the same. In addition, **Uds., ellos,** and **ellas** share common verb forms. This is true for all verbs in all tenses.

- The infinitive of Spanish verbs consists of a stem (such as **habl-**) and an ending (such as **-ar**).

- The stem **habl-** does not change. The endings change with the subject.

> **LEARNING TIP**
>
> In Lesson 1 you were introduced to the verb **ser**. Realize now that the **-ar** verbs *conjugate* those same persons (**yo, tú/Ud.,** and **él/ella**) and number (the singular or plural forms of each person). In fact, all verbal tenses in Spanish (present, past, future) conjugate according to the very same categories: person and number.

- The Spanish present tense is equivalent to three English forms.

Yo **hablo** inglés.

> I speak English.
> I do speak English.
> I am speaking English.

- Because the verb endings indicate who is performing the action, the subject pronouns are frequently omitted.

Necesito un lápiz.	I need a pencil.
Estudiamos inglés.	We study English.
Hoy **trabajo.**	I work today.

- Subject pronouns can, however, be used for emphasis or clarification.

—¿**Ellos** hablan inglés?   *"Do they speak English?"*
—**Ella** habla inglés y **él** habla   *"She speaks English, and he speaks*
    alemán.   *German."*

- In Spanish, as in English, when two verbs are used together, the second verb remains in the infinitive.

—¿Con quién necesita **hablar** Ud.?   *"With whom do you need to speak?"*
—Necesito **hablar** con el Sr. Vega.   *"I need to speak with Mr. Vega."*

¿Lo sabía Ud.?

El español es el idioma vernáculo (*native*) de más de 430.000.000[1] de personas.

- ¿Cuántas personas cree Ud. que hablan inglés en el mundo (*world*)?

ACE the Test

Práctica

iLrn

A. Complete the following dialogues, using the present indicative of the verbs given. Then act them out with a partner.

1. estudiar
   —¿Qué _____ Uds.?
   —_____ chino.

2. trabajar
   —¿Tú _____ en el hospital por la noche?
   —No, _____ por la tarde.

3. regresar
   —¿Cuándo _____ Uds.?
   —Yo _____ el lunes y Jorge _____ el miércoles.

iLrn   **Un dicho**

El trabajo dignifica.

Work dignifies.

---

[1]*430 millions.* Note that, in Spanish numbers, a period is used instead of a comma to indicate thousands.

4. practicar

—¿Uds. _____ el español todos los días?

—No.

5. hablar

—¿Qué idioma _____ ellos?

—Carlos _____ español y Michele _____ francés.

—¿Cuántos idiomas _____ tú?

_____ tres: español, italiano y portugués.

6. necesitar

—¿Qué _____ Uds.?

—_____ unos marcadores.

7. tomar

—¿Cuántas clases _____ Ud.?

—Yo _____ cinco clases.

8. llegar

—¿A qué hora _____ a tu casa (*home*)?

—Yo _____ a las ocho de la noche.

9. anotar

—¿Qué _____ tú?

—_____ la dirección de Eva.

B. What language do these people speak?

1. Jean-Pierre, que (*who*) es de París.

2. Mao, que enseña (*teaches*) en la Universidad de Beijing.

3. María Mercedes, que trabaja en la Pequeña Habana.

4. Vittorino y Gina, que estudian en Florencia.

5. Carolyn, que es de Toronto, Canadá.

6. João, que trabaja en Río de Janeiro, Brasil.

C. With a partner, talk about what is going on in these drawings, using the subject pronouns given and the verbs **trabajar, hablar, necesitar, regresar, tomar,** and **estudiar.**

1.

2.

3.
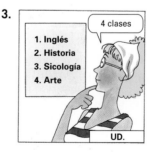

4.

5.

6.

A. Dos estudiantes conversan. With a partner, take turns asking and answering the following questions.

1. ¿Dónde trabajas? ¿Qué días trabajas?
2. ¿Qué idiomas hablas tú?
3. ¿Qué idioma estudias? ¿Te gusta? ¿Es fácil o difícil?
4. ¿Estudias por la mañana, por la tarde o por la noche? ¿Cuántas horas (*hours*) estudias?
5. ¿Qué necesitas? ¿Cuánto dinero necesitas?
6. ¿A qué hora llegas (*do you arrive*) a la universidad?

B. Now each student will share some information about his/her partner with the rest of the class.

6. Negative and interrogative sentences (*Oraciones negativas e interrogativas*)

A. Negative sentences

◆ To make a sentence negative, simply place the word **no** in front of the verb.

Yo trabajo en el hospital.	*I work at the hospital.*
Yo **no** trabajo en el hospital.	*I don't work at the hospital.*
Ella habla inglés.	*She speaks English.*
Ella **no** habla inglés.	*She doesn't speak English.*

◆ If the answer to a question is negative, the word **no** will appear twice: at the beginning of the sentence, as in English, and in front of the verb.

—¿Habla Ud. español?	*"Do you speak Spanish?"*
—**No,** yo **no** hablo español.	*"No, I don't speak Spanish."*

The subject pronoun may be omitted.

—No, no hablo español.	*"No, I don't speak Spanish."*

  El saber no ocupa lugar.

Equivalent: One can never know too much.

B. Interrogative sentences

◆ In Spanish, there are several ways of asking a question to elicit a *yes* or *no* answer.

¿**Ud.** habla español?	
¿Habla **Ud.** español?	**Sí**, yo hablo español.
¿Habla español **Ud.**?	

◆ These three questions ask for the same information and have the same meaning. The subject may be placed at the beginning of the sentence, after the verb, or at the end of the sentence.

◆ Note that written questions in Spanish begin with an inverted question mark.

◆ Another common way to ask a question in Spanish is to add tag questions such as **¿no?** and **¿verdad?** at the end of a statement.

Ud. habla español, **¿verdad?**   *You speak Spanish, don't you?*

◆ Questions that ask for information begin with an interrogative word, and the verb, not the subject, is placed after the interrogative word.

¿Dónde **trabajas** tú?	*Where do you work?*
¿Cuándo **regresan** ellos?	*When do they return?*
¿Qué **necesita** Ud.?	*What do you need?*
¿Quién **es** el profesor?	*Who is the professor?*

¡Atención! Spanish does not use an auxiliary verb, such as *do* or *does,* in negative or interrogative sentences.

Práctica

ACE the Test

A. Write the questions that will elicit each of the following answers.

1. —_____
   —Sí, nosotros estudiamos inglés.

2. —_____
   —No, yo no trabajo en el hospital hoy.

3. —_____
   —Somos de Colombia.

4. —_____
   —No, nosotros no hablamos francés.

5. —_____
   —Ellos necesitan los bolígrafos.

6. —_____
   —Ella trabaja en la universidad.

7. —_____
   —Carlos regresa a las ocho de la noche.

8. —_____
   —No, no soy profesora.

B. With a partner, take turns answering the following questions in the negative.

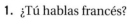
1. ¿Tú hablas francés?
2. ¿Tú trabajas en un hospital? ¿Trabajas en la universidad?
3. ¿Tú necesitas el libro de español?
4. ¿Tú regresas a la clase a las cinco?
5. ¿Tú estudias por la noche? ¿Estudias mucho?
6. ¿Tú eres de Madrid?

Un nuevo amigo With a partner, work together to formulate ten questions about the following information on David.

▲ David Rojas

Yo soy cubanoamericano y estudio en la Universidad Internacional de la Florida. Tomo cuatro clases por la mañana, trabajo por la tarde y estudio por la noche; los sábados y los domingos no trabajo.

Hablo tres idiomas: español, inglés y un poco de francés, y ahora deseo estudiar portugués. Trabajo mucho porque necesito dinero.

HINT: Be aware of these interrogative words.

¿Dónde? (*Where?*)
¿Qué? (*What?*)
¿Cuándo? (*When?*)
¿Cuántos(-as)? (*How many?*)
¿Quién(-es)? (*Who?*)
¿Por qué? (*Why?*) (porque = *because*)

Some of the questions may require a "yes" or "no" answer. After completing the questions, join another group to ask your questions and answer theirs.

7. Possession with *de* (*El caso posesivo*)

◆ The **de** + *noun* construction is used to express possession or relationship. Spanish does *not* use the apostrophe.

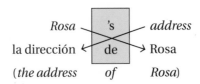

la clase **de la Dra. Peña**   *Dr. Peña's class*
el libro **de Dora**   *Dora's book*

¡Atención! Note the use of the definite article before the words **dirección, clase,** and **libro.**

—¿Quién es Francisco Acosta?   *"Who is Francisco Acosta?"*
—Es **el profesor de Carmen.**   *"He is Carmen's professor."*

—¿Cuál es **la dirección de Irene?**   *"What is Irene's address?"*
—Calle Magdalena, número seis.   *"Six Magdalena Street."*

◀ Una fotografía de Nora, **la hermana** (*sister*) **de Gloria.**

Práctica

ACE the Test

 With a partner, look carefully at the illustrations and then take turns answering the questions that follow.

1.

2.

3.

4.

5.

6.

1. ¿Quiénes son las amigas de Sergio?
2. ¿Qué necesita Olga?
3. ¿Qué necesita Luis?
4. ¿Quién es el Sr. Soto?
5. ¿Quién es de Cuba?
6. ¿Quiénes son Pedro y José?

Para conversar

 ¿Lo necesita o no? (*Do you need it or not?*) Take turns asking other members of the class if they need certain things.

◆ **MODELO:** —*Marta, ¿tú necesitas el libro de Raúl?*
—*Sí, yo necesito el libro de Raúl. (No, yo no necesito el libro de Raúl.)*

 **Un dicho**

En casa del herrero, cuchillo de palo.

Equivalent: The shoemaker's son always goes barefoot.

Así somos

Estrategia **Listening for specifics and guessing intelligently** Often when listening, you have specific information in mind that you want to know or that you expect to hear. Concentrating on these specifics helps your understanding and allows you to "discard" unrelated information. For example, if your Spanish-speaking housemate wants you to buy some things on your way home, you automatically listen for the items you need to buy. If he or she asks you to pick up **café, pan, leche y huevos,** by guessing intelligently you know you're expected to buy **leche** and **huevos** even if you aren't sure what they are.

Necesitamos muchas cosas Julio and Carmen need to make some classroom-related purchases. Listen to their conversation and mark only the items they need to buy. Read the list before listening. If you hear an unknown word, make an intelligent guess about it.

____ tablilla de anuncios	____ tiza
____ cesto de papeles	____ calculadora
____ mochila	____ carpetas
____ reloj	____ sacapuntas
____ mapas	____ bolígrafos
____ archivo	____ pizarras

Al conversar...

Estrategia **Asking for repetition** Conversing is a negotiating process. Be ready to ask the person you are speaking with, for instance, to repeat whenever there's something important you didn't understand or didn't hear well. Here are some phrases you can use in these situations.

- ◆ **¿Cómo?** (*What?*) or **¿Perdón?** (*I beg your pardon?*)
- ◆ **Repite, por favor** (*informal*) or **Repita, por favor** (*formal*). (*Please repeat.*)
- ◆ **Más despacio, por favor.** (*Slower, please.*)
- ◆ **Otra vez, por favor.** (*Once more, please.*)

¿Cómo? With a partner, take turns asking about each other's classes. Find out which classes he or she takes, on what days, and who the professor is. Use the phrases you've just learned to ask for repetitions when necessary.

¿Qué dice Ud.? What would you say in the following situations? What might the other person say? Act out scenes with a partner. Take turns playing each role.

1. You ask a friend if he/she wishes to study with you in the library tonight. Ask at what time.
2. Tell a friend when you study and when you work and also the days you don't work. Ask him/her about his/her schedule.
3. Ask your professor how to say in Spanish a word that you don't know.

4. Ask a classmate what his/her address is and give him/her your phone number.
5. Ask your professor if he/she speaks other languages.
6. Your friend thinks he speaks Chinese because he can order Chinese food. Tell him that, in that case, you speak Italian.

 Para conocernos mejor To do this activity, work with a classmate whom you would like to get to know. Take turns asking each other these questions.

1. ¿Qué idiomas hablas tú? ¿Deseas estudiar otro idioma? ¿Cuál?
2. ¿Cuántas clases tomas? ¿A qué hora es tu primera clase? ¿Es una clase fácil o difícil?
3. ¿Tú estudias en la biblioteca o en tu casa? ¿Cuántas horas estudias?
4. ¿Dónde trabajas? ¿Trabajas los sábados y los domingos?
5. ¿Necesitas dinero? ¿Cuánto?
6. ¿Cuál es tu dirección? ¿Cuál es tu número de teléfono?
7. ¿Tú practicas el español todos los días? ¿Con quién? ¿Necesitas practicar más tiempo?
8. ¿Necesitas más tiempo para estudiar o para trabajar?
9. ¿Qué hora es?
10. ¿A qué hora regresas a tu casa hoy? ¿Y mañana?

 Una encuesta Interview your classmates to identify who fits the following descriptions. Include your instructor, but remember to use the **Ud.** form when addressing him/her. After finishing the survey, get together with two or three classmates and discuss the results.

Nombre

1. Trabaja en la universidad. _____
2. Trabaja los sábados. _____
3. Necesita dinero. _____
4. Estudia por la noche. _____
5. Necesita estudiar más. _____
6. Desea estudiar otro idioma. _____
7. Habla con sus amigos en la cafetería. _____
8. Regresa a su casa por la noche. _____

 Para crear In groups of three, look at this photo and use your imagination to create a story about the person in the picture. Who is he? Give him a name. Is he a student? Where is he from? Does he work? What might he be saying to the other person on the phone? In general, what's the story behind the photo?

¡Vamos a leer!

Estrategia **Guessing the meaning of unknown words** When you read you can often guess the meaning of some of the words you don't know by paying attention to the context. Look at the words surrounding the unknown word. Are there cognates, familiar words, or explanation or information that give clues to the meaning of the word? If a word seems important to the general meaning of a passage, try to make logical guesses about its meaning based on context before you consult a dictionary.

¿Qué significa? Read the following sentences and choose the definition that best fits the context.

1. El profesor Griego **enseña** ciencias políticas en la universidad.
   - **a.** learns
   - **b.** teaches
   - **c.** supervises

2. La señora Jiménez es profesora de literatura española en el departamento de **lenguas.**
   - **a.** languages
   - **b.** humanities
   - **c.** arts

3. El estudiante **ayuda** a sus amigos a estudiar para el examen de cálculo porque las matemáticas son fáciles para él.
   - **a.** helps
   - **b.** tests
   - **c.** demands

A leer

 ORGANIZACIÓN DE ESTUDIANTES HISPANOS

La profesora del año

La Dra. Isabel Junco, de La Habana, Cuba, que es profesora de Literatura Latinoamericana en el Departamento de Lenguas, acaba de publicar° un libro sobre la poesía° de José Martí.

    La Dra. Junco es una profesora excelente, admirada y respetada por todos sus estudiantes. Además° de enseñar, Isabel Junco trabaja como voluntaria en una organización dedicada a ayudar° a los refugiados° cubanos.

acaba... has just published / poetry

Besides
to helping / refugees

 Comprensión Now, as you read the article about Dra. Isabel Junco, find the answers to the following questions.

1. ¿De dónde es la Dra. Junco?
2. ¿Qué enseña? ¿En qué departamento?
3. ¿Qué acaba de publicar?
4. ¿Es una buena profesora?
5. ¿A quiénes ayuda como voluntaria?

¡Vamos a escribir!

Antes de escribir

Estrategia **Conducting and reporting an interview** To prepare an effective interview, use your knowledge of the person you plan to interview and what readers might want to know about the person or the subject the interviewee will talk about as a guide to the types of questions you ask.

- Include questions that ask for information, not just questions than can be answered yes or no.
- Prepare more questions than you think you need.
- Organize your questions in a logical sequence.
- When you write the interview, you can eliminate the least interesting responses.

 Una entrevista (*An interview*) You write a column about new students for the school paper and must interview a Spanish-speaking student for your next article. Brainstorm eight to ten questions you might ask and organize them in a logical sequence. Then, interview a Spanish-speaking student or a classmate playing the role of a Spanish speaker.

Al escribir el informe

Now write a draft (**borrador**) of your interview article. Sequence the information you obtained so that it flows smoothly and weed out any uninteresting responses. Do not include the questions.

Después de escribir

Before writing the final version of your interview, exchange your first draft with a classmate and peer edit each other's work. Use the following guidelines.

- noun-adjective and noun-article agreement (in gender and number)
- subject-verb agreement (in person and number)
- logical sequence of information

Después de leer... desde su mundo

 In small groups, talk about your favorite professor, whom you want to select as professor of the year.

Improve Your Grade
Web Search

Los cubanoamericanos

◆ Los cubanos son el 5% de los hispanos de este país, y como buena parte de ellos vinieron (*came*) por razones políticas, no económicas, son los inmigrantes hispanos más conservadores, con mayor nivel de escolaridad y mayor ingreso (*income*) per capita. Entre los más conocidos se destacan: en la política, Ileana Ros-Lehtinen, Representante al Congreso de los Estados Unidos y Mel Martínez, Senador por la Florida; en el cine, Andy García y Eva Mendes; y en la música, Jon Secada, Gloria Estefan y Celia Cruz (1925–2003), la reina (*queen*) de la salsa.

◆ En la Pequeña Habana, un barrio (*neighborhood*) cubano de la ciudad de Miami, muchos de los bancos, cafés, restaurantes, mercados y tiendas son de propiedad cubana, y el español es el idioma más hablado (*spoken*).

La política

◄ Ileana Ros-Lehtinen (1952–), primera mujer hispana elegida (*elected*) al Congreso de Estados Unidos (1989–presente)

◄ Mel Martínez, Senador por la Florida, primer senador cubanoamericano de los Estados Unidos

El entretenimiento

▲ Andy García, famoso actor cubano

▲ La bella actriz cubanoamericana, Eva Mendes, en una entrega de premios en Berlín, Alemania

▲ Jon Secada, famoso cantante

Los negocios[1]

◄ Jeff Bezos, presidente fundador (*founder*) de la empresa (*company*) Amazon

▲ Los pequeños comerciantes (*Small business sector*): Café de la Pequeña Habana

Nuestro panorama cultural

In groups of three, answer the following questions about your home state, region, or country.

1. ¿Quién es el representante de su estado (*state*) al Congreso?
2. ¿Quiénes son los senadores de su estado?
3. ¿Cuál es su actor favorito?
4. ¿Cuál es su cantante favorito(-a)?
5. ¿Conoce Ud. (*Do you know*) otros cantantes de origen cubano?
6. ¿Es popular la salsa en los Estados Unidos?
7. ¿Cuál es el grupo minoritario más numeroso en su ciudad?
8. ¿Hay algún (*any*) restaurante cubano en su ciudad?
9. ¿Cómo se llama el barrio de Ud.?
10. ¿Celebran algún festival especial en su ciudad? ¿Cuándo?

---

[1]**negocios** = *business*

Lección

3

▲ Una chica usa su teléfono celular.

Objetivos

Comunicación

You will learn vocabulary used to describe people and activities and to make and receive phone calls.

Pronunciación

Linking

Estructuras

◆ Possessive adjectives
◆ Cardinal numbers 101–1,000
◆ Descriptive adjectives: Forms, position, and agreement with articles and nouns
◆ Present indicative of regular **-er** and **-ir** verbs
◆ Present indicative of the irregular verbs **tener** and **venir**
◆ The personal **a**

Cultura

◆ Hispanics in the U.S.
◆ Answering the phone in different Spanish-speaking countries

Panorama hispánico

◆ Los puertorriqueños en los Estados Unidos

Estrategias

Listening: Taking a phone call
Speaking: Using stock phrases
Reading: Activating background knowledge
Writing: Analyzing writing models

Por teléfono

Los puertorriqueños

Los puertorriqueños son el segundo grupo más grande (*largest*) de hispanos en los Estados Unidos. Como Puerto Rico es un Estado Libre Asociado a este país, los puertorriqueños son ciudadanos estadounidenses y no necesitan pasaporte ni visa para entrar en el país.

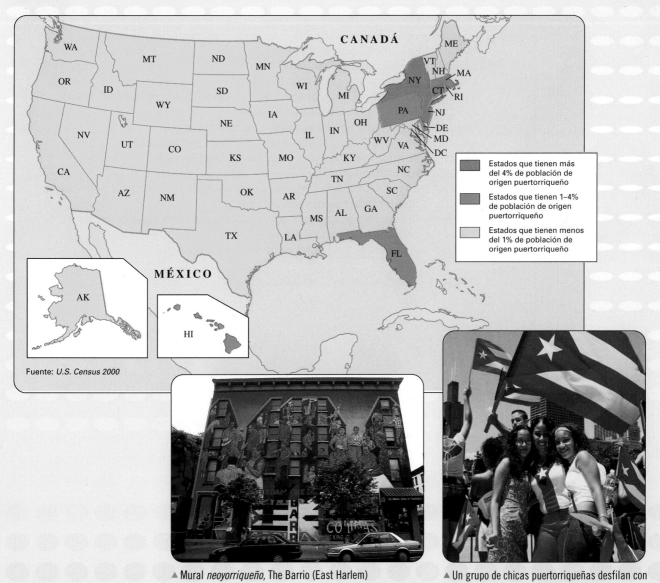

CANADÁ

WA, MT, ND, MN, OR, ID, SD, WI, MI, WY, IA, NE, IL, IN, OH, NV, UT, CO, KS, MO, KY, CA, AZ, NM, OK, AR, TN, NC, MS, AL, GA, SC, TX, LA, FL, ME, VT, NH, MA, NY, CT, RI, PA, NJ, DE, MD, DC, WV, VA

MÉXICO

AK, HI

Estados que tienen más del 4% de población de origen puertorriqueño

Estados que tienen 1–4% de población de origen puertorriqueño

Estados que tienen menos del 1% de población de origen puertorriqueño

Fuente: *U.S. Census 2000*

▲ Mural *neoyorriqueño,* The Barrio (East Harlem)

▲ Un grupo de chicas puertorriqueñas desfilan con la bandera de su país, en Chicago, Illinois.

63

Olga Carrera y su compañera de cuarto, Mariana Zayas, conversan en la sala de su apartamento mientras comen sándwiches y beben café. Las chicas viven en Nueva York, donde trabajan y asisten a la universidad de CUNY.[1] Olga es morena, alta, bonita y muy inteligente. Mariana es baja, rubia y muy simpática.

Mariana	Tengo que llenar la solicitud de empleo de la compañía Sandoval. Necesito ganar más dinero.
Olga	Pero tú no tienes conocimiento de computadoras... y no tienes la experiencia necesaria...
Mariana	¡Pero tengo problemas económicos! A ver... (*Lee el anuncio en el periódico.*) Debe hablar, leer y escribir portugués...
Olga	Tú no hablas portugués.
Mariana	Pero recibo mensajes electrónicos de mi amiga de Brasil... y no son en castellano.
Olga	Oye, el teléfono...

Al teléfono.

Mariana	Hola.
Rafael	Hola. ¿Está Mariana?
Mariana	Sí, con ella habla. ¿Rafael?
Rafael	Sí. ¿Cómo estás, Mariana?
Mariana	Más o menos. ¿Qué hay de nuevo?
Rafael	No mucho. Oye, mañana tenemos el examen parcial en la clase de historia. ¿Estudiamos esta noche?
Mariana	Sí. ¿Por qué no vienes aquí, a mi apartamento?
Rafael	Buena idea. Nos vemos a las seis. Oye... ¿está Olga?
Mariana	Sí, un momento. (*Llama a Olga.*) ¡Olga! ¡Tu novio!
Olga	¿Qué tal, mi amor?
Rafael	Bien. Oye, mi vida... Mariana y yo tenemos que estudiar, pero después... ¿deseas beber algo en el café París?
Olga	Bueno... tengo que escribir un informe para mi clase de literatura, pero... ¡acepto tu invitación! ¡Chau!
Mariana	¡Ajá! ¡Con razón Rafael viene a estudiar conmigo!

Después de estudiar, Rafael lleva a Olga y a Mariana a tomar algo.

¿Lo sabía Ud.?

Contestando el teléfono (*Answering the phone*):
En España (*Spain*): "Diga", "Dígame", "¿Sí?"
En Cuba y en otras regiones del Caribe: "Oigo"
En México: "Bueno"
En Argentina: "¿Sí?", "Hable", "Hola", "Aló"

♦ ¿Cómo se contesta el teléfono en este país (*this country*)?

---

[1]**CUNY** = *City University of New York*

Mariana

Olga

Rafael

ACE the Test

 ¿Quién lo dice?   Identify the person who said the following in the dialogues.

1. Oye, mañana tenemos el examen parcial en la clase de historia   _____
2. Pero recibo mensajes electrónicos de mi amiga de Brasil.   _____
3. ¡Acepto tu invitación!   _____
4. Pero tú no tienes conocimiento de computadoras.   _____
5. Tengo que llenar la solicitud de empleo de la compañía Sandoval.   _____
6. Buena idea. Nos vemos a las seis. Oye… ¿está Olga?   _____
7. ¿Deseas beber algo en el café París?   _____
8. Tú no hablas portugués.   _____
9. ¡Ajá! ¡Con razón Rafael viene a estudiar conmigo!   _____

¿Lo sabía Ud.?

"Español" y "castellano" son equivalentes.

◆ ¿Hay mucha diferencia entre el inglés que hablan en Inglaterra (*England*) y el que se habla en este país?

Hablemos.   With a partner, take turns asking and answering the following questions. Base your answers on the dialogue and on your own circumstances.

En el diálogo	¿Y tú?
1. ¿Quién es la compañera de cuarto de Olga?	¿Tú tienes compañero(-a) de cuarto o vives con tu familia? (Yo tengo…)
2. ¿Dónde conversan las chicas?	¿Dónde conversas tú con tus amigos?
3. ¿Cómo es Olga?[1] ¿Cómo es Mariana?	¿Cómo eres tú?
4. ¿Mariana tiene dinero o problemas económicos?	¿Ganas mucho dinero?
5. ¿Mariana tiene conocimiento de computadoras?	¿Tú tienes conocimiento de computadoras?
6. ¿Qué recibe Mariana de Brasil?	¿Recibes muchos mensajes electrónicos?
7. ¿Qué tienen Rafael y Mariana mañana?	¿Cuándo tienes examen?
8. ¿Qué tiene que escribir Olga?	¿Qué tienes que escribir tú?
9. ¿Acepta Olga la invitación de Rafael?	¿Tú recibes muchas invitaciones?
10. ¿Rafael viene o no a estudiar con Mariana?	¿Tú estudias con un(-a) amigo(-a) o estudias solo(-a)?

---

[1]*What is Olga like?*

Vocabulario

Improve Your Grade
Audio Flashcards

Cognados

el apartamento apartment	**inteligente** intelligent
el café cafe	**la invitación** invitation
la compañía company	**la literatura** literature
la computadora[1] computer	**el momento** moment
el examen exam	**necesario(-a)** necessary
la experiencia experience	**puertorriqueño(-a)** Puerto Rican
la historia history	**el sándwich** sandwich

Nombres

el anuncio, el aviso ad	**el mensaje electrónico** e-mail
el café coffee	**la novia** girlfriend
el (la) compañero(-a) de cuarto roommate	**el novio** boyfriend
el conocimiento knowledge	**el periódico, el diario** newspaper
el empleo, el trabajo job	**la sala** living room
el examen parcial midterm examination	**la solicitud** application, application form
el informe report	**— de empleo** job application

Verbos

aceptar to accept	**llamar** to call
asistir (a) to attend	**llenar** to fill out
beber, tomar to drink	**llevar** to take (*someone or something someplace*)
comer to eat	
deber must, should	**recibir** to receive
escribir to write	**tener** to have
ganar to earn	**venir** to come
leer to read	**vivir** to live

Adjetivos

alto(-a) tall
bajo(-a) short
bonito(-a), lindo(-a) pretty
económico(-a) financial
moreno(-a) dark, brunette
rubio(-a) blond(e)
simpático(-a) nice, charming

---

[1] **el ordenador** (*Spain*)

A ver... Let's see . . .
al teléfono on the phone
aquí here
beber, tomar (comer) algo to have something to drink (eat)
Con él (ella) habla. This is he (she) speaking.
con razón no wonder
después later, afterwards
¿Está... (nombre)? Is . . . (name) there?
mañana tomorrow

más o menos more or less
mi amor my love, darling
mi vida darling (my life)
mientras while
para for
por qué[1] why
por teléfono on the phone
tener que + *infinitivo* to have to + *infinitive*

Vocabulario adicional

EMPRESAS VALDÉS ▪ URB. CAPARRA ▪ SAN JUAN ▪ PR ▪ 00920

SOLICITUD DE TRABAJO

Nombre y apellidos: Nora López Rivera
(First/Last names)

Fecha de nacimiento: **Día:** 9 **Mes:** 10 **Año:** 86
(Date of birth) *(Day)* *(Month)* *(Year)*

Número de identidad: 534-78-9078
(I.D. number)

Edad: 22 años
(Age)

Dirección: Calle 5, 456 Urb. La Arboleda[2]
(Address)

Ciudad: Carolina **Zona postal:** 00979
(City) *(Zip code)*

Teléfono: 675-8902

Nacionalidad: puertorriqueña

Lugar de nacimiento: San Juan, Puerto Rico
(Place of birth)

Ciudadanía: estadounidense

Estado civil: ● Soltero(-a) ○ Casado(-a) ○ Divorciado(-a) ○ Viudo(-a)
(Marital status) *(Single)* *(Married)* *(Divorced)* *(Widowed)*

Sexo: ○ Masculino ● Femenino

Educación: **Institución:** Universidad de Río Piedras **Años:** 2003-2007
 North Jersey High **Años:** 1999-2003

Experiencia: **Compañía:** Hotel Plaza de Armas **Años:** 2007 (seis meses)

Características

amable, cortés polite, courteous
antipático(-a) unpleasant
delgado(-a) thin, slender
encantador(-a) charming
feo(-a) ugly
gordo(-a) fat

guapo(-a) handsome, good-looking
optimista[3] optimist
pelirrojo(-a) red-headed
pesimista[3] pessimist
realista[3] realist
terco(-a) stubborn

Datos personales (*Personal data*)

lugar donde trabaja place of employment
número de la licencia de conducir driver's license number
número de seguro social social security number
ocupación occupation
profesión profession

---

[1]**porque** = *because*
[2]Given that the postal system in Puerto Rico is that of the United States, there have been trends toward reversing the street name and number so as to conform to American conventions. Remember, though: this is just in the case of Puerto Rico.
[3]The ending of this kind of adjective (**-ista**) does not change, regardless of gender: **un chico optimista; una chica optimista.**

Práctica

A. Match the questions in column A with the responses in column B.

A	B
1. ¿Qué tienes que llenar? ____	**a.** En un apartamento.
2. ¿Qué beben las chicas? ____	**b.** Es viudo.
3. ¿Está Mariana? ____	**c.** No, es alto y delgado.
4. ¿Dónde viven los chicos? ____	**d.** Más o menos.
5. ¿Javier es bajo y gordo? ____	**e.** Un anuncio en el diario.
6. ¿Es simpática? ____	**f.** Con ella habla.
7. ¿Luis es soltero o casado? ____	**g.** Un informe para la clase de historia.
8. ¿Qué lees? ____	**h.** La solicitud de empleo.
9. ¿Qué tienen que escribir? ____	**i.** No, es antipática. ¡Y terca!
10. ¿Cómo estás? ____	**j.** Café.

B. Supply the items of information required, according to the personal data provided.

SOLICITUD DE EMPLEO

_____ : Ana Alicia Vega Ruiz

_____ : 13 de agosto de 1983

_____ : calle Bértoli, número 103

_____ : Ponce

_____ : puertorriqueña

_____ : San Juan, Puerto Rico

_____ : casada

_____ : femenino

_____ : Compañía Lux

C. Complete the following exchanges, using vocabulary from this lesson.

1. ¿Daniel es rubio o _____?

Es pelirrojo.

¿Es guapo?

No... es _____, pero es muy amable y simpático.

2. ¿Cuál es su _____?

Soy profesor de literatura.

3. ¿Las muchachas son de San Juan?

Sí, son _____.

4. ¿Tiene _____ de computadoras?

Un poco... pero no tiene la _____ necesaria.

D. Write the word or phrase that corresponds to the following.

1. clase en la que estudiamos a Shakespeare _____
2. empleo _____
3. beber _____
4. persona de Puerto Rico _____
5. bonita _____
6. opuesto de **moreno** _____
7. cortés _____
8. anuncio _____
9. opuesto de **pesimista** _____
10. *Folgers,* por ejemplo _____
11. tipo de mensaje que recibimos en la computadora _____
12. opuesto de **hoy** _____
13. lo que llenamos para solicitar algo (*something*) _____
14. diario _____
15. clase en la que estudiamos a Lincoln _____
16. verbo: invitar nombre: _____

Para conversar

¿Sí o no? With a partner, take turns asking each other at least six questions starting with **¿Deseas...?** or **¿Necesitas...?,** and using the vocabulary presented in this lesson as much as possible.

◆ MODELOS: *¿Deseas tomar café?*
¿Necesitas el periódico?

Pronunciación

Linking

◆ In Spanish, a final consonant is always linked with the next initial vowel sound.

Es el amigo de Rafael.

◆ When two identical consonants are together, they are pronounced as one.

Ellos son nativos.

◆ When two identical vowels are together, they are pronounced as one long vowel.

¿Está Ana Acosta?

◆ The final vowel of one word is linked with the initial vowel of the following word to form one syllable.

La amiga de Olga es rubia.

Aspectos culturales

En imágenes (*Las telecomunicaciones*)

▲ Teléfonos públicos en una ciudad hispana

▲ Una estudiante del Maine Community College habla por teléfono al terminar sus clases.

Ubíquese... y búsquelo

 Improve Your Grade
Web Search

As part of an assignment for her Latin American history class, Olga has to go to the Museo del Barrio, and she has asked Mariana to accompany her. Go to **www.cengage .com/highered** to find out more about the Museo del Barrio. What kind of information or exhibits will Olga and Mariana find there? In the next class, team up with two classmates to discuss your findings.

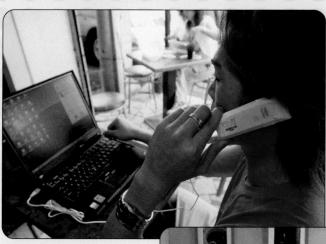

▲ Un joven usa un teléfono de Internet (Skype) y una microcomputadora.

▲ Unos estudiantes usan sus microcomputadoras en un café de Nueva York.

▲ Una estudiante universitaria usa una computadora portátil en un café de Internet.

Estructuras

1. Possessive adjectives (*Los adjetivos posesivos*)

Forms of the Possessive Adjectives		
Singular	**Plural**	
mi	mis	*my*
tu	tus	*your* (fam.)
su	sus	*your* (form.) *his* *her* *its* *their*
nuestro(-a)	nuestros(-as)	*our*
vuestro(-a)	vuestros(-as)	*your* (fam.)

◆ Possessive adjectives always precede the nouns they introduce. They agree in number with the nouns they modify.

| Yo | necesito | mi | libro. |
| | | | pluma. |

| Yo | necesito | mis | libros. |
| | | | plumas. |

◆ **Nuestro** and **vuestro** are the only possessive adjectives that have the feminine endings **-a** and **-as.** The others take the same endings for both genders.

| Nosotros | necesitamos | nuestro | libro. |
| | | nuestra | pluma. |

| Nosotros | necesitamos | nuestros | libros. |
| | | nuestras | plumas. |

◆ Possessive adjectives agree in gender with the thing possessed and *not* with the possessor. For example, two male students referring to their female professor will say *nuestra* **profesor***a*.

◆ Because **su** and **sus** each have several possible meanings, the form **de él** (or **de ella, de ellos, de ellas, de Ud.,** or **de Uds.**) can be substituted to avoid confusion. The "formula" is: *article* + *noun* + **de** + *pronoun*.

sus plumas ⟶ las plumas **de él** (**ella, Ud.,** *etc.*)
su libro ⟶ el libro **de él** (**ella, Ud.,** *etc.*)

—¿De dónde son **tus** amigos?　　　　*"Where are your friends from?"*
—**Mis** amigos son de Puerto Rico.　　*"My friends are from Puerto Rico."*

—¿Quién es la profesora **de Uds.**?　　*"Who is your professor?"*
—**Nuestra** profesora es la doctora Paz　*"Our professor is Dr. Paz."*

 **Un dicho** 　 *Mi casa es su casa.*

Práctica

A. Complete the following exchanges, using the corresponding possessive adjectives. Then act them out with a partner.

1. Raquel, ¿de dónde es _____ novio?
   _____ novio es de Caracas.
   ¿Y el novio de Marta?
   El novio _____ es de San Salvador.

2. ¿De dónde es el profesor de Uds.?
   _____ profesor es de la República Dominicana.
   ¿Y de dónde es la profesora de Uds.?
   _____ profesora es de Santiago, Chile.

3. Sr. Álvarez, ¿_____ hijos (*children*) hablan francés?
   Sí, _____ hijos hablan francés y alemán.

4. ¿Los estudiantes de Uds. estudian por la noche?
   No, _____ estudiantes estudian por la mañana.

5. ¿De dónde es _____ amiga, Srta. Burgos?
   _____ amiga es de Tegucigalpa. ¿Y de dónde son _____ amigas, Rosita?
   _____ amigas son de Cádiz.

6. ¿Las hijas (*daughters*) de Uds. trabajan?
   No, _____ hijas no trabajan.

B. Answer the following questions *in the negative*, using the appropriate possessive adjectives.

1. ¿Lorena es la novia de Alberto?
2. ¿Necesitas tu libro de español?
3. ¿La profesora de Uds. es de México?
4. ¿Carlos y Daniel son tus amigos?
5. ¿El Dr. Paz y la Dra. Ruiz son profesores de Uds.?
6. ¿Tú necesitas mis cuadernos?
7. ¿Tú necesitas la dirección de los chicos?
8. ¿Marisa y Olga son las amigas de Claudia?

Para conversar

Deseamos saber... (*We want to know . . .*) With a classmate, prepare six questions you want to ask Olga and Mariana about their apartment, their friends, their classes, etc. Some of the questions should be addressed to both of them, and some to one of them. Make sure you use the appropriate possessive adjectives.

2. Cardinal numbers 101–1,000 (*Los números cardinales 101–1.000*)

101	**ciento uno** (*and so on*)	600	**seiscientos**
200	**doscientos**	700	**setecientos**
300	**trescientos**	800	**ochocientos**
400	**cuatrocientos**	900	**novecientos**
500	**quinientos**	1.000	**mil**

- When counting beyond 100 (101 to 199), **ciento** is used.

- **Y** appears only in numbers between 16 and 99. It is not used to separate thousands, hundreds, and tens from each other: **mil quinientos ochenta y seis.**

- In Spanish, one does not count in hundreds beyond 1,000; thus, 1,100 is expressed as **mil cien.** After 1,000, thousands are counted **dos mil, tres mil,** and so on. Note that Spanish uses a period rather than a comma to indicate thousands.

—¿Cuál es su fecha de nacimiento?	*"What is the date of your birthday?"*
—El tres de abril de mil novecientos ochenta y dos.	*"April third, nineteen (hundred and) eighty-two."*

- When modifying a feminine noun, the feminine form is used: **doscientas sillas.**

- To ask how much a single item costs, say, **"¿Cuánto cuesta?"** For multiple items, use **"¿Cuánto cuestan?"**

—¿Cuánto cuesta el escritorio?	*"How much does the desk cost?"*
—Cuesta **ciento cincuenta** dólares.	*"It costs a hundred and fifty dollars."*
—¿Cuánto cuestan las ventanas?	*"How much do the windows cost?"*
—Cuestan **mil cien** dólares.	*"They cost eleven hundred dollars."*

ACE the Test

Práctica

A. Complete the following series of numbers.

1. cien, doscientos, trescientos, ... mil
2. diez mil, veinte mil, treinta mil, ... cien mil
3. ciento diez, doscientos veinte, trescientos treinta, ... mil cien

B. With a partner, look at the illustrations and ask how much each item costs.

- MODELO: —¿Cuánto cuesta la silla?
  —La silla cuesta trescientos trece dólares.

Para conversar

A. En el año... (*In the year . . .*) In groups of three, determine in which year each of the events mentioned took place.

1. Los Juegos Olímpicos de Barcelona
2. La Primera Guerra Mundial (*World War I*)
3. El descubrimiento de América
4. La independencia de los Estados Unidos
5. La Guerra Civil
6. Shakespeare publica *Romeo y Julieta.*
7. El nuevo milenio
8. La fundación de Jamestown
9. Las fechas de nacimiento de Uds. tres

B. Buscamos apartamento. (*We're looking for an apartment.*) In groups of three or four, try to figure out how much a one-room, two-room, and a three-room apartment costs. Discuss different locations.

HINT: un apartamento
- de una habitación
- de dos habitaciones
- de tres habitaciones

3. Descriptive adjectives: Forms, position, and agreement with articles and nouns (*Adjetivos calificativos: formas, posición y concordancia con artículos y nombres*)

A. Forms of adjectives

◆ Descriptive adjectives identify characteristics or qualities such as color, size, and personality. In Spanish, these adjectives agree in gender and number with the nouns they modify. Adjectives ending in **-o** are made feminine by changing the **-o** to **-a.**

el muchach**o** cuban**o**   la muchach**a** cuban**a**
el chic**o** rubi**o**   la chic**a** rubi**a**
el lápiz roj**o**   la plum**a** roj**a**

Un dicho

A palabras necias, oídos sordos.

Equivalent: Take no notice of the stupid things people say.

- Adjectives ending in **-e** or in a consonant have the same form for the masculine and the feminine.

el chico inteligent**e**	la chica inteligent**e**
el esposo feli**z**	la esposa feli**z**
el libro fáci**l**	la clase fáci**l**

- Adjectives of nationality that end in a consonant add an **-a** in the feminine.

el muchacho españo**l**	la muchacha español**a**
el señor inglé**s**	la señora ingles**a**

- Adjectives ending in **-or, -án, -ón,** or **-ín** add an **-a** in the feminine.

el alumno trabajad**or**

la alumna trabajad**ora**

the hard-working student

> **¡Atención!** Adjectives that have an accent in the last syllable of the masculine form drop it in the feminine: **inglés → inglesa.**[1]

- To form the plural, adjectives follow the same rules as nouns. Adjectives ending in a vowel add **-s**; adjectives ending in a consonant add **-es**; adjectives ending in **-z** change the **-z** to **c** and add **-es.**

norteamerican**a**	norteamerican**as**
españo**l**	español**es**
feli**z**	felic**es**

B. Position of adjectives

- Descriptive adjectives generally follow the noun.

Miguel es un chico **inteligente.**	*Miguel is an intelligent boy.*
Necesito dos plumas **rojas.**	*I need two red pens.*

- Adjectives denoting nationality always follow the noun.
El profesor **mexicano** trabaja en la universidad.

C. Agreement of articles, nouns, and adjectives

- In Spanish, the article, noun, and adjective agree in gender and number.

un muchach**o alto**	**una** muchach**a alta**
los muchach**os altos**	**las** muchach**as altas**

- When an adjective modifies two or more nouns, the plural form is used.

la sill**a** y la mes**a rojas**

- If two nouns described together are of different genders, the masculine plural form of the adjective is used.

la chic**a** mexican**a**

el chic**o** mexican**o**

la chic**a** y el chic**o** mexican**os**

---

[1]For rules on accent marks, see Appendix A.

Dos cantantes famosos

▲ El famoso cantante puertorriqueño Chayanne es un hombre muy guapo.

▲ La famosa cantante y actriz de ascendencia puertorriqueña Jennifer Lopez es una mujer muy guapa.

Práctica

ACE the Test

A. You are acquainted with these famous people. With a partner, take turns matching them with their nationalities. Be sure to make any necessary changes to the adjectives.

mexicano	norteamericano	dominicano	colombiano
español	cubano	inglés	francés

1. Margaret Thatcher y Tony Blair
2. Shakira
3. el presidente Felipe Calderón
4. Gloria Estefan y Celia Cruz
5. Julio y Enrique Iglesias
6. Hillary Swank
7. Jean Paul Sartre y Albert Camus
8. Sammy Sosa

B. With a partner, take turns asking and answering the following questions. In your answers, contradict what is stated.

◆ **MODELO:** —¿Rosaura es alta?
   —*No, es baja.*

1. ¿El novio de Adriana es rubio?
2. ¿Las mujeres son gordas?
3. ¿Los muchachos son bajos?
4. ¿La novia de Roberto es pesimista?
5. ¿La novia de Daniel es fea?
6. ¿Tú eres optimista?
7. ¿El hermano de Olga es antipático?
8. ¿Las chicas son morenas?

C. With a partner, take turns describing the following people, places or things, using as many descriptive adjectives as possible.

1. Julia Roberts
2. Antonio Banderas
3. Roseanne
4. Brad Pitt
5. tu mejor amigo(-a)
6. las chicas de la clase
7. los chicos de la clase
8. Sandra Bullock

Para conversar

A. Características Get together in groups of three or four and, with the characteristics listed for all the signs of the zodiac, decide whether or not they correspond to your personalities. Then each person in the group will think of someone he or she knows and check out that person's sign. Do the characteristics fit that person?

Aries: valientes, dinámicos, interesantes y un poco impacientes

Tauro: prácticos, pacientes, leales (*loyal*) y un poco tercos

Géminis: inteligentes, enigmáticos, no muy religiosos y un poco superficiales

Cáncer: amistosos, afectuosos, hogareños (*family oriented*) y muy sensibles

Leo: optimistas, románticos, divertidos y un poco egoístas

Virgo: inteligentes, eficientes, generosos y un poco inseguros

Libra: amables, diplomáticos, idealistas y un poco indecisos

Escorpión: valientes, leales, trabajadores y un poco sarcásticos

Sagitario: lógicos, optimistas, encantadores y un poco egoístas

Capricornio: maduros, disciplinados, trabajadores y muy reservados

Acuario: compasivos, independientes, un poco excéntricos y un poco tercos

Piscis: creativos, espirituales, compasivos y un poco indecisos

B. El hombre ideal... la mujer ideal With a classmate, list ten characteristics that make a man or a woman the ideal partner. When you have finished, join another group and compare your lists. How are they the same? How do they differ? Then each person reads one characteristic they find most important in a man or a woman (**El hombre ideal es...; La mujer ideal es...**).

4. Present indicative of regular *-er* and *-ir* verbs (*Presente de indicativo de los verbos regulares que terminan en -er y en -ir*)

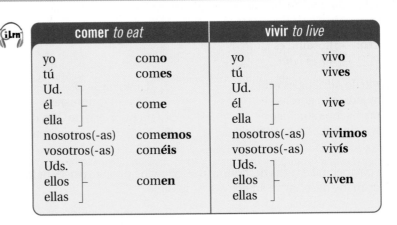

comer *to eat*		vivir *to live*	
yo	com**o**	yo	viv**o**
tú	com**es**	tú	viv**es**
Ud.		Ud.	
él	com**e**	él	viv**e**
ella		ella	
nosotros(-as)	com**emos**	nosotros(-as)	viv**imos**
vosotros(-as)	com**éis**	vosotros(-as)	viv**ís**
Uds.		Uds.	
ellos	com**en**	ellos	viv**en**
ellas		ellas	

◆ Other verbs conjugated like **comer:**

aprender *to learn*   **beber** *to drink*
creer *to believe, to think*   **vender** *to sell*
leer *to read*   **deber** *must, should*
correr *to run*

—¿Dónde **comen** ustedes?   *"Where do you eat?"*
—Eva y yo **comemos** en la cafetería   *"Eva and I eat in the cafeteria and Anabel*
  y Anabel **come** en su apartamento.   *eats in her apartment."*

—¿Tú **crees** que Marcos es simpático?   *"Do you think Marcos is nice?"*
—Sí, yo **creo** que es muy simpático.   *"Yes, I think that he's very nice."*

—¿Qué periódico **lee** Ud., señorita?   *"What newspaper do you read, miss?"*
—Yo **leo** el *New York Times.*   *"I read The New York Times."*

◆ Other verbs conjugated like **vivir:**

asistir *to attend*   **escribir** *to write*
abrir *to open*   **decidir** *to decide*
recibir *to receive*

—¿Dónde **viven** Uds.?   *"Where do you live?"*
—Nosotros **vivimos** en la calle Seis.   *"We live on Six Street."*

—¿Tú **escribes** con lápiz o con   *"Do you write with a pencil or with*
pluma?   *a pen?"*
—**Escribo** con bolígrafo.   *"I write with a ballpoint pen."*

Un proverbio   ## No sólo de pan vive el hombre.

Man does not live by bread alone.

Práctica

ACE the Test

A. In the school cafeteria, you overhear the following exchanges. You and your
partner play the roles of the people talking.

1. comer   —¿Dónde _____ ustedes los sábados?
              —Nosotros _____ en nuestra casa. ¿Dónde
              _____ tú?
              —Yo _____ en mi apartamento.

2. vivir   —¿Dónde _____ tú?
              —Yo _____ en la calle Quinta.
              —¿Y Ana y Lupe?
              —Ellas _____ en la calle Magnolia.

3. recibir   —¿Cuánto dinero _____ ustedes?
              —Yo _____ quinientos dólares y Tomás _____
              setecientos.

4. leer   —¿Qué periódico _____ ellos?
              —El *New York Times.* ¿Qué periódico _____ tú?
              —Yo _____ el *Wall Street Journal.*

5. vender   —¿Dónde _____ (ellos) sándwiches?
   creer / abrir —En el café "El Yunque", pero yo _____ que (ellos) no
              _____ hasta (*until*) las siete.

6. beber   —¿Qué _____ ustedes?
              —Nosotros _____ Coca-Cola y Celia _____ Pepsi.

7. deber   —¿Qué idioma _____ estudiar yo?
              —Usted _____ estudiar portugués.

8. escribir   —¿Ustedes _____ en inglés?
              —No, nosotros _____ en español.

9. correr   —¿Alberto _____ en el parque?
              —Sí, y yo _____ con él.

B. ¿Qué hacemos? (*What do we do?*) With a partner, complete the following sentences by describing what one or both of you do or don't do. Use regular **-er** and **-ir** verbs in your answers.

◆ MODELOS: _____ el diario por la mañana.
Yo (no) leo el diario por la mañana.
or *Nosotros (no) leemos el diario por la mañana.*

1. _____ mucho (*a lot of*) café.
2. _____ en la cafetería de la universidad.
3. _____ mucho dinero.
4. _____ a la universidad.
5. _____ en Arizona.
6. _____ estudiar más (*more*).
7. _____ español.
8. _____ en Santa Claus.
9. _____ por la mañana.
10. _____ en el cuaderno.
11. _____ la puerta de la clase.
12. _____ en un apartamento.

 Un dicho

*Debes comer para vivir,
no vivir para comer.*

You should eat to live, not live to eat.

Para conversar

A. Dime... (*Tell me . . .*) With a partner, take turns asking and answering the following questions.

1. ¿Dónde vives? ¿Vives en una casa o en un apartamento?
2. ¿Dónde comes? ¿A qué hora comes? ¿Comes con un(-a) amigo(-a) o comes solo(-a)?
3. ¿Tú y tus amigos comen sándwiches? ¿Comen comida (*food*) mexicana?
4. ¿Tú bebes Sprite o Pepsi? ¿Bebes café?
5. ¿Aprendes mucho en la clase de español? ¿Debes estudiar más?
6. ¿Tú lees periódicos en español?
7. ¿Lees bien el español?[1] ¿Escribes en español o en inglés?
8. ¿Vendes tus libros? ¿Los estudiantes reciben mucho dinero por (*for*) sus libros?
9. ¿Debes trabajar mañana o debes estudiar?
10. ¿Reciben tus amigos muchos mensajes electrónicos? ¿Y tú?

B. ¿Estás de acuerdo? (*Do you agree?*) In groups of three, express your opinion about each of the following (**Yo creo que...**). The others agree (**Estoy de acuerdo**) or disagree (**No estoy de acuerdo**).

HINT: caro = *expensive*   bueno = *good*
              barato = *inexpensive*   malo = *bad*

1. la clase de español
2. el presidente
3. Bill O'Reilly
4. París
5. Britney Spears
6. Leonardo Di Caprio
7. los profesores de la universidad
8. la universidad

---

[1]The definite article is used with names of languages except after the prepositions **en** and **de**, or after the verbs **hablar** and usually **estudiar**.

5. Present indicative of the irregular verbs *tener* and *venir*
(*Presente de indicativo de los verbos irregulares* **tener** *y* **venir**)

tener *to have*		**venir** *to come*	
yo	**tengo**	yo	**vengo**
tú	**tienes**	tú	**vienes**
Ud.		Ud.	
él	**tiene**	él	**viene**
ella		ella	
nosotros(-as)	**tenemos**	nosotros(-as)	**venimos**
vosotros(-as)	**tenéis**	vosotros(-as)	**venís**
Uds.		Uds.	
ellos	**tienen**	ellos	**vienen**
ellas		ellas	

¿Tú crees que **tengo que estudiar** más...?

—¿Cuántas clases **tienen** Uds.?　　　*"How many classes do you have?"*
—**Tenemos** dos. ¿Cuántas **tienes** tú?　*"We have two. How many do you have?"*
—Yo **tengo** cuatro.　　　　　　　　*"I have four."*

> **¡Atención!**　**Tener que** means *to have to,* and it is followed by an infinitive: Olga **tiene que trabajar** hoy. / *Olga has to work today.*

—¿A qué hora **vienen** Uds. a la universidad?　　　　　　*"What time do you come to the university?"*
—Yo **vengo** a las ocho y Teresa **viene** a las diez.　　　　*"I come at eight and Teresa comes at ten."*
—¿Las chicas **vienen** los sábados?　*"Do the girls come on Saturdays?"*
—Sí, y nosotras **venimos** con ellas.　*"Yes, and we come with them."*

Práctica

ACE the Test

A. Using the present indicative of **tener** and **venir,** as appropriate, write statements about each person by combining elements from columns A and B. Several alternatives are possible. Join one or two of your classmates and compare statements.

A	B
1. Mi papá	a. por la mañana
2. Yo	b. problemas económicos
3. Los profesores	c. a clase los lunes
4. Mis amigos y yo	d. muchas clases
5. Tú	e. a la universidad solo(-a)
6. Ustedes	f. la solicitud
	g. mucho dinero
	h. un empleo muy bueno
	i. un examen parcial
	j. a la universidad los sábados

B. Work with a partner. Using **tener que** + *infinitive*, say what the following people have to do, according to each circumstance.

1. Silvia tiene un examen parcial mañana.
2. John tiene una amiga de Madrid que no habla inglés.
3. Nosotros necesitamos dinero.
4. Yo necesito escribir y no tengo pluma.
5. Necesito hablar con Marta y ella no está en su casa por la mañana.

Para conversar

 Entrevista With a partner, take turns asking and answering these questions.

1. ¿Tú tienes mi número de teléfono? ¿Tienes mi dirección?
2. ¿El (La) profesor(-a) tiene tu número de teléfono? ¿Tiene tu número de seguro social?
3. ¿Tú y tus amigos vienen a la universidad los sábados? ¿Vienen los domingos?
4. ¿Tú tienes problemas económicos? ¿Tienes que trabajar más?
5. ¿A qué hora vienes tú a tu primera clase?
6. ¿Qué días vienes a la universidad?
7. ¿Tienes compañero(-a) de cuarto o vives solo(-a)?
8. ¿Tu mejor amigo(-a) tiene conocimiento de computadoras? ¿Y tú?

6. The personal *a* (*La a personal*)

- The preposition **a** is used in Spanish before a direct object[1] referring to a specific person or persons. It is called "the personal **a**" and has no equivalent in English.

| Yo llamo **a** mi amiga. | Nosotros llamamos **a** los estudiantes. |
| D.O. | D.O. |

| *I* | *call* | *my friend.* | *We* | *call* | *the students.* |
| | | D.O. | | | D.O. |

- The personal **a** is *not* used when the direct object is not a person.

Yo llamo un taxi.   *I call a taxi.*
Nosotros llevamos los   *We take the books to the library.*
    libros a la biblioteca.

- The verb **tener** generally does not take the personal **a,** even if the direct object is a person.

Yo tengo muchos amigos.   *I have many friends.*

—¿Tú llevas **a** tu novia a la   *"Do you take your girlfriend*
    universidad?   *to the university?"*
—Yo no tengo novia. Llevo   *"I don't have a girlfriend. I take Jorge*
    a Jorge y **a** Luis.   *and Luis."*

> **¡Atención!** When there is a series of direct object nouns referring to people, the personal **a** is repeated: **Llevo *a* Jorge y *a* Luis.**

---

[1]See **Lección 6** for further explanation of the direct object.

Práctica

A. Match the items in column A with the ones in column B.

A		B
1. Nosotros tenemos	_____	**a.** el informe para mi clase de historia.
2. Miguel llama	_____	**b.** a su mamá.
3. Yo escribo	_____	**c.** a su mamá a la biblioteca.
4. Mi novio lleva	_____	**d.** muchos mensajes electrónicos.
5. Yo debo llamar	_____	**e.** un taxi.
6. Los niños (*kids*) necesitan	_____	**f.** a sus pacientes (*patients*).
7. El profesor Paz tiene	_____	**g.** cien estudiantes en su clase.
8. Yo recibo	_____	**h.** muchos amigos puertorriqueños.
9. El doctor Peña debe llamar	_____	**i.** a nuestros amigos a la fiesta.
10. Nosotros invitamos	_____	**j.** a su novia por la tarde.

B. Use the personal **a** when needed to complete the following exchanges. Then act them out with a partner.

1. —¿Tu amigo lleva _____ Rosa a la biblioteca?

  —No, lleva _____ su novia.

2. —¿Cuántos compañeros de cuarto tienes?

  —Tengo _____ dos compañeros de cuarto.

3. —¿Usted llama _____ Amelia o _____ Rogelio?

  —Llamo _____ Rogelio.

4. —¿Rafael lleva _____ su novia a tomar algo?

  —Sí, lleva _____ su novia y _____ Mariana.

5. —¿Adónde lleva usted _____ los libros?

  —A la biblioteca.

6. —¿Qué lees?

  —Leo _____ mi libro de español.

Para conversar

¡Una fiesta! (*A party!*) With a partner, decide which members of the class you want to take or invite (**invitar**) to a party next Saturday. Give reasons for your choices.

Así somos

Estrategia **Taking a phone call** In a very broad sense, most listening has a purpose, whether to get specific information such as movie times or store hours, follow a lecture for the important points, or simply to provide an ear for a friend. When you get a phone call, you generally expect the caller to let you know the reason for the call, which then tells you how to respond and what specific information to listen for or ask about as the conversation continues.

Hola Javier calls his friend Marta. Listen to their conversation and answer the first question to identify the reason for his call. Then listen a second time for the specifics and answer the remaining questions.

1. ¿Por qué llama a Marta?
2. ¿Qué hay mañana?
3. ¿Dónde estudian Javier y Marta? ¿A qué hora?
4. ¿Para qué clase tiene que escribir un informe Marta?

Al conversar...

Estrategia **Using stock phrases** Having a repertoire of phrases that you can use in particular situations can help take the pressure off speaking, especially when you are beginning to learn a language. It also lets you concentrate on listening and understanding. Here are some phrases you can use.

To show agreement:	**Buena idea.** (*Good idea.*) **Es verdad.** (*It's true.*)
	Por supuesto. (*Of course.*) **Está bien.** (*That's fine/good.*)
To apologize:	**Lo siento.** (*I'm sorry.*)
To decline or make an excuse:	**No puedo.** (*I can't.*) **Tengo que...**

 ¿Estudiamos el lunes? With a partner, agree on a day, time, and place to study Spanish together. Use some of the preceding phrases in your conversation as you try to find a day and time that's convenient for both of you.

 ¿Qué dice Ud.? What would you say in the following situations? What might the other person say? Act out the scenes with a partner. Take turns playing each role.

1. Describe your best (**mejor**) friend as completely as possible. Add any pertinent information about him/her you deem important.
2. You have agreed to pick up a classmate on your way to school. Inform him/her at what time you come to class in the morning and get the following information:
   a. where he/she lives
   b. at what time he/she returns home in the evening.
3. Your phone rings and you answer it. The call is for you. You and the caller, a friend, make plans for him/her to come to your house to study.
4. You tell a friend three things you have to do tomorrow afternoon.
5. Ask your friend if he/she wants to have something to drink after studying.

Para conocernos mejor

 To do this activity, work with a classmate whom you would like to get to know. Take turns asking each other these questions.

1. ¿Vives con tus padres? ¿Dónde vive tu mejor (*best*) amigo(-a)?
2. ¿Tú vienes a la universidad los sábados? ¿Qué días vienes? ¿Vienes por la mañana o por la tarde?
3. ¿Tienes conocimiento de computadoras? ¿Recibes muchos mensajes electrónicos? ¿De quiénes?
4. ¿Tienes que estudiar mañana? ¿A qué hora?
5. ¿Tienes exámenes parciales en tus clases? ¿Son difíciles?
6. ¿Deseas comer o beber algo después de la clase?

Una encuesta

 Interview your classmates to identify who fits the following descriptions. Include your instructor, but remember to use the **Ud.** form when addressing him/her. After finishing the survey, get together with two or three classmates and discuss the results.

Nombre

1. Vive en un apartamento. _____
2. Tiene un compañero (una compañera) de cuarto. _____
3. Tiene un novio muy guapo (una novia muy bonita). _____
4. Es un poco terco(-a). _____
5. Es un poco impaciente. _____
6. Lee el periódico los domingos. _____
7. Bebe café por la mañana. _____
8. Corre todos los días. _____

Para crear

Get together in groups of three and "create" the scenario for this photo. Who are the people? Give them names. What is the relationship they have with each other? Where are they from? What might they say to each other? What plans might they make?

¡Vamos a leer!

Estrategia **Activating background knowledge** Bringing your own experiences to a new reading helps prepare you for the kinds of information you may encounter. By thinking about what you know of a topic before reading, you will be better able to anticipate the content of a text and understand more of what you read.

 Un mensaje electrónico Aurora Paz and Sergio Guzmán have recently met in a chat room. Before reading an e-mail from Aurora to Sergio, discuss with a partner what information you would give about yourself to a new cyberfriend and what questions you would ask to get to know someone.

A leer

Comprensión As you read the e-mail, find the answers to the following questions.

1. ¿Qué desea Sergio?
2. ¿Aurora es rubia?
3. ¿Qué características positivas tiene?
4. ¿Qué dice la mamá de Aurora?
5. ¿Qué actividades tiene Aurora todos los días?
6. Los sábados, ¿trabaja o sale con sus amigos?
7. ¿Qué ciudades puertorriqueñas menciona Aurora?

El mensaje de Aurora

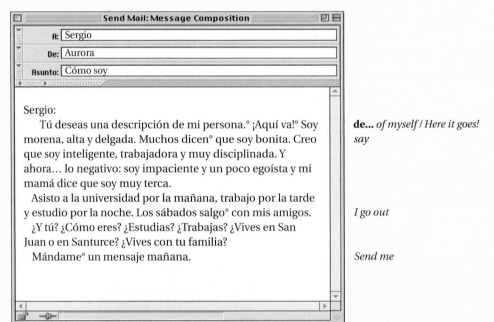

Send Mail: Message Composition

A: Sergio
De: Aurora
Asunto: Cómo soy

Sergio:

Tú deseas una descripción de mi persona.° ¡Aquí va!° Soy morena, alta y delgada. Muchos dicen° que soy bonita. Creo que soy inteligente, trabajadora y muy disciplinada. Y ahora… lo negativo: soy impaciente y un poco egoísta y mi mamá dice que soy muy terca.

Asisto a la universidad por la mañana, trabajo por la tarde y estudio por la noche. Los sábados salgo° con mis amigos.

¿Y tú? ¿Cómo eres? ¿Estudias? ¿Trabajas? ¿Vives en San Juan o en Santurce? ¿Vives con tu familia?

Mándame° un mensaje mañana.

de... of myself / Here it goes!
say

I go out

Send me

¡Vamos a escribir!

Antes de escribir

Estrategia **Analyzing writing models** A model or written sample is often an excellent aid for your development as a writer in Spanish. By examining how a letter, an article, or other piece of writing is organized and what words are used, you can gain helpful ideas about how to construct your own writing.

Un mensaje electrónico Look at the e-mail in **¡Vamos a leer!** and ask yourself the following questions.

1. What is the main idea that groups together the sentences in each paragraph?
2. How does Aurora describe herself? How would you describe yourself?
3. What activities does she talk about in the second paragraph?
4. What questions does she ask Sergio in the third paragraph? What questions would you ask?

A escribir un mensaje electrónico

You have a new cyberacquaintance. Write the first draft (**primer borrador**) of an e-mail to send to this person, following the organization of Aurora's e-mail to Jorge. You may want to use some of the questions that you brainstormed for the pre-reading activity in **¡Vamos a leer!**

Después de escribir

Before writing the final version of your e-mail, exchange your first draft with a class-mate and peer edit each other's work using the following guidelines:

- ◆ noun-adjective-article agreement (in gender and and number)
- ◆ subject-verb agreement (in person and number)
- ◆ clear organization and use of the model

Después de leer... desde su mundo

In groups of three or four, talk about your chat-room habits.

Panorama hispánico

Los puertorriqueños en los Estados Unidos

▲ El desfile puertorriqueño de Nueva York, segundo domingo de junio

◆ En total, más de 2.700.000 puertorriqueños viven en los Estados Unidos, el 70% de ellos en Nueva York y Nueva Jersey. Más puertorriqueños viven en Nueva York que en San Juan, la capital de Puerto Rico.

Nueva York: epicentro de la vida puertorriqueña en los Estados Unidos

▲ El Nuyorican Poets Café, una de varias (*several*) instituciones neoyorriqueñas

◆ La mayoría de los puertorriqueños llegaron (*arrived*) a este país después de la Segunda Guerra Mundial (*Second World War*) y, para muchos, fue (*it was*) muy difícil adaptarse a la vida de la gran ciudad. En las últimas décadas, han llegado de Puerto Rico miles de profesionales, artistas y gente de negocios (*businesspeople*). Hoy hay puertorriqueños famosos en todos los campos. Son buenos ejemplos de estos éxitos Nydia Velázquez y José Serrano, congresistas; la familia Unanue, dueños de los famosos productos Goya; Ricky Martin y Chayanne, cantantes; Rosalyn Sanchez, Benicio del Toro y muchos más, artistas de Hollywood; Félix (Tito) Trinidad, ex triple campeón de boxeo, etc.

La política

◀ Nydia Velázquez (1953–), primera mujer puertorriqueña elegida al Congreso de EEUU (1992–presente)

◀ José Serrano, representante de origen puertorriqueño

Personalidades

El mundo del espectáculo

▲ Benicio del Toro, famoso actor puertorriqueño

▲ Daddy Yankee, ganador (*winner*) del premio (*award*) "Artista del Año" del MTV latino, 2006

▲ Zuleyka Rivera, Miss Puerto Rico, fue elegida Miss Universo en el año 2006

Nuestro panorama cultural

In groups of three, answer the following questions about your home state, region, or country.

1. ¿Hay diversidad cultural y étnica en la ciudad donde Ud. vive? ¿Qué grupos hay? ¿Qué nacionalidades están representadas?
2. Un norteamericano, ¿necesita visa para viajar a Canadá?
3. ¿Hay muchos puertorriqueños en la ciudad donde Ud. vive?
4. En su ciudad, ¿celebran el cuatro de julio con desfiles?
5. ¿Cuál es la música típica de su país?
6. Además (*Besides*) de las personalidades mencionadas, ¿puede Ud. (*can you*) nombrar otros artistas puertorriqueños?
7. ¿Qué familias norteamericanas son importantes en el mundo de los negocios?

For the next class: Go to the World Wide Web and find photos from your hometown, state, region, or country. Use the questions from **Nuestro panorama cultural** above as guidelines for choosing them. Be ready to present the photos to your classmates.

Self-Test

Take this test. When you have finished, check your answers in the answer key provided in Appendix D. Then use a red pen to correct any mistakes you may have made. Are you ready?

Lección 1

A. The alphabet Spell the following last names in Spanish.

1. Vargas
2. Mena
3. Botero
4. Peña
5. Juárez
6. Chávez
7. Dávila
8. Félix
9. Quiroz

B. Cardinal numbers (0–30) Write the following numbers in Spanish.

1. 11
2. 17
3. 30
4. 20
5. 15
6. 13
7. 28
8. 19
9. 12
10. 14
11. 16
12. 22

C. Colors What colors come to mind when you think of the following?

1. grass
2. a pumpkin
3. a banana
4. rosy cheeks
5. coal
6. a plum
7. a tree trunk
8. the American flag

D. Days of the week Give the days of the week that come *before* the ones mentioned here.

1. lunes
2. jueves
3. sábado
4. miércoles
5. domingo
6. viernes
7. martes

E. Months and seasons Give the months and seasons that come *before* the ones mentioned here.

1. diciembre
2. abril
3. agosto
4. febrero
5. junio
6. octubre
7. invierno
8. verano
9. enero

F. Subject pronouns and the present indicative of the verb *ser*
Complete the following dialogue, using the present indicative of the verb **ser.**

—¿De dónde _____ ustedes?
—Nosotros _____ de California. ¿De dónde _____ tú?
—Yo _____ de Tejas.
—¿Y Carlos y Amelia?
—Carlos _____ de Arizona y Amelia _____ de Nuevo México.
—¿De dónde _____ los profesores?
—De Nueva Jersey.

G. Just words . . . Match each question in column A with the best response in column B.

A		B
1. ¿Cómo están Uds.?	_____	a. No, martes.
2. ¿Cómo te llamas?	_____	b. Sí, es mi cumpleaños.
3. ¿Qué hay de nuevo?	_____	c. Cuatro-dos-seis-cinco-ocho-nueve-cero.
4. ¿Hay una fiesta hoy?	_____	
5. ¿Uds. son norteamericanos?	_____	d. De Tejas.
6. ¿De dónde eres tú?	_____	e. Bien, gracias.
7. ¿Qué día es hoy?	_____	f. No, estudiantes.
8. ¿Hoy es lunes?	_____	g. No, somos mexicanos.
9. ¿Cuál es tu número de teléfono?	_____	h. Ana María Belgrano.
10. ¿Uds. son profesores?	_____	i. Miércoles.
		j. Nada.

H. Culture Answer the following questions, based on information from this lesson.

1. ¿Cuál es un nombre muy popular en España y en Latinoamérica?
2. ¿Cuál es el sobrenombre de Dolores? ¿Y de Enrique?
3. ¿Cuántos millones de hispanos hay en los Estados Unidos?
4. ¿Quién es Sandra Cisneros?

Lección 2

A. Gender and number and definite articles Write **el, la, los,** or **las** before each noun.

1. _____ pizarra
2. _____ luz
3. _____ lápices
4. _____ día
5. _____ lección
6. _____ relojes
7. _____ mapa
8. _____ universidades
9. _____ pared
10. _____ bolígrafos
11. _____ amistad (*friendship*)
12. _____ problemas

B. Gender and number and indefinite articles Write **un, una, unos,** or **unas** before each noun.

1. _____ programas
2. _____ borradores
3. _____ mano
4. _____ hombres
5. _____ mujer
6. _____ secretario
7. _____ profesores
8. _____ papel
9. _____ decisión
10. _____ ciudad

C. Cardinal numbers (31–100) Write the following numbers in Spanish.

1. 38
2. 100
3. 91
4. 85
5. 72
6. 57
7. 46
8. 63
9. 77

D. Telling time Use the cues given to say at what time the following classes are.

1. la clase de español / 9:10 A.M.
2. la clase de inglés / 1:15 P.M.
3. la clase de literatura / 8:25 P.M.

E. Present indicative of -ar verbs and negative and interrogative sentences Complete the following dialogues, using the verbs given.

1. —¿Dónde _____ (trabajar) tú?
   —Yo _____ (trabajar) en la universidad.
   —¿A qué hora _____ (regresar) a tu casa?
   —A las cuatro.

2. —¿Uds. _____ (estudiar) por la mañana?
   —No, nosotros _____ (estudiar) por la tarde.
   —¿Cuántas clases _____ (tomar) ustedes?
   —Yo _____ (tomar) cuatro y Estrella _____ (tomar) cinco.

3. —¿Qué _____ (necesitar) Carlos y Aurora?
   —Carlos _____ (necesitar) lápices y Aurora _____ (necesitar) libros.

4. —¿Tú _____ (desear) llamar más tarde, Anita?
   —Sí, yo _____ (desear) llamar a las cinco.

5. —¿Uds. _____ (hablar) inglés en clase?
   —No, nosotros _____ (hablar) español.

 F. Possession with _de_ Form sentences with the items given.

1. la señorita / estudiantes / norteamericanos
2. Amanda / profesor / mexicano
3. Paco / amigos / de California

 G. Just words . . . Complete the following sentences using vocabulary from **Lección 2.**

1. Estudiamos en la _____.
2. Mi _____ es: Calle Olmos, número 96.
3. ¿Cómo se _____ _"door"_ en español?
4. ¿Qué _____ decir "borrador"?
5. ¿_____ estudias? ¿Los sábados?
6. En Roma hablan _____ y en París hablan _____.
7. El español es un _____ difícil.
8. Necesitas practicar _____ los días.
9. ¡En ese _____, yo hablo chino!
10. Pedro habla un _____ de portugués.

 H. Culture Answer the following questions, based on information from this lesson.

1. Si usamos el sistema de 24 horas, ¿qué hora es cuando decimos (_when we say_) "las diecinueve horas"?
2. ¿Cuántos cubanos viven en Miami?
3. ¿Qué es "la Pequeña Habana"?

Lección 3

A. Possessive adjectives Complete these sentences with the appropriate possessive adjectives. Make sure they agree with the subjects.

1. Yo necesito _____ libro y _____ bolígrafos.
2. Nosotros hablamos con _____ profesora y ellos hablan con _____ profesor.
3. ¿Tú vives con _____ padres (*parents*)?
4. Jorge come con _____ amigos.
5. Nosotros vivimos en _____ casa con _____ padres.
6. ¿Usted necesita _____ computadora, Srta. Mejías?

B. Cardinal numbers (101–1,000) Write the following numbers in Spanish.

1. 195
2. 286
3. 371
4. 460
5. 553
6. 644
7. 732
8. 827
9. 918
10. 1.513

C. Descriptive adjectives Change the articles and the adjectives according to the nouns in parentheses.

1. El chico es alto. (*chica*)
2. La pizarra es pequeña. (*escritorios*)
3. Los chicos son norteamericanos. (*chicas*)
4. Es un hombre muy simpático. (*mujer*)
5. Necesito los lápices rojos. (*plumas*)

D. Present indicative of regular -*er* and -*ir* verbs Complete the following sentences, using the verbs in the list.

deber	aprender	vender	comer	escribir
abrir	creer	leer	recibir	beber

1. Nosotros _____ mucho en la clase de español.
2. ¿Tú _____ en la cafetería?
3. Yo _____ que Elena habla portugués.
4. ¿Ustedes _____ muchos libros?
5. Carlos _____ café.
6. Usted _____ estudiar más.
7. Ellos _____ sus libros por (*for*) treinta dólares.
8. Yo _____ las ventanas.
9. Ellos _____ mensajes electrónicos.
10. Nosotros _____ con lápiz.

E. The verbs *tener* and *venir*   Complete the following sentences using the present indicative of **tener** or **venir.**

1. Yo no _____ a la universidad los viernes porque no _____ clases.
2. ¿Tú _____ la dirección de Julio? Él no _____ a clase los lunes.
3. Nosotros _____ a la biblioteca con Amanda porque no _____ auto (*car*).
4. Rogelio _____ a las ocho y ellos _____ a las diez.
5. ¿Ellos _____ tu número de teléfono?

F. The personal *a*   Form sentences, using the elements provided. Include the personal **a** when necessary.

1. yo / llamar / Rosa / a las tres
2. nosotros / llevar / los libros / a la universidad
3. ellos / llevar / Julio / y su novia / a la biblioteca
4. nosotros / tener / muchos amigos

G. Just words . . .   Match the questions in column A with the answers in column B.

A		B
1. ¿Ana es tu novia?	____	a. No, soy realista.
2. ¿Tienes problemas económicos?	____	b. Sí, ¡y muy simpática!
3. ¿Estudian hoy?	____	c. Menéndez.
4. ¿Cómo estás?	____	d. No, es muy guapo.
5. ¿Es bonita?	____	e. Secretaria.
6. ¿Está Jorge?	____	f. Sí, necesito dinero.
7. ¿Eres pesimista?	____	g. No, es rubia.
8. ¿Es feo?	____	h. No, es muy antipática.
9. ¿Es simpática?	____	i. No, mañana.
10. ¿Cuál es su apellido?	____	j. El anuncio.
11. ¿Estado civil?	____	k. Más o menos.
12. ¿Ocupación?	____	l. No, es bajo.
13. ¿Es morena?	____	m. No, es una amiga.
14. ¿Es alto?	____	n. Soltero.
15. ¿Qué leen?	____	o. Con él habla.

H. Culture   Answer the following questions, based on information from this lesson.

1. ¿Cómo contestan el teléfono en México?
2. ¿Cuál es un sinónimo de "español"?
3. ¿Qué no necesitan los puertorriqueños para entrar en los Estados Unidos?
4. ¿Quién es Chayanne?

4

▲ Preparativos para una cena de cumpleaños

Objetivos

Comunicación

You will learn vocabulary related to planning weekend activities, needs and preferences, and states of mind.

Pronunciación

The Spanish **b, v, d,** and **g** (before **a, o,** or **u**)

Estructuras

- Pronouns as objects of prepositions
- Contractions
- Present indicative of the irregular verbs **ir, dar,** and **estar**
- **Ir a** + *infinitive*
- Present indicative of **e:ie** stem-changing verbs
- Expressions with **tener**

Cultura

- Relationships
- Customs
- Certain Hispanic celebrations

Panorama hispánico

- México

Estrategias

Listening: Listening to voice mail
Speaking: Asking for additional information
Reading: Identifying text formats
Writing: Writing an e-mail

Costumbres y tradiciones

México

México, con más de cien millones de habitantes, ocupa por su población el primer lugar entre los países del mundo hispano, y tiene casi tres veces el área de Tejas. Su capital, la Ciudad de México, D.F. (Distrito Federal), con unos 24 millones de habitantes, es el centro urbano más grande del mundo.

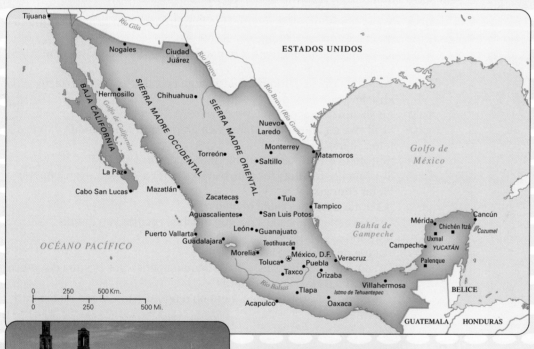

▲ La Plaza de las Tres Culturas, en Tlatelolco (hoy parte de la Ciudad de México), ciudad azteca fundada en el siglo XIV (*14th century*)

▲ Una chica baila con su papá en su fiesta de quinceañera. Las chicas hispanas celebran sus 15 años en vez de (*instead of*) los 16, como en los Estados Unidos.

▲ Vista del Monumento a la Independencia en la Ciudad de México

Julia Lara, una chica mexicoamericana que vive en Colorado con su familia, visita México por primera vez. Acaba de llegar del aeropuerto con sus primos y ahora está en la casa de sus tíos, que están muy contentos con la llegada de la muchacha. Julia va a pasar la Navidad y el Año Nuevo con ellos.

Doña Luz	¡Bienvenida, hijita! ¡Ay! ¡Dame un abrazo! ¿Cómo estás? ¿Y cómo está mi hermano... tu papá...? ¿Tienes hambre?
Lupita	¡Mamá! ¡Una pregunta a la vez! ¡La pobre Julia está aturdida!
Julia	(*Abraza a su tía.*) Estoy bien, gracias, tía. Y su hermano... está bien, también. Y no tengo hambre, pero tengo mucha sed...
Doña Luz	(*A su hijo Mario*) Mario, una soda para tu prima.
Julia	Prefiero un vaso de agua, tía.
Don Rodolfo	¿Cómo estás, sobrina? ¿Qué tal el viaje?
Julia	Muy bien, tío. Estoy un poco cansada, pero estoy muy contenta de estar aquí, con ustedes.

Por la noche, Julia está en el cuarto de Lupita. Las dos primas conversan.

Lupita	Mañana vamos a ir al parque de Chapultepec y por la noche vamos a ir al cine con unos amigos.
Julia	¡Perfecto! También quiero ir a una tienda por la tarde. Oye, ¿qué vamos a hacer pasado mañana?
Lupita	Pasado mañana damos una fiesta aquí en casa. Es el santo de mi abuelo.
Julia	Ah sí, don Gustavo.
Lupita	Sí, él vive con nosotros. Mamá va a preparar mucha comida y vamos a tener mariachis...
Julia	¡Entonces quiero sacar muchas fotos! ¿Vamos a bailar?
Lupita	Sí... Muchos de nuestros amigos van a venir a la fiesta y van a querer bailar contigo.
Julia	¿Cuántas personas están invitadas?
Lupita	Unas cincuenta... o más, porque muchos vecinos van a venir también...
Julia	¿Y cuándo empiezan las posadas?
Lupita	La semana que viene. Este fin de semana pensamos ir a una discoteca de la Zona Rosa... Oye... es tarde.
Julia	Tienes razón. ¡Son las once! ¡Pero no tengo sueño! Quiero platicar un rato más...

¿Lo sabía Ud.?

En España y en Latinoamérica, no existe tanta (*as much*) separación entre (*among*) generaciones como en los Estados Unidos. Los niños, los padres y los abuelos frecuentemente van juntos a fiestas y celebraciones.

◆ **¿Qué celebraciones tienen las familias de este país?**

Doña Luz

Lupita

Julia

Don Rodolfo

 ¿Quién lo dice? Identify the person who said the following in the dialogues.

ACE the Test

1. Pasado mañana damos una fiesta aquí en casa. _____
2. Entonces quiero sacar muchas fotos. _____
3. Mario, una soda para tu prima. _____
4. ¡Pero no tengo sueño! Quiero platicar un rato más. _____
5. ¡Bienvenida, hijita! ¡Ay! ¡Dame un abrazo! _____
6. ¡La pobre Julia está aturdida! _____
7. ¡Mamá! ¡Una pregunta a la vez! _____
8. ¿Cómo estás, sobrina? ¿Qué tal el viaje? _____
9. Y su hermano está bien, también. _____

¿Lo sabía Ud.?

En México, durante la época de Navidad, celebran las posadas, que representan el viaje de María y José desde Nazaret a Belén y su búsqueda (*search*) de alojamiento (*lodging*). Empiezan el 16 de diciembre y terminan el 24 de diciembre.

◆ **¿Celebran las posadas en algún barrio mexicano en la ciudad donde Ud. vive?**

 **Hablemos.** With a partner, take turns asking and answering the following questions. Base your answers on the dialogue and on your own circumstances.

En el diálogo	**¿Y tú?**
1. ¿Dónde va a pasar Julia la Navidad?	¿Dónde vas a pasar tú la Navidad?
2. ¿Julia tiene hambre o tiene sed?	¿Tú tienes hambre?
3. ¿Qué quiere beber Julia?	¿Qué quieres beber tú?
4. ¿Adónde van a ir Julia y Lupita mañana?	¿Adónde vas a ir tú?
5. ¿Es el santo o el cumpleaños del abuelo de Lupita?	¿Cuándo es tu cumpleaños?
6. ¿Quiénes van a venir a la fiesta?	¿Tú vas a dar una fiesta?
7. ¿Cuándo empiezan las posadas?	¿Adónde vas a ir tú la semana que viene?
8. ¿Julia tiene sueño?	¿Tienes sueño o estás cansado(-a)?

¿Lo sabía Ud.?

Los hispanos generalmente celebran el cumpleaños y también el día de su "santo", que corresponde al santo de su nombre en el calendario católico. Por ejemplo, si un niño nace (*is born*) en junio, y sus padres lo llaman Miguel, celebra su cumpleaños en junio y celebra el día de su "santo" el 29 de septiembre, que es el día de San Miguel.

◆ **En este país, ¿las personas celebran el día de su santo?**

Vocabulario

Improve Your Grade
Audio Flashcards

Cognados

el aeropuerto airport
la discoteca discotheque
la familia family
la foto, fotografía photo, photograph

el parque park
la persona person
la soda soda[1]
la tradición tradition

Nombres

el abrazo hug
la abuela grandmother
el abuelo grandfather
el agua water
el Año Nuevo New Year
el cine movies, movie theatre
la comida food
la costumbre custom
el cuarto, la habitación room
la hermana sister
el hermano brother
la hija daughter
el hijo son
la llegada arrival

la Navidad Christmas
la pregunta question
el (la) primo(-a) cousin
el santo saint's day
la semana week
la sobrina niece
el sobrino nephew
la tía aunt
la tienda store
el tío uncle
el vaso glass
el (la) vecino(-a) neighbor
la vez time (*in a series*)
el viaje trip

Verbos

abrazar to hug
bailar to dance
dar to give
empezar, comenzar (e:ie) to begin,
   to start
hacer (yo hago) to do
ir to go
llegar to arrive

pasar to spend (*time*)
pensar (e:ie) to think
pensar + *infinitive* to plan (*to do
   something*)
preferir (e:ie) to prefer
preparar to prepare
querer (e:ie) to want, to wish
visitar to visit

Adjetivos

aturdido(-a) dazed, confused
bienvenido(-a) welcome
cansado(-a) tired
contento(-a) happy
invitado(-a) invited
pobre poor

[1]also **la gaseosa** (*Colombia*), **el refresco** (*Caribbean and other regions*)

Otras palabras y expresiones

a la vez at a time

acabar de + *infinitive* to have just (*done something*)

ahora now

contigo with you (*familiar*)

dame give me

don a title of respect, used with a man's first name

doña a title of respect, used with a lady's first name

en casa at home

entonces then (in that case)

este fin de semana this weekend

hijita (darling) daughter (*a term of endearment*)

pasado mañana the day after tomorrow

por primera vez for the first time

que that, who

sacar (tomar) una foto to take a picture

la semana que viene, la semana próxima next week

tener hambre to be hungry

tener razón to be right

tener sed to be thirsty

tener sueño to be sleepy

un poco a little

un rato a while

Vocabulario adicional

Actividades para un fin de semana

ir a un concierto to go to a concert

ir a la montaña mountain

ir al museo museum

ir al parque de diversiones amusement park

ir a un partido (o juego) de... game

ir a la playa beach

ir al teatro theatre

ir al zoológico zoo

Para describir cómo estamos

aburrido(-a) bored

alegre joyful

animado(-a) animated

enfermo(-a) sick

enojado(-a), enfadado(-a) angry

entusiasmado(-a) enthused

frustrado(-a) frustrated

nervioso(-a) nervous

ocupado(-a) busy

preocupado(-a) worried

triste sad

La fiesta de Navidad (*Christmas*)

el árbol de Navidad

Ellos cantan.

¡Salud!

el brindis

el equipo estereofónico

el reproductor de discos

el disco compacto

la mesa

el ponche

el vino

Práctica

A. Match the questions in column A with the responses in column B.

A		B
1. ¿La Sra. Pérez es tu abuela? ____		**a.** A las nueve.
2. ¿Qué quieres beber? ____		**b.** En su cuarto.
3. ¿Adónde vamos a ir? ____		**c.** No, no estamos invitados.
4. ¿Dónde está tu prima? ____		**d.** La semana que viene.
5. ¿Elena es tu sobrina? ____		**e.** No, pasado mañana.
6. ¿Cuándo llega tu tío? ____		**f.** No, preferimos conversar.
7. ¿La fiesta es mañana? ____		**g.** Al cine.
8. ¿A qué hora comienza la fiesta? ____		**h.** En México.
9. ¿Quieren bailar? ____		**i.** Sí, es la mamá de mi papá.
10. ¿Van Uds. a la fiesta? ____		**j.** Sí, es la hija de mi hermana.
11. ¿Dónde vas a pasar la Navidad? ____		**k.** No, estoy un poco cansado.
12. ¿No vas a trabajar? ____		**l.** Un vaso de agua.

B. Write the words or phrases that correspond to the following.

1. opuesto de **alegre** _____

2. enojado _____

3. Mount Everest, por ejemplo _____

4. lugar (*place*) donde vamos a bailar _____

5. Disneylandia, por ejemplo _____

6. que tiene mucho entusiasmo _____

7. partido _____

8. lugar donde hay muchos animales _____

9. el Louvre, por ejemplo _____

10. cuarto _____

C. Complete the following sentences, using vocabulary from this lesson.

1. Voy a _____ muchas fotografías.

2. ¡Bienvenida! ¡ _____ un abrazo!

3. Hoy vamos al _____ de Chapultepec.

4. Vamos a ir a una _____ a bailar.

5. ¡Feliz Año _____!

6. La Sra. Fuentes es mi _____; es la hermana de mi mamá.

7. Nosotros _____ ir a la universidad el sábado.

8. _____ Oscar y _____ María van a ir a México la semana que viene.

9. Mamá va a _____ mucha comida para la fiesta.

10. ¡ _____ Julia! Está cansada...

Para conversar

A. Planes With a partner, tell each other about what you plan to do and what you don't plan to do at different times in the near future.

◆ **MODELO:** (*No*) *pienso ir a...*

B. Una fiesta You and a partner play the roles of two friends who are planning a party and cannot agree on anything: the day, the time, the place, whom to invite, what to serve, etc.

◆ **MODELO:** —*¿Damos una fiesta el sábado?*
　　　　　　 —*No... yo tengo planes para el sábado.*

Pronunciación

A. The Spanish *b* and *v*

The Spanish **b** and **v** are pronounced exactly alike. Both sound like a weak English *b*, as in the word *Abe*. In Spanish, they are even weaker when pronounced between vowels. The lips don't quite touch. Never pronounce these consonants like the English *v*. Listen to your instructor and repeat the following words.

Beto **v**ive en **B**ogotá.

Bien**v**enida a **B**olivia.

Don Gusta**v**o es mi a**b**uelo.

B. The Spanish *d*

The Spanish **d** is slightly softer than the *d* in the English word *day*. When pronounced between two vowels or at the end of a word, it is similar to the *th* in the English word *they*. Listen to your instructor and repeat the following words.

Doña **D**elia es **d**e Colora**d**o.

¿Uste**d**es están cansa**d**os?

Davi**d** está invita**d**o.

C. The Spanish *g* (before *a, o,* or *u*)

◆ When followed by **a, o,** or **u,** the Spanish **g** is similar to the *g* in the English word *guy*. Listen to your instructor and repeat the following words.

Gustavo es **g**ordo.

◆ When pronounced between vowels, the Spanish **g** is much softer. Repeat after your instructor.

Mi ami**g**o es uru**g**uayo.

◆ In the combinations **gue** and **gui,** the **u** is silent. Repeat after your instructor.

Guillermo **G**uevara toca la **g**uitarra.

Aspectos culturales

En imágenes (*Fiestas y celebraciones en México y en Centroamérica*)

▲ México: El Día de los Muertos

OCÉANO PACÍFICO

▲ La Quema del Diablo (*burning of the Devil*) es una celebración muy popular en Guatemala.

Ubíquese... y búsquelo

Improve Your Grade
Web Search

As part of her visit to Mexico City, Julia's family is taking her to the **Parque de Chapultepec.** Go to **www.cengage.com/highered** to research the **Parque.** What attractions will Julia find there? What are some other parks in Mexico City that she could visit? In the next class, team up with two classmates to discuss your findings.

▲ En los países hispanos los niños reciben juguetes (*toys*) de los Tres Reyes Magos, Melchor, Gaspar y Baltasar, el 6 de enero.

▲ Celebración religiosa en Honduras el día de Año Nuevo

▲ Nicaragua: Festival de Santo Domingo

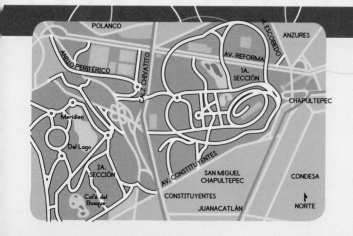

Estructuras

1. Pronouns as objects of prepositions (*Pronombres usados como objetos de preposición*)

◆ The object of a preposition is the noun or pronoun that immediately follows it: **La fiesta es para María (ella). Ellos van con nosotros.**

Singular		Plural	
mí	*me*	**nosotros(-as)**	*us*
ti	*you* (fam.)	**vosotros(-as)**	*you* (fam.)
Ud.	*you* (form.)	**Uds.**	*you* (form.)
él	*him*	**ellos**	*them* (masc.)
ella	*her*	**ellas**	*them* (fem.)

Un dicho

Hoy por ti, mañana por mí.

Equivalent: One hand washes the other.

◆ Only the first- and second-person singular, **mí** and **ti,** are different from regular subject pronouns.

◆ **Mí** and **ti** combine with **con** to become **conmigo** (*with me*) and **contigo** (*with you*), respectively.

—¿Hablan de **mí**?
—No, no hablamos de **ti;**
hablamos de **ella.**

"Are you talking about me?"
"No, we are not talking about you; we're talking about her."

—¿Estudias **conmigo**
o con Carlos?
—No estudio **contigo;**
estudio **con él.**

*"Are you studying with me
or with Carlos?"*
*"I'm not studying with you; I'm studying
with him."*

ACE the Test

Práctica

Complete the following dialogues, using the Spanish equivalent of the words in parentheses. Then act them out with a partner, adding a sentence or two to each dialogue.

1. —¿Carlos habla _____? (*with me*)

—No, no habla _____; habla _____. (*with you / with her*)

2. —¿Para quién son los libros, Paco? ¿ _____ o _____? (*For him / for her*)

—Son _____. (*for me*)

—¿ _____? (*For you*)

—Sí, señor.

3. —¿El vino es _____? (*for you, pl.*)

—No, es _____. (*for them, fem.*)

Para conversar

 ¡Habla con tu compañero! Interview a classmate, using the following questions and two questions of your own. When you have finished, switch roles. Use the appropriate prepositions and pronouns in your responses.

1. ¿Hablas con tus amigos en la clase?
2. ¿Deseas estudiar español conmigo?
3. ¿Trabajas para tus padres?
4. ¿Vives cerca de (*near*) tus abuelos?
5. ¿Hablas mucho con tus amigos por teléfono?
6. ¿Tus amigos vienen a la universidad contigo?

2. Contractions (*Contracciones*)

◆ There are only two contractions in Spanish: **al** and **del**. Both the preposition **a** (*to, toward*) and the personal **a** followed by the article **el** contract to **al**.

Llamo	**a**	+	**el**	profesor.
Llamo		**al**		profesor.

◆ The preposition **de** (*of, from*) followed by the article **el** contracts to **del**.

Tiene los libros	**de**	+	**el**	profesor.
Tiene los libros		**del**		profesor.

—¿Llevas **al** amigo de Ana?   *"Are you taking Ana's friend?"*
—No, llevo **a las** primas de Eva.   *"No, I'm taking Eva's cousins."*

—¿La casa es **de la** Sra. Vega?   *"Is it Mrs. Vega's house?"*
—No, es **del** Sr. Parra.   *"No, it's Mr. Parra's."*

> **¡Atención!** **A + el** and **de + el** must always be contracted to **al** and **del**. None of the other combinations (**de la, de las, de los, a la, a las, a los**) is contracted: **Llaman a los hijos de los profesores.**

Práctica

 ACE the Test

 **A.** Complete the following dialogues, using **de la, de las, del, de los, a la, a las, al,** or **a los.** Then act them out with a partner.

1. —¿De dónde vienes? ¿_____ aeropuerto?
   —No, vengo _____ discoteca.
2. —¿A qué hora llamas _____ chicas?
   —_____ dos.
3. —¿Los mapas son _____ Sr. Vega?
   —No, son _____ Srta. Ruiz.
4. —¿Tienes que ir _____ apartamento de Julia?
   —No, tengo que ir _____ biblioteca.
5. —¿Adónde llevas _____ chicos?
   —_____ clase _____ Sr. Peña.

 **Un dicho**

Al pan, pan y al vino, vino.

Equivalent: To call a spade a spade.

B. With a partner, take turns asking and answering the following questions, using the cues provided.

1. ¿De quién son los libros? (profesor)
2. ¿De quién es el escritorio? (Srta. Paz)
3. ¿A quiénes llevas a la universidad? (chicos)
4. ¿A quién invitan ustedes? (Sr. Vega)
5. ¿A quiénes llaman los chicos? (muchachas)
6. ¿Adónde llevan a las muchachas? (parque)
7. ¿De dónde vienen ustedes? (aeropuerto)
8. ¿Los libros son de los muchachos? (no, muchachas)

Para conversar

¿Qué pasa aquí? In a hotel lobby, you and your partner observe what is going on. Take turns asking each other who is calling whom, where people are coming from, how they relate to each other, etc.

3. Present indicative of the irregular verbs *ir*, *dar*, and *estar*
(*Presente de indicativo de los verbos irregulares **ir**, **dar** y **estar***)

	ir to go	**dar** to give	**estar** to be
yo	**voy**	**doy**	**estoy**
tú	**vas**	**das**	**estás**
Ud.			
él	**va**	**da**	**está**
ella			
nosotros(-as)	**vamos**	**damos**	**estamos**
vosotros(-as)	**vais**	**dais**	**estáis**
Uds.			
ellos	**van**	**dan**	**están**
ellas			

—Susana **da** una fiesta hoy.
 ¿Tú **vas**?
—No, no **voy** porque **estoy**
 muy cansada.
—Entonces **voy** con Ana y Beto.
 ¿Dónde **están** ellos?
—**Están** en la universidad.
 Vienen a las tres.

"Susana is giving a party today.
 Are you going?"
"No, I'm not going because I am very
 tired."
"Then I'm going with Ana and Beto.
 Where are they?"
"They're at the college.
 They're coming at three."

♦ The verb **estar**, *to be,* is used here to indicate current condition (**Estoy muy cansada.**) and location (**Está en la universidad.**). **Ser,** another equivalent of the English verb *to be,* has been used up to now to refer to origin (**Él es de México.**), nationality (**Ellas son mexicanas.**), characteristics (**Jorge es rubio.**), profession (**Elsa es profesora.**), and time (**Son las doce.**).

♦ Other frequent uses of **dar** are **dar un examen, dar una conferencia** (*lecture*), and **dar una orden** (*order*).

Práctica

ACE the Test

A. Complete the following conversation, using the appropriate forms of the verbs **ir, dar,** and **estar.** Then act out the dialogue with a partner.

José Rosa, ¿tú _____ a la fiesta que _____ Estrella el sábado?

Rosa Sí, _____ con Inés. ¿Tú _____ también?

José Sí. Oye, ¿estudiamos esta noche? El Dr. Vargas y la Dra. Soto _____ exámenes mañana.

Rosa Ay, José, yo _____ muy cansada.

José Pero, Rosa, ¡tú siempre _____ cansada!

Rosa No siempre. ¿Por qué no estudias con Jorge y Raúl? Ellos no _____ al cine esta noche.

José Buena idea. ¿Dónde _____ ellos ahora?

Rosa _____ en la tienda.

 ¿Lo sabía Ud.?

En los países hispanos, las chicas y los muchachos generalmente van en grupos a fiestas, al teatro y a conciertos.

♦ En este país, ¿los chicos prefieren salir en grupos o en parejas (*couples*)?

B. Complete the following statements in a logical manner.

1. Roberto está en el parque y nosotros...
2. Yo doy una fiesta esta noche y tú...
3. Tú vas al museo y yo...
4. Yo estoy muy enojado(-a) y ellos...
5. Nosotros damos una fiesta de Navidad y él...
6. Ellos van hoy y nosotros...
7. Ella está nerviosa y su novio...
8. Julia está aburrida y yo...

Para conversar

A. **¡Habla con tu compañero!** Interview a classmate, using the following questions. When you have finished, switch roles.

1. ¿Cómo estás?
2. ¿Quién no está en clase hoy?
3. ¿Está muy ocupado(-a) el profesor (la profesora)?
4. ¿El profesor (La profesora) da exámenes fáciles o difíciles?
5. ¿Adónde vas los sábados por la noche con tus amigos?
6. ¿Van Uds. a un club? (¿A cuál?)
7. ¿Das muchas fiestas en tu casa?
8. ¿Das una fiesta de fin de año? ¿De Navidad?

B. **¿Adónde vamos?** Imagining that you or you and one classmate are walking around town, walk around the class. You will bump into several of your classmates. Ask them where they are going now. Here is a list of places that people go to.

la playa	el cine	el parque
el parque de diversiones	el concierto	el zoológico
el teatro	el museo	la tienda

◆ **MODELO:** —¡Hola! ¿Adónde vas?
—*Voy al cine. ¿Y tú?*
—*Yo voy a la tienda.*

After everyone sits down, the instructor will ask where everyone is going.

4. *Ir a* + infinitive (*Ir a* + *infinitivo*)

◆ **Ir a** + *infinitive* is used to express future action. It is equivalent to the English expression *to be going (to)* + *infinitive*. The "formula" is as follows.

ir (*conjugated*)	+ a +	*infinitive*
Voy	**a**	**trabajar.**
I am going		*to work.*

—¿Con quién **vas a bailar** en la fiesta?   *"With whom are you going to dance at the party?"*
—**Voy a bailar** contigo.   *"I'm going to dance with you."*

—¿Uds. **van a cantar?**   *"Are you going to sing?"*
—No, **vamos a bailar.**   *"No, we're going to dance."*

Práctica

What do you think these people are going to do? Consider where they are and what time of day it is.

◆ **MODELO:** José / en la tienda / por la tarde
José va a trabajar en la tienda por la tarde.

1. Yo / en mi casa / por la noche
2. Los estudiantes / en la clase / por la mañana
3. Nosotros / en la discoteca / por la noche
4. Tú / en la cafetería / a las doce
5. Susana / en su casa / por la mañana
6. Uds. / en la fiesta / por la noche

Para conversar

A. ¡Habla con tu compañero! Interview a classmate, using the following questions. When you have finished, switch roles.

1. ¿Dónde vas a comer hoy? ¿Con quién vas a comer?
2. ¿A qué hora van a comer Uds.?
3. ¿Qué van a comer? ¿Qué van a tomar?
4. ¿Qué vas a hacer (*to do*) mañana por la tarde?
5. ¿Qué van a estudiar tú y tus amigos?
6. ¿Qué van a hacer Uds. por la noche?
7. ¿Dónde vas a trabajar mañana?
8. ¿Tu amigo(-a) va a trabajar también?

B. ¿Qué van a hacer? What are these people going to do? With a partner, take turns asking and answering questions, using the information in the illustrations.

◆ **MODELO:** —*¿Con quién va a bailar Marisol?*
—*Va a bailar con Tito.*

▲ Marisol

▲ 1. Roberto

▲ 2. Elisa

▲ 3. Julio y Estrella

▲ 4. Daniel

▲ 5. Eduardo

▲ 6. Graciela

5. Present indicative of *e:ie* stem-changing verbs
(*Presente de indicativo de los verbos que cambian en la raíz* **e:ie**)

◆ Some Spanish verbs undergo a stem change in the present indicative. For these verbs, when **e** is the last stem vowel and it is stressed, it changes to **ie** as follows.

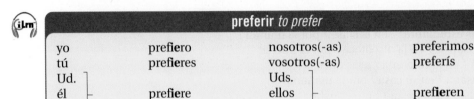

preferir *to prefer*			
yo	pref**ie**ro	nosotros(-as)	preferimos
tú	pref**ie**res	vosotros(-as)	preferís
Ud.		Uds.	
él	pref**ie**re	ellos	pref**ie**ren
ella		ellas	

—¿A qué hora **piensas** ir a la fiesta?　　*"What time are you planning to go to the party?"*

—**Prefiero** ir a las diez. ¿Y tú?　　*"I prefer to go at ten. And you?"*
—Yo **no quiero** ir. Estoy cansado.　　*"I don't want to go. I'm tired."*

—¿A qué hora **empiezan** a[1] estudiar Uds.?　　*"What time do you start to study?"*
—**Empezamos** a las tres.　　*"We start at three."*

◆ Note that the stem vowel is not stressed in the verb forms used with **nosotros (-as)** and **vosotros(-as);** therefore, the **e** does not change to **ie.**
◆ Stem-changing verbs have the same endings as regular **-ar, -er,** and **-ir** verbs.
◆ Some verbs that undergo this change:

cerrar *to close*
comenzar *to begin, to start*
empezar *to begin, to start*
entender *to understand*
pensar *to think*
pensar (+ *infinitive*) *to plan* (*to do something*)
perder *to lose*
querer *to want, to wish, to love*

 **Ojos que no ven, corazón que no siente.**
Equivalent: Out of sight, out of mind.

Práctica

A. Complete the following dialogues, using the verbs given. Then act them out with a partner, expanding each dialogue by adding one or two sentences.

1. preferir　—¿Dónde _____ comer Uds.? ¿En la cafetería o en su casa?
　　　　　—(Nosotros) _____ comer en nuestra casa.

2. querer　—¿Qué _____ comer Uds.?
　　　　　—Rosa _____ comer pollo y Oscar y yo _____ comer langosta (*lobster*).

---

[1]The preposition **a** is used after **empezar** and **comenzar** when they are followed by an infinitive.

3. pensar   —¿Adónde _____ ir Uds. el domingo?

—_____ ir al partido de fútbol.

4. cerrar   —¿No _____ (ellos) la cafetería los sábados?

—No, creo que no _____ la cafetería los sábados.

5. perder   —Cuando Uds. van a Las Vegas, ¿_____ mucho dinero?

—Sí, _____ mucho.

6. empezar   —¿A qué hora _____ Uds. a trabajar?

—Nosotros _____ a las ocho y Luis _____ a las nueve.

B. You have just enrolled at a new university, and some current students are helping to orient you. Compare their routines and preferences with your own.

1. Comenzamos las clases a las nueve.
2. No entendemos inglés.
3. Pensamos trabajar mañana.
4. Queremos ir al zoológico.
5. Preferimos beber ponche.
6. No cerramos las ventanas por la noche.

Para conversar

¡Habla con tu compañero! Interview a classmate, using the following questions. When you have finished, switch roles.

1. ¿Entiendes una conversación en español? ¿Entiendes la lección?
2. ¿Quieres beber algo? ¿Prefieres Coca-Cola o Sprite?
3. ¿Quieres comer en tu casa o en la cafetería? ¿Qué quieres comer?
4. ¿Piensas ir a un baile el sábado? ¿Adónde piensas ir el domingo?
5. ¿Prefieres ir al cine o al teatro? ¿Te gusta ir a la playa? ¿Al parque?
6. ¿Qué piensas hacer hoy? ¿Y mañana?

Now get together with another classmate and tell each other about your respective partners.

Muchos productos norteamericanos como la Coca-Cola, por ejemplo, son muy populares en los países hispanos.

♦ **¿Qué productos extranjeros (foreign) son populares en este país?**

6. Expressions with *tener* (*Expresiones con* ***tener***)

♦ Many useful idiomatic expressions that use *to be* + *adjective* in English are formed with **tener** + *noun* in Spanish.

tener (mucho) frío	*to be (very) cold*
tener (mucha) sed	*to be (very) thirsty*
tener (mucha) hambre	*to be (very) hungry*
tener (mucho) calor	*to be (very) hot*
tener (mucho) sueño	*to be (very) sleepy*
tener (mucha) prisa	*to be in a (great) hurry*
tener (mucho) miedo	*to be (quite) afraid, scared*
tener cuidado	*to be careful*
tener razón	*to be right*
no tener razón[1]	*to be wrong*
tener... años de edad	*to be . . . years old*

---

[1]Incorrectness is also conveyed by the expression **estar equivocado(-a).**

—¿**Tienes calor?**   *"Are you hot?"*
—Sí, y también **tengo** mucha **sed.**   *"Yes, and I'm also very thirsty."*

—¿Deseas comer pollo?   *"Do you want to eat chicken?"*
—No, gracias, no **tengo hambre.**   *"No, thank you, I'm not hungry."*

—¿Cuántos **años tienes?**   *"How old are you?"*
—**Tengo** diecinueve **años.**   *"I'm nineteen years old."*

—Tenemos que trabajar más.   *"We have to work harder (more)."*
—**Tienes razón...**   *"You're right . . ."*

> **¡Atención!** Note that Spanish uses **mucho(-a)** (*adjective*) + *noun* (as in **mucha hambre**) the way English uses *very* + *adjective* (as in *very hungry*).

Un dicho

Donde hay hambre no hay pan duro.

Equivalent: Beggars can't be choosers.

Práctica

ACE the Test

A. ¿Qué tienen?

1. Jorge

2. Yo

3. Tú

4. La profesora

5. Ud.

6. Felipe

7. Marisa y Elena

8. Ella

 B. Which expression with **tener** would you use in each of the following situations?

1. You are in the Sahara desert in the middle of summer.
2. A big dog is chasing you.
3. You have only a minute to get to your next class.
4. You are in Alaska in the middle of winter.
5. You haven't eaten for an entire day.
6. You got up at four A.M. and it is now midnight.
7. You just ran for two hours in the sun.
8. You are blowing out thirty candles on your birthday cake.

Para conversar

 A. ¡Habla con tu compañero! Interview a classmate, using the following questions. When you have finished, switch roles.

1. ¿Qué bebes cuando tienes sed? ¿Y cuando tienes frío?
2. ¿Qué comes cuando tienes hambre?
3. ¿Cuántos años tienes?
4. ¿Cuántos años tiene tu mamá? ¿Y tu papá?
5. En tu familia, ¿quién tiene razón siempre? ¿Y en la clase?
6. ¿Tienes miedo a veces (*sometimes*)?

 B. Tenemos huéspedes. (*We have guests.*) Imagine that Mr. and Mrs. Vega and their two children, Anita and Luisito, are staying with you and your partner. Take turns asking them individually and/or collectively whether they are hungry, thirsty, etc. When possible, ask them also if they want a drink, etc.

¿Lo sabía Ud.?

En español se dice "¡Salud!" (*Cheers*) para brindar. En España también dicen "Salud, amor, y pesetas[1]" (*Health, love, and pesetas*).

---

[1]Pesetas were the monetary unit in Spain before the use of the Euro.

Así somos

Al escuchar...

Listening to voice mail When you listen to recorded announcements, such as a voice mail message or an announcement about an upcoming event or a sale at a store, it's important to grasp the basic information: the *who, what, when*, and *where*. As you listen, try to focus on the main facts rather than trying to understand everything you hear.

 Un mensaje telefónico A relative of your Spanish-speaking housemate has left a voice mail on your phone system. Listen to the message and make a note of the specifics of the call for your housemate. Listen to the message as many times as necessary.

1. ¿Quién llama?
2. ¿Quiénes vienen?
3. ¿Cuándo vienen?
4. ¿Dónde van a estar?
5. ¿Qué quieren hacer el sábado?

Al conversar...

Estrategia **Asking for additional information** When conversing, you often ask questions to learn more about a topic or statement. Asking questions also lets the person you are talking with know that you are interested in what he or she is saying. Here are some question words you can use when you want more information.

¿qué?	¿con quién?	¿para qué? (*what for?*)	¿cuál?
¿cuándo?	¿dónde?	¿por qué?	¿cuánto?

 ¿Y qué más? For each of the following statements write two or three questions you might ask to get more information.

1. Ana viene.
2. Necesito dinero.
3. Quiero libros.

 ¿Qué dice Ud.? What would you say in the following situations? What might the other person say? Act out the scenes with a partner. Take turns playing each role.

1. Someone offers you something to eat. Decline, saying that you are not hungry because you have just been eating.
2. You are planning a weekend with a friend. Ask where he/she wants to go; offer as many choices as possible.
3. A friend of yours is obviously upset. Try to find out what's wrong by asking him/her whether he/she is angry, nervous, etc.
4. You have three days off. Tell a friend what you are going to do for fun and ask him/her what he/she is going to do.
5. You are talking to an acquaintance from Mexico. Tell him/her what you and your friends do when you give a party.

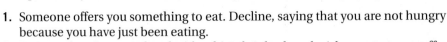

Para conocernos mejor To do this activity, work with a classmate whom you would like to get to know. Take turns asking and answering these questions.

1. ¿Cuántos años tienes? ¿Cuándo es tu cumpleaños?
2. ¿Estás invitado(-a) a una fiesta? ¿Asistes a muchas fiestas?
3. En una fiesta, ¿prefieres bailar o platicar con un amigo? ¿Bailas bien?
4. ¿Dónde vas a pasar el Año Nuevo? ¿Vas a dar una fiesta?
5. ¿Qué piensas hacer este fin de semana? ¿Adónde piensas ir?
6. ¿Prefieres ir a un museo o a un parque de diversiones? ¿A la playa o a la montaña?
7. ¿Tienes hambre o acabas de comer? ¿Quieres beber algo?
8. ¿Tienes hermanos? ¿Tienes muchos primos? ¿Tienes sobrinos?
9. ¿Estás contento(-a) o triste hoy? ¿Estás cansado(-a)?
10. ¿Dónde vas a estar mañana por la mañana? ¿Y por la tarde?

 Una encuesta Interview your classmates to identify who fits the following descriptions. Include your instructor, but remember to use the **Ud.** form when addressing him/her. After finishing the survey, get together with two or three classmates and discuss the results.

Nombre

1. Da fiestas frecuentemente. _____
2. Va a ir a una fiesta la semana que viene. _____
3. Celebra su cumpleaños con sus amigos. _____
4. Tiene muchos discos compactos. _____
5. Piensa ir a un concierto este fin de semana. _____
6. Tiene un equipo estereofónico muy bueno. _____
7. Va al parque a veces (sometimes). _____
8. Va al cine frecuentemente. _____

 Para crear Get together in groups of three or four and "create" the scenario for this photo. Who are the people in it? Give them names and describe them. What is their relationship to each other? What kind of party is it? Add any other pertinent details.

¡Vamos a leer!

Estrategia   **Identifying text formats** Before reading a text, it is useful to look at the title, subtitles, photos or illustrations, and format to get a general idea of the nature of the text. For example, is it an informative article, a calendar of events, an advertisement, or an interview? Recognizing formats can help orient you to the type of information to expect.

¿De qué habla? Look at the reading that follows. Have you come across similar types of texts? Where did this reading possibly appear? What is the title? Who is featured? Why? What might be said about them? Use this information to help you decipher the specifics of this reading.

A leer

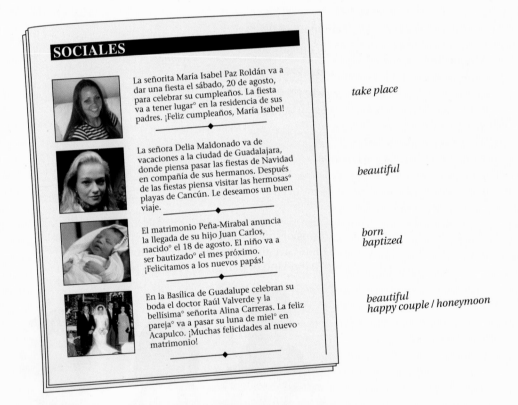

SOCIALES

La señorita María Isabel Paz Roldán va a dar una fiesta el sábado, 20 de agosto, para celebrar su cumpleaños. La fiesta va a tener lugar° en la residencia de sus padres. ¡Feliz cumpleaños, María Isabel!

take place

La señora Delia Maldonado va de vacaciones a la ciudad de Guadalajara, donde piensa pasar las fiestas de Navidad en compañía de sus hermanos. Después de las fiestas piensa visitar las hermosas° playas de Cancún. Le deseamos un buen viaje.

beautiful

El matrimonio Peña-Mirabal anuncia la llegada de su hijo Juan Carlos, nacido° el 18 de agosto. El niño va a ser bautizado° el mes próximo. ¡Felicitamos a los nuevos papás!

born
baptized

En la Basílica de Guadalupe celebran su boda el doctor Raúl Valverde y la bellísima° señorita Alina Carreras. La feliz pareja° va a pasar su luna de miel° en Acapulco. ¡Muchas felicidades al nuevo matrimonio!

beautiful
happy couple / honeymoon

 Comprensión As you read the **Sociales** section of the newspaper, find the answers to the following questions.

1. ¿Qué día va a dar una fiesta María Isabel? ¿Qué va a celebrar?
2. ¿Dónde va a tener lugar la fiesta?
3. ¿A qué ciudad va de vacaciones la Sra. Maldonado?
4. ¿Qué fiestas va a pasar allí (*there*)? ¿Con quiénes?
5. ¿Adónde va a ir después?
6. ¿Qué anuncia el matrimonio Peña-Mirabal? ¿Cuándo va a ser bautizado el niño?
7. ¿Quién es la esposa del doctor Valverde?
8. ¿Adónde va a ir de luna de miel la pareja?

¡Vamos a escribir!

Antes de escribir

Estrategia **Writing an e-mail** Although e-mails are more informal than letters, they follow a similar pattern.

- Greeting: **Querido(-a)...: Hola...:** (Use a colon after the name.)
- Body: one or more paragraphs that include the purpose of the message, the information you want to convey, and questions you want to ask
- Closing: **Bueno, nos vemos el día..., Besos, Tu amigo(-a)...**

Una invitación You will write an e-mail in which you invite a friend to spend a weekend with you. Before writing, jot down the information you want to include.

- When will it be? When should your friend arrive?
- What are the general plans and schedule of activities for the weekend? What are you going to do each day?
- Ask your friend if he or she prefers or wants to do one activity or another.

A escribir la invitación

Write your **primer borrador** of the message. Remember to use an appropriate greeting and closing.

Después de escribir

Before writing the final version, exchange your first draft with a classmate and peer edit each other's work using the following guidelines.

- use of **ir a** + *infinitive*
- formation of **e:ie** stem-changing verbs
- form of the e-mail: greeting, body, and closing

Después de leer... desde su mundo

In groups of three or four, talk about your plans for several holidays in the year.

Panorama hispánico

México

- La economía tradicional de México está basada en el petróleo y la agricultura, pero en las últimas décadas la industria, el turismo y el dinero que los emigrantes en los Estados Unidos envían a su casa, son la principal fuente de ingreso (*source of income*).

- La importancia del turismo se debe a (*is due to*) la abundancia de bellezas naturales y de reliquias históricas y al servicio eficiente de sus centros turísticos. Playas famosas como Acapulco, Cancún y Puerto Vallarta; ruinas arquitectónicas como Teotihuacán, Chichén Itzá y Tulúm, y la arquitectura de muchas ciudades atraen a turistas de todo el mundo. En México, D.F. coexisten restos arquitectónicos de la ciudad prehistórica Tenochtitlán, fundada en 1325 por los aztecas, edificios coloniales y modernas estructuras.

▲ La pirámide del Mago, parte de la ciudad maya de Uxmal (Yucatán), de los siglos VII a XIII

▲ El mariachi nació (*was born*) en Guadalajara, pero hoy es la música mexicana más popular en todo el mundo (*world*).

- Otras ciudades de gran interés turístico son Guadalajara, la segunda ciudad más grande del país, origen del mariachi y del tequila; Guanajuato, famosa por sus momias, y San Miguel de Allende, residencia de artistas de todo el mundo.

- En el mundo del arte, se destacan (*stand out*) pintores como Diego Rivera, José Clemente Orozco, David Alfaro Siqueiros y Frida Kahlo. Su música es popular en todo el mundo y las obras (*works*) de muchos de sus escritores están traducidas a muchas lenguas. Las telenovelas mexicanas son populares en muchos países, incluyendo aquéllos (*those*) donde no se habla español. Otro producto mexicano que ahora es internacional es su comida. En los Estados Unidos la salsa mexicana se vende hoy más que el "ketchup", y los tacos, las enchiladas, los burritos y el guacamole son parte de los menús de muchas escuelas.

Las artes plásticas, la literatura y el cine

◄ Mural de Diego Rivera
(1886–1957)

▲ Los famosos pintores mexicanos
Diego Rivera y Frida Kahlo

▲ La bellísima actriz mexicana, Salma Hayek,
en la entrega de los premios Grammy Latinos,
en Los Ángeles, California

▲ Octavio Paz (1914–1998), pensador e
intérprete de la cultura mexicana, Premio Nobel
de Literatura, 1990

Nuestro panorama cultural

In groups of three, answer the following questions about your home state, region, or country.

1. ¿Qué culturas indígenas existen en su país?
2. ¿Qué centros turísticos hay en el estado donde Ud. vive?
3. ¿Qué pintores famosos hay en su país?
4. ¿Cuál es la capital del estado donde Ud. vive?
5. ¿Qué tradiciones celebran Ud. y su familia en diciembre?
6. ¿Qué tipos de música tienen su origen en las ciudades de Nueva Orleáns y Nashville?

For the next class: Go to the World Wide Web and find photos from your home-town, state, region, or country. Use the questions from **Nuestro panorama cultural** above as guidelines for choosing them. Be ready to present the photos to your class-mates.

5

▲ Vista de un restaurante en la Zona Viva en la Ciudad de Guatemala

Objetivos

Comunicación

You will learn vocabulary related to restaurants, menus, ordering meals, and paying the bill. You will also learn to talk about the weather.

Pronunciación

The Spanish **p**, **t**, **c** (in the combinations **ca, co, cu**), and **q**

Estructuras

◆ Comparative forms
◆ Irregular comparative forms
◆ Present indicative of **o:ue** stem-changing verbs
◆ Present progressive
◆ Uses of **ser** and **estar**
◆ Weather expressions

Cultura

◆ Customs related to mealtimes and restaurants
◆ Currency of Hispanic countries
◆ Some regional foods and dishes

Panorama hispánico

◆ Guatemala
◆ El Salvador
◆ Aportaciones hispanas a la cocina norteamericana

Estrategias

Listening: Listening for details I
Speaking: Providing supporting details
Reading: Expanding your vocabulary through reading
Writing: Solidifying and repurposing what you learn

Las comidas

Recursos

Guatemala y El Salvador

Guatemala

Guatemala es uno de los países centroamericanos que fue (*was*) parte del imperio maya. Aunque el español es el idioma oficial, sólo lo habla el 60% de la población; el resto habla alguna lengua maya.

Guatemala es un país de volcanes, montañas y bellos paisajes. Su clima es muy agradable y por eso se conoce como "el país de la eterna primavera".

El Salvador

El Salvador es el país más pequeño de Centroamérica, pero es el más densamente poblado. Tiene más de seis millones de habitantes en un área aproximadamente del tamaño (*size*) del estado de Massachusetts.

En El Salvador hay más de 200 volcanes, y por eso lo llaman "la tierra (*land*) de los volcanes".

▲ Palacio de Gobierno en la Ciudad de Guatemala

▲ El volcán Izalco

◄ Tikal, ciudad maya que llegó a tener (*reached*) 100.000 habitantes.

Fernando Madera es de El Salvador, pero vive en la Ciudad de Guatemala. Es contador y trabaja en una fábrica. Fernando es casado y su esposa Cristina es guatemalteca, de la ciudad de Antigua. Él es delgado y de estatura mediana. No es muy guapo, pero es inteligente y simpático. Cristina es un poco más baja que él, y es muy hermosa.

En este momento están en un restaurante. Cristina está leyendo el menú.

Cristina	Arroz con pollo… biftec con papas al horno o puré de papas, ensalada… pescado frito…
Fernando	Yo a veces almuerzo aquí. Preparan una ensalada de camarones muy rica. También tienen langosta…
Cristina	La langosta cuesta 80 quetzales.[1] Es un poco cara…

El camarero viene a la mesa.

Camarero	¿Qué desean comer?
Cristina	Pollo a la parrilla con ensalada y una papa al horno. Para beber, agua mineral. (*A Fernando*) Tengo que contar calorías.
Camarero	(*Anota el pedido.*) Muy bien, señora. ¿Y usted, señor?
Fernando	Tráigame biftec con papas fritas y sopa de verduras. Para beber, vino tinto. (*A Cristina*) Las papas fritas tienen más sabor que las papas asadas…

El mozo va hacia la cocina.

Cristina	Voy a llamar a mamá para ver qué están haciendo los niños. Estoy un poco preocupada…
Fernando	¡Cristina! ¡Están en su casa, con su abuela! ¡Están bien! ¡Eres imposible!

Cristina habla por teléfono y después vuelve a la mesa.

Cristina	Amanda está estudiando, Fernandito está durmiendo y mamá está mirando su telenovela. Hay un mensaje electrónico de tu hermano. Lo están pasando muy bien en Cancún. Hace sol, pero no hace calor…
Fernando	¡Perfecto! Oye, voy a pedir flan con crema de postre.
Cristina	Y yo voy a pedir helado de chocolate…
Fernando	¿No estás contando calorías?
Cristina	Sí, pero el helado no tiene muchas calorías. Además… hoy es un día especial.
Fernando	¿Un día especial…?
Cristina	¡Sí! Estamos solos… podemos conversar… Creo que voy a pedir un pedazo de torta y después, café. Mañana vuelvo a mi dieta…

Fernando paga la cuenta y deja una buena propina.

---

[1]Guatemalan currency. Rate of exchange can vary.

Cristina

Fernando

Camarero

ACE the Test

¿Quién lo dice? Identify the person who said the following in the dialogues.

1. Tráigame biftec con papas fritas y sopa de verduras. _____
2. Mañana vuelvo a mi dieta. _____
3. Voy a llamar a mamá para ver qué están haciendo los niños. _____
4. Las papas fritas tienen más sabor que las papas asadas. _____
5. Yo a veces almuerzo aquí. Preparan una ensalada de camarones muy rica. _____
6. ¡Están bien! ¡Eres imposible! _____
7. ¿Que desean comer? _____
8. Pollo a la parrilla con ensalada y una papa al horno. _____
9. Tengo que contar calorías. _____

Hablemos. With a partner, take turns asking and answering the following questions. Base your answers on the dialogue and on your own circumstances.

En el diálogo	¿Y tú?
1. ¿Fernando es contador o profesor?	¿Tú deseas ser contador(-a)?
2. ¿Dónde trabaja Fernando?	¿Tú trabajas? ¿Dónde?
3. ¿Cómo es Fernando?	¿Tú eres bajo(-a), alto(-a) o de estatura mediana?
4. ¿Qué está leyendo Cristina?	¿Tú lees mucho?
5. ¿Cuánto cuesta la langosta?	¿Tú comes langosta o prefieres los camarones?
6. ¿Qué va a comer Cristina y qué va a beber?	¿Qué bebes tú en las comidas?
7. ¿Por qué prefiere Fernando comer papas fritas?	¿Tú prefieres papas fritas o papas al horno?
8. ¿A quién va a llamar Cristina? ¿Para qué?	¿A quién vas a llamar tú mañana?
9. ¿Qué están haciendo los niños? ¿Qué está haciendo la mamá de Cristina?	¿Tú miras telenovelas?
10. ¿Qué va a pedir Cristina de postre? ¿Cuándo vuelve a su dieta?	¿Qué comes tú de postre generalmente?

ⓘ Vocabulario

Cognados

las calorías calories	**especial** special
el chocolate chocolate	**guatemalteco(-a)** Guatemalan
la crema cream	**imposible** impossible
la dieta diet	**el menú** menu
la ensalada salad	**la sopa** soup

Nombres

el agua mineral mineral water	**el helado** ice cream
el arroz rice	**la langosta** lobster
el biftec, el bistec steak	**el (la) niño(-a)** child
el (la) camarero(-a), el mozo waiter, waitress	**la papa** potato
los camarones shrimp	**el pedazo, el trozo** piece
la cocina kitchen	**el pedido** order
la comida meal	**el pescado** fish
el (la) contador(-a) accountant	**el pollo** chicken
la cuenta bill, check	**la propina** tip
la esposa, la mujer wife	**el puré de papas** mashed potatoes
el esposo, el marido husband	**el sabor** flavor
la fábrica, la factoría factory	**la telenovela** soap opera
el flan caramel custard	**la torta** cake
	la verdura, la legumbre vegetable

Verbos

almorzar (o:ue) to have lunch	**mirar** to look (at), to watch (*e.g., TV*)
contar (o:ue) to count	**pagar** to pay
costar (o:ue) to cost	**pedir (e:i)** to order
dejar to leave (behind)	**poder (o:ue)** can, to be able to
dormir (o:ue) to sleep	**volver (o:ue), regresar** to return

Adjetivos

asado (-a) baked, roasted
caro(-a) expensive
frito(-a) fried
hermoso(-a) beautiful
rico(-a), sabroso(-a) tasty
solo(-a) alone
tinto red (*when referring to wine*)

Otras palabras y expresiones

a la parrilla grilled
además besides
al horno baked, cooked in the oven
de estatura mediana of medium height
de postre for dessert
en este momento at this moment
Hace calor. It's hot.

Hace sol. It's sunny.
hacia towards
para beber to drink
para ver to see
pasarlo bien to have a good time
tráigame bring me

¿Lo sabía Ud.? En los países hispanos el café se sirve después del postre. Generalmente es café tipo expreso, y se sirve en tazas muy pequeñas.

◆ **¿Se bebe mucho café en este país? ¿Qué tipo de café es muy popular aquí ahora?**

Vocabulario adicional

Para comer

el arroz con leche rice pudding
el cordero lamb
los frijoles beans
la hamburguesa hamburger
el jamón ham

el lechón pork
el pastel pastry
el pavo turkey
el perro caliente hot dog
el queso cheese
la sopa de fideos noodle soup

Bebidas (*Drinks*)

la cerveza beer
el champán champagne
el chocolate caliente hot chocolate
el jugo de frutas fruit juice
la leche milk
el refresco soft drink, soda pop
el té frío (helado) iced tea

Para poner la mesa (*To set the table*)

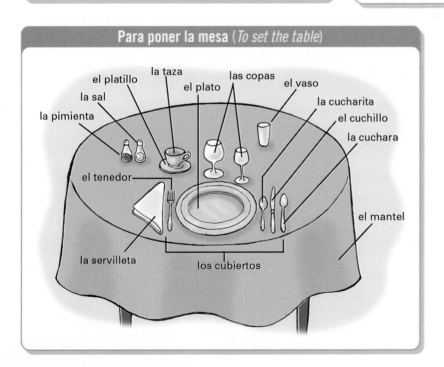

Práctica

 A. Choose the word or phrase that best completes each sentence.

1. Para beber quiero (cordero, cerveza, queso).
2. De postre queremos (pavo, lechón, arroz con leche).
3. Necesito (un cuchillo, una cuchara, un tenedor) para la sopa.
4. ¿Dónde está (el mantel, la cocina, el camarero)? Voy a poner la mesa.
5. Quiero (té, jugo, refresco) de frutas.
6. Voy a tomar (un plato, una copa, una taza) de café.
7. ¿Vienes con tus amigos o vienes (solo, caro, bajo)?
8. ¿Prefieres vino blanco o vino (rojo, delgado, tinto)?
9. Quiero un sándwich de (jamón, pastel, frijoles) y queso.
10. Necesito la sal y la (servilleta, pimienta, cucharita) para el biftec.

B. Write the words or phrases that correspond to the following.

1. lo que cuenta una persona que está a dieta _____
2. persona de Guatemala _____
3. opuesto de **posible** _____
4. Perrier, por ejemplo _____
5. factoría _____
6. marido _____
7. trozo _____
8. salmón, por ejemplo _____
9. regresar _____
10. rico _____

¿Lo sabía Ud.?

Después de comer, los hispanos se quedan sentados (*remain seated*) alrededor de la mesa y conversan. A esto se le llama "hacer la sobremesa".

◆ **¿Se hace la sobremesa en este país?**

C. Complete the following exchanges, using vocabulary from this lesson.

1. —¿Quieres _____ caliente?
   —No, prefiero _____ helado.
2. —¿Qué quieren de _____?
   —Flan con _____ y helado.
3. —¿Qué vas a pedir?
   —Pescado _____ y _____ de papas, ¿y tú?
   —Pollo a la _____, una papa al _____ y verduras.
4. —¿Qué desea comer, señora?
   —Sopa de _____, langosta y biftec.
5. —¿Dónde están los niños en _____ momento?
   —En el zoológico. Ellos lo _____ muy bien allí.
6. —¿Tú miras la _____ *Todos tus hijos*?
   —No, yo no _____ mirar televisión. Estoy muy ocupada.

Para conversar

 Tráigame… With a partner, take turns playing a customer and a waiter (waitress). The waiter (waitress) recommends things to eat, things for dessert, and things to drink (**Yo le recomiendo…**). The customer has other ideas and orders something else (**No, tráigame…**).

En los países hispanos, la propina generalmente es del 10%. Con frecuencia la propina está incluida en la cuenta. Si Ud. no está seguro de esto, debe preguntar (*ask*), **¿Está incluido el servicio?**

◆ **Generalmente, ¿cuánto se deja de propina en un restaurante en este país?**

Pronunciación

A. The Spanish *p*

The Spanish **p** is pronounced like the English *p* in the word *sparks*, but with no expulsion of air. Listen to your instructor and repeat the following phrases.

> **P**aco **p**refiere **p**apas fritas.
>
> Mi es**p**osa está un **p**oco **p**reocu**p**ada.
>
> **P**iden **p**ollo y **p**astel.

B. The Spanish *t*

The Spanish **t** is pronounced by placing the tongue against the upper teeth, as in the English word *stop*. Listen to your instructor and repeat the following phrases.

> Cris**t**ina es**t**á en Gua**t**emala.
>
> **T**ambién **t**ienen **t**orta.
>
> **T**i**t**o es**t**á a die**t**a.

C. The Spanish *c*

The Spanish sound for the letter **c** in the combinations **ca**, **co**, and **cu** is /k/, pronounced as in the English word *scar*, but with no expulsion of air. Listen to your instructor and repeat the following phrases.

> **C**arlos **c**ome **c**amarones.
>
> ¿**C**uánto **c**uesta el **c**afé?
>
> **C**armen A**c**osta está en **C**ancún.

D. The Spanish *q*

The Spanish **q** is always followed by a **u**; it is pronounced like the *c* in the English word *come*, but without any expulsion of air. Listen to your instructor and repeat the following phrases.

> ¿**Q**ué **q**uiere **Q**uique?
>
> Ro**q**ue **Q**uintana come **q**ueso.
>
> ¿**Q**uién **q**uiere **q**uesadillas?

Aspectos culturales

En imágenes (*Algunos alimentos¹ regionales y platos típicos*)

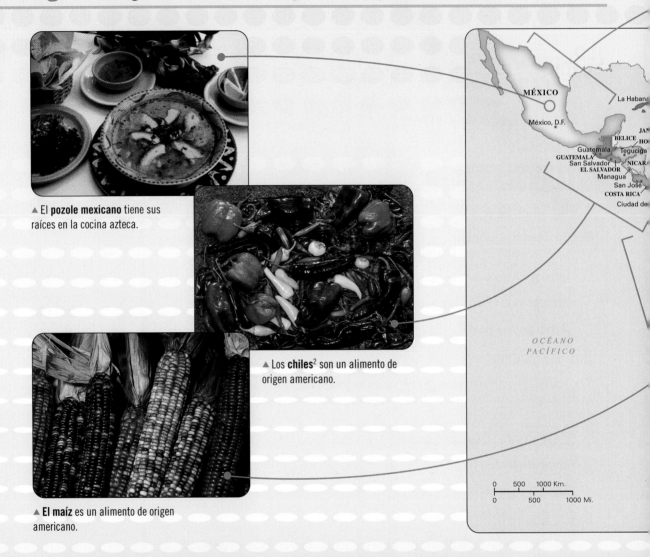

▲ El **pozole mexicano** tiene sus raíces en la cocina azteca.

▲ Los **chiles**² son un alimento de origen americano.

▲ El **maíz** es un alimento de origen americano.

Ubíquese... y búsquelo

Improve Your Grade
Web Search

You are helping Fernando show his mother, who is visiting from El Salvador, around Guatemala City, and you are looking for a good restaurant. Go to **www.cengage .com/highered** and research some of Guatemala City's restaurants online and find one where you would like to eat. Which restaurant did you choose? What kinds of foods or dishes do they serve there? In the next class, team up with two classmates to discuss your findings.

¹**alimentos** = *food*
²**ají (ajíes)** (*América del Sur, Puerto Rico*), **guindillas** (*España*)

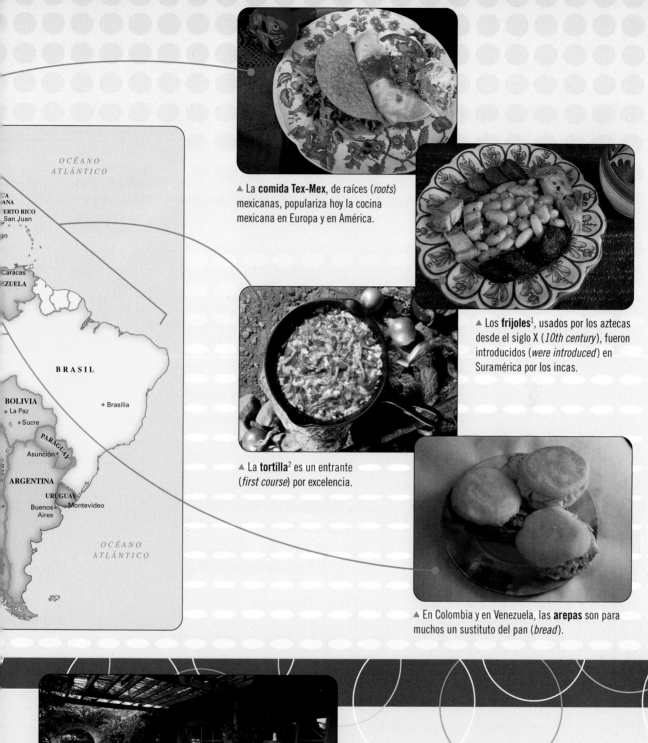

▲ La **comida Tex-Mex**, de raíces (*roots*) mexicanas, populariza hoy la cocina mexicana en Europa y en América.

▲ Los **frijoles**[1], usados por los aztecas desde el siglo X (*10th century*), fueron introducidos (*were introduced*) en Suramérica por los incas.

▲ La **tortilla**[2] es un entrante (*first course*) por excelencia.

▲ En Colombia y en Venezuela, las **arepas** son para muchos un sustituto del pan (*bread*).

[1]**habichuelas** (*Puerto Rico*), **porotos** (*Argentina*), **judías** (*España*), **caraotas** (*Venezuela*) [2]**tortilla española** (*América*)

Estructuras

1. Comparative forms (*Formas comparativas*)

A. Comparisons of inequality

◆ In Spanish, the comparative of inequality of most adjectives, adverbs, and nouns is formed by placing **más** (*more*) or **menos** (*less*) before the adjective, the adverb, or the noun and **que** (*than*) after it.

más (*more*)		*adjective*		
	+	*or adverb* +	**que** (*than*)
menos (*less*)		*or*		
		noun		

—¿Tú eres **más alta que** Ana? *"Are you taller than Ana?"*
—Sí, ella es mucho **más baja que** yo. *"Yes, she is much shorter than I."*

> **¡Atención!** **De** is used instead of **que** before a numerical expression of quantity or amount.

Luis tiene **más de** treinta años. *Luis is over thirty years old.*

Hay **menos de** veinte estudiantes aquí. *There are fewer than twenty students here.*

Es agradable ser importante, pero es más importante ser agradable.

It is nice to be important, but it's more important to be nice.

B. Comparisons of equality

◆ To form comparisons of equality with adjectives and adverbs in Spanish, use the adverb **tan… como.**

When comparing adjectives or adverbs:

tan (*as*) ⟨ bonita / tarde ⟩ **+ como**

—Luis es **tan** inteligente **como** Sergio. *"Luis is as intelligent as Sergio."*
—Sí, pero él no es **tan** guapo **como** Sergio. *"Yes, but he is not as handsome as Sergio."*
—Carol habla muy bien el español. *"Carol speaks Spanish very well."*
—Tú hablas **tan** bien **como** ella. *"You speak as well as she (does)."*

No es tan fiero el león como lo pintan.

Equivalent: His bark is worse than his bite.

C. The superlative

◆ The superlative construction is similar to the comparative. It is formed by placing the definite article before the person or thing being compared.

| definite article | + | (noun) | + | más or menos | + | adjective | + | de |

—¿Quieres ir a Antigua? "Do you want to go to Antigua?"
—Sí, es **la ciudad más hermosa de** Guatemala. "Yes, it's the most beautiful city in Guatemala."

—Juan no es muy inteligente. "Juan is not very intelligent."
—No, es **el**[1] **menos inteligente de** la familia. "No, he is the least intelligent (one) in the family."

¡Atención! Note that the Spanish **de** translates to the English *in* after a superlative.

Es la ciudad más hermosa **de** Guatemala. *It's the most beautiful city in Guatemala.*
Es la chica más bonita **de** la clase. *She is the prettiest girl in the class.*

Un dicho

Amigo y vino, el más antiguo.

Equivalent: Old friends and old wine are best.

Práctica

ACE the Test

A. With a partner, compare the people in the picture to each other.

1. María es _____ Rosa.
2. Rosa es _____ María.
3. Carlos es _____ Rosa y que María.
4. Carlos es _____ Juan.
5. Juan es _____ Carlos.
6. Juan es _____ María.
7. Juan es el _____ de todos.
8. Carlos es el _____ de todos.

Carlos   Rosa   María   Juan

B. Establish comparisons between the following people and things, using the adjectives provided and adding any necessary words.

1. Michael Jordan / Danny De Vito (alto)
2. El Salvador / Canadá (pequeño) (*small*)
3. La clase de español / inglés (difícil)
4. Julia Roberts / Penélope Cruz (bonita)
5. Guatemala / Argentina (grande) (*big*)
6. Jim Carrey / Antonio Banderas (guapo)

Now find a partner and take turns comparing more people and things.

---

[1]As in English, the noun may be omitted.

A. **¡A conocernos mejor!** With a partner, take turns asking each other the following questions.

1. ¿Tú eres tan inteligente como tus padres? ¿Quién es el (la) más inteligente de la familia? ¿Tú eres más inteligente que tu mejor (*best*) amigo(-a)?
2. ¿Tú eres más alto(-a) que yo? ¿Tú eres más alto(-a) que tu mamá? ¿Quién es el más alto de la familia?
3. ¿Tú bailas tan bien como Ricky Martin? ¿Cantas tan bien como él?
4. ¿Tú eres tan guapo como Brad Pitt? (¿Tan bonita como Jennifer López?) ¿Quién es el más guapo de tus amigos? ¿La más bonita de tus amigas?

 B. **¡Vamos a comparar!** (*Let's compare!*) In groups of three or four, make comparisons between each one of you and other members of the class. You might want to include the instructor. Decide who is the tallest, the most intelligent, the most charming, etc.

2. Irregular comparative forms (*Formas comparativas irregulares*)

◆ The following adjectives and adverbs have irregular comparative and superlative forms in Spanish.

Adjective	Adverb	Comparative	Superlative
bueno	bien	**mejor**	**el (la) mejor**
malo	mal	**peor**	**el (la) peor**
grande		**mayor**	**el (la) mayor**
pequeño		**menor**	**el (la) menor**

> **LEARNING TIP**
>
> Think of hotels and restaurants in your city. Which ones are the best? The worst? Compare some of your friends and relatives to you. Who are older? Who are younger?

—El restaurante El Dorado es muy **malo.**
—Sí, pero la cafetería de la universidad es **peor.**

"*The El Dorado Restaurant is very bad.*"
"*Yes, but the university's cafeteria is worse.*"

—Eva es una **buena** estudiante.
—Sí, es **la mejor** de la clase.

"*Eva is a good student.*"
"*Yes, she's the best in the class.*"

◆ When the adjectives **grande** and **pequeño** refer to size, the regular forms are generally used.

Tu casa es **más grande** que la de Carolina.

Your house is bigger than Carolina's.

◆ When these adjectives refer to age, the irregular forms are used.

Ella es **mucho mayor** que yo.   *She is much older than I.*
Teresa es **menor** que Carlos.   *Teresa is younger than Carlos.*
Ella es **la menor** de todos.   *She is the youngest of all.*

Yo soy un poco **mayor** que mi novio.

Práctica

 Answer the following questions with complete sentences.

1. Mi sobrina tiene siete años y mi sobrino tiene cinco. ¿Quién es mayor? ¿Quién es menor?
2. Mi tío tiene cuarenta años y mi tía tiene treinta y ocho. ¿Quién es menor? ¿Quién es mayor?
3. ¿Quién habla mejor el español, tú o el profesor (la profesora)?
4. Pedro tiene una "B" en inglés; Antonio tiene una "C"; y José tiene una "F". ¿Quién es el peor estudiante? ¿Quién es el mejor estudiante?

Now write three original comparative situations, using the ones you have just completed as models. When you have finished, take turns giving and responding to situations with a partner.

Para conversar

¡Habla con tu compañero! Interview a classmate, using the following questions. When you have finished, switch roles.

1. ¿Tú eres mayor o menor que tu mejor amigo(-a)?
2. ¿Tu mamá es menor que tu papá?
3. ¿Quién cocina (*cooks*) mejor, tú o tu mamá?
4. ¿Quién crees tú que es el (la) mejor estudiante de la clase?
5. ¿Cuál crees tú que es la mejor película (*film*) del año? ¿Y la peor?
6. De los restaurantes de la ciudad donde vives, ¿cuál es el mejor? ¿Y el peor?
7. ¿Cuál crees tú que es la mejor universidad de tu país?
8. ¿Quiénes crees tú que manejan (*drive*) mejor: los hombres o las mujeres?

3. Present indicative of *o:ue* stem-changing verbs (*Presente de indicativo de los verbos que cambian en la raíz o:ue*)

♦ Some verbs undergo a stem change in the present indicative. For these verbs, when **o** is the last stem vowel and it is stressed, it changes to **ue**.

poder *to be able*	
puedo	podemos
puedes	podéis
puede	**pue**den

—**¿Puedes** ir conmigo al restaurante?　*"Can you go with me to the restaurant?"*
—No, no **puedo**. No tengo dinero.　*"No, I can't. I don't have (any) money."*

♦ Other verbs that undergo this change:[1]

almorzar *to have lunch*　　　**llover** (impersonal) *to rain*
contar *to tell, to count*　　　**morir** *to die*
costar *to cost*　　　　　　　**recordar** *to remember*
dormir *to sleep*　　　　　　**volar** *to fly*
encontrar *to find*　　　　　**volver** *to return*

—¿A qué hora **vuelven** Uds.?　　*"At what time are you returning?"*
—**Volvemos** a las doce.　　　　*"We'll return at twelve o'clock."*
—Entonces **almorzamos** a　　　*"Then we'll have lunch at*
　las doce y media.　　　　　　　*twelve-thirty."*

Aquí **llueve** mucho.

Note that the stem vowel is not stressed in the verb forms used with **nosotros(-as)** and **vosotros(-as);** therefore, the **o** does not change to **ue.**

---
[1]For a complete list of stem-changing verbs, see Appendix B.

Práctica

 A. Marité is talking to her roommate, who is sound asleep. Complete the story, supplying the missing (**o:ue**) verbs. Then read it aloud.

Marité ¡Teresa, me voy! No _____ mis libros. ¿Dónde están? No _____ ir a mi clase sin (*without*) mis libros. ¡Oye! Hoy _____ con Pedro en la cafetería; no tengo dinero y los sándwiches en la cafetería _____ tres dólares. ¡Ay, Teresa!, hoy tengo que llamar a Marta y no _____ su número de teléfono. ¡Teresa!, ¿tú _____ el número de Marta? ¡Oye! ¿Roberto _____ a San Salvador hoy? ¿Vas al aeropuerto con él? (*Mira por la ventana.*) ¡Ay, cómo _____ ! Necesito tu impermeable (*raincoat*). ¡Ah!, hoy _____ a casa a las cinco. (*Abre la puerta de Teresa.*) ¡Teresa! ¡Teresa! ¿Por qué no contestas (*answer*)?

Teresa (*Mmm…*) Nunca _____ dormir cuando tú estás en casa.

Marité Tú _____ mucho. No necesitas dormir más. Me voy. Nos vemos.

 B. Arnaldo is very nosy and is always asking questions. Here are the answers. What are his questions?

1. ¿ _____? Mi equipo estereofónico cuesta $1.000.
2. ¿ _____? Nosotros almorzamos en el restaurante.
3. ¿ _____? Volvemos a casa a las cinco.
4. ¿ _____? No, yo no duermo mucho.
5. ¿ _____? No, no recuerdo el número de teléfono de Ana.
6. ¿ _____? Vuelo a Guatemala los domingos.
7. ¿ _____? No, no puedo ir a tu casa esta noche.

 C. With a classmate, prepare four or five questions to ask your instructor, using stem-changing (**o:ue**) verbs.

Para conversar

A. **¡Habla con tu compañero!** Interview a classmate, using the following questions. When you have finished, switch roles.

1. ¿Almuerzas en la cafetería, en tu casa o en un restaurante? ¿Con quién almuerzas? ¿A qué hora?
2. ¿Cuánto cuesta un sándwich de jamón y queso en la cafetería? ¿Y uno de ensalada de pollo? ¿Son caros? ¿Son buenos?
3. ¿Duermes bien? ¿Cuántas horas duermes? ¿Cuentas ovejas (*sheep*) para dormir?
4. ¿Hasta (*Up to*) qué número puedes contar en español?
5. ¿Encuentras fácil o difícil la clase de español? ¿Recuerdas todo el vocabulario? ¿Te gusta el español?
6. ¿A qué hora vuelves a tu casa hoy? ¿A qué hora vuelves mañana? Generalmente, ¿vuelves temprano (*early*)?
7. ¿Llueve mucho en tu ciudad? ¿En qué mes llueve más? ¿Tú vienes a la universidad cuando llueve mucho?
8. ¿Recuerdas el número de teléfono de tus amigos? ¿Y el de tus padres?

B. **Compañeros de cuarto** You are interviewing a prospective roommate. Tell him/her how much the apartment costs and ask pertinent questions about his/her schedule and routine. Give details about yours.

4. Present progressive (*Estar* + *gerundio*)

◆ The present progressive describes an action that is in progress. It is formed with the present tense of **estar** and the **gerundio,** which is equivalent to the English present participle (the *-ing* form of the verb).

Gerundio		
hablar	*comer*	*escribir*
habl -**ando**	com -**iendo**	escrib -**iendo**
speaking	*eating*	*writing*

—¿Qué **estás tomando**?   *"What are you drinking?"*
—**Estoy tomando** chocolate caliente.   *"I am drinking hot chocolate.*
    Y tú, ¿qué **estás comiendo?**   *And you, what are you eating?"*
—**Estoy comiendo** un pedazo de pastel.   *"I'm eating a piece of pie."*

—¿Qué **están haciendo** los niños?   *"What are the children doing?"*
—**Están escribiendo.**   *"They are writing."*

◆ The following forms are irregular.

pedir: **pidiendo**   dormir: **durmiendo**
decir: **diciendo**   traer: **trayendo**
servir: **sirviendo**   leer: **leyendo**

—¿Daniel **está leyendo**?   *"Is Daniel reading?"*
—No, **está durmiendo**.   *"No, he's sleeping."*

—¿Qué **está sirviendo** el camarero?   *"What is the waiter serving?"*
—**Está sirviendo** las bebidas.   *"He's serving the drinks."*

—¿Daniel **está pidiendo** champán?   *"Is Daniel ordering champagne?"*
—No, porque el champán   *"No, because champagne*
    cuesta 70 quetzales.   *costs 70 quetzales."*

◆ Note that as shown with **traer** and **leer,** the i of **-iendo** becomes **y** between vowels.

¡Atención!   In Spanish, the present progressive is never used to indicate a future action. The present tense is used in future expressions that would require the present progressive in English.

Trabajo mañana.   *I'm working tomorrow.*

Some verbs, such as **ser, estar, ir,** and **venir,** are rarely used in the progressive construction.

El **quetzal** es la unidad monetaria de Guatemala. Argentina, Chile, Colombia, Cuba, México, República Dominicana y Uruguay usan el **peso.** Otras unidades monetarias de los países de habla hispana son: el **boliviano** en Bolivia, el **colón** en Costa Rica y El Salvador[1], el **dólar** en Ecuador, Panamá y Puerto Rico, el **lempira** en Honduras, el **córdoba** en Nicaragua, el **nuevo sol** en Perú, el **guaraní** en Paraguay, el **bolívar** en Venezuela y el **euro** en España. El valor de estas monedas no es estable y su equivalencia con el dólar varía frecuentemente.

◆ **¿Cuál es la unidad monetaria de este país?**

---
[1]The dollar is legal tender in this country.

Práctica

 A. With a partner, take turns asking each other what the following people are doing (**haciendo**).

1. Tú…

2. Yo…

3. Raúl y Sara…

4. Eva…

5. La profesora…

6. Nosotros… y el chico…

 B. Complete the following dialogues, using the present progressive of the verbs given. Then act them out with a partner, adding a sentence or two to each dialogue.

1. comer   —¿Qué _____ tú?

   —Yo _____ ensalada.

2. leer   —¿Qué libro _____ Uds.?

   —_____ *Don Quijote.*

3. servir   —¿Qué _____ Uds.?

   —Yo _____ refrescos y Luisa _____ vino.

4. decir   —¿Qué _____ Juan Carlos?

   —_____ que está muy preocupado.

5. estudiar   —¿José _____?

   dormir   —No, _____.

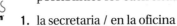

C. With a partner, discuss what you think these people are doing. Give two or three possibilities for each situation.

1. la secretaria / en la oficina
2. los estudiantes / en la clase
3. los chicos / en la cafetería
4. el profesor / en la universidad

5. los muchachos y las muchachas / en la fiesta
6. el Sr. Vega / en su cuarto
7. el camarero / en el restaurante
8. la Srta. Barrios / en su apartamento

Para conversar

 ¿Qué están haciendo? The instructor will play the role of house-parent in a dorm. He/She will leave the classroom for one minute, then return and ask each student what he/she is doing. Each person will claim to be doing something worthwhile and accuse another student of doing something naughty. The student will deny it and say he/she is doing something else.

HINT: fumar *to smoke*

5. Uses of *ser* and *estar* (*Usos de* **ser** *y* **estar**)

The English verb *to be* has two Spanish equivalents, **ser** and **estar**. As a general rule, **ser** expresses *who* or *what* the subject is *essentially*, and **estar** indicates *state* or *condition*. **Ser** and **estar** are *not* interchangeable.

A. Uses of *ser*

Ser expresses a fundamental quality and identifies the essence of a person or thing.

♦ It describes the basic nature or character of a person or thing. It is also used with expressions of age that do not refer to a specific number of years.

   Amanda **es** hermosa y muy inteligente. **Es** joven (*young*), pero **es** muy madura.

♦ It is used to denote nationality, origin, and profession or trade.

   Amanda **es** guatemalteca. **Es** de la ciudad de Guatemala. **Es** estudiante.

♦ It is used to indicate relationship or possession.

   Amanda **es** la sobrina del Sr. Álvarez. Los discos compactos **son** de Amanda.

♦ It is used with expression of time and with dates.

   Son las cuatro y cuarto de la tarde. Hoy **es** miércoles, cuatro de abril.

♦ It is used with events as the equivalent of *taking place*.

   La fiesta **es** en la casa de Amanda.

No todo lo que brilla es oro.

All that glitters is not gold.

♦ It describes the material that things are made of.

   La mesa **es** de metal.

Práctica

ACE the Test

Interview a classmate, using the following questions and two of your own. When you have finished, switch roles.

1. ¿Eres norteamericano(-a)? ¿De dónde eres?
2. ¿De qué ciudad eres?
3. ¿Cómo es tu mamá? ¿Cómo es tu papá?
4. ¿Quién es tu mejor amigo(-a)?
5. ¿Es alto(-a) o bajo(-a)?
6. ¿Eres optimista?
7. ¿Dónde son tus clases?
8. ¿Qué día es hoy?
9. ¿Qué fecha es hoy?
10. ¿Qué hora es?

B. Uses of *estar*

Estar is used to express more transitory qualities and often implies the possibility of change.

♦ It indicates place or location.

   Mi prima no **está** aquí. ¿**Está** en el restaurante?

♦ It is used to indicate condition.

   Mis amigos **están** muy cansados.
   El contador **está** enfermo.

♦ With personal reactions, it describes what is perceived through the senses—that is, how a person or thing seems, looks, tastes, or feels.

   El ponche **está** muy sabroso.

♦ It is used in the present progressive tense.

   Yo **estoy** estudiando y Ana **está** leyendo.

Práctica

A. Imagine that you and a friend are at a party at a club, and answer the following questions. Work with a partner.

1. ¿En qué calle está el club?
2. ¿Los amigos de Uds. están en el club?
3. ¿Sus amigos están contentos o tristes?
4. ¿Cómo está la comida? ¿Rica?

5. ¿Quiénes están bailando?
6. ¿Tu mamá está en la fiesta?
7. ¿Tú estás conversando?
8. ¿Lo estás pasando bien?

B. Complete the following dialogues, using the appropriate forms of **ser** or **estar.** Then act them out with a partner.

1. —¿De dónde _____ tu mamá? ¿_____ guatemalteca?

   —Sí, pero ahora _____ en San Salvador.

   —¿Tu mamá _____ profesora?

   —No, _____ contadora.

2. —¿Olga _____ tu prima?

   —No, _____ mi hermana.

   —¿Cómo _____ ella?

   —_____ alta, morena y delgada. _____ muy bonita.

   —¿Dónde _____ ella ahora?

   —_____ en su casa.

3. —¿Qué hora _____?

   —_____ las siete.

   —¿Dónde _____ la fiesta de Navidad?

   —_____ en el club. ¿Tú vas a ir?

   —No, _____ muy cansada.

4. —¿Qué _____ comiendo tú?

   —_____ comiendo arroz con pollo.

   —¿ _____ rico?

   —Sí, _____ muy sabroso.

5. —¿Ése (*That*) _____ tu escritorio?

   —Sí, _____ mi escritorio.

   —¿ _____ de metal?

   —No, _____ de madera (*wood*).

C. Answer the following questions according to what you see in the illustration. Take turns responding with a partner.

1. ¿Qué día es hoy? ¿Qué fecha es hoy? ¿Qué hora es?
2. ¿Luis es casado o soltero?
3. ¿Ud. cree que Eva es la esposa o la mamá de Luis?
4. ¿Eva es bonita o fea? ¿Cómo es Luis?
5. ¿Dónde están Eva y Luis?
6. ¿Qué está comiendo Luis? ¿Está sabrosa la langosta?
7. ¿Quién es José?
8. ¿Qué está sirviendo José?
9. ¿En qué está pensando José? ¿Dónde es la fiesta?
10. ¿Isabel está contenta o triste?

Para conversar

¿Quién es? With two or three other students, prepare a description of a famous person. Include as much information as possible (nationality, profession, physical characteristics, etc.). Read your description to the rest of the class and see who can identify your subject.

En la mayoría de los países hispanos, los restaurantes no sirven la cena hasta las nueve de la noche. A las cuatro de la tarde, la gente merienda (*has an afternoon snack*).

◆ **¿A qué hora empiezan a servir la cena los restaurantes en este país?**

6. Weather expressions (*Expresiones para describir el tiempo*)

◆ In the following expressions, Spanish uses the verb **hacer,** *to make,* followed by a noun.

▲ Es el 13 de agosto. Eva está en Phoenix, Arizona. **Hace sol** y **hace** mucho **calor.**

▲ Es el 20 de enero. Luis está en Alaska. **Hace** mucho **frío.**

▲ Ana y Raúl están en Chicago en octubre. Hoy **hace** mucho **viento.**

◆ To ask about the weather, say, **"¿Qué tiempo hace?"** (*What's the weather like?*).

—¿**Qué tiempo hace** hoy?   *"What's the weather like today?"*
—**Hace** buen (mal) tiempo.   *"The weather is good (bad)."*

◆ The following words used to describe the weather do not combine with **hacer;** they are impersonal verbs used only in the infinitive, present participle, past participle, and third person singular forms of all tenses.

llover (**o:ue**) *to rain*   **Llueve.** *It rains.*
nevar (**e:ie**) *to snow*   **Nieva.** *It snows.*

▲ Está lloviendo.   ▲ Está nevando.

◆ Other weather-related words are **lluvia** (*rain*) and **niebla** (*fog*).

—¿**Hace frío** en Guatemala?   *"Is it cold in Guatemala?"*
—No, Guatemala es el país de   *"No, Guatemala is the country*
     la eterna primavera.   *of eternal spring."*

—¿Vas a volar hoy a San Salvador?   *"Are you going to fly to San Salvador today?"*
—No, porque **hay niebla.**   *"No, because it's foggy."*

ACE the Test

Práctica

A. Study the words in the following list, then complete the dialogues.

el paraguas *umbrella*
el impermeable *raincoat*
el sombrero *hat*
el abrigo *coat*
el suéter *sweater*

1. —¿Necesitas un paraguas?
    —Sí, porque en Oregón _____ mucho.

2. —¿No necesitas un abrigo?
    —No, porque _____.

3. —¿Por qué no quieres llevar el suéter?
    —¡Porque _____!

4. —¿Vas a llevar el sombrero?
    —Sí, porque _____.

5. —¿Necesitas un suéter y un abrigo?
    —Sí, porque _____.

6. —¿Un impermeable? ¿Por qué? ¿Está lloviendo?
    —No, pero _____.

7. —¡Qué lluvia! Necesito un _____ y un _____.
    —¡Yo también!

B. Say what the weather will be like in different locations at different times of the year.

1. Portland, Oregón—el 2 de enero
2. Anchorage, Alaska—el 25 de diciembre
3. Phoenix, Arizona—el 13 de agosto
4. Londres (*London*)—el 5 de febrero
5. Chicago—el 6 de marzo

 **A mal tiempo, buena cara.**

Equivalent: **Keep a stiff upper lip.**

Para conversar

  A. De visita (*Visiting*) A visiting professor from Guatemala is planning a weekend visit to your hometown. What questions is he or she likely to ask about the weather there and what clothes to bring? How will you respond? Act out the scene with a partner. Say at least five lines each.

 B. El pronóstico del tiempo (*The weather forecast*) You and a classmate are in charge of preparing the weather report for a local TV station. Discuss the weather in your area today.

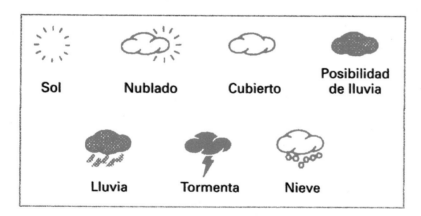

Sol   Nublado   Cubierto   Posibilidad de lluvia

Lluvia   Tormenta   Nieve

LEARNING TIP

Note that when talking about weather conditions, the normal Spanish sentence structure is modified. Instead of the general *subject* + *verb* + *object* structure, one uses **Hace** or **Hay** (impersonal forms of **hacer** and **haber**—that is, in this construction the verb is not conjugated) + the particular weather expression, or just the impersonal weather-related verb such as **Llueve** or **Nieva**. The repertory of sentence structures in Spanish, just as in English, goes beyond the basic one you know. Start recognizing any variant structure (syntactic) patterns.

Así somos

Al escuchar...

> **Estrategia** **Listening for details I** In the preceding lessons, you have practiced listening for the main idea and for specific information in different types of oral texts. When listening for details, draw on the strategies you've already learned and concentrate on the specific information you want to obtain, such as the what, where, and when. Also use your knowledge of the topic and format (voice mail, ad, public service announcement, etc.) to anticipate the kind of information you will hear. This will help you understand more of the details.

 Un anuncio de radio You hear a commercial about a new restaurant that has just opened near where you live. You want to know what it's like, its menu, the hours, specific location, prices of dishes, etc. Listen attentively and jot down the following information. Listen a second time for any details you missed.

nombre del restaurante _____

dirección _____

tipo de comida _____

horas del almuerzo _____

horas de la cena _____

cómo son los precios _____

Al conversar...

> **Estrategia** **Providing supporting details** To express a point of view effectively, give an explanation, or inform others about a topic, you need to include details or information that makes the topic interesting to your listener, helps him or her understand it, and that supports and expands on your basic idea.

 Un restaurante nuevo You're interested in going to the new restaurant you have just heard about (or your favorite restaurant). Tell two friends about it, giving as much information as you can about the restaurant to explain why it's a good choice. Answer their questions about the food, the specialties (**especialidades**), the prices, etc., and find out if they want to try it.

 ¿Qué dice Ud.? What would you say in the following situations? What might the other person say? Act out the scenes with a partner. Take turns playing each role.

1. You describe your mother and a friend describes his/hers. Make comparisons between them.
2. You and a friend are at a restaurant. Order a complete meal, including drinks and dessert.
3. You tell your dining companion that you can pay the bill and ask if he/she can leave the tip.
4. You are cooking a gourmet dinner. Ask your roommate to set the table. Name the utensils and other items you want. Your roommate doesn't know where things are.
5. You are hosting a party at your home. Some of your guests have brought children. Offer a selection of beverages.

Para conocernos mejor To do this activity, work with a classmate whom you would like to get to know. Take turns asking and answering these questions.

1. ¿Prefieres comer una hamburguesa o un perro caliente? ¿Prefieres beber leche, té helado o chocolate caliente?
2. ¿Tú almuerzas en un restaurante a veces? ¿Cuál es el mejor restaurante de tu ciudad? ¿Es muy caro?
3. Generalmente, ¿almuerzas con tu familia? ¿Vives con tus padres o vives solo(-a)?
4. ¿Eres el más alto (la más alta) de tu familia? ¿Quién es el más bajo?
5. ¿Tu mamá es mayor o menor que tu papá? ¿Cuál de los dos tiene razón siempre (*always*)?
6. ¿Quién es tu mejor amigo(-a)? ¿Cómo es? ¿Dónde está ahora?
7. ¿Qué tiempo hace hoy? Cuando llueve, ¿prefieres usar (*to wear*) impermeable o paraguas? Cuando hace frío, ¿usas abrigo o suéter?
8. ¿Te gusta vivir en un lugar donde hace frío o donde hace calor? En la ciudad donde viven tus padres, ¿generalmente hace buen tiempo o mal tiempo?

Una encuesta Interview your classmates to identify who fits the following descriptions. Include your instructor, but remember to use the **Ud.** form when addressing him/her. After finishing the survey, get together with two or three classmates and discuss the results.

	Nombre
1. Come pollo a la parrilla.	_____
2. Come pescado frito, a veces.	_____
3. Come arroz con frijoles.	_____
4. Come puré de papas.	_____
5. Cuenta calorías.	_____
6. Bebe leche con las comidas.	_____
7. Bebe chocolate caliente cuando hace frío.	_____
8. Generalmente almuerza solo(-a).	_____

 Para crear Get together in groups of three and "create" the scenario for this photo. Who are the people in it? Are they celebrating? What? What are they ordering for dessert? What are they going to drink after dessert? What are they going to do later?

¡Vamos a leer!

Antes de leer

Estrategia **Expanding your vocabulary through reading** Just as in English, a purpose of reading in any language is to increase your vocabulary. Some ways of doing this are by looking for cognates, for word families (**comer-comida-comedor**), and for words that pertain to topics of interest to you.

Una dieta balanceada The following reading about healthful eating habits contains numerous words that are unfamiliar to you. As you answer these questions, make it a goal to learn at least five new words.

1. Look at the highlighted words. Which are easily understood cognates? Consider the context of the paragraph. Can you make an intelligent guess about the meaning of the remaining highlighted words?
2. Scan the text for unfamiliar words that you think refer to foods. Select three whose meaning you can't guess but want to learn and look them up in a dictionary.

A leer

 Comprensión As you read the article, find the answers to the following questions.

1. ¿Qué porcentaje de la energía de la dieta debe venir de los hidratos de carbono?
2. ¿Qué porcentaje debe venir de las proteínas y de las grasas?
3. ¿Qué otros elementos debe proporcionar (*furnish*) la dieta?
4. ¿Cuántas raciones de alimentos lácteos debemos consumir diariamente (*daily*)?
5. ¿A cuántas tazas de cerezas (*cherries*) o fresas (*strawberries*) equivale una rodaja de piña (*slice of pineapple*)?
6. ¿Cuáles son los alimentos proteicos? ¿Qué farináceos podemos comer?

¿Qué hemos de comer cada día?

Según los expertos el 55–60% de la energía de la dieta debe proceder de los **hidratos de carbono**, el 10–15% de las **proteínas** y el 30–35% de las **grasas**. Además, la dieta ha de proporcionar la cantidad de **fibra, vitaminas y minerales** que nuestro organismo necesite. Pero, ¿con qué alimentos se cubren estas cantidades?

- 2–4 raciones de lácteos diarios: Una ración = un vaso de leche, o 2 yogures, o 40 g de queso duro, o 80–100 g de queso fresco.

- 2 raciones de frutas: Una ración = una pieza de fruta, o una taza de cerezas o fresas, o una rodaja de piña o de melón.

- 2 raciones de alimentos proteicos: Una ración = 100–125 g de carne, o 1/4 de pollo, o dos huevos, o 130–150 g de pescado blanco, o 100–120 g de pescado azul.

- 3-5 raciones de farináceos: Una ración = 60–100 g de pasta, o arroz, o 80–100 g de legumbres, o 60–80 g de pan.

- 2 raciones de verduras: Una ración = 2 tomates, o 2 zanahorias, o un plato de ensalada.

¡Vamos a escribir!

Estrategia **Solidifying and repurposing what you learn** You were asked to use the reading activity for the goal of increasing your vocabulary on the basic subjects of food and health. To add new words to those you already use, you need to practice and reuse them whenever you can.

A. ¿Qué comes? In preparation for inviting your classmates to dinner, interview two classmates about their food preferences and general eating habits. Ask for their preferred sources of carbohydrates, protein, fiber, etc., to find out about the kinds of food and drinks they like. Be sure to use some of the words you learned from the reading and don't forget to ask about dessert! Take notes.

B. Un menú sabroso You are planning to invite two classmates to an evening of fine and healthy dining at your place! Before writing an e-mail invitation, use your notes from the preceding activity to plan the menu. Also, organize the paragraphs of your e-mail according to what you will communicate in each, including the occasion, comments about the menu, day, time, and place.

A escribir un mensaje electrónico

Write your **primer borrador** of the e-mail invitation. Remember the greetings and closings presented in **Lección 4.** You may want to begin by saying: **Quiero invitarlos** (*invite you*) **a cenar en mi casa...**

Después de escribir

Before writing the final version, exchange your first draft with a classmate and peer edit each other's work, using the following guidelines.

- ◆ spelling of foods
- ◆ formation and subject-verb agreement of verbs, especially stem-changing and irregular verbs
- ◆ completeness of information (when, what time, where)

Después de leer... desde su mundo

In groups of three or four, discuss your preferences for specific dishes and foods.

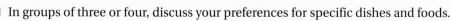

Panorama hispánico

Guatemala

◆ En Guatemala encontramos selvas tropicales (*jungles*), hermosas playas e innumerables centros arqueológicos. Uno de los más famosos es la ciudad maya de Tikal, que por su valor arqueológico fue declarada Patrimonio de la Humanidad por la UNESCO.

◆ La economía del país se basa en la agricultura. Los principales productos de exportación son café, bananas, algodón (*cotton*) y madera. En sus bosques hay numerosos pájaros (*birds*), entre ellos el quetzal, que le da nombre a la moneda del país, y que es el símbolo nacional de Guatemala.

◆ Una ciudad muy interesante de este país es Antigua, que fue la capital hasta 1776. Ciudad de Guatemala, la capital actual es, en su mayor parte, una ciudad moderna, aunque todavía hay algunas construcciones antiguas.

◆ Entre las personas famosas de este país podemos citar al escritor Miguel Ángel Asturias, que recibó el Premio Nobel de Literatura en 1967, y a la activista Rigoberta Menchú, ganadora del Premio Nobel de la Paz en 1992.

Monumentos de la civilización maya

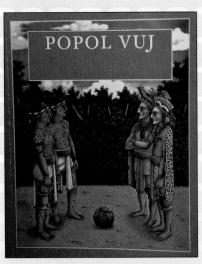

◄ El *Popol-Vuh*, uno de los pocos (*few*) libros de los mayas que aun se conservan

Letras y derechos[1] humanos

▲ Rigoberta Menchú (1959–), famosa activista guatemalteca que ganó el Premio Nobel de la Paz en 1992

---
[1]**derechos** = *rights*

El Salvador

◆ El Salvador tiene unos 300 kilómetros de costa, y sus playas están entre las más hermosas de América. El "surfing" es el deporte que más se practica en las playas.

◆ El clima del país es tropical, con dos estaciones: la estación de las lluvias (de mayo a octubre) y la estación de la seca (*dry season*) (de noviembre a abril).

◆ La capital de El Salvador es San Salvador, la ciudad más industrializada de América Central. Los principales productos industriales que se producen en el país son textiles y artículos de cuero, madera y metal. La agricultura también es importante en El Salvador; entre los productos agrícolas que exporta el país están el café y las bananas.

Del conflicto a la democracia

◀ El arzobispo (*archbishop*) Oscar Romero, baja (*casualty*) de la guerra civil de los años ochenta (*1980s*)

Aportaciones[1] hispanas a la cocina[2] norteamericana

Nuestro panorama cultural

In groups of three, answer the following questions about your home state, region, or country.

1. ¿Cuáles son los edificios más antiguos de su ciudad?
2. ¿Cuáles son algunas de las ciudades más antiguas de su país?
3. ¿Qué frutas se cultivan en la región donde Ud. vive?

For the next class: Go to the World Wide Web and find photos from your hometown, state, region, or country. Use the questions from **Nuestro panorama cultural** above as guidelines for choosing them. Be ready to present the photos to your classmates.

---

[1]**Aportaciones** = *Contributions*
[2]**cocina** = *cuisine*

Lección

6

▲ Actualmente (*Nowadays*), los hombres latinos ayudan más con los quehaceres de la casa.

Objetivos

Comunicación

You will learn vocabulary related to household chores, family relationships, and various parts of a house.

Pronunciación

The Spanish **j**, **g** (before **e** or **i**), and **h**

Estructuras

◆ Demonstrative adjectives and pronouns
◆ Present indicative of **e:i** stem-changing verbs
◆ Affirmative and negative expressions
◆ Verbs with irregular first-person forms
◆ **Saber** vs. **conocer**
◆ Direct object pronouns

Cultura

◆ Use of last names and maiden names
◆ Alphabetization of names
◆ Concept of family
◆ Housekeeping and gender roles

Panorama hispánico

◆ Honduras
◆ Nicaragua
◆ El concepto de la "república bananera"

Estrategias

Listening: Listening for details II
Speaking: Reporting
Reading: Scanning and purpose in reading
Writing: Summarizing

Los quehaceres de la casa

Honduras y Nicaragua

Honduras

 Cuando Colón llegó a la costa de esta región de Centroamérica, quedó sorprendido por la profundidad (*depth*) de las aguas junto a la tierra, así que llamó al lugar Honduras. Aquí floreció el gran imperio maya unos 500 años antes de la llegada de los conquistadores.

Nicaragua

 Nicaragua, con un área un poco mayor que la del estado de Nueva York, es el país más extenso de la América Central, pero menos de una décima parte de su territorio es cultivable.

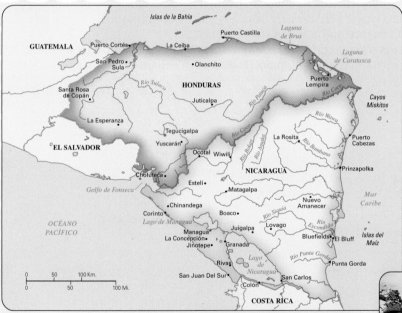

▲ Ruinas mayas en Copán, Honduras

▲ Un grupo folclórico nicaragüense baila para los turistas de un crucero.

▲ Vista panorámica de Tegucigalpa

151

La familia Núñez Arzuaga, de Tegucigalpa, Honduras, está esperando la llegada de doña Nora, la hermana mayor del señor Núñez. Ella vive en Managua y siempre viene a visitarlos en el verano. Hoy Ester y sus hijos están haciendo los trabajos de la casa.

Ester   ¡Amalia! Yo estoy cocinando. Tú tienes que lavar los platos y barrer la cocina. ¿Dónde está la escoba?

Amalia   ¿Y qué va a hacer Celia mientras yo hago todo el trabajo? ¡Ella nunca hace nada!

Celia   ¡Ja! ¡Eso no es verdad! Yo estoy planchando las camisas de papá...

Ester   Sí, y después va a hacer las camas y va a cambiar las sábanas.

Amalia   ¿Y Daniel? ¿Está haciendo algo? Él nunca nos ayuda.

Ester   Él está arreglando su cuarto...

Celia   ¡Ay, mamá! ¿Desde cuándo? Para él, arreglar su cuarto es esconderlo todo debajo de la cama.

Ester   Pues esta vez tiene que poner las cosas en su lugar, porque tu tía Nora va a usar ese cuarto y Daniel va a dormir en el sofá de la sala.

Amalia   ¿Quién va a hacer las compras en el mercado?

Ester   Tu papá. (*Llama a su esposo.*) ¡Pedro! Tienes que ir al Mercado Municipal. Y a ver si esta vez consigues carne buena... Aquí tengo la lista...

Pedro   ¡No la necesito! Yo sé lo que tengo que comprar. En seguida vuelvo. (*Sale del cuarto.*)

Ester   ¡Quién sabe lo que va a traer! (*Suspira.*) ¡Qué trabajo tenemos cuando mi cuñada viene a visitarnos...!

Amalia   El año próximo, nosotros podemos visitarla a ella. Yo quiero conocer Managua.

Celia   ¡Estoy de acuerdo! Yo también quiero ir a Managua.

Amalia   ¿Papá va a ir a buscar a tía Nora a la parada de autobuses?

Ester   No, ella dice que es mejor tomar un taxi...

Celia   ¡Tocan a la puerta! (*Mira por la ventana.*) ¡Es tía Nora! (*Recoge un montón de revistas.*) ¡Daniel! ¡Rápido! ¡Todo esto va debajo de la cama!

¿Lo sabía Ud.?

En una guía telefónica en español, alfabetizan los nombres según los dos apellidos; por ejemplo:

     Núñez Arzuaga, Pedro
     Núñez Lara, Inés

◆ ¿Cómo alfabetizan los nombres en una guía telefónica en este país?

Ester

Amalia

Celia

Pedro

ACE the Test

¿Quién lo dice? Identify the person who said the following in the dialogues.

1. Yo sé lo que tengo que comprar. _____

2. Y a ver si esta vez consigues carne buena. _____

3. ¿Y qué va a hacer Celia mientras yo hago todo el trabajo? _____

4. ¡Pedro! Tienes que ir al Mercado Municipal. _____

5. ¿Papá va a ir a buscar a tía Nora a la parada de autobuses? _____

6. Yo estoy planchando las camisas de papá. _____

7. No, ella dice que es mejor tomar un taxi. _____

8. ¿Quién va a hacer las compras en el mercado? _____

9. ¡Qué trabajo tenemos cuando mi cuñada viene a visitarnos! _____

¿Lo sabía Ud.?

En los países de habla hispana, el concepto de familia es más amplio e incluye a todos los parientes: tíos, primos, sobrinos, etc. Generalmente, la relación entre ellos es muy estrecha (*close*).

◆ Generalmente, ¿con qué miembros de la familia tienen los americanos una relación estrecha?

Hablemos. With a partner, take turns asking and answering the following questions. Base your answers on the dialogue and on your own circumstances.

En el diálogo	¿Y tú?
1. ¿De dónde es la familia Núñez Arzuaga?	¿De dónde es tu familia?
2. ¿Qué están haciendo Ester y sus hijos?	¿Qué trabajos de la casa no te gusta hacer?
3. ¿Qué tiene que hacer Amalia?	¿Qué tienes que hacer tú hoy?
4. ¿Qué está haciendo Celia?	¿Tú planchas la ropa?
5. ¿Qué va a hacer Celia después?	¿Qué días cambias las sábanas de tu cama?
6. ¿Dónde va a dormir Nora? ¿Y Daniel?	¿Dónde duermes tú?
7. ¿Quién va a hacer las compras en el mercado?	En tu familia, ¿quién hace las compras?
8. ¿Qué ciudad quiere conocer Amalia?	¿Qué ciudad quieres conocer tú?
9. ¿Va a ir Pedro a la parada de autobuses a buscar a Nora?	¿Tú vienes a la universidad en autobús?
10. ¿Dónde va a poner Daniel las revistas?	¿Qué revistas te gusta leer?

Vocabulario

Cognados

el autobús, el bus, el ómnibus bus   **el sofá** sofa
la lista list   **el taxi** taxi

Nombres

la cama bed
la camisa shirt
la carne meat
la cosa thing
la cuñada sister-in-law
el cuñado brother-in-law
la escoba broom
el lugar place

el mercado market
la parada de autobuses bus stop
los quehaceres (trabajos) de la casa housework
la revista magazine
la sábana sheet
la verdad truth

Verbos

arreglar to tidy up, to fix
ayudar to help
barrer to sweep
buscar to get, to pick up, to look for
cambiar to change
cocinar to cook
comprar to buy
conocer (yo conozco) to know, to be acquainted with
conseguir (e:i) to get, to obtain
decir (e:i) (yo digo) to say, to tell
esconder to hide

esperar to wait for, to expect
lavar los platos, fregar (e:ie) to wash dishes
planchar to iron
poner (yo pongo) to put
recoger to pick up
saber (yo sé) to know (*a fact; how to*)
salir (yo salgo) to leave, to go out
suspirar to sigh
tomar to take (*e.g., a taxi or a bus*)
traer (yo traigo) to bring
usar to use

Adjetivos

próximo(-a) next
todo(-a) all

Otras palabras y expresiones

algo something, anything
debajo (de) under
desde since
en seguida right away
En seguida vuelvo. I'll be right back.
ese, esa that
eso that (*neutral*)
esta vez this time
estar de acuerdo to agree, to be in agreement
esto this (*neutral*)
hacer las compras to do the shopping

lo que what, that which
mirar por la ventana to look out the window
nunca never
pues... well . . .
¡Rápido! Quick!
siempre always
tocar a la puerta to knock on the door
un montón de a bunch of

Vocabulario adicional

Otros quehaceres de la casa

cortar el césped to cut (mow) the grass
doblar la ropa to fold clothes
lavar la ropa to wash the clothes (do laundry)
limpiar (el cuarto de baño) to clean (the bathroom)
pasar la aspiradora to vacuum

sacar la basura to take out the trash
sacudir los muebles to dust the furniture
secar (los platos) to dry (the dishes)
trapear el piso to mop the floor

Los parientes

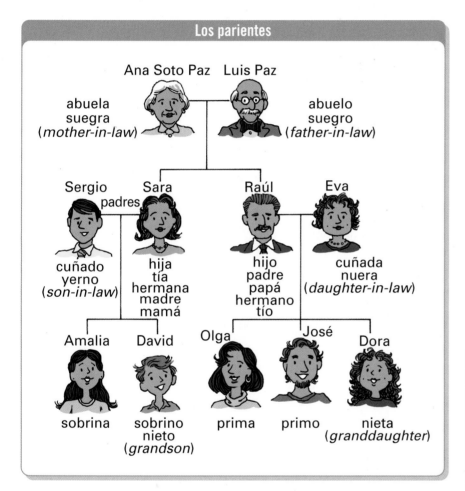

LEARNING TIP

Especially when learning concrete actions (verbs) such as **arreglar, barrer, recoger, cocinar, lavar, planchar,** etc., you might want to reinforce their meaning in your mind by stating which ones you do and what is done by other people. For example: **Yo arreglo mi cuarto. Mi mamá plancha la ropa.**

La casa

el comedor dining room
el dormitorio, la recámara (*Méx.*) bedroom
el garaje garage
el (cuarto de) baño bathroom
la sala de estar family room
el sótano basement

¿Lo sabía Ud.?

Actualmente muchos hombres hispanos, especialmente los más jovenes, ayudan a sus esposas con los trabajos de la casa. Esto es debido a que a menudo los dos trabajan fuera de la casa.

◆ **Generalmente, ¿ayudan los hombres norteamericanos a sus esposas con los quehaceres de la casa?**

Práctica

A. Match the questions in column A with the responses in column B.

A	B
1. ¿Qué está haciendo Rosa? ____	**a.** Debajo del sofá.
2. ¿Qué vas a comprar? ____	**b.** En la sala de estar.
3. ¿Qué no te gusta hacer? ____	**c.** De lo que tiene que hacer.
4. ¿Beto está en la parada de autobuses? ____	**d.** Sí, desde las seis.
5. ¿Dónde escondes las revistas? ____	**e.** Los quehaceres de la casa.
6. ¿Cuándo viene tu cuñado? ____	**f.** Sí, aquí tengo la lista.
7. ¿De qué está hablando Ana? ____	**g.** Está arreglando su cuarto.
8. ¿Dónde vas a poner el sofá? ____	**h.** La semana próxima.
9. ¿Felipe está aquí? ____	**i.** Sí, está esperando a Nora.
10. ¿Vas a ir al mercado? ____	**j.** Carne.

B. Write the words or phrases that correspond to the following.

1. ómnibus _____
2. la hermana de mi esposo _____
3. *Newsweek,* por ejemplo _____
4. comprar _____
5. opuesto de **llevar** _____
6. opuesto de **siempre** _____
7. parte de la casa donde comemos _____
8. recámara _____
9. lavar los platos _____
10. la usamos para barrer _____

C. Complete the following sentences, using vocabulary from the lesson.

1. Necesito las _____ para mi cama.
2. Tengo que lavar y _____ las camisas.
3. Tocan a la _____. Voy a abrir.
4. Voy al mercado. En _____ vuelvo.
5. Elsa cree que Julio es inteligente, pero yo no estoy de _____.
6. Estoy muy ocupado. Tengo que hacer un _____ de cosas.
7. Voy a _____ el césped. ¿Tú puedes pasar la _____?
8. Teresa va a _____ los muebles y Susana va a _____ el piso. _____ vez vamos a hacer _____ el trabajo.

Para conversar

A. **Relaciones familiares** With a partner, look at the family tree on page 155 and ask each other questions about the relationship of the people in the illustration.

HINT: ¿Cuál es la relación que existe entre _____ y _____?

B. **¿Quién puede ayudarme?** With a partner, take turns asking for help and saying that you can't help. Say what you have to do.

◆ **MODELO:** —*¿Puedes ayudarme a...?*
　　　　　　—*No puedo; tengo que...*

C. Prefiero hacer otra cosa. "I prefer to do something else." With a partner, take turns indicating what you frankly *hate* to do, and stating what you *would rather* do.

◆ **MODELO:** *Francamente, yo odio pasar la aspiradora; prefiero sacudir los muebles.*

Pronunciación

A. The Spanish *j*

The Spanish **j** sounds somewhat like the *h* in the English word *hit*. It is never pronounced like the English *j* in *John* or *James*. Listen to your instructor and repeat the following phrases.

Julia y **J**avier traba**j**an hoy.

Juan **J**osé viene el **j**ueves.

Juana de**j**a a su hi**j**o aquí.

B. The Spanish *g* (before *e* or *i*)

When followed by **e** or **i**, the Spanish **g** sounds like the Spanish **j** mentioned above. Listen to your instructor and repeat the following phrases.

Gerardo reco**g**e a **G**enaro.

Eva **G**il es inteli**g**ente.

El **g**eneral **G**inés está en Ar**g**entina.

C. The Spanish *h*

The Spanish **h** is always silent. Listen to your instructor and repeat the following phrases.

Humberto **H**ernández **H**errera es de **H**onduras.

Tu **h**ermano está en el **h**otel.

Hilda es la **h**ija de **H**ugo.

¿Lo sabía Ud.?

En la mayoría de los países de habla hispana, cuando una mujer se casa (*gets married*) retiene su apellido de soltera (*maiden name*). Puede también añadir (*add*) el apellido de su esposo. Por ejemplo, Ana Soto está casada con Luis Paz y su nombre completo es Ana Soto (de) Paz. La mayoría de los hispanos usan dos apellidos: el del padre y el de la madre, en ese orden. Por ejemplo, el nombre completo de Raúl (el hijo de Ana y Luis) es Raúl Paz Soto.

◆ **Cuando las mujeres americanas se casan, ¿usan el apellido del esposo? ¿Usan su apellido de soltera?**

Aspectos culturales

En imágenes (*Quehaceres y tiendas*)

▲ Colmado (*Small grocery store*), Puerto Rico

▲ En un hotel de Managua, una empleada hace la cama.

▲ Mercado al aire libre en Tegucigalpa, Honduras

Ubíquese... y búsquelo

 Improve Your Grade
Web Search

Pedro has been sent to the market to prepare for Nora's visit. Go to **www.cengage .com/highered** and research markets in Tegucigalpa. What kind of market would Pedro be likely to visit to do his shopping? Are there other types of markets in Tegucigalpa? What kinds of things do they sell there? In the next class, team up with two classmates to discuss your findings.

▲ Comprando medicinas en una farmacia en San José, Costa Rica

▲ Supermercado en Mérida, Yucatán, México

▲ Un empleado atiende a un cliente (*customer*) que quiere comprar un equipo estereofónico en Yucatán, México.

Estructuras

1. Demonstrative adjectives and pronouns (*Los adjetivos y los pronombres demostrativos*)

aquel hombre

aquella chica

esa chica

esta chica

A. Demonstrative adjectives

♦ Demonstrative adjectives point out persons or things. Like all other adjectives, they agree in gender and number with the nouns they modify. The forms of the demonstrative adjectives are as follows.

Masculine		Feminine		
Singular	*Plural*	*Singular*	*Plural*	
este	estos	esta	estas	*this, these*
ese	esos	esa	esas	*that, those*
aquel	aquellos	aquella	aquellas	*that, those* (at a distance in space or time)

—¿Qué vas a fregar?
—**Este** plato, **esas** tazas y **aquellos** vasos.

"What are you going to wash?"
"This dish, those cups, and those glasses (over there)."

B. Demonstrative pronouns

- The forms of the demonstrative pronouns are as follows.

Masculine		Feminine		Neuter	
Singular	*Plural*	*Singular*	*Plural*		
éste	**éstos**	**ésta**	**éstas**	**esto**	*this* (one), *these*
ése	**ésos**	**ésa**	**ésas**	**eso**	*that* (one), *those*
aquél	**aquéllos**	**aquélla**	**aquéllas**	**aquello**	*that* (one), *those* (at a distance)

- The masculine and feminine demonstrative pronouns are the same as the demonstrative adjectives, except that they have a written accent.

- Each demonstrative pronoun has a neuter form. They are **esto, eso,** and **aquello.** The neuter forms, which do not change in number or gender, are used to refer to situations, ideas, and nonspecific objects or things, equivalent to the English *this, that matter; this, that business;* and *this, that stuff.*

—¿Entiendes **eso**?   *"Do you understand that?"*
—No, es muy difícil.   *"No, it's very difficult."*

—¿Qué es **esto**?   *"What's this?"*
—¿Quién sabe?   *"Who knows?"*

Práctica

ACE the Test

A. Amalia and Celia are still trying to do housework. With a partner, complete this conversation using demonstrative adjectives. Then play the roles of the two girls.

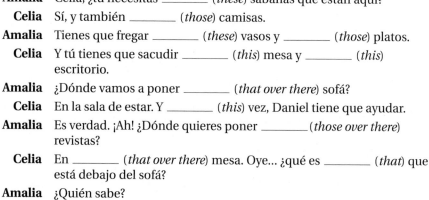

Amalia   Celia, ¿tú necesitas _____ (*these*) sábanas que están aquí?

Celia   Sí, y también _____ (*those*) camisas.

Amalia   Tienes que fregar _____ (*these*) vasos y _____ (*those*) platos.

Celia   Y tú tienes que sacudir _____ (*this*) mesa y _____ (*this*) escritorio.

Amalia   ¿Dónde vamos a poner _____ (*that over there*) sofá?

Celia   En la sala de estar. Y _____ (*this*) vez, Daniel tiene que ayudar.

Amalia   Es verdad. ¡Ah! ¿Dónde quieres poner _____ (*those over there*) revistas?

Celia   En _____ (*that over there*) mesa. Oye... ¿qué es _____ (*that*) que está debajo del sofá?

Amalia   ¿Quién sabe?

B. With a partner, play the roles of two friends. Take turns asking and answering the questions. The one who answers always rejects the objects indicated and wants the ones far from both.

1. ¿Quieres estas revistas?
2. ¿Vas a usar esta aspiradora?
3. ¿Vas a lavar este mantel?
4. ¿Vas a fregar estos vasos?

¡Habla con tu compañero! With a partner, take turns asking each other who the other students in the class are. Respond, using the appropriate demonstrative adjectives, and a description.

◆ **MODELO:** —*¿Quién es Sandra?*
—*Es aquella chica rubia.*

2. Present indicative of *e:i* stem-changing verbs (*Presente de indicativo de los verbos que cambian en la raíz e:i*)

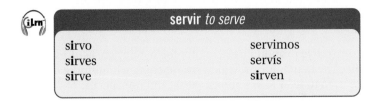

servir *to serve*	
sirvo	servimos
sirves	servís
sirve	sirven

◆ Some **-ir** verbs undergo a special stem change in the present indicative. For these verbs, when **e** is the last stem vowel and it is stressed, it changes to **i.**

—¿Qué **sirven** Uds. en sus fiestas? *"What do you serve at your parties?"*
—**Servimos** champán. *"We serve champagne."*

◆ Note that the stem vowel is not stressed in the **nosotros(-as)** and **vosotros(-as)** verb forms; therefore, the **e** does not change to **i.**

◆ Other verbs that undergo this change:[1]

conseguir *to get, to obtain*
decir *to say, to tell*
pedir *to ask for, to request, to order*
seguir *to follow, to continue*

◆ The verb **decir** undergoes the same change, but in addition it has an irregular first-person singular form: **yo digo.**

◆ Note that in the present tense **seguir** and **conseguir** drop the **u** before **a** or **o: yo sigo, yo consigo.**

Summary of the present indicative of stem-changing verbs			
e:ie	*o:ue*		*e:i*
cerrar	almorzar	morir	conseguir
comenzar	contar	mostrar	decir
empezar	costar	poder	pedir
entender	dormir	recordar	seguir
pensar	encontrar	volar	servir
perder	llover	volver	
preferir			
querer			

Add to this list as you learn other stem-changing verbs.

---

[1]For a complete list of stem-changing verbs, see Appendix B.

Práctica

A. Form complete sentences by combining the words in the three columns in sequence, starting with A. Use each subject and each verb at least once.

A	B	C
yo	decir	la comida
nosotros	servir	un cuarto
Amalia y Celia	pedir	que necesitamos un sofá nuevo
mis padres	conseguir	revistas
tú	seguir	información sobre Honduras
mi cuñado		a mis amigos
		estudiando español

B. Complete the following dialogues, using the verbs given. Then act them out with a partner, adding a sentence or two to each dialogue.

1. decir ¿Tú _____ que ese sofá es caro?

   Sí, yo _____ que es caro, pero Carmen _____ que es barato (*inexpensive*).

2. servir ¿Qué _____ Uds. en sus fiestas?

   _____ pollo y refrescos. ¿Qué _____ tú?

   Yo _____ sándwiches y cerveza.

3. pedir ¿Qué _____ Uds. cuando van a un restaurante mexicano?

   Yo _____ tacos y Ernesto _____ enchiladas.

4. conseguir Yo no _____ trabajo.

   Tú no _____ trabajo porque no hablas dos idiomas.

Para conversar

A. ¡Habla con tu compañero! Interview a classmate, using the following questions. When you have finished, switch roles.

1. ¿En qué restaurante de tu ciudad sirven buena comida mexicana? ¿Italiana? En un restaurante, ¿qué pides para beber?
2. ¿A qué hora sirven la cena (*dinner*) en tu casa? ¿Quién cocina?
3. ¿Tú consigues revistas en español? ¿Dónde consiguen los estudiantes libros en español?
4. En general, ¿sigues la moda (*fashion*)? ¿Y tus amigos?
5. ¿Tú dices que el español es fácil o difícil? ¿Tú siempre dices la verdad?

B. Para comer y beber With a partner, take turns asking each other two things: what you order when you go to ethnic restaurants and what you serve to eat and drink at your parties.

El que la sigue, la consigue.

Equivalent: If at first you don't succeed, try, try again.

3. Affirmative and negative expressions (*Expresiones afirmativas y negativas*)

Affirmative	Negative
algo *something, anything*	**nada** *nothing, not anything*
alguien *someone, somebody, anyone*	**nadie** *nobody, no one, not anyone*
alguno(-a), algún *any, some*	**ninguno(-a), ningún** *no, none, not any*
a veces *sometimes*	**nunca, jamás** *never*
siempre *always*	
también *also, too*	**tampoco** *neither, not either*
o *or*	**ni... ni** *neither . . . nor*
o... o *either . . . or*	

—¿Necesita Ud. **algo** más?   *"Do you need anything else?"*
—No, no necesito **nada** más.   *"No, I don't need anything else."*

—¿Tienes **algunos** amigos de Nicaragua?   *"Do you have any friends from Nicaragua?"*
—No, no tengo **ningún** amigo nicaragüense.[1]   *"No, I don't have any Nicaraguan friends."*

—¿Hay **alguien** en tu cuarto?   *"Is there anybody in your room?"*
—No, no hay **nadie.**   *"No, there's no one."*

—¿Quieres café **o** té?   *"Do you want coffee or tea?"*
—Yo no bebo **ni** café **ni** té.   *"I don't drink either coffee or tea."*

¡Atención!   Note that **alguno(-a)** may be used in the plural forms, but **ninguno(-a)** is not pluralized.

¡Atención!   **No** is never used as an adjective, as it sometimes is in English (*No person could do all that.*).

- **Alguno** and **ninguno** drop the **-o** before a masculine singular noun: *algún* niño, *ningún* niño; but *alguna* niña, *ninguna* niña.

- Spanish sentences frequently use a double negative form to express a degree of negation: the adverb **no** is placed before the verb and the second negative word either follows the verb or appears at the end of the sentence. If, however, the negative word precedes the verb, **no** is never used.

    No hablo español **nunca.**

    or: **Nunca** hablo español.   *I never speak Spanish.*

    No compro **nada nunca.**

    or: **Nunca** compro **nada.**   *I never buy anything.*

- Note that Spanish often uses several negatives in one sentence.

    Yo **no** quiero **nada tampoco.**   *I don't want anything either.*

---

[1]In some cases before an **e** or **i**, the **u** is not silent. To indicate this, a **diéresis** (two dots) is added over the **u** (**pingüino, Mayagüez**).

Práctica

Your friend Oscar always gets the facts wrong when he talks about other people. Set him straight!

◆ **MODELO:** Ana necesita algo.
Ana no necesita nada.

1. Delia siempre va a Managua.
2. En esa ciudad hay muchos lugares bonitos.
3. Silvia a veces sale con Eduardo y Eva sale con él también.
4. Doña Teresa nunca dobla la ropa.
5. No hay nadie en el baño.
6. Marta tiene algunas amigas hondureñas.
7. Raquel limpia el baño o la cocina.
8. Pedro necesita algo más.
9. La suegra de Luis nunca habla con nadie.
10. Siempre hay alguien en la casa de Ernesto.

Un dicho

Nadie es profeta en su tierra.

Equivalent: A prophet is not recognized in his own land.

Para conversar

A. **¡Habla con tu compañero!** Interview a classmate, answering the following questions in the negative. Use the expressions you have just learned. When you have finished, switch roles.

1. ¿Quieres ir a Nicaragua o a Honduras?
2. ¿Tienes algunos amigos en Managua?
3. Yo no hablo portugués. ¿Y tú?
4. ¿Siempre vas a restaurantes chinos?
5. ¿Siempre vienes con alguien aquí?
6. ¿Compras algo cuando vas de vacaciones?

B. **Siempre... a veces... nunca** With a partner, tell each other four things that you always do, four things that you sometimes do, and four things that you never do. Compare notes.

C. **Quejas** (*Complaints*) With a partner, write a list of complaints frequently heard on campus. Use the expressions you have just learned.

◆ **MODELO:** *Nunca podemos comer nada en la cafetería.*

4. Verbs with irregular first-person forms (*Verbos irregulares en la primera persona*)

◆ The following verbs are irregular in the first-person singular of the present tense.

Verb	yo form	Regular forms
salir (*to go out*)	**salgo**	sales, sale, salimos, salís, salen
hacer (*to do, make*)	**hago**	haces, hace, hacemos, hacéis, hacen
poner (*to put, place*)	**pongo**	pones, pone, ponemos, ponéis, ponen
traer (*to bring*)	**traigo**	traes, trae, traemos, traéis, traen
conducir (*to drive*)	**conduzco**	conduces, conduce, conducimos, conducís, conducen
traducir (*to translate*)	**traduzco**	traduces, traduce, traducimos, traducís, traducen
conocer (*to know*)	**conozco**	conoces, conoce, conocemos, conocéis, conocen
caber (*to fit*)	**quepo**	cabes, cabe, cabemos, cabéis, caben
ver (*to see*)	**veo**	ves, ve, vemos, veis, ven
saber (*to know*)	**sé**	sabes, sabe, sabemos, sabéis, saben

—¿Qué haces los domingos?   *"What do you do on Sundays?"*
—No **hago** nada.   *"I don't do anything."*

—¿Estás mirando por la ventana?   *"Are you looking out the window?"*
—Sí, pero no **veo** nada.   *"Yes, but I don't see anything."*

ACE the Test

Práctica

 A. Compare this information about Celia to you, by completing the following sentences.

1. Celia sale de su casa a las siete y yo...
2. Celia conduce un Ford y yo...
3. Celia ve a sus amigos los sábados y yo...
4. Celia conoce a muchos estudiantes y yo...
5. Celia trae a su hermana a la universidad y yo...
6. Celia cabe en un coche (*car*) muy pequeño y yo...
7. Celia sabe hablar portugués y yo...
8. Celia no hace nada los domingos y yo...

 B. Read this paragraph about Amalia's preparations for her trip to Nicaragua and then rewrite it as if you were Amalia, starting with **Yo...**

Amalia sale para Nicaragua esta noche. Va con su amiga Susan. Conduce al banco para comprar cheques de viajero (*traveler's checks*), regresa a su casa, pone todos los documentos en su bolso de mano (*handbag*) y después hace las maletas (*packs*). Como sabe que hay mucho tráfico, sale de su casa a las cinco para ir al aeropuerto. Cuando llega al aeropuerto, ve que Susan está esperando.

Para conversar

¡Habla con tu compañero! Your classmate is traveling to Tegucigalpa. Here is a list of questions you want to ask in order to help him/her prepare for the trip.

1. ¿Conoces Tegucigalpa? ¿Sabes a qué distancia está de los Estados Unidos?
2. ¿Sabes cuál es la moneda (*currency*) de Honduras? ¿Sabes a cómo está el cambio de moneda (*rate of exchange*)?
3. ¿Haces la reservación del hotel antes de salir de viaje? ¿Dónde pones el pasaporte?
4. El día del viaje, ¿sales de casa con tiempo? ¿Conduces tu coche para ir al aeropuerto?
5. ¿Conoces a alguien en Tegucigalpa?
6. ¿Traes muchas cosas para tu familia? ¿Compras algo para ti?

5. *Saber* vs. *conocer*

Spanish has two verbs that mean *to know*, **saber** and **conocer**.

A. *Saber* means:

◆ to know something by heart.

Yo **sé** un poema de Rubén Darío.

◆ to know a fact.

Yo **sé** que Rubén Darío es un poeta nicaragüense.

◆ to know how to do something.

Yo **sé** bailar salsa.

B. *Conocer* means:

- to be familiar or acquainted with a person.
  Nosotros **conocemos** a Ester Núñez.

- to be acquainted with a place.
  Ellos **conocen** Honduras.

- to be acquainted with an artist or writer's work.
  ¿Tú **conoces** la poesía de Rubén Darío?

Yo no **sé** bailar muy bien.

Práctica

Complete the following dialogues, using **saber** or **conocer** as appropriate. Then act them out with a partner.

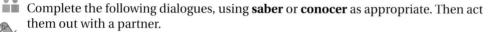

ACE the Test

1. Yo _____ al abuelo de Olga.
   ¿Tú _____ dónde vive?
   No, pero _____ su número de teléfono.

2. Tú _____ Brasil, ¿no?
   Sí, pero no _____ hablar portugués.

3. ¿Tú _____ los poemas de Bécquer?
   Sí, _____ muchos de memoria (*by heart*).

4. ¿Tú _____ qué hora es?
   Sí, son las ocho.

5. Jorge conduce muy mal.
   Sí, no _____ conducir bien.

Para conversar

A. ¡Habla con tu compañero! Interview a classmate, using the following questions. When you have finished, switch roles.

1. ¿Cuántos idiomas sabes hablar? ¿Cuáles son?
2. ¿Conoces a los padres de tu mejor amigo(-a)?
3. ¿Sabes dónde viven?
4. ¿Qué sabes hacer?
5. ¿Sabes tocar (*play*) el piano? ¿la guitarra? ¿el violín?
6. ¿Sabes preparar una sangría?
7. ¿Conoces un buen restaurante? ¿Dónde está?
8. ¿Conoces a un actor famoso? ¿Quién es? ¿Cómo es?
9. ¿Conoces las novelas de Hemingway? ¿Cuáles?
10. ¿Sabes bailar salsa? ¿Qué sabes bailar?

B. ¿Qué sabes? o ¿Qué conoces? With a partner, talk about the places you are familiar with and the ones you want to know, some people you know, facts you know about your college, city or state, and things you know how to do. Compare notes!

6. Direct object pronouns (*Pronombres usados como complemento directo*)

A. The direct object

◆ In addition to a subject, most sentences have an object that directly receives the action of the verb.

Ellos	compran	el libro.
S.	V.	D.O.

In the preceding sentence, the subject (**Ellos**) performs the action, while **el libro,** the direct object, directly receives the action of the verb. The direct object of a sentence may be either a person or a thing.

◆ The direct object can be easily identified as the answer to the questions *whom?* and *what?* about what the subject is doing.

Ellos compran **el libro.**	*What are they buying?*
Pepe visita a **su primo.**	*Whom is Pepe visiting?*

◆ Direct object pronouns may be used in place of the direct object.

B. Forms of the direct object pronouns

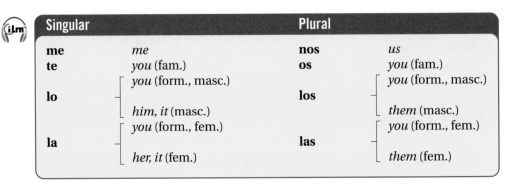

Singular		Plural	
me	*me*	**nos**	*us*
te	*you* (fam.)	**os**	*you* (fam.)
lo	*you* (form., masc.) *him, it* (masc.)	**los**	*you* (form., masc.) *them* (masc.)
la	*you* (form., fem.) *her, it* (fem.)	**las**	*you* (form., fem.) *them* (fem.)

—¿Tienes **la lista?**	*"Do you have the list?"*
—Sí, **la** tengo.	*"Yes, I have it."*

—¿Seca Ud. **los platos?**	*"Do you dry the dishes?"*
—Sí, **los** seco.	*"Yes, I dry them."*

C. Position of direct object pronouns

◆ In Spanish, object pronouns are normally placed before a conjugated verb.

	D.O.			D.O.	
Ellos sirven	**la comida.**		*They serve the meal.*		
Ellos	**la**	sirven.	*They serve it.*		

◆ In negative sentences, the **no** must precede the object pronoun.

		D.O.			D.O.	
Ellos sirven		**la comida.**		*They serve the meal.*		
Ellos		**la**	sirven.	*They serve it.*		
Ellos	**no**	**la**	sirven.	*They don't serve it.*		

♦ When an infinitive is used with a conjugated verb, the direct object pronoun may either be attached to the infinitive or be placed before the conjugated verb. The same principle applies with the present participle in progressive constructions.

Puedo leer**lo**.
⎱
⎰ *I can read it.*
Lo puedo leer.

Estoy leyéndo**lo**.
⎱
⎰ *I am reading it.*
Lo estoy leyendo.

> **¡Atención!** When a direct object pronoun is attached to a present participle (**leyéndolo**), an accent mark is added to maintain the correct stress.

Práctica

ACE the Test

A. Complete the following dialogue, using the appropriate direct object pronouns. Then act it out with a partner.

Julio   ¿Tú me puedes llevar a casa hoy?
Delia   Sí, puedo llevar____ a las tres.
Julio   ¡Ah! Necesito la maleta (*suitcase*) de mamá. ¿Tú ____ tienes?
Delia   Sí, yo la tengo. ¿Tú quieres llevar____ a Tegucigalpa?
Julio   Sí. También necesito comprar cheques de viajero...
Delia   Podemos comprar____ esta tarde.
Julio   Rosa y yo tenemos que estar en el aeropuerto a las ocho de la noche. ¿Tú ____ puedes llevar?
Delia   Sí, yo ____ puedo llevar...
Julio   ¡Ah! Las sobrinas de Rosa quieren ir al aeropuerto con nosotros. ¿Tú ____ puedes traer a mi casa a las siete?
Delia   ¡No! ¡Yo no tengo un servicio de taxi!

B. You and your roommates are doing chores. Volunteer to do the following tasks yourself.

♦ MODELO: —¿Quién lava las sábanas?
—*Yo las lavo.*

1. ¿Quién barre el garaje?
2. ¿Quién friega los platos?
3. ¿Quién limpia el cuarto de baño?
4. ¿Quién corta el césped?
5. ¿Quién pasa la aspiradora?
6. ¿Quién sacude los muebles?
7. ¿Quién va a lavar la ropa?
8. ¿Quién prepara la comida?

¿Dónde está tu camisa?

La estoy planchando.

Los quehaceres de la casa   ♦   ciento sesenta y nueve **169**

C. With a partner, take turns answering the following questions. Use direct object pronouns and the cues provided to indicate what people do differently.

◆ **MODELO:** —Yo pongo las revistas en la mesa (Teresa / en su escritorio)
—*Teresa las pone en su escritorio.*

1. Don Manuel consigue la carne en el supermercado.
   (nosotros / en la carnicería)
2. Yo voy a llevar a Tito a su casa.
   (Elena / a la parada de autobuses)
3. Yo plancho las camisas en la cocina.
   (Julio / en su dormitorio)
4. Nosotros hacemos las compras los viernes.
   (Mis padres / los sábados)
5. Elisa trapea el piso dos veces por semana.
   (tú / todos los días)
6. Nosotros sabemos el número de teléfono de Irene.
   (yo / no)

D. With a partner, take turns answering the questions on page 171, basing your answers on the illustrations. Use direct object pronouns in your responses.

Juan

Eva

1. ¿A qué hora llama Sara a Luis?
2. ¿Cuándo tiene que llamar Luis a Sara?
3. ¿Pepe puede llevar a los chicos a casa?
4. ¿Dónde tiene Pepe los libros?
5. ¿Quién abre la puerta?
6. ¿Quién sirve el café?
7. ¿Quién bebe el refresco?
8. ¿Quién tiene las cartas?

Para conversar

A. ¡Habla con tu compañero! You and your partner play the roles of two roommates that are planning their weekend activities. Take turns answering the following questions, using appropriate direct object pronouns.

1. ¿Quieres dar la fiesta el viernes o el sábado?
2. ¿Vamos a invitar a los chicos de la clase?
3. ¿Tú puedes comprar las bebidas?
4. Mi auto no funciona. ¿Puedes llevarme al mercado?
5. Vamos a tener que limpiar la casa. ¿Quién puede ayudarnos?
6. ¿Quién va a preparar el postre?
7. Yo no puedo ir contigo a la iglesia (*church*) el domingo. ¿Alguien puede llevarte?
8. Mis amigos y yo queremos ver el partido de fútbol por la tarde. ¿Y tú?

B. ¿Quién lo hace? With a partner, ask each other who does what around the house with other members of the family, etc.

◆ **MODELO:** —*¿Quién friega los platos?*
　　　　　　—*Mi mamá los friega.*

Un dicho

A quien madruga, Dios lo ayuda.

Equivalent: The early bird catches the worm.

Así somos

Al escuchar...

Listening for details II Remember what you have learned in preceding lessons about focusing your listening. Anticipate the kinds of information you will hear, concentrate on listening for the details you want to know, and ignore extraneous information.

 Un anuncio de radio Everybody in your household has been discussing the need for extra cleaning help as you are all very busy. You hear a radio commercial on cleaning services. Listen once and make notes of the following details so that you can report to your housemates in the **Al conversar...** activity.

1. nombre del servicio
2. dos servicios que ofrece
3. el número de teléfono

Al conversar...

Estrategia **Reporting** When you tell something you hear to another person, you can use **decir** (**Ramón dice que va a limpiar**) or you can simply report the information without specifying the source. When restating what you hear, use the language you know.

 Un servicio fenomenal Get together with two classmates. Today they happen to be your housemates also! You all heard the radio ad for a cleaning service and now take turns telling the others what you recall about the services offered and what cleaning help you think you need. Decide what help you most need and who's going to call for prices.

 ¿Qué dice Ud.? What would you say in the following situations? What might the other person say? Act out the scenes with a partner. Take turns playing each role.

1. You and your roommate are trying to divide household chores. Volunteer for those chores that you want to do.
2. Tell a friend about two or three members of your family and make comparisons between them and yourself. Talk about age, physical characteristics, etc.
3. You complain about chores that certain people in your family don't do.
4. You are trying to sell or rent your house or apartment. Describe it to a prospective buyer, by giving as many details as possible.

 Para conocernos mejor To do this activity, work with a classmate whom you would like to get to know. Take turns asking and answering these questions.

1. ¿Te gusta hacer los quehaceres de la casa? ¿Cuáles no te gusta hacer?
2. En tu casa, ¿quién friega los platos? ¿Quién barre la cocina? ¿Quién saca la basura?
3. ¿Te ayuda alguien a arreglar tu cuarto? ¿Quién? ¿Siempre pones las cosas en su lugar?
4. ¿Te gusta hacer las compras en el mercado? ¿Qué días las haces?
5. ¿Prefieres pasar la aspiradora o trapear el piso?
6. ¿Prefieres cortar el césped o limpiar el baño?

7. ¿Algunos de tus parientes viven en otras ciudades? ¿Vas a visitarlos? ¿Ellos te visitan?
8. ¿Tienes primos? ¿Tienes sobrinos? ¿Tienes cuñados?
9. ¿Tú sabes tocar algún instrumento musical? ¿Te gusta el piano o prefieres la guitarra?
10. ¿Qué ciudades norteamericanas conoces? ¿Cuáles quieres conocer?

Una encuesta Interview your classmates to identify who fits the following descriptions. Include your instructor, but remember to use the **Ud.** form when addressing him/her. After finishing the survey, get together with two or three classmates and discuss the results.

Nombre

1. Hace su cama todos los días.
2. Cambia las sábanas de su cama una vez por semana.
3. Arregla su cuarto los fines de semana.
4. Sacude los muebles de su cuarto.
5. Tiene un montón de revistas en su cuarto.
6. Plancha su ropa.
7. Hace las compras en el mercado los sábados.
8. Cocina muy bien.

Para crear In groups of three or four, look at the photo and use your imagination to create a story about the people in the picture. Give them names and ages. What is their relationship to each other? What are they doing?

¡Vamos a leer!

Antes de leer

Estrategia **Scanning and purpose in reading** When you set out to read a magazine or newspaper you can scan its contents, for example, by previewing the table of contents or by leafing through the pages to zero in on the articles that you'd like to read. Then, when you read an article, you might read it lightly for the main ideas or in depth for a thorough understanding of the information. Having a purpose when reading enables you to read more efficiently because your mind is focused.

Una entrevista Before reading the complete interview with Andy García, scan the interviewer's questions to find out in which paragraph the actor will talk about Miami and in which he mentions his parents. Then skim the reading with the purpose of learning what it is about.

A leer

Comprensión As you read the article, find the answers to the following questions.

1. ¿Qué dice Andy García de Miami?
2. ¿Cuántos primos tienen sus hijos en Miami?
3. ¿Qué otra persona de su familia vive allí (*there*)?
4. ¿Qué placer le dan sus hijos?
5. ¿Qué usa como ejemplo para sus hijos?
6. ¿Cuál es el legado más importante que aspira a dejarles?
7. ¿Cuál es el principal deber de un padre?

Con el son en las venas

Fragmento de una entrevista con Andy García en la revista Selecciones.

often **Selecciones:** Viene a Miami a menudo,° ¿qué significa esta ciudad para usted?

García: Es mi centro, el núcleo familiar para mí y mis hijos. Si no estoy trabajando en el verano, siempre vengo porque las muchachas están de vacaciones. Aquí mis hijos tienen 21 primos, en

city blocks un radio de diez manzanas.° Para mí es muy importante mantener esa conexión porque

far vivimos lejos.° Mi madre aún vive aquí, y además hay una alta concentración de cultura cubana e hispana, que disfruto° mucho. Además,

I enjoy tengo amigos y me gusta compartir con ellos.

joy **Selecciones:** ¿Qué es lo que más gusto° le ha dado en la vida?

García: Mi familia y mis hijos son los que me dan el placer más grande. Verlos florecer, verlos

grow crecer° y tener una buena relación con ellos. Como padre, ésa es la relación más fuerte y

life verdadera que tengo en mi vida.°

Selecciones: ¿Qué lección de sus padres trata de transmitirles a sus hijos?

García: Obviamente, les inculco los valores que me dieron mis padres. Quizá° lo más importante Perhaps
es que trato de darles un ejemplo con mi propia° own
vida.

Selecciones: ¿Cuál es el legado más importante que aspira a dejarles?

García: Haber sido° un buen padre. Estar cuando Having been
me necesitan y ser parte de su vida. Ése es el
principal deber° de un padre. duty

¡Vamos a escribir!

Antes de escribir

> **Estrategia** **Summarizing** A summary includes the main ideas of a reading or of something you hear, without all the details. When preparing a summary, you can start by making notes of the main ideas. Often the first sentence of a paragraph contains the main idea; however, you'll also need some of the supporting information. When summarizing, use your own words to restate ideas more concisely. This will also aid your understanding. To support your statements, an important device you can use is to quote someone's speech:
>
> **El artículo (periódico, periodista) dice que...**
> **El señor X dice: "..."**
> **En la entrevista se dice que...** (*it is said that . . .*)

Un resumen (*A summary*) You are going to summarize the interview with Andy García in your own words. Reread the interview and make notes of the main themes and ideas. Find one quote to include.

A escribir el resumen

Write your **primer borrador** of the summary. Use one or two sentences for each paragraph.

Después de escribir

Before writing the final version, exchange your first draft with a classmate and peer edit each other's work using the following guidelines.

- use of the personal **a**
- direct object pronouns
- use of **ser** and **estar**
- presence of main points from the interview in writer's words

Después de leer... desde su mundo

Interview a classmate about his or her family. You may want to adapt some of the questions asked of Andy García to your classmate's circumstances.

Panorama hispánico

Honduras

- Hoy Honduras, con un área un poco mayor que la del estado de Tennessee, tiene más de 5 millones y medio de habitantes.

- Honduras es el único país centroamericano que no tiene volcanes, pero esto no es favorable para el país, pues las tierras volcánicas son, por lo general, fértiles y buenas para la agricultura. Como la economía del país se basa en la agricultura,

Honduras es hoy uno de los países más pobres de América. Sin embargo, Honduras tiene el mayor bosque de pinos.

- La capital de Honduras es Tegucigalpa. La mayor atracción turística del país es Copán, una ciudad maya que existió hace unos dos mil años y de la que sólo quedan ruinas.

La imaginación artística

De la escuela pictórica paisajista (*landscape painting*) a la cinematografía hondureña.

▲ Pintura (*Painting*) de José Antonio Velázquez, *San Antonio de Oriente,* ciudad clave (*key*) para comprender (*understand*) la obra del autor

▲ Max Hernández, fotógrafo de fama internacional

Nicaragua

- Nicaragua es la tierra de los lagos (*lakes*) y de los volcanes. El lago Nicaragua es uno de los mayores largos de agua dulce (*fresh*) de todo el mundo, y en él hay tiburones (*sharks*) y otros peces que sólo viven en agua salada en otras regiones.

- La mayor parte de su población vive en el oeste del país, junto a los lagos Nicaragua y Managua, y al océano Pacífico. Allí están las tres ciudades más

importantes del país: Managua, la capital, León y Granada.

- La economía de Nicaragua se basa en la agricultura, y sus principales productos de exportación son café, algodón (*cotton*), carne de res (*beef*) y madera (*wood*). El país tiene una selva virgen mucho más extensa que la de Costa Rica, pero no está debidamente (*duly*) protegida contra su explotación excesiva.

Impacto universal de las letras nicaragüenses

▲ Rubén Darío (1867–1916), iniciador del Modernismo, movimiento literario iberoamericano

▲ La conocida (*well known*) poeta nicaragüense Claribel Alegría

El concepto de la "república bananera"[1]

◄ Lavando y pesando (*weighing*) bananas

Nuestro panorama cultural

In groups of three, answer the following questions about your home state, region, or country.

1. ¿Vive Ud. cerca del mar o de algún río o lago?
2. ¿Cuál es la región más poblada de su estado?
3. ¿Cuáles son los productos típicos de su región?
4. ¿Los turistas visitan mucho su región? ¿Cuáles son las atracciones principales?
5. ¿Tiene un artista favorito? ¿Quién es?
6. ¿Qué personas de su ciudad son famosas?

For the next class: Go to the World Wide Web and find photos from your hometown, state, or country. Use the questions from **Nuestro panorama cultural** above as guidelines for choosing them. Be ready to present the photos to your classmates.

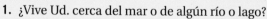

[1]**"república bananera"** = "banana republic"

Self-Test

Take this test. When you have finished, check your answers in the answer key provided in Appendix D. Then use a red pen to correct any mistakes you may have made. Are you ready?

Lección 4

 A. Pronouns as objects of prepositions Complete the following sentences, using the Spanish equivalent of the words in parentheses.

1. La comida es para _____. (*me*)
2. Eduardo habla mucho de _____. (*you, fam.*)
3. Hay dos libros para _____. (*them*)
4. Los vasos son para _____. (*us*)
5. ¿Quieres comer _____? (*with me*)
6. Voy a dejar (*leave*) los discos compactos _____. (*with you, fam.*)

B. Contractions Complete the following sentences, using the Spanish equivalent of the words in parentheses.

1. Necesito llamar _____. (*Mr. Estrada*)
2. Yo vengo _____. (*from the hospital*)
3. ¿Tú vienes _____? (*from the beach*)
4. Eduardo lleva _____ a la fiesta. (*the girls*)
5. El vaso es _____. (*Mr. Soto's*)

C. Present indicative of the irregular verbs *ir, dar,* and *estar* Complete the following sentences, using the present indicative of **ir, dar,** or **estar,** as appropriate.

1. Yo no _____ al concierto con mis amigos.
2. Nosotros _____ una fiesta aquí hoy.
3. Mi hermana _____ en su casa.
4. ¿Dónde _____ el ponche?
5. Las chicas _____ a la fiesta con sus amigos.
6. Tus primos no _____ mucho dinero para los pobres (*poor*).
7. Yo _____ cansado.
8. ¿Adónde _____ tus padres hoy?
9. ¿Dónde _____ tú ahora?
10. Yo no _____ mi número de teléfono.

 D. *Ir a* + infinitive Form sentences that tell what is and is not going to happen. Use the given elements.

1. yo / no hablar / con mi mamá / hoy
2. mis hijos / estudiar / en Guadalajara
3. mi amiga / leer / libro
4. Uds. / traer / los discos compactos
5. tú / bailar / en la fiesta
6. nosotros / no brindar / con vino

E. Present indicative of *e:ie* stem-changing verbs Complete the following sentences, using the present indicative of the verbs in the list, as necessary.

entender	cerrar	empezar	preferir
pensar	querer	perder	comenzar

1. Mi primo no _____ beber café.
2. Nosotros no _____ la Lección 2.
3. Ella siempre _____ mucho dinero en Las Vegas.
4. ¿Tú _____ la ventana?
5. Las clases _____ hoy.
6. Nosotros _____ a bailar ahora.
7. Yo no _____ trabajar el domingo.
8. Luis y yo _____ beber café.

F. Expressions with *tener* Write the Spanish equivalent of the words in parentheses.

1. Mis primos _____. (*are in a hurry*)
2. Yo _____, pero _____. (*am not hungry / am very thirsty*)
3. Nosotros vamos a abrir la ventana porque _____. (*we are hot*)
4. Las chicas _____. (*are very sleepy*)
5. ¿Tú _____, Anita? (*are afraid*)
6. Ud. _____, Srta. Peña. María _____. (*are right / is ten years old*)

G. Just words . . . Choose the word or phrase that best completes each sentence.

1. Yo voy a (dar, pasar, abrazar) cinco días en Puerto Rico.
2. Las dos chicas hablan (entonces, a la vez, bienvenidas).
3. La fiesta (prepara, piensa, empieza) a las nueve de la noche.
4. Tengo sed. Quiero (comida, abrazo, agua).
5. Mi (abuela, hija, tía) Marta es la hermana de mi mamá.
6. Voy a hablar con mi (sobrino, cuarto, habitación).
7. Quiero ir a un (teatro, concierto, partido) de fútbol.
8. Estamos (cansados, aturdidos, invitados) a la fiesta de Navidad.
9. Trabaja mucho; siempre está (triste, ocupado, aburrido).
10. Voy a (bailar, pensar, sacar) una foto.

H. Culture Circle the correct answer, based on information from this lesson.

1. En Latinoamérica y en España (existe, no existe) mucha separación entre las generaciones.
2. Además del cumpleaños, muchos hispanos celebran su (baile, santo).
3. La segunda ciudad más grande de México es (Guanajuato, Guadalajara).
4. Diego Rivera es un famoso (pintor, músico) mexicano.

Lección 5

A. Comparative forms Form sentences, using the elements provided. Use the comparative or the superlative, as appropriate.

1. mi hermano / estudiante / más / inteligente / clase
2. la Lección 2 / menos / interesante / la Lección 7
3. mi novia / más / bonita / tu novia
4. mi primo / más / guapo / familia
5. el profesor Paz / tener / menos / veinte estudiantes
6. mi sobrino / tan / alto / yo

B. Irregular comparative forms Complete the following sentences, using regular or irregular comparative forms, as appropriate.

1. Un hotel es _____ que una casa.
2. El profesor Alvarado habla español _____ que sus estudiantes.
3. Eva tiene "A" en literatura; Beto tiene "C" y Cora tiene "F". Eva es la _____ estudiante y Cora es la _____ estudiante.
4. Yo tengo treinta años y Raquel tiene doce años. Yo soy _____ que Raquel; ella es _____ que yo.
5. Un libro es _____ que un escritorio.

C. Present indicative of *o:ue* stem-changing verbs Complete the following sentences, using the present indicative of the verbs in the list, as appropriate.

recordar	almorzar	costar	dormir
contar	volver	poder	llover

1. ¿Cuánto _____ el libro?
2. Ellos no _____ ir hoy.
3. ¿ _____ Ud. cuál es el número de teléfono de Claudia?
4. Yo _____ de uno a veinte en francés.
5. Tengo hambre. ¿A qué hora _____ (nosotros)?
6. ¿Cuándo _____ tú a Guatemala?
7. En Oregón _____ mucho.
8. ¿ _____ usted bien, señora?

D. Present progressive Write sentences saying what *is happening*, using the verbs in the list.

pedir	comer	hablar	leer	decir	dormir

1. ella / que nosotros necesitamos más dinero
2. yo / con mi abuela en español
3. nosotros / un libro muy bueno
4. ¿qué / tú? / ¿Biftec?
5. Luis / en su cuarto
6. los chicos / dinero

E. Uses of *ser* and *estar* Form sentences, using the elements provided and the appropriate forms of **ser** or **estar**. Add the necessary connectors.

1. Elsa / mamá / Marcela
2. restaurante Miramar / calle Siete
3. ¡Mmmm! / el pollo / delicioso
4. Roberto / de México / pero ahora / en Guatemala
5. café / frío
6. escritorio / metal
7. hoy / lunes
8. Elvira / profesora de español
9. fiesta / casa / Armando
10. Mariana / muy inteligente
11. ellos / cansados
12. mi suegra / guatemalteca

F. Weather expressions Complete the following sentences appropriately.

1. Necesito un paraguas. _____ mucho en este momento.
2. ¿No te vas a poner el abrigo? ¡Brrr! _____.
3. No necesito el suéter. ¡ _____ !
4. En Alaska _____ mucho en el invierno.
5. Necesitas el sombrero. Hoy _____.
6. No quiero vivir en Oregón porque allí llueve mucho y no me gusta la _____.

G. Just words . . . Choose the word or phrase that does not belong in each group.

1. frito / al horno / de postre
2. lechón / trozo / pedazo
3. torta / pescado / helado
4. esposo / primo / marido
5. verdura / pollo / legumbre
6. camarones / langosta / arroz
7. cuchara / tenedor / cuenta
8. mantel / vaso / copa
9. rico / hermoso / sabroso
10. pavo / cordero / leche
11. platillo / sal / pimienta
12. fábrica / camarero / factoría

H. Culture Complete the following sentences, based on the information from this lesson.

1. En los países hispanos, el café se sirve después del _____.
2. Con frecuencia, la _____ está incluida en la cuenta.
3. Guatemala es el país de la eterna _____.
4. El Salvador es el país más _____ de Centroamérica.

Lección 6

A. Demonstrative adjectives and pronouns Complete the following sentences, using the appropriate demonstrative adjectives and pronouns.

1. Yo necesito _____ escritorio, _____ silla y _____ mapas. (*this / this / those*)
2. _____ señor es el profesor de inglés y _____ chicas son sus estudiantes. Ellas estudian tres horas por día. _____ es muy importante. (*That over there / those over there / That*)

B. Present indicative of *e:i* stem-changing verbs Complete the following sentences, using the present indicative of the verbs in the list, as needed.

decir (2)　　　servir　　　seguir　　　pedir (2)　　　conseguir

1. ¿A qué hora _____ ustedes la cena?
2. Nosotros siempre _____ biftec cuando vamos a ese restaurante. ¿Qué _____ tú?
3. Yo _____ libros en español en la universidad.
4. ¿Los chicos _____ en la clase de español?
5. Yo siempre _____ que Alejandro es guapo, pero Elba _____ que es feo.

C. Affirmative and negative expressions Change the following sentences to the affirmative.

1. Ellos no van a querer nada.
2. No hay nadie en la clase.
3. No tengo ningún amigo español.
4. Ellos nunca dicen nada.
5. Yo tampoco ceno a las nueve.
6. Jamás tiene los libros que necesita.
7. No puedes ir ni al cine ni al teatro.
8. Ellos nunca quieren nada tampoco.

D. Verbs with irregular first-person forms Complete the following sentences, using the present indicative of the verbs in the list, as needed.

traducir　　　hacer　　　conocer　　　saber　　　salir
poner　　　caber　　　ver　　　traer　　　conducir

1. Yo _____ un Ford, modelo 2000.
2. Yo no _____ dónde está el hotel.
3. Yo no _____ en este taxi. ¡Hay ocho personas!
4. Yo siempre _____ de mi casa a las siete de la mañana.
5. Yo _____ las lecciones del inglés al portugués.
6. Yo no _____ los pasaportes. ¿Dónde están?
7. Yo no _____ nada los domingos.
8. Yo nunca _____ las sillas aquí.
9. Yo no _____ California.
10. Yo _____ a mi amigo Carlos a la universidad.

E. *Saber* vs. *conocer* Form sentences, using **saber** or **conocer.**

1. nosotros / que ella es su novia
2. yo / a Teresa / pero / no / dónde vive
3. Peter / Madrid / pero / no / hablar español
4. los chicos / no / los poemas / de memoria

F. Direct object pronouns Answer the following questions in the negative. Substitute direct object pronouns for the direct objects.

1. ¿Tú quieres comprar el libro?
2. ¿Tú llamas a tus amigos todos los días?
3. ¿Uds. sirven la cena a las siete?
4. ¿Tú tienes los pasaportes de Héctor?
5. ¿Sergio te va a llevar a la fiesta?
6. ¿Ustedes pueden llevarme a la casa de mis padres? (*Use* **tú** *form.*)
7. ¿Tú conoces a las primas de Isabel?
8. ¿Tú necesitas las sábanas blancas?
9. ¿El profesor los lleva a Uds. a la biblioteca?
10. ¿Tú puedes llevarnos a mí y a Jorge a la casa del profesor?

G. Just words . . . Match the questions in column A with the answers in column B.

A		B
1. ¿Para qué quieres la escoba?	____	a. Sí, es la esposa de mi hermano.
2. ¿Qué estás planchando?	____	b. Sí, y tú puedes doblarla.
3. ¿Tocan a la puerta?	____	c. Sí, pero yo no estoy de acuerdo.
4. ¿Qué vas a comprar en el mercado?	____	d. La revista de Eva.
5. ¿Elisa es tu cuñada?	____	e. Porque estoy triste...
6. ¿Qué estás leyendo?	____	f. ¡Nunca!
7. ¿Cuándo viene Julián?	____	g. Sí, voy a abrir.
8. ¿Ana dice que él es guapo?	____	h. Sí, es la hija de mi hermana Nora.
9. ¿Vas a lavar la ropa?	____	i. Los muebles de mi dormitorio.
10. ¿Cuándo te ayuda Luis?	____	j. Para barrer la cocina.
11. ¿Por qué suspiras?	____	k. La semana próxima.
12. ¿Qué vas a sacudir?	____	l. Para la sala de estar.
13. ¿Es tu sobrina?	____	m. Las camisas de papá.
14. ¿Para dónde es el sofá?	____	n. Sí, ¡y yo soy su nieta favorita!
15. ¿La Sra. Paz es tu abuela?	____	o. Carne.

H. Culture Answer the following questions, based on the information from this lesson.

1. En los países de habla hispana, ¿qué retiene una mujer cuando se casa?
2. ¿Qué gran imperio floreció en Honduras 500 años antes de la llegada de los españoles?
3. Honduras no tiene volcanes. ¿Por qué no es esto favorable para el país?
4. ¿Cuál es la capital de Honduras?
5. ¿Cuál es la mayor atracción turística de Honduras?

Lección

7

▲ El Hotel Born, en Palma de Mallorca, Islas Canarias, España

Objetivos

Comunicación

You will learn vocabulary related to checking in at a hotel, asking about accommodations, and about tourism.

Pronunciación

The Spanish **ll** and **ñ**

Estructuras

◆ Indirect object pronouns
◆ Constructions with **gustar**
◆ Time expressions with **hacer**
◆ Preterit of regular verbs
◆ Ordinal numbers

Cultura

◆ Travel and currency
◆ Types of accommodations
◆ Customs related to travel
◆ Floor-numbering conventions

Panorama hispánico

◆ Costa Rica
◆ Panamá

Estrategias

Listening: Listening to authentic language
Speaking: Simplifying ideas through paraphrasing
Reading: Guessing meaning from context
Writing: Selecting topics and organizing the information

En un hotel

Recursos

Costa Rica y Panamá

Costa Rica

Costa Rica, llamada "la Suiza de América" por su estabilidad política, es una nación progresista y democrática. El país no tiene ejército (*army*), y la educación es obligatoria y gratuita (*free*). El 95% de su población sabe leer y escribir. La mayoría de los ticos (como se les llama a los costarricenses) es de origen español.

Panamá

Panamá está situado en el istmo que une la América del Norte con la América del Sur. Panamá fue (*was*) una provincia de Colombia hasta 1903 y, por lo tanto (*so*), es la república hispanoamericana de más reciente creación.

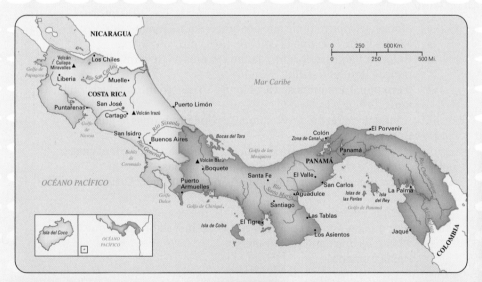

▲ Jungla en Costa Rica

▲ El Canal de Panamá

▲ Niños en una carreta típica, en Costa Rica

Rubén Saldaña, su esposa Beatriz y sus hijas Paola y Ariana están en un hotel en San José, la capital de Costa Rica. El Sr. Saldaña es un hombre de negocios y su esposa es maestra. Paola y Ariana son adolescentes.

Empleado	¿En qué puedo servirle, señor?
Rubén	Me llamo Rubén Saldaña. Mi familia y yo necesitamos una habitación para cuatro personas, con dos camas dobles. Tenemos reservación. Yo llamé anteayer para confirmarla.
Empleado	A ver... Rubén Saldaña... Sí, señor. Su habitación está en el tercer piso.
Ariana	¿Los cuartos tienen televisor? Yo quiero ver mi programa favorito.
Paola	¿Tienen servicio de Internet? Yo necesito mandarle un mensaje instantáneo a Carolina. Hace mucho tiempo que no hablamos.
Beatriz	Hablaste con ella ayer. ¡Y anoche le mandaste una tarjeta postal! Ahora tenemos que llevar el equipaje al cuarto.
Empleado	Tiene que dejarnos el número de su tarjeta,[1] señor. El botones puede llevar las maletas a su cuarto. (*Le da la llave.*) Aquí tiene la llave. Debe dejarla con nosotros en la recepción si sale del hotel.
Rubén	¿El hotel tiene servicio de habitación?
Empleado	Sí, señor. Sirven la cena hasta las once de la noche.
Beatriz	Rubén... ya cenamos... ¡Y tú comiste muchísimo!
Rubén	Sí, pero me gusta comer algo antes de dormir...
Beatriz	Vamos a nuestro cuarto. ¿Dónde está el ascensor? Estoy cansada.
Ariana	Yo voy a usar la escalera. Necesito hacer ejercicio.
Paola	¿El hotel tiene piscina? Yo quiero nadar un rato.

En el cuarto

Ariana	Mamá, ¿el cuarto tiene aire acondicionado? Tengo calor.
Paola	No me gusta la cama. El colchón no es muy cómodo...
Rubén	Es tarde. Vamos a dormir. Mañana vamos a ir al jardín Lankester y al parque Braulio Carrillo.
Ariana	¡Pero papá! ¡Estamos de vacaciones! Yo quiero mirar televisión hasta tarde...
Beatriz	Ariana tiene razón. A ver, Rubén... ¿Qué programas te gustan?
Rubén	Bueno...
Ariana	A Paola y a mí nos gusta la película que pasan en el canal cuatro.
Rubén	Bueno... a mí me gusta más mirar las noticias...
Beatriz	A las chicas les gusta la película... ¡Y a mí también! Yo la vi el mes pasado.
Rubén	Buenas noches...
Beatriz	¿Por qué no miras la película con nosotras? Te prometo que te va a gustar. Es una comedia romántica...
Rubén	Hasta mañana...

¿Lo sabía Ud.?

En muchos países hispanos, especialmente en los pueblos pequeños, hay hoteles donde las habitaciones no tienen baño privado. Generalmente tienen uno o dos baños por piso.

◆ ¿Cuál es la situación en los *bed and breakfasts* de este país?

---

[1]**Tarjeta** here means **tarjeta de crédito** = *credit card*. To be introduced in **Lección 8**.

el empleado

Rubén

Ariana

Paola

Beatriz

LEARNING TIP

Take advantage of any opportunity you may have to interact in conversation with a native Spanish speaker.

¿Quién lo dice? Identify the person who said the following in the dialogues.

1. El botones puede llevar las maletas a su cuarto. _____
2. A mí me gusta más mirar las noticias. _____
3. Yo quiero mirar televisión hasta tarde. _____
4. Rubén... ya cenamos... ¡Y tú comiste muchísimo! _____
5. No me gusta la cama. El colchón no es muy cómodo. _____
6. ¿En qué puedo servirle, señor? _____
7. ¿El hotel tiene servicio de habitación? _____
8. Yo necesito mandarle un mensaje instantáneo a Carolina. _____
9. ¿Por qué no miras la película con nosotras? _____
10. Yo voy a usar la escalera. Necesito hacer ejercicio. _____

Hablemos. With a partner, take turns asking and answering the following questions. Base your answers on the dialogue and on your own circumstances.

En el diálogo	¿Y tú?
1. ¿Dónde están Rubén Saldaña y su familia?	¿Tú conoces Costa Rica? ¿Adónde vas de vacaciones generalmente?
2. ¿Qué pide la familia Saldaña en el hotel?	En tu cuarto, ¿tienes una cama doble o una cama sencilla?
3. ¿En qué piso está la habitación de la familia Saldaña?	En un hotel, ¿prefieres una habitación en el primer piso o en el décimo (*tenth*) piso?
4. ¿A quién quiere mandarle un mensaje instantáneo Paola?	Cuando tú estás viajando, ¿les mandas mensajes electrónicos a tus amigos? ¿Les mandas tarjetas postales?
5. ¿Quién lleva las maletas al cuarto?	En un hotel, ¿quién lleva tus maletas al cuarto: tú o el botones?
6. En el hotel, ¿hasta qué hora sirven la cena?	¿A qué hora cenas tú?
7. ¿Ariana va a usar la escalera o el ascensor? ¿Por qué?	¿Tú prefieres usar el elevador o la escalera mecánica (*escalator*)?
8. ¿Qué quiere hacer Paola en la piscina?	¿Tu casa tiene piscina? ¿Sabes nadar?
9. ¿Qué dice Paola del colchón?	¿Tu colchón es cómodo?
10. ¿Qué quieren mirar Beatriz y las chicas? ¿Qué quiere mirar Rubén?	¿Tú prefieres mirar una película o mirar las noticias?

Vocabulario

Cognados

la comedia comedy	**instantáneo(-a)** instant
doble double	**la reservación, la reserva** reservation
favorito(-a) favorite	**el servicio** service
el hotel hotel	**las vacaciones**[1] vacation

Nombres

el (la) adolescente teenager	**el Internet, la Red** World Wide Web
el aire acondicionado air conditioner	**el jardín** garden
el almuerzo lunch	**la llave** key
el ascensor, el elevador elevator	**el (la) maestro(-a)** teacher
el botones bellhop	**la maleta, la valija** suitcase
el canal channel	**la noticia** piece of news
la cena dinner, supper	**la película** movie, film
el colchón mattress	**la piscina, la alberca** (*Méx.*) swimming pool
el desayuno breakfast	**el piso** floor
el equipaje luggage	**el servicio de habitación (cuarto)** room service
la escalera stairs	**la tarjeta postal** postcard
el hombre de negocios[2] businessman	**el televisor** TV set

Verbos

cenar to have dinner, to dine	**mandar, enviar** to send
confirmar to confirm	**nadar** to swim
gustar to like, to be pleasing to	**prometer** to promise

Adjetivos

cómodo(-a) comfortable
pasado(-a) last
tercero(-a) third

Otras palabras y expresiones

anoche last night	**hacer ejercicio** to exercise
anteayer the day before yesterday	**hasta** until
antes (de) before	**muchísimo** a lot
ayer yesterday	**mucho tiempo** a long time
¿En qué puedo servirle? How may I help (serve) you?	**pasar (dar) una película** to show a movie
estar de vacaciones to be on vacation	**ya** already
Hace mucho tiempo que no hablamos. We haven't talked for a long time.	

---

[1]**Vacaciones** is always used in the plural in Spanish.
[2]**la mujer de negocios** = *businesswoman*

Vocabulario adicional

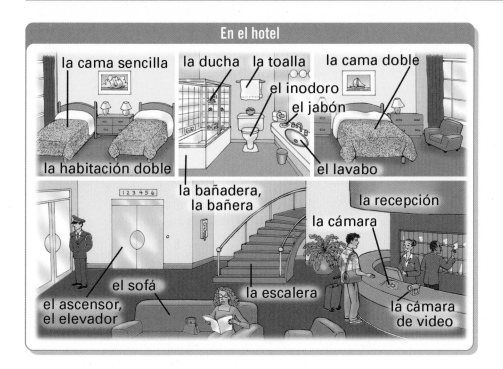

En el hotel

la cama sencilla
la ducha
la toalla
la cama doble
el inodoro
el jabón
la habitación doble
el lavabo
la bañadera, la bañera
la recepción
la cámara
el sofá
la escalera
el ascensor, el elevador
la cámara de video

Las comidas

el desayuno breakfast
el almuerzo lunch

la merienda snack, luncheon
la cena dinner, supper

Para hablar de turismo

¿A cómo está el cambio de moneda?
  What is the rate of exchange?
la aduana customs
cancelar to cancel
con vista a overlooking
el consulado consulate
desocupar el cuarto to vacate the room
la embajada embassy
la escalera mecánica escalator

libre vacant
la lista de espera waiting list
el mar sea
el pasaporte passport
pasar por la aduana to go through customs
la habitación sencilla single room
la tarjeta de turista tourist card
viajar to travel

¿Lo sabía Ud.?

Lo que en los Estados Unidos es el primer piso es la planta baja en los países hispanos. Entonces, el primer piso en España, por ejemplo, corresponde al segundo piso en los Estados Unidos.

◆ **En los hoteles, ¿cómo llaman en este país a la planta baja?**

Práctica

A. Circle the word or phrase that doesn't belong in each group.

1. almuerzo / cena / escalera
2. jardín / conserje / botones
3. ducha / llave / bañadera
4. equipaje / jabón / toalla
5. almorzar / cenar / nadar
6. recepción / inodoro / reservación
7. cama / canal / colchón
8. televisor / película / maestro
9. pasado / doble / sencillo
10. hacer ejercicio / prometer / correr

B. Match the questions in column A with the answers in column B.

A	B
1. ¿Tienen reservación? _____	**a.** No, le mandé un mensaje instantáneo.
2. ¿Vas a mirar tu programa? _____	**b.** No, la dejé en la recepción.
3. ¿Llamaste a tu novia? _____	**c.** Sí, la vi el mes pasado.
4. ¿Le dejaste la tarjeta de crédito? _____	**d.** No, mi cuarto no tiene televisor.
5. ¿Llevaste la llave? _____	**e.** Sí, necesito hacer ejercicio.
6. ¿Vas a usar la escalera? _____	**f.** Sí, tienen catorce años.
7. ¿Viste esa película? _____	**g.** Sí, yo la confirmé ayer.
8. ¿Son adolescentes? _____	**h.** No, solamente el número.

C. Write the words or phrases that correspond to the following.

1. persona de 15 años, por ejemplo _____
2. elevador _____
3. valija _____
4. alberca _____
5. opuesto de **cancelar** _____
6. opuesto de **mañana** _____
7. documento que usamos para viajar _____
8. bañera _____
9. opuesto de **drama** _____
10. la primera comida del día _____

D. Complete the following sentences, using vocabulary from this lesson.

1. El hotel tiene aire _____.
2. Hace mucho _____ que no hablamos.
3. ¿En qué _____ servirle, señora?
4. Vamos a _____ de vacaciones en agosto.
5. ¿A cómo está el _____ de _____?
6. Tenemos que pasar por la _____ con el equipaje.
7. Quiero una habitación con _____ al mar.
8. Mi cuarto está en el tercer _____.
9. ¿Vas a llevar la cámara _____ o la cámara de _____?
10. Él es un hombre de _____ y su esposa es maestra.

Para conversar

A. **¿En qué puedo servirle?** With a partner, take turns playing the part of a hotel employee and a customer who wants to find out about specific accommodations that the hotel has to offer. The employee's answers will determine what kind of hotel it is.

B. **Quejas** (*Complaints*) With a partner, play the roles of two guests who complain about everything when staying at a hotel. Discuss everything that you find wrong with the place and the service.

◆ **MODELO:** *No hay suficientes toallas en el baño.*

Pronunciación

A. The Spanish ll

In most countries, the Spanish **ll** has a sound similar to the *y* in the English word *yes*. Listen to your instructor and repeat the following sentences.

Me **ll**amo Raúl A**ll**ende.

E**ll**os **ll**evan las **ll**aves.

El Dr. **Ll**anes vive en la ca**ll**e Porti**ll**o.

Las **ll**amas **ll**egaron del Ca**ll**ao.

B. The Spanish ñ

The Spanish **ñ** is similar to the *ny* in the English word *canyon*. Listen to your instructor and repeat the following sentences.

El se**ñ**or Salda**ñ**a está en Espa**ñ**a.

La se**ñ**orita Nú**ñ**ez viene ma**ñ**ana.

La se**ñ**ora Pe**ñ**a tiene treinta a**ñ**os.

La ni**ñ**a sue**ñ**a con ir a la monta**ñ**a.

Al seleccionar un hotel en Latinoamérica hay que tener en cuenta (*keep in mind*) que los precios que dan no incluyen los impuestos (*taxes*) que, en la mayoría de los países, son muy altos.

◆ **En este país, los precios que dan los hoteles, ¿incluyen los impuestos?**

En un hotel ◆ ciento noventa y uno **191**

Aspectos culturales

En imágenes (*Hoteles para viajes de negocios y de gran turismo*)

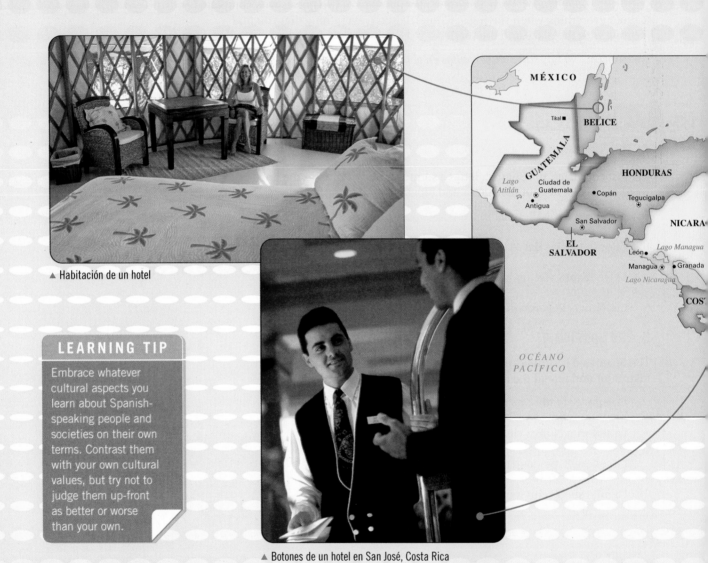

▲ Habitación de un hotel

▲ Botones de un hotel en San José, Costa Rica

Ubíquese... y búsquelo

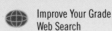 Improve Your Grade
Web Search

The Saldaña family is staying in a hotel in San José while they visit Costa Rica. Go to **www.cengage.com/highered** to find some information about hotels in San José. Find some hotels that you could recommend to the Saldañas, taking location, price, and amenities into account. In the next class, team up with two classmates to discuss your findings.

OCÉANO
ATLÁNTICO

Mar Caribe

Canal de Panamá
Colón
Panamá

NAMÁ

COLOMBIA

▲ Vista de una playa, Costa Rica

▲ Salón de conferencias de un hotel

CAMINO REAL INTER-CONTINENTAL

Estructuras

1. Indirect object pronouns (*Pronombres usados como complemento indirecto*)

♦ In addition to a subject and a direct object, a sentence may have an indirect object.

Él **te** da **el libro.**	*He gives you the book.*
I.O. D.O.	I.O. D.O.

♦ An indirect object describes *to whom* or *for whom* an action is done. An indirect object pronoun can be used in place of an indirect object. In Spanish, the indirect object pronoun includes the meaning *to* or *for*: **Yo les** mando los libros **(a los estudiantes).**

♦ The forms of the indirect object pronouns are as follows. Notice that the indirect object pronouns are the same as the direct object pronouns, except in the third person.

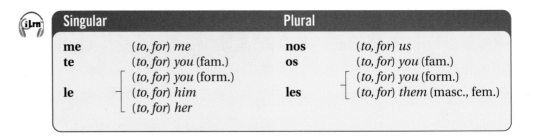

Singular		Plural	
me	(*to, for*) *me*	**nos**	(*to, for*) *us*
te	(*to, for*) *you* (fam.)	**os**	(*to, for*) *you* (fam.)
le	(*to, for*) *you* (form.) (*to, for*) *him* (*to, for*) *her*	**les**	(*to, for*) *you* (form.) (*to, for*) *them* (masc., fem.)

♦ Indirect object pronouns are usually placed in front of the conjugated verb.

—¿Qué **te** está diciendo el empleado?
—Que puedo pagar con dólares.

"What is the employee saying to you?"
"That I can pay with dollars."

—¿En qué idioma **les** hablan sus padres a ustedes?
—Ellos **nos** hablan en español.

"In what language do your parents speak to you?"
"They speak to us in Spanish."

¡Guau, guau!

Siempre **les** habla en español.

◆ In sentences with a conjugated verb followed by an infinitive, the indirect object pronoun may either be placed in front of the conjugated verb or be attached to the infinitive.

Le quiero dar dinero. ⎱
Quiero dar**le** dinero. ⎰   *I want to give him money.*

◆ When used in sentences with the present progressive, an indirect object pronoun may either be placed in front of the conjugated verb or be attached to the present participle.

Nos está diciendo   que viene hoy. ⎱   *He is telling us that*
Está diciéndo**nos**[1]   que viene hoy. ⎰   *he is coming today.*

> **¡Atención!** The indirect object pronouns **le** and **les** sometimes require clarification when the person to whom they refer is not specified. Spanish provides clarification (or emphasis) by using the preposition **a** + *personal pronoun or noun.*

     Le doy el pasaje.   *I am giving the ticket . . .* (to him? to her? to you?)
but: **Le** doy el pasaje **a ella.**   *I am giving the ticket to her.*

Note, however, that the prepositional phrase is optional, while the indirect object pronoun must always be used.

     Le traigo un libro a **Roberto.**   *I am bringing a book to Roberto.*
     ¿Les vas a dar el dinero **a ellas?**   *Are you going to give the money to them?*

Práctica

ACE the Test

A. You are at a hotel waiting for a friend to arrive and you overhear some people making the following comments. Complete their sentences with the appropriate indirect object pronouns.

1. _____ dan las llaves. (a nosotros)
2. _____ doy el equipaje. (a ellos)
3. _____ doy la maleta. (a él)
4. _____doy las tarjetas postales. (a ella)
5. _____ traigo la cámara fotográfica. (a Uds.)
6. _____ piden el pasaporte. (a ella)
7. _____ traigo la cámara de video. (a ti)
8. _____ traen el periódico. (a él)
9. _____ decimos "gracias". (a ellos)
10. _____ dan las bebidas. (a mí)

B. Add the appropriate indirect object pronouns to the following exchanges, and then act them out with a partner.

1. —¿Quién _____ va a traer las tarjetas de turista a Uds.?
   —Rogelio, y yo voy a dar_____ el pasaporte a él.
2. —¿ _____ vas a escribir a tus padres, Rosita?
   —Sí, _____ voy a mandar una tarjeta postal.
3. —¿En qué idioma _____ hablan tus padres a ti?
   —_____ hablan en portugués.
4. —¿Qué _____ vas a traer a Sergio y a mí, tía Isabel?
   —_____ voy a traer dos cámaras fotográficas.
   —¿Y a Elsa?
   —A ella voy a traer_____ una cámara de video.

---

[1]When an indirect object pronoun is attached to a present participle, an accent mark is added to maintain the correct stress.

C. With a partner, take turns asking each other what the people depicted here do or are going to do. Remember to use the appropriate indirect object pronouns in your questions and answers.

Eva y Sara

Juan

1. dar

Olga

Andrés

2. dar

Paco   Ana

3. dar

Paco   sus padres

4. dar

el camarero

Pedro

5. traer

el camarero

Nora   Luis

6. traer

D. The following people are going on a trip and need certain items. Say who is going to give, bring, or buy the things they need.

◆ **MODELO:** Oscar necesita un mapa.
El papá de Oscar le va a traer (comprar, dar) el mapa.

tu mamá	el amigo de...	mi hermano	el novio de...
nuestros amigos	el papá de...	la abuela de...	su esposo(-a)
los chicos			

1. Yo necesito las maletas.
2. Teresa necesita el pasaporte.
3. Tú necesitas una valija.
4. Ana y yo necesitamos ropa.
5. Carlos necesita una cámara de video.
6. Los chicos necesitan una cámara fotográfica.
7. Olga y Pedro necesitan dinero.
8. Ud. necesita una tarjeta postal.

Un dicho

Les das la mano y te agarran el pie.

Equivalent: You give them an inch
and they take a mile.

Para conversar

A. **¡Habla con tu compañero!** You are going on a trip to Panamá to visit your aunt and uncle. Discuss with a classmate what you are doing now and what you are going to do once you get there.

1. ¿Les estás escribiendo a tus tíos de Panamá?
2. ¿Qué les estás diciendo?
3. ¿Qué les vas a llevar a tus tíos?
4. ¿Tu papá te va a dar su cámara fotográfica?
5. ¿Nos vas a escribir desde (*from*) Panamá?
6. ¿Me vas a dejar la llave de tu casa?
7. ¿Qué les vas a traer a tus padres?
8. ¿Qué me vas a traer a mí?

B. **De Costa Rica** You and your partner are going on a trip to Costa Rica. Ask each other what you are going to bring people as gifts.

1. a tu mamá
2. a tus hermanos
3. a tu mejor amigo(-a)
4. a tus compañeros de clase
5. a tus tíos favoritos

2. Constructions with *gustar* (*Construcciones con* **gustar**)

◆ The verb **gustar** means *to like* (literally, *to be pleasing to*). **Gustar** is always used with an indirect object pronoun (**me** in the following example).

Me gusta tu casa.	*I like your house.*
I.O. V. S.	S. V. D.O.
	Your house is pleasing to me.
	S. V. I.O.

◆ The two most commonly used forms of **gustar** are the third-person singular form, **gusta,** used if the subject is singular or if **gustar** is followed by one or more infinitives; and the third-person plural form, **gustan,** used if the subject is plural.

Indirect object pronouns

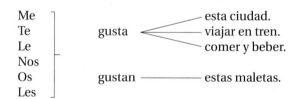

Me
Te
Le   gusta   ⟨ esta ciudad.
Nos   viajar en tren.
Os   gustan ——— estas maletas.
Les   comer y beber.

◆ Note that the verb **gustar** agrees with the *subject* of the sentence—that is, with the person or thing being liked.

Me gust**a** **Lima.**	*I like Lima.*
No me gust**an esas maletas.**	*I don't like those suitcases.*

> **¡Atención!** When what is liked is an activity, **gustar** is followed by the infinitive.

Me gust**a ir** al cine.	*I like to go to the movies.*

> **LEARNING TIP**
>
> The construction with **gustar** is one of the cases in which Spanish expresses something in a way quite different from English. This structure will require some understanding on its own terms.
> Spanish: **Me gusta...**
> (*. . . appeals to me*)
> English: *I like . . .*

◆ The person who does the liking is the indirect object.

Me gustan los hoteles de esta ciudad.
I.O.

—¿**Te** gusta Panamá?   *"Do you like Panamá?"*
—Sí, **me** gusta **mucho** Panamá,   *"Yes, I like Panamá very much, but I like*
pero **me** gusta **más** Guatemala.   *Guatemala better."*
—A Eva **le** gusta México y   *"Eva likes México and we like Costa Rica."*
a nosotros nos gusta Costa Rica.

> **¡Atención!**   Note that the words **mucho** and **más** (*better*) immediately follow **gustar**.

◆ The preposition **a** + *noun* or *pronoun* may be used to emphasize or specify the name of the person referred to by the indirect object pronoun.

A Eva (A ella) le gusta nadar y **a mí**   *Eva (She) likes to swim and I like*
me gusta bailar.   *to dance.*

Práctica

 A. You have used certain constructions with **gustar (me gusta, te gusta)**. To review, get together with a partner and ask each other whether or not you like the following things.

1. la comida mexicana (italiana / china)
2. la cerveza (el vino)
3. el rojo (el azul)
4. la playa (la montaña)
5. nadar (correr)
6. ir al cine (ir al teatro)
7. cantar (bailar)
8. el béisbol (el tenis)

If you address someone as **usted, le** is used instead of **te.** Now choose questions from the list above to ask your instructor.

B. Rewrite the following sentences, using constructions with **gustar.**

◆ **MODELO:** Yo prefiero Punta Arenas.
             *A mí **me gusta más** Punta Arenas.*

1. Yo prefiero las ciudades grandes.
2. Marcelo prefiere los hoteles pequeños.
3. Ellos prefieren pasar las vacaciones en México.
4. ¿Ud. prefiere viajar en autobús o en avión (*plane*)?
5. Adela prefiere ir al zoólogico.
6. Nosotras preferimos ir al teatro.
7. ¿Uds. prefieren la comida italiana?
8. Nosotros preferimos comer comida mexicana.

 C. Interview a classmate to find out what the following members of his or her family like and don't like to do on weekends. When you have finished, switch roles.

◆ **MODELO:** —*A tus hermanas, ¿qué les gusta hacer? ¿Qué no les gusta hacer?*
             —*A mi hermana le gusta muchísimo ir a bailar. No le gusta trabajar.*

1. a ti   4. a Uds.
2. a tus hermanos   5. a tus primos
3. a tu padre   6. a tu mamá

D. Look at the illustrations below and say what these people like (or don't like) and what they like (or don't like) to do.

◆ MODELO:

Juan

A Juan le gusta leer.

Inés

1. _____

Jorge

Mario

2. _____

Yo

3. _____

Nosotras

4. _____

Tú

5. _____

Carmen

6. _____

Ud.

7. _____

A. ¡Habla con tu compañero! Interview a classmate, using the following questions. When you have finished, switch roles.

1. ¿Dónde te gusta pasar tus vacaciones?
2. ¿Te gustan más las ciudades grandes o las ciudades pequeñas?
3. ¿Te gusta más ir a un museo o a un parque de diversiones?
4. ¿Qué les gusta hacer a tus amigos los fines de semana?
5. ¿A Uds. les gusta bailar? ¿cantar?
6. ¿A tu mejor amiga le gustan las canciones de Enrique Iglesias?
7. ¿Qué estación del año te gusta más?
8. ¿Qué te gusta hacer cuando llueve?

B. ¿Y a usted? With a partner, prepare four questions to ask your instructor about his or her likes and dislikes.

C. Para comparar Compare your likes and dislikes with those of two classmates. Consider your tastes in food, music, weekend activities, classes, and travel.

3. Time expressions with *hacer* (*Expresiones de tiempo con el verbo hacer*)

LEARNING TIP

Note that just as with some weather expressions (**hace calor**, **hace frío**, etc.), **hace** is used with time expressions in Spanish (**hace mucho tiempo**, **hace tres meses**, and so on).

♦ English uses the present perfect progressive or the present perfect tense to express how long something has been going on.

*I **have been living** here **for** twenty years.*

♦ Spanish uses the following construction.

| **Hace** | + | *length of time* | + | **que** | + | *verb* (in the present tense) |
| Hace | | veinte años | | que | | vivo aquí. |

—**¿Cuánto tiempo hace que** Ud. estudia español?
"How long have you been studying Spanish?"

—**Hace** tres meses **que** estudio español.
"I have been studying Spanish for three months."

—¿Tienes mucha hambre?
"Are you very hungry?"

—¡Sí! **Hace** ocho horas **que** no como.
"Yes! I haven't eaten for eight hours."

¡Atención! To ask how long something has been going on, use the expression **¿Cuánto tiempo hace que...?**

Práctica

  Tell how long each action depicted below has been going on. Use **hace... que** and the length of time specified.

1. veinte minutos

2. tres años

3. una hora

4. dos horas

5. siete horas

6. quince días

Para conversar

A. ¡Habla con tu compañero! Interview a classmate, using the following questions and two questions of your own. When you have finished, switch roles.

1. ¿Cuánto tiempo hace que vives en la misma (*same*) casa?
2. ¿Cuánto tiempo hace que estudias aquí?
3. ¿Cuánto tiempo hace que trabajas en esta ciudad?
4. ¿Cuánto tiempo hace que hablas español?
5. ¿Cuánto tiempo hace que no comes?
6. ¿Cuánto tiempo hace que no ves a tus padres?
7. ¿Cuánto tiempo hace que conoces a tu mejor amigo(-a)?
8. ¿Cuánto tiempo hace que no tienes vacaciones?

B. Queremos saber... In groups of three, prepare six questions to ask your instructor, using time expressions with **hacer.** You may want to use the verb **enseñar** (*to teach*) in your questions.

4. Preterit of regular verbs (*Pretérito de verbos regulares*)

- Spanish has two simple past tenses: the preterit and the imperfect. (The imperfect tense will be studied in **Lección 10.**) The preterit tense is used to refer to actions or states that the speaker views as completed in the past.

- The preterit of regular verbs is formed as follows. Note that the endings for the **-er** and **-ir** verbs are the same.

-ar verbs **tomar** *to take*	-er verbs **comer** *to eat*	-ir verbs **escribir** *to write*
tom**é**	com**í**	escrib**í**
tom**aste**	com**iste**	escrib**iste**
tom**ó**	com**ió**	escrib**ió**
tom**amos**	com**imos**	escrib**imos**
tom**asteis**	com**isteis**	escrib**isteis**
tom**aron**	com**ieron**	escrib**ieron**

—¿**Hablaste** con Silvia ayer?   *"Did you speak with Silvia yesterday?"*
—Sí, **comí** con ella en la cafetería.   *"Yes, I ate with her in the cafeteria."*

—¿Le **escribió** Roberto?   *"Did Roberto write to her?"*
—Sí, **recibió** una tarjeta de él ayer.   *"Yes, she received a card from him yesterday."*

- The first-person plural of **-ar** and **-ir** verbs is identical to the present tense forms.

—¿A qué hora salieron Uds.?   *"What time did you leave?"*
—**Salimos** de casa a las seis y no **llegamos** hasta las siete.   *"We left home at six, and we didn't arrive until seven."*

- Verbs ending in **-gar, -car,** and **-zar** change g to **gu,** c to **qu,** and z to **c** before **-é** in the first-person singular of the preterit: **pagar → pagué; buscar** (*to look for*) → **busqué; empezar → empecé.**

—¿A qué hora **llegaste** a la pensión?   *"What time did you arrive at the boarding house?"*
—**Llegué** a las ocho y **empecé** a trabajar enseguida.   *"I arrived at eight and I started to work right away."*

- Certain **-er** and **-ir** verbs with the stem ending in a vowel change **i** to **y** in the third-person singular and plural endings: **leer → leyó, leyeron; creer → creyó, creyeron.**

Él lo **leyó** en el periódico, pero no lo **creyó.**

- Verbs of the **-ar** and **-er** groups that are stem-changing in the present indicative are regular in the preterit.

Rosa **volvió** a las seis y **cerró** las puertas.   *Rosa returned at six o'clock and closed the doors.*

¿Lo sabía Ud.?

Las pensiones son muy populares en los países de habla hispana. Son más económicas que los hoteles y generalmente el precio incluye el cuarto y las comidas.

- Los *bed and breakfast* que hay en este país, ¿son equivalentes a las pensiones?

◆ Spanish has no equivalent for the English word *did* used as an auxiliary verb in questions and negative sentences.

—¿Encontraste el dinero?   *"Did you find the money?"*
—No lo busqué.   *"I didn't look for it."*

—¿Dejaste una buena propina?   *"Did you leave a good tip?"*
—Sí, dejé el 20 por ciento.   *"Yes, I left 20 percent."*

Práctica

ACE the Test

A. Complete the following dialogues, using the verbs given. Then act them out with a partner.

1. hablar / hablar / llamar / charlar
   —¿Tú _____ por teléfono con tus suegros ayer?
   —Sí, _____ con ellos. Los _____ por la mañana y _____ hasta las once.

2. volver / volver / volver / volver
   —¿A qué hora _____ Uds.?
   —Yo _____ a las cuatro y Mario _____ a las seis. ¿A qué hora _____ tú?
   —A las siete.

3. recibir / mandar / recibir
   —¿_____ (tú) las tarjetas que yo te _____?
   —No, no las _____.

4. llegar / llegar / comenzar
   —¿A qué hora _____ Ud., señorita?
   —_____ a las nueve y _____ a trabajar a las nueve y media.

5. cerrar / cerrar / abrir
   —¿_____ Uds. las puertas?
   —Sí, _____ las puertas y _____ las ventanas.

B. With a partner, ask each other questions about what the following people purchased and how much each item cost.

◆ **MODELO:** Tú
—¿Qué compraste tú?
—*Compré una blusa* (blouse).
—¿Cuánto te costó?
—*Me costó cuarenta dólares.*

$40,00

$120,00

$1.500,00

$83,00

1. Tú   2. Uds.   3. Rafael

$1,20

$358,00

4. Ana y Eva   5. Alicia

Un dicho

Salió de Guatemala y entró en Guatepeor.

Equivalent: He went from bad to worse.

Para conversar

A. ¡Habla con tu compañero! With a partner, take turns asking and answering the following questions.

1. ¿Qué comiste ayer?
2. ¿Qué bebiste?
3. ¿Estudiaste español anoche?
4. ¿A qué hora saliste de tu casa?
5. ¿A qué hora llegaste a tu primera clase?
6. ¿Trabajaron tus amigos ayer?
7. ¿Dónde almorzó tu mejor amigo(-a)?
8. ¿A qué hora volviste a tu casa?
9. ¿Leíste el periódico ayer?
10. ¿A qué hora cenaste ayer?

B. ¿Qué hiciste tú...? With a partner, use the verbs listed to ask each other what you did yesterday and last night (**anoche**).

◆ MODELO: —¿Dónde almorzaste ayer?
—Almorcé en la cafetería.

almorzar	escribir	mirar	trabajar	volver
cenar	leer	pagar	ver	mandar
cerrar	llegar	practicar	buscar	salir
conversar				

5. Ordinal numbers (*Números ordinales*)

primero(-a)[1]	*first*	**sexto(-a)**	*sixth*
segundo(-a)[1]	*second*	**séptimo(-a)**	*seventh*
tercero(-a)[1]	*third*	**octavo(-a)**	*eighth*
cuarto(-a)	*fourth*	**noveno(-a)**	*ninth*
quinto(-a)	*fifth*	**décimo(-a)**	*tenth*

◆ Ordinal numbers agree in gender and number with the nouns they modify.

el segundo **chico**   la segunda **chica**
los primeros **días**   las primeras **semanas**

◆ Ordinal numbers are seldom used after **décimo** (*tenth*).

> **¡Atención!** The ordinal numbers **primero** and **tercero** drop the final **-o** before masculine singular nouns.

el **primer**[2] día   el **tercer**[3] año

—Nosotros estamos en el   *"We are on the second floor. And you?"*
   segundo piso. ¿Y Uds.?

—Estamos en el **tercer** piso.   *"We are on the third floor."*

---

[1]abbreviated 1°, 2°, 3°, and so on
[2]abbreviated 1er
[3]abbreviated 3er

Práctica

ACE the Test

A. Write the ordinal numbers that correspond to the following cardinal numbers.

◆ **MODELO:** ocho *octavo*

1. nueve _____
2. cinco _____
3. uno _____
4. siete _____
5. dos _____
6. tres _____
7. seis _____
8. cuatro _____
9. diez _____

B. Complete the following sentences with the appropriate ordinal numbers.

1. Según la Biblia, Adán fue (*was*) el _____ hombre y Eva fue la _____ mujer.
2. Febrero es el _____ mes del año y mayo es el _____ mes.
3. En el calendario hispano el miércoles es el _____ día de la semana y el domingo es el _____ día.
4. El Día de Acción de Gracias es el _____ jueves de noviembre.
5. El _____ mes del año es junio y el _____ mes es octubre.

C. Concurso de belleza (*Beauty contest*)   In a beauty contest, these are the ten finalists. With a partner, put their names in order, according to the points that they have accumulated.

◆ **MODELO:** *Maribel Fuentes es la primera; Isabel Reyes…*

1. Lucía Ayala: 450 pts.
2. Teresa Peñarol: 560 pts.
3. Ana Luisa Peña: 380 pts.
4. Maribel Fuentes: 850 pts.
5. Silvia Torres: 600 pts.
6. Mireya Vargas: 760 pts.
7. María Inés Valles: 490 pts.
8. Isabel Reyes: 800 pts.
9. Marcela Vigo: 700 pts.
10. Gloria Calderón: 500 pts.

Para conversar

¿En qué piso están?   Imagine that the whole class is staying at a hotel in Costa Rica. Your classmates were assigned rooms on different floors. With a partner, take turns saying who is on what floor.

Un dicho

Los últimos serán los primeros.

The last shall be first.

Así somos

Estrategia   **Listening to authentic language**   When listening to authentic programs and commercials, listen as attentively as you can, but don't feel frustated if you don't understand everything. Seek out opportunities to listen to Spanish speakers or Spanish-language television and try to identify what the subject of conversation or discussion is; catch as many words and phrases as you can. With time and continued practice, your comprehension level *will* improve.

Turismo local   You will listen three times to a fragment from a Costa Rican TV program on local tourism.

1. Escuche por primera vez y conteste: ¿De qué trata (*deals with*) este fragmento?
2. Escuche por segunda vez y conteste:
   a. ¿Cuántas habitaciones tiene el hotel?
   b. ¿Dónde está el hotel? ¿Cuántas personas trabajan en el hotel?
   c. ¿Qué tipos de restaurantes hay en la zona?
3. Escuche por tercera vez y conteste: ¿Hacia qué lugar dan (*overlook*) las habitaciones del hotel?

Al conversar...

Estrategia   **Simplifying ideas through paraphrasing**   An important skill in conversation is to be able to bring the interaction to a manageable level so you can participate. Paraphrasing and simplifying ideas is one technique that enables you to engage with others in discussion. For instance, when talking with someone, you can demonstrate your understanding of a statement by expressing it in simpler words.

  ¿Cómo?   You will hear a series of sentences on familiar topics. Listen and express an approximation of the message of each one. Then compare your responses with those of a classmate to determine whether you've understood the essence of the message.

◆ **MODELO:**   *You hear:* Para quienes les gusta la comida internacional hay una gran cantidad de restaurantes en la zona entre los cuales escoger.
   Sample paraphrase: Si te gusta la comida internacional, hay muchos restaurantes aquí que la sirven.

 ¿Qué dice Ud.?   What would you say in the following situations? What might the other person say? Act out the scenes with a partner. Take turns playing each role.

1. You have just checked into a hotel. You want to know what time they serve breakfast, and whether they have room service.
2. You are a hotel clerk. Someone calls to reserve a single room with a private bathroom, but it is July, and you don't have any. Tell the person you can put his or her name on a waiting list but don't have any vacant rooms.
3. You tell a traveling companion that you want to go to your room for a while because they are showing a good movie on channel four.
4. You are checking in at a hotel in Costa Rica. Ask about prices and accommodations. Make sure you get a room with an ocean view.
5. You ask the concierge two questions: what time you have to vacate the room and where the American embassy or consulate is.
6. You are a hotel employee and ask a guest what you can do for him/her.

Para conocernos mejor To do this activity, work with a classmate whom you would like to get to know. Take turns asking each other these questions.

1. Cuando viajas, ¿haces reservaciones para el hotel antes de salir de viaje? ¿Prefieres una habitación interior o con vista a la calle (al mar)? ¿Cuál es tu hotel favorito?

2. ¿Prefieres un cuarto en el segundo piso o en el décimo piso? Si el cuarto no tiene baño privado, ¿lo aceptas?

3. Cuando viajas, ¿les mandas tarjetas postales a tus amigos? ¿Sacas muchas fotografías cuando viajas? ¿Prefieres llevar una cámara fotográfica o una cámara de video?

4. ¿Prefieres cenar en tu cuarto si el hotel tiene servicio de habitación o te gusta más ir a un restaurante? ¿Cuál es tu restaurante favorito? ¿Es muy caro?

5. Cuando estás de viaje, ¿miras televisión? ¿Qué tipos de programas te gustan más? ¿Tienes un canal favorito? ¿Cuál? ¿Viste alguna película anoche? ¿Te gustó?

6. ¿Qué lugares te gusta visitar cuando estás de vacaciones? ¿Te gusta más viajar solo(-a), con tus amigos o con tu familia? ¿Cuándo son tus próximas vacaciones? ¿Adónde piensas ir? ¿Cuánto tiempo hace que no viajas?

Una encuesta Interview your classmates to identify who fits the following descriptions. Include your instructor, but remember to use the **Ud.** form when addressing him/her. After finishing the survey, get together with two or three classmates and discuss the results.

Nombre

1. Tiene un cuarto con vista a la calle. _____
2. Tiene ducha y bañadera en su baño. _____
3. Tiene televisor en su cuarto. _____
4. Le gusta mirar la tele mientras cena. _____
5. Vio una película anoche. _____
6. Prefiere las comedias románticas. _____
7. Tiene piscina en su casa. _____
8. Hace ejercicio por la mañana. _____

 De viaje (*Traveling*) Get together with a couple of your classmates and plan a trip to a Spanish-speaking country. Visit a Web site to obtain information about the country you are going to visit. Find out about hotels, rate of exchange, places of interest, and so on. Discuss how and when you will be leaving, how much spending money you'll bring, what cities and special sites you intend to visit, and what you will need to take with you.

 Para crear Get together in groups of three and "create" the scenario for this photo. Who are the people in it? Give them names and say where they are coming from and where they are going. Where are they going to stay? What places of interest are they going to visit? What kind of accommodations do they want?

¡Vamos a leer!

Antes de leer

> **Estrategia** **Guessing meaning from context** In **Lección 2,** you practiced guessing the meaning of unknown words by examining the surrounding context. Remember to look for clues such as cognates, other familiar words, and to make logical guesses based on what you know.

El turismo Before reading a brief article on Costa Rican tourism, in pairs, guess the meaning of the highlighted words in these sentences. Can you explain what helped you guess?

1. El presidente inauguró un terminal de **cruceros** en la costa del Caribe.
2. Ampliamos la operación del muelle (*dock*): en lugar de un crucero, ahora el muelle va a poder **atender** dos cruceros.
3. El ministerio de Turismo dice que 500.000 visitantes van a **ingresar** al país por mar.
4. En cada crucero viaja un **promedio** de 2.000 pasajeros.

A leer

 Comprensión As you read the article, find the answers to the following questions.

1. ¿Qué inauguró el presidente costarricense? ¿Qué busca incrementar?
2. ¿Cuánto costó la obra?
3. ¿Qué capacidad tiene el muelle? ¿Cuántos barcos van a llegar este año?
4. ¿Cuántos cruceros van a usar el nuevo muelle?
5. Como promedio, ¿cuántas personas viajan en cada crucero?
6. ¿Con qué lugares turísticos tratan de competir los costarricenses?

Costa Rica busca aumentar la entrada de cruceros

San José (AP).— El presidente costarricense inauguró el lunes un nuevo terminal de cruceros en la costa del Caribe del país, que busca incrementar la llegada de turistas a esa zona.

La obra costó un poco más de 3 millones y va a permitir recibir dos cruceros de forma simultánea en Puerto Limón, a 160 kilómetros de San José.

"Inauguramos la operación del muelle de cruceros ampliado y con capacidad para atender dos cruceros... Con ello reducimos el tiempo de espera y mejoramos la condición de Limón como destino turístico," destacó° el presidente.

emphasized

Aumentan las visitas de cruceros

Las visitas de cruceros a Costa Rica se aumentaron en los últimos años; este año van a llegar unos 255 barcos, 45 más que en el 2001.

Para la temporada siguiente sólo para Puerto Limón ya está confirmada la llegada de 122 cruceros que van a utilizar el nuevo muelle.°

dock

El ministerio de Turismo (ICT) dice que este año van a ingresar al país unos 500.000 visitantes por los puertos tanto del Caribe como del Pacífico. En cada crucero viajan como promedio 2.000 personas.

Con la remodelación del muelle caribeño, las autoridades costarricenses intentan competir en mejores condiciones con Colón, en Panamá, Cartagena, en Colombia, Cancún, en México y todas las islas caribeñas, principales destinos de las rutas de cruceros.

Del periódico *El Nuevo Día* (Puerto Rico)

¡Vamos a escribir!

Antes de escribir

Estrategia **Selecting topics and organizing the information** When writing multiple paragraphs, it's important to organize your thoughts so that the reader can clearly follow them from beginning to end. This generally means that each paragraph revolves around one distinct idea, which is often the topic sentence or **tema,** and that the ideas transition well from one to the next. When selecting or deciding on the central idea of each paragraph, it is helpful to brainstorm a number of topics and then choose those you think will be most interesting to your reader.

Una carta (*A letter*) You will be writing an e-mail to a friend from Costa Rica that you met in a chat room. He or she will be visiting you and wants to know something about your area.

1. Decide on the area (your region, state, or hometown) you will write about and select two to four topics about which you wish to write. If needed, research information online.
2. Brainstorm the specifics you want to present for each topic. Try to include varied aspects about the area and remember to use language that you know.
3. Decide how you will organize the topics.

A escribir un mensaje electrónico

Write your **primer borrador** of the letter. Use an appropriate greeting and farewell formula.

Saludos: Querido(-a)...: Estimado(-a)...: (*especially a man to another man*)
Despedidas: Saludos de, Afectuosamente,

Después de escribir

Before writing the final version of your letter, exchange your first draft with a classmate and peer edit each other's work, using the following guidelines.

- ◆ formation of all verbs and subject-verb agreement
- ◆ noun-adjective agreement
- ◆ clear topic in each paragraph

Después de leer... desde su mundo

In groups of three or four, discuss your preferred vacation (**vacaciones preferidas**). Find out more details about your classmates' travel and accommodation preferences.

Panorama hispánico

Costa Rica

◆ Costa Rica tiene una de las mejores economías de Centroamérica, aunque el 60% de sus ingresos proviene de la agricultura. El país produce principalmente café, bananas, caña de azúcar (*sugar cane*) y flores. Su segunda fuente de ingresos es el ecoturismo. Costa Rica tiene 24 parques nacionales y reservas ecológicas y en sus selvas tropicales viven más de 100.000 especies de flora y de fauna.

◆ San José, la capital, no es una gran ciudad, pero tiene lugares muy interesantes como el Teatro Nacional, el Museo de Jade, el Museo del Oro, el Parque Nacional de Diversiones, el Jardín Botánico de Lankester, etc.

◆ En la música popular de Costa Rica se notan sus raíces (*roots*) españolas, y sus instrumentos musicales más populares (la guitarra, la mandolina y el acordeón) también llegaron de España.

▲ Riquezas[1] naturales: El Jardín de Lankester

▲ Niñez[2] y educación costarricenses: Estudiantes en un laboratorio

Panamá

◆ La principal fuente de ingreso de Panamá proviene del famoso Canal de Panamá, que divide su territorio y une los océanos Atlántico y Pacífico. El Canal fue propiedad de los Estados Unidos hasta 1999. Ahora pertenece (*it belongs*) a Panamá. Junto al Canal están las dos ciudades más grandes del país: Ciudad de Panamá, su capital, y Colón, la segunda ciudad más importante del país.

◆ Los turistas están comenzando a descubrir las bellezas ecológicas de Panamá, especialmente sus selvas tropicales, la gran cantidad de arrecifes (*reefs*) de coral de sus costas y la extraordinaria variedad de peces (*fish*) que viven en ellos.

◆ La cultura panameña es una mezcla (*mixture*) de las tradiciones españolas, africanas, indias y norteamericanas, como muestra su variada música que incluye la cumbia, el jazz, la salsa y el reggae.

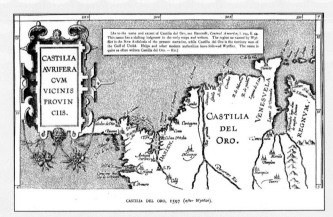

▲ Los territorios del actual (*present-day*) Panamá fueron llamados (*were named*) **Castilla del Oro** por el Rey Fernando de España (1508).

---

[1]**Riquezas** = *Riches; Resources*
[2]**Niñez** = *Childhood*

▲ Mujer cuna, grupo indígena conocido por su autosuficiencia (*self-sufficiency*) y perspectiva democrática.

▲ Laura Chinchilla, vicepresidenta de Costa Rica, durante una conferencia en Zambrano, Honduras

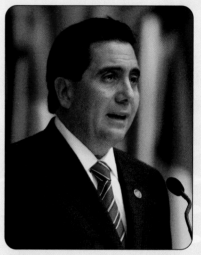

▲ El presidente de Panamá, Martín Torrijos, dando una conferencia en La Habana, Cuba

Nuestro panorama cultural

In groups of three, answer the following questions about your home state, region, or country.

1. ¿Es obligatoria la educación en su país? ¿Hasta qué nivel o grado? ¿Es gratuita?
2. ¿Cuáles son algunos animales y plantas típicos de su región?
3. ¿La capital de su estado tiene edificios altos? ¿Cuáles son los lugares de interés?
4. ¿Su país tiene canales? ¿Dónde están?
5. ¿Qué deportes son populares donde Ud. vive? ¿Qué deportes le gustan a Ud.?
6. ¿Cómo se llama el presidente de su país?
7. ¿Qué tipos de vegetación y de climas hay en su país?

For the next class: Go to the World Wide Web and find photos from your hometown, state, region, or country. Use the questions from **Nuestro panorama cultural** above as guidelines for choosing them. Be ready to present the photos to your classmates.

Lección

8

▲ Cliente saliendo de un banco de Renata, Chile

Objetivos

Comunicación

You will learn vocabulary related to banking and running errands. You will also be able to talk about flowers and pets.

Pronunciación

The Spanish **l**, **r**, **rr**, and **z**

Estructuras

- ◆ Direct and indirect object pronouns used together
- ◆ Preterit of **ser**, **ir**, and **dar**
- ◆ Preterit of **e:i** and **o:u** stem-changing verbs
- ◆ Uses of **por** and **para**
- ◆ Formation of adverbs

Cultura

- ◆ Banks and banking
- ◆ Bad-luck day
- ◆ Living with parents until marriage

Panorama hispánico

- ◆ Puerto Rico

Estrategias

Listening: Guessing meaning from context
Speaking: Paraphrasing practice I
Reading: Rereading critically
Writing: Writing journal entries

Haciendo diligencias

Recursos

Puerto Rico

Puerto Rico, "la isla del encanto", es la menor de las islas que forman el archipiélago de las Antillas Mayores. Los indios la llamaban *Boriquén,* y aún hoy muchos la llaman así, y llaman *boricuas* a sus habitantes.

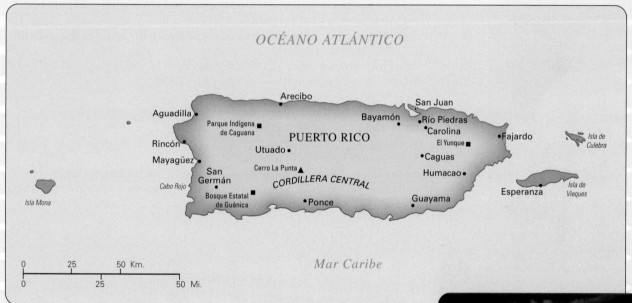

OCÉANO ATLÁNTICO

Arecibo · San Juan
Aguadilla · Bayamón · Río Piedras
Parque Indígena · Carolina
de Caguana · PUERTO RICO · El Yunque · Fajardo
Rincón · Utuado · Caguas
Mayagüez · Humacao
Cerro La Punta ▲
San · CORDILLERA CENTRAL
Germán
Cabo Rojo · Ponce · Guayama
Bosque Estatal
de Guánica

Isla Mona

Isla de Culebra

Isla de Vieques

Esperanza

Mar Caribe

| 0 | 25 | 50 Km. |
| 0 | 25 | 50 Mi. |

▲ La playa Flamenco en Culebra, Puerto Rico

▲ El Castillo del Morro, situado en la Bahía de San Juan, Puerto Rico

▲ Una calle en el Viejo San Juan, en Puerto Rico

En una casa de la Avenida Ponce de León, en San Juan, Puerto Rico, vive la familia Burgos Trinidad: Sara y Luis Burgos y su hijo Edwin. Edwin tiene mucho sueño hoy porque anoche no durmió muy bien. Ahora está desayunando y hablando con su mamá. Le está contando todo lo que le pasó ayer.

Mamá   ¿Fuiste a la tintorería a recoger tus pantalones?

Edwin   Sí... Ése fue mi primer problema... Estacioné la motocicleta frente a una boca de incendios y un policía me dio una multa.

Mamá   ¡Pobrecito! Y después... ¿fuiste al banco?

Edwin   Sí, deposité dinero en mi cuenta de ahorros y en mi cuenta corriente. Después pedí un préstamo, pero no me lo dieron.

Mamá   Tu papá tampoco consiguió el préstamo que pidió... ¡Qué mala suerte!

Edwin   Después compré dos peces de colores para Martita pero... murieron... Creo que les di demasiada comida...

Mamá   Probablemente. ¿Compraste el regalo para tu novia?

Edwin   Sí, pero no se lo di.

Mamá   ¿Por qué no? Le compraste un diccionario, ¿no? Un buen regalo para una chica que estudia para maestra...

Edwin   Sí, pero su ex novio le regaló una enciclopedia. En fin... fui a la florería y le compré un ramo de rosas.

Mamá   ¡Perfecto! Estoy segura de que le encantaron.

Edwin   Bueno... desgraciadamente es alérgica a las flores...

Mamá   ¡Ay, Edwin! ¡Qué desastre!

Edwin   ¡Eso no es todo! Ahora tengo que ahorrar dinero para comprar una motocicleta.

Mamá   Pero tú tienes una moto casi nueva...

Edwin   ¡Se la presté a Raúl y se la robaron!

Mamá   ¡Ay, bendito![1] ¡Ya sé por qué ocurrió todo eso! ¡Ayer fue martes trece!

Edwin   Ay, mamá... Yo no soy supersticioso... ¡Pero el próximo martes trece no salgo de casa!

¿Lo sabía Ud.?

En los países hispanos por lo general los jóvenes (*young people*) viven con su familia hasta que se casan (*get married*), pero esto está cambiando un poco, especialmente en las ciudades grandes.

◆ Generalmente, ¿hasta qué edad viven con sus padres los jóvenes de este país?

---

[1]**¡Ay, bendito!** = *Oh, my goodness!* (A common phrase in Puerto Rico)

Mamá

Edwin

¿Quién lo dice? Identify the person who said the following in the dialogue.

1. ¿Fuiste a la tintorería a recoger tus pantalones? _____
2. Después pedí un préstamo, pero no me lo dieron. _____
3. Tu papá tampoco consiguió el préstamo que pidió. _____
4. Después compré dos peces de colores para Martita. _____
5. ¿Compraste el regalo para tu novia? _____
6. Sí, pero su ex novio le regaló una enciclopedia. _____
7. En fin... fui a la florería y le compré un ramo de rosas. _____
8. Pero tú tienes una moto casi nueva. _____
9. ¡Ya sé por qué ocurrió todo eso! ¡Ayer fue martes trece! _____
10. ¡Pero el próximo martes trece no salgo de casa! _____

Hablemos. With a partner, take turns asking and answering the following questions. Base your answers on the dialogue and on your own circumstances.

En el diálogo	¿Y tú?
1. ¿Edwin durmió bien anoche?	¿Cómo dormiste tú?
2. ¿Qué le está contando Edwin a su mamá?	¿A quién le cuentas tú tus problemas?
3. ¿Para qué fue Edwin a la tintorería?	¿Tú mandas tu ropa a la tintorería?
4. ¿Por qué le dio el policía una multa a Edwin?	¿Te dieron una multa alguna vez (ever)?
5. ¿En qué cuentas depositó Edwin dinero?	¿Qué cuentas tienes tú en el banco?
6. ¿Consiguió el papá de Edwin el préstamo que pidió?	¿Tú piensas pedir un préstamo?
7. ¿Qué compró Edwin para Martita? ¿Qué les pasó a los peces?	¿Tú tienes animales? ¿Cuáles?
8. ¿Qué compró Edwin en la florería?	¿Te gustan las rosas?
9. ¿Para qué tiene que ahorrar dinero Edwin?	¿Tú puedes ahorrar? ¿Para qué?
10. ¿Qué no piensa hacer Edwin el próximo martes trece?	¿Tú eres supersticioso(-a)?

¿Lo sabía Ud.?

En los países hispanos el día de "mala suerte" es el martes trece y no el viernes trece. Dice un dicho, "Martes trece ni te cases ni te embarques" (*Don't get married or get on a boat [travel] on Tuesday the 13th*).

◆ **¿En este país toman muy en serio la idea de que el viernes trece es un día de mala suerte?**

⟨iLrn⟩ Vocabulario

Improve Your Grade
Audio Flashcards

Cognados

alérgico(-a) allergic
el banco bank
el desastre disaster
el diccionario dictionary
la enciclopedia encyclopedia

la motocicleta, la moto motorcycle
el policía[1] policeman
probablemente probably
la rosa rose
supersticioso(-a) superstitious

Nombres

la boca de incendios, el hidrante fire hydrant
la cuenta account
— **corriente** checking account
— **de ahorros** savings account
la flor flower
la florería flower shop
el incendio, el fuego fire
la multa fine, ticket

los pantalones pants, trousers
el pez de color goldfish
el (la) pobrecito(-a) poor thing
el préstamo loan
el ramo bouquet
el regalo present
la suerte luck
la tintorería dry cleaner's

Verbos

ahorrar to save (*e.g., money*)
contar (o:ue) to tell (*e.g., a story*)
depositar to deposit
estacionar, aparcar, parquear to park

pasar, ocurrir to happen
prestar to lend
regalar to give (as a gift)
robar to steal

Adjetivos

demasiado(-a) too
seguro(-a) sure

Otras palabras y expresiones

casi almost
dar (poner) una multa to fine
desgraciadamente, por desgracia, desafortunadamente unfortunately
en fin... anyway . . .
encantarle a uno to love

frente a in front of
hacer diligencias to run errands
pedir (solicitar) un préstamo to apply for a loan
¡Qué mala suerte! Such bad luck!
salir de casa to leave the house
todo all, everything

¿Lo sabía Ud.?

Cada nación latinoamericana tiene un banco central encargado de (*in charge of*) emitir el dinero y de controlar la actividad de los bancos comerciales. En algunos países hay también sucursales (*branches*) de bancos extranjeros.

◆ **En este país, ¿qué institución está encargada de emitir el dinero?**

---

[1]**policewoman** = *la agente de policía*

Vocabulario adicional

En el banco

a plazos on installments

al contado in cash

el cheque de viajero traveler's check

abrir una cuenta to open an account

el cajero automático automatic teller (ATM)

cobrar un cheque to cash a check

la cuenta conjunta joint account

en efectivo in cash

fechar to date (*a check, a letter, etc.*)

la firma signature

firmar to sign

gratis free of charge

la libreta de ahorros savings passbook

el talonario de cheques,
    la chequera checkbook

la tarjeta de crédito credit card

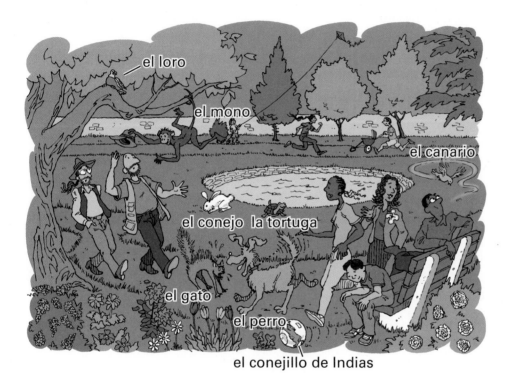

el loro

el mono

el canario

el conejo la tortuga

el gato

el perro

el conejillo de Indias

Otras flores

la camelia camellia

el clavel carnation

el geranio geranium

la lila lilac

la margarita daisy

la orquídea orchid

el pensamiento pansy

el tulipán tulip

la violeta violet

¿Lo sabía Ud.?

El uso de cheques no es tan común en América Latina como en los Estados Unidos y en Canadá, pero muchos bancos tienen sus propias (*own*) tarjetas de crédito.

◆ Generalmente ¿cómo paga la gente de este país cuando va de compras?

Práctica

 A. Match the questions in column A with the responses in column B.

A		B	
1. ¿Cuál es tu flor favorita?	____	**a.** Del cajero automático.	
2. ¿Vas a ir al banco?	____	**b.** Sí, me puso una multa.	
3. ¿Dónde estacionaste la moto?	____	**c.** No, a plazos.	
4. ¿Hablaste con el policía?	____	**d.** Sí, se lo di anoche.	
5. ¿Compraste el regalo para Olga?	____	**e.** No, de ahorros.	
6. ¿Adónde llevaste los pantalones?	____	**f.** Frente a una boca de incendios.	
7. ¿De dónde sacaste el dinero?	____	**g.** No, un canario.	
8. ¿Tienes cuenta corriente?	____	**h.** La margarita.	
9. ¿Lo compraste al contado?	____	**i.** A la tintorería.	
10. ¿Tienes un loro?	____	**j.** Sí, voy a solicitar un préstamo.	

B. Write the words or phrases that correspond to the following.

1. que tiene alergia _____
2. lugar donde venden flores _____
3. fuego _____
4. aparcar _____
5. pasar _____
6. por desgracia _____
7. gustarle mucho a uno _____
8. poner la fecha _____
9. chequera _____
10. Morris, por ejemplo _____

C. Complete the following sentences, using vocabulary from this lesson.

1. Por _____ me robaron la motocicleta. ¡Qué mala _____!
2. Hoy tengo que hacer muchas _____. Voy a salir de _____ a las ocho.
3. Mi esposa y yo vamos a _____ una cuenta _____.
4. Le regalé un _____ de rosas y unos _____ de colores.
5. Van a comprar la _____ *Británica* y un diccionario.
6. No va a hacer nada el martes _____ porque es muy _____.
7. Carlitos no puede ir a la fiesta porque está enfermo. ¡_____!
8. Me gusta muchísimo Puerto Rico. Me _____.
9. Creo que puedes ahorrar dinero allí, pero no estoy _____.
10. Voy a _____ el cheque y voy a _____ el dinero en el banco.

Para conversar

A. Problemas y más problemas With a partner, take turns indicating what these people can do about all the problems they had last week.

◆ **MODELO:** Anita compró dos peces de colores y los dos murieron.
Anita puede comprar otros peces de colores y preguntarle al empleado cómo cuidarlos (take care of them).

1. Paloma pidió un préstamo en el banco y no se lo dieron.
2. Roberto tiene que comparle un regalo de cumpleaños a su novia y no tiene mucho dinero.
3. Beto quiere comprar un ramo de flores para una chica, pero no sabe qué flores le gustan a ella.
4. Julio quiere ahorrar dinero para comprar una motocicleta pero él gana (*earns*) muy poco.
5. A Marisa le robaron el coche el sábado pasado y ella no sabe cómo va a ir a la universidad.

B. **¡Cuántas diligencias!** With a partner, play the roles of two roommates who were supposed to run several errands yesterday. You ask each other whether or not you did certain things, including follow-up questions as much as possible (**¿Fuiste a...?, ¿Compraste...?,** etc.).

Pronunciación

A. The Spanish *l*

The Spanish **l** is pronounced like the *l* in the English word *lean*. The tip of the tongue must touch the palate. Listen to your instructor and repeat the following sentences.

Laura y Silvia le dan el regalo.

Luis vuela a la capital el lunes.

El policía le dio una multa a Lola.

B. The Spanish *r*

The Spanish **r** sounds something like the *dd* in the English word *ladder*. Listen to your instructor and repeat the following sentences.

Sara Burgos fue a la tintorería.

El teatro abre a las tres y cuarto.

Teresa Vera compró flores en la florería.

C. The Spanish *rr*

The Spanish **rr** is spelled **r** at the beginning of the words and **rr** between vowels. It is a strong trill. Listen to your instructor and repeat the following sentences.

Rosa Romero está aburrida.

El arroz está rico.

Roberto Reyes come con Rita.

D. The Spanish *z*

In Latin America the Spanish **z** is pronounced like the *ss* in the English word *pressing*. In Spain it is pronounced like the *th* in the English word *think*. Avoid using the buzzing sound of the English *z* in the words *zoo* and *zebra*. Listen to your instructor and repeat the following sentences.

La taza azul es de Zoila.

El lápiz es del mozo.

Zulema Pérez fue al zoológico.

Aspectos culturales

▲ Mercado al aire libre

▲ Frutería

▲ Policías municipales

Ubíquese... y búsquelo

Improve Your Grade
Web Search

You are in Metropolitan San Juan using the **Tren Urbano,** a new rail transit system, as your means of transportation. Go to **www.cengage.com/highered** to find out about some of the places for sightseeing and for running different errands at several **Tren Urbano** stations. In the next class, team up with two classmates to discuss your findings.

▲ Correo Central, Puerto Rico

▲ Cajero automático (*ATM*)

Estructuras

1. Direct and indirect object pronouns used together (*Pronombres de complemento directo e indirecto usados juntos*)

♦ When an indirect object pronoun and a direct object pronoun are used together, the indirect object pronoun always comes first.

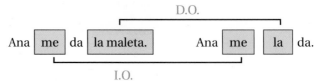

♦ With an infinitive, the pronouns can either be placed before the conjugated verb or be attached to the infinitive.

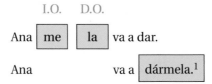

♦ With the present progressive, the pronouns can either be placed before the conjugated verb or be attached to the gerund.

♦ If both pronouns begin with **l,** the indirect object pronoun (**le** or **les**) is changed to **se.**

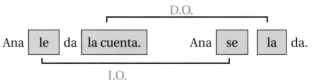

For clarification, it is sometimes necessary to add **a él, a ella, a Ud., a Uds., a ellos,** or **a ellas.**

—¿A quién le da la cuenta Ana?
—**Se la** da **a él.**

---

[1]Note the use of the written accent, which follows the rules for accentuation. See Appendix A.

Práctica

A. Complete the following exchanges, using direct and indirect object pronouns. Then act them out with a partner, adding a sentence or two to each dialogue.

1. —¿Le dejaste la chequera a Raúl?

—Sí, _____ dejé en su escritorio.

2. —¿Uds. nos van a traer los cheques?

—Sí, _____ vamos a traer ahora.

3. —¿El banco les va a dar el préstamo a Uds.?

—Sí, va a _____ hoy.

4. —¿El empleado te trae el talonario de cheques?

—Sí, _____ trae.

5. —¿Me vas a dar las tarjetas de crédito?

—No, no _____ puedo dar. Lo siento.

6. —¿Le vas a prestar el dinero a Mario?

—Sí, _____ voy a prestar.

B. You have a friend who is always willing to help others. Explain how, using the information provided.

◆ **MODELO:** Yo necesito un diccionario. (comprar)
*Mi amigo **me lo** compra.*

1. Tú necesitas los cheques. (traer)
2. Yo necesito dos tarjetas. (comprar)
3. Nosotros necesitamos un préstamo. (dar)
4. Elsa necesita cheques de viajero. (comprar)
5. Mis hermanos necesitan dinero. (prestar)
6. Ud. necesita la chequera. (traer)
7. Yo quiero el talonario de cheques. (buscar)
8. Mi prima quiere unas flores. (comprar)

C. With a partner, take turns asking and answering questions about what the following people want and whether you can help them. Use the verbs **mandar, dar, prestar, comprar,** and **traer.**

◆ **MODELO:**
—*¿Qué quiere Elisa?*
—*Quiere dinero. ¿Tú se lo puedes mandar?*
—*No, lo siento. Yo no puedo mandárselo.*

Elisa

2. Ana y Paco

3. Javier

4. Lidia

5. Lucía

1. Carlos

D. You are in a bad mood, and people keep asking you to do things you don't want to do. Tell them you can't do the favors they are requesting.

◆ **MODELO:** —¿Puedes traerme las violetas?
—*No, no puedo traér**telas.***

1. ¿Puedes comprarle el regalo a mamá?
2. ¿Puedes buscarme la chequera?
3. ¿Puedes llevarle las flores a Luisa?
4. ¿Puedes darle los cheques de viajero a Raúl?
5. ¿Puedes traernos los pantalones de la tintorería?
6. ¿Puedes comprarnos un perro?

E. Now repeat Exercise D, following the model below.

◆ **MODELO:** —¿Puedes traerme las violetas?
—*No, no **te las** puedo traer.*

Para conversar

A. **¡Habla con tu compañero!** Interview a classmate, using the following questions and two questions of your own. When you have finished, switch roles.

1. Cuando tú necesitas dinero, ¿a quién se lo pides?
2. Cuando tú les pides dinero a tus padres, ¿te lo dan?
3. Si yo necesito tu libro de español, ¿me lo prestas?
4. Si Uds. no entienden algo, ¿se lo preguntan (*ask*) a su profesor(-a)?
5. Si tú y yo somos amigos(-as) y yo necesito tu coche, ¿tú me lo prestas?
6. Necesito tu pluma. ¿Puedes prestármela?
7. Necesito cheques de viajero. ¿Tú me los puedes conseguir?
8. Yo no tengo el número de teléfono del profesor (de la profesora). ¿Tú se lo puedes pedir?

B. **¿Qué necesitamos?** In groups of three, talk about what each of you needs. Then ask a member of the group whether he/she can lend you, give you, or send you the needed item.

Camarón que se duerme,
se lo lleva la corriente.

Equivalent: Don't rest on your laurels.

2. Preterit of *ser, ir,* and *dar* (*Pretérito de los verbos **ser, ir** y **dar***)

◆ The preterit forms of **ser, ir,** and **dar** are irregular.

ser *to be*	**ir** *to go*	**dar** *to give*
fui	fui	di
fuiste	fuiste	diste
fue	fue	dio
fuimos	fuimos	dimos
fuisteis	fuisteis	disteis
fueron	fueron	dieron

◆ Note that **ser** and **ir** have identical forms in the preterit.

—Ayer **fue** el cumpleaños   *"Yesterday was Lucía's birthday,*
de Lucía, ¿no?   *right?"*
—Sí, Ana y yo **fuimos** a su casa y   *"Yes, Ana and I went to her house and gave*
le **dimos** los regalos.   *her the presents."*
—¿**Fuiste** a la fiesta que **dio** Sara?   *"Did you go to the party that Sara gave?"*
—Sí, **fui. Fue** la mejor fiesta   *"Yes, I went. It was the best party of*
del año.   *the year."*

Práctica

ACE the Test

 Complete the following exchanges, using the preterit of **ser, ir,** or **dar** as appropriate. Then act them out with a partner, adding a sentence or two to each dialogue.

1. —¿Adónde _____ tú ayer?

   _____ a la tienda. Compré un pantalón y se lo _____ a mi esposo.

2. —¿_____ Uds. a casa de tía Eva ayer?

   —Sí, _____ y le _____ el libro que tú mandaste para ella.

3. —¿Uds. _____ estudiantes del Dr. Paz?

   —Carlos _____ su estudiante, pero Raquel y yo _____ estudiantes de la Dra. Guerra.

4. —¿A quién le _____ (tú) la orquídea?

   —Se la _____ a Susana.

5. —¿Adónde _____ Uds. anoche?

   —_____ al teatro. Los padres de Dora nos _____ el dinero para ir.

Para conversar

¡**Habla con tu compañero!** Interview a classmate, using the following questions. When you have finished, switch roles.

1. ¿Quién fue tu profesor(-a) favorito(-a) el año pasado? ¿La clase fue fácil o difícil?
2. ¿Fuiste a la cafetería ayer? ¿A qué hora? ¿Alguien fue contigo o fuiste solo(-a)?
3. ¿Adónde fuiste el sábado? ¿Con quién fuiste?
4. ¿Tus amigos fueron a visitarte o tú fuiste a visitarlos a ellos?
5. ¿Dieron tus amigos una fiesta para celebrar tu cumpleaños? ¿Cuándo la dieron? ¿Dónde?
6. ¿Diste una fiesta el viernes pasado? ¿Alguien dio una fiesta el sábado?
7. ¿A quién le diste un abrazo ayer? ¿Alguien te dio un beso (*kiss*)?
8. ¿Quién fue tu primer amor?

 **Todo tiempo pasado fue mejor.**

Equivalent: **Those were the good old days.**

3. Preterit of *e:i* and *o:u* stem-changing verbs (*Pretérito de los verbos que cambian en la raíz: e:i y o:u*)

◆ Verbs of the **-ir** conjugation that have a stem change in the present tense change **e** to **i** and **o** to **u** in the third-person singular and plural of the preterit.[1]

preferir *to prefer*		**dormir** *to sleep*	
preferí	preferimos	dormí	dormimos
preferiste	preferisteis	dormiste	dormisteis
prefirió	prefirieron	durmió	durmieron

◆ Other verbs that follow the same pattern:

pedir	seguir
mentir (*to lie*)	conseguir
servir	morir
repetir (*to repeat*)	

—¿Cómo **durmieron** Uds. anoche?   *"How did you sleep last night?"*
—Nosotros **dormimos** bien,   *"We slept well, but Paco didn't*
    pero Paco no **durmió** muy bien.   *sleep very well."*

—¿Qué **pidieron** ellos?   *"What did they order?"*
—Raúl **pidió** camarones   *"Raúl ordered shrimp and Rosa*
    y Rosa **pidió** langosta.   *ordered lobster."*

—Beba dice que Ada salió   *"Beba says that Ada went out with your*
    con tu novio.   *boyfriend."*
—Te **mintió.**   *"She lied to you."*

¿**Durmió** bien anoche, señorita...?

---

[1]Remember that the **-ar** and **-er** stem-changing verbs are regular in the preterit: **él cerró, ellos volvieron.** Exceptions are **poder** and **querer,** which are explained in **Lección 9.**

A. With a partner, take turns describing what the following people did last night. Use the verbs given (or similar).

1. Arturo (preferir)

2. Ernesto (pedir)

3. Paco (seguir)

4. Rosa (dormir)

5. el mozo (servir)

6. Pilar (conseguir)

 B. Find out what Andrés did yesterday by adding the correct form of the missing verbs.

1. Yo _____ (ir) a visitar a mi padre y le _____ (pedir) dinero.

2. _____ (Conseguir) revistas en español.

3. _____ (Salir) con otra chica y le _____ (mentir) a mi novia.

4. Nosotros _____ (ir) a un restaurante y yo _____ (pedir) pollo frito; ella _____ (pedir) langosta.

5. Yo _____ (volver) a mi casa y _____ (dormir) dos horas.

6. Mis padres me _____ (invitar) a una fiesta, pero yo _____ (preferir) no ir.

7. Por la noche, yo _____ (dar) una fiesta y _____ (servir) ponche.

Para conversar

 A. Queremos saber... Now, using the information above, prepare questions to ask your classmates about what Andrés did.

 B. ¡Qué mala suerte! With two classmates, imagine that you have a friend who had really bad luck last Friday the 13th. Brainstorm to come up with all the bad things that happened to him. Use the verbs studied in this section.

4. Uses of *por* and *para* (*Usos de* **por** *y* **para**)

A. Uses of *por*

The preposition **por** is used to express the following concepts.

♦ motion or approximate location (*through, around, along, by*)

Luis salió **por** la ventana.	*Luis went out through the window.*
Enrique va **por** la calle Juárez.	*Enrique is going down Juárez Street.*
Gustavo pasó **por** el hotel.	*Gustavo went by the hotel.*

♦ cause or motive of an action (*because of, on account of, on behalf of*)

Llegamos tarde **por** la lluvia.	*We were late because of the rain.*
Lo hago **por** ellos.	*I do it on their behalf.*

♦ means, manner, unit of measure (*by, for, per*)

Siempre viajamos **por** tren.	*We always travel by train.*
Van a 100 kilómetros **por** hora.	*They're going 100 kilometers per hour.*

♦ *in exchange for*

Te doy 50 dólares **por** esa cámara.	*I'll give you 50 dollars for that camera.*

♦ period of time during which an action takes place (*during, in, for*)

Ella trabaja **por** la mañana.	*She works in the morning.*
Va a estar aquí **por** dos meses.	*He's going to be here for two months.*

♦ *in search of, for*

Voy a venir **por** ti a las siete.	*I'll come by for you at seven.*

ACE the Test

Práctica

Interview a classmate, using the following questions. When you have finished, switch roles.

1. ¿Tienes una clase por la mañana? ¿Y por la noche?
2. Antes de ir a clase, ¿vas por tus amigos? ¿Alguien viene por ti?
3. ¿Cuánto pagaste por tu libro de español?
4. ¿Pasaste por mi casa anoche?
5. Si tú pierdes la llave de tu casa, ¿entras por la ventana?
6. ¿Tus padres hacen mucho por ti?
7. ¿Tú les escribes a tus padres o prefieres llamarlos por teléfono?
8. ¿Prefieres viajar por tren o por avión (*plane*)? ¿Por qué?

Podemos estar con Uds. **por** un mes.

Un dicho

El pez muere por la boca.

Equivalent: Engage brain before putting mouth in gear.

B. Uses of *para*

The preposition **para** is used to express the following concepts.

◆ destination

Mañana salgo **para** San Juan.	*Tomorrow I am leaving for San Juan.*
¿A qué hora hay autobuses **para** Río Piedras?	*What time are there buses for Río Piedras?*

◆ goal for a point in the future (*by* or *for* a certain time)

Quiero el dinero **para** el sábado.	*I want the money for Saturday.*
Debo estar allí **para** el mes de noviembre.	*I must be there by the month of November.*

◆ whom or what something is for

Compré una mesa **para** mi cuarto.	*I bought a table for my room.*
Compramos los libros **para** Fernando.	*We bought the books for Fernando.*

◆ *in order to*

Necesito mil dólares **para** pagar el viaje.	*I need a thousand dollars in order to pay for the trip.*
Vamos al teatro **para** celebrar mi cumpleaños.	*We are going to the theater (in order) to celebrate my birthday.*

◆ objective or goal

Mi novio estudia **para** médico.	*My boyfriend is studying to be a doctor.*

Práctica

ACE the Test

A. Look at the illustrations and describe what is happening, using **por** or **para**.

1. Fuimos _____ a la capital.

2. Daniel salió _____.

Gracias.

Ana

3. La torta es _____.

4. Luisa va a estar en San Juan _____.

Jorge

5. Jorge pagó _____ el vino.

6. Eva sale mañana _____.

B. Imagine that you and your partner are planning a trip to Puerto Rico. Take turns asking and answering the following questions.

1. ¿Cuánto dinero necesitan Uds. para pagar el viaje?
2. ¿Van a pedirles dinero a sus padres para el viaje?
3. ¿Para qué día quieren los pasajes (*tickets*)?
4. ¿A qué hora sale el avión para San Juan?
5. ¿Por cuánto tiempo piensan estar en Puerto Rico?
6. ¿Van a traer regalos para su familia?
7. ¿Van Uds. a Puerto Rico para practicar el español?
8. John estudia para profesor de español y quiere visitar San Juan. ¿Puede ir con Uds.?

C. Complete the following description of a trip to Mexico, using **por** or **para.**

Roberto y yo salimos _____ Cancún la semana próxima. Vamos a viajar _____ avión. Tenemos pasajes _____ el sábado _____ la mañana. Pagamos tres mil dólares _____ el pasaje, pero como pensamos pasar _____ Guatemala, donde vamos a estar _____ unos días, no es muy caro. Mañana _____ la tarde vamos a la tienda _____ comprar algunos regalos _____ nuestros amigos mexicanos. Desde Guatemala vamos a llamar _____ teléfono a nuestros amigos en Cancún y ellos van a ir al aeropuerto _____ nosotros.

Para conversar

De viaje Plan a trip to Puerto Rico with a classmate. Using the paragraph in Exercise C (above) as a model, describe your travel plans.

5. Formation of adverbs (*La formación de los adverbios*)

◆ Most Spanish adverbs are formed by adding **-mente** (the equivalent of the English *-ly*) to the adjective.

especial	*special*	especial**mente**	*especially*
reciente	*recent*	reciente**mente**	*recently*
general	*general*	general**mente**	*generally*
probable	*probable*	probable**mente**	*probably*

◆ Adjectives ending in **-o** change the **-o** to **-a** before adding **-mente.**

lento	*slow*	lent**amente**	*slowly*
rápido	*rapid*	rápid**amente**	*rapidly*
desafortunado	*unfortunate*	desafortunad**amente**	*unfortunately*

◆ If two or more adverbs are used together, both change the **-o** to **-a,** but only the last adverb takes the **-mente** ending.

Habló clara y **lentamente.**　　　*He spoke clearly and slowly.*

◆ If the adjective has an accent, the adverb retains it.

fácil　　　　　**fácilmente**

Camina **lentamente.**

Práctica

A. Change the following adjectives to adverbs.

1. fácil
2. feliz
3. claro (*clear*)
4. raro (*rare*)
5. necesario
6. frecuente (*frequent*)
7. triste
8. trágico (*tragic*)
9. alegre (*merry*)
10. desgraciado

B. Complete the following sentences with appropriate adverbs.

1. Ellos hablaron _____ y _____.
2. Mis padres vienen a verme _____.
3. Jaime llegó _____.
4. El muchacho me habló _____.
5. _____ me levanto a las siete.
6. Los muchachos cantan _____.
7. _____ no tengo dinero.
8. Compré estas flores _____ para ti.
9. _____ no voy a poder ir a San Juan con ellos.
10. _____ están en casa por la noche.

C. Interview a classmate, using the following questions and two of your own. Include adverbs in your responses. When you have finished, switch roles.

1. ¿A qué hora te levantas tú?
2. ¿Tú y tu familia van de compras juntos?
3. ¿Tú ves a tus abuelos a menudo (*often*)?
4. ¿Vas al teatro a menudo?
5. ¿Tú tienes mucho dinero?

Para conversar

Lo que hacemos. With a partner, discuss what you frequently do, rarely do, and what, unfortunately, you can't do.

◆ **MODELO:** *Yo raramente visito a mis abuelos.*

Un dicho

Lo que fácilmente se consigue, a menudo se pierde fácilmente.

That which is easily obtained is often easily lost.

Así somos

Estrategia **Guessing meaning from context** When you listen to speech, you can use informed guesswork to figure out the approximate meaning of an unknown word or phrase, just as you have been learning to do when reading. Use your knowledge of the topic and the words you do know to help you decipher unfamiliar words.

  ¿Qué significa? You will listen to three commercials on different products and services. Guess the meaning of the following words and phrases.

Commercial 1:
  a. mándale
  b. va a quedar encantada

Commercial 2:
  a. perrito
  b. gatito
  c. venga
  d. cuidarlos

Commercial 3:
  a. bancarios
  b. estamos a su disposición

── Al conversar... ──

Estrategia **Paraphrasing practice I** In **Al conversar...** of **Lección 7,** you were introduced to the technique of simplifying statements in your own words. This helps you manage a conversation by confirming that you understand. The following is the first of four activities in which you will practice paraphrasing what you hear.

 ¿Qué dice? Listen to the following sentences and restate them in a simpler way in your own words. Then compare your responses with those of a classmate.

  ◆ MODELO: *You hear:* Me resulta imposible sacar dinero del cajero automático. Parece que está roto o fuera de servicio.
  Sample paraphrase: No puedo sacar dinero del cajero automático porque no funciona.

  ¿Qué dice Ud.? What would you say in the following situations? What might the other person say? Act out the scenes with a partner. Take turns playing each role.

  1. Mention four transactions that people can make at a bank.
  2. You ask Mrs. López if she got the loan that she asked for at the bank.
  3. You work at a pet store. Tell a customer what pets you have for sale.
  4. A young man wants to send flowers to his girlfriend. Make suggestions about what kind of flowers to send.
  5. You are talking to a friend about your activities last week. Mention several things you did and places you went to.

Para conocernos mejor To do this activity, work with a classmate whom you would like to get to know. Take turns asking each other these questions.

1. ¿A qué hora desayunaste esta mañana? ¿Qué comiste? ¿Qué tomaste? ¿Desayunaste solo(-a)?
2. ¿Fuiste a la tintorería la semana pasada? Generalmente, ¿llevas tu ropa a la tintorería o la lavas en tu casa?
3. ¿Fuiste al banco la semana pasada? ¿Depositaste dinero? ¿Sacaste dinero del cajero automático? ¿Abriste una cuenta?
4. ¿Compraste algún regalo el mes pasado? ¿Para quién? ¿Le gustó a esa persona el regalo?
5. ¿Compras flores frecuentemente? ¿Cuáles son tus flores favoritas?
6. ¿Tú eres alérgico(-a) a los animales? ¿A las flores? ¿A algún tipo de comida?
7. ¿Te gustan los animales? ¿Tienes alguna mascota (*pet*)? ¿Qué animales prefieres?
8. ¿Te gustan las motocicletas? ¿Tienes una? Muchas personas dicen que las motocicletas son peligrosas (*dangerous*); ¿tú piensas lo mismo?

Una encuesta Interview your classmates to identify who fits the following descriptions. Include your instructor, but remember to use the **Ud.** form when addressing him/her. After finishing the survey, get together with two or three classmates and discuss the results.

Nombre

1. Fue al banco la semana pasada. _____
2. Pidió un préstamo en el banco. _____
3. Tiene una cuenta conjunta. _____
4. Siempre paga con tarjeta de crédito. _____
5. Siempre tiene su chequera con él (ella). _____
6. Prefiere pagar en efectivo. _____
7. Cobró un cheque la semana pasada. _____
8. Le prestó dinero a alguien. _____

Para crear Get together in groups of three and "create" the scenario for this photo. Who are the people? Give them names. Talk about what the employee and the customer do and want to do. Include as many banking transactions as possible.

¡Vamos a leer!

Antes de leer

Estrategia **Reading critically** Interacting with a reading engages you personally with the text. A reading might generate questions, as well as positive and negative reactions. When you read critically, try to think about your impressions of what you read and why a reading evokes particular thoughts. Does what you read ring true or make sense? Do you agree with the writer's point of view, ideas, or the information conveyed? Why?

La suerte Find out what day of the week you were born and read what the following text says about that day. In pairs, tell your partner your impression of what you read. Answer this question: **¿Es cierto lo que se dice de tu día?**

A leer

 Comprensión As you read the article, find the answers to the following questions.

1. ¿Por qué es importante en su vida el día de la semana en que Ud. nació?
2. ¿Qué debe aprender a hacer una mujer que nació el lunes? ¿Y un hombre?
3. ¿Qué debe recordar una mujer que nació un martes? ¿Qué debe aprender a hacer un hombre que nació ese día?
4. ¿Qué debe hacer una mujer que nació un miércoles? ¿Y un hombre?
5. Si una mujer nació un jueves, ¿qué debe combatir? ¿Qué debe aceptar un hombre que nació ese día?
6. ¿Qué gran poder tiene una mujer que nació un viernes? ¿Qué debe aprender a aceptar un hombre que nació ese día?
7. ¿Qué deben hacer las mujeres y los hombres que nacieron un sábado?
8. ¿Qué le va a ser difícil a una mujer que nació un domingo? ¿Por qué no debe preocuparse un hombre que nació ese día?

El día de la semana en que nació marcó su suerte

Según el profesor Waffman, mucho de lo que sucede en su vida depende del día de su nacimiento.

Si nació un lunes...
Ella: Sus problemas se deben a hechos° anteriores, pero luego se estabilizan. Si aprende a confiar,° será feliz.
Él: Tiene excelentes posibilidades de éxito en su vida si sabe aprovecharlas° y no lo deja todo para último momento.

Si nació un martes...
Ella: Recuerde que su mejor defensa está en el cariño° que da y que recibe.
Él: Aprenda a comprender y a compartir° para vivir en armonía.

Si nació un miércoles...
Ella: Tendrá problemas en su vida conyugal, pero no van a durar si usted resuelve las tensiones diarias.
Él: Tiene posibilidades de éxito personal y profesional. Evite las situaciones que ponen en peligro su felicidad.

Si nació un jueves...
Ella: Trate de combatir la depresión y escuche los consejos° de personas realistas.
Él: Para lograr los objetivos deseados, trabaje y acepte las cosas como vienen. No se desespere, pues todo llega.

Si nació un viernes...
Ella: Usted tiene un gran poder de recuperación.
Él: Planee el futuro junto a la mujer que ama. En el plano profesional tendrá éxito si acepta la realidad como es.

Si nació un sábado...
Ella: Usted puede encontrar la felicidad si sabe aprovechar todas las oportunidades.
Él: Si quiere conseguir la felicidad, use sus habilidades para destacarse.°

Si nació un domingo...
Ella: El triunfo profesional le va a ser difícil.
Él: No se preocupe por los conflictos familiares que no están vinculados con usted.

events
trust

to take advantage of them

love

share

advice

to stand out

¡Vamos a escribir!

Antes de escribir

Estrategia **Writing journal entries** Diary or journal writing allows you to freely express yourself however you want, for however long you want. You can use a journal to record events, whether large or small, or to think about something you read or heard or a problem you're working to resolve. Whatever your purpose, just let the ideas flow. Writing frequently will help you become a better writer, and journal writing is particularly useful because you can write freely without being overly concerned about form.

Querido diario Before writing journal entries for two days, jot down some ideas or events you want to write about. Will you report mainly things that happened or will you also write about your ideas or difficulties you might be facing?

A escribir el diario

Write journal entries for two days. You can include whatever you like: people you saw, interesting things you did, a troublesome encounter, a special achievement, etc. Remember to let the thoughts flow.

Después de escribir

Review what you wrote and add any additional thoughts you might have. Because a journal is a personal rather than a formal piece of writing, you won't be asked to peer edit it for grammar. Exchange your journal entries with a classmate and comment only on general content, reacting to what your classmate wrote. Some useful phrases: **¡Qué interesante! ¡Qué bien! ¡Qué divertido** (*fun*)**! Lo siento. ¡Qué mala suerte!** (*What bad luck!*)

Después de leer... desde su mundo

Reread the descriptions for every day for your gender. In groups of three, discuss your impressions of the nature and validity of the descriptions. Answer these questions: **¿Son apropiadas para cualquier** (*any*) **persona? ¿Por qué?**

Panorama hispánico

Puerto Rico

◆ Puerto Rico es una de las áreas más densamente pobladas del mundo. En la pequeña isla, con menos de 3.500 millas cuadradas de superficie, viven cerca de (*around*) 4 millones de habitantes. El país tiene solamente unas 100 millas de largo. Desde 1952 Puerto Rico es un Estado Libre Asociado de los Estados Unidos.

◆ San Juan, la capital de la isla, es la ciudad más grande y más poblada de Puerto Rico. Su parte antigua, el Viejo San Juan, es un centro de atracción turística por sus hermosas plazas, sus interesantes museos, sus edificios coloniales y las fortalezas (*fortresses*) de El Morro y San Cristóbal. El Morro fue construido por los españoles durante la época colonial para defender el puerto de los ataques de los corsarios (*privateers*) y piratas. Hoy también muchos turistas visitan San Juan por su intensa vida nocturna. Ponce es la segunda ciudad más importante del país. Fuera de la capital, son puntos de interés turístico las hermosas playas y el Yunque, un bosque (*forest*) tropical situado al este de San Juan. En el bosque hay más de 225 especies de árboles y muchas especies de animales.

◆ Igual que en Cuba, se nota la influencia de España, de África y de los Estados Unidos en el arte y en la música. De los deportes, el más popular es el béisbol. Muchos puertorriqueños se han distinguido en el mundo del espectáculo y en la literatura. Tito Puente, Raúl Juliá, Ricky Martin, Rosalyn Sanchez y Benicio del Toro son artistas muy conocidos. Julia de Burgos ha alcanzado (*has achieved*) fama internacional como poeta.

▲ Parque en el Viejo San Juan, en Puerto Rico

Imágenes de la historia y de la economía puertorriqueñas

▲ Carrera de bicicletas en una calle de San Juan, Puerto Rico

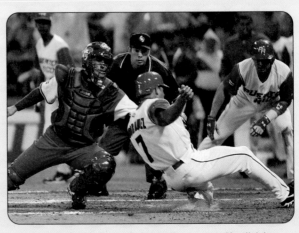

▲ Jugada (*Play*) sensacional durante el Campeonato Mundial de Béisbol entre Cuba y Puerto Rico, 2006

La política

▲ Luis Muñoz Marín (1898–1980), gobernador de 1948 a 1964, hizo realidad (*made possible*) el actual estado (*status*) constitucional del Puerto Rico de hoy: el Estado Libre Asociado de los Estados Unidos (1952).

Otras personalidades

▲ Tito Trinidad (1973–), cinco veces (*times*) campeón mundial (*world champion*) de boxeo

Nuestro panorama cultural

In groups of three, answer the following questions about your home state, region, or country.

1. ¿Cuáles son algunas de las actividades típicas de la vida nocturna en su ciudad?
2. ¿Cuáles son las industrias de la región donde Ud. vive?
3. ¿Conoce Ud. a algunos latinos famosos?
4. ¿Ha estado (*Have you been*) alguna vez en Puerto Rico?
5. ¿Qué tipos de música y de bailes le gustan a Ud.?

For the next class: Go to the World Wide Web and find photos from your hometown, state, region, or country. Use the questions from **Nuestro panorama cultural** above as guidelines for choosing them. Be ready to present the photos to your classmates.

Lección

9

Objetivos

Comunicación

You will learn vocabulary related to shopping for groceries, meal preparation, and daily routines.

Pronunciación

La entonación

Estructuras

◆ Reflexive constructions
◆ Some uses of the definite article
◆ Possessive pronouns
◆ Irregular preterits
◆ **Hace...** meaning *ago*

Cultura

◆ Roles of senior family members
◆ Specialty stores and open-air markets
◆ Intergenerational attitudes among family members

Panorama hispánico

◆ Cuba
◆ La República Dominicana

Estrategias

Listening: Dealing with fast speech
Speaking: Using pauses to manage conversation
Reading: Skimming
Writing: Sequencing steps for a recipe

▲ Una familia cubana, residente en Santo Domingo, celebra el cumpleaños del abuelo.

Una cena de cumpleaños

Cuba y la República Dominicana

Cuba

Cuba es la mayor de las islas del archipiélago de las Antillas. Su figura es similar a la de un cocodrilo y, como es larga y estrecha (*narrow*), tiene extensas costas en las cuales hay playas de gran belleza (*beauty*). Muchos llaman a Cuba "la Perla de las Antillas".

La República Dominicana

La República Dominicana ocupa las dos terceras partes de la isla que Colón descubrió en su primer viaje y a la que llamó La Española. La parte occidental de la isla está ocupada por la República de Haití.

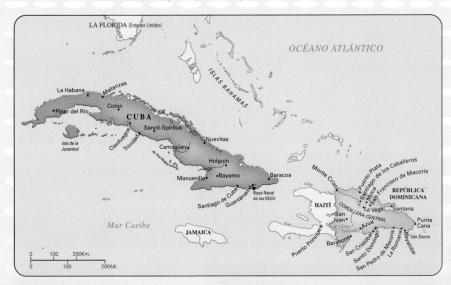

▲ La Catedral (construida entre 1748 y 1767), La Habana Vieja

▲ El río Ozama en Santo Domingo, capital de la República Dominicana

▲ Vista de la hermosa playa de Punta Cana, en la República Dominicana

En el Mar Caribe hay una isla que comparten dos países: Haití y la República Dominicana. La capital de la República Dominicana es Santo Domingo. A esta ciudad llegaron muchos cubanos hace muchos años, después de la revolución castrista.[1] Entre ellos vinieron Rogelio Peña, su esposa Isabel y sus hijos, César y Graciela. La esposa de don Rogelio falleció hace tres años, de modo que él vive con su hija, su yerno y sus nietos, Mario y Magali. Hoy don Rogelio cumple setenta años y su familia está preparando una cena para festejar su cumpleaños.

Graciela	Magali, ¿trajiste el arroz y los frijoles para preparar el congrí?[2] Tu tío César va a hacer el lechón asado.
Magali	Sí, y traje lechuga, tomates, cebollas, pepinos y zanahorias para la ensalada. Lo puse todo en el refrigerador.
Graciela	¿Y tú, Mario? ¿Qué hiciste?
Mario	Yo tuve que levantarme muy temprano para ir a la pescadería para comprar un pargo, el pescado que le gusta a abuelo.
Magali	¡Ay, pobrecito! Yo me levanté a las cinco, a pesar de que anoche no me acosté hasta las once.
Mario	Porque estuviste hablando con Ramón hasta muy tarde... ¡Ah! ¿Te acordaste de comprar las frutas para la ensalada? Necesito naranjas, mangos, plátanos, manzanas y uvas. Es mi receta especial.
Magali	Es la receta de la señora Torales...
Mario	¡Pero yo la mejoré! Yo le pongo azúcar, y la sirvo con crema.
Magali	¡Ay, caramba! Me olvidé de comprar café, dulce de leche, pan y mantequilla, y leche para el flan.
Graciela	Y dos latas de salsa de tomate... Aquí tengo mi lista.
Magali	Yo dejé la mía en el supermercado. Mamá, ¿a qué hora es la cena?
Graciela	A las ocho. ¡Ay! Todavía tengo que bañarme, lavarme la cabeza y vestirme.
Magali	Yo también. Oye, ¿dónde está abuelo? Voy a ver si está en su cuarto.

En el cuarto de don Rogelio

Magali	¿Qué estás haciendo, abuelo?
Don Rogelio	Estoy leyendo unos poemas de José Martí.
Magali	Extrañas Cuba, ¿verdad?
Don Rogelio	Mucho. Extraño los lugares donde pasé mi infancia y mi juventud: La Habana, Camagüey... Pinar del Río...
Magali	Abuelo, ¿por qué no tocas la guitarra y cantamos nuestra canción favorita?

Don Rogelio toma su guitarra y los dos cantan "La Guantanamera".

"Yo soy un hombre sincero, de donde crece la palma..."

¿Lo sabía Ud.?

En los países hispanos frecuentemente hay dos o más generaciones que viven en la misma (*same*) casa. Los abuelos, por ejemplo, muchas veces viven con sus hijos y contribuyen al cuidado (*care*) de los niños. Muy raramente las personas mayores viven en una casa de ancianos (*nursing home*).

◆ **En este país, ¿las personas mayores generalmente viven con sus hijos o en una casa de ancianos?**

---

[1]de Fidel Castro, líder de la revolución
[2]comida típica cubana

Graciela

Magali

Mario

Don Rogelio

 ¿Quién lo dice? Identify the person who said the following in the dialogues.

1. Yo tuve que levantarme muy temprano para ir a la pescadería. _____

2. Extraño los lugares donde pasé mi infancia y mi juventud. _____

3. Tu tío César va a hacer el lechón asado. _____

4. Yo le pongo azúcar y la sirvo con crema. _____

5. ¿Qué estás haciendo, abuelo? _____

6. ¡Ay, pobrecito! Yo me levanté a las cinco. _____

7. Estoy leyendo unos poemas de José Martí. _____

8. Todavía tengo que bañarme, lavarme la cabeza y vestirme. _____

 Hablemos. With a partner, take turns asking and answering the following questions. Base your answers on the dialogue and on your own circumstances.

En el diálogo	¿Y tú?
1. ¿Cuántos años cumple don Rogelio?	¿Cuántos años vas a cumplir tú? ¿Siempre festejas tu cumpleaños?
2. ¿Qué trajo Magali para preparar el congrí?	¿Tú preparas alguna comida típica? ¿Te gusta cocinar?
3. ¿Qué trajo Magali para la ensalada?	¿Tú comes mucha ensalada? ¿Qué ingredientes usas para la ensalada?
4. ¿A qué hora tuvo que levantarse Mario? ¿Adónde fue? ¿Qué compró?	¿Tú compras pescado a veces? ¿Dónde lo compras?
5. ¿A qué hora se levantó Magali? ¿A qué hora se acostó? ¿Con quién estuvo hablando?	¿Con quién hablaste tú anoche?
6. ¿Qué frutas necesita Mario?	¿Qué frutas te gustan a ti?
7. ¿Qué se olvidó de comprar Magali?	¿Tú prefieres mantequilla o margarina? ¿Tú tomas café con leche?
8. ¿Dónde está don Rogelio? ¿Qué está haciendo?	¿Te gusta leer poemas? ¿Quién es tu poeta favorito?
9. ¿Qué extraña don Rogelio? ¿Qué ciudades recuerda?	¿Dónde pasaste tú tu niñez?
10. ¿Qué instrumento toca don Rogelio?	¿Tú tocas algún instrumento? ¿Cuál es tu favorito?

Vocabulario

Improve Your Grade
Audio Flashcards

Cognados

la **fruta** fruit
la **guitarra** guitar
la **isla** island
el **mango** mango
la **palma** palm, palm tree

la **revolución** revolution
sincero(-a) sincere
el **supermercado** supermarket
el **tomate** tomato

Nombres

el **azúcar** sugar
la **canción** song
la **cebolla** onion
la **infancia** childhood
la **juventud** youth
la **lata, el bote** (*Méx.*) can
la **lechuga** lettuce
la **mantequilla** butter
la **manzana** apple
la **naranja** orange

el **país** country
el **pan** bread
el **pepino** cucumber
la **pescadería** fish store
el **plátano, la banana** banana
la **receta** recipe
la **salsa** sauce
las **uvas** grapes
la **zanahoria** carrot

Verbos

acordarse (o:ue) (de) to remember
acostarse (o:ue) to go to bed
bañarse to bathe
compartir to share
crecer (yo crezco) to grow
cumplir to turn (. . . years old)
extrañar to miss

fallecer (yo fallezco) to pass away
festejar, celebrar to celebrate
levantarse to get up
mejorar to improve
olvidarse (de) to forget
tocar to play (*e.g., a musical instrument*)
vestirse (e:i) to get dressed

Adjetivo

asado(-a) barbecued, roasted

Otras palabras y expresiones

a pesar de que in spite of the fact that
de modo que, de manera que so
entre among, between
lavarse la cabeza to wash one's hair
temprano early

Vocabulario adicional

Para hacer compras

la carnicería meat market
la farmacia pharmacy
la ferretería hardware store
la joyería jewelry store
la panadería bakery
la zapatería shoe store

Instrumentos musicales

la batería drums
el clarinete clarinet
el contrabajo bass
la flauta flute
el piano piano
la trompeta trumpet
el violín violin

Cosas del supermercado

el apio

el durazno, el melocotón

el aceite

el vinagre

la sandía

la margarina

la piña

el repollo

las fresas

el papel higiénico

¿Lo sabía Ud.?

Aunque en la actualidad los supermercados son muy populares en los países de habla hispana, todavía es costumbre comprar en pequeñas tiendas especializadas en uno o dos productos: panadería, pescadería, etc. La mayoría de los pueblos tienen un mercado central, con pequeñas tiendas. Mucha gente todavía prefiere comprar en estos mercados donde los precios son más bajos y los clientes pueden regatear (*bargain*) con los vendedores (*merchants*).

◆ ¿Hay en su ciudad pequeñas tiendas que se especializan en dos o más productos? ¿Hay mercados al aire libre?

[1] *Answer:* dos naranjas

Práctica

A. Write the words or phrases that correspond to the following.

1. fruta cítrica _____
2. banana _____
3. celebrar _____
4. de modo que _____
5. durazno _____
6. lugar donde compramos pescado _____
7. lugar donde compramos carne _____
8. similar a la mantequilla _____
9. lugar donde compramos pan _____
10. lugar donde compramos medicinas _____

B. Select the word or phrase that does not belong in each group.

1. niñez / juventud / contrabajo
2. uvas / lata / sandía
3. mar / piña / isla
4. morir / fallecer / extrañar
5. lechuga / fresas / apio
6. país / pepino / cebolla
7. lavarse la cabeza / bañarse / acordarse
8. compartir / levantarse / acostarse

C. Complete the following sentences, using vocabulary from this lesson.

1. Tengo que ir al _____ para comprar frutas.
2. Él _____ el piano y el violín.
3. Vamos a _____ el cumpleaños de mi hermano.
4. Necesito un _____ de salsa de _____.
5. Voy a pedir lechón _____, a _____ de que no me gusta mucho.
6. Necesito _____ y _____ para la ensalada.
7. Tengo que comprar papel _____ para el baño.
8. Yo no le pongo _____ al café.
9. Yo puedo bañarme y _____ en cinco minutos.
10. Jorge tocó el clarinete y Amelia cantó una _____ cubana.

Para conversar

¿Qué te olvidaste de traer?   With a partner, play the roles of two roommates who ask each other whether or not they brought certain items from the supermarket. Each one will answer saying that he/she did not bring the particular item, but another, and indicate where he/she put those items: in the refrigerator, on the table, or in the pantry (**la alacena**).

◆ **MODELO:**   —¿Trajiste... ?
    —No, pero traje... Lo/La/Los/Las puse en...

Pronunciación

La entonación

Intonation refers to the variations in the pitch of your voice when you are talking. Intonation patterns in Spanish are different from those in English. Note the following regarding Spanish intonation.

1. For normal statements, the pitch generally rises on the first stressed syllable.

Yo compré el regalo para Elena.

2. For questions eliciting information, the pitch is highest on the stressed syllable of the interrogative pronoun.

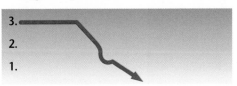

¿Cómo está tu mamá?

3. For questions that can be answered with **sí** or **no,** the pitch is generally highest on the last stressed syllable.

¿Fuiste al mercado ayer?

4. In exclamations, the pitch is highest on the first stressed syllable.

¡Qué bonita es esa alfombra!

Aspectos culturales

En imágenes (*Vínculos[1] familiares entre generaciones*)

▲ Una familia puertorriqueña celebra el bautizo de dos bebés

LA FLORIDA (Estados Unidos)

Islas Baha...

La Habana ✪ Matanzas
Pinar del Río
Morón
Cienfuegos
Camagüey **CUBA**
Isla de la Juventud Guantán...
Santi...
de Cu...

JAMAICA

▲ Tres generaciones de cubanos

Ubíquese... y búsquelo

🌐 Improve Your Grade
Web Search

Besides La Habana, don Rogelio mentions two other places that he misses from his youth in Cuba: Camagüey and Pinar del Río. Go to **www.cengage.com/highered** to figure out what they are and where they are in relation to La Habana. Which one would you rather visit? Why? In the next class, team up with two classmates to discuss your findings.

---

[1]**Vínculos** = *Ties, Bonds*

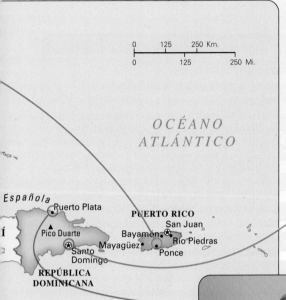

▲ Familia dominicana sentada (*seated*) a la mesa durante la cena de Navidad

▲ Abuelo y nieto dominicanos

Estructuras

1. Reflexive constructions (*Construcciones reflexivas*)

A. Reflexive pronouns

Subjects		Reflexive pronouns
yo	**me**	*myself, to (for) myself*
tú	**te**	*yourself, to (for) yourself* (**tú** form)
nosotros(-as)	**nos**	*ourselves, to (for) ourselves*
vosotros(-as)	**os**	*yourselves, to (for) yourselves* (**vosotros** form)
Ud.		*yourself, to (for) yourself* (**Ud.** form)
Uds.		*yourselves, to (for) yourselves* (**Uds.** form)
él	**se**	*himself, to (for) himself*
ella		*herself, to (for) herself*
		itself, to (for) itself
ellos, ellas		*themselves, to (for) themselves*

◆ Reflexive pronouns are used whenever the direct or indirect object is the same as the subject of the sentence.

◆ Note that except for **se,** the reflexive pronouns have the same forms as the direct and indirect object pronouns.

◆ The third-person singular and plural **se** is invariable.

◆ Reflexive pronouns are positioned in the sentence in the same manner as object pronouns. They are placed in front of a conjugated verb: **Yo *me* levanto;** or they may be attached to an infinitive or to a present participle: **Yo voy a levantar*me*. Yo estoy levantándo*me*.**

B. Reflexive verbs

◆ Many verbs can be made reflexive in Spanish, that is, they can be made to act upon the subject, by the use of a reflexive pronoun.

lavarse *to wash oneself*	
Yo **me lavo**	*I wash* (*myself*)
Tú **te lavas**	*You wash* (*yourself*) (**tú** form)
Ud. **se lava**	*You wash* (*yourself*) (**Ud.** form)
Él **se lava**	*He washes* (*himself*)
Ella **se lava**	*She washes* (*herself*)
Nosotros(-as) **nos lavamos**	*We wash* (*ourselves*)
Vosotros(-as) **os laváis**	*You wash* (*yourselves*) (**vosotros** form)
Uds. **se lavan**	*You wash* (*yourselves*) (**Uds.** form)
Ellos **se lavan**	*They* (masc.) *wash* (*themselves*)
Ellas **se lavan**	*They* (fem.) *wash* (*themselves*)

Un dicho

Lo que no se ve, pronto se olvida.

Equivalent: Out of sight, out of mind.

▲ Julia baña al perro.

▲ Julia se baña.

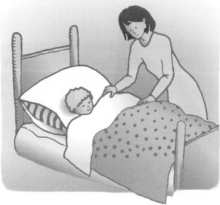

▲ Elsa acuesta a su hijo a las siete.

▲ Elsa se acuesta a las diez.

◆ In addition to the verbs included in the vocabulary list, the following verbs are commonly used in reflexive constructions.

afeitarse *to shave*
despertarse (e:ie) *to wake up*
desvestirse (e:i) *to get undressed*
peinarse *to comb one's hair*
preocuparse (por) *to worry* (*about*)
quejarse *to complain*
sentarse (e:ie) *to sit* (*down*)
sentirse (e:ie) *to feel* (mood or physical condition)

—¿A qué hora **se acuestan** Uds.?	*"What time do you go to bed?"*
—Yo **me acuesto** a las diez y Ana **se acuesta** a las doce.	*"I go to bed at ten and Ana goes to bed at twelve."*
—¿Cómo **te sientes?**	*"How do you feel?"*
—**Me siento** bien, gracias.	*"I feel fine, thank you."*

¡Atención! The Spanish reflexives are seldom translated using the reflexive pronouns in English: **Yo me acuesto** = *I go to bed.*

◆ The following verbs have different meanings when they are used with reflexive pronouns.

acostar (o:ue) *to put to bed*	**acostarse** *to go to bed*
dormir (o:ue) *to sleep*	**dormirse** *to fall asleep*
ir *to go*	**irse** *to go away, leave*
levantar *to raise, lift*	**levantarse** *to get up*
llamar *to call*	**llamarse** *to be called*
poner *to put, place*	**ponerse** *to put on*
probar (o:ue) *to try; to taste*	**probarse** *to try on*
quitar *to take away*	**quitarse** *to take off*

—¿**Te** vas a **acostar**?	*"Are you going to go to bed?"*
—Sí, pero primero voy a **acostar** a los niños.	*"Yes, but first, I'm going to put the children to bed."*
—¿A qué hora **se levantaron** Uds.?	*"What time did you get up?"*
—**Nos levantamos** muy temprano.	*"We got up very early."*
—¿Ya **te vas**?	*"Are you leaving already?"*
—Sí, tengo que ir al mercado.	*"Yes, I have to go to the market."*

Summary of Personal Pronouns

Subject	Direct object	Indirect object	Reflexive	Object of prepositions
yo	me	me	me	mí
tú	te	te	te	ti
usted (*fem.*)	la			usted
usted (*masc.*)	lo	le	se	usted
él	lo			él
ella	la			ella
nosotros(-as)	nos	nos	nos	nosotros(-as)
vosotros(-as)	os	os	os	vosotros(-as)
ustedes (*fem.*)	las			ustedes
ustedes (*masc.*)	los	les	se	ustedes
ellos	los			ellos
ellas	las			ellas

ACE the Test

Práctica

A. Say what you and your relatives normally do by adding the correct form of the missing verbs.

1. Mi tía siempre _____ (despertarse) tarde.
2. Yo _____ (levantarse) muy temprano.
3. Mi padre _____ (afeitarse) en el baño.
4. Nosotros _____ (bañarse) por la mañana.
5. Mi hermana _____ (lavarse) la cabeza todos los días.
6. Mis primos _____ (vestirse) en diez minutos.
7. Yo _____ (desvestirse) y _____ (acostarse).
8. Mi mamá _____ (preocuparse) mucho cuando yo llego tarde.
9. En la cafetería, yo _____ (sentarse) con mis amigos.
10. Ellos _____ (probarse) los pantalones.

B. Say what these people are doing.

1. María _____ bien.

2. Los estudiantes _____ en la clase.

3. Juan le _____ el dinero al niño.

4. Pepito _____ el suéter.

5. Yo _____ la _____ en la clase.

6. Yo _____ a las seis.

7. Rosa _____ el _____ en la _____.

8. Rosa _____ el _____

9. Sergio _____ a Eva.

10. El muchacho _____ _____ Sergio Paz.

C. With a partner, take turns saying what these people do according to the time and the circumstances.

1. A las seis de la mañana, yo _____.

2. En el baño, Carlos _____ con champú.

3. Antes de salir, tú te bañas y te _____.

4. En la tienda, antes de comprar un vestido (*dress*), Rocío _____.

5. Cuando hace mucho frío, yo _____ un suéter.

6. Frente al espejo (*mirror*), mi hermana _____.

7. Mi papá _____ con una máquina de afeitar (*razor*).

8. Cuando yo vuelvo a mi casa muy tarde, mis padres _____.

9. En la clase, cuando están aburridos, los estudiantes _____.

10. A las once de la noche, Uds. _____.

A. ¡Habla con tu compañero! Interview a classmate, using the following questions and two questions of your own. When you have finished, switch roles.

1. ¿A qué hora te levantas tú generalmente? ¿Y los sábados? ¿A qué hora te levantaste hoy?
2. ¿A qué hora te acuestas? ¿A qué hora te acostaste anoche? ¿Dormiste bien?
3. ¿Puedes bañarte y vestirte en diez minutos? ¿Te lavas la cabeza cuando te bañas? ¿Te bañas por la mañana o por la tarde?
4. ¿Te miras en el espejo para peinarte?
5. ¿Te acordaste de traer el libro de español hoy? ¿A veces te olvidas de traerlo?
6. ¿Cómo se llama tu mejor amigo(-a)? ¿Cómo se llama tu abuelo? ¿Y tu abuela?
7. ¿Se preocupan tus padres por ti? ¿Tú te preocupas por alguien? ¿Por quién?
8. ¿Qué te pones cuando hace frío, un suéter o un abrigo? Cuando llueve, ¿te pones un impermeable o usas un paraguas?

B. Nuestra rutina diaria With a partner, ask each other about your daily routines, beginning in the morning until the time you go to bed. Compare notes.

2. Some uses of the definite article (*Algunos usos del artículo definido*)

The definite article has the following uses in Spanish.

- The possessive adjective is often replaced by the definite article. An indirect object pronoun or a reflexive pronoun (if the subject performs the action upon himself or herself) usually indicates who the possessor is. Note the use of the definite article in Spanish in the following specific situations indicating possession.

- With parts of the body

Voy a cortar**le el pelo.**	*I'm going to cut his hair.*
Me lavé **las manos.**	*I washed my hands.*

- With articles of clothing and personal belongings

¿**Te** quitaste **el abrigo?**	*Did you take off your coat?*
Ellos **se** quitaron **el suéter.**	*They took off their sweaters.*

> **¡Atención!** The number of the subject and verb generally does not affect the number of the thing possessed. Spanish uses the singular to indicate that each person has only one of any particular object.

Ellas se quitaron **el abrigo.**	*They took off their coats.*
(Each one has one coat.)	
but: Ellas se quitaron **los zapatos.**	*They took off their shoes.*
(Each one has two shoes.)	

Un dicho *Yo me lavo las manos.*

I wash my hands.

- The definite article is used with abstract and generic nouns.

Me gusta **el té,** pero prefiero **el café.**	*I like tea, but I prefer coffee.*
Las madres siempre se preocupan por sus hijos.	*Mothers always worry about their children.*
La educación es muy importante.	*Education is very important.*

- The definite article is used with certain nouns, including **cárcel** (*jail*), **iglesia** (*church*), and **escuela** when they are preceded by a preposition.

—¿Vas a **la iglesia** los domingos?	*"Do you go to church on Sundays?"*
—No, voy a **la iglesia** los sábados.	*"No, I go to church on Saturdays."*
—¿Dónde están los chicos?	*"Where are the children?"*
—Están en **la escuela.**	*"They're at school."*
—¿Jorge está en **la cárcel?**	*"Is Jorge in jail?"*
—Sí, lo visito todas las semanas.	*"Yes, I visit him every week."*

- Remember that the definite article is also used with days of the week, when indicating titles in indirect address, and when telling time.

El Sr. Vega viene **el sábado** a **las tres** de la tarde.	*Mr. Vega is coming on Saturday at three o'clock in the afternoon.*

Práctica

ACE the Test

Supply the Spanish equivalents of the words in parentheses. Then act out the dialogues with a partner.

1. —¿Qué están haciendo _____ Paz y _____ Díaz? (*Miss / Mrs.*)

   —Se están poniendo _____. (*their coats*)

2. —¿Qué estás haciendo, Paquito?

   —Me estoy lavando _____. (*my hands*)

3. —_____ son más inteligentes que _____. (*Women / men*)

   —_____ siempre dicen eso. (*Women*)

4. —¿Él está en _____? (*school*)

   —Sí, pero su hermano está en _____. (*church*)

5. —¿Qué dice _____ Peña? (*Dr.*)

   —Ella dice que _____ es muy importante. (*education*)

6. —¿Cuándo llega _____ Roca? (*Mister*)

   —_____, _____ cinco. (*On Thursday / at*)

Un dicho

El amor todo lo puede.

Equivalent: Love conquers all.

Para conversar

¡Habla con tu compañero! With a partner, take turns asking and answering the following questions.

1. ¿Qué te gusta más, el pescado o la carne? ¿Te gustan más las manzanas o las uvas?
2. ¿Qué te gusta más, el café o el té? ¿El agua mineral o los refrescos?
3. ¿Te lavas la cabeza todos los días? ¿Qué champú usas?
4. ¿Te quitas los zapatos cuando llegas a tu casa? ¿Te cambias de ropa?
5. ¿Te gustan los idiomas extranjeros (*foreign*)? ¿Te gusta más el francés o el español?
6. ¿Vas a la iglesia los domingos? ¿A qué hora vas? ¿Con quién vas?
7. ¿Qué es más importante para ti, el amor o el dinero?
8. ¿Quiénes conducen mejor, los hombres o las mujeres? ¿Quiénes son más eficientes?

3. Possessive pronouns (*Pronombres posesivos*)

	Singular		Plural		
	Masculine	*Feminine*	*Masculine*	*Feminine*	
	el mío	la mía	los míos	las mías	*mine*
	el tuyo	la tuya	los tuyos	las tuyas	*yours* (fam.)
	el suyo	la suya	los suyos	las suyas	*yours* (form.) *his* *hers*
	el nuestro	la nuestra	los nuestros	las nuestras	*ours*
	el vuestro	la vuestra	los vuestros	las vuestras	*yours* (fam.)
	el suyo	la suya	los suyos	las suyas	*yours* (form.) *theirs*

◆ In Spanish, possessive pronouns agree in gender and number with the thing possessed. They are generally used with the definite article.

—Aquí están **mis maletas.** ¿Dónde están **las tuyas?**
—**Las mías** están en mi cuarto.

"Here are my suitcases. Where are yours?"
"Mine are in my room."

—**Nuestro profesor** es de Colombia.
—**El nuestro** es de Venezuela.

"Our professor is from Colombia."
"Ours is from Venezuela."

—**Mi apartamento** está en la calle Palma.
—**El mío** está en la calle Estrella.

"My apartment is on Palma Street."
"Mine is on Estrella Street."

¡Atención! After the verb **ser,** the definite article is frequently omitted.

—¿Estos billetes son **suyos,** señor?
—No, no son **míos.**

"Are these tickets yours, sir?"
"No, they're not mine."

◆ Because the third-person forms of the possessive pronouns (**el suyo, la suya, los suyos, las suyas**) can be ambiguous, they can be replaced by the pronouns below for clarification.

el de	Ud.			
la de	él	el [libro]	de él	
los de	ella	el	**de él**	
las de	Uds.			
	ellos	Es **suyo.** (*unclarified*)		
	ellas	Es **el de él.** (*clarified*)		

—Estas maletas son de Eva y de Jorge, ¿no?
—Bueno, la maleta azul es **de ella** y la maleta marrón es **de él.**

"These suitcases are Eva's and Jorge's, aren't they?"
"Well, the blue suitcase is hers, and the brown suitcase is his."

—¿El piano es **de Uds.?**
—No, es **de ellos.**

"Is the piano yours?"
"No, it's theirs."

Un dicho

Lo que es tuyo es mío y lo que es mío es tuyo.

What's yours is mine and what's mine is yours.

Práctica

A. Provide the correct possessive pronoun for each subject.

◆ **MODELO:** Yo tengo una tarjeta postal. Es...
Es mía.

1. Mario tiene una revista. Es...
2. Nosotros tenemos dos guitarras. Son...
3. Tú tienes un violín. Es...
4. Inés tiene dos diccionarios. Son...
5. Yo tengo dos casas. Son...
6. Ud. tiene un perro. Es...
7. Ellas tienen los abrigos. Son...
8. Paco tiene una trompeta. Es...

B. Complete the following dialogue using the correct possessive pronoun.

1. —Mis revistas están aquí. ¿Dónde están _____, Anita? (*yours*)

   —_____ están en mi cuarto, pero Pedro no tiene _____.
   (*Mine / his*)

2. —Yo no tengo maletas, pero Ana me va a prestar una de _____. (*hers*)

   —O yo puedo prestarte una de _____. (*mine*)

   —¡Pero tú vas a necesitar todas _____! (*yours*)

   —Yo tengo tres maletas...

3. —Mis hijos están en Santo Domingo. ¿Dónde están _____, señor
   Fuentes? (*yours*)

   —_____ están en La Habana. (*Mine*)

C. With a partner, make comparisons between the objects and people described
and those in your own experience. Use appropriate possessive pronouns when
asking each other questions.

◆ **MODELO:** —El hermano de Teresa tiene quince años. ¿Y el tuyo?
—*El mío tiene dieciocho.*

1. Los mejores amigos de Rosa son de Cuba.
2. El apartamento de Ana tiene cuatro cuartos.
3. Los padres de Ramiro viven en Pinar del Río.
4. El cumpleaños de Jorge es en septiembre.
5. Las maletas de Alina son verdes.
6. La hermana de Rafael es muy bonita.
7. El idioma de Hans es alemán.
8. Las primas de Enrique son dominicanas.

Para conversar

Así es la vida. (*Such is life.*) In groups of three, compare some aspects of your
lives, such as your room or apartment, relatives, classes, jobs, and so on.

4. Irregular preterits (*Pretéritos irregulares*)

- The following Spanish verbs are irregular in the preterit.

tener:	tuve, tuviste, tuvo, tuvimos, tuvisteis, tuvieron
estar:	estuve, estuviste, estuvo, estuvimos, estuvisteis, estuvieron
poder:	pude, pudiste, pudo, pudimos, pudisteis, pudieron
poner:	puse, pusiste, puso, pusimos, pusisteis, pusieron
saber:	supe, supiste, supo, supimos, supisteis, supieron
hacer:	hice, hiciste, hizo,[1] hicimos, hicisteis, hicieron
venir:	vine, viniste, vino, vinimos, vinisteis, vinieron
querer:	quise, quisiste, quiso, quisimos, quisisteis, quisieron
decir:	dije, dijiste, dijo, dijimos, dijisteis, dijeron[2]
traer:	traje, trajiste, trajo, trajimos, trajisteis, trajeron[2]
conducir:	conduje, condujiste, condujo, condujimos, condujisteis, condujeron[2]
traducir:	traduje, tradujiste, tradujo, tradujimos, tradujisteis, tradujeron[2]

—¿Por qué no **viniste** anoche?	*"Why didn't you come last night?"*
—No **pude; tuve** que trabajar. Y tú, ¿qué **hiciste**?	*"I wasn't able to; I had to work. And you, what did you do?"*
—Yo **estuve** en casa toda la noche.	*"I was home all night."*
—¿Qué me **trajeron** Uds.?	*"What did you bring me?"*
—Te **trajimos** una cámara.	*"We brought you a camera."*
—¿Dónde la **pusieron**?	*"Where did you put it?"*
—La **pusimos** en tu cuarto.	*"We put it in your room."*

¡Atención!   The preterit of **hay** (impersonal form of **haber**) is **hubo** (*there was, there were*).

Anoche **hubo** un concierto.	*Last night there was a concert.*

Papá, hoy **conduje** tu auto...

---

[1]Note that in the third-person singular form, **c** changes to **z** in order to maintain the soft sound.
[2]Note that in the third-person plural ending of these verbs, the **i** is omitted.

Práctica

A. Elsa and David are arguing. Complete their dialogue, using the preterit of the verbs given. Then act it out with a partner.

Elsa ¿Dónde _____ (estar) (tú) anoche? ¡ _____ (Venir) muy tarde!

David ¡Te lo _____ (decir)! _____ (Estar) en casa de mamá. _____ (Tener) que hablar con papá. No te llamé porque no _____ (poder).

Elsa ¿No _____ (poder) o no _____ (querer)?

David Bueno. ¿Dónde _____ (poner) tú los documentos que yo _____ (traducir) ayer en la oficina?

Elsa ¡Tú no _____ (traer) ningún documento!

David No... los empleados los _____ (traer) cuando _____ (venir) ayer.

Elsa Ellos no me _____ (decir) nada. ¡Son unos idiotas!

B. Read what the following people typically do. Then, using your imagination, say what everyone did differently yesterday.

1. Yo estoy en mi casa por la mañana.
2. Tú vienes a la universidad a las diez de la mañana.
3. Paquito hace ejercicio por la tarde.
4. Julio tiene que trabajar en el mercado.
5. Nosotros traemos a nuestros hijos a la escuela.
6. Ellos traducen las lecciones al inglés.
7. María se pone el suéter azul.
8. Yo conduzco mi coche.

Para conversar

A. **¡Habla con tu compañero!** With a partner, take turns asking each other the following questions.

1. ¿Qué tuviste que hacer ayer? ¿Tuviste mucho trabajo? ¿Estuviste muy ocupado(-a)?
2. ¿Qué hicieron tú y tus amigos ayer? ¿Qué hicieron el sábado?
3. ¿Dónde estuvieron tú y tu familia anoche? ¿Qué hicieron tus padres?
4. ¿Hubo una fiesta en tu casa el mes pasado? ¿Quiénes vinieron?
5. ¿Tuviste que limpiar la casa ayer? ¿Alguien te ayudó? ¿Quién?
6. ¿Viniste a clase la semana pasada? ¿Viniste solo(-a)? ¿Qué días viniste?
7. ¿Pudiste venir temprano a la universidad ayer? ¿A qué hora viniste? ¿Alguien vino contigo?
8. ¿Condujiste tu auto ayer o viniste en autobús?

B. **¿Qué hiciste?** In groups of three, ask each other about what you did yesterday, last night, or last week. Use irregular preterit forms in your questions. Ask for as many details as possible.

5. *Hace...* meaning *ago* (*Hace...* como equivalente de ago)

◆ In sentences using the preterit and in some cases the imperfect, **hace** + *period of time* is the equivalent of the English *ago*. When **hace** is placed at the beginning of the sentence, the construction is as follows.

Hace + *period of time* + **que**
Hace + dos años + **que** la conocí.

—¿Cuánto tiempo hace que conociste a tu novia?   *"How long ago did you meet your girlfriend?"*
—**Hace tres años que** la conocí.   *"I met her three years ago."*

—**Hace diez años que** ellos vinieron a los Estados Unidos. ¿Y tú?   *"They came to the United States ten years ago. And you?"*
—Yo llegué **hace cuatro años.**   *"I arrived four years ago."*

¡Sí! Hace dos minutos que llegaron.

Hace dos horas que llegaron.

¡Atención! Note that it is also possible to say: **Yo llegué hace cuatro años.**

ACE the Test

Práctica

 Say how long ago everything happened, according to the information provided.

1. Preparamos la ensalada de frutas a las dos. Son las dos y media.
2. Ellos fueron a Santo Domingo en agosto. Estamos en diciembre.
3. Tú viste a tu abuelo el lunes. Hoy es viernes.
4. Empecé a trabajar a las diez. Son las diez y cuarto.
5. Yo vine de Cuba el 15 de junio. Hoy es el 30 de junio.
6. Carlos compró la casa en el año 2000. Estamos en el año 2009.

Para conversar

A. Dime... With a partner, take turns asking and answering these questions.

1. ¿Cuánto tiempo hace que empezaste a estudiar en esta universidad?
2. ¿Cuánto tiempo hace que conociste a tu primer(-a) novio(-a)?
3. ¿Cuánto tiempo hace que hablaste con tu mejor amigo(-a)?
4. ¿Cuánto tiempo hace que te compraste ropa?
5. ¿Cuánto tiempo hace que le mandaste un mensaje electrónico a alguien?
6. ¿Cuánto tiempo hace que comiste?

B. ¡Hace mucho tiempo! With a partner, take turns asking each other how long ago you did each of the following things.

1. ir a la playa
2. ir al dentista
3. dar una fiesta
4. ir de compras
5. ir al cine
6. empezar a estudiar español
7. ver a sus padres
8. ir de vacaciones
9. llamar a su mejor amigo(-a)
10. levantarse

C. Acontecimientos importantes With a partner, prepare two questions about how long ago an important event took place. Then join another pair and ask them your questions and answer theirs.

¿Lo sabía Ud.?

La palabra *salsa* (sauce, spice) se usa también para referirse a la música caribeña. Actualmente este ritmo, basado en la música afrocubana, es muy popular en muchos países.

◆ ¿Cuáles son los ritmos típicos de este país?

Así somos

Al escuchar...

Estrategia **Dealing with fast speech** Listening to speech when you can't ask the speaker to slow down or repeat is especially challenging in a foreign language, particularly if the language is spoken at what seems to be a fast pace. In such instances, try to listen for familiar words to understand what the topic is, or to get the gist of what is said. When dealing with fast speech in a classroom setting—with video or lab activities, for instance— you can often listen more than once and thus train yourself to become a better listener.

 ¿Qué dijeron? Listen to a conversation between Ester and Raúl and answer the following questions when you feel you can provide the answer or make a guess.

1. ¿Qué festejan hoy Ester y Raúl?
2. ¿Qué necesita Ester para la ensalada?
3. ¿Qué va a comprar Raúl en la pescadería?
4. ¿Quién va a traer el postre?
5. ¿Para qué debe ir Raúl a la joyería?

Al conversar...

Estrategia **Using pauses to manage conversation** In addition to asking for repetition or clarification (**Lección 2**), and restating something you hear in your own words (**Lecciones 7** and **8**), you can create pauses during a conversation in order to gain time to organize your thoughts and reply. The following words and expressions, most of which you have seen in previous lessons, are commonly used as pausing devices.
- Gaining time: **Bueno..., A ver...**
- Asking for your listener's attention: **Oye... (Óyeme...), Mira...**
- Reacting to what you hear: **¡Caramba!**
- Fillers: **Este..., Eh...** (*Uh . . ., Ummm . . .*)
- Correcting or clarifying what you are saying: **Es decir...** (*That is to say . . .*)

 Este... Take turns telling a classmate about the last birthday you celebrated. Your goal is to describe the celebration as fully as you can. Tell whose birthday you celebrated, where, how many people attended, and talk about the food, gifts, etc. Use some of the phrases above when you need to pause or gain time to think.

 ¿Qué dice Ud.? What would you say in the following situations? What might the other person say? Act out the scenes with a partner. Take turns playing each role.

1. You and your roommate are going to decide what you need from the grocery store. Don't forget to include fruits and vegetables.
2. You are talking to a prospective roommate and want to know about his/her daily routine. Ask him/her pertinent questions.
3. You are in Santo Domingo. Your Dominican friend is going to accompany you downtown to do some shopping. Tell him/her which stores you have to go to. You want to buy nails, shoes, a bracelet, medicine, etc. Say what time you want to leave.
4. Last night you called your friend Fernando and he wasn't home. Ask him where he was, what he had to do, whether or not he was able to speak with his parents, and what they said about the party.

Para conocernos mejor To do this activity, work with a classmate whom you would like to get to know. Take turns asking and answering these questions.

1. ¿Cuánto tiempo hace que empezaste a estudiar en esta universidad? ¿Te gusta la universidad? ¿Tienes muchos amigos aquí?
2. ¿Tu español está mejorando? ¿El profesor (La profesora) comparte tu opinión? ¿Sabes algún poema en español? ¿Alguna canción?
3. ¿Hiciste algo de interés anteayer? ¿Adónde fuiste? ¿Con quién estuviste? ¿Tuviste que trabajar?
4. ¿Qué hiciste anoche para cenar? ¿Tienes alguna receta especial? ¿Dónde la conseguiste?
5. ¿A qué hora te despertaste hoy? ¿A qué hora te levantas generalmente? ¿Te gusta acostarte temprano o tarde?
6. Generalmente, ¿te bañas por la mañana o por la tarde? ¿Qué jabón usas? ¿Necesitas mucho tiempo para vestirte?
7. ¿Tomas café? ¿Le pones azúcar y crema? ¿Lo tomas después de las comidas o con las comidas?
8. ¿Dónde creciste? ¿Extrañas el lugar donde pasaste tu niñez? ¿Extrañas a tus amigos de la escuela?

 Una encuesta Interview your classmates to identify who fits the following descriptions. Include your instructor, but remember to use the **Ud.** form when addressing him/her. After finishing the survey, get together with two or three classmates and discuss the results.

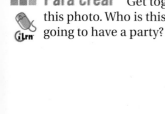

Nombre

1. Usa recetas para cocinar.
2. Compró una lata de salsa de tomate ayer.
3. Comió una ensalada de lechuga y tomate ayer.
4. Le pone aceite y vinagre a la ensalada.
5. Hizo una ensalada de frutas la semana pasada.
6. Compró manzanas cuando fue al supermercado.
7. Comió mucha sandía el verano pasado.
8. Come pan con mantequilla con la comida.

Para crear Get together in groups of three or four and "create" the scenario for this photo. Who is this person? What is he buying? What does he like to eat? Is he going to have a party?

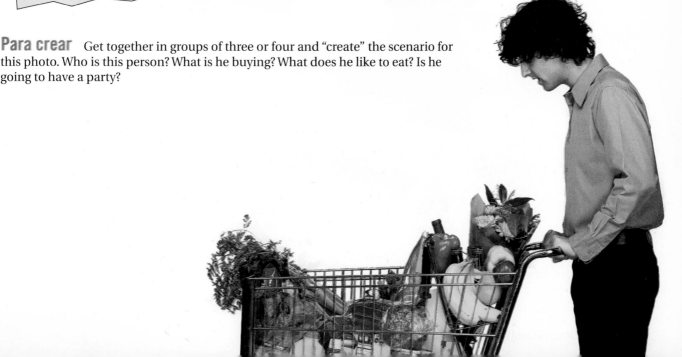

¡Vamos a leer!

Antes de leer

Estrategia **Skimming** When skimming, you look over a text quickly to get the gist or a general idea of its content. Skimming is especially useful if you want to decide whether you're interested in a text before reading it more thoroughly. Scanning is a similar technique often used along with skimming; however, when scanning, you look for very specific information. For example, you might scan a TV listing to locate a basketball game you know is on.

La receta You will be reading a recipe for **flan,** one of the most widespread dessert dishes in the Spanish-speaking world. Imagine that you have promised to make a dessert for dinner at a friend's. You don't have a lot of time so you first skim the recipe to decide whether it's relatively easy and quick to make.

1. ¿Hay muchos o pocos ingredientes? ¿Son fáciles o difíciles de encontrar?
2. ¿Cuánto tiempo tiene que cocinar en el horno?
3. ¿Vas a preparar un flan? ¿Por qué sí o por qué no?

A leer

 Comprensión As you read the recipe, find the answers to the following questions.

1. ¿Cuáles son los ingredientes del flan?
2. ¿Qué hacemos con el azúcar para hacer el caramelo? ¿Qué color va a tener el azúcar?
3. ¿Con qué cubrimos el molde?
4. Después de batir los huevos, ¿qué agregamos (*add*)?
5. ¿Cómo debemos cocinar el flan? ¿A qué temperatura?
6. ¿Qué tenemos que hacer para saber si ya está cocinado?
7. ¿Qué hacemos después de sacarlo del horno?
8. ¿Qué debemos hacer antes de servirlo?

Sección de cocina

Si Ud. quiere servir un postre sabroso y elegante en su próxima fiesta, le ofrecemos una magnífica idea: sirva un flan, que es sin lugar a dudas el postre más popular entre los hispanos. Siga las instrucciones de doña Laura, que le dice cómo prepararlo.

 FLAN

Ingredientes:

Para el flan
2 tazas de leche evaporada
4 huevos
8 cucharadas de azúcar
1 cucharadita de vainilla

Para el caramelo
3 cucharadas de azúcar

melt	
golden	
let it cool / Beat	
Add / stir it	
double boiler / oven	
clean	
turn over	

Preparación: En el molde donde va a hacer el flan, poner[1] a derretir° al fuego tres cucharadas de azúcar. Después de unos minutos el azúcar va a tener un color dorado.° Mover el molde para cubrirlo todo con el caramelo y dejarlo enfriar.° Batir° los huevos. Agregar° el azúcar y la vainilla y revolverlo° bien. Ponerlo todo en el molde y cocinarlo a Baño María° en el horno° a 350 grados por una hora. (Para saber si ya está cocinado, introducir un cuchillo en el flan, y si sale limpio,° ya está listo.) Sacarlo del horno y dejarlo enfriar. Ponerlo en el refrigerador. Antes de servirlo, voltear° el molde en un plato.

---

[1]In Spanish the infinitive is often used as commands to give instructions or directions.

¡Vamos a escribir!

Antes de escribir

Estrategia **Sequencing steps for a recipe** When following a recipe, the preparation process generally requires a precise order of steps. The sequence of a well written recipe can save preparation time as well as ensure a tasty final result. Here are some sequencing words you can use: **primero, luego, después, finalmente.**

Una receta You will be sharing with the class how you make one of your favorite dishes. First, make a list of the steps to follow in the order in which they should be completed. With the help of a bilingual dictionary, look up only the words you absolutely need. Here are some verbs commonly used in recipes.

agregar to add	**revolver (o:ue)** to mix	**freír (e:i)** to fry
batir to beat	**cocinar** to cook	**hervir (e:ie)** to boil

A escribir la receta

Write your **primer borrador** of the recipe, using the **flan** recipe as a model and being sure to sequence the steps carefully.

Después de escribir

A. Mi receta Before writing the final version, exchange your first draft with a classmate and peer edit each other's work using the following guidelines.

- use of infinitives in cooking instructions
- subject-verb agreement
- clear and logical sequence of steps

B. Del libro de cocina de... ¡la clase de español! Prepare a cookbook with the recipes from the entire class.

C. ¡Una fiesta para comer y charlar! Confer as a class to set aside a day or an evening to gather socially and cook recipes from your class cookbook! Take the opportunity to mingle and chat in Spanish with your classmates.

Después de leer... desde su mundo

¿Te gusta...? In groups of three or four, find out who likes to cook and what types of dishes your classmates like to make. Do they have a favorite dish? Also find out who's an adventurous eater and likes to try new and sometimes unusual foods.

Panorama hispánico

Cuba

- Hoy Cuba exporta azúcar, níquel, tabaco y frutas. El tabaco cubano tiene fama mundial. Sin embargo, las principales fuentes de ingreso del país son el turismo y el dinero que les envían a sus familiares más de un millón de cubanos que viven en el extranjero.

- La Habana es la capital y la ciudad más grande del Caribe. La Habana vieja (*old*), su sección antigua, se caracteriza por sus iglesias, plazas, fortalezas y edificios coloniales, como la Catedral y su plaza, y las fortalezas de El Morro y la Cabaña. En la Habana nació José Martí, escritor, poeta y el más famoso de los patriotas cubanos. De su libro *Versos sencillos* proviene la letra de la canción "La Guantanamera".

- La música cubana o afrocubana es muy popular en todo el mundo. De Cuba salieron el son, el danzón, la rumba, la conga, el cha cha cha, el mambo y, en buena parte, la salsa. Muchos músicos y cantantes cubanos triunfan hoy en el extranjero (*abroad*); entre ellos, Gloria Estefan y Jon Secada. El deporte más popular en el país es el béisbol, que los cubanos llaman "la pelota". En la actualidad varios "peloteros" cubanos juegan en las Grandes Ligas de los Estados Unidos. Los más famosos son Rafael Palmeiro y los hermanos Liván y Orlando (el Duque) Hernández. Por otra parte, son exponentes de la cultura cubana contemporánea escritores de fama internacional como Guillermo Cabrera Infante, Zoé Valdés y Daína Chaviano.

La Habana

▲ Vista de La Habana hacia finales (*toward the end*) del siglo XX

La República Dominicana

- La extensión de la República Dominicana es más o menos igual a la mitad (*half*) de la superficie de Kentucky. Su economía se basa en la agricultura, pero el turismo comienza a ser una buena fuente de ingresos para el país. Sus principales atracciones son sus construcciones coloniales y sus hermosas playas, como las de los centros turísticos de La Romana y Puerto Plata, donde se puede disfrutar de muchas actividades al aire libre.

- La música típica del país es el merengue, pero además son populares otros ritmos del Caribe como la rumba y la salsa. Como en Cuba y en Puerto Rico, el béisbol es el deporte más popular de la isla. La República Dominicana es el país extranjero mejor representado en las Grandes Ligas. El más conocido de todos los jugadores dominicanos es Sammy Sosa.

- Casi la mitad de la población del país vive en la capital, Santo Domingo, la primera ciudad europea fundada en el Nuevo Mundo. Aquí se encuentran algunas de las construcciones coloniales más antiguas de América, como las ruinas del Monasterio de San Francisco y la Catedral de Santa María la Menor, la más antigua del continente americano, donde muchos creen que están enterrados (*buried*) los restos de Cristóbal Colón.

▲ Pórtico (*Entrance*) de la Catedral Santa María de la Encarnación, primera de América, construida (*built*) de 1520 a 1540

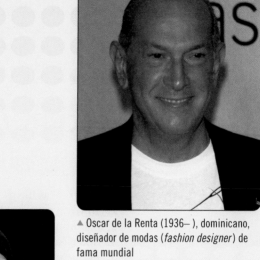
▲ Oscar de la Renta (1936–), dominicano, diseñador de modas (*fashion designer*) de fama mundial

▲ Juan Luis Guerra (1956–), dominicano, es un famoso compositor y cantante (*singer*) de merengue

▲ José Martí (1853–1895), cubano, es uno de los grandes escritores de Latinoamérica

▲ Celia Cruz (1925–2003), cubana y legendaria Reina (*Queen*) de la Salsa

Nuestro panorama cultural

In groups of three, answer the following questions about your home state, region, or country.

1. ¿Qué productos exporta su país?
2. ¿Hay centros religiosos históricos en su país? ¿Dónde están?
3. ¿Hay fortalezas históricas en su país?
4. ¿Vive algún miembro de su familia en el extranjero? ¿Dónde vive?
5. ¿Cuáles son algunos diseñadores de moda famosos de su país?
6. ¿Qué ritmos son autóctonos de (*originate in*) su país o región? ¿Cuál prefiere Ud.?

For the next class: Go to the World Wide Web and find photos from your hometown, state, region, or country. Use the questions from **Nuestro panorama cultural** above as guidelines for choosing them. Be ready to present the photos to your classmates.

Self-Test

Take this test. When you have finished, check your answers in the answer key provided in Appendix D. Then use a red pen to correct any mistakes you may have made. Are you ready?

Lección 7

A. Indirect object pronouns Rewrite the following sentences, using indirect object pronouns to replace the words in italics.

1. Ella trae las llaves *para ellos*.
2. Yo voy a preparar la cena *para ti*.
3. El botones trae el equipaje *para Ud.*
4. Ana va a comprar las tarjetas *para mí*.
5. Él trae el desayuno *para nosotros*.
6. Traen las maletas *para ellas*.

B. Constructions with *gustar* Tell who likes what.

1. Nosotros / más / esta película
2. Ellos / mucho / ese hotel
3. Tú / nadar
4. Yo / hacer ejercicio
5. Ella / no / usar la escalera mecánica

C. Time expressions with *hacer* Form sentences with the elements provided, using the expression **hace... que.** Follow the model.

◆ **MODELO:** una hora / él / trabajar
Hace una hora que él trabaja.

1. dos días / yo / no dormir
2. un mes / tú / no llamarme
3. media hora / nosotras / estar / aquí
4. un año / ellos / vivir / Panamá
5. doce horas / Eva / no comer

D. Preterit of regular verbs Rewrite the following sentences to describe things that already happened.

1. Mañana Leo y yo vamos a comprar las valijas. (ayer)
2. La semana próxima yo voy a viajar. (la semana pasada)
3. Hoy ella va a cancelar la reservación. (ayer)
4. ¿Van a confirmar Uds. el viaje hoy? (ayer)
5. Esta tarde ellos van a hablar con el empleado. (al mediodía)
6. Voy a darle las maletas ahora. (anoche)

E. Ordinal numbers   Complete the following sentences.

1. Marzo es el _____ mes del año.
2. Mayo es el _____ mes del año.
3. Abril es el _____ mes del año.
4. El _____ mes del año es octubre.
5. Agosto es el _____ mes del año.
6. Enero es el _____ mes del año.

F. Just words . . .   Complete the following sentences, using vocabulary from Lección 7.

1. El cuarto tiene _____ acondicionado.
2. El _____ lleva el equipaje al cuarto.
3. No voy a usar la escalera. Voy a usar el _____.
4. Sirven el _____ a las siete de la mañana y el _____ al mediodía.
5. El baño tiene ducha y _____.
6. No tiene una habitación sencilla; tiene una habitación _____.
7. Ayer compré una _____ de video.
8. En este hotel no hay servicio de _____.
9. Voy a _____ en la piscina.
10. ¿En qué puedo _____, señor?
11. ¿A cómo está el _____ de moneda?
12. Ud. tiene que _____ el número de su tarjeta.

G. Culture   Complete the following sentences, based on the Panorama hispánico section.

1. La segunda fuente de ingresos de Costa Rica es el _____.
2. En Costa Rica la educación es _____ y gratuita.
3. El Canal de Panamá une los océanos _____ y _____.
4. El Canal de Panamá fue propiedad de _____ hasta 1999.

Lección 8

A. Direct and indirect object pronouns used together Answer the following questions, using the cues provided, substituting direct object pronouns for the underlined words, and making any necessary changes.

1. ¿Cuándo le van a mandar <u>las flores</u> a Elena? (mañana)
2. ¿Quién te va a comprar <u>el perro</u>? (mi mamá)
3. ¿Quién les va a prestar <u>el dinero</u> a Uds.? (Luis)
4. ¿Cuándo me vas a traer <u>la chequera</u>? (esta tarde)
5. ¿Quién les va a dar <u>el diccionario</u> a Uds.? (la profesora)

B. Preterit of *ir, ser,* and *dar* Complete the following sentences, using the preterit of **ir, ser,** or **dar.**

1. Nosotros _____ al banco y le _____ el dinero al empleado.
2. Ellos _____ mis estudiantes el año pasado.
3. ¿A quién le _____ tú la cuenta?
4. Ayer, yo _____ a la florería y compré rosas.
5. Ellos no nos _____ el préstamo.
6. Ellas _____ de vacaciones a México.
7. La doctora Vega _____ mi profesora.
8. Yo _____ al hotel y le _____ las maletas al botones.

C. Preterit of *e:i* and *o:u* stem-changing verbs Complete the following sentences, using the preterit tense of the verbs listed below, as needed.

| mentir | dormir | seguir | conseguir |
| pedir | repetir | morir | servir |

1. ¿ _____ ellos en el hotel el jueves?
2. Los chicos _____ a sus amigos a la tienda.
3. Nosotros _____ sándwiches de jamón y queso.
4. Ella me _____ . No tiene veinte años.
5. ¿No _____ Ud. el dinero para ir de vacaciones?
6. ¿Qué le _____ los niños a Santa Claus?
7. El hombre _____ en un accidente.
8. Ella me _____ la pregunta.

D. Uses of *por* and *para*   Complete the following sentences with **por** or **para**, as needed.

1. Voy a llamar a Ana _____ teléfono _____ decirle que necesito el dinero _____ el sábado _____ la mañana.

2. Mañana salimos _____ San Juan. Vamos _____ tren y pensamos estar allí _____ dos semanas. Vamos a visitar a Pedro, que estudia _____ médico.

E. Formation of adverbs   Give the Spanish equivalent of the adverbs in parentheses.

1. Me gustan las flores, _____ las rosas. (*especially*)
2. Yo _____ voy a conciertos. (*frequently*)
3. El profesor habló _____ y _____. (*slowly and clearly*)
4. Vino a verme _____. (*recently*)
5. _____ voy al banco los sábados. (*Generally*)
6. _____ no tengo dinero. (*Unfortunately*)

F. Just words . . .   Choose the word that best completes each sentence.

1. Voy a llevar los pantalones a la (tintorería, florería).
2. Fui al banco para pedir un (fuego, préstamo).
3. Me (pasaron, robaron) la motocicleta ayer.
4. El policía me puso (una multa, un ramo) anoche.
5. No tengo que pagar por los cheques porque son (seguros, gratis).
6. Estas (margaritas, violetas) son moradas.
7. Tienes que (contar, fechar) el cheque.
8. Voy a comprarle un (incendio, regalo) para su cumpleaños.
9. Me gusta mucho ese loro. Me (encanta, solicita).
10. Le voy a (prestar, aparcar) 100 dólares.

G. Culture   Complete the following sentences, based on the **Panorama hispánico** section.

1. La capital de Puerto Rico es _____.
2. _____ es la segunda ciudad más importante del país.
3. Puerto Rico forma parte del archipiélago de las _____.
4. El deporte más popular de Puerto Rico es el _____.

Lección 9

A. Reflexive constructions Form sentences with the elements provided, using reflexive constructions.

1. Tú / vestirse / muy bien
2. Ellos / afeitarse / todos los días
3. Nosotros / acostarse / a las once
4. ¿Uds. / preocuparse / por sus hijos?
5. Yo / ponerse / la camisa
6. Juan / sentarse / aquí
7. Ella / lavarse / la cabeza todos los días
8. Él / quitarse / el suéter
9. Yo no / acordarse / de eso
10. Uds. / irse
11. ¿Cómo / llamarse / tú?
12. Daniel no / despertarse / hasta las diez

B. Some uses of the definite article Form sentences with the elements given, adding the necessary connectors. Use verbs in the present tense. Follow the model.

◆ **MODELO:** yo / ponerse / los pantalones
Yo me pongo los pantalones.

1. ¿Tú / quitarse / abrigo?
2. ellos / estar / escuela
3. mi mamá / lavarme / cabeza
4. Uds. / no lavarse / manos
5. padres / preocuparse / por / sus hijos
6. nosotros / preferir / café
7. educación / ser / lo más importante

C. Possessive pronouns Give the Spanish equivalent of the pronouns in parentheses.

1. El vestido de Nora está aquí. _____ está en mi cuarto. (*Mine*)
2. Mis revistas están aquí. ¿Dónde están _____, Sr. Vega? (*yours*)
3. Ellos van a enviar sus cartas (*letters*) hoy. ¿Cuándo vamos a enviar _____?
   (*ours*)
4. No tengo maletas. ¿Puedes prestarme _____, Anita? (*yours*)
5. Aquí están los regalos de Jorge. ¿Dónde están _____? (*ours*)
6. Juan necesita tu cuaderno, Eva. _____ está en la universidad. (*His*)

D. Irregular preterits
Complete the following sentences, using the preterit of the verbs given.

1. Yo _____ (tener) una fiesta anoche y todos mis amigos _____ (estar) allí.
2. Ellos _____ (traer) las fresas y las _____ (poner) en la mesa.
3. María _____ (venir) anoche y _____ (traducir) los documentos.
4. Él no _____ (poder) ir porque _____ (tener) que trabajar.
5. Nosotros no les _____ (decir) nada.
6. ¿Cuándo lo _____ (tú) (saber)? ¿Anoche?
7. Ellos no _____ (venir) porque no _____ (querer).
8. ¿Ellas _____ (conducir) tu coche?
9. Andrés _____ (hacer) todo el trabajo.

E. *Hace...* meaning *ago*
Answer the following questions, using the cues provided.

1. ¿Cuánto tiempo hace que conociste a tu mejor amigo(-a)? (cuatro años)
2. ¿Cuánto tiempo hace que tú y tus amigos fueron de vacaciones? (seis meses)
3. ¿Cuánto tiempo hace que Uds. fueron a la playa? (tres días)
4. ¿Cuánto tiempo hace que tus padres volvieron de Cuba? (una semana)
5. ¿Cuánto tiempo hace que llegaste a tu casa? (quince minutos)

F. Just words . . .
Match the questions in column A with the answers in column B.

A		B
1. ¿Qué le pones al café?	____	a. La guitarra.
2. ¿Cuántos años cumples?	____	b. En el supermercado.
3. ¿Qué instrumento tocas?	____	c. Mi país.
4. ¿Quieres mantequilla?	____	d. No, tarde.
5. ¿Qué extrañas?	____	e. No, margarina.
6. ¿Qué le pones a la ensalada?	____	f. No, me olvidé de traerla.
7. ¿Dónde compraste los mangos?	____	g. No, el piano.
8. ¿Él sabe tocar el violín?	____	h. Azúcar.
9. ¿Te acostaste temprano?	____	i. Aceite y vinagre.
10. ¿Trajiste la receta?	____	j. Veinte.

G. Culture
Complete the following sentences, based on the **Panorama hispánico** section.

1. Cuba es la _____ de las islas de las Antillas.
2. El _____ cubano tiene fama mundial.
3. La música típica de la República Dominicana es el _____.
4. Santo Domingo fue la _____ ciudad europea fundada en el Nuevo Mundo.

▲ Edificio de apartamentos llamado "las Torres Gemelas" en Caracas, Venezuela

Objetivos

Comunicación

You will learn vocabulary related to renting an apartment, the various parts of a house, home furniture, and appliances.

Pronunciación

Pronunciation in context

Estructuras

◆ The imperfect
◆ The preterit contrasted with the imperfect
◆ Verbs that change meaning in the preterit
◆ The relative pronouns **que** and **quien**

Cultura

◆ Housing
◆ Word **barrio**
◆ Housekeeping assistance

Panorama hispánico

◆ Venezuela

Estrategias

Listening: Training yourself to listen for units of meaning
Speaking: Paraphrasing practice II
Reading: Activating background knowledge
Writing: Using models to write classified ads

Buscando apartamento

Recursos

Venezuela

Cuando los conquistadores españoles llegaron al lago Maracaibo, las construcciones de los indígenas a orillas del lago les recordaron las de Venecia, y por eso llamaron al país Venezuela, nombre que significa "pequeña Venecia".

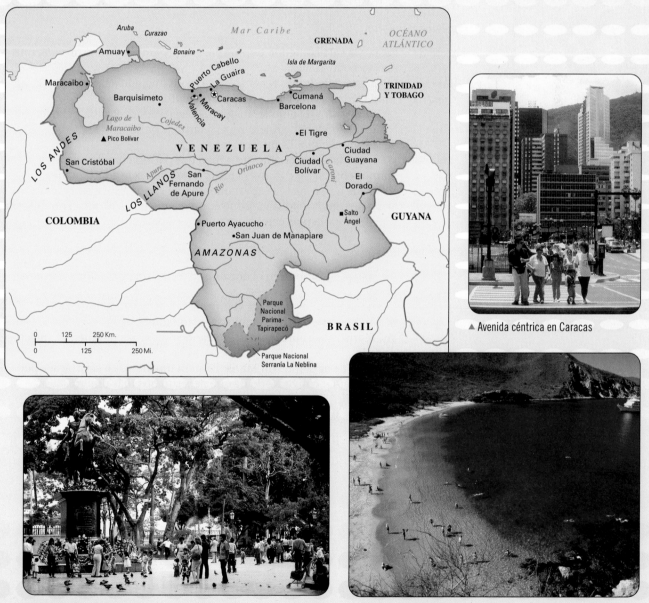

▲ Avenida céntrica en Caracas

▲ Parque en la ciudad de Caracas

▲ Parque Nacional Mochima

273

Silvia, Marisol y Cristina son tres chicas de Mérida, Venezuela, que vinieron a Caracas el mes pasado para asistir a la universidad. Silvia y Marisol son primas, pero ellas conocieron a Cristina cuando estaban en la escuela. Ahora están en una pensión, pero quieren mudarse a un apartamento.

Silvia	¿Llamó Cristina?
Marisol	Sí, y me dijo que podía encontrarse con nosotras a las tres para ver el apartamento.
Silvia	¿Te dio la dirección?
Marisol	Sí, aquí la tengo. Nosotras podemos ir en el metro y Hugo dijo que él iba a llevar a Cristina en su coche.
Silvia	El apartamento tiene que estar amueblado porque no tenemos muebles.
Marisol	Bueno... tenemos bolsas de dormir.
Silvia	Vamos, que es tarde. ¿Dónde pusiste la llave?
Marisol	Te la di esta mañana... ¡Ah no! Está en mi bolso.

En el apartamento

Encargado	Ésta es la sala comedor. Como ven, es muy amplia. Tiene un sofá, una mesa y cuatro sillas.
Marisol	(*A Cristina*) Podemos tener solamente un invitado a la vez.
Cristina	¡Shh! Vamos a ver el resto del apartamento.
Silvia	(*Al encargado*) ¿El alquiler incluye la electricidad, el agua y el teléfono?
Encargado	No, el teléfono, no. ¿Quiere ver el cuarto de baño?
Silvia	Sí. (*Desde el baño*) Es muy chico...
Marisol	¿Te acuerdas de la criada que tenían mis padres cuando nosotras éramos chicas? Su cuarto era más grande que este apartamento.
Cristina	Yo sé que a ti te gustó el apartamento que vimos anteayer.
Marisol	Sí, yo no quería ver éste porque tampoco me gusta el barrio donde está y el otro estaba más cerca de la universidad. Éste está muy lejos.

Silvia viene adonde están las chicas.

Silvia	¡No hay una cómoda en el dormitorio! Y hay solamente una mesita de noche.
Marisol	Cuando veníamos para acá vi un edificio de apartamentos mucho mejor que éste. Y había algunos desocupados...
Cristina	¡Ay, Marisol! Siempre la misma. Cuando eras chica también te quejabas de todo.
Silvia	¡Yo estoy de acuerdo con Marisol! Ahora mismo voy a escribirle a papá para tratar de convencerlo de que necesitamos más dinero.
Marisol	¡Chévere![1]
Encargado	Entonces, ¿no piensan alquilar el apartamento?
Marisol	¡Le vamos a avisar!

---

[1]**¡Chévere!** = *Great!* (used in Venezuela and the Caribbean)

Silvia

Marisol

el encargado

Cristina

¿Quién lo dice? Identify the person who said the following in the dialogue.

1. Cuando eras chica también te quejabas de todo. _____
2. Cuando veníamos para acá vi un edificio de apartamentos mucho mejor que éste. _____
3. Vamos, que es tarde. ¿Dónde pusiste la llave? _____
4. Yo sé que a ti te gustó el apartamento que vimos anteayer. _____
5. Entonces, ¿no piensan alquilar el apartamento? _____
6. El apartamento tiene que estar amueblado porque no tenemos muebles. _____
7. Bueno... tenemos bolsas de dormir. _____
8. Ésta es la sala comedor. Como ven, es muy amplia. _____

Hablemos. With a partner, take turns asking and answering the following questions. Base your answers on the dialogue and on your own circumstances.

En el diálogo	¿Y tú?
1. ¿De qué ciudad vinieron Silvia, Marisol y Cristina?	¿De qué ciudad eres tú?
2. ¿Dónde conocieron Silvia y Marisol a Cristina?	¿Dónde conociste tú a tu mejor amigo(-a)?
3. ¿A qué hora dijo Cristina que podía encontrarse con sus amigas?	¿Tú te vas a encontrar con alguien mañana?
4. ¿Cómo van a ir las chicas al apartamento?	¿Cómo vienes tú a la universidad?
5. ¿Dónde puso Marisol la llave?	¿Tú pierdes tus llaves a veces?
6. ¿Qué incluye el alquiler?	¿Tú tienes casa o alquilas un apartamento?
7. ¿Cómo es el baño del apartamento?	¿Cuántos baños hay en tu casa o apartamento?
8. ¿Marisol conocía a Cristina cuando las dos eran chicas?	¿Tú conocías a tu mejor amigo(-a) cuando eras chico(-a)?
9. ¿Qué dice Marisol del barrio donde está el apartamento?	¿A ti te gusta tu barrio?
10. ¿Qué va a hacer Silvia enseguida?	Cuando tú necesitas dinero, ¿a quién se lo pides?

Vocabulario

Cognados

la **electricidad** electricity
el **resto** rest

Nombres

el **alquiler** rent
el **barrio**, la **vecindad** neighborhood
la **bolsa (el saco) de dormir** sleeping bag
el **bolso**, la **cartera** handbag
el **coche**, el **carro**, el **auto**, el **automóvil** car
la **cómoda** chest of drawers
la **criada** maid
el **edificio** building

el (la) **encargado(-a)** super
la **escuela**[1] school
el (la) **invitado(-a)** guest
la **mesita de noche** night table
el **metro**, el **subterráneo** subway
los **muebles** furniture
la **pensión** boarding house

Verbos

alquilar to rent
avisar to let know, to advise
conocer to meet (*for the first time*)
convencer to convince

encontrarse (o:ue) to meet (*someone somewhere*)
incluir[2] to include
mudarse to move (*from one house to another*)
quejarse to complain

Adjetivos

amplio(-a) large, ample
amueblado(-a) furnished
chico(-a) small

desocupado(-a) vacant
mismo(-a) same

Otras palabras y expresiones

acá here
cerca close, near
desde from

lejos far
solamente, sólo only

¿Lo sabía Ud.?

La palabra "barrio" equivale simplemente al inglés *neighborhood*, pero en muchos lugares de los Estados Unidos y en algunos países latinoamericanos tiene una connotación negativa.

◆ ¿Le gusta a Ud. el barrio donde vive?

---

[1]**escuela primaria** = *elementary school;* **escuela secundaria** = *secondary school*
[2]present indicative: **incluyo, incluyes, incluye, incluimos, incluís, incluyen**

Vocabulario adicional

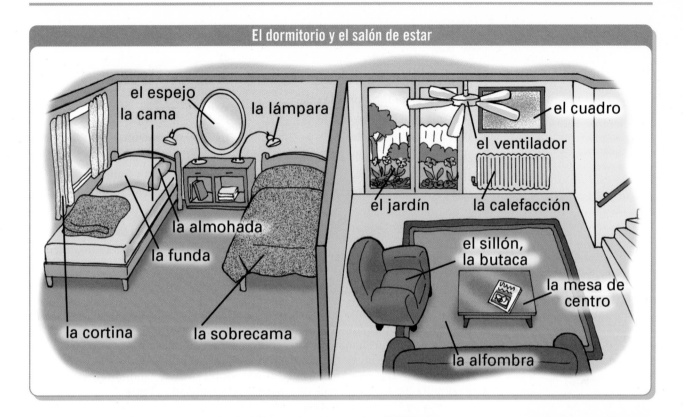

El dormitorio y el salón de estar

- el espejo
- la cama
- la lámpara
- el cuadro
- el ventilador
- el jardín
- la calefacción
- la almohada
- la funda
- el sillón, la butaca
- la mesa de centro
- la cortina
- la sobrecama
- la alfombra

Aparatos electrodomésticos y batería de cocina
(*Home appliances and cookware*)

la cacerola pot
la cafetera coffee pot, coffee-maker
el horno oven
la lavadora washing machine
la licuadora blender

el microondas microwave (oven)
la plancha iron
la sartén frying pan
la secadora clothes dryer
la tostadora toaster

¿Lo sabía Ud.?

En los países hispanos, muchas familias de la clase alta y de la clase media tienen criadas. Frecuentemente la criada vive en la casa donde trabaja. Cuando lleva muchos años trabajando en la misma casa, es considerada prácticamente como un miembro de la familia.

◆ **En general, ¿las familias de este país tienen criadas?**

Práctica

A. Match the questions in column A with the responses in column B.

A	B
1. ¿Qué compraste para tu casa? ____	a. No, en la secadora.
2. ¿Qué vas a comprar para la sala? ____	b. La criada.
3. ¿La ropa está en la lavadora? ____	c. No, muy cerca.
4. ¿Vas a usar la cacerola? ____	d. En la escuela secundaria.
5. ¿Está lejos? ____	e. Con el encargado.
6. ¿Están en un hotel? ____	f. Sábanas y fundas.
7. ¿Quién limpió el baño? ____	g. No, me voy a mudar.
8. ¿Con quién hablaste? ____	h. No, la sartén.
9. ¿Dónde lo conociste? ____	i. No, en una pensión.
10. ¿No te gusta tu casa? ____	j. Una mesa de centro.

B. Select the word or phrase that best completes each sentence.

1. Compré (una licuadora, cortinas, un espejo) para la ventana de la sala.
2. Puse el pollo en (la cómoda, el horno, el ventilador).
3. La almohada está en mi (cama, microondas, tostadora).
4. Tengo muchas rosas en mi (lámpara, calefacción, jardín).
5. Voy a pasarle la aspiradora (al cuadro, a la sobrecama, a la alfombra).
6. El alquiler (incluye, se queja, convence) la electricidad y el agua.
7. Me voy a sentar en esa (cómoda, silla, tabla de planchar).
8. Ese edificio tiene muchos apartamentos (desocupados, mismos, asados).
9. ¿Vas a comprar la casa o la vas a (avisar, alquilar, convencer)?
10. Voy a tratar de llamarte (desde, hacia, entre) mi casa.

C. Write the words or phrases that correspond to the following.

1. barrio _____
2. metro _____
3. coche _____
4. bolso _____
5. sólo _____
6. que no está ocupado _____
7. la usamos para planchar _____
8. sillón _____
9. la usamos para hacer café _____
10. que tiene muebles _____

D. Complete the following, using appropriate vocabulary.

1. Necesitamos tres _____ de dormir, pero tenemos _____ una.
2. Mi _____ es un Ford del año 1994, pero no me _____ porque hay muchos estudiantes que tienen que tomar el autobús…
3. Compré una mesa de _____ y dos mesitas de _____.
4. David quiere _____ a la hermana de Julio, pero a Julio no le gusta la idea porque todos dicen que David es un Casanova. ¿Tú crees que David va a _____ a Julio? Yo no sé…

5. ¿Hay algún apartamento _____ en ese edificio? Nosotros necesitamos un apartamento _____ porque no tenemos muebles.

6. Ellos consiguieron un apartamento que está muy _____ de la universidad. Viven allí _____ mayo.

Para conversar

A. Mañana nos mudamos. With a partner, play the roles of two people who are moving into a new house or apartment. Ask each other whether or not you have certain pieces of furniture, appliances, or kitchen utensils. You each answer that you do, and mention what you have to buy.

◆ **MODELO:** —¿Tenemos...?
—Sí, tenemos..., pero tenemos que comprar...

B. No estamos de acuerdo. You and a partner play the roles of two roommates looking for a new apartment. One likes everything and the other finds fault with everything.

◆ **MODELO:** —Las cortinas son muy bonitas.
—No me gusta el color...

Pronunciación

Pronunciation in context

In this lesson, there are some new words or phrases that may be challenging to pronounce. For further pronunciation practice of Spanish sounds, listen to your instructor and repeat the following sentences.

1. **Ahora** están en una **pensión.**

2. **Hugo** dijo que él iba a **llevar** a Cristina.

3. Podemos tener un solo **invitado** a la vez.

4. El **alquiler** incluye la **electricidad.**

5. A ti te gustó el apartamento que vimos **anteayer.**

6. Cuando **veníamos** para acá, vi un **edificio** de apartamentos.

7. Voy a tratar de **convencerlo.**

8. ¿No piensan **alquilar** el apartamento?

Aspectos culturales

En imágenes (*Algunos tipos de vivienda[1] en el mundo hispano*)

▲ Una estudiante usa su computadora personal en su casa, en México

▲ Famoso edificio La Pedrera (Casa Milà) 1906–1910, Barcelona, España

▲ Casa típica en Córdoba, España

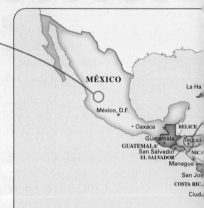

Ubíquese... y búsquelo

Improve Your Grade
Web Search

Silvia, Marisol, and Cristina will be attending school in the **Ciudad Universitaria** neighborhood. They want to live close to school or be able to reach it by the **Metro de Caracas.** Using the metro map, go to **www.cengage.com/highered** to search for likely neighborhoods where the three roommates could live. In the next class, team up with two classmates to discuss your findings.

---

[1]**vivienda** = *housing*

▲ Casa típica de ciudad, Tegucigalpa, Honduras

▲ Casas-palafito (*lake houses*), vivienda tradicional de los indígenas Warao, Venezuela

▲ Arrabal (*slums*), Caracas, Venezuela

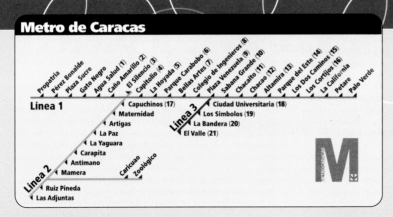

Estructuras

1. The imperfect (*El imperfecto de indicativo*)

There are two simple past tenses in the Spanish indicative: the preterit, which you studied in **Lecciones 7, 8,** and **9,** and the imperfect.

A. Regular forms

◆ To form the regular imperfect, add the following endings to the verb stem.

-ar verbs		*-er* and *-ir* verbs			
hablar		*comer*		*vivir*	
habl-	**aba**	com-	**ía**	viv-	**ía**
habl-	**abas**	com-	**ías**	viv-	**ías**
habl-	**aba**	com-	**ía**	viv-	**ía**
habl-	**ábamos**	com-	**íamos**	viv-	**íamos**
habl-	**abais**	com-	**íais**	viv-	**íais**
habl-	**aban**	com-	**ían**	viv-	**ían**

◆ Note that the endings of the **-er** and **-ir** verbs are the same, and that there is a written accent on the first **í** of the endings of the **-er** and **-ir** verbs.

◆ The Spanish imperfect tense is equivalent to three English forms.

Yo **vivía** en Caracas.
I used to live in Caracas.
I was living in Caracas.
I lived in Caracas.

◆ The imperfect is used to refer to habitual or repeated actions in the past, with no reference to when they began or ended.

—¿Uds. **tenían** una casa en Caracas? *"Did you have a house in Caracas?"*
—No, **vivíamos** en un apartamento. *"No, we lived in an apartment."*

◆ The imperfect is also used to refer to actions, events, or conditions that the speaker views as *in the process* of happening in the past, again with no reference to when they began or ended.

—**Veníamos** para casa cuando vimos a Raúl. *We were coming home when we saw Raúl.*

¿Lo sabía Ud.?

En las grandes ciudades españolas y latinoamericanas, la mayoría de la gente vive en apartamentos, que en España se llaman "pisos". Los apartamentos se alquilan o se compran. Muchos edificios tienen oficinas o tiendas en la planta baja y apartamentos en los otros pisos.

◆ En la ciudad donde Ud. vive, ¿la mayoría de la gente vive en casas o en apartamentos?

B. Irregular forms

♦ Only three verbs are irregular in the imperfect tense: **ser, ver,** and **ir.**

ser	ver	ir
era	veía	iba
eras	veías	ibas
era	veía	iba
éramos	veíamos	íbamos
erais	veíais	ibais
eran	veían	iban

—¿**Ibas** mucho a casa de tus abuelos cuando **eras** niño?
—Sí, los **veía** todos los sábados.

"Did you often go to your grandparents' house when you were a child?"
"Yes, I used to see them every Saturday."

—¿Adónde **iban** Uds. de vacaciones cuando eran niños?
—**Íbamos** a la playa o a las montañas.

"Where did you go on vacation when you were children?"
"We used to go to the beach or to the mountains."

Práctica

ACE the Test

A. Ten years ago, María wrote this composition about herself and her family. Rewrite her composition, using the imperfect tense.

Mi familia y yo vivimos en Caracas. Mi padre trabaja para la compañía Sandoval y mi madre enseña en la universidad. Es una profesora excelente. Mis hermanos y yo asistimos a la escuela. Generalmente pasamos las vacaciones en isla Margarita. Allí vamos a la playa y nadamos. Mis abuelos viven en Maracaibo y no los vemos mucho, pero siempre les escribimos.

B. Now write a paragraph about your own childhood, using Exercise A as a model.

C. Compare your teenage years with those of a classmate by taking turns completing the following sentences.

1. Cuando yo era adolescente...
2. Mi familia y yo siempre...
3. Mis abuelos...
4. Mi mejor amigo(-a)...
5. Frecuentemente nosotros...
6. Cuando yo tenía dieciséis años...
7. En la escuela, yo...
8. Todos los fines de semana, mis amigos y yo...
9. En el verano...
10. Cuando yo quería salir con mis amigos, mis padres...

Para conversar

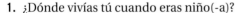

A. ¡Habla con tu compañero! Interview a classmate, using the following questions and two of your own. When you have finished, switch roles.

1. ¿Dónde vivías tú cuando eras niño(-a)?
2. ¿Vivías en una casa o en un apartamento?
3. ¿Te gustaba estudiar? ¿Eras buen estudiante?
4. ¿Adónde iban tú y tu familia de vacaciones? ¿Qué les gustaba hacer?
5. ¿Preferías pasar las vacaciones en el campo (*country*) o en la ciudad?
6. ¿Qué hacías cuando ibas de vacaciones?
7. ¿Veías mucho a tus abuelos?
8. ¿Vivías cerca de tus abuelos?

B. Recuerdos Get together with a partner and compare your high school years. Ask pertinent questions.

2. The preterit contrasted with the imperfect (*El pretérito contrastado con el imperfecto*)

◆ The difference between the preterit and the imperfect can be visualized in the following way.

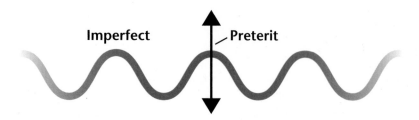

The wavy line representing the imperfect shows an action or event taking place over a period of time in the past. There is no reference to when the action began or ended. The vertical line representing the preterit shows an action or event as completed in the past.

In many instances, the choice between the preterit and the imperfect depends on how the speaker views the action or event. The following table summarizes some of the most important uses of both tenses.

Preterit	Imperfect
1. Reports past actions that the speaker views as finished and completed. Yo **estuve** allí el año pasado. Ayer **compré** una bolsa de dormir.	1. Describes past actions in the process of happening, with no reference to their beginning or end. **Iba** a la biblioteca cuando lo vi.
2. Sums up a condition or state viewed as a whole (and no longer in effect). Me **sentí** mal todo el día.	2. Refers to repeated or habitual actions or events: *used to ...* Cuando **era** niña **iba**[1] de vacaciones a Montevideo.
	3. Describes a physical, mental, or emotional state or condition in the past. Me **sentía** muy mal.
	4. Expresses time in the past. **Eran** las ocho de la noche cuando llegaron a su casa.
	5. Is generally used in indirect discourse. Me dijo que **podía** encontrarse con nosotras.
	6. Describes age in the past. Cuando **tenía** veinte años, vivía en Chile.
	7. Describes or sets the stage in the past. **Hacía** frío y **llovía.**

[1]Note that this use of the imperfect also corresponds to the English *would* used to describe a repeated action in the past: *When I was a child, I used to go to Montevideo on vacation.* = *When I was a child, I would go to Montevideo on vacation.*

Preterit or Imperfect ... ?

1. Eran las siete de la mañana cuando Beto salió de su casa.

2. ¡Brrr! Llovía y hacía frío.

3. Cuando Beto iba por la calle Lima, vio un accidente. CALLE LIMA

4. Beto llegó a la biblioteca. 2º PISO Subió al 2º piso.

5. En el 2º piso, Beto vio a Eva.

6. Beto le preguntó si quería ir a la cafetería, pero ella le dijo que no podía ir. ¿Quieres ir a la cafetería? No puedo ir.

7. Beto fue a la cafetería solo. Se sentía muy triste... CAFETERÍA

8. Beto comió solo. Cuando Beto era pequeño, siempre comía solo.

9. Beto volvió a su casa.

10. Beto cenó con su familia.

11. Eran las nueve cuando Beto se acostó.

12. Beto no pudo dormir porque le dolió la cabeza toda la noche.

Práctica

ACE the Test

A. Complete the following dialogues. Then act them out with a partner.

1. —¿Cuántos años _____ (tener) tú cuando _____ (venir) a vivir a Caracas?
   —_____ (Tener) doce años.

2. —¿Qué te _____ (decir) el encargado ayer?
   —Me _____ (decir) que yo _____ (deber) volver mañana.

3. —¿Qué tiempo _____ (hacer) cuando Uds. _____ (salir) de casa esta mañana?
   —_____ (Hacer) frío y _____ (nevar).

4. —¿Adónde _____ (ir) Uds. de vacaciones cuando _____ (ser) niños?
   —Siempre _____ (ir) a la playa, pero un verano mis padres _____ (decidir) alquilar una casa en las montañas y ésas _____ (ser) nuestras mejores vacaciones.

5. —¿Qué hora _____ (ser) cuando tú _____ (llegar) a casa ayer?
   —_____ (Ser) las ocho.
   —¿ _____ (Ir) a la tienda?
   —Sí, _____ (ir) con Nora. Cuando nosotras _____ (ir) para la tienda, _____ (ver) un accidente en la calle.
   —¿ _____ (Morir) alguien?
   —No, por suerte no _____ (morir) nadie.

B. This interview takes place in Caracas. Play the role of a reporter interviewing a famous star from Spain.

—_____

—Yo nací (*I was born*)¹ en Sevilla, y no te digo cuándo.

—_____

—Yo tenía diez años cuando nos fuimos a vivir a Madrid.

—_____

—Cuando era niña era fea y un poco gorda.

—_____

—Sí, tenía un perro que se llamaba Chispita.

—_____

—Cuando era niña me gustaba ir a la playa y nadar.

—_____

—Estudié en la Escuela de Arte Dramático.

—_____

—Empecé a trabajar en televisión en 1995.

—_____

—Vine a Caracas en el año 2000.

—_____

—Sí, el año pasado estuve en París y trabajé en un club nocturno.

—_____

—Estuve allí por tres meses.

C. With a partner, go to the illustration on page 285 and prepare questions about what Beto's day was like. Take turns asking and answering the questions.

D. Preterit versus imperfect   As you know, the preterit *advances* the story, while the imperfect adds information about what was happening at that moment. With a partner, create clauses using the imperfect tense to provide descriptions, to talk about what was going on when something else took place, to tell what someone was saying, etc. Be creative! Then get together with another group to compare stories.

◆ **MODELO:**   —Me levanté a las seis y miré por la ventana.
　　　　　　　—*Estaba nevando y no había nadie en la calle.*

1. Desayuné con mi familia. Comimos cereal con leche y panqueques.
2. Me bañé y me vestí. Salí de mi casa a las siete.
3. Decidí ir a la universidad a pie. Fui por el parque. En el parque vi a Marisol. Hablamos por unos diez minutos.
4. Llegué a la universidad a las ocho.
5. El profesor de historia nos dio un examen muy difícil.
6. A las once y media, almorcé en la cafetería. La comida no me gustó.
7. A la una, comencé a sentirme enfermo.
8. Volví a mi casa y hablé con mi mamá.
9. No cené. Me acosté a las nueve, pero no pude dormir en toda la noche.

_____

¹**Nacer** is a regular verb in the preterit.

Para conversar

A. ¡Habla con tu compañero!   Interview a classmate, using the following questions and two of your own. When you have finished, switch roles.

1. ¿Cuántos años tenías cuando aprendiste a nadar?
2. ¿Adónde ibas de vacaciones?
3. ¿Te divertías durante el verano?
4. ¿Qué te gustaba hacer cuando eras niño(-a)?
5. ¿Cómo era tu primer(-a) novio(-a)?
6. ¿Qué hiciste ayer?
7. ¿A qué hora te levantaste esta mañana?
8. ¿Qué tiempo hacía cuando saliste de tu casa?
9. ¿Qué hora era cuando llegaste a la universidad?
10. ¿Tomaste una clase de inglés el año pasado?

B. Cuando era adolescente...   In groups of four or five, prepare five to six questions to ask your instructor about his or her life as a teenager.

3. Verbs that change meaning in the preterit (*Verbos que cambian de significado en el pretérito*)

- Some Spanish verbs change meaning when they are used in the preterit. Note the usage of the verbs in the following examples.

conocer:	conocí (preterit)	*I met*
	conocía (imperfect)	*I knew (was acquainted or familiar with)*
	Anoche **conocí** a una chica muy simpática.	(*I met her for the first time.*)
	Yo no **conocía** la ciudad.	(*I wasn't familiar with the city.*)
saber:	supe (preterit)	*I found out, I learned*
	sabía (imperfect)	*I knew*
	Lo **supe** cuando él me lo dijo.	(*I found it out.*)
	Yo no **sabía** que te gustaba.	(*I wasn't aware of it.*)
no querer:	no quise (preterit)	*I refused*
	no quería (imperfect)	*I didn't want*
	Raúl **no quiso** ir.	(*didn't want to and refused*)
	Rita **no quería** ir, pero después decidió ir.	(*didn't want to at the time*)

—¿Tú **conocías** al cuñado de Carmen? *"Did you know Carmen's brother-in-law?"*
—No, lo **conocí** anoche. *"No, I met him last night."*

—¿Y Roberto? ¿No vino? *"And Roberto? Didn't he come?"*
—No, **no quiso** venir. *"No, he refused to come."*
—Yo tampoco **quería** venir, pero vine para traer a Anita. *"I didn't want to come either, but I came to bring Anita."*

Práctica

ACE the Test

 Act out the following scene from a soap opera with a partner, providing the missing verbs.

Adrián ¿Tú _____ que Rosaura estaba embarazada (*pregnant*)?

Sara No, lo _____ anoche.

Adrián ¡Qué horrible! Dicen que su esposo es un idiota. Los padres de ella no _____ ir a la boda (*wedding*). Ese día se fueron a Europa.

Sara Pero, ¿dónde _____ Rosaura a Lorenzo?

Adrián En una fiesta. Rosaura no _____ ir, pero Olga la llevó.

Sara ¿Olga _____ a Lorenzo?

Adrián Sí, Olga es la ex esposa de Lorenzo...

Para conversar

A. ¡Habla con tu compañero! Interview a classmate, using the following questions and at least two of your own. When you have finished, switch roles.

1. ¿Conocías tú al profesor (a la profesora) antes de empezar esta clase?
2. ¿Cuándo lo (la) conociste?
3. ¿Sabías tú la nacionalidad del profesor (de la profesora)?
4. ¿Cuándo la supiste?
5. Yo no quería venir a clase hoy. ¿Y tú?
6. La última vez (*last time*) que no viniste a clase, ¿fue porque no pudiste o porque no quisiste?
7. ¿Cuándo conociste a tu mejor amigo(-a) o novio(-a)?
8. De niño(-a), ¿conocías a alguien interesante? ¿A quién?
9. ¿Cuándo supiste que Santa Claus no traía los regalos?
10. De niño(-a), ¿qué cosas no querías comer?

B. La próxima escena With a partner, write and act out the scene that follows the one you read in the **Práctica.** Some words you might use: **divorciarse, el (la) amante** (*lover*), **irse de casa, los problemas económicos,** etc.

4. The relative pronouns *que* and *quien* (*Los pronombres relativos que y quien*)

Relative pronouns are used to combine two sentences that have a common element, usually a noun or a pronoun.

A. The relative pronoun *que*

¿Dónde está **el dinero**?	Trajiste **el dinero.**

common element

¿Dónde está el dinero **que** trajiste?

R.P.

La chica se llama Rosa.	**La chica** vino esta mañana.

common element

La chica **que** vino esta mañana se llama Rosa.

R.P.

- The relative pronoun **que** not only helps to combine the two sentences in the examples, but also replaces the nouns **el dinero** and **la chica** in the combined sentences.

- The relative pronoun **que** is invariable and is used for both persons and things. It is the Spanish equivalent of *that, which,* and *who.* Unlike its English equivalent, the Spanish **que** is never omitted.

—¿Para quién es el sofá **que** compraste?   *"For whom is the sofa that you bought?"*

—Es para la señora **que** alquiló el apartamento.   *"It is for the lady who rented the apartment."*

B. The relative pronoun *quien*

—¿La muchacha **con quien** hablabas es americana?   *"Is the girl with whom you were talking an American?"*

—No, es venezolana.   *"No, she's a Venezuelan."*

—¿Quiénes son esos señores?   *"Who are those gentlemen?"*

—Son los señores **de quienes** te habló José.   *"They are the gentlemen about whom José spoke to you."*

- The relative pronoun **quien** is used only with persons.

- The plural of **quien** is **quienes**. **Quien** does not change for gender.

- **Quien** is generally used after prepositions, e.g., **con quien, de quienes.**

- **Quien** is the Spanish equivalent of *whom* and *that.*

Práctica

ACE the Test

 Complete the following dialogues, using **que, quien,** or **quienes.** Then act them out with a partner.

1. —¿Quién es el señor _____ alquiló el apartamento?

   —Es el papá de Marisa, la chica con _____ trabajo.

2. —¿Dónde están las sillas _____ compré ayer?

   —En la cocina.

3. —Las chicas con _____ salimos anoche llamaron esta mañana.

   —¿Qué dijeron?

   —Que nos van a traer los libros _____ necesitamos.

4. —¿Con quién vas al museo?

   —Con María Luisa, la chica de _____ te hablé.

5. —¿Ella es la muchacha _____ trabaja contigo?

   —No, es la chica con _____ estudio.

 *El que ríe último, ríe mejor.*

He who laughs last, laughs best.

Para conversar

 ¡Habla con tu compañero!   Interview a classmate, using the following questions. When you have finished, switch roles.

1. ¿Cómo se llama la persona a quien más admiras?
2. ¿Cómo se llama el profesor o la profesora que enseña tu clase favorita?
3. ¿Quiénes son las personas que viven contigo?
4. ¿Cómo se llaman las personas con quienes vas a salir el sábado?
5. ¿Quién es la persona que más te quiere?
6. ¿Cuál es la comida que más te gusta?
7. ¿Cuál es el color que más te gusta?
8. ¿Dónde está el banco en el que tienes tu cuenta corriente?

Así somos

Al escuchar...

Estrategia **Training yourself to listen for units of meaning** One of the most challenging aspects of listening to native speech as a beginning Spanish learner is telling where a word or a part of a sentence ends and the next one begins. Linking, which you read about in **Lección 3**, can contribute to the challenge of hearing words or phrases distinctly. Remember that if two adjacent letters are the same (for example, la**s** **s**opas or v**a** **a** tomar), they sound almost like one in speech. Be aware of this and listen for logical phrases or groups of words.

En busca de un apartamento You will listen to several sentences that are transcribed below without spacing between words. Listen as many times as needed and mark the divisions between the words.

1. elapartamentoquevimosenesteedificionotienecalefacción
2. nopiensanalquilareseapartamentoporquenoestáamueblado
3. megustamáselotroapartamentoporqueestácercadelmetro
4. levanaavisarmañanasipuedemudarseestasemana
5. ellosquedaronenencontrarseenlauniversidadalauna

Al conversar...

Estrategia **Paraphrasing practice II** When paraphrasing, remember that your goal is to simplify what you hear using words that you know. Developing this skill can be useful in conversation as well as in writing to summarize and report or explain something that you have heard or read.

  ¿Qué dijo? You will hear five sentences. Listen and restate them in your own words. Then compare your responses with those of a classmate.

 ¿Qué dice Ud.? What would you say in the following situations? What might the other person say? Act out the scenes with a partner. Take turns playing each role.

1. You are talking to a real estate agent. You are looking for a house in a good neighborhood, with five bedrooms, air conditioning, and a three-car garage.
2. You and your friend are going to share an apartment. Describe one that you have just seen, and tell him/her why you should take the apartment. Your friend doesn't think it is a good idea.
3. You are going to give a bridal shower for a friend who has nothing. Decide what appliances and other necessities you think that your guests can buy.
4. You ask the super of an apartment building if the rent includes electricity, water, and phone.

Para conocernos mejor To do this activity, work with a classmate whom you would like to get to know. Take turns asking and answering these questions.

1. La escuela secundaria a la que tú asistías, ¿estaba cerca o lejos de tu casa? ¿Cómo ibas a la escuela? ¿A qué hora empezaban las clases? ¿Almorzabas en la cafetería con tus amigos?
2. ¿Dónde te encontrabas con tus amigos los fines de semana? ¿Qué hacían? ¿Iban al cine a veces?
3. ¿Tú vives en una casa o en un apartamento? ¿Cuántos dormitorios tiene? ¿Te gusta tu barrio? ¿Vives cerca o lejos de la universidad?
4. ¿Qué muebles tienes en tu dormitorio? ¿Qué muebles hay en la sala? ¿Qué aparatos electrodomésticos hay en la cocina?
5. ¿Qué tuviste que hacer ayer? ¿Qué hora era cuando saliste de tu casa esta mañana? ¿Qué tiempo hacía? ¿A qué hora piensas volver a tu casa hoy?

 Una encuesta Interview your classmates to identify who fits the following descriptions. Include your instructor, but remember to use the **Ud.** form when addressing him/her. After finishing the survey, get together with two or three classmates and discuss the results.

Nombre

1. Tiene alfombra en toda su casa. _____
2. Tiene una cómoda en su dormitorio. _____
3. Tiene un ventilador en su cuarto. _____
4. Usa dos almohadas para dormir. _____
5. Tiene una bolsa de dormir. _____
6. Tiene invitados frecuentemente. _____
7. Compró un coche el año pasado. _____
8. Tenía una criada cuando era niño(-a). _____

 Para crear Get together in groups of three or four and "create" the scenario for this photo. Imagine that the couple is talking to a real estate agent about renting an apartment. What do they want? What is everybody saying? Add any other pertinent details.

¡Vamos a leer!

Estrategia **Activating background knowledge** Thinking about what you know of a topic before reading in order to anticipate or predict content can be applied to almost any type of text. For instance, you can draw on your knowledge of a subject such as national parks or the Caribbean, and you also can use your knowledge of a text type to predict the kinds of words and information it will contain. Remember that bringing your own experiences to a reading improves your understanding of the text.

Avisos clasificados You will be reading classified ads for places for rent and for sale. Think of and jot down eight to ten words in Spanish that you would expect to find in this kind of classified ad. Then scan the ads to see how many of these words are in the ads.

A leer

Comprensión As you read the ads, find the answers to the following questions.

1. ¿Cómo es el apartamento que se alquila?
2. ¿Qué se puede ver desde el apartamento?
3. ¿Cuántos dormitorios tiene? ¿Qué más tiene?
4. ¿Tiene aire acondicionado?
5. ¿Qué está incluido en el alquiler?
6. ¿A qué hora se puede llamar para tener información?
7. ¿Dónde está situada la casa que se vende?
8. ¿Qué tiene además de jardín y piscina?
9. ¿Qué comodidades tiene la casa?
10. ¿Para cuántos coches es el garaje?

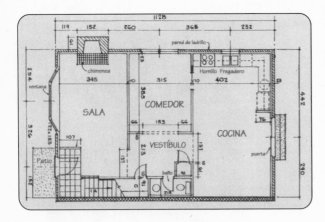

SE ALQUILA

- Apartamento amplio y cómodo, con vista panorámica de la ciudad.
- Tres dormitorios, sala-comedor, cocina y dos baños.
- Calefacción y aire acondicionado. Electricidad y agua incluidas en el alquiler.
- Situado a cinco minutos del metro. Lugar de estacionamiento.

Información: Edificio Rivera
Teléfono 342-2704   Llamar de 8 a 5

Se vende

- Casa en barrio residencial, con jardín, piscina y patio con árboles frutales.
- Cuatro habitaciones, sala y comedor, dos baños completos y cocina grande con horno y microondas.
- Instalaciones para lavadora y secadora. Garaje para dos coches.

Precio razonable. **Para verla**, llame al tel. 483-7590 de 2 a 5.

¡Vamos a escribir!

Antes de escribir

Estrategia **Using models to write classified ads** Models are especially useful when writing ads because they provide a reference for format, the type of information to include, and the kinds of words to use.

Avisos clasificados Imagine that you own a real estate agency (**agencia de bienes raíces** or **agencia inmobiliaria**, in Spain). You will be writing two classified ads for the following properties. First, look at the models in **¡Vamos a leer!** and make a list of words you can use. Add additional words, including adjectives or phrases designed to interest prospective renters or buyers. Try to use words you already know, but consult a dictionary if needed.

- ◆ For rent: an inexpensive but very functional apartment
- ◆ For sale: the most beautiful but impractical house you can create

A escribir los avisos clasificados

Write your **primer borrador** of the ads, using the models provided in **¡Vamos a leer!** and your list of words.

Después de escribir

Before writing your final version, exchange your first draft ads with a classmate and peer edit each other's work using the following guidelines.

- ◆ noun-adjective agreement
- ◆ use of adjectives and descriptive phrases to create appealing ads

Después de leer... desde su mundo

In pairs, take turns describing the apartment or house where you live. If you live in a dorm, talk about your family's house. Tell what rooms it has and mention two or three characteristics or special features. Refer to the ads for ideas.

Panorama hispánico

Venezuela

- Venezuela tiene dos veces el área de California, más de 350.000 millas cuadradas, y más de 23 millones de habitantes.

- El país es uno de los diez mayores exportadores de petróleo del mundo. Más de la octava parte del petróleo importado por los Estados Unidos viene de Venezuela. La mayor parte de su gran reserva de petróleo se encuentra debajo del lago Maracaibo. Este lago es el mayor de Venezuela y de toda la América del Sur.

- La principal atracción turística del país es el Salto Ángel, diecisiete veces más alto que las cataratas del Niágara.

- Caracas, la capital de Venezuela, es el centro gubernamental, financiero, cultural y artístico del país. Es una ciudad en que se mezclan lo ultramoderno con lo antiguo, y el lujo (*luxury*) con la pobreza (*poverty*). En Caracas nació Simón Bolívar, llamado el Libertador de América porque luchó (*fought*) por la independencia de cinco países de América del Sur: Colombia, Venezuela, Ecuador, Perú y Bolivia. Otras ciudades importantes del país son Maracaibo, el centro petrolero de Venezuela, Valencia y Barquisimeto.

- Venezuela es la patria del gran novelista Rómulo Gallegos. La música típica venezolana es el joropo, pero son populares todos los ritmos caribeños.

La industria petrolera

▲ Pozos (*Wells*) petroleros en el lago Maracaibo

Personalidades del *glamour*

▲ Carolina Herrera, diseñadora de modas (*fashion designer*)

▲ Miss Venezuela, Srta. Universo 1996

Riquezas naturales venezolanas

▲ Salto Ángel, las cataratas (*waterfalls*) más altas del mundo

▲ Isla Margarita

Nuestro panorama cultural

In groups of three, answer the following questions about your home state, region, or country.

1. ¿Cuáles son los lagos más grandes de su país?
2. ¿Cuáles son algunos de los parques nacionales de su país? ¿En qué estado están?
3. ¿Hay transportación pública en su ciudad? Donde Ud. vive, ¿cuál es la forma más eficiente de viajar?
4. ¿Hay muchas universidades en su región? ¿Cuál es la más grande?
5. ¿Le gustan los concursos de belleza? ¿Qué tipo de concursos hay donde Ud. vive?

For the next class: Go to the World Wide Web and find photos from your hometown, state, region, or country. Use the questions from **Nuestro panorama cultural** above as guidelines for choosing them. Be ready to present the photos to your classmates.

Lección

11

▲ Aeropuerto en Bogotá, Colombia

Objetivos

Comunicación

You will learn vocabulary related to travel.

Pronunciación

Pronunciation in context

Estructuras

◆ The subjunctive mood
◆ The subjunctive with verbs of volition
◆ The subjunctive with verbs of emotion

Cultura

◆ Engagements
◆ Family
◆ Role of godparents

Panorama hispánico

◆ Colombia

Estrategias

Listening: Recognizing linking or transition words
Speaking: Using courtesy expressions and common phrases
Reading: Predicting
Writing: Describing a trip

En una agencia de viajes

Colombia

Colombia es la única nación nombrada en honor de Cristóbal Colón. Su extensión es algo mayor que las de los estados de California y Tejas juntos. Es el cuarto país suramericano en tamaño (*size*), y es el único con costas en el Pacífico y en el mar Caribe.

▲ Fundada en 1533, Cartagena de Indias es hoy Patrimonio de la Humanidad (*World Heritage*), así declarada (*thus declared*) por la UNESCO.

▲ Vista panorámica de Bogotá

▲ Un avión de la línea aérea colombiana Avianca, la más antigua de Hispanoamérica

297

Gustavo Cisneros y Victoria Villareal son de Chía, un pueblo que está cerca de Bogotá. Hoy están en una agencia de viajes de la ciudad capital. Planean casarse el mes que viene y quieren decidir dónde van a pasar la luna de miel. La mamá de Gustavo, que es argentina, espera que vayan a Buenos Aires. Los padrinos de Victoria les sugieren que viajen a Costa Rica porque a ellos les encanta ese país.

Victoria	Mi amor, si tú quieres ir a Buenos Aires, no hay problema. A mí me encantan las ciudades grandes.
Gustavo	Bueno, la verdad es que yo quiero conocer los bosques de Costa Rica. Estos folletos describen unos paquetes buenísimos, que incluyen los pasajes, el hospedaje y algunas excursiones.
Victoria	Sí, pero éstos que yo tengo también describen viajes muy interesantes que incluyen Río de Janeiro... ¡Ah! El agente nos está llamando. Ojalá que podamos reservar los pasajes hoy.

Con el agente de viajes

Gustavo	Vamos a necesitar que usted nos aconseje sobre cuál es el lugar ideal para pasar la luna de miel. Espero que nos dé buenas ideas.
Agente	Yo les recomiendo que hagan un crucero por el Mediterráneo. ¡Viajar en barco es muy romántico! Y después, una semana en Italia.
Gustavo	Bueno... temo que eso sea un poco caro. Mi prometida y yo preferimos quedarnos en este continente.
Agente	¡Tengo una idea brillante! Les sugiero que visiten Canadá. Pueden ir en avión hasta Toronto y después viajar en tren hasta Vancouver...
Victoria	Sí, todo eso es muy bonito, ¡pero no tenemos tanto dinero! Queremos dos pasajes de ida y vuelta a San José, en clase turista. ¿Tienen vuelos directos? Preferimos no hacer escala en ninguna parte...
Agente	Sí, señorita. ¡Excelente idea!
Gustavo	¿Estás segura, mi amor?
Victoria	Sí, estoy segura, pero el año próximo... ¡me llevas a Buenos Aires!

¿Lo sabía Ud.?

En los países hispanos las parejas (*couples*) generalmente están comprometidas durante años, porque no se casan hasta terminar los estudios o tener un buen puesto (*job*). Muchos esperan hasta tener un apartamento amueblado o una casa.

◆ Por lo general, ¿las parejas de este país están comprometidas por mucho tiempo antes de casarse?

Victoria

Gustavo

el agente

¿Quién lo dice? Identify the person who said the following in the dialogue.

1. Bueno... temo que eso sea un poco caro. _____
2. Les sugiero que visiten Canadá. _____
3. Mi prometida y yo preferimos quedarnos en este continente. _____
4. A mí me encantan las ciudades grandes. _____
5. Pueden ir en avión hasta Toronto. _____
6. Estos folletos describen unos paquetes buenísimos. _____
7. Queremos dos pasajes de ida y vuelta a San José, en clase turista. _____
8. Yo les recomiendo que hagan un crucero por el Mediterráneo. _____
9. Mi amor, si tú quieres ir a Buenos Aires, no hay problema. _____

Hablemos. With a partner, take turns asking and answering the following questions. Base your answers on the dialogue and on your own circumstances.

En el diálogo	¿Y tú?
1. ¿Cuándo planean casarse Victoria y Gustavo?	¿Algún amigo tuyo planea casarse pronto? ¿Quién? ¿Cuándo?
2. ¿Qué están tratando de decidir Gustavo y Victoria?	¿Cuál crees tú que es un buen lugar para pasar la luna de miel?
3. ¿Qué les sugieren los padrinos de Victoria?	¿Qué país (lugar) te encanta a ti?
4. ¿Qué incluyen los paquetes que describen los folletos?	Antes de viajar, ¿tú tratas de conseguir información sobre los lugares adonde piensas viajar? ¿Dónde consigues esa información?
5. ¿Qué espera Victoria que puedan hacer hoy?	¿Con cuánta anticipación (*How far in advance*) reservas tú los pasajes?
6. ¿Qué les recomienda el agente que hagan?	¿Tú prefieres hacer un crucero por el Mediterráneo o un viaje en tren por Canadá?
7. ¿Qué decide hacer Victoria?	¿Tú viajas en clase turista o en primera clase? ¿Por qué?
8. ¿Por qué prefieren Victoria y Gustavo un vuelo directo?	¿Tú prefieres un vuelo directo o un vuelo con escala? ¿Por qué?

Vocabulario

Improve Your Grade
Audio Flashcards

Cognados

la agencia agency	**la excursión** excursion
argentino(-a) Argentinian	**ideal** ideal
el continente continent	**interesante** interesting
directo(-a) direct	**romántico(-a)** romantic
excelente excellent	

Nombres

la agencia de viajes travel agency	**el padrino**[1] godfather
el agente de viajes travel agent	**el paquete** package
el avión plane	**el pasaje, el billete** ticket
el barco ship	— **de ida** one-way ticket
el bosque, la selva forest, jungle	— **de ida y vuelta** round-trip ticket
la clase turista tourist class	**el (la) prometido(-a)** fiancé(e)
el folleto brochure	**el pueblo** town
el hospedaje lodging	**el tren** train
la luna moon	**el vuelo** flight
— **de miel** honeymoon	

Verbos

aconsejar to advise	**planear** to plan
casarse to get married	**quedarse** to stay
describir to describe	**sugerir (e:ie)** to suggest
esperar to hope	**temer** to fear, to be afraid

Adjetivos

brillante brilliant
buenísimo(-a) extremely good
tanto(-a) so much

 **¿Lo sabía Ud.?**

Cuando se bautiza a un hijo o a una hija, los padres invitan a dos amigos o parientes para ser los padrinos de sus hijos. Los padrinos se convierten en **compadre** y **comadre** de los padres del niño (de la niña); el niño o niña que se bautiza es ahora el **ahijado** o **ahijada** de sus padrinos. La relación entre los compadres, los ahijados y los padrinos es generalmente muy estrecha. Los padrinos son considerados como parte de la familia.

◆ **Cuando se bautiza a un niño en este país, ¿siempre tiene padrinos?**

---

[1]**la madrina** = *godmother*

Otras palabras y expresiones

en ninguna parte, en ningún lado nowhere
hacer escala to make a stopover
hacer un crucero to take a cruise
el mes que viene the coming month, next month

ojalá I hope (God grant)
sobre about

Vocabulario adicional

En el aeropuerto / En el avión

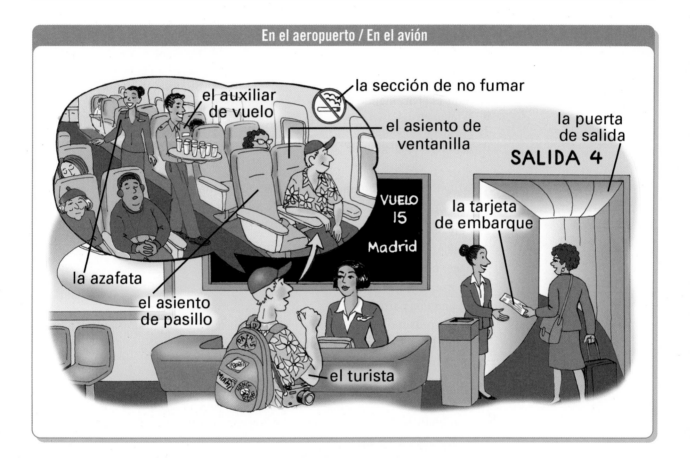

De viaje

la aerolínea airline
¡Buen viaje! Have a nice trip!
la entrada entrance
facturar el equipaje to check luggage
la fila row
hospedarse to stay, to lodge (*e.g., at a hotel*)

pagar exceso de equipaje to pay excess baggage
la primera clase first class
la salida exit, departure
tener... de retraso (atraso) to be . . . behind schedule
el (la) viajero (-a) traveler

Note: **La azafata** is feminine only.

ACE the Test

Práctica

A. Select the word or phrase that does not belong in each group.

1. aconsejar / sugerir / temer
2. ventanilla / tarjeta / pasillo
3. avión / barco / folleto
4. amiga / novia / prometida
5. hospedaje / hotel / tren
6. viajar / quedarse / hacer un crucero
7. bosque / casarse / luna de miel
8. brillante / hacer escala / vuelo directo

B. Match the questions in column A with the answers in column B.

A

1. ¿Sabes que hoy salgo para Caracas? ____
2. ¿Te sientas en la sección de fumar? ____
3. ¿Llegó el avión? ____
4. ¿Cuándo llega Marité? ____
5. ¿Luis es el prometido de Eva? ____
6. ¿Viajan en avión? ____
7. ¿Te gusta ese hotel? ____
8. ¿Es una ciudad grande? ____

B

a. No, van a hacer un crucero.
b. No, tiene una hora de retraso.
c. No, es un pueblo pequeño.
d. Sí, se casan en junio.
e. Sí. ¡Es buenísimo!
f. Sí. ¡Buen viaje!
g. El mes que viene.
h. No. Yo no fumo.

C. Write the words or phrases that correspond to the following.

1. Asia, por ejemplo _____
2. muy bueno _____
3. pasaje _____
4. hacer una descripción _____
5. no irse _____
6. en ninguna parte _____
7. el mes próximo _____
8. lo que le decimos a una persona que va a viajar _____
9. auxiliar de vuelo _____
10. persona que viaja _____

D. Complete the following sentences, using vocabulary from this lesson.

1. Trabaja en una agencia de _____.
2. Sandra es _____; es de Buenos Aires.
3. ¿Uds. viajan en primera clase o en clase _____ ?
4. Quiero un billete de ida y _____ en la sección de no _____, en la _____ "F".
5. Tiene que darle la tarjeta de _____ a la auxiliar de _____.
6. ¿En qué hotel van a _____ Uds.?
7. ¿Cuál es la _____ de salida?
8. ¿Vas a México? ¡Buen _____!
9. El avión tiene quince minutos de _____. Va a llegar tarde.
10. Ésta no es la salida; es la _____.

A. ¡Buen viaje! With a partner, play the roles of two travelers planning every step of a trip, from going to the travel agency and deciding where they will travel, to buying the tickets and then getting to the airport and boarding the plane. Give details.

B. En el avión With a partner, play the roles of a difficult traveler and a very patient flight attendant.

Pronunciación

Pronunciation in context

In this lesson, there are some new words or phrases that may be challenging to pronounce. For further pronunciation practice of Spanish sounds, listen to your instructor and repeat the following sentences.

1. Gustavo **Cisneros** y Victoria **Villarreal** están en una **agencia** de viajes.

2. Quieren **decidir** dónde van a pasar la luna de miel.

3. Los padrinos les **sugieren** que viajen a Costa Rica.

4. Los **paquetes incluyen** los pasajes y el **hospedaje**.

5. **Ojalá** que podamos **reservar** los pasajes hoy.

6. Les **recomiendo** que hagan un **crucero** por el **Mediterráneo**.

7. ¡Tengo una **idea** brillante!

8. **Preferimos** no hacer escala en **ninguna** parte.

Un dicho

Antes de casarte, abre bien los dos ojos. Después de casarte... ¡cierra uno!

Before getting married, keep both eyes open wide. After marrying... close one!

Aspectos culturales

En imágenes (*De viaje: destinos, transportes, agentes de aeropuertos*)

▲ Facturando (*Checking in*) equipaje en el Aeropuerto Internacional de las Américas, República Dominicana

▲ El *AVE* (Tren de Alta Velocidad) de Madrid a Sevilla, España

Ubíquese... y búsquelo

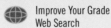

Improve Your Grade
Web Search

After speaking with the travel agent, Gustavo and Victoria wish to do some local tourism in Bogotá. They go to La Candelaria, the old part of the city. There are historic landmarks, government buildings, and quaint streets to discover, and places to eat and to shop. Go to **www.cengage.com/highered** to find out the places in La Candelaria that you would like to explore. In the next class, team up with two classmates to discuss your findings.

▲ Xcaret, parque ecológico situado al sur de Playa del Carmen, en Quintana Roo, México

▲ Tren para ir de Cuzco (capital del imperio Inca a la llegada de los españoles) a Machu Picchu, Perú

▲ Una hermosa playa en el centro turístico de Mar del Plata, Argentina

Estructuras

1. The subjunctive mood (*El modo subjuntivo*)

A. Introduction to the subjunctive

Until now, you have been using verbs in the indicative mood. The indicative is used to express factual, definite events. By contrast, the subjunctive is used to reflect the speaker's feelings or attitudes toward events, or when the speaker views events as uncertain, unreal, or hypothetical.

◆ The Spanish subjunctive is most often used in subordinate or dependent clauses.

◆ The subjunctive is also used in English, although not as often as in Spanish. Consider the following sentence:

*I suggest that he **arrive** tomorrow.*

The expression that requires the use of the subjunctive is in the main clause, *I suggest*. The subjunctive appears in the subordinate clause, *that he **arrive** tomorrow*. The subjunctive is used because the action of arriving is not real; it is only what is *suggested* that he do.

B. Present subjunctive forms of regular verbs

◆ To form the present subjunctive, add the following endings to the stem of the first-person singular of the present indicative after dropping the **o.**

-ar verbs		*-er* verbs		*-ir* verbs	
habl	**-e**	com	**-a**	viv	**-a**
habl	**-es**	com	**-as**	viv	**-as**
habl	**-e**	com	**-a**	viv	**-a**
habl	**-emos**	com	**-amos**	viv	**-amos**
habl	**-éis**	com	**-áis**	viv	**-áis**
habl	**-en**	com	**-an**	viv	**-an**

◆ Note that the endings for **-er** and **-ir** verbs are identical.

◆ The following table shows how to form the first-person singular of the present subjunctive. The stem is the same for all persons.

Verb	First-person singular present indicative	Subjunctive stem	First-person singular present subjunctive
camin**ar**	camin**o**	camin-	**camine**
aprend**er**	aprend**o**	aprend-	**aprenda**
escrib**ir**	escrib**o**	escrib-	**escriba**
dec**ir**	dig**o**	dig-	**diga**
hac**er**	hag**o**	hag-	**haga**
tra**er**	traig**o**	traig-	**traiga**
sac**ar**	sac**o**	sac-	**saque**[1]
lleg**ar**	lleg**o**	lleg-	**llegue**[1]
empez**ar**	empiez**o**	empiez-	**empiece**[1]

---

[1]Remember that in verbs ending in **-gar, -car,** and **-zar, g** changes to **gu, c** changes to **qu,** and **z** changes to **c** before **e.**

Práctica

Give the present subjunctive of the following verbs.

1. *yo:* solicitar, recibir, traer, decir, caminar, comer, ver
2. *tú:* escribir, cobrar, decidir, regresar, venir, barrer, aparcar
3. *él:* aconsejar, hacer, mandar, salir, anotar, esperar
4. *nosotros:* cocinar, depositar, leer, poner, pagar
5. *ellos:* caminar, deber, robar, conocer, vender, salir, empezar

C. Subjunctive forms of stem-changing verbs

◆ Verbs that end in **-ar** and **-er** undergo the same stem changes in the present subjunctive as in the present indicative.

recomendar (e:ie) *to recommend*		recordar (o:ue) *to remember*	
recom**ie**nde	recomend**emos**	rec**ue**rde	record**emos**
recom**ie**ndes	recomend**éis**	rec**ue**rdes	record**éis**
recom**ie**nde	recom**ie**nden	rec**ue**rde	rec**ue**rden

entender (e:ie) *to understand*		devolver (o:ue) *to return (something)*	
ent**ie**nda	entend**amos**	dev**ue**lva	devolv**amos**
ent**ie**ndas	entend**áis**	dev**ue**lvas	devolv**áis**
ent**ie**nda	ent**ie**ndan	dev**ue**lva	dev**ue**lvan

◆ In stem-changing verbs that end in **-ir,** the unstressed **e** changes to **i** and the unstressed **o** changes to **u** in the first- and second-person plural (**nosotros** and **vosotros**) forms. The other persons follow the same pattern as the indicative.

mentir (e:ie) *to lie*		dormir (o:ue) *to sleep*	
m**ie**nta	m**i**nt**amos**	d**ue**rma	d**u**rm**amos**
m**ie**ntas	m**i**nt**áis**	d**ue**rmas	d**u**rm**áis**
m**ie**nta	m**ie**ntan	d**ue**rma	d**ue**rman

D. Verbs that are irregular in the subjunctive

◆ The following verbs are irregular in the subjunctive.

dar	estar	saber	ser	ir
dé	esté	sepa	sea	vaya
des	estés	sepas	seas	vayas
dé	esté	sepa	sea	vaya
demos	estemos	sepamos	seamos	vayamos
deis	estéis	sepáis	seáis	vayáis
den	estén	sepan	sean	vayan

¡Atención! The subjunctive of **hay** (impersonal form of **haber**) is **haya.**

Práctica

Give the present subjunctive of the following verbs.

1. *yo:* dormir, mentir, recomendar, dar, pensar, ir
2. *tú:* volver, estar, ser, preferir, recordar, morir, ver, pedir
3. *él:* cerrar, saber, perder, probar, dar, servir, seguir
4. *nosotros:* sentir, ir, dar, dormir, perder, cerrar, saber, ser
5. *ellos:* estar, ser, recordar, saber, encontrar, repetir

E. Uses of the subjunctive

There are four main concepts that call for the use of the subjunctive in Spanish.

◆ **Volition:** demands, wishes, advice, persuasion, and other attempts to impose will

Ella **quiere** que yo **viaje** hoy.	*She wants me to travel today.*
Te **aconsejo** que no **vayas** a esa agencia.	*I advise you not to go to that agency.*
Les **ruego** que no se **vayan.**	*I beg you not to leave.*

◆ **Emotion:** pity, joy, fear, surprise, hope, and so on

Espero que **lleguen** temprano.	*I hope they arrive early.*
Siento que no **puedas** ir a Costa Rica.	*I'm sorry you can't go to Costa Rica.*
Me **sorprende** que no **vayas** a Río de Janeiro.	*It surprises me that you're not going to Río de Janeiro.*

◆ **Doubt:** disbelief, denial, uncertainty, and negated facts

Dudo que se **casen** hoy.	*I doubt they'll get married today.*
No creo que ella sea **argentina.**	*I don't think she is Argentinian.*
No es verdad que Ana **esté** en Bogotá.	*It isn't true that Ana is in Bogotá.*

◆ **Unreality:** indefiniteness and nonexistence

¿Hay alguien que **tenga** los pasajes?	*Is there anyone who has the tickets?*
No hay nadie que **quiera** ir.	*There's nobody that wants to go.*

2. The subjunctive with verbs of volition (*El subjuntivo con verbos que indican voluntad o deseo*)

◆ All impositions of will, as well as indirect or implied commands, require the subjunctive in subordinate clauses. The subject in the main clause must be different from the subject in the subordinate clause.

◆ Note the sentence structure for this use of the subjunctive in Spanish.

Él **quiere**	que yo **estudie**
He wants	*me to study.*
main clause	subordinate clause

—¿Quiere que le **dé** el número de mi cuenta?	*"Do you want me to give you my account number?"*
—Sí, y también necesito que **firme** la tarjeta.	*"Yes, and I also need you to sign the card."*
—Roberto quiere que tú **vayas** a la fiesta.	*"Robert wants you to go to the party."*
—Sí, pero yo no quiero **ir.**	*"Yes, but I don't want to go."*

> **¡Atención!** Notice that the infinitive is used after a verb of volition if there is no change of subject: **Yo no quiero** *ir.*

◆ Some verbs of volition are:

aconsejar *to advise*
desear *to want*
mandar *to order*
necesitar *to need*
pedir (e:i) *to ask for, request*

querer (e:ie) *to want*
recomendar (e:ie) *to recommend*
rogar (o:ue) *to beg, plead*
sugerir (e:ie) *to suggest*

¿**Quieres** que te **mande** una tarjeta postal?

ACE the Test

Práctica

A. Tell the following people that you want them to do something other than what they'd like to do.

◆ **MODELO:** Yo quiero viajar el martes. (el sábado)
Yo te sugiero que viajes el sábado.

1. Nosotros queremos ir en avión. (en tren)
2. Ellos quieren hablar con su padrino. (madrina)
3. Ana quiere casarse en mayo. (junio)
4. Uds. quieren quedarse una semana. (5 días)
5. Yo quiero hacer un crucero por el Mediterráneo. (Caribe)
6. Nosotros queremos empezar a las ocho. (a las diez)
7. Yo quiero volver en tren. (en coche)
8. Ellos quieren almorzar en la cafetería. (en un restaurante)

LEARNING TIP

Try to personalize the uses of the subjunctive. Think of people you know. What do they want you to do (or not to do)? What do you want them to do (or not to do)? Think of as many examples as possible. Remember: Practice makes perfect!

B. Describe what the following people want each person to do, using the present subjunctive.

◆ **MODELO:**

¡Tienes que estudiar!
Sí, mamá.

Anita
La mamá de Anita quiere que ella estudie.

Tienes que llevarlos a la tintorería.
Sí, abuelita.

1. Tito

Tienes que depositar $300.
Sí, papá.

2. Julia

Tienes que ir al banco.
Sí, tía.

3. Beto

Tienen que estar en la clase a la una.
Sí, profesor.

4. Los estudiantes

Tienes que acostarte temprano.
Sí, mamá.

5. Hugo

C. Your friends are always coming to you with their problems. Tell them what you suggest, recommend, or advise for each situation.

◆ **MODELO:** Mañana tengo un examen. ¿Qué me aconsejas que haga?
Te aconsejo que estudies mucho.

1. Yo no puedo lavar mis pantalones en casa. ¿Adónde me sugieres que los lleve?
2. Un Porsche es muy caro para mí. ¿Qué coche me recomiendas que compre?
3. A mi hermano le regalaron mil dólares. ¿Qué le sugieres que haga con el dinero?
4. Mi prima no tiene suficiente dinero para ir al teatro. ¿Le aconsejas que se lo pida prestado a su papá o a su novio?
5. Alguien nos robó las maletas. ¿Adónde nos aconsejas que vayamos?
6. Tengo hambre. ¿Qué me recomiendas que coma?
7. Mi tía está enferma. ¿Qué le aconsejas que haga?
8. Los chicos tienen sed. ¿Qué les sugieres que tomen?
9. A mi hermana no le gusta cocinar. ¿Qué le sugieres que haga?
10. Mañana es el cumpleaños de mi padre. ¿Qué me sugieres que le regale?

D. With a classmate, look at the list of errands that must be done tomorrow. Then take turns saying what you want each other to do, and give different reasons why you can't do it.

◆ **MODELO:** Comprar la medicina para Ernesto.
—*Yo quiero que tú compres la medicina para Ernesto.*
—*Yo no puedo comprarla porque tengo que estudiar.*

1. Llevar los pantalones a la tintorería.
2. Pagar los pasajes.
3. Depositar el cheque en el banco.
4. Llevar la motocicleta al taller (*shop*).
5. Comprar las bebidas para la fiesta.
6. Llevar los discos compactos a casa de Ana.
7. Alquilar un video.
8. Comprar los billetes para la excursión.
9. Ir a la oficina de turismo para pedir la lista de hoteles.
10. Comprar el regalo para Eva.

Para conversar

A. Todos me dan órdenes. Discuss with a classmate things that important people in your life (parents, relatives, friends, professors, etc.) want you to do. List at least five things, and then compare your results with another group.

B. Problemas y soluciones Write two or three problems on a slip of paper. Then, form a small group with two or three classmates. Switch slips within the group and take turns offering solutions to each other's problems.

Un consejo

Si quieres que los demás te respeten... ¡empieza por respetar a los demás!

If you want others to respect you, start by respecting others.

3. The subjunctive with verbs of emotion (*El subjuntivo con verbos de emoción*)

◆ In Spanish, the subjunctive is always used in subordinate clauses when the verb in the main clause expresses any kind of emotion, such as fear, joy, pity, hope, pleasure, surprise, anger, regret, sorrow, likes and dislikes, and so forth.

—**Siento** que Julia no **venga** hoy.	*"I'm sorry that Julia is not coming today."*
—**Espero** que pueda **venir** mañana.	*"I hope she can come tomorrow."*
—Ramón no tiene dinero para comprar un coche.	*"Ramón doesn't have money to buy a car."*
—**Ojalá** que **consiga** un préstamo.	*"I hope that he obtains a loan."*

¡Atención!   **Ojalá** is always followed by the subjunctive.

◆ If there is no change of subject, the infinitive is used instead of the subjunctive.

Me alegro de estar aquí.
(**Yo** me alegro—**yo** estoy aquí.) ⎤ *I'm glad to be here.*

◆ Some verbs and expressions that express emotion are:

alegrarse (de) *to be glad*	**temer** *to fear*
esperar *to hope*	**es una lástima** *it's a pity*
sentir (e:ie) *to be sorry, to regret*	**ojalá** *I hope*
sorprender *to surprise*	

Ojalá que no **traiga** a su perro.

Práctica

ACE the Test

A. You are talking to a classmate. Say whether you are glad (**Me alegro de que...**) or sorry (**Siento que...**) about what is happening to your classmate and his or her family.

◆ **MODELO:** Estoy enferma.
  Siento que estés enferma.

1. Yo quiero salir, pero tengo que quedarme en casa.
2. Mi hermano y yo no nos sentimos bien.
3. Mi mamá estaba enferma, pero ahora está mejor.
4. Mi hijo es muy inteligente.
5. Mi hermana sabe cocinar muy bien.
6. No hay suficiente dinero en mi cuenta corriente.
7. Mis padres van a Barranquilla.
8. Mis profesores me dan muchos problemas.

B. Complete the following sentences to express how you feel, using the infinitive or the subjunctive as appropriate.

1. Yo me alegro mucho de...
2. Yo me alegro mucho de que mis amigos...
3. Yo temo no...
4. Yo temo que mi papá [mamá, hijo(-a)] no...
5. Yo siento...
6. Yo siento que el profesor (la profesora, los profesores)...
7. Yo espero...
8. Yo espero que mis padres (Ud.)...
9. Ojalá que...
10. Es una lástima que tú...

Para conversar

¿Qué tal nos va?   In groups of three, tell each other about things that are going on in your life, some positive and some negative. Everyone should react appropriately.

Así somos

Al escuchar...

> **Estrategia** **Recognizing linking or transition words** Different classes of words contribute to convey different aspects of meaning orally or in writing. For example, nouns, adjectives, and verbs provide the bulk of the "picture" that is being communicated in words. There are other classes of words, such as linking or transition words that hold the ideas together, indicate sequence, and establish transitions or relationships among the elements in the picture.
>
> ◆ Linking ideas: **y, también, además (de)**
> ◆ Comparing or contrasting: **pero, como** (*like*)
> ◆ Establishing sequence: **primero, luego, antes, después, finalmente**
> ◆ Expressing a result: **entonces** (*so then*), **por eso, como resultado, de modo que**

 Unas vacaciones Raúl and Rita are talking about where to go on vacation. Listen to their conversation and try to list at least six words you hear that serve to link ideas and/or create a transition.

Al conversar...

> **Estrategia** **Using courtesy expressions and common phrases** Interacting with others requires being able to express your reactions and emotions in a sensitive way. Learning courtesy phrases and other common expressions allows you to show your empathy and interest in what others have to say. Here are some common phrases for a variety of situations.

To wish a friend well	To react with certain emotions
¡Que te mejores! *Get better!*	**¡Cuánto me alegro!** *I'm so glad!*
¡Que te vaya bien! *May it all go well (for you)!*	**Temo que no.** *I'm afraid not.*
	Espero que sí (no). *I hope so (not).*
¡Que te diviertas! *Have fun!*	**¡Cuánto lo siento!** *I'm so sorry!*
¡Que pases un buen fin de semana! *Have a good weekend!*	**¡Qué lástima!** *What a pity (shame)!*
	¡Qué sorpresa! *What a surprise!*

 Situaciones With a partner, react to the following situations. Then, take turns telling your partner something about your own life and react to each other's news.

1. Una amiga te dice que sale de viaje a México mañana.
2. Un amigo perdió su vuelo para Cancún.
3. Un compañero quiere que le hagas un favor. No sabes si quieres hacerlo.
4. A tu hermana le ofrecieron el trabajo que quería para el verano.

 ¿Qué dice Ud.? What would you say in the following situations? What might the other person say? Act out the scenes with a partner. Take turns playing each role.

1. Two of your friends are getting married and ask your advice about the wedding date, the reception, and where to spend their honeymoon. Give suggestions and recommendations.

2. At a travel agency you ask whether the package they offer includes the tickets, lodging, and excursions.
3. You tell your traveling companion that you have to check your luggage.
4. You tell a friend what you hope will happen in your life this year.

 Para conocernos mejor   To do this activity, work with a partner whom you would like to get to know. Take turns asking and answering these questions.

1. Cuando tú viajas, ¿dónde compras los pasajes? ¿Prefieres pasar tus vacaciones en una selva, en una playa o en una ciudad grande?
2. Generalmente, ¿cuánto tiempo tienes de vacaciones? ¿Prefieres tener vacaciones en el verano o en el invierno? ¿Qué te gusta hacer? ¿Adónde planeas ir en tus próximas vacaciones?
3. ¿Tú prefieres hacer un crucero o pasar una semana en un balneario (*resort*)? ¿Qué es más romántico para una luna de miel?
4. Si alguien no sabe adónde ir de vacaciones, ¿adónde le sugieres que vaya? ¿Le aconsejas que compre los pasajes en una agencia de viajes o por el Internet? ¿Por qué?
5. Cuando tú viajas, ¿llevas mucho equipaje? ¿Llevas cámara fotográfica o cámara de video cuando viajas? ¿Les mandas tarjetas postales a tus amigos?

 Una encuesta   Interview your classmates to identify who fits the following descriptions. Include your instructor, but remember to use the **Ud.** form when addressing him/her. After finishing the survey, get together with two or three classmates and discuss the results.

Nombre

1. Planea viajar el mes que viene.
2. Teme no poder ir a ningún lado en sus vacaciones.
3. Nunca viaja en primera clase.
4. Prefiere un asiento de ventanilla.
5. Prefiere viajar en la sección de no fumar.
6. A veces tiene que pagar exceso de equipaje.
7. Viaja en clase turista.
8. No fue a ningún lado el verano pasado.

Para crear   Get together in groups of three and "create" the scenario for this photo. Who are the people? Give them names. Where does the woman on the left want to travel? Why is she traveling? What kind of ticket is she buying? What places of interest is she going to visit?

¡Vamos a leer!

Antes de leer

Estrategia **Predicting** Like activating background knowledge, predicting allows you to anticipate the content of a text and helps prepare you for reading. You can first look over a text—its format, headings, and any visuals—to get an idea of the topic and then predict what ideas or information you might encounter.

Viajar en avión Before reading the following suggestions about air travel, with a partner, read the title and the two lines that appear beside it. Then make four or five predictions about what tips you might encounter.

A leer

 Comprensión As you read the article, find the answers to the following questions.

1. Según el artículo, ¿qué vuelos se cancelan con más frecuencia? ¿Por qué?
2. ¿Por qué es mejor tomar un vuelo directo?
3. ¿Qué recomienda el artículo en relación con el equipaje?
4. ¿Qué cosas debemos tener en cuenta (*keep in mind*) al elegir un asiento?
5. ¿Qué debemos llevar en un bolso de mano? ¿Por qué es importante esto?
6. ¿Qué nos va a ayudar a pasar el tiempo mientras esperamos?
7. La última vez que Ud. viajó, ¿hizo Ud. algo de lo que se recomienda en el artículo? ¿Qué hizo?
8. ¿Qué recomendaciones cree Ud. que son las más importantes?

Si viaja en avión...

Si usted quiere viajar en avión, es mejor que aprenda a volar en forma confortable. Para eso, le sugerimos que...

1. ...trate de viajar durante las primeras horas del día, pues muchas veces las líneas aéreas cancelan los últimos° vuelos si no tiene suficientes pasajeros.

2. ...evite° las escalas en ruta porque frecuentemente causan retrasos.

3. ...compre maletas de buena calidad.

4. ...no escriba su dirección en la etiqueta de identificación del equipaje.

5. ...ponga una tarjeta de identificación dentro° de la maleta.

6. ...consiga información sobre otros vuelos de regreso con distintas° compañías en caso de que cancelen su vuelo.

7. ...llegue al aeropuerto por lo menos dos horas antes de su vuelo para reservar asiento.

8. ...pida un asiento en la primera fila si quiere tener sitio° para estirar° las piernas.°

9. ...no escoja° un asiento cerca de los lavabos porque el ir y venir de la gente no le va a permitir descansar.°

10. ...lleve en su bolso de mano lo que necesita para poder pasar un día o dos sin usar lo que tiene en sus maletas.

11. ...lleve algo para leer o para escuchar° para no aburrirse mientras espera.

12. ...sea tolerante con los demás° y tenga paciencia para aceptar algunos inconvenientes.

Y ahora... ¡le deseamos que tenga un buen viaje y que lo pase muy bien!

last

avoid

inside

different

room / stretch / le[gs]

choose

to rest

to listen to

others

¡Vamos a escribir!

Antes de escribir

Estrategia **Describing a trip** When telling about a trip—whether one you have taken or one you are planning to take—you need to use a variety of strategies.

- ◆ Brainstorm the basics: who, what, how, when, where.
- ◆ Select the activities that will be most interesting or unusual in order to make your experience memorable for your reader. These might even include a mishap or unexpected incident.
- ◆ Organize your ideas in a logical sequence. You can follow a chronological organization or one dictated by the types of activities or the sights you saw or plan to see.

Un viaje perfecto To create your ideal trip, in Spanish, brainstorm where you want to go, with whom you will be traveling, what type of accommodations and transportation you want, and what you want to see or do, etc.

A escribir sobre un viaje perfecto

Write your **primer borrador,** describing your trip. Incorporate the ideas from your brainstorming.

Después de escribir

Before writing the final version of your description, exchange your draft with a classmate and peer edit each other's work, using the following guidelines.

- ◆ use and formation of the subjunctive or indicative
- ◆ noun-adjective agreement
- ◆ memorable experience(s) that would interest a reader

Después de leer... desde su mundo

In groups of three, talk about your favorite mode of traveling. Include the advantages (**ventajas**) and disadvantages (**desventajas**) of traveling by plane, car, ship, train, or bus. Do travelers have more problems nowadays? Why?

Panorama hispánico

Colombia

- Colombia produce y exporta café, bananas, flores y petróleo. El café colombiano tiene fama mundial por su alta calidad. Para el país, también es importante la ganadería (*livestock*), especialmente en la región de los llanos orientales. Colombia es también famosa por sus esmeraldas, consideradas las mejores del mundo. El 90% de todas las esmeraldas provienen de este país.

- La música típica de Colombia es muy variada. Incluye la cumbia y el vallenato, que han alcanzado fama internacional. Además, son populares todos los ritmos latinos y aún los norteamericanos. Shakira y Carlos Vives son cantantes populares en los Estados Unidos: ella cultiva el rock, y él, el vallenato.

- El deporte más popular en todo el país es el fútbol (*soccer*), y Colombia es uno de los cuatro países latinoamericanos donde se celebran corridas de toros (*bullfights*).

- La cultura colombiana se destaca por el esmerado cultivo de la lengua española de sus más famosos escritores: Jorge Isaacs y Gabriel García Márquez, Premio Nobel de Literatura, entre otros. También ha ganado fama internacional el pintor y escultor Fernando Botero.

- La capital de Colombia es Bogotá, una ciudad rodeada (*surrounded*) de montañas, por lo que el transporte entre ella y el resto del país es principalmente por vía aérea. Bogotá es la base de Avianca, la primera y más antigua línea aérea de América. En Bogotá encontramos modernos rascacielos (*skyscrapers*) junto a (*next to*) iglesias y otros edificios muy antiguos, algunos del siglo XVI. En la ciudad hay muchos museos, pero el más famoso de ellos es el Museo del Oro, que tiene una de las mejores colecciones de la artesanía precolombina, incluidos unos 30.000 objetos de oro.

- Cerca de Bogotá están las famosas minas de sal de Zipaquirá, donde se encuentra la famosa Catedral de Sal, que tiene sus columnas, paredes y estatuas hechas (*made*) de sal.

Personalidades

▲ Gabriel García Márquez, escritor colombiano, ganó el Premio Nobel de Literatura en 1982 por su novela *Cien años de soledad*.

▲ Shakira, famosa cantante colombiana, durante un concierto en la pirámide de Giza, en El Cairo, Egipto

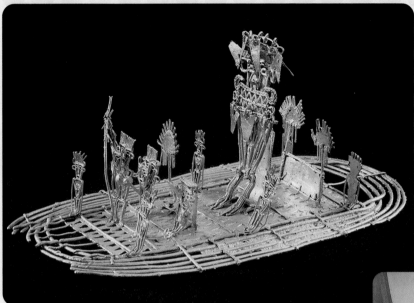

▲ Importante pieza de artesanía precolombina, Museo del Oro

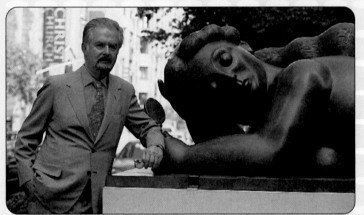

▲ Fernando Botero (1932–) junto a una de sus esculturas

▲ Otra obra de Botero: *La familia presidencial*

Nuestro panorama cultural

In groups of three, answer the following questions about your home state, region, or country.

1. ¿Cuál es el museo más famoso de su ciudad? ¿Del país?
2. ¿Le gusta el café? ¿Qué bebidas toman en su país en el desayuno? ¿En el almuerzo y en la cena?
3. ¿Su región tiene montañas? ¿Lagos? ¿Ríos? ¿Cuáles son las características físicas del estado donde Ud. vive?
4. En el lugar donde Ud. vive, ¿hay edificios antiguos o modernos? ¿O una mezcla de ambos (*both*)? ¿Es grande el pueblo donde vive?

For the next class: Go to the World Wide Web and find photos from your hometown, state, region, or country. Use the questions from **Nuestro panorama cultural** above as guidelines for choosing them. Be ready to present the photos to your classmates.

Lección 12

▲ Vista del tráfico en una avenida de Quito, Ecuador, a la hora de salida del trabajo

Objetivos

Comunicación

You will learn vocabulary related to automobiles, service stations, and road emergencies.

Pronunciación

Pronunciation in context

Estructuras

◆ The **Ud.** and **Uds.** commands
◆ The subjunctive to express doubt, disbelief, and denial
◆ Constructions with **se**

Cultura

◆ Use of vehicles in Latin America
◆ Use of the metric system

Panorama hispánico

◆ Perú
◆ Ecuador

Estrategias

Listening: Recognizing spatial markers
Speaking: Paraphrasing practice III
Reading: Anticipating content
Writing: Writing based on a visual

El automóvil

Perú y Ecuador

Perú

Perú es el tercer país más grande de Suramérica. Su territorio es un poco menor que el de Alaska, y su población es de unos 28 millones de habitantes. La moneda del país es el nuevo sol.

Ecuador

Ecuador debe su nombre a su posición geográfica. El país está situado justamente sobre la línea del ecuador. Su territorio, incluidas las islas Galápagos, es un poco menor que el de Nevada, y su población es de unos 13,5 millones de habitantes.

▲ Vista de Machu Picchu, ciudadela (*fortress-city*) y palacio de retiro (*retreat*) de los reyes incas

▲ Tortuga (*Turtle*) galápago, de las islas del mismo (*same*) nombre

▲ Monumento La Mitad del Mundo, situado en la línea del ecuador

319

Se venden coches usados

En el Distrito de Miraflores de Lima, Perú, vive la familia Ugarte, de Guayaquil, Ecuador. Liliana, una sobrina de la Sra. Ugarte, y su esposo Ramiro, están viviendo con ellos por un tiempo. Ramiro trabaja y va a asistir a la Universidad de San Marcos. Ahora están en el comedor, bebiendo café, leyendo el diario y hablando.

Ramiro	Creo que voy a necesitar un carro si tengo que ir al trabajo después de mi última clase...
Liliana	Bueno... aquí dice que se venden coches usados, pero dudo que podamos comprar uno con el dinero que tenemos.
Ramiro	A ver... (*Mira el anuncio.*) Coche compacto de dos puertas, de cambios mecánicos... mmm... Me gustan más los carros automáticos.

Don José Ugarte entra en el comedor, se sirve una taza de café y se sienta a hablar con Liliana y Ramiro.

Don José	Buenos días. ¿Están leyendo los avisos clasificados?
Ramiro	Sí. Dígame, don José, ¿usted cree que necesitamos comprar un carro?
Don José	Francamente, no creo que valga la pena. Escuchen lo que me pasó la semana pasada: El lunes por la mañana, mi auto no arrancó.
Liliana	Porque necesitaba un acumulador nuevo, ¿no?
Don José	No... Llamé una grúa, que llevó el coche al taller de mecánica. El arreglo me costó un ojo de la cara...
Liliana	Pero tía Marta dice que usted sabe arreglar carros.
Don José	No, no es verdad que yo sepa arreglar nada. Los coches modernos son muy complicados.
Ramiro	¿Cuántas veces al mes va a una gasolinera para comprar gasolina, don José?
Don José	Tres veces... cuatro... Eso es porque Marta me obliga a ir a pie a todas partes...
Ramiro	(*Se ríe.*) En serio... ¿su carro se descompone a menudo?
Don José	¡Sí! Funciona un día sí y otro no.
Liliana	¡Ay! Tengo que ir al correo y después a la peluquería. Necesito un corte de pelo. ¿A qué hora se cierra el correo? ¿A las seis?

Caminan hacia la puerta de calle.

Don José	Dudo que esté abierto hasta las seis, pero váyanse ahora. Si toman el ómnibus, a lo mejor pueden llegar. Sigan derecho por la calle Esperanza hasta llegar a la avenida José Larco. Doblen a la izquierda y ahí pueden tomar el ómnibus.
Liliana	Vamos, Ramiro. Tenemos que acostumbrarnos a usar colectivos...
Don José	(*Bromeando*) Si quieren, les vendo mi coche...
Ramiro	No, gracias. ¡Prefiero una bicicleta!

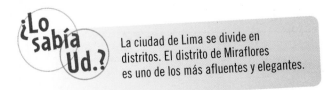

¿Lo sabía Ud.? La ciudad de Lima se divide en distritos. El distrito de Miraflores es uno de los más afluentes y elegantes.

Ramiro

Liliana

don José

ACE the Test

¿Quién lo dice?   Identify the person who said the following in the dialogue.

1. Me gustan más los carros automáticos. _____

2. Eso es porque Marta me obliga a ir a pie a todas partes. _____

3. Pero tía Marta dice que usted sabe arreglar carros. _____

4. No, gracias. ¡Prefiero una bicicleta! _____

5. ¿Usted cree que necesitamos comprar un carro? _____

6. Tenemos que acostumbrarnos a usar colectivos. _____

7. No, no es verdad que yo sepa arreglar nada. _____

8. ¡Ay! Tengo que ir al correo y después a la peluquería. _____

9. Llamé una grúa, que llevó el coche al taller de mecánica. _____

Hablemos.   With a partner, take turns asking and answering the following questions. Base your answers on the dialogue and on your own circumstances.

En el diálogo	¿Y tú?
1. ¿Adónde tiene que ir Ramiro después de su última clase?	¿Adónde vas tú después de esta clase?
2. ¿Liliana y Ramiro planean comprar un coche nuevo o usado?	¿Tú crees que es mejor comprar un coche nuevo o usado? ¿Por qué?
3. ¿Qué tipo de carro prefiere Ramiro?	¿Qué tipo de coche prefieres tú?
4. ¿Don José cree que vale la pena comprar un coche?	¿Tú crees que es mejor tener coche o usar colectivos?
5. ¿Por qué tuvo que llamar una grúa don José?	¿Alguna vez tuviste que llamar una grúa?
6. ¿Le costó a don José mucho dinero el arreglo del coche?	¿Tú sabes arreglar coches?
7. ¿Cuántas veces al mes compra gasolina don José?	¿Tú tienes que comprar gasolina? (¿Cuántas veces al mes?)
8. ¿Qué dice don José que su esposa lo obliga a hacer?	¿Cómo vienes tú a la universidad?
9. ¿Adónde tiene que ir Liliana? ¿Por qué?	¿Adónde tienes que ir tú hoy?
10. ¿Qué duda don José?	¿Hasta qué hora está abierto el correo en tu barrio?
11. ¿A qué tienen que acostumbrarse Liliana y Ramiro?	¿Tú usas el autobús a veces (*sometimes*)?
12. ¿Qué dice don José que puede venderles?	¿Tú tienes bicicleta? ¿Cuándo la usas?

Vocabulario

Cognados

automático(-a) automatic	**francamente** frankly
la avenida avenue	**la gasolina** gasoline
clasificado(-a) classified	**moderno(-a)** modern
compacto(-a) compact	**usado(-a)** used
complicado(-a) complicated	

Nombres

el acumulador, la batería battery	**la gasolinera, la estación de servicio** gas (service) station
el arreglo repair	
la bicicleta bicycle	**la grúa, el remolcador** tow truck
el colectivo bus	**la peluquería, el salón de belleza** beauty salon
el comedor dining room	
el correo, la oficina de correos post office	**la puerta de calle** front door
el corte de pelo haircut	**el taller de mecánica** car repair shop

Verbos

acostumbrarse (a) to get used (to)	**doblar** to turn
arrancar to start (*e.g., a motor*)	**dudar** to doubt
arreglar to repair	**entrar** to enter, to come in
bromear to kid, to joke	**escuchar** to listen (to)
caminar to walk	**funcionar** to work, to function
descomponerse to break down (*e.g., a motor*)	**obligar** to force, to make
	reírse[1] to laugh

Adjetivo

abierto(-a) open

¿Lo sabía Ud.?

En las grandes ciudades como Madrid, Bogotá, la Ciudad de México y Buenos Aires, hay muchísimos automóviles y autobuses, lo cual (*which*) está causando graves problemas de contaminación del aire. Sin embargo, en muchas zonas rurales de los países hispanos, particularmente en Hispanoamérica, hay muy pocos automóviles, ya que no hay carreteras, o las que existen están en muy malas condiciones.

◆ ¿En qué ciudades de este país hay mucha contaminación del aire?

---

[1]present indicative: **me río, te ríes, se ríe, nos reímos, os reís, se ríen**

a la izquierda² to the left	**costar un ojo de la cara** to cost an arm and a leg
a lo mejor may be	**de cambios mecánicos** standard shift
a menudo, frecuentemente often, frequently	**ir a pie, ir caminando** to go on foot, to walk
a pie on foot	**por un tiempo** for a while
a todas partes, a todos lados everywhere	**seguir derecho** to continue straight ahead
al mes, por mes a month, per month	**valer (merecer) la pena** to be worth it

Vocabulario adicional

En el taller de mecánica

Para hablar del coche

la bocina horn	**el neumático pinchado, la llanta pinchada** flat tire
la bolsa de aire air bag	**la pieza de repuesto** spare part
descompuesto(-a) out of order, not working	**el tanque** tank
el freno brake	**vacío(-a)** empty
lleno(-a) full	**la velocidad máxima** speed limit
la milla mile	

---

²**a la derecha** = *to the right*

Práctica

ACE the Test

A. Select the word or phrase that does not belong in each group.

1. corte de pelo / arreglo / taller de mecánica
2. ir a pie / ir en coche / ir caminando
3. acostumbrarse / descomponerse / no funcionar
4. neumático / bocina / llanta
5. ventanilla / capó / parabrisas
6. bicicleta / carro / puerta de calle
7. maletero / cajuela / volante
8. costar muy caro / costar poco / costar un ojo de la cara

B. Match the items in column A with the ones in column B.

A		B
1. ¿Cuánto te costó el arreglo? _____		**a.** No, vamos a pie.
2. ¿Tu coche no arranca? _____		**b.** Piezas de repuesto.
3. ¿Van en coche? _____		**c.** El mecánico.
4. ¿Quién va a arreglar el coche? _____		**d.** No, tiene que seguir derecho.
5. ¿El coche funciona? _____		**e.** No, está vacío.
6. ¿Qué necesitas? _____		**f.** Un ojo de la cara.
7. ¿El tanque está lleno? _____		**g.** No, está descompuesto.
8. ¿Tengo que doblar? _____		**h.** No, necesito un remolcador.

C. Write the words or phrases that correspond to the following.

1. lugar donde se compra gasolina _____
2. batería _____
3. lo necesitamos para cambiar una llanta _____
4. correo _____
5. grúa _____
6. peluquería _____
7. opuesto de "a la izquierda" _____
8. frecuentemente _____
9. a todas partes _____
10. tener dudas _____

D. Complete the following sentences, using vocabulary from this lesson.

1. La _____ máxima en la autopista es de 65 _____ por hora.
2. Ellos tienen que _____ a levantarse temprano ahora que van a trabajar.
3. Yo siempre tengo mi teléfono _____ conmigo.
4. Cuando mi coche se descompone, lo llevo al _____ de mecánica.
5. ¿Tengo que doblar a la _____ o a la izquierda? ¿O tengo que seguir _____?
6. No vale la _____ arreglar el coche. Es mejor comprar uno nuevo.
7. Vamos a vivir en esta casa por un _____.
8. ¿Es una calle o una _____?
9. Estoy leyendo los avisos _____.
10. Francamente, yo _____ que tú puedas _____ a tu hijo a trabajar.

Para conversar

A. **¿Vale la pena arreglarlo?** With a partner, play the roles of two family members who are trying to decide what has to be done with a car that is frequently broken and is very old. Decide also who can fix it, how much it's going to cost, etc.

B. **Tenemos mucho que hacer.** Someone wants you and your partner to do some chores tomorrow morning. Take turns telling this person you can't help him or her and say what you have to do and where you have to go tomorrow. Think of several excuses.

Pronunciación

Pronunciation in context

In this lesson, there are some new words or phrases that may be challenging to pronounce. For further pronunciation practice of Spanish sounds, listen to your instructor and repeat the following sentences.

1. La familia **Ugarte** es de **Guayaquil**.

2. Es un coche **compacto** de cambios **mecánicos**.

3. **Necesitaba** un **acumulador** nuevo.

4. La grúa llevó el coche al **taller** de **mecánica**.

5. No es **verdad** que yo sepa **arreglar** nada.

6. ¿Su coche se **descompone** a **menudo**?

7. Tengo que ir al **correo** y después a la **peluquería**.

8. Doblen a **la izquierda** y **ahí** pueden tomar el autobús.

Aspectos culturales

En imágenes (*El coche, las motocicletas... ¡y el tránsito!*[1])

▲ Congestión de tráfico, San José, Costa Rica

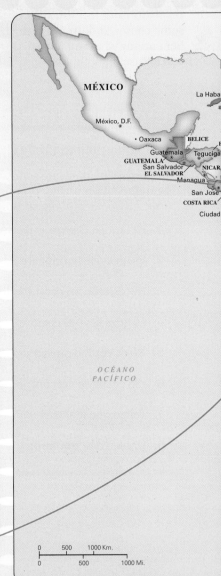

▲ Mujer en moto, Lima, Perú. En la ciudad, la motocicleta es otro medio de transporte personal motorizado.

Ubíquese... y búsquelo

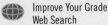 Improve Your Grade
Web Search

The Ugarte family lives in Miraflores, Lima. Go to **www.cengage.com/highered** to find out something about that section of town. In addition to working, Ramiro attends the University of San Marcos. Try to locate it within metropolitan Lima. In the next class, team up with two classmates to discuss your findings.

---

[1]**tránsito** = *traffic*

▲ Carretera en las montañas al sur de Ciales, en Puerto Rico.

▲ Embotellamiento de tráfico (*Traffic jam*), Buenos Aires, Argentina

Estructuras

1. The *Ud.* and *Uds.* commands (*Formas del imperativo para **Ud.** y **Uds.***)

The command forms for **Ud.** and **Uds.**[1] are identical to the corresponding present subjunctive forms.

A. Regular forms

		Endings of the Formal Commands			
		Ud.		**Uds.**	
-ar verbs	cantar	cant	**-e**	cant	**-en**
-er verbs	beber	beb	**-a**	beb	**-an**
-ir verbs	vivir	viv	**-a**	viv	**-an**

LEARNING TIP

Think of as many **-ar** verbs as you can and use them to give commands: ***Estudie** más. **Cierre** la puerta.* Repeat this activity using **-er** and **-ir** verbs.

—¿Cuándo volvemos?
—**Vuelvan** mañana y **traigan** los documentos.

"When do we return?"
"Come back tomorrow and bring the documents."

—¿Sigo derecho?
—No, no **siga** derecho. **Doble** a la izquierda.

"Do I keep going straight ahead?"
"No, don't keep going straight ahead. Turn left."

¡Atención! To give a negative **Ud./Uds.** command, place **no** in front of the verb: **No siga** derecho.

B. Irregular forms

◆ The command forms of the following verbs are irregular.

	dar	estar	ser	ir
Ud.	dé	esté	sea	vaya
Uds.	den	estén	sean	vayan

—¿Adónde tengo que ir?
—**Vaya** a la gasolinera.

"Where do I have to go?"
"Go to the gas station."

—¿A qué hora tenemos que estar aquí?
—**Estén** aquí a las ocho. ¡**Sean** puntuales!

"At what time do we have to be here?"
"Be here at eight. Be punctual!"

¿Lo sabía Ud.?

En la mayoría de los países hispanos, la gasolina y los automóviles son mucho más caros que en los Estados Unidos. Por esta razón es muy popular la motocicleta, especialmente entre la gente joven.

◆ ¿Qué medio de transporte prefiere usar la gente joven en la ciudad donde Ud. vive?

---

[1]**Tú** commands will be studied in **Lección 13.**

What commands would these people give?

1. Don José a sus sobrinos:
   a. leer los anuncios de coches
   b. ir al correo
   c. seguir derecho por la calle Lima
   d. doblar a la izquierda en la calle 8
   e. tomar el ómnibus allí
   f. no volver muy tarde
2. El cliente (*customer*) al mecánico:
   a. cambiar la llanta pinchada
   b. revisar el carburador
   c. pedir una pieza de repuesto
   d. poner un acumulador nuevo
   e. arreglar las luces
   f. instalar una bomba de agua nueva

Un dicho

Si toma, no maneje. Si maneja, no tome.

If you drink, don't drive. If you drive, don't drink.

Para conversar

¿Cómo vamos?   Claudia and Silvia, two girls from Quito, have decided to visit a few places of interest in Lima, but don't know how to get to them. Using the map, you and your partner are going to give them directions. (Note: In Peru, **jirón** = **calle.**)

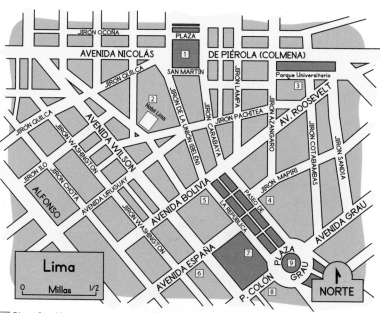

1 Plaza San Martín
2 Hotel Lima
3 Universidad de San Marcos
4 Palacio de Justicia
5 Centro Cívico
6 Embajada de los Estados Unidos
7 Museo de Arte Italiano
8 Museo Nacional de Arte
9 Plaza Grau

1. del Hotel Lima a la Plaza San Martín
2. de la Plaza San Martín a la Universidad de San Marcos
3. de la Universidad de San Marcos al Palacio de Justicia
4. del Palacio de Justicia al Centro Cívico
5. del Centro Cívico al Museo de Arte Italiano
6. del Museo de Arte Italiano a la Plaza Grau
7. de la Plaza Grau a la Embajada de los Estados Unidos
8. de la embajada al hotel

C. Position of object pronouns with direct commands

◆ In all direct *affirmative* commands, the object pronouns are placed *after* the verb and attached to it.

Ud. form		Uds. form	
Hága**lo.**	*Do it.*	Cómpren**lo.**	*Buy it.*
Díga**les.**	*Tell them.*	Díga**nle.**	*Tell him/her.*
Tráiga**nosla.**	*Bring it to us.*	Tráigan**selo.**	*Bring it to him/her.*
Quéde**se.**	*Stay.*	Quéden**se.**	*Stay.*

¡Atención! Note the use of the written accent, which follows the rules for accentuation. See Appendix A.

◆ In all *negative* commands, the pronouns are placed *in front of the verb.*

Ud. form		Uds. form	
No **lo** haga.	*Don't do it.*	No **lo** hagan.	*Don't do it.*
No **le** hable.	*Don't speak to him/her.*	No **le** hablen.	*Don't speak to him/her.*
No **se lo** dé.	*Don't give it to him/her.*	No **se lo** den.	*Don't give it to him/her.*

◆ Remember that when an indirect and a direct object pronoun are used together in the same sentence, the indirect object always precedes the direct object.

Vístanme despacio, porque tengo prisa.

Equivalent: When you rush, you make mistakes.

¡No **se** vayan! ¡Quéden**se** un mes más!

Grrr...

Práctica

ACE the Test

A. Using the direct commands, tell your younger brothers to do the following.

1. Levantarse a las siete, bañarse y vestirse.
2. Hacer unos sándwiches y ponerlos en el refrigerador.
3. Escribirle una carta a su madrina.
4. Mandarle un paquete a Teresa.
5. Llamar a la Dra. Peña, pero no llamarla antes de las tres.
6. Comprarle el regalo a mamá, pero no dárselo hoy.
7. Decirle a Marta que la fiesta es mañana, pero no decírselo a Raúl.
8. No acostarse muy tarde.

B. With a partner, take turns telling two people what to do about the items given.

 ◆ **MODELO:** los avisos clasificados
    Léanlos.

1. el tanque
2. la bicicleta
3. la grúa
4. el gato
5. el coche descompuesto
6. la bomba de agua
7. las llantas
8. el teléfono celular

C. You are having dinner at a fancy restaurant. Tell the waiter what you want or don't want him to do.

 ◆ **MODELO:** ¿Le traigo el menú?
    Sí, tráigamelo, por favor. (No, no me lo traiga.)

1. ¿Le traigo la lista de vinos?
2. ¿Le sirvo la ensalada primero?
3. ¿Le pongo pimienta a la ensalada?
4. ¿Abro la botella de vino ahora?
5. ¿Le traigo el postre?
6. ¿Le sirvo el café?
7. ¿Le traigo la cuenta ahora?

Para conversar

ACE the Test

Querida Zulema... You and your partner are going to be the "ghost" advice columnist behind Zulema. Decide what advice you are going to give each of the following people. Be sure to use commands.

Querida Zulema

1. Tengo 29 años y vivo con mis padres. Quiero comprarme un coche, pero mi padre dice que no vale la pena y no quiere prestarme el dinero. **¿Qué hago?**

    Incomprendida

2. Mi esposa y yo le compramos a nuestro vecino un coche usado que funciona un día sí y otro no. ¡Siempre está en el taller! Queremos que nos devuelva *(return)* el dinero, pero él se niega. **¿Qué podemos hacer?**

    Dos víctimas

3. Pienso dar una fiesta solamente para adultos. Invité a mis vecinos y ellos insisten en traer a sus dos niños. **¿Cómo les pido que no los traigan?**

    Tímida

4. Yo quiero ir a pasar una semana en Lima, donde vive mi novia, pero tengo un amigo que siempre insiste en ir conmigo a todas partes. Esta vez yo prefiero ir solo. **¿Cómo se lo digo para no ofenderlo?**

    Preocupado

2. The subjunctive to express doubt, disbelief, and denial (Uso del subjuntivo para expresar duda, incredulidad y negación)

A. Doubt

- In Spanish, the subjunctive is always used in a subordinate clause when the verb of the main clause expresses doubt or uncertainty.

—Vamos al correo.	*"Let's go to the post office."*
—**Dudo** que **esté** abierto a esta hora.	*"I doubt that it's open at this time."*
—Estoy seguro de que abren a las ocho.	*"I'm sure that they open at eight."*

> **¡Atención!** When *no doubt* is expressed and the speaker is certain of the reality (**Estoy seguro[-a], No dudo**), the indicative is used: **Estoy seguro** de que **abren** a las ocho.

B. Disbelief

- The verb **creer** is followed by the subjunctive in negative sentences, where it expresses disbelief.

—¿Uds. van a la peluquería hoy?	*"Are you going to the beauty parlor today?"*
—No, **no creo** que **tengamos** tiempo...	*"No, I don't think we'll have time ..."*
—Yo creo que pueden ir, si salen temprano.	*"I think you can go if you leave early."*

LEARNING TIP

Make a list of descriptive adjectives and think of them as being applied to you. Then indicate whether each statement is true or not. For example: *Es verdad* que yo soy muy alto. (No es verdad que yo sea muy alto.)

> **¡Atención!** **Creer** is followed by the indicative when it expresses belief or conviction: **Yo creo** que **pueden** ir.

C. Denial

- When the main clause expresses denial of what is said in the subordinate clause, the subjunctive is used.

—¡Tú siempre llegas tarde!	*"You always arrive late!"*
—**No es verdad** que siempre **llegue** tarde. No niego que a veces llego un poco tarde, pero a veces soy puntual.	*"It's not true that I always arrive late. I don't deny that sometimes I arrive a little late, but sometimes I'm punctual."*

¡**No es verdad** que **estés** ocupado!

> **¡Atención!** When the main clause does *not* deny, but rather confirms what is said in the subordinate clause, the indicative is used: **No niego** que a veces **llego** un poco tarde.

A. Say whether the following statements are true or not. If a statement is false, correct it.

1. Texas es más grande que Maine.
2. Hace más calor en Alaska que en Arizona.
3. Quito es la capital de Perú.
4. El 25 de diciembre celebramos la independencia de nuestro país.
5. Necesitamos un documento de identidad para comprar un coche.
6. Arreglan coches en un taller de mecánica.
7. Una bicicleta es más cara que un auto.
8. Los coches modernos tienen bolsas de aire.

B. You and a friend are spending the weekend in a very small town. Your friend wants to know about things to do, places to go, and so on. Answer, expressing belief or disbelief, doubt, or certainty.

1. ¿Tú crees que hay habitaciones libres en el hotel?
2. ¿Tú crees que un cuarto cuesta menos de cien dólares la noche?
3. ¿Tú crees que aceptan cheques de viajero en el hotel?
4. ¿Tú crees que hay un aeropuerto aquí?
5. ¿Podemos alquilar un coche?
6. Son las siete; ¿tú crees que el correo está abierto?
7. Vamos al centro. Quiero ir a una tienda elegante.
8. Tengo el pelo muy largo. Dicen que aquí hay peluquerías excelentes.
9. Quiero ir a cenar a un restaurante francés.
10. ¿Tú crees que vamos a volver aquí algún día?

C. Complete the following sentences logically, using the subjunctive or the indicative as appropriate.

1. Yo dudo que en mi cuenta de ahorros...
2. Estoy seguro(-a) de que el banco...
3. No creo que la oficina de correos...
4. Estoy seguro(-a) de que la estación del metro...
5. No es verdad que yo...
6. Yo no niego que mis padres...
7. Creo que un Cadillac...
8. No dudo que un buen mecánico...
9. Es verdad que nosotros...
10. No es cierto que mi coche...

¿Lo sabía Ud.?

En muchos países hispanos es necesario tener una cédula (*document*) de identidad como identificación y es necesario llevarla en todo momento.

◆ ¿Qué documento de identificación es el equivalente, en su país, a la cédula de identidad?

¡Habla con tu compañero! With a partner, take turns asking each other the following questions.

1. ¿Tú crees que un Honda cuesta mucho más que un Chevrolet?
2. ¿Es verdad que un Cadillac cuesta un ojo de la cara?
3. ¿Es verdad que los coches modernos son muy complicados?
4. ¿Tú crees que un coche automático gasta menos gasolina que un coche de cambios mecánicos?
5. ¿Crees que pronto los coches no van a necesitar gasolina o dudas que esto pueda pasar?
6. ¿Crees que las estaciones de servicio están abiertas a esta hora?
7. Si tu coche se descompone, ¿crees que puedes arreglarlo?
8. ¿Crees que tu mamá sabe cambiar una llanta?
9. ¿Es verdad que tú vienes a la universidad a pie?
10. ¿Es verdad que tú lees los anuncios clasificados todos los días?

3. Constructions with *se* (*Construcciones con se*)

◆ In Spanish the pronoun **se** + *the third-person singular or plural form of the verb* is used as an impersonal construction. It is equivalent to the English passive voice, in which the person doing the action is not specified. It is also equivalent to English constructions that use the impersonal subjects *one, they, people,* and *you* (indefinite). The impersonal construction is widely used in Spanish.

Se habla español en Lima.	*Spanish is spoken in Lima.* *They speak Spanish in Lima.*
—¿A qué hora **se abren** las peluquerías? —**Se abren** a las nueve de la mañana.	*"What time do the beauty salons open?"* *"They open at nine A.M."*
—**Se dice** que la gasolina es barata aquí. —Sí, pero los coches son muy caros.	*"It's said that gasoline is inexpensive here."* *"Yes, but cars are very expensive."*

◆ The impersonal **se** is often used in ads, instructions, or directions.

FOR SALE

NO SMOKING

EXIT TO THE RIGHT

Práctica

ACE the Test

A. In groups of three, draw signs with the following information on them.

1. No parking
2. Exit to the left
3. Spanish spoken here
4. No littering (*to litter:* **tirar basura**)
5. Apartments for rent
6. No swimming
7. Cars for sale

B. With a partner, take turns telling different people what is inappropriate, according to what they are doing.

◆ **MODELO:** A teenager is using a swear word.
   ¡Eso no se dice!

1. A child is eating spaghetti with his/her hands.
2. A little boy is trying to eat dirt.
3. Someone wears white after Labor Day[1]. (*to wear:* **usar**)
4. A child is touching the salad on your plate. (*to touch:* **tocar**)
5. Someone is about to drink mouthwash.

Un dicho

Se sufre, pero se aprende.

One suffers, but one learns.

Para conversar

El turista necesita saber...   With a partner, act out a scene between a tourist in Lima and a resident of the city who responds to the tourist's questions about the city. Use constructions with **se** in your conversation.

1. ... el horario (*schedule*) de los bancos, del correo y de las tiendas.
2. ... qué idiomas habla la gente.
3. ... qué y dónde comen.
4. ... si venden objetos de oro (*gold*) y de plata (*silver*).
5. ... dónde alquilan coches.

---

[1] *Labor Day* = **Día del Trabajo**

Así somos

Al escuchar...

Estrategia   **Recognizing spatial markers**   In **Lección 11** you reviewed transition words that hold together and establish relationships between ideas in a sentence. Prepositions such as **en, entre,** and **hacia** and phrases indicating location are another category of words that serve to mark the spatial relationship of elements in a sentence. Some common phrases that indicate location are:

al lado de next to, beside	**debajo de** underneath, below	**detrás de** behind
cerca de near	**encima de** on top of	**frente a** in front of

Un aviso comercial   You are going to hear a commercial from a car-towing business. Listen for and write the four words or phrases that indicate spatial relationships. There is one phrase that you have probably never heard. Can you identify it?

Al conversar...

Estrategia   **Paraphrasing practice III**   You have already read that paraphrasing, in speech or writing, can be a useful tool for showing that you understand what is said, as well as for reporting or summarizing what you hear.

¿Qué dijeron?   You will hear a series of sentences related to everyday situations. Listen and restate each in your own words. Then compare your responses with those of a classmate.

¿Qué dice Ud.?   What would you say in the following situations? What might the other person say? Act out the scenes with a partner. Take turns playing each role.

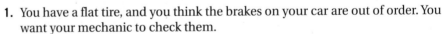

1. You have a flat tire, and you think the brakes on your car are out of order. You want your mechanic to check them.
2. Tell a tourist that he or she can buy gasoline at the service station located at the next corner (**esquina**).
3. You are a police officer, and you have stopped a motorist. The car doesn't have a license plate, and the lights aren't working. Ask to see the motorist's driver's license.
4. Your car won't start, and you're going to need a tow truck. Someone passes by as you fiddle with the ignition.
5. Your friend bought a car that was a lemon, and then spent three thousand dollars to have it fixed. You tell him it wasn't worth it.

Para conocernos mejor
To do this activity, work with a classmate whom you would like to get to know. Take turns asking and answering these questions.

1. ¿Prefieres los coches automáticos o los coches de cambios mecánicos? ¿Los coches grandes o los compactos? ¿Los de dos puertas o los de cuatro puertas? ¿Prefieres comprar un coche nuevo o un coche usado?

2. ¿Qué haces tú cuando tu coche no arranca? Si tienes una llanta pinchada, ¿sabes cambiarla? ¿Tú crees que es fácil hacerlo? ¿Siempre llevas un gato en el maletero de tu coche? ¿Es verdad que tú sabes arreglar coches? Si un coche se descompone a menudo, ¿crees que vale la pena arreglarlo?

3. Cuando vienes a la universidad, ¿vienes en coche, en autobús o a pie? Si haces un viaje largo, ¿prefieres ir en avión o en coche?

4. ¿Cuántas veces al mes vas al correo? La oficina de correos, ¿está cerca o lejos de tu casa? ¿Tú sabes a qué hora se abre el correo? ¿A qué hora se cierra?

5. ¿A qué peluquería vas cuando necesitas un corte de pelo? ¿Vas a menudo? ¿Cuánto pagas? ¿Es verdad que un corte de pelo te cuesta a veces un ojo de la cara?

Una encuesta
Interview your classmates to identify who fits the following descriptions. Include your instructor, but remember to use the **Ud.** form when addressing him/her. After finishing the survey, get together with two or three classmates and discuss the results.

	Nombre
1. Conduce desde los dieciséis años.	_____
2. Usa su teléfono celular cuando maneja.	_____
3. No le gusta conducir en la autopista.	_____
4. Vive a más de diez millas de la universidad.	_____
5. Tiene un coche que costó un ojo de la cara.	_____
6. Compra gasolina cuatro o cinco veces al mes.	_____
7. Lleva su coche al taller de mecánica a menudo.	_____
8. Va a todas partes en bicicleta.	_____

Para crear
Get together in groups of three and "create" the scenario for this photo. Who are the people? Give them names. What kind of car do they want? What kind of car is the salesman (**vendedor**) trying to sell them? Discuss prices, colors, and so on.

¡Vamos a leer!

Antes de leer

Estrategia **Anticipating content** Activating background knowledge, or thinking about what you know of a topic, and predicting are two techniques you have practiced in order to anticipate the content of a reading. Asking questions is also a useful means of approaching a text to prepare for its content. For example, before reading an interview, you might think of the questions that are likely to be asked. Or, before reading an article on hybrid cars, you can write the questions you hope will be answered.

 ¿Compro un coche? Before reading a brochure about buying a car, with a partner, write six to eight questions you would ask when buying a car. Then, when you read the brochure, compare your questions with those in the reading.

A leer

Comprensión As you read the text, find the answers to the following questions.

1. Antes de comprar un automóvil, ¿qué se debe determinar primero?
2. ¿Con cuántos comerciantes debe consultar antes de tomar una decisión?
3. ¿Qué ventajas (*advantages*) tiene hacer las preguntas que sugiere el artículo?
4. ¿De qué hay que asegurarse?
5. ¿Qué debe Ud. hacerle saber al vendedor?
6. ¿Qué debe hacer si el precio no le parece (*seem*) justo (*fair*)?

Cuando vaya a comprar un automóvil, ¡pregunte!

Ciertas preguntas le ahorrarán dinero.

Determine primero qué automóvil necesita y cuánto dinero puede invertir.

Consulte por lo menos con tres comerciantes de automóviles antes de decidir a cuál le comprará.

Pregunte:

• ¿Qué garantía tiene el automóvil?

• Si el automóvil se descompone, ¿quién va a componerlo?

• ¿El automóvil será aprobado en la inspección del Estado?

¡Pregunte el precio!

• ¿Qué precio de reventa° tendrá el automóvil cuando Ud. quiera venderlo?

• ¿Está el automóvil en perfectas condiciones?

• ¿Le dejarán probar° el automóvil antes de entregárselo?

• Si el automóvil necesita ser reparado, ¿quién pagará la reparación?

Recuerde hacer estas preguntas y ahorrará mucho dinero.

Asegúrese de que el vendedor no lo engañe.° Muchos vendedores tratarán de engañarlo para hacer la venta.

Hágale saber al vendedor que Ud. ya conoce los precios de otros competidores.

Recuerde que los vendedores a veces pueden cambiar el precio. No cierre el trato° si el precio que le ofrecen no le parece correcto o justo.

Recuerde, es su dinero.

resale

test drive

lo... *doesn't deceive you*

deal

Después de leer... desde su mundo

 Prepare a skit in which a partner and you enact a situation between a car dealer and a prospective buyer.

¡Vamos a escribir!

Estrategia **Writing based on a visual** Using a drawing, a cartoon, or other visual as the basis for writing provides a ready-made source of inspiration from which to build a story. Whether you use dialogue or prose to tell the story of the visual, think of an interesting ending or punch line.

- Brainstorm possible scenarios. Who are the people? What are the circumstances? What is happening and what happened leading up to this moment? Let your imagination go.
- If you are writing dialogue, think of what type of language best suits the characters. Do you need formal address? Will the tone be light or serious?, etc.
- Plan your ending. Will your dialogue or story have an end or will you leave the conclusion hanging?

Un diálogo dramático You will be writing a dialogue to accompany a drawing. First, look at the scene and brainstorm the possible situations you can create and imagine how each one came about. What are the circumstances?

A escribir un diálogo dramático

Write the **primer borrador** of your dialogue. Try to provide an interesting ending.

Después de escribir

 Before writing the final version, exchange your first draft with a classmate and peer edit each other's work using the following guidelines.

- question formation
- use and formation of the preterit, subjunctive, indicative
- formation of **Ud.** commands
- connection between the dialogue story and the drawing

Panorama hispánico

Perú

- La principal fuente de riqueza de Perú continúa siendo la industria pesquera, a pesar de los grandes daños sufridos a consecuencia de El Niño. También son importantes para la economía de Perú las industrias minera y textil, y la agricultura. Perú exporta petróleo, oro (*gold*), cobre (*copper*), zinc, café y algodón (*cotton*).

- Entre los animales típicos de la fauna de Perú están las llamas, alpacas y vicuñas. De su lana dependen muchas de las artesanías del país. La llama, además, se usa como animal de carga y para el transporte.

- Las principales atracciones turísticas del país son Cuzco, la antigua capital de los incas, y las impresionantes ruinas de Machu Picchu, situadas en las montañas cerca de Cuzco a una altura de 2.350 metros. Machu Picchu fue una fortaleza incaica que después de la conquista quedó perdida hasta 1911, cuando fue descubierta por el arqueólogo norteamericano Hiram Bingham.

- La capital de Perú, Lima, fue fundada en 1535 por el explorador español Francisco Pizarro, y es hoy el centro comercial e industrial del país. En su arquitectura se mezclan lo antiguo y lo moderno. En la ciudad se encuentran la Universidad de San Marcos (la más antigua de Suramérica), la iglesia de San Francisco (notable por la influencia árabe en su arquitectura), el Museo del Oro (con una gran cantidad de objetos precolombinos de oro y de plata) y el Museo Nacional de Antropología y Arqueología.

◄ Plaza San Martín, Lima. José de San Martín (1778–1850) es considerado el libertador de Argentina, Chile y Perú.

Historia y literatura peruanas

◄ Dibujo (*Drawing*) del quipu, de un manuscrito colonial. El quipu se utilizaba para contar y quizás (*perhaps*) era también método de escritura de los incas.

◄ Mario Vargas Llosa (1936–), escritor perteneciente (*belonging*) al llamado (*so-called*) "boom" literario latinoamericano [décadas de los sesenta (*1960s*) y setenta (*1970s*)], que incluye a escritores muy distintos (*different*) como Gabriel García Márquez, de Colombia; Carlos Fuentes, de México; Jorge Luis Borges, de Argentina, y Pablo Neruda, de Chile.

Ecuador

- La lengua oficial de Ecuador es el español, pero también se hablan algunas lenguas indígenas. Ecuador fue el primer país latinoamericano que le concedió el voto a la mujer, en el año 1929.

- La economía de Ecuador depende principalmente de la producción de petróleo, madera y pescado. Los bosques cubren casi la mitad del país, a pesar de la gran deforestación de los últimos años.

- Debido a la inestabilidad del sucre, su antigua moneda, en septiembre de 2000 el país adoptó el dólar de Estados Unidos como su moneda oficial.

- Quito, la capital de Ecuador, está situada en las laderas (*hillsides*) del volcán Pichincha, a más de 9.000 pies de altura sobre el nivel del mar. Por eso, aunque la ciudad está muy cerca de la línea del ecuador, su clima es templado (*mild*) y agradable. Quito es la capital más antigua de la América del Sur, y todavía mantiene su aspecto colonial, con sus calles estrechas (*narrow*) y sus viejas iglesias.

- A 22 millas de Quito, cerca de la villa de San Antonio, está el monumento La Mitad del Mundo, que marca el sitio exacto por donde pasa la línea del ecuador.

- La artesanía de Ecuador se caracteriza por los colores vivos y los diseños de sus tejidos y confecciones, que se venden en los mercados de artesanías. El más conocido de éstos es el de Otavalo.

- Las islas Galápagos, situadas frente a las costas de Ecuador, son una de las zonas ecológicas mejor conservadas del mundo. En ellas encontramos numerosas especies de animales y plantas, muchas de las cuales son exclusivas de allí. Las islas deben su nombre a sus tortugas gigantes, llamadas galápagos.

▲ Iglesia de San Francisco, Quito (terminada [*finished*] en 1534)

Otros lugares de Ecuador

▲ Otavalo, pueblo conocido (*known*) por su mercado y artesanías

▲ El Chimborazo, de una altitud (*height*) de 20.700 pies (*feet*) (ó 6.310 metros) es la montaña más alta de Ecuador.

Nuestro panorama cultural

In groups of three, answer the following questions about your home state, region, or country.

1. ¿Hay algún tipo de arquitectura típica en su ciudad?
2. ¿Cómo es el clima en el lugar donde Ud. vive? ¿Le gusta?
3. ¿Va de compras muy a menudo? ¿Dónde prefiere hacer sus compras?
4. ¿Se hablan muchos idiomas en su ciudad? ¿Qué idiomas se hablan?
5. ¿Hay volcanes en su país? ¿Hay islas? ¿Dónde están?

For the next class: Go to the World Wide Web and find photos from your hometown, state, region, or country. Use the questions from **Nuestro panorama cultural** above as guidelines for choosing them. Be ready to present the photos to your classmates.

Self-Test

Take this test. When you have finished, check your answers in the answer key provided in Appendix D. Then use a red pen to correct any mistakes you may have made. Are you ready?

Lección 10

A. The imperfect Complete the following exchanges, using the imperfect of the verbs in the list.

quejarse (1)	gustar (1)	ir (1)
vivir (3)	ser (4)	ver (1)

1. —¿Qué hora _____ cuando tú llegaste a casa?

   — _____ las dos y media.

2. —¿Dónde _____ tú cuando _____ chico?

   —Yo _____ en Lima, pero todos los años mi familia y yo _____ de vacaciones a Venezuela.

   —¿Tú _____ a tus abuelos frecuentemente?

   —No, porque ellos _____ en Chile.

3. —Cuando Rita _____ chica siempre se _____ de todo.

   —¿Por qué?

   —Porque a ella no le _____ nada.

B. The preterit contrasted with the imperfect Complete the following sentences, using the preterit or the imperfect of the verbs in parentheses.

1. Anoche Alberto me _____ (decir) que _____ (necesitar) alquilar un apartamento, pero que no _____ (poder) ser muy caro porque él no _____ (tener) mucho dinero.

2. Ayer mi hermana y yo _____ (comprar) dos bolsas de dormir para las vacaciones. Cuando nosotras _____ (ser) niñas siempre _____ (llevar) bolsas de dormir cuando _____ (ir) de vacaciones.

3. Cuando yo _____ (tener) diez años, mi familia y yo _____ (venir) a los Estados Unidos a vivir. Nosotros _____ (hablar) inglés y español.

4. —¿Cómo te _____ (ir) anoche en la fiesta de Silvia?

   —No muy bien. (Yo) _____ (tener) que irme a las diez porque no me _____ (sentir) bien.

5. Cuando Amalia _____ (ir) a la biblioteca, _____ (ver) un accidente en la calle Quinta. Dos personas _____ (morir).

C. Verbs that change meaning in the preterit
Answer the following questions, using the cues provided.

1. ¿Dónde conoció Beto a Marisa? (en la universidad)
2. ¿Marisa conocía a la hermana de Beto? (sí)
3. ¿Tú querías venir a clase hoy? (no)
4. ¿Uds. sabían que hoy había examen? (no)
5. ¿Cuándo lo supieron? (anoche)
6. David se quedó en su casa hoy. ¿No quiso venir? (no)

D. The relative pronouns *que* and *quien*
Rewrite the following, using **que, quien,** or **quienes.**

1. Ésta es la señora. La señora vino ayer.
2. Éstos son los niños. Yo te hablé de los niños.
3. Ésa es la profesora. Nosotros compramos los libros para la profesora.
4. Ésa es la chica. La chica trajo la licuadora.

E. Just words . . .
Complete the following sentences, using vocabulary from **Lección 10.**

1. No me gusta esta casa; me voy a _____ a otra.
2. El alquiler _____ el agua y la _____.
3. Necesitamos alquilar un apartamento _____ porque no tenemos muebles.
4. No vive cerca; vive muy _____.
5. Su cuarto no es _____. Es muy chico.
6. En este _____ no hay ningún apartamento _____. Todos están alquilados.
7. Necesito una mesa de _____ para la sala y una _____ de noche para el dormitorio.
8. La casa tiene aire acondicionado y _____.
9. Compré unas _____ para las ventanas y un espejo.
10. Saqué la ropa de la lavadora y la puse en la _____.

F. Culture
Answer the following questions, based on the **Panorama hispánico** section.

1. ¿Cuál es la capital de Venezuela?
2. ¿Qué significa el nombre Venezuela?
3. ¿Cuál es el principal producto de exportación del país?
4. ¿Cuál es la principal atracción turística de Venezuela?

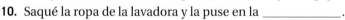

Lección 11

A. The subjunctive mood Give the present subjunctive of the following verbs, according to each subject.

1. estar: nosotros
2. caminar: tú
3. sacar: yo
4. sugerir: ella
5. dar: ellos
6. saber: usted
7. volver: tú
8. quejarse: yo
9. ser: ustedes
10. ir: usted
11. recoger: él
12. recibir: yo

B. The subjunctive with verbs of volition Complete the following exchanges, using the infinitive or the present subjunctive of the verbs in parentheses.

1. —¿Tú quieres _____ (ir) a Colombia?

   —Sí, pero mi esposa quiere que (nosotros) _____ (ir) a Chile.

2. —¿A qué hora me aconsejas que _____ (venir)?

   —Yo te sugiero que _____ (estar) aquí a las dos.

3. —¿Tienes que _____ (ir) a la agencia de viajes?

   —Sí, mi madre quiere que yo _____ (comprar) los pasajes hoy.

4. —Yo les recomiendo que _____ (hacer) un crucero por el Caribe.

   —No, nosotros preferimos _____ (visitar) Canadá.

5. —Yo te sugiero que _____ (viajar) en avión.

   —No, yo quiero _____ (viajar) en tren.

C. The subjunctive with verbs of emotion Rewrite the following sentences, according to the new beginnings.

1. Ellos van a hacer una excursión.
   Me alegro de que ellos...
2. Julio va a venir este verano.
   Espero que Julio...
3. ¿Tú sabes cuánto cuesta el vuelo?
   Me sorprende que tú...
4. Ada está enferma.
   Temo que Ada...
5. Nosotros no podemos ir en ese viaje.
   Es una lástima que nosotros...
6. Ellos van a Colombia.
   Ojalá que ellos...

D. Just words . . . Match the questions in column **A** with the answers in column **B**.

A		B
1. ¿Carmen es de Buenos Aires?	_____	**a.** En Canadá.
2. ¿Vas a viajar en avión?	_____	**b.** En un hotel.
3. ¿Van a hacer escala?	_____	**c.** En Delta.
4. ¿Qué me sugieres?	_____	**d.** Sí, tengo cinco maletas.
5. ¿En qué aerolínea viajan?	_____	**e.** Que hagas un crucero.
6. ¿Quieres un asiento de pasillo?	_____	**f.** No, en clase turista.
7. ¿Dónde te vas a hospedar?	_____	**g.** Sí, es argentina.
8. ¿Viajas en primera clase?	_____	**h.** No, el vuelo es directo.
9. ¿Tienes que pagar exceso de equipaje?	_____	**i.** No, de ventanilla.
10. ¿Dónde vas a pasar la luna de miel?	_____	**j.** No, en barco.

E. Culture Complete the following sentences, based on the **Panorama hispánico** section.

1. Colombia es el único país con _____ en el Pacífico y en el mar Caribe.

2. El _____ colombiano tiene fama mundial.

3. Las _____ de Colombia son las mejores del mundo.

4. _____ es una famosa cantante colombiana.

5. _____ es la línea aérea más antigua de Hispanoamérica.

A. The *Ud.* and *Uds.* commands Complete the following sentences, using the Spanish equivalent of the words in parentheses.

1. _____ en la oficina de correos a las ocho, señoras. (*Be*)
2. Necesito el acumulador. _____ esta tarde, señor. (*Bring it to me*)
3. _____ por aquí, señoritas. (*Go out*)
4. ¿La licencia para conducir? _____ hoy, señora. (*Give it to him*)
5. _____ al taller de mecánica, señores. (*Go*)
6. _____ aquí, señor López. (*Stay*)
7. Necesitamos las piezas de repuesto. _____ mañana, señor. (*Send them to us*)
8. ¿Los neumáticos? No _____ allí, señor. (*put them*)

B. The subjunctive to express doubt, disbelief, and denial Complete the following sentences, using the present subjunctive or the present indicative of the verbs in parentheses.

1. Yo no creo que ella _____ (ser) peruana.
2. Dudo que la gasolinera _____ (estar) abierta ahora.
3. No es verdad que Uds. _____ (necesitar) ir por la autopista.
4. Creo que Cuzco _____ (estar) a cien kilómetros de aquí.
5. Estoy seguro de que ellas _____ (encontrarse) en la peluquería.
6. Es verdad que yo _____ (necesitar) un corte de pelo.
7. No dudo que el arreglo _____ (costar) un ojo de la cara.
8. Yo no niego que no me _____ (gustar) conducir.

C. Constructions with *se* Form questions with the elements given, adding the necessary connectors. Follow the model.

◆ **MODELO:** a qué hora / abrir / las tiendas
¿A qué hora se abren las tiendas?

1. qué idiomas / hablar / Perú
2. a qué hora / cerrar / las gasolineras
3. a qué hora / abrir / la peluquería
4. dónde / vender / gasolina
5. por dónde / salir / de aquí

D. Just words . . . Choose the word or phrase in parentheses that best completes each sentence.

1. Voy a la (peluquería, estación de servicio) porque necesito un corte de pelo.
2. Voy a llamar una grúa porque mi coche no (bromea, arranca).
3. Prefiero los coches (de cambios mecánicos, abiertos).
4. Es muy caro. Me (costó, pagó) un ojo de la cara.
5. Tienes que (funcionar, doblar) a la izquierda.
6. No pude parar porque (los frenos, las bocinas) no funcionaban.
7. El número de la (chapa, luz) de mi coche es SB-456.
8. Ponga el gato en (la cajuela, el volante) del coche.
9. El tanque del auto está (vacío, descompuesto).
10. Yo le dije que no (valía, reía) la pena comprarlo.

E. Culture Complete the following sentences, based on the **Panorama hispánico** section.

1. La moneda de Perú es el _____.
2. Las principales atracciones turísticas de Perú son _____ y _____.
3. Quito es la capital más _____ de la América del Sur.
4. Una de las zonas ecológicas mejor conservadas del mundo son las _____.

Lección

13

▲ Elegante centro comercial en Santiago, Chile

Objetivos

Comunicación
You will learn vocabulary related to clothing and shopping.

Pronunciación
Pronunciation in context

Estructuras
◆ The familiar commands (**tú**)
◆ **¿Qué?** and **¿cuál?** used with **ser**
◆ The subjunctive to express indefiniteness and nonexistence

Cultura
◆ Department stores and specialty shops
◆ Manner of addressing people in stores
◆ Clothing sizes

Panorama hispánico
◆ Chile

Estrategias
Listening: Listening for the order of events
Speaking: Expressing ideas and opinions
Writing: Supporting opinions
Rincón literario: Reading poetry

En un centro comercial

Recursos

Chile

Chile es un país largo y estrecho. El país tiene dos veces el área de Montana y su población es de unos 16 millones de habitantes. De éstos, el 80% vive en las ciudades. En Santiago, la capital, vive casi la tercera parte de los habitantes del país.

▲ Vista panorámica de Santiago, Chile

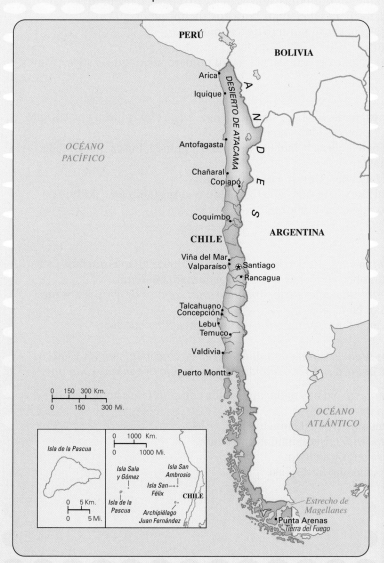

PERÚ

BOLIVIA

Arica

Iquique

DESIERTO DE ATACAMA

OCÉANO
PACÍFICO

A
N
D
E
S

Antofagasta

Chañaral
Copiapó

Coquimbo

ARGENTINA

CHILE

Viña del Mar
Valparaíso ⊛ Santiago
• Rancagua

Talcahuano
Concepción
Lebu
Temuco

Valdivia

Puerto Montt

0   150   300 Km.
0   150   300 Mi.

Isla de la Pascua

0   1000 Km.
0   1000 Mi.

Isla Sala
y Gómez   Isla San
               Ambrosio
         Isla San
         Félix   CHILE
0   5 Km.
        Isla de la
0   5 Mi. Pascua
         Archipiélago
         Juan Fernández

OCÉANO
ATLÁNTICO

Estrecho de
Magallanes

• Punta Arenas
Tierra del Fuego

▲ La cordillera del Paine en los Andes, Chile

▲ Modernos edificios bancarios y de comercio en Santiago, Chile

Ángela y Rebeca Montoya son dos hermanas que viven con sus padres en Santiago, Chile. Asisten a la misma universidad, trabajan en la misma oficina y muchas veces salen juntas. Hoy, por ejemplo, van de compras con Fernando, el novio de Ángela, y Gonzalo, el novio de Rebeca. Primero, los cuatro van a almorzar.

En un restaurante de comida rápida

Ángela	Fernando, ¿qué te parece si Rebeca y yo vamos a los Almacenes París y Gonzalo y tú van a la zapatería?
Fernando	Buena idea. Yo quiero cambiar un par de botas que me quedan chicas y Gonzalo necesita zapatos.
Gonzalo	También quiero ir a la librería, y después voy a tratar de encontrar algún disco compacto que le guste a mi hermanita.
Rebeca	Oye, ¿no dijiste que necesitabas calcetines y zapatos de tenis? Cómpralos hoy, que tienes la oportunidad.
Fernando	Sí, y yo necesito una camiseta... Dime, Ángela, ¿cuánto tiempo crees tú que van a tardar en hacer sus compras?
Ángela	Por lo menos dos horas, quizás tres... Yo tengo mi teléfono celular. Llámame para saber a qué hora nos encontramos.
Fernando	A ver... ¿cuál es tu número de teléfono?
Ángela	¡¿Qué?!
Rebeca	(*Se ríe.*) No te preocupes. Él sabe tu número mejor que el suyo. ¡Vamos!

En la tienda

Ángela	Ven acá, Rebeca. Mira esta falda. Hace juego con la blusa que compré ayer. Y este vestido... ¿no es precioso?
Rebeca	¡Pruébatelo! Pero la falda te va a quedar grande. Busca una en talla mediana.
Ángela	Aquí hay una. ¿Dónde está el probador?
Rebeca	Allí, al lado de la caja. Yo tengo algunas cosas también... ¡Es que no tengo nada que ponerme!

En la zapatería

Fernando	(*Al empleado*) ¿Tienen botas como éstas que sean más anchas? Éstas son un poco estrechas... Yo calzo el número cuarenta.
Gonzalo	(*Al empleado, que le está probando unos zapatos de tenis*) Éstos me quedan bien.
Empleado	Y le van a durar, porque son de una marca muy buena.

A las cuatro, todos se encuentran a la salida del centro comercial. Ángela y Rebeca están cargadas de paquetes, pero Fernando y Gonzalo sólo tienen uno cada uno.

Fernando	(*A su novia*) No hay nadie que pueda comprar tanto como ustedes dos en un par de horas.
Ángela	Hazme un favor... ¡Llama un taxi!
Gonzalo	(*Bromeando*) ¡Necesitamos un camión!
Rebeca	No exageres y ayúdame...
Fernando	¡Ahí viene uno libre! ¡Taxi!

Ángela

Fernando

Gonzalo

Rebeca

¿Quién lo dice? Identify the person who said the following in the dialogues.

1. También quiero ir a la librería.   _____
2. Llámame para saber a qué hora nos encontramos.   _____
3. ¡Pruébatelo! Pero la falda te va a quedar grande.   _____
4. Yo quiero cambiar un par de botas que me quedan chicas.   _____
5. Mira esta falda. Hace juego con la blusa que compré ayer. _____
6. No te preocupes. Él sabe tu número mejor que el suyo.   _____
7. ¡Necesitamos un camión!   _____
8. A ver... ¿cuál es tu número de teléfono?   _____

Hablemos. With a partner, take turns asking and answering the following questions. Base your answers on the dialogue and on your own circumstances.

En el diálogo	¿Y tú?
1. ¿Con quiénes van de compras Ángela y Rebeca?	¿Con quién vas de compras tú?
2. ¿Qué quiere cambiar Fernando?	¿Tú prefieres usar botas o zapatos?
3. ¿Qué quiere comprar Fernando para su hermanita?	¿Tienes algún disco compacto en español?
4. ¿Cuánto tiempo van a tardar las chicas en hacer sus compras?	Cuando tú vas de compras, ¿cuánto tiempo tardas generalmente?
5. ¿Qué quiere Ángela que haga Fernando?	¿Tú tienes teléfono celular?
6. ¿Con qué hace juego la falda?	¿Con qué hacen juego tus zapatos?
7. ¿Qué talla usa Ángela?	¿Qué talla usas tú?
8. ¿Qué problema tiene Rebeca?	¿Qué haces tú cuando no tienes nada que ponerte?
9. ¿Qué número calza Fernando?	¿Qué número calzas tú?
10. ¿Qué le dice Gonzalo de los tenis al empleado?	¿De qué marca son tus zapatos de tenis?
11. ¿Quiénes compraron más?	Generalmente, ¿quiénes compran más, los hombres o las mujeres?
12. ¿Qué dice Gonzalo que necesitan para llevar todos los paquetes?	¿Tú exageras a veces?

🎧 Vocabulario

Cognados

la blusa blouse	**la oportunidad** opportunity
las botas boots	**el par** pair
la oficina office	

Nombres

el almacén, la tienda por departamentos
  department store
la caja cash register
los calcetines socks
el camión truck
la camiseta T-shirt
el centro comercial shopping mall
el (la) empleado(-a) clerk
la falda skirt
la hermanita[1] little sister

la librería bookstore
la marca brand
el número size (*of shoes*)
el probador fitting room
la ropa clothing
la talla, la medida size (*in clothing*)
el vestido dress
los zapatos shoes
  — de tenis tennis shoes

Verbos

calzar to wear (*a certain size shoe*)	**parecer (yo parezco)** to seem
cambiar to exchange	**preocuparse** to worry
durar to last	**tardar** to take (*time to do something*)
exagerar to exaggerate	

Adjetivos

ancho(-a) wide	**libre** available, free
estrecho(-a), angosto(-a) narrow	**mediano(-a)** medium
cargado(-a) (de) loaded (with)	**precioso(-a)** pretty, beautiful
juntos(-as) together	**rápido(-a)** quick, fast

🎧

Aunque la mona se vista de seda, mona se queda.

Equivalent: You can't make a silk purse out of a sow's ear.

---

[1]**el hermanito** = *little brother*

al lado de   next to
cada   each
es que...   the fact is . . .
hacer juego (con), combinar (con)   to match
no tener nada que ponerse   to have nothing to wear
por ejemplo   for example
por lo menos   at least
¿Qué les parece si...?   What do you think about . . .?

quedarle chico(-a) (grande) a uno
   to be too small (big) on one
quizás   perhaps
vamos de compras   let's go
   shopping

Vocabulario adicional

Mirando vidrieras (*Window shopping*)

el vestido de noche
la blusa de lunares
las pantimedias
la corbata
el traje
estampado(-a)
el anillo
la ropa interior
las joyas
la camisa de rayas
el camisón
el collar
el pañuelo
la camisa de cuadros
los aretes
la billetera
los calcetines
los guantes
la pulsera
la ropa interior

Más sobre las tiendas

barato(-a)   inexpensive
el cuero   leather
el departamento de caballeros
   men's department
el departamento de damas
   women's department

devolver (o:ue) (algo)   to return
   (*something*)
la ganga   bargain
la rebaja, la liquidación   sale
rebajar   to mark down

Tipos de tela

el algodón   cotton
el hilo, el lino   linen
la lana   wool
el poliéster   polyester
el rayón   rayon
la seda   silk

Práctica

A. Select the word or phrase that does not belong in each group.

1. ancho / estrecho / libre
2. calcetines / marca / zapatos
3. número / vestido / falda
4. barato / ganga / algodón
5. camión / seda / rayón
6. collar / rebaja / aretes
7. tienda por departamentos / almacén / caja
8. liquidación / ropa / probador

B. Select the word or phrase that best completes each sentence.

1. Pedro trabaja en una (marca, librería, billetera).
2. Ana necesita comprar (ropa interior, la caja, la medida).
3. ¿Conduce un coche o un (camisón, camión, pañuelo)?
4. ¿Puedes ayudarme a llevar estos (paquetes, probadores, departamentos)?
5. ¿Cuánto tiempo van a (parecer, tardar, durar) en hacer las compras?
6. Necesitamos un taxi. ¡Ah! Ahí viene uno (cargado, mismo, libre).
7. Ana vive (al lado de, cada, es que) mi casa.
8. Estela se va a poner el (vestido de noche, calcetín, anillo) negro para ir a la fiesta.
9. ¿La blusa es estampada o (de cuadros, una ganga, de seda)?
10. Yo calzo el número seis y estos zapatos son el número ocho. Me quedan (bien, chicos, grandes).

C. Match the questions in column A with the answers in column B.

A	B
1. ¿Qué te vas a poner con la falda blanca? _____	a. El treinta y seis.
2. ¿Te vas a poner las botas? _____	b. Sí, porque no tengo nada que ponerme.
3. ¿Dónde trabaja Elena? _____	c. No, yo voy sola.
4. ¿Qué número calzas? _____	d. No, una pulsera.
5. ¿No te gusta el vestido? _____	e. En un centro comercial.
6. ¿Tú y Roberto van juntos? _____	f. No, de seda.
7. ¿Vas a comprar ropa? _____	g. La blusa roja.
8. ¿Cuánto dinero necesitas? _____	h. No, lo voy a cambiar.
9. ¿La camisa es de algodón? _____	i. Por lo menos cien dólares.
10. ¿Eva te compró aretes? _____	j. No, los zapatos negros.

D. Write the words or phrases that correspond to the following.

1. tienda donde venden libros _____
2. talla _____
3. opuesto de **ancho** _____
4. ni grande ni pequeño _____
5. hermoso _____
6. combinar _____
7. a lo mejor _____
8. hilo _____
9. rebaja _____
10. joya que se usa en el dedo _____

Para conversar

A. Buenas ideas Get together with a partner. Play the roles of two friends who are telling each other what clothes and footwear to buy for some members of their families. Include details like the material things are made of, etc. (**A tu...,** **cómprale... / regálale...**).

B. De compras With your partner, play the roles of a customer and a store clerk. Discuss sizes, colors, prices, etc. The customer should buy clothes and shoes.

C. Mirando vidrieras You and a partner are standing in front of the store window shown on page 353. Take turns saying what you are going to buy for yourselves and for a relative or friend.

Pronunciación

Pronunciation in context

In this lesson, there are some new words or phrases that may be challenging to pronounce. For further pronunciation practice of Spanish sounds, listen to your instructor and repeat the following sentences.

1. ¿Qué te **parece** si Rebeca y yo vamos a los **Almacenes** París?

2. Quiero **cambiar** un par de botas que me **quedan** chicas.

3. ¿No **dijiste** que necesitabas **calcetines?**

4. Yo tengo mi **teléfono celular.**

5. **Hace juego** con la blusa que compré ayer.

6. Yo **calzo** el **número** cuarenta.

7. Le van a **durar** porque son de una marca muy buena.

8. Todos se **encuentran** a la salida del centro **comercial.**

¿Lo sabía Ud.? Actualmente (*Nowadays*), los empleados de las tiendas a menudo tutean (*use the tú form of address*) a los clientes en España y en algunos países de Hispanoamérica.

Aspectos culturales

En imágenes (*De compras por el mundo hispano*)

▲ Mercado prehispánico, de México-Tenochtitlán, capital del imperio azteca
a la llegada (*upon arrival*) de los españoles

▲ El Rastro de Madrid, España, mercado al aire libre los domingos por la mañana

Ubíquese... y búsquelo

 Improve Your Grade
Web Search

Ángela, Rebeca, and their boyfriends went to Almacenes París, a well-known department store in Santiago, Chile. There are several other malls and shopping centers that they (or you) could visit and shop at in metropolitan Santiago. Go to **www.cengage.com/highered** to find out where these malls are. In the next class, team up with two classmates and report your findings. What stores can you find in the mall(s) that you searched? Are there special services that are convenient and activities other than shopping that you would like to do?

▲ Catedral de La Habana, Cuba, un edificio característico de la arquitectura colonial española

▲ Mercado al aire libre, Cuzco, Perú

▲ De compras en Buenos Aires, Argentina

OCÉANO ATLÁNTICO

REPÚBLICA DOMINICANA
PUERTO RICO
San Juan
Santo Domingo
HAITÍ
Mar Caribe

* Caracas
VENEZUELA

* Bogotá
COLOMBIA

PERÚ

BRASIL

* Lima

BOLIVIA
* La Paz
* Sucre

* Brasília

PARAGUAY
Asunción

CHILE

ARGENTINA

URUGUAY
Santiago *   * Buenos Aires   * Montevideo

OCÉANO ATLÁNTICO

Estructuras

1. The familiar commands (*tú*) (*Las formas imperativas de* *tú*)

Unlike other commands in Spanish, the familiar affirmative command does not use the subjunctive.

A. *Tú* commands[1]

◆ The affirmative command form for **tú** has exactly the same form as the third-person singular form of the present indicative.

Verb	Present Indicative	Familiar Command (*tú*)[1]
hablar	él habla	**habla** (tú)
comer	él come	**come** (tú)
abrir	él abre	**abre** (tú)
cerrar	él cierra	**cierra** (tú)
volver	él vuelve	**vuelve** (tú)

—Teresa, **trae** el vestido.
—**Espera** un momento. Estoy ocupada.

"Teresa, bring the dress."
"Wait a moment. I'm busy."

—Me voy.
—**Vuelve** temprano y **cierra** la puerta de calle.

"I'm leaving."
"Return early and close the front door."

◆ Spanish has eight irregular **tú** command forms.

decir	**di**	salir	**sal**
hacer	**haz**	ser	**sé**
ir	**ve**	tener	**ten**
poner	**pon**	venir	**ven**

—Carlitos, **ven** aquí; **hazme** un favor. **Ve** a la casa de Rita y **dile** que la fiesta es hoy.

"Carlitos, come here. Do me a favor. Go to Rita's house and tell her the party is today."

—¿Dónde pongo el anillo?
—**Ponlo** en el tocador.

"Where shall I put the ring?"
"Put it on the dresser."

Un dicho

Crea fama y acuéstate a dormir.

Equivalent: Once you build a reputation, it stays forever.

---

[1]The affirmative command form for **vosotros** is formed by changing the final **r** of the infinitive to **d:** hablar → **hablad,** comer → **comed,** vivir → **vivid.**

B. Negative forms

◆ The negative **tú**[1] commands use the corresponding forms of the present subjunctive.

No cantes victoria antes de tiempo.

Equivalent: Don't count your chickens before they're hatched.

hablar	no **hables** tú
vender	no **vendas** tú
decir	no **digas** tú

—¿Voy con Julia?	*"Shall I go with Julia?"*
—No, no **vayas** con ella.	*"No, don't go with her."*

—¿Pongo las faldas aquí?	*"Do I put the skirts here?"*
—No, no las **pongas** aquí.	*"No, don't put them here."*

¡Atención! Object and reflexive pronouns are positioned with familiar commands just as they are with the formal commands.

Pon**lo** aquí.	*Put it here.*
No **lo** pongas allí.	*Don't put it there.*

Vénde**nosla.**	*Sell it to us.*
No **nos la** vendas.	*Don't sell it to us.*

Práctica

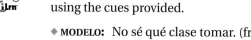

ACE the Test

A. Play the role of an older sibling giving instructions to a younger brother or sister, using the cues provided.

1. levantarse temprano
2. estudiar y no hablar por teléfono con sus amigos
3. hacer la tarea y no mirar televisión
4. escribirle una carta a la abuela
5. bañar al perro
6. ir al mercado y comprar frutas
7. recoger la ropa de la tintorería
8. llamar por teléfono a Carlos y decirle que traiga los discos compactos
9. lavar el mantel y las servilletas pero no lavar las sábanas
10. limpiar su cuarto
11. poner la mesa
12. barrer la cocina pero no pasarle la aspiradora a la alfombra

B. Juana always has a hard time deciding what to do. Give her some suggestions, using the cues provided.

◆ **MODELO:** No sé qué clase tomar. (francés)
Toma una clase de francés.

1. No sé adónde ir esta noche. (cine)
2. No sé con quién salir. (Mauricio)
3. No sé qué hacer mañana. (ir de compras)
4. No sé qué comprar. (un traje de baño)
5. No sé qué regalarle a papá. (una corbata)
6. No sé qué comprarle a mamá. (un vestido)
7. No sé qué hacer para comer. (sopa y pollo)
8. No sé qué decirle a Jorge. (que te lleve al centro comercial)
9. No sé en qué banco poner mi dinero. (en el Banco Nacional)
10. No sé qué hacer con las botas. (cambiarlas)

---

[1]The negative **vosotros** commands also use the present subjunctive: **no habléis.**

C. Say two commands, one affirmative and one negative, that the following people would be likely to give.

1. una madre a su hijo de quince años
2. un(-a) estudiante a su compañero(-a) de cuarto
3. una muchacha a su novio
4. un hombre a su esposa
5. un profesor a un estudiante

 D. Lucía and David are moving into their new apartment and some friends are helping them. Based on the illustration, what does Lucía tell each person to do? Use familiar commands.

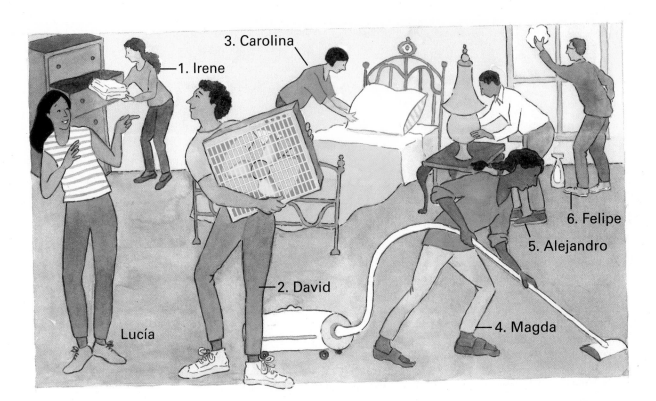

Para conversar

De compras With a partner, play the role of two friends who are at a shopping mall helping a third friend shop for clothes, shoes, jewelry, etc., and telling him/her what to do and what not to do.

¿Lo sabía Ud.?

Aunque ahora hay muchos grandes almacenes, todavía existen en los países hispanos muchas tiendas pequeñas especializadas en un solo producto. Por ejemplo, se vende perfume en la **perfumería**, joyas en la **joyería** y relojes en la **relojería**.

◆ En este país, ¿la mayoría de las tiendas especializadas están en centros comerciales o en edificios independientes?

2. ¿Qué? and ¿cuál? used with *ser* (*Qué* y *cuál* usados con el verbo *ser*)

◆ *What* translates as **¿qué?** when it is used as the subject of the verb and it asks for a definition.

—¿**Qué** es el pisco?　　　　　　*"What is pisco?"*
—Es una bebida chilena.　　　　　*"It's a Chilean drink."*

◆ *What* translates as **¿cuál?** when it is used as the subject of a verb and it asks for a choice. **Cuál** conveys the idea of selection from among several or many available objects, ideas, and so on.

—¿**Cuál** es su número de teléfono?　*"What is your phone number?"*
—792–4856.　　　　　　　　　　*"792–4856."*

—¿**Cuál** es tu tienda favorita?　　*"Which is your favorite store?"*
—La tienda París, pero yo tengo una　*"The Paris Store, but I have a dressmaker."*
modista.

¿Lo sabía Ud.?

En las ciudades hispanas hay excelentes tiendas donde se puede comprar ropa hecha (*ready-to-wear*), pero muchas personas prefieren utilizar los servicios de un sastre (*tailor*) o de una modista (*dressmaker*).

◆ En general, ¿dónde prefieren comprar la ropa los norteamericanos?

Práctica

ACE the Test

 Write the questions you would ask to get the following information. Use **qué** or **cuál**, as needed.

1. —_____
   —Mi apellido es Velázquez.

   —_____
   —Calle Rosales, número 420.

   —_____
   —835–2192.

2. —¿Quiere un pisco?

   —_____
   — Es una bebida chilena. ¿Quiere comer una cazuela de ave?

   —_____
   —Es un plato chileno que se prepara con pollo.

Para conversar

 ¡Habla con tu compañero! With a partner, take turns asking and answering the following questions.

1. ¿Cuál es la fecha de tu cumpleaños?
2. ¿Cuál es tu color favorito?
3. ¿Cuál es la estación del año que más te gusta?
4. ¿Cuál es tu programa de televisión favorito?
5. ¿Cuál es el título de tu libro favorito?
6. ¿Cuál es la ciudad más grande de tu estado?
7. ¿Cuál es la tienda que más te gusta?
8. ¿Cuál es tu día favorito?

3. The subjunctive to express indefiniteness and nonexistence
(*El subjuntivo para expresar lo indefinido y lo inexistente*)

◆ The subjunctive is always used when the subordinate clause refers to someone or something that is indefinite, unspecified, or nonexistent.

Quiero una cartera que **haga** juego con estos zapatos.	*I want a purse that matches these shoes.*
Busco un disco compacto que le **guste** a Eva.	*I'm looking for a CD that Eva will like.*
No hay ninguna blusa que **sea** de mi talla.	*There is no blouse that's my size.*

◆ If the subordinate clause refers to existing, definite, or specific persons or things, the indicative is used instead of the subjunctive.

Tengo una cartera que **hace** juego con estos zapatos.	*I have a purse that matches these shoes.*
Busco el disco que le **gusta** a Eva.	*I'm looking for the CD that Eva likes.*
Hay una blusa que **es** de mi talla.	*There is a blouse that's my size.*

Busco a alguien que sea... grande, fuerte, ágil... y que prefiera vivir cerca de la naturaleza.

La computadora te va a encontrar el novio perfecto.

  Práctica

ACE the Test

A. Indicate that there is nobody in your class to whom the circumstances below apply. Follow the model.

◆ MODELO: En mi clase...
... hay una chica que baila flamenco.
En mi clase no hay nadie que baile flamenco.

En mi clase...

1. ... hay dos chicas que son de Paraguay.
2. ... hay un muchacho que conduce un Mercedes Benz.
3. ... hay un muchacho que habla francés.
4. ... hay tres estudiantes que tienen solamente quince años.
5. ... hay una chica que sabe tocar el violín.
6. ... hay dos muchachos que dan fiestas todos los sábados.
7. ... hay una chica que va a Europa todos los veranos.
8. ... hay dos muchachas que vienen a la universidad los domingos.
9. ... hay tres estudiantes que siempre están ocupados.
10. ... hay una chica que sale de su casa a las cinco de la mañana.

B. With a partner, play the roles of a newcomer to Santiago and a helpful long-time resident who is able to offer solutions to all of the newcomer's needs. Follow the model.

◆ **MODELO:** una casa – tener piscina
—*Quiero (Necesito, Busco) una casa que tenga piscina.*
—*En mi barrio hay una casa que tiene piscina.*

1. una casa – tener tres dormitorios
2. una casa – estar cerca de la universidad
3. una casa – no costar un ojo de la cara
4. un coche – tener aire acondicionado
5. muebles – ser baratos
6. un empleo – pagar bien
7. alguien – ayudarme a mudarme
8. un restaurante – servir hamburguesas

C. A friend of yours is planning to move to your city or town and wants some information about it. Answer his or her questions as completely as possible.

1. ¿Hay alguna casa en un buen barrio que sea barata?
2. ¿Hay alguna casa que tenga piscina?
3. ¿Hay algún apartamento que esté cerca del centro (*downtown*)?
4. Yo necesito una secretaria. ¿Conoces a alguien que sepa hablar alemán y japonés?
5. A mí me gusta la comida chilena. ¿Hay algún restaurante que sirva comida chilena?
6. A mis padres les gusta la comida mexicana. ¿Hay algún restaurante que sirva comida mexicana?

D. Complete the following sentences logically, using the subjunctive or indicative as appropriate.

1. Necesito unos zapatos que...
2. En esta tienda no hay ningún pantalón que...
3. Aquí venden unas botas que...
4. Rosa tiene una falda que...
5. Busco una tienda que...
6. En esta clase no hay nadie que...
7. Mi novio(-a) necesita un empleo que...
8. ¿Hay alguien aquí que...?

En la mayoría de los países hispanos, la talla de la ropa se basa en el sistema métrico.

◆ **¿Se usa el sistema métrico en este país?**

┌ Para conversar ──────────────────

Díganme... You and your classmates want to know more about each other. Take turns asking whether there is anybody there who speaks German, vacations in a foreign country, needs new clothes, jewelry, etc.

Así somos

Al escuchar...

Estrategia **Listening for the order of events** You have already read about the words **primero, luego, después,** and **finalmente** to indicate sequence and have used them in writing a recipe. When listening to a narration of events, biographical information, or other text in which a series of events come into play, pay particular attention to sequencing words in order to understand the chronology of events.

La cronología You are going to hear a short narration about a shopping trip. Listen and number the activities according to the order in which they occurred. Then listen again and write the sequencing word or phrase used to indicate the order of each event. There may be a sequencing phrase that you have not heard before. Can you identify it?

_____ Fueron a la zapatería.   _____

_____ Fueron a la tienda La Francia.   _____

_____ Fueron a la joyería.   _____

_____ Almorzaron.   _____

Al conversar...

Estrategia **Expressing ideas and opinions** Here is a series of phrases and expressions that are useful for discussing ideas and introducing your opinions or point of view on a topic.

Introducing an opinion or idea:

(No) Me parece que...
(No) Creo que...   + subjunctive for doubt / indicative for certainty
(No) Pienso que...

Adding ideas or changing the direction of a conversation:

Sin embargo,... *However, . . .*
Por el contrario... *On the contrary . . .*
Por otro lado... *On the other hand . . .*

Reacting to ideas:

De acuerdo. *I'm in agreement.*
¡Ya lo creo! *I'll say!*
No exactamente. *Not exactly.*
No creo eso por lo siguiente: ... *I don't think so for the following reason: . . .*
No creo eso porque... *I don't think so because . . .*
No estoy de acuerdo contigo (en eso, en ese punto, con esa idea). *I disagree with you (on that, on that point, with that idea).*

A discutir In groups of three or four, discuss the following issue for five minutes. Use the phrases for expressing opinions and be ready to report at least two arguments in favor and two against to the class.

¿Vivimos en una sociedad demasiado consumista (*consumerist*)?

¿Qué dice Ud.? What would you say in the following situations? What might the other person say? Act out the scenes with a partner. Take turns playing each role.

1. You are shopping in a large department store. You need a pair of gloves, panty-hose, a wallet, and an evening gown. You also see a brown suit that you like, and you want to know how much it costs.
2. You are a clerk. A customer is admiring a pink nightgown. Ask her what size she wears, and tell her the fitting room is on the left next to the cash register.
3. A clerk at a shoe store wants to sell you a pair of boots. The ones he is showing you are too expensive and too tight on you.
4. Your friend is going to the store. Ask her to buy you a pair of socks and a T-shirt for your little sister.

 Para conocernos mejor To do this activity, work with a classmate whom you would like to get to know. Take turns asking and answering these questions.

1. ¿Prefieres comprar tu ropa en una boutique o en una tienda por departamentos? ¿Prefieres usar ropa de algodón, de seda o de rayón? ¿Gastas mucho dinero en ropa?
2. Para el cumpleaños de tu mejor amiga, ¿planeas regalarle aretes, un collar o una pulsera? ¿Recibiste muchos regalos en tu cumpleaños? ¿Cuál te gustó más? ¿Quién te lo regaló?
3. ¿Usas talla grande, pequeña o mediana? ¿Qué número calzas? ¿Tus zapatos son de cuero? Si te gustan mucho unos zapatos, pero te quedan anchos o estrechos, ¿los compras?
4. Si tienes la oportunidad de ir de compras o al cine, ¿adónde vas? ¿Prefieres ir de compras solo(-a) o con un(-a) amigo(-a)? ¿Vas de compras por lo menos una vez al mes? Generalmente, ¿la ropa te dura mucho tiempo?

 Una encuesta Interview your classmates to identify who fits the following descriptions. Include your instructor, but remember to use the **Ud.** form when addressing him/her. After finishing the survey, get together with two or three classmates and discuss the results.

Nombre

1. Va de compras cada semana. _____
2. Solamente va de compras cuando hay rebajas. _____
3. Siempre dice que no tiene nada que ponerse. _____
4. Se encuentra con sus amigos en el centro comercial. _____
5. Tiene mucho dinero en la cartera (en la billetera). _____
6. Usa zapatos de tenis todos los días. _____
7. A veces consigue buenas gangas. _____
8. A menudo devuelve las cosas que le regalan. _____

 Para crear Get together in groups of three or four and "create" the scenario for this photo. Who are these children? What is their relationship to each other? What are they wearing? Whose clothes are they wearing? Are they having fun? etc.

¡Vamos a escribir!

Estrategia **Supporting opinions** When expressing a point of view or opinion, you need to defend your position, especially if you are aiming to convince others of your view. Information that supports your opinion can take numerous forms: examples, data or statistics, personal experiences, statements by experts. Using supporting information can aid in maintaining a neutral or objective tone, which often is more convincing than an emotional defense.

Un mensaje electrónico You are going to write an e-mail to a Spanish-speaking friend about the importance of fighting consumerism. Make a list of ideas that you can include in your message.

◆ Try to find some data online (such as effects of consumerism, ways of reducing consumption, and efforts or groups that address conservation) that you can cite to support your views.

◆ Include a personal experience in support of your ideas.

A escribir el mensaje electrónico

Write the **primer borrador** of your e-mail message. Select the most convincing facts and ideas to support your opinions. Refer to the preceding **Al conversar...** section for useful phrases you can include to express your ideas.

Después de escribir

Before writing the final version of your e-mail, exchange your first draft with a classmate and peer edit each other's work using the following guidelines.

◆ use of the subjunctive and the indicative

◆ subject-verb agreement in main and subordinate clauses

◆ at least two types of information to support the opinion

Gabriela Mistral (*Chile: 1889–1957*)

Gabriela Mistral es una de las poetisas más famosas de Hispanoamérica. En su obra se refleja su amor por la humanidad, especialmente por los niños. Los temas principales de su poesía son la maternidad (*motherhood*), el dolor (*pain*) del amor y la justicia. En 1945 recibió el Premio Nobel de Literatura, siendo (*being*) la primera entre los escritores latinoamericanos en recibirlo.

Gabriela Mistral no sólo (*not only*) fue una gran escritora, sino que también (*but also*) ocupó cargos (*positions*) importantes como educadora y como diplomática en varios países de América y de Europa.

Antes de leer

> **Estrategia** **Reading poetry** When reading poetry you can use some of the same strategies you have used with other types of texts. Looking at the title and skimming the poem for the main idea or recurring phrases can provide clues to the subject of the poem. Remember that poetry often conveys strong feelings and frequently makes use of images and symbols. Here are a few elements to look for to aid your comprehension and appreciation of a poem.
>
> - **la rima** (*rhyme*) or **el verso libre** (*blank verse*)
> - **la repetición:** of sounds, words, or phrases
> - **los símbolos** or **las imágenes** (*images*)
> - **el ritmo** (*rhythm*)

Un poema With a partner, do the following.

1. Read the title of the poem. What do you think it means?
2. Skim the poem. Three verbs plus their direct object pronouns are highlighted in this poem.
   a. Which of the poet's major themes might this poem represent?
   b. Whom do you think the direct object pronouns refer to in relation to the speaker in the poem (the poetic **yo**)?
3. This poem has the structure of a lullaby (**canción de cuna**). Certain words repeat throughout the stanzas (**estrofas**). What is the same in all the stanzas?

A leer

Comprensión Read each stanza and answer the following questions.

1. Primera estrofa: ¿Desde dónde hasta dónde es la noche desamparo?
2. Segunda estrofa: ¿Cuándo hay en el cielo desamparo?
3. Tercera estrofa: ¿Cómo van los seres humanos (*human beings*) por el mundo?

Yo no tengo soledad

Es la noche desamparo°
de las sierras° hasta el mar.
Pero yo, la que **te mece,**°
¡yo no tengo soledad!°

Es el cielo desamparo
si la luna cae° al mar.
Pero yo, la que **te estrecha**°
¡yo no tengo soledad!

Es el mundo desamparo
y la carne° triste va.
Pero yo, la que **te oprime,**°
¡yo no tengo soledad!

abandonment
mountains
te... *rocks you*
loneliness

falls
te... *holds you*

flesh
te... *holds you tightly against*

Después de leer... reflexiones

Poetry should be recited aloud. Go to your in-text audio to listen to the poem. Try to learn it by heart.

Más sobre Gabriela Mistral

Gabriela Mistral es un *pseudónimo* o nombre de pluma (*pen name*). El verdadero nombre de la poetisa era Lucila Godoy. Nació en Vicuña, Chile. Dejó una amplia obra tanto en (*both in*) prosa como en (*and in*) verso, en la que se reflejan su bondad (*kindness*), su ternura (*tenderness*) y su amor por la humanidad. Además del libro *Ternura* (1924), donde muestra su inmenso amor por los niños y de donde es el siguiente poema, Gabriela Mistral escribió también otros libros de poemas famosos: *Desolación* (1922), *Tala* (1938) y *Lagar* (1954). Otros temas de su poesía son la soledad, la muerte y Dios.

Antes de leer

El lenguaje poético   In this poem a mother rocks a baby. With a partner, skim the poem on the next page and identify the words or phrases that repeat in each stanza. What impression or sensation do you think this might convey?

Comprensión As you read the poem, find the answers to the following questions.

1. ¿A quién está dedicado este poema?
2. Mientras el **yo** del poema mece a su niño, ¿qué mecen el mar y el viento?
3. ¿Qué mece Dios Padre?
4. ¿Qué siente la madre que mece a su niño?

Meciendo

El mar sus millares° de olas°
mece,° divino.
Oyendo a los mares amantes°
mezo a mi niño.

El viento errabundo° en la noche
mece los trigos.°
Oyendo a los mares amantes
mezo a mi niño.

Dios° Padre sus miles de mundos
mece sin ruido.°
Sintiendo su mano en la sombra°
mezo a mi niño.

thousands / waves
rocks
loving

wandering
wheat

God
sin... *silently*
shadow

Después de leer... reflexiones

In groups of three, have a conversation using the following questions as guidelines.

1. ¿Por qué sentimos ternura al mecer a un niño?
2. ¿Qué sensación recordamos al pensar en el mar y en las olas?
3. ¿Experimentamos alguna vez una noche de tranquilidad y de silencio, lejos de los ruidos de la ciudad?
4. El **yo** del poema "siente" una "mano en la sombra". ¿Sentimos algunas veces una presencia que no podemos explicar?
5. ¿En qué ocasiones nos sentimos parte de la naturaleza?

Panorama hispánico

Improve Your Grade
Web Search

Chile

- En Chile encontramos algunas de las montañas más altas de Suramérica, y por eso son muy populares los deportes de invierno. La cordillera de los Andes atraviesa (*goes through*) el país de norte a sur. Por sus bellos paisajes de montaña, algunos llaman a Chile "la Suiza de América del Sur".

- La educación es muy importante para los chilenos, y el 95% de ellos saben leer y escribir. Hasta 1970, la economía de Chile dependía principalmente de la exportación de cobre, pero hoy en día el país exporta, además de minerales, productos agrícolas, pescados y mariscos, y productos industriales. Por su gran producción y exportación de frutas, algunos llaman a Chile "la frutería del mundo". Sus vinos tienen fama internacional, y sus exportaciones de pescado y mariscos están entre las primeras del mundo.

- Chile forma parte del tratado de libre comercio MERCOSUR, y tiene también tratados similares con Canadá, la Unión Europea y los Estados Unidos.

- Santiago, la capital, es el centro industrial y cultural del país. Aunque Santiago es una ciudad moderna, aún conserva algunos edificios de la época colonial. Entre sus centros de atracción turística están el Museo Precolombino, el Parque de Artesanías y los mercados de artesanía. En Viña del Mar, el más conocido de los balnearios (*resorts*) de Chile, todos los años se celebra el Festival Internacional OTI de la Voz y la Canción.

- Chile es la cuna de Pablo Neruda, Premio Nobel de Literatura en 1971, y de Gabriela Mistral, Premio Nobel de Literatura en 1945, dos de los poetas hispanos más famosos del siglo pasado. Otra escritora chilena de gran fama es Isabel Allende, autora de *La casa de los espíritus* y muchas otras novelas.

Tierra de grandes escritores, ...

▲ Isabel Allende, escritora chilena, autora de la novela *La casa de los espíritus,* entre otras

▲ Pablo Neruda (1904–1973), famoso poeta chileno, Premio Nobel de 1971

... de música, ...

◄ Este nativo toca la quena, un tipo de flauta. Durante la dictadura de Pinochet (1973–1990), se prohibió tocar este instrumento.

... y de voluntad[1] democrática ejemplar

◄ Chile, después del dictador Augusto Pinochet: manifestación (*demonstration*) de protesta

Paisaje campestres[2]

▲ Viñedos (*Vineyards*). Actualmente (*Presently*) el vino chileno se exporta a unos 100 países de cinco continentes.

Nuestro panorama cultural

In groups of three, answer the following questions about your home state, region, or country.

1. En la región donde Ud. vive, ¿hay oportunidades de hacer actividades al aire libre? ¿Hay más cosas que hacer en el verano o en el invierno?
2. ¿Hay viñedos en su país?
3. ¿Hay festivales anuales en su ciudad o en su país? ¿Cuándo son y cómo se celebran?
4. ¿Ha leído recientemente obras de algún autor popular? ¿De quién? ¿De qué tratan esas obras?
5. ¿Su país tiene mercados al aire libre? ¿Qué venden?

For the next class: Go to the World Wide Web and find photos from your hometown, state, region, or country. Use the questions from **Nuestro panorama cultural** above as guidelines for choosing them. Be ready to present the photos to your classmates.

---

[1]**voluntad** = *will*
[2]**campestres** = *rural, country*

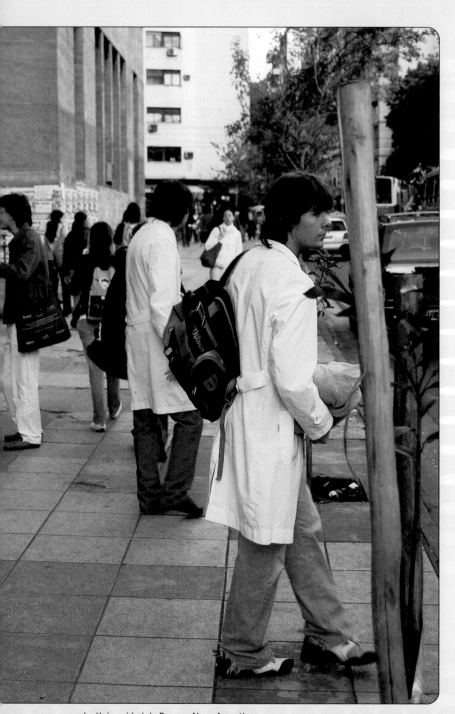

▲ La Universidad de Buenos Aires, Argentina

Objetivos

Comunicación

You will learn vocabulary related to college activities and careers.

Pronunciación

Pronunciation in context

Estructuras

◆ The subjunctive or indicative after certain conjunctions
◆ The past participle
◆ The present perfect and the past perfect (pluperfect)

Cultura

◆ Aspects of higher education
◆ Grading system

Panorama hispánico

◆ Argentina

Estrategias

Listening: Guessing meaning practice I
Speaking: Paraphrasing practice IV
Writing: Writing a presentation
Rincón literario: Reading literature

Las carreras universitarias

Argentina

Argentina, por su extensión, es el país de habla española más grande del mundo, y ocupa el octavo lugar entre los países más extensos. Sin embargo, la población del país es de sólo unos 40 millones de habitantes, la mayor parte de origen europeo, principalmente italianos, alemanes, ingleses y españoles.

▲ Un gaucho con su ganado (*cattle herd*)

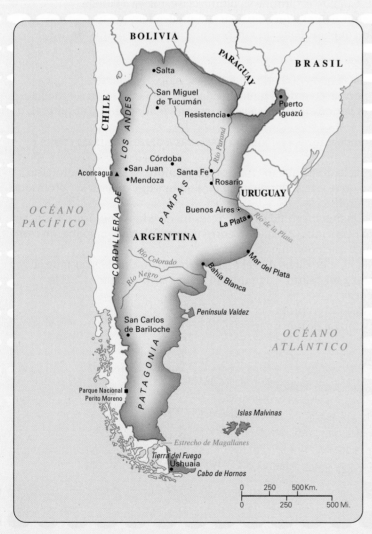

▲ Vista de la avenida 9 de julio y el Obelisco

▲ Vista de la Plaza de Mayo, donde se pueden ver la Casa Rosada y la Pirámide de Mayo

Mónica Valenzuela, una chica norteamericana de ascendencia mexicana, se graduó de la escuela secundaria en mayo y decidió escapar del calor de Arizona y volar a Buenos Aires. Allí visita a su amiga porteña,[1] Norma Benedetti, que había pasado un año con ella y su familia. Mónica tuvo que llevar suéteres y un abrigo porque el 21 de junio empieza el invierno en Argentina. Hoy las dos muchachas están sentadas en un café de la avenida de Mayo, mirando pasar a la gente y hablando de sus planes para el futuro.

Mónica	Tú empezaste a asistir a la Facultad de Medicina en marzo, ¿no? ¿Qué tal te va?
Norma	Me va bastante bien. Las clases son interesantísimas y pronto vamos a comenzar a trabajar en el hospital.
Mónica	Yo empiezo las clases en septiembre. Ya estoy matriculada en inglés, matemáticas, química, sicología y sociología. ¡Cinco requisitos!
Norma	¿Qué otras materias son requisito?
Mónica	Física, biología, comunicación pública... Depende en parte de la especialización del estudiante. Oye, ¿no vamos a encontrarnos con tu hermano?
Norma	Más tarde. Cuando él termine su última clase, me va a llamar.
Mónica	¡Ay! Tengo que llamar a mi mamá en cuanto lleguemos a tu casa esta noche, para que me diga si puede comprarme los libros que voy a necesitar.
Norma	¿Ya has decidido cuál va a ser tu especialización?
Mónica	Bueno, todavía no he tomado ninguna decisión... Mi padre se enoja conmigo porque cuando él tenía mi edad, ya había decidido ser médico. Me gusta el periodismo, pero a veces quiero ser abogada... o arquitecta, o escritora...
Norma	Bueno, cuando empieces a tomar clases, vas a darte cuenta de cuáles te gustan.
Mónica	Hasta ahora, lo único que me ha gustado siempre ha sido ir al gimnasio.
Norma	Bueno, eso no te va a servir de mucho, ¡a menos que quieras ser profesora de educación física!
Mónica	¡Me has dado una magnífica idea! ¡Profesora de educación física! ¡Y quizás experta en nutrición! ¿Por qué no corremos en Palermo[2] mañana, en caso de que tenga que ponerme en forma?
Norma	¡No, no, no! Ya te he dicho que el único ejercicio que yo hago es ir de la sala de estar a mi cuarto... ¿Por qué no invitas a mi hermano? A él le encanta correr.
Mónica	¡Perfecto! Se lo voy a proponer en cuanto lo vea.
Norma	¡Bárbaro![3] Con tal de que no insistas en que yo corra...

¿Lo sabía Ud.?

En la mayoría de las universidades hispanas no existe el concepto de *"major"* usado en los Estados Unidos. Los estudiantes españoles y latinoamericanos toman muy pocas clases optativas (*electives*), ya que la mayoría comienza a especializarse en la universidad a partir de su primer año.

◆ ¿Cuáles son algunas clases optativas que se toman en la universidad?

---

[1]**porteña** = *from Buenos Aires; literally, from the port (of Buenos Aires)*
[2]*a big park*
[3]**¡Bárbaro!** (Argentina) = *Great!*

Mónica

Norma

¿Quién lo dice?   Identify the person who said the following in the dialogue.

1. Oye, ¿no vamos a encontrarnos con tu hermano? _____

2. Me gusta el periodismo, pero a veces quiero ser abogada. _____

3. Pronto vamos a comenzar a trabajar en el hospital. _____

4. Lo único que me ha gustado siempre ha sido ir al gimnasio. _____

5. ¿Por qué no invitas a mi hermano? A él le encanta correr. _____

6. Con tal de que no insistas en que yo corra... _____

7. ¡Me has dado una magnífica idea! ¡Profesora de educación física! _____

8. El único ejercicio que yo hago es ir de la sala de estar a mi cuarto. _____

Hablemos.   With a partner, take turns asking and answering the following questions. Base your answers on the dialogue and on your own circumstances.

En el diálogo	¿Y tú?
1. ¿En qué mes se graduó Mónica de la escuela secundaria?	¿Cuándo te graduaste tú?
2. ¿Dónde están sentadas las chicas y de qué están hablando?	¿Con quién hablas tú de tus planes para el futuro?
3. ¿Qué empezó a hacer Norma en marzo?	¿Cuándo empezaste tú a asistir a la universidad?
4. ¿Cómo le va a Norma en las clases?	¿Cómo te va a ti en tus clases?
5. ¿Cuántos requisitos está tomando Mónica?	¿Cuántos requisitos estás tomando tú?
6. ¿Cuándo va a llamar Mónica a su mamá?	¿Qué vas a hacer tú en cuanto llegues a tu casa?
7. ¿Ha decidido Mónica cuál va a ser su especialización?	¿Cuál va a ser tu especialización?
8. ¿Por qué se enoja el padre de Mónica con ella a veces?	¿Quién se enoja a veces contigo?
9. ¿Qué es lo único que siempre le ha gustado a Mónica?	¿Qué es lo que siempre te ha gustado a ti?
10. ¿Qué quiere hacer Mónica mañana?	¿Tú corres para ponerte en forma?
11. ¿Cuál es el único ejercicio que hace Norma?	¿Tú crees que es mejor caminar o correr?
12. ¿A quién va a invitar Mónica?	¿Tú prefieres hacer ejercicio solo(-a) o con un(-a) amigo(-a)?

¿Lo sabía Ud.?

En España y en Latinoamérica, las universidades se dividen en "facultades", donde los estudiantes toman clases directamente relacionadas con su especialización (por ejemplo, la Facultad de Medicina, la Facultad de Ingeniería, la Facultad de Arquitectura, etc.). No existen requisitos generales, pues éstos se toman en la escuela secundaria.

◆ **¿Cuáles son algunos de los requisitos generales que se toman en las universidades de su país?**

Vocabulario

Cognados

el (la) arquitecto(-a) architect
la biología biology
el (la) experto(-a) expert
la física physics
el futuro future

el gimnasio gym
las matemáticas math, mathematics
la nutrición nutrition
la sicología psychology
la sociología sociology

Nombres

el (la) abogado(-a) lawyer
la ascendencia ancestry
la carrera career
el calor heat
la edad age
la educación física physical education
el (la) escritor(-a) writer

la especialización major
la facultad college, school
la materia, la asignatura subject (*in school*)
el (la) médico(-a) doctor, M.D.
el periodismo journalism
la química chemistry
el requisito requirement

Verbos

comparar to compare
depender to depend
enojarse to get angry
escapar to escape
graduarse to graduate

insistir (en) to insist (on)
matricularse to register
proponer (yo propongo) to propose
terminar to finish, to end

Adjetivos

magnífico(-a) excellent, great
matriculado(-a) registered
sentado(-a) seated, sitting
universitario(-a) (having to do with) college

Otras palabras y expresiones

a menos que unless
bastante quite
con tal (de) que provided that, as long as
darse cuenta (de) to realize
en caso de que in case
en parte in part
hasta ahora up to now

lo único the only thing
no servir de mucho not to be much good
ponerse en forma to get in shape
pronto soon
¿Qué tal te va? How's it going for you?
si if
tomar una decisión to make a decision

Vocabulario adicional

Para hablar de los estudios

la administración de empresas business administration
aprobar (o:ue) to pass (*an exam or course*)
la beca scholarship
el (la) bibliotecario(-a) librarian
la ciencia science
el (la) consejero(-a) advisor
la contabilidad accounting
entregar to turn in, to deliver
el horario schedule

la investigación research
el laboratorio laboratory
mantener to maintain (*conj. like* **tener**)
la matrícula registration, tuition
la nota grade
el promedio grade point average
quedar suspendido(-a) to fail (*an exam or course*)
sacar to get, to receive (*a grade*)
el título title

Profesiones y oficios (*Trades*)

▲ **el (la) vendedor(-a)** salesperson

▲ **el (la) carpintero(-a)** carpenter

▲ **el (la) cocinero(-a)** cook, chef

▲ **el (la) electricista(-a)** electrician

▲ **el (la) ejecutivo(-a)** executive

▲ **el (la) ingeniero(-a)** engineer

▲ **el (la) plomero(-a)** plumber

▲ **el (la) programador(-a)** programmer

Práctica

A. Select the word or phrase that does not belong in each group.

1. tan pronto como / con tal que / en cuanto
2. hacer ejercicio / ponerse en forma / proponer
3. sentado / muy bueno / magnífico
4. plomero / bañadera / edad
5. enojarse / darse cuenta / entender
6. física / sicología / química
7. dar / entregar / escapar
8. comparar / tomar una decisión / decidir

B. Match the questions in column A with the answers in column B.

A		B
1. ¿Aprobaste el examen? _____		a. Sí, de ascendencia mexicana.
2. ¿Cuál es tu especialización? _____		b. No muy bien.
3. ¿Tú eres norteamericano? _____		c. No, es médico.
4. ¿Tú eres mayor que Nora? _____		d. Una A-.
5. ¿Tu papá es abogado? _____		e. ¡No! ¡Acabo de empezar!
6. ¿Qué propones tú? _____		f. Biología.
7. ¿Qué tal te va en la clase? _____		g. Pronto.
8. ¿Terminaste? _____		h. Que estudiemos juntos.
9. ¿Qué nota sacaste? _____		i. No, quedé suspendido.
10. ¿Cuándo se casan? _____		j. No, somos de la misma edad.

C. Write the words or phrases that correspond to the following.

1. materia _____
2. clases que todos los estudiantes deben tomar _____
3. opuesto de **empezar** _____
4. opuesto de **quedar suspendido** _____
5. persona que trabaja en una biblioteca _____
6. persona que cocina en un restaurante _____
7. persona que vende _____
8. la especialización de un futuro contador _____

D. Complete the following sentences, using the vocabulary from this lesson.

1. Es profesor de _____ física.
2. Elsa sabe mucho de vitaminas y proteínas porque es experta en _____.
3. Hemingway fue un gran _____ norteamericano.
4. Esteban estudia en la _____ de Medicina.
5. ¿Cuál es tu _____? ¿Sicología?
6. Hasta _____, no hay nadie que pueda enseñar la clase.
7. Lo _____ que sé es que no voy a _____ una "A" en esta clase.
8. Tiene una "A" y una "C". Su _____ es "B".
9. Vamos a ir a la biblioteca para hacer _____.
10. Ese título no _____ de mucho.
11. Tengo que _____ un buen promedio, porque tengo una _____.
12. Marisol estudia _____ de empresas.

Para conversar

A. Aquí, en los Estados Unidos... With a partner, play the roles of two counselors talking to two students from Argentina who are attending your college. Tell them what classes to take (**Pueden tomar...**) and suggest some extracurricular activities. Also, ask them what professions or trades they like.

B. Nuestras clases... You and your partner discuss your class schedule, and talk about your favorite classes and the classes you don't like. Give reasons. Talk also about the classes you plan to take next semester.

C. Profesiones Taking into account the professions and trades presented on page 377, discuss, with a partner, the ones you like and don't like, and say why. Give details.

Un pensamiento

La educación empieza en la cuna y termina en la tumba.

Equivalent: Education begins in the womb and ends in the tomb.

Pronunciación

Pronunciation in context

In this lesson, there are some new words or phrases that may be challenging to pronounce. For further pronunciation practice of Spanish sounds, listen to your instructor and repeat the following sentences.

1. Mónica **Valenzuela** es una chica norteamericana de **ascendencia** mexicana.

2. Ya estoy **matriculada** en **química** y **sicología.**

3. Depende de la **especialización** del estudiante.

4. Todavía no he tomado **ninguna decisión.**

5. Cuando él tenía mi **edad,** ya había **decidido** ser médico.

6. A veces quiero ser **abogada** o **arquitecta.**

7. Lo **único** que me ha gustado siempre ha sido ir al **gimnasio.**

8. Me has dado una **magnífica idea.**

Aspectos culturales

En imágenes (*Profesionales del mundo hispánico*)

▲ Maestra bilingüe de escuela

▲ Dentista latina

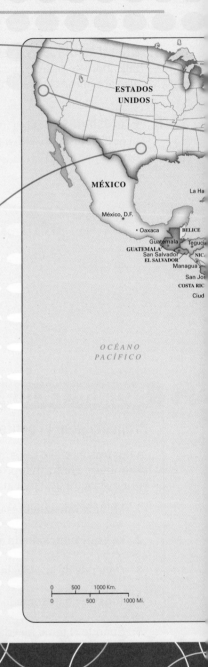

ESTADOS
UNIDOS

MÉXICO

La Ha

México, D.F.

• Oaxaca   BELICE

Guatemala   Teguci

GUATEMALA   San Salvador   NIC.
EL SALVADOR   Managua

San Jos
COSTA RIC
Ciud

OCÉANO
PACÍFICO

| 0 | 500 | 1000 Km. |
| 0 | 500 | 1000 Mi. |

Ubíquese... y búsquelo

Improve Your Grade
Web Search

You plan to study abroad in Buenos Aires next summer or during the next academic year. Go to **www.cengage.com/highered** and find information about programs available at colleges and universities in Buenos Aires. In the next class, team up with two classmates and discuss your findings. What institutions and what programs of study will best suit your career goals?

▲ La vida de Jaime Escalante, profesor de física boliviano-estadounidense, es el tema (*subject*) de la película *Stand and Deliver* (1988).

▲ La mujer hispana se destaca cada vez más en el mundo de los negocios. Aquí vemos a una ejecutiva firmando documentos.

Estructuras

1. The subjunctive or indicative after certain conjunctions
(*El subjuntivo o el indicativo después de ciertas conjunciones*)

A. Conjunctions that are always followed by the subjunctive

◆ Some conjunctions, by their meaning, imply uncertainty or condition. They are, therefore, always followed by the subjunctive. Here are some of them.

en caso de que *in case*
sin que *without*
con tal (de) que *provided that*
a menos que *unless*
para que *in order that*
antes de que *before*

—Voy a ir al gimnasio **con tal que** los chicos **vayan** conmigo.
"I'm going to go to the gym provided the boys go with me."

—Llámelos **antes de que salgan.**
"Call them before they leave."

—No me van a dar la beca **a menos que** ella me **dé** una carta.
"They're not going to give me the scholarship unless she gives me a letter."

—Yo puedo dársela **en caso de que** ella no **quiera** hacerlo.
"I can give it to you in case she doesn't want to do it."

—Te voy a dar dinero **para que puedas** matricularte.
"I'm going to give you money so that you can register."

—No puedo matricularme **sin que** el consejero **firme** la tarjeta.
"I can't register without the advisor signing the card."

B. Conjunctions that are followed by the subjunctive or indicative

◆ The subjunctive follows certain conjunctions when the main clause refers to the future or is a command. Some of these conjunctions are:

cuando *when*
hasta que *until*
tan pronto como, en cuanto *as soon as*

—¿Lo van a esperar?
"Are you going to wait for him?"

—Sí, **hasta que llegue.**
"Yes, until he arrives."

—**En cuanto llegue,** díganle que me llame.
"As soon as he arrives, tell him to call me."

◆ If there is no indication of a future action, the conjunction of time is followed by the indicative.

—¿Siempre lo esperan?
"Do you always wait for him?"

—Sí, **hasta que llega.**
"Yes, until he arrives."

Lo voy a comprar **en cuanto tenga** $40.000...

Práctica

A. Complete the following dialogue between two roommates who are expecting a houseguest, using **con tal que, sin que, en caso de que, a menos que, para que,** and **antes de que** and the verbs given. Then act it out with a partner, adding two original lines.

—Tenemos que limpiar el apartamento _____ (llegar) él.

—Yo voy a preparar unos sándwiches _____ (tener) hambre.

—Sí, ¿y por qué no compras unos refrescos _____ (poder) tomar algo en cuanto llegue?

—Bueno, pero yo no puedo ir al supermercado _____ tú me _____ (dar) el dinero.

—Está bien. Yo te voy a dar el dinero _____ tú me lo _____ (devolver) mañana.

—Voy ahora mismo. Voy a salir _____ me _____ (ver) Paco porque va a querer ir conmigo.

— _____

— _____

B. Change the following, according to the new beginning.

1. Todos los días yo llamo a mi amiga en cuanto llego a casa. Mañana,...
2. Generalmente esperamos al profesor hasta que llega. El próximo viernes,...
3. Todos los días, tan pronto como termina la clase, vamos a la cafetería. Esta tarde...
4. Ud. se lo dice a los estudiantes cuando los ve. Dígaselo a los estudiantes...
5. Cuando él va al laboratorio siempre se queda dos horas. La semana próxima...

Para conversar

¡Habla con tu compañero! With a partner, ask each other the following questions.

1. Generalmente, ¿qué haces en cuanto llegas a tu casa? ¿Qué vas a hacer hoy en cuanto llegues?
2. ¿Tú puedes pagar la matrícula sin que tus padres te presten el dinero?
3. ¿Qué promedio tienes que mantener para que te den una beca? ¿Una "A" o una "B"?
4. ¿Tú puedes estudiar conmigo antes de que el profesor nos dé el próximo examen?
5. Por lo general, ¿adónde vas cuando termina la clase? ¿Adónde vas a ir hoy cuando termine la clase?
6. ¿Con quién puedo dejar un mensaje en caso de que tú no estés cuando yo te llame?

> **LEARNING TIP**
>
> Personalize each of these statements by talking about what *you* usually do and what *you* are going to do. For example: *Todos los días yo como algo en cuanto llego a casa.*

¿Lo sabía Ud.? En lugar de letras, el sistema de calificaciones (*grading system*) en las universidades hispanas usa números. Por lo general, se califica asignando notas de 1 a 5 en Hispanoamérica y de 1 a 10 en España. Una nota de 3 ó de 6 es normalmente la nota mínima para aprobar una clase o un examen.

◆ En su país, ¿cuál es la nota mínima para aprobar una clase o un examen?

 ACE the Test

2. The past participle (*El participio pasado*)

A. Forms of the past participle

Past Participle Endings		
-ar *verbs*	-er *verbs*	-ir *verbs*
habl-**ado** (*spoken*)	com-**ido** (*eaten*)	decid-**ido** (*decided*)

◆ The following verbs have irregular past participles.

abrir	**abierto**	*opened*
cubrir	**cubierto**	*covered*
decir	**dicho**	*said*
hacer	**hecho**	*done, made*
escribir	**escrito**	*written*
morir	**muerto**	*died*
poner	**puesto**	*put*
romper	**roto**	*broken*
ver	**visto**	*seen*
volver	**vuelto**	*returned* (somewhere)
devolver	**devuelto**	*returned* (something)
envolver	**envuelto**	*wrapped*

¡Atención! Verbs ending in **-er** and **-ir** whose stem ends in a strong vowel require an accent mark on the **i** of the **-ido** ending.

creer	**creído**	*believed*
leer	**leído**	*read*
oír[1]	**oído**	*heard*
traer	**traído**	*brought*

ACE the Test

Práctica

Supply the past participle of each of the following verbs.

1. tener	9. romper	17. abrir
2. traer	10. cubrir	18. escribir
3. cerrar	11. cambiar	19. ver
4. decir	12. sentir	20. aceptar
5. aprovechar	13. entrar	21. devolver
6. apretar	14. salir	22. leer
7. cortar	15. hacer	23. dar
8. volver	16. poner	24. sacar

B. Past participles used as adjectives

◆ In Spanish, most past participles may be used as adjectives. As such, they agree in number and gender with the nouns they modify.

La biblioteca está **abierta** hoy.	*The library is open today.*
El gimnasio está **abierto** hoy.	*The gym is open today.*
Las bibliotecas están **abiertas** hoy.	*The libraries are open today.*
No dejen los libros **abiertos.**	*Don't leave the books open.*
Le mandé dos tarjetas **escritas** en inglés.	*I sent him two cards written in English.*

---

[1]Present tense: **oigo, oyes, oye, oímos, oís, oyen.**

Práctica

Complete the description of each illustration, using the verb **estar** and the appropriate past participle.

1. El coche _____ en la esquina.

2. Los niños _____.

3. La puerta _____.

4. La ventana _____.

5. El restaurante _____.

6. La carta _____ en español.

7. Los vestidos _____ en México.

8. El cuaderno _____.

9. La señora _____ cerca de la ventana.

Para conversar

¿Cómo están...? In groups of three, talk about the state of the following things. After you finish, you may brainstorm and propose other possibilities.

1. En mi casa: la puerta, las ventanas, los muebles...
2. En la clase: el profesor, los estudiantes, los libros...
3. En la ciudad: el correo, los bancos, las tiendas...

3. The present perfect and the past perfect (pluperfect)
(*El pretérito perfecto y el pluscuamperfecto*)

A. The present perfect

◆ The present perfect tense is formed by using the present indicative of the auxiliary verb **haber** with the past participle of the verb that expresses the action or state. This tense is equivalent to the English present perfect (*have* + *past participle*, as in *I have spoken.*).

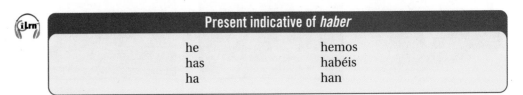

Present indicative of *haber*	
he	hemos
has	habéis
ha	han

Formation of the Present Perfect Tense			
	hablar	*tener*	*venir*
yo	**he** hablado	**he** tenido	**he** venido
tú	**has** hablado	**has** tenido	**has** venido
Ud. él ella	**ha** hablado	**ha** tenido	**ha** venido
nosotros(-as)	**hemos** hablado	**hemos** tenido	**hemos** venido
vosotros(-as)	**habéis** hablado	**habéis** tenido	**habéis** venido
Uds. ellos ellas	**han** hablado	**han** tenido	**han** venido

—¿**Has pagado** más de mil dólares por la matrícula? — *"Have you paid more than one thousand dollars for the tuition?"*
—No, nunca **he pagado** tanto dinero. — *"No, I've never paid that much money."*

—¿**Has visto** a Teresa? — *"Have you seen Teresa?"*
—No, no la **he visto.** — *"No, I haven't seen her."*

Note that when the past participle is part of a perfect tense, it is invariable. The past participle only changes in form when it is used as an adjective.

Ella ha escrit**o** la cart**a.** — *She has written the letter.*
La cart**a** está escrit**a.** — *The letter is written.*

In the Spanish present perfect tense the auxiliary verb **haber** can never be separated from the past participle as it can in English.

Yo nunca **he estado** en Lima. — *I have never been in Lima.*

◆ Remember that when reflexive or object pronouns are used with compound tenses, the pronouns are placed immediately before the auxiliary verb.

Le ha dado mucho dinero a su hijo. — *He has given a lot of money to his son.*
María y José **se** han ido. — *María and José have left.*

A. Look at the following illustrations and describe what these people have done today, using the present perfect.

1. Tú

2. Tú y yo

3. Los chicos

4. Yo

5. Mi mamá

6. Uds.

B. With a partner, take turns asking each other what you have done lately.

> ◆ MODELO: ir al cine / con quién
> —¿Has ido al cine últimamente?
> —Sí, he ido.
> —¿Con quién?
> —Con mi novio(-a).

1. comprar ropa / dónde
2. ver alguna película / cuál
3. dar alguna fiesta / dónde
4. mandar algún mensaje electrónico / a quién
5. tomar algún examen / en qué clase
6. visitar algún lugar interesante / cuál
7. escribir una carta / a quién
8. poner dinero en el banco / en cuál
9. leer un libro / cuál
10. recibir algún regalo / de quién

¡Quien no ha vista Sevilla, no ha visto maravilla!

Equivalent: If you haven't seen Sevilla, you've missed out on something wonderful.

Para conversar

 Nuestras experiencias With a partner, discuss five things that you or your family and friends have never done and five things you have done many times. Compare your own experiences with those of your partner.

◆ **MODELO:** —*Yo nunca he estado en Buenos Aires.*
   —*Yo tampoco he estado en Buenos Aires.*
   (Yo he estado en Buenos Aires dos veces.)

B. The past perfect (pluperfect)

◆ The past perfect tense is formed by using the imperfect tense of the auxiliary verb **haber** with the past participle of the verb that expresses the action or state.

◆ This tense is equivalent to the English past perfect (*had* + past participle, as in *I had spoken*). Generally, the past perfect tense expresses an action that had taken place before another action in the past.

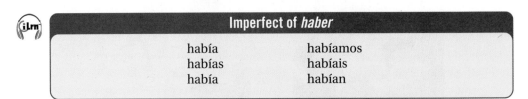

Imperfect of *haber*	
había	habíamos
habías	habíais
había	habían

Formation of the Past Perfect Tense			
	estudiar	*beber*	*ir*
yo	**había** estudiado	**había** bebido	**había** ido
tú	**habías** estudiado	**habías** bebido	**habías** ido
Ud. él ella	**había** estudiado	**había** bebido	**había** ido
nosotros(-as)	**habíamos** estudiado	**habíamos** bebido	**habíamos** ido
vosotros(-as)	**habíais** estudiado	**habíais** bebido	**habíais** ido
Uds. ellos ellas	**habían** estudiado	**habían** bebido	**habían** ido

—¿No hablaste con tu abogada?   *"Didn't you speak with your lawyer?"*
—No, cuando yo llegué, ella ya se **había ido.**   *"No, when I arrived, she had already left."*

—¿Uds. ya **habían estado** en Buenos Aires?   *"Had you been in Buenos Aires?"*
—No, nunca **habíamos estado** allí.   *"No, we had never been there."*

Práctica

A. One of your brothers is never around when there is work to be done. Say what had already been done by the time he got home last night.

◆ **MODELO:** nosotros / lavar los platos
Cuando él llegó, nosotros ya habíamos lavado los platos.

1. yo / barrer la cocina
2. los chicos / pasarle la aspiradora a la alfombra
3. Roberto y yo / hacer la comida
4. Elsa / planchar la ropa
5. tú / limpiar el refrigerador
6. Carmen y Elena / bañar al perro
7. Anita / poner la mesa
8. Raúl y Carlos / comprar las bebidas
9. Mirta / lavar las sábanas
10. Raúl y yo / envolver los regalos

B. Complete the following sentences logically, using the pluperfect tense.

1. Antes de venir a esta universidad, yo nunca...
2. Antes de tomar esta clase, mis compañeros y yo nunca...
3. Hasta el año pasado, mis amigos y yo siempre...
4. Hasta el semestre pasado, los estudiantes de esta clase nunca...
5. Hasta que yo cumplí dieciséis años, yo nunca...
6. Hasta el verano pasado, mi familia y yo siempre...
7. Antes de vivir en esta ciudad, yo nunca...
8. Antes de cumplir dieciocho años, yo siempre...

Para conversar

A. ¡Habla con tu compañero! With a partner, ask each other the following questions.

1. Cuando llegaste a tu casa anoche, ¿las otras personas ya habían cenado?
2. A las once de la noche, ¿ya te habías acostado?
3. Cuando te levantaste esta mañana, ¿alguien te había preparado el desayuno?
4. Cuando yo llegué a clase, ¿ya habías llegado tú?
5. Cuando llegaste a clase hoy, ¿ya habías hecho todos los ejercicios de esta lección?
6. ¿Ya habías tomado español antes de tomar esta clase?

B. Antes de cumplir los 16 años With a partner, discuss things you had done before you turned sixteen. Then talk to another classmate and tell him/her about your partner's experience.

Así somos

Estrategia **Guessing meaning practice I** You have already practiced guessing meaning from context while listening and reading. Remember to use cognates, word families (**aprender–aprendizaje–aprendiz**), the words you know, and the surrounding ideas to make informed guesses about unfamiliar words.

Tres avisos You are going to hear three brief commercials on institutions of higher learning and guess the meaning of the following words or phrases. Listen to each commerical first for the gist and then listen again for the specific words.

Aviso 1: 1. diseñados 2. extranjeras 3. enseñanza 4. docente
Aviso 2: 1. calendario 2. a partir de 3. publicada 4. avanzados
Aviso 3: 1. aprendizaje 2. sustituir 3. a través de

Al conversar...

Estrategia **Paraphrasing practice IV** When paraphrasing, remember that your goal is to simplify what you hear while capturing the main idea. Aim to apply this technique in the future in speech and in writing when you report, summarize, or explain what you hear or read.

¿Qué dijeron? Listen to five sentences and restate each in your own words. Then compare your responses with those of a classmate.

¿Qué dice Ud.? What would you say in the following situations? What might the other person say? Act out the scenes with a partner. Take turns playing each role.

1. Carlos is a new classmate. Ask him what his major is, what his favorite subjects are, and when he plans to graduate. Ask also how he's doing in his classes.
2. You tell a friend that you want to take a physical education class because you realize you need to get in shape.
3. A freshman asks you what courses to take. Find out something about his or her interests and plans, and make sure he/she takes the appropriate courses. Be sure to mention some of your school's requirements.
4. You are talking to a friend about classes you like, classes you don't like, and the reasons why.

Para conocernos mejor To do this activity, work with a classmate whom you would like to get to know. Take turns asking and answering these questions.

1. ¿Prefieres tomar una clase de matemáticas, una clase de nutrición o una clase de contabilidad? ¿Has tomado una clase de biología? ¿Cuál es tu asignatura favorita? ¿Cuál es la materia que menos te gusta?
2. ¿Has pensado en el futuro? ¿En qué año te vas a graduar? ¿Qué carrera te gusta? ¿Te gusta más la idea de ser ingeniero(-a), arquitecto(-a), bibliotecario(-a) o profesor(-a)?

3. ¿Qué tal te va en tus estudios hasta ahora? ¿Tienes un buen horario? ¿Qué requisitos has tomado? ¿Has aprobado todos tus exámenes o has quedado suspendido(-a) en alguno?

4. ¿Te enojas a veces con tus profesores? ¿Por qué? ¿Con qué otras personas te enojas a veces?

5. ¿Ya estás matriculado(-a) para el semestre que viene? ¿Qué clases vas a tomar?

Una encuesta Interview your classmates to identify who fits the following descriptions. Include your instructor, but remember to use the **Ud.** form when addressing him/her. After finishing the survey, get together with two or three classmates and discuss the results.

Nombre

1. Ha conseguido una beca. _____

2. Mantiene un buen promedio. _____

3. Saca buenas notas en todas sus clases. _____

4. Está haciendo investigación para una clase. _____

5. Ha tomado clases de Educación Física. _____

6. Ha hablado con un consejero últimamente. _____

7. Se va a graduar pronto. _____

8. Piensa estudiar periodismo. _____

Para crear In groups of three or four, make up a story about the people in the photo. Say who they are, what subjects they are taking, their majors, their grade point averages, when they will graduate, and so forth. The woman in the middle is an advisor.

¡Vamos a escribir!

Antes de escribir

Una presentación You will write a presentation about yourself in which you describe your life as a student. First brainstorm the following topics, jotting down all the ideas that come to you. Then select the ideas you want to use and decide how you want to organize the ideas.

1. your studies: your major (if you have one) and the classes you are taking
2. your living situation and job (if you have one)
3. what you do outside class to relax and for fun
4. your thoughts about what you like and don't like about campus life

Here are some possible ways in which you could organize your presentation:

Option 1: Discuss your studies first, then your living situation and job, and finally other interesting aspects of your life.

Option 2: Discuss personal preferences and how these affect your choices at school regarding studies, work, and activities.

Option 3: Talk about the major aspects of your work chronologically, say, from Monday through Sunday.

A escribir la presentación

Write the **primer borrador** of your presentation.

Después de escribir

Before writing the final version of your presentation, exchange your first draft with a classmate and peer edit each other's work using the following guidelines.

- use and formation of the subjunctive and indicative
- subject-verb agreement in main and subordinate clauses
- noun-adjective agreement
- clear organization

Enrique Anderson-Imbert (*Argentina: 1910–2000*)

Enrique Anderson-Imbert se conoce internacionalmente sobre todo como cuentista y crítico de literatura. En 1965 la Universidad de Harvard creó (*created*) la cátedra (*faculty appointment*) de literatura hispanoamericana para este distinguido estudioso y creador literario.

Anderson-Imbert escribió cuentos muy breves de tipo fantástico, en los que la realidad se mezcla con la fantasía. El cuento que Ud. va a leer muestra ambas (*shows both*) cualidades.

Antes de leer

Estrategia **Reading literature** As with poetry, many of the strategies you have employed with other types of texts are useful when reading literature. Predicting, guessing meaning from context, anticipating content as you read, and reading critically all contribute to understanding a text. In addition, for short stories or prose narrations, it may be important to identify who is telling the story. Is the narrator the writer or a character? Is the narration first or third person? This will determine whether you see a character only through his or her thoughts and speech or from the perspective of an observer and the point of view of others.

Estrategias Before reading the complete story, you will look at different aspects with different goals for each.

1. Predicting: Read the title. What does it suggest?
2. Predicting: Read the first two sentences of the story. In pairs, list three possible things that could happen to Costa, the murderer. Who is the narrator? How might this affect how the story unfolds?
3. Creating context by establishing key connections: Skim the story and try to figure out why it was entitled "Sala de espera." Were your earlier predictions helpful?

A leer

Comprensión Read the story and find the answers to the following questions.

1. ¿Qué hacen Costa y Wright y qué pasa después?
2. ¿Qué sucede en la sala de espera?
3. ¿Con quién conversa la señora?
4. ¿Por qué no puede Costa tomar el tren?
5. ¿Es lógico el final de este cuento? ¿Por qué?

Sala de espera (Adaptado)

Costa y Wright roban una casa. Costa
asesina a Wright y se queda con° la valija
llena de joyas y dinero. Va a la estación para
escaparse en el primer tren. En la sala de espera, una señora se sienta a su izquierda y le
da° conversación. Fastidiado,° Costa finge°
con un bostezo que tiene sueño y que va a
dormir, pero oye que la señora continúa
conversando. Abre entonces los ojos y ve,
sentado a la derecha, el fantasma° de Wright.
La señora atraviesa° a Costa de lado a lado
con la mirada y charla con el fantasma,
quien contesta con simpatía.° Cuando llega
el tren, Costa trata de levantarse, pero no
puede. Está paralizado, mudo y observa
atónito° cómo el fantasma toma tranquila-
mente la valija y camina con la señora hacia
el andén,° ahora hablando y riéndose.
Suben, y el tren parte.° Costa los sigue con
los ojos. Viene un hombre y comienza a
limpiar la sala de espera, que ahora está
completamente desierta. Pasa la aspiradora
por el asiento donde está Costa, invisible.

(De su colección *El gato Cheshire*)

se... keeps

*engages him in /
Annoyed / pretends*

ghost
transfixes

charm

aghast

platform
leaves

Después de leer... reflexiones

 A. In groups of four, discuss the following questions.

1. ¿Qué pensaron Ud. y sus compañeros(-as) que le iba a pasar a Costa en la sala de espera?
2. ¿Alguna de sus posibilidades se acerca a lo que le ocurrió a Costa según el des-enlace (*according to the ending*) del cuento? Comparta sus ideas con la clase.

 B. In pairs, write an equally surprising alternative ending to the story.

Frases célebres

Sobre la convivencia°

El respeto al derecho ajeno° es la paz.
Benito Juárez (México: 1806–1872)

Si te sientes muy solo, busca la compañía de otras almas° y frecuéntalas.° Pero no olvides que cada alma está especialmente construida para la soledad.°
Juan José Arreola (México: 1918–2001)

El primero de los deberes° es dar buen ejemplo.
Cecilia Böhl de Faber (España: 1796–1877)

Los hombres van en dos bandos°: los que aman y fundan, los que odian y destruyen.
José Martí (Cuba: 1853–1895)

coexistence

al... *the other person's right*

souls
be with them
solitude

duties

groups

Comentarios...

A. With a partner, take turns reading the **Frases célebres,** and say which one appeals to you the most. Give reasons for your choice.

B. Can you think of any famous sayings in English about this topic?

Panorama hispánico

Argentina

- La economía tradicional de Argentina se basa en la producción y exportación de carne y de cereales que se cultivan en grandes extensiones de terreno (*land*) fértil de sus llanuras o pampas. La economía actual, sin embargo, depende principalmente de la industria y del sector de servicios.

- Para muchos, Argentina es la tierra del tango, de Evita y de los gauchos, pero hoy la música argentina es muy variada, Evita es el símbolo de una época que no todos admiran, y los gauchos sólo se encuentran en las regiones aisladas del país y en los espectáculos para turistas.

- La ciudad más importante del país es Buenos Aires, la capital, la ciudad más grande del mundo hispano después de México. En la capital vive casi la mitad de la población argentina. Buenos Aires ha sido llamada "el París de Suramérica" porque muchos de sus edificios tienen un estilo similar al de París. La ciudad tiene amplias avenidas, entre ellas la avenida Nueve de Julio, una de las más anchas del mundo. Su nombre recuerda el día de la independencia del país.

- Son atracciones turísticas de la capital El Museo de Bellas Artes, el Teatro Colón, la calle Florida (donde están algunas de las tiendas más elegantes del país) y el barrio de la Boca, famoso por su tradición italiana, sus casas de múltiples colores y su famoso **Caminito,** que inspiró uno de los tangos más populares. Atracciones turísticas en el resto del país son las cataratas de Iguazú, el famoso balneario Mar del Plata, el centro turístico de deportes invernales Bariloche y el glaciar Perito Moreno.

◄ Hermosa vista del glaciar Perito Moreno, en la Patagonia, Argentina

Cumbres[1] de la literatura mundial contemporánea

▲ Jorge Luis Borges (1899–1986), maestro del relato (*short story*) y del ensayo (*essay*)

▲ Julio Cortázar (1914–1984), máximo exponente (*representative*) de la literatura fantástica

[1]**Cumbres** = *Pinnacles*

Estampas[1] de la vida cotidiana porteña

▲ Galerías Pacífico, elegante centro comercial

▲ La famosa calle Florida, arteria (*artery*) comercial y cultural de la ciudad a partir de (*since*) 1900

El espectáculo y las artes

▲ El tango se origina en los suburbios de la ciudad porteña a finales (*end*) del siglo XIX, adonde llegaban y se mezclaban inmigrantes de Europa y del interior (*provinces*).

Nuestro panorama cultural

In groups of three, answer the following questions about your home state, region, or country.

1. ¿Puede Ud. nombrar algunos escritores famosos de su país?
2. ¿Qué otras culturas influyen en la formación cultural de su país? ¿Puede dar algunos ejemplos?
3. ¿De dónde vienen sus antepasados (*ancestors*)? ¿Son de diferentes países?
4. ¿Sabe bailar el tango o ha visto cómo se baila? ¿Le gusta?

For the next class: Go to the World Wide Web and find photos from your hometown, state, region, or country. Use the questions from **Nuestro panorama cultural** above as guidelines for choosing them. Be ready to present the photos to your classmates.

---

[1]**Estampas** = *Images*

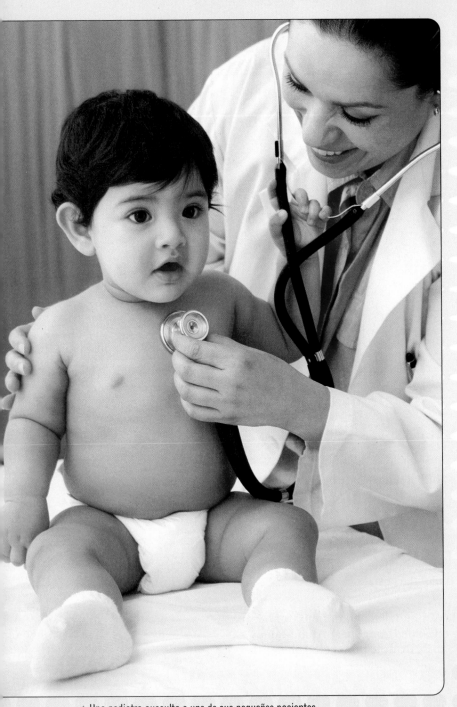

Objetivos

Comunicación

You will learn vocabulary related to health problems.

Pronunciación

Pronunciation in context

Estructuras

◆ The future
◆ The conditional
◆ The future perfect and the conditional perfect

Cultura

◆ Hospitals and clinics
◆ Urban vs. rural medical care
◆ Over-the-counter drugs
◆ Conventional and traditional medicine

Panorama hispánico

◆ Paraguay
◆ Bolivia

Estrategias

Listening: Recognizing transitions
Speaking: Practicing extended conversation
Writing: Writing to persuade
Rincón literario: Poetic language and the dictionary

▲ Una pediatra ausculta a uno de sus pequeños pacientes.

Problemas de salud

Paraguay y Bolivia

Paraguay

Paraguay es casi tan grande como el estado de California, pero su población es de menos de 6 millones de habitantes. La mayoría de los paraguayos hablan dos idiomas: el español y el guaraní.

Bolivia

Bolivia, llamada así en honor del Libertador Simón Bolívar, es un país de superlativos. Tiene la capital (La Paz), el aeropuerto y el lago navegable (el lago Titicaca) que son los más altos del mundo. También tiene unas de las ruinas más antiguas en Tiahuanaco.

▲ Ruinas de las misiones jesuitas, que aparecen en la película *The Mission* de 1986 (con Robert DeNiro y Jeremy Irons).

▲ Una farmacéutica en La Paz, Bolivia

▲ El Panteón de los Héroes, en Asunción, Paraguay

399

La familia Vargas, de Villarrica, Paraguay, vive ahora en Asunción, en una casa de tipo colonial, con árboles frutales en el patio y un jardín enorme. Adriana, la hija menor, está en la sala, hablando por teléfono con una compañera de la universidad.

Adriana   ¿Anabel? Habla Adriana. Hoy no quiero ir a la facultad, de modo que le voy a decir a mi mamá que no me siento bien. ¿Te gustaría venir a visitarme esta tarde? Podríamos mirar la tele y comer algo. Bueno... ¡te espero a eso de las cuatro! ¡Chau!

Adriana se acuesta en el sofá de la sala y llama a su mamá.

Adriana   Mamá, tendré que quedarme en casa hoy. Creo que tengo catarro... o gripe... o pulmonía... Me duele la cabeza, me duele la garganta, ¡y tengo fiebre! (*Tose.*)

Doña Eva   ¡Tienes tos! Sería una buena idea llevarte al médico. El doctor Viñas está en su consultorio...

Adriana   No, no será necesario que me vea. Me quedaré en casa, tomaré dos aspirinas y mañana estaré perfectamente bien. ¡Ya verás!

Doña Eva   Bueno, mi hija, pero tendrás que acostarte y tomar una taza de té bien caliente, con miel de abeja. Voy a llamar al médico para que te recete algún antibiótico.

Más tarde suena el timbre. La criada abre la puerta.

Criada   Señora, aquí hay un joven que quiere hablar con la señorita Adriana.

Doña Eva   ¡Ignacio! ¡Qué gusto de verte! De haber sabido que venías, habría preparado algo para merendar. ¿Un cafecito?

Ignacio   No, gracias, señora. ¡No se moleste! Vine a preguntarle a Adriana si le gustaría ir a una fiesta en la embajada de Bolivia esta noche.

Doña Eva   ¡Ay, qué lástima! Adriana está enferma. Tiene una temperatura de 39 grados, creo... Supongo que lo que tiene es contagioso... ¡Menos mal que hoy es viernes! Para el lunes ya se habrá curado y podrá volver a la universidad.

Adriana   ¡No, mamá! Para esta noche ya habré tomado un montón de remedios, y me sentiré mejor...

Ignacio   No, Adriana... podrías empeorarte. Necesitas descansar... Voy a llamar a Carolina, a ver si ella puede ir conmigo. ¡Ojalá que te mejores pronto!

¿Lo sabía Ud.?

En los países de habla hispana se mide la temperatura en grados Celsius, a los que también se les llama Centígrados. En la escala Celsius, 0° (temperatura de fusión del hielo) corresponde a 32° Fahrenheit. Por ejemplo, 40° Celsius corresponde a 104° Fahrenheit.

◆ **¿Sabe Ud. convertir grados Fahrenheit a Centígrados?**

Adriana

doña Eva

ACE the Test

criada

Ignacio

 ¿Quién lo dice? Identify the person who said the following in the dialogues.

1. No, gracias, señora. ¡No se moleste! _____
2. ¡Ojalá que te mejores pronto! _____
3. Para el lunes ya se habrá curado y podrá volver a la universidad. _____
4. Mamá, tendré que quedarme en casa hoy. _____
5. Voy a llamar a Carolina, a ver si ella puede ir conmigo. _____
6. ¡Ignacio! ¡Qué gusto de verte! _____
7. ¿Te gustaría venir a visitarme? _____
8. Señora, aquí hay un joven que quiere hablar con la señorita Adriana. _____
9. Sería una buena idea llevarte al médico. _____
10. Bueno... ¡te espero a eso de las cuatro! ¡Chau! _____

Hablemos. With a partner, take turns asking and answering the following questions. Base your answers on the dialogue and on your own circumstances.

En el diálogo	¿Y tú?
1. ¿Qué hay en el patio de la familia Vargas?	¿Tu casa tiene árboles frutales?
2. Para no ir a la facultad, ¿qué le va a decir Adriana a su mamá?	¿Qué excusa das tú cuando no quieres venir a clase?
3. ¿Qué síntomas dice Adriana que tiene?	¿Qué síntomas tienes tú cuando tienes gripe?
4. ¿Qué tomará Adriana para mejorarse?	¿Qué tomas tú cuando te duele la cabeza?
5. ¿Qué dice la mamá de Adriana que su hija tendrá que tomar?	¿Qué le pones tú al té?
6. ¿Quién abre la puerta cuando suena el timbre?	¿Tú y tu familia tienen criada?
7. ¿Qué habría hecho doña Eva de haber sabido que Ignacio venía?	¿Tú meriendas a veces? ¿Qué comes?
8. ¿Qué quiere preguntarle Ignacio a Adriana?	¿Has ido a una fiesta últimamente?
9. ¿Cuándo dice doña Eva que Adriana podrá volver a la universidad?	Si tú tienes algo contagioso, ¿vienes a la universidad?
10. ¿Qué dice Ignacio que Adriana necesita hacer?	¿Qué haces tú cuando no te sientes bien?

Vocabulario

Cognados

el antibiótico antibiotic
la aspirina aspirin
colonial colonial
contagioso(-a) contagious
enorme enormous

perfectamente perfectly
el síntoma symptom
la temperatura temperature
el tipo type

Improve Your Grade
Audio Flashcards

Nombres

la ambulancia ambulance
los árboles frutales fruit trees
el cafecito small (cup of) coffee
el catarro, el resfriado, el resfrío cold
el chequeo checkup
el consultorio doctor's office
la fiebre fever
la garganta throat
el grado degree

la gripe influenza, flu
el (la) joven young man (woman)
la miel de abeja honey
el patio backyard
la pulmonía pneumonia
el remedio, la medicina medicine
la salud health
el timbre doorbell
la tos cough

Verbos

curarse to cure oneself, to get better
descansar to rest
doler[1] (o:ue) to hurt
empeorarse to get worse
enyesar to put in a cast
mejorarse to get better

merendar (e:ie) to have an afternoon snack
molestarse to bother (doing something)
preguntar to ask (a question)
recetar to prescribe
sonar (o:ue) to ring
toser to cough

Otras palabras y expresiones

a eso de at about
bien caliente nice and hot
de haber sabido had I known
menos mal it's a good thing
¡Qué gusto de verte! How nice to see you!
¡Qué lástima! What a pity!
¡Ya verás! You'll see!

 ¿Lo sabía Ud.?

Especialmente en las grandes ciudades hispanas, la medicina está muy adelantada (*advanced*), pero en muchos pueblos remotos no hay médicos ni hospitales. En ese caso, mucha gente recurre a (*turn to*) los servicios de un curandero (*healer*). Muchas mujeres tienen sus bebés con la ayuda de una partera (*midwife*).

◆ La mayoría de las mujeres de este país, ¿tienen su bebé en un hospital o en casa, con la ayuda de una partera?

---

[1]Same construction as **gustar: Me duele** la cabeza. **Me duelen** los pies.

Vocabulario adicional

El cuerpo

la oreja
el pelo
la cara
la cabeza
el ojo
la nariz
el cuello
la boca
el oído
los dientes
la lengua
el pecho
la espalda
el estómago
el dedo
la mano
la rodilla
el tobillo
el dedo del pie
el pie

En el consultorio del médico

el chequeo, el examen check-up
embarazada pregnant
hacer una radiografía to take an X-ray
la inyección antitetánica tetanus shot

poner una inyección to give a shot
la receta prescription
la sala de rayos X X-ray room

En el hospital

el accidente accident
el ataque al corazón heart attack
la emergencia emergency
romperse, quebrarse to break
la silla de ruedas wheelchair

¿Lo sabía Ud.?

En España y en algunos países latinoamericanos, las farmacias venden principalmente medicinas. En algunos países hispanos es posible comprar ciertas medicinas —como la penicilina— sin tener receta médica.

◆ ¿En este país se pueden comprar antibióticos sin receta médica?

ACE the Test

Práctica

 A. Select the word or phrase that does not belong in each group.

1. gripe / pulmonía / miel de abeja
2. grado / consultorio / fiebre
3. árbol frutal / puerta de calle / timbre
4. pies / tobillos / oídos
5. cabello / dientes / lengua
6. espalda / rodilla / cuello
7. comer / merendar / recetar
8. boca / nariz / dedo
9. ojo / oreja / pecho
10. estómago / cabeza / cara

 B. Match the questions in column A with the answers in column B.

A		B
1. ¿El médico te recetó un antibiótico? _____		**a.** La espalda.
2. ¿Tiene fiebre? _____		**b.** ¡Sí! ¡Menos mal!
3. ¿Qué te duele? _____		**c.** ¡No! ¡Pulmonía!
4. ¿Te mejoraste? _____		**d.** Si quería merendar.
5. ¿Tiene gripe? _____		**e.** Miel de abeja.
6. ¿Eva está mejor? _____		**f.** Sí, tiene una temperatura de 104 grados.
7. ¿Qué le pones al té? _____		**g.** No, gracias. No te molestes.
8. ¿Qué le preguntaste? _____		**h.** De un ataque al corazón.
9. ¿Quieres que te traiga un cafecito? _____		**i.** Sí, porque tengo una infección.
10. ¿De qué murió? _____		**j.** No, me empeoré.

 C. Write the words or phrases that correspond to the following.

1. la penicilina, por ejemplo _____
2. la tomamos para el dolor de cabeza _____
3. muy grande _____
4. resfriado _____
5. medicina _____
6. opuesto de **mejorarse** _____
7. chequeo _____
8. lo que nos da el médico para comprar medicina _____
9. romperse _____
10. opuesto de **trabajar** _____

 D. Complete the following sentences, using vocabulary from this lesson.

1. La fiebre es un _____ de la gripe.
2. Se quebró la pierna y se la van a _____.
3. No puedo hablar porque me _____ la _____.
4. Marta está enferma. ¡Qué _____!
5. Está _____; va a tener el bebé (*baby*) en junio.
6. En el _____ de la casa hay _____ frutales.
7. La fiesta empieza a _____ de las nueve.
8. Quiero un cafecito bien _____.
9. ¡Qué _____ de verte!
10. Salió de la sala de _____ X en una silla de _____.

Para conversar

 A. **¡Ay!** (*Ouch!*)   With a partner, play the roles of a doctor and a patient who is a hypochondriac. The patient describes symptoms and says what he/she thinks the problem is (**Yo creo que tengo...**). The doctor tells the patient what to do or what he/she is going to prescribe (**Tiene que.../Le voy a recetar**).

 B. **¿Qué haces tú?**   With a partner, take turns asking each other what you do when different parts of your body hurt. When you answer, give some details.

 C. **¡Bienvenido(-a)!**   With a partner, play the roles of a guest and a gracious host (hostess). Express happiness at seeing each other. The host (hostess) offers something to eat and drink, including an afternoon snack. Use vocabulary from previous lessons.

Pronunciación

Pronunciation in context

In this lesson, there are some new words or phrases that may be challenging to pronounce. For further pronunciation practice of Spanish sounds, listen to your instructor and repeat the following sentences.

1. Son de **Villarrica,** pero ahora **viven** en **Asunción.**

2. Tendré que **quedarme** en casa hoy.

3. El doctor **Viñas** está en su **consultorio.**

4. Voy a llamar al médico para que te **recete** algún **antibiótico.**

5. Hay un **joven** que quiere hablar con la señorita **Adriana.**

6. Tiene una **temperatura** de treinta y nueve grados.

7. Ya **habré** tomado un montón de **remedios.**

8. **¡Ojalá** te mejores pronto!

 *Salud, amor y pesetas...
y tiempo para gastarlas.*

Health, love, and money ...
and the time to enjoy them.

Aspectos culturales

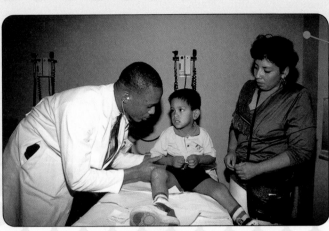

▲ Doctor atendiendo a un niño que está acompañado (*accompanied*) de la madre, Nueva Jersey

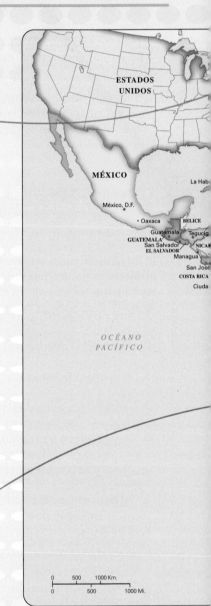

▲ Remedios naturales (hierbas medicinales) a la venta en un mercado de La Paz, Bolivia

Ubíquese... y búsquelo

Improve Your Grade
Web Search

Ignacio comes to visit Adriana hoping that she can go with him to a dance at the Bolivian embassy in Asunción. Go to **www.cengage.com/highered** to find out about embassies in Asunción. In the next class, team up with two classmates and report your findings. What embassies did you find? Did you find the embassy of your country? What are some of the services offered there?

▲ Farmacia de Humacao, Puerto Rico

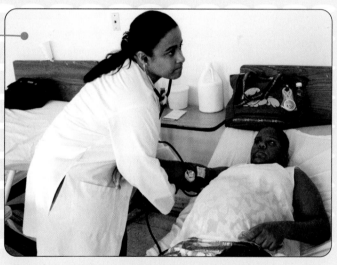

▲ Una enfermera atiende a un paciente en un hospital en Bolivia

Estructuras

1. The future (*El futuro*)

♦ Most Spanish verbs are regular in the future tense. The infinitive serves as the stem of almost all of them, and the endings are the same for all three conjugations.

The Future Tense					
Infinitive		*Stem*		*Ending*	
trabajar	yo	trabajar-	**é**	trabajar**é**	
aprender	tú	aprender-	**ás**	aprender**ás**	
escribir	Ud.	escribir-	**á**	escribir**á**	
hablar	él	hablar-	**á**	hablar**á**	
decidir	ella	decidir-	**á**	decidir**á**	
dar	nosotros(-as)	dar-	**emos**	dare**mos**	
ir	vosotros(-as)	ir-	**éis**	ir**éis**	
caminar	Uds.	caminar-	**án**	caminar**án**	
perder	ellos	perder-	**án**	perder**án**	
recibir	ellas	recibir-	**án**	recibir**án**	

¡Atención! Note that all the endings, except the one for the **nosotros** form, have written accents.

—¿**Irás** al médico?   *"Will you go to the doctor?"*
—Sí, y ya **verás** que pronto me   *"Yes, and you'll see that soon I'll feel better."*
   sentiré mejor.

The English equivalent of the Spanish future is *will* or *shall* + a verb. As you have already learned, Spanish also uses the construction **ir a** + *infinitive* or the present tense with a time expression to express future action, very much like the English present tense or the expression *going to*.

Vamos a ir al hospital esta noche.   ⎤ *We're going (We'll go) to the hospital*
or: **Iremos** al hospital esta noche.   ⎦ *tonight.*

Anita **toma** el examen mañana.   ⎤ *Anita is taking (will take) the exam*
or: Anita **tomará** el examen   ⎦ *tomorrow.*
   mañana.

¡Atención! The Spanish future is *not* used to express willingness, as is the English future. In Spanish, this is expressed with the verb **querer**.

¿**Quieres** llamar a Tomás?   *Will you call Tomás?*

¿Lo sabía Ud.?

En la mayoría de los países de habla hispana, los hospitales son gratis y subvencionados (*subsidized*) por el gobierno. Hay clínicas privadas para la gente de mejor posición económica que no quiere ir a un hospital público.

♦ **En este país, ¿los hospitales son gratis?**

◆ A small number of verbs are irregular in the future. These verbs use a modified form of the infinitive as a stem, but have the same endings as the regular verbs.

Irregular Future Stems		
Infinitive	*Modified form (Stem)*	*First-person singular*
decir	dir-	**diré**
hacer	har-	**haré**
querer	querr-	**querré**
saber	sabr-	**sabré**
poder	podr-	**podré**
caber	cabr-	**cabré**
poner	pondr-	**pondré**
venir	vendr-	**vendré**
tener	tendr-	**tendré**
salir	saldr-	**saldré**
valer[1]	valdr-	**valdré**

—¿Qué les **dirás** a tus padres?
—Les **diré** que no **podremos** venir en enero y que **vendremos** en febrero.

"What will you tell your parents?"
"I will tell them that we won't be able to come in January and that we will come in February."

¡Atención! The future of **hay** (impersonal form of **haber**) is **habrá**.

¿Habrá una fiesta? *Will there be a party?*

Práctica

ACE the Test

 A. Say what the following people will do after next week, using the future tense.

1. Jorge / ir al consultorio del médico
2. Mis padres / venir a visitarme / agosto
3. Ud. / ponerse / una inyección antitetánica
4. Uds. / pasar dos días / Asunción
5. Marta y yo / tener que hacer una radiografía
6. Yo tomar / medicina todos los días
7. Tú / visitar / un amigo en el hospital
8. Yo / salir para La Paz

B. Say what the following people *will do* in each situation.

1. Mauricio tiene pulmonía.
2. Eva y yo tenemos tos.
3. El doctor tiene dos pacientes que tienen gripe.
4. Yo tengo una temperatura de 103 grados de fiebre.
5. El médico cree que uno de sus pacientes se rompió una pierna.
6. A Paco y a Raquel les duele la garganta.

  Un dicho **Dime con quién andas y te diré quién eres.**

Equivalent: You are known by the company you keep.

[1]**valer** = *to be worth*

C. You and a friend will be attending a special program in Paraguay next year. Take turns asking and answering these questions about your trip.

1. ¿A qué ciudad irán?
2. ¿Cuándo saldrán de viaje?
3. ¿Viajarán en barco o en avión?
4. ¿Cuánto tiempo estarán estudiando?
5. ¿Podrán visitar muchas ciudades?
6. ¿Qué lugares visitarán? (Hint: *see Internet*)
7. ¿Les enviarán tarjetas postales a sus amigos?
8. ¿Cuánto dinero necesitarán para el viaje?
9. ¿Se lo pedirán a sus padres?
10. ¿Cuándo volverán?

Para conversar

A. ¿Cuáles son tus planes?   Now, use the questions in Exercise C as a model to ask a classmate about his or her upcoming travel plans.

B. Tu horóscopo   You and your partner are in charge of the astrology section in a newspaper. Using the future tense, write predictions for each sign. Compare notes with other members of the class.

Aries	Tauro	Géminis	Cáncer	Leo	Virgo

Libra	Escorpión	Sagitario	Capricornio	Acuario	Piscis

---

2. The conditional (*El condicional*)

◆ The conditional tense in Spanish is equivalent to the conditional in English, expressed by *should* or *would* + *a verb*.[1] Like the future tense, the conditional uses the infinitive as the stem and has only one set of endings for all three conjugations.

The Conditional Tense

Infinitive		Stem	Ending	
trabajar	yo	trabajar-	**ía**	trabajar**ía**
aprender	tú	aprender-	**ías**	aprender**ías**
escribir	Ud.	escribir-	**ía**	escribir**ía**
ir	él	ir-	**ía**	ir**ía**
ser	ella	ser-	**ía**	ser**ía**
dar	nosotros(-as)	dar-	**íamos**	dar**íamos**
hablar	vosotros(-as)	hablar-	**íais**	hablar**íais**
servir	Uds.	servir-	**ían**	servir**ían**
estar	ellos	estar-	**ían**	estar**ían**
preferir	ellas	preferir-	**ían**	preferir**ían**

---

[1]The conditional is never used in Spanish as an equivalent of *used to*.
Cuando era pequeño siempre **iba a la playa.** *When I was little I would always go to the beach.*

◆ All of the conditional endings have written accents.

—Él dijo que **tomaría** esta medicina.   *"He said that he would take this medicine."*
—Sí, y también dijo que **hablaría**   *"Yes, and he also said that he would speak*
con el médico.   *with the doctor."*

No sé... yo no lo **lavaría** aquí.

◆ The conditional is also used as the future of a past action. The future states what *will* happen; the conditional states what *would* happen.

Future	Conditional
(states what *will* happen)	(states what *would* happen)
Él **dice** que **estará** aquí mañana.	Él **dijo** que **estaría** aquí mañana.
He says that he will be here tomorrow.	*He said that he would be here tomorrow.*

◆ The verbs that have irregular stems in the future tense are also irregular in the conditional. The endings are the same as those for regular verbs.

Irregular Conditional Stems		
Infinitive	*Modified form (Stem)*	*First-person singular*
decir	dir-	**diría**
hacer	har-	**haría**
querer	querr-	**querría**
saber	sabr-	**sabría**
poder	podr-	**podría**
caber	cabr-	**cabría**
poner	pondr-	**pondría**
venir	vendr-	**vendría**
tener	tendr-	**tendría**
salir	saldr-	**saldría**
valer	valdr-	**valdría**

—¿A qué hora te dijo que **vendría**?   *"What time did he tell you he would come?"*
—Dijo que **saldría** de casa a las dos.   *"He said he would leave home at two."*

¡Atención!   The conditional of **hay** (impersonal form of **haber**) is **habría**.

Dijo que **habría** un examen   *He said there would be an exam tomorrow.*
mañana.

ACE the Test

Práctica

 A. Nobody would do the things that Carlos does. With a partner, take turns saying what the following people would do instead.

     ◆ **MODELO:** Carlos come en la cafetería. (yo)
          Yo no comería en la cafetería; comería en mi casa.

Carlos...

1. se levanta a las cinco. (Uds.)
2. estudia por la mañana. (Ana y Luis)
3. viene a la universidad en ómnibus. (nosotros)
4. toma clases de alemán. (yo)
5. se baña por la noche. (Elsa)
6. se acuesta a las nueve de la noche. (Ud.)
7. va a las montañas los fines de semana. (ellos)
8. sale con Margarita. (tú)

 B. Describe what you would do in the following situations, using the conditional.

1. Su amigo(-a) le pide consejos sobre la carrera que debe seguir.
2. Su equipo de fútbol americano favorito juega hoy.
3. Un compañero quiere que Ud. lo ayude con su informe.
4. Sus amigos lo (la) invitan a ir al cine esta noche y Ud. tiene que trabajar mañana.
5. Una persona muy antipática lo (la) invita a salir.
6. Usted tiene que estar en la universidad a las siete de la mañana.
7. Usted tiene una beca y necesita mantener un buen promedio.
8. Ud. va a matricularse y no sabe qué asignaturas debe tomar.

Para conversar

 A. Buenos consejos Using the following advice from a magazine article, take turns with your partner indicating what each person in the list said he/she would or wouldn't do after reading it.

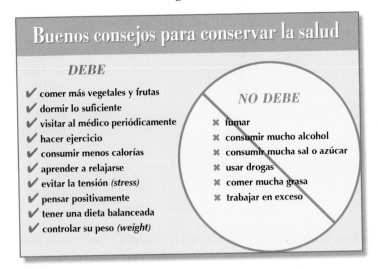

Buenos consejos para conservar la salud

DEBE
- ✔ comer más vegetales y frutas
- ✔ dormir lo suficiente
- ✔ visitar al médico periódicamente
- ✔ hacer ejercicio
- ✔ consumir menos calorías
- ✔ aprender a relajarse
- ✔ evitar la tensión *(stress)*
- ✔ pensar positivamente
- ✔ tener una dieta balanceada
- ✔ controlar su peso *(weight)*

NO DEBE
- ✖ fumar
- ✖ consumir mucho alcohol
- ✖ consumir mucha sal o azúcar
- ✖ usar drogas
- ✖ comer mucha grasa
- ✖ trabajar en exceso

1. El Sr. Vega toma diez cervezas todos los días.
2. La Srta. Díaz está siempre sentada, mirando la televisión.
3. Elsa come muchos dulces *(sweets)*.
4. El Dr. Álvarez trabaja catorce horas cada día.
5. La Sra. Carreras duerme sólo cuatro horas cada noche.
6. Estela se preocupa constantemente por todo.

7. Adela siempre come papas fritas, hamburguesas, mantequilla, pollo frito, etc.
8. Hace cinco años que Carlos no va a ver a su médico.
9. La dieta de Eduardo es de 5.000 calorías al día.
10. Raúl pesa (*weighs*) 300 libras (*pounds*).
11. Raquel solamente come carne y pastas.
12. A Jorge le gustan mucho los cigarrillos.

B. ¡Gané la lotería! With a partner, take turns telling each other what you would do if you won a million dollars in the lottery. Say at least five things each, and then compare your responses with those of other classmates.

3. The future perfect and the conditional perfect (*El futuro perfecto y el condicional perfecto*)

A. The future perfect

◆ The future perfect in Spanish corresponds closely in formation and meaning to the same tense in English. The Spanish future perfect is formed with the future tense of the auxiliary verb **haber** + *the past participle* of the main verb.

Future tense of *haber*	
habré	habremos
habrás	habréis
habrá	habrán

Formation of the Future Perfect Tense		
yo	**habré terminado**	*I will have finished*
tú	**habrás vuelto**	*you will have returned*
Ud. él ella	**habrá comido**	*you (he, she) will have eaten*
nosotros(-as)	**habremos escrito**	*we will have written*
vosotros(-as)	**habréis dicho**	*you (fam.) will have said*
Uds. ellos ellas	**habrán salido**	*you (they) will have left*

◆ Like its English equivalent, the future perfect is used to indicate an action that will have taken place by a certain time in the future.

—¿Tus padres estarán aquí para el dos de junio?
—Sí, para esa fecha ya **habrán vuelto** de Madrid.

"Will your parents be here by June second?"
"Yes, by that date they will have returned from Madrid."

¿Habrás terminado para las seis?

ACE the Test

Práctica

Complete the following dialogues, using the future perfect forms of the verbs listed. Then act them out with a partner.

acostarse	salir	limpiar
cenar	terminar (2)	volver (2)

1. —Esta noche a las once voy a llamar a Quique.

   —¿Estás loco(-a)? Para esa hora él ya _____. Llámalo mañana a las siete.

   —Para esa hora ya _____ de su casa.

2. —¿Uds. _____ de México para el 4 de julio?

   —No, no _____ todavía. Vamos a estar allí hasta agosto.

3. —Tú y yo podemos salir para España el 12 de diciembre porque ya estaremos de vacaciones.

   —Bueno, tú _____ las clases para entonces, pero yo no las _____ todavía.

4. —No podemos traer a mis amigos esta noche porque la casa está muy sucia (*dirty*).

   —No te preocupes. Para cuando Uds. vengan, las chicas ya la _____.

5. —¿Quieres cenar con nosotros hoy?

   —Gracias, pero para cuando yo vuelva, Uds. ya _____.

Para conversar

Para entonces With a partner, discuss things that you will or will not have done by the following times.

1. para las once de la noche
2. para mañana a las cinco de la mañana
3. para mañana a las seis de la tarde
4. para el sábado próximo
5. para junio del año próximo
6. para el año 2012
7. para diciembre
8. para el mes próximo
9. para el verano que viene
10. para el año 2020

B. The conditional perfect

♦ The conditional perfect is formed with the conditional tense of the auxiliary verb **haber** + *the past participle* of the main verb.

Conditional tense of *haber*	
habría	habríamos
habrías	habríais
habría	habrían

Formation of the Conditional Perfect Tense		
yo	**habría vuelto**	*I would have returned*
tú	**habrías comido**	*you would have eaten*
Ud.		
él	**habría salido**	*you (he, she) would have left*
ella		
nosotros(-as)	**habríamos estudiado**	*we would have studied*
vosotros(-as)	**habríais hecho**	*you* (fam.) *would have done*
Uds.		
ellos	**habrían muerto**	*you (they) would have died*
ellas		

Yo **habría comprado** una talla más grande.

◆ Like the English conditional perfect, the Spanish conditional perfect is used to indicate an action that would have taken place but didn't.

—Lo llevé al hospital en mi coche. *"I took him to the hospital in my car."*
—Yo **habría llamado** una ambulancia. *"I would have called an ambulance."*

Práctica

ACE the Test

Last summer, my family, a friend, and I took a trip to New York. Based on what I tell you about our trip, say what you and each member of your family would have done differently, if anything.

◆ **MODELO:** Mi padre llevó tres maletas.
Mi padre habría llevado una maleta.

1. Nosotros fuimos a Nueva York.
2. Viajamos en tren.
3. Yo me senté en la sección de no fumar.
4. Mi mamá preparó sándwiches para el viaje.
5. Mi amigo y yo bebimos refrescos en el café del tren.
6. En Nueva York, mi amigo se quedó en casa de su abuelo.
7. Nosotros nos quedamos en un hotel.
8. Mis padres fueron a ver una comedia musical.
9. Yo fui a bailar.
10. Nosotros visitamos el Museo de Arte Moderno.
11. Mi amigo visitó la Estatua de la Libertad.
12. Estuvimos en Nueva York por dos semanas.

Para conversar

¡No los esperábamos! You and your family had unannounced guests last Saturday. You were not prepared! Say what you and other members of your family would have done, had you known that they were coming.

◆ **MODELO:** mi mamá
De haber sabido que vendrían, mi mamá habría limpiado la casa.

1. yo
2. mi papá
3. mi hermana y yo
4. mis hermanos
5. mis padres
6. mi mamá y yo
7. la criada
8. mi tía

Summary of the Tenses of the Indicative			
Simple Tenses			
	-ar	*-er*	*-ir*
Presente	habl**o**	com**o**	viv**o**
Pretérito	habl**é**	com**í**	viv**í**
Imperfecto	habl**aba**	com**ía**	viv**ía**
Futuro	hablar**é**	comer**é**	vivir**é**
Condicional	hablar**ía**	comer**ía**	vivir**ía**
Compound Tenses			
Pretérito perfecto	**he** habl**ado**	**he** com**ido**	**he** viv**ido**
Pretérito pluscuamperfecto	**había** habl**ado**	**había** com**ido**	**había** viv**ido**
Futuro perfecto	**habré** habl**ado**	**habré** com**ido**	**habré** viv**ido**
Condicional perfecto	**habría** habl**ado**	**habría** com**ido**	**habría** viv**ido**

Así somos

Al escuchar...

> **Estrategia** **Recognizing transitions** You have already seen that certain words establish links or transitions between one idea and the next. Review the transition words listed in **Al escuchar..., Lección 11.** Here are other transition words you have seen. The lesson number where each was introduced is shown in parentheses.
>
> | | | |
> |---|---|---|
> | bueno (1) | a pesar de (esto, lo anterior) (9) | en cuanto (14) |
> | en ese caso (2) | es que (13) | si (14) |
> | en fin (8) | por ejemplo (13) | de haber(lo) sabido (15) |

 Estoy muy mal. Listen to a conversation between Rosa and Sergio. Listen specifically for the transitional markers and write them on a piece of paper. Try to list ten different ones.

Al conversar...

> **Estrategia** **Practicing extended conversation** As you continue your study of Spanish, it is important that you develop your conversational skills beyond brief oral exchanges. When you make a statement, try to elaborate with details. For example, on the topic **Hoy voy al médico,** you can talk about the time of the appointment, why you are going, your symptoms, how long you have had the problem, etc.

 Anécdotas personales Think of three simple statements to tell your partner and expand on each with as much information as you can. You might talk about something you plan to do, a friend, a recent medical problem, a movie you saw, etc.

 ¿Qué dice Ud.? What would you say in the following situations? What might the other person say? Act out the scenes with a partner. Take turns playing each role.

1. You tell a friend that you were sick but the doctor has prescribed some medicine, and you are now feeling perfectly well.
2. You tell a friend that an ambulance has taken his dad to the emergency room because he had a heart attack.
3. You inform a man that his son has had an accident. Add that you asked the doctor how he is and he is O.K.
4. Someone offers to do something for you. Tell him/her not to bother.

 Para conocernos mejor To do this activity, work with a classmate whom you would like to get to know. Take turns asking and answering these questions.

1. ¿Has tenido algún problema últimamente? ¿Cuántas veces al año vas al médico? ¿Cuándo fue la última vez que te hicieron un chequeo? ¿Cómo se llama tu médico? ¿Cómo te sientes hoy?
2. ¿Tú te quedas en tu casa cuando estás enfermo(-a)? ¿Has tenido pulmonía alguna vez? ¿Cuándo fue la última vez que tuviste catarro? ¿Qué hiciste?
3. ¿Tú eres alérgico(-a) a alguna medicina? ¿Qué tomas cuando tienes tos? ¿Tu médico te receta antibióticos a veces? ¿Cuáles?

4. ¿Te han enyesado una pierna o un brazo alguna vez? ¿Cuándo fue la última vez que te hicieron una radiografía? ¿De qué parte del cuerpo? ¿Te pusieron alguna inyección antitetánica? ¿Cuándo?

5. ¿Te habrás acostado para las once de la noche? ¿Tomarás algo antes de acostarte? ¿Qué?

 Una encuesta   Interview your classmates to identify who fits the following descriptions. Include your instructor, but remember to use the **Ud.** form when addressing him/her. After finishing the survey, get together with two or three classmates and discuss the results.

Nombre

1. Tiene buena salud.
2. Necesita descansar más.
3. Toma una taza de té cuando no se siente bien.
4. Le gustaría tomar un cafecito bien caliente.
5. A veces le duele la espalda.
6. Toma aspirina cuando le duele la cabeza.
7. Se habrá acostado para las once de la noche.
8. Tendrá que quedarse en su casa este fin de semana.

Para crear   Get together in groups of three or four and "create" the scenario for this photo. Who are the people? Give them names. What is their relationship to each other? What happened to the young man, and what did the doctor do? What symptoms is the patient describing? What is the doctor saying? What will he prescribe?

¡Vamos a escribir!

Antes de escribir

Estrategia **Writing to persuade** One of the functions of writing is persuading someone to agree with your point of view. To be as convincing as possible, think through the reasons that justify or support your point of view. Think of the reader's possible reactions and use logic to present your case. Provide a statement of your position and include ideas that support it, such as benefits of a course of action and information or facts regarding the possible outcome of an action.

Una nota para excusarse You will write a note to your instructor explaining that you cannot take an exam because you are sick. You want to persuade your instructor to allow you to take a make-up exam.

◆ Brainstorm about the symptoms you have in order to make a case for not taking the exam.
◆ Brainstorm why you should take a make-up exam and how it will benefit you and the instructor. How will you counter possible objections your instructor might have?
◆ Select what you think are the most convincing ideas.

A escribir la nota

Write the **primer borrador** of your excuse note. Be sure to mention when you would be able to take the make-up exam and thank your instructor for considering your request!

Después de escribir

Before writing the final version of your note, exchange your first draft with a classmate and peer edit each other's work using the following guidelines.

◆ use of the subjunctive and indicative, especially after conjunctions
◆ formation and use of all tenses, especially the future and conditional
◆ convincing presentation of ideas

Hugo Rodríguez-Alcalá (*Paraguay: 1917–*)

El autor paraguayo Hugo Rodríguez-Alcalá escribe poesía, cuentos y ensayos. Publicó sus dos primeros libros en 1939: *Poemas* y *Estampas de la guerra.* Este último influyó más tarde en la literatura de su país, evocadora de la Guerra del Chaco, librada (*fought*) con Bolivia.

Este escritor ha publicado gran número de estudios literarios en revistas del norte y del sur del continente a partir de 1950, pero la mayoría de sus libros han aparecido en México. Entre los más importantes figuran el libro de poemas *Abril que cruza el mundo* y el libro dedicado al gran escritor mexicano Juan Rulfo, *El arte de Juan Rulfo.*

Hugo Rodríguez-Alcalá fue catedrático de la Universidad de California en Riverside, y durante su estancia allí, escribió varios libros de poemas donde refleja su vivencia en este estado. El siguiente poema es un ejemplo de esta poesía.

Antes de leer

Estrategia   **Poetic language and the dictionary**   Poets use very precise language. Sometimes a poet uses a rather obscure word to create a specific effect. When you encounter an unfamiliar word, you can try to extract its meaning from context; however, often it may be necessary to look up the word in a dictionary to better understand the nuance and mood or tone the poet is conveying. When consulting a dictionary, you may need to consider the context in which the word appears in order to select the correct meaning.

Lenguaje poético   Go to your dictionary, find the definition of the following words, and write them on a piece of paper. Then, to help you remember the word, give a simpler approximate word you know that conveys the same general concept.

1. columbrar (una casa)
2. tembloroso
3. (a la) vera
4. verter (hojas de un árbol, *leaves of a tree*)

A leer

Read the first stanza of the poem. In pairs, try to determine what the direct object pronoun **lo** refers to. Then read the complete poem.

Jacarandá en California

Cuando regreso a la casa
y **lo columbro** de lejos,
todo vestido de gala°
y enamorado del viento,

con el lila de sus ramos
tembloroso de deseo,
se me figura impaciente,
como si fuera un velero°
queriendo soltar amarras°
y navegar por el cielo.°

Bajo del coche y avanzo
por la escalera de piedra,°
y a su **vera** me detengo
para admirar su belleza.

Y él se me antoja° que inclina
su copa de primavera
y que a mis pies, saludando,
vierte sus flores más tiernas.

vestido... *dressed up*

sailboat
soltar... *untie lines*
sky

stone

se... *it seems to me*

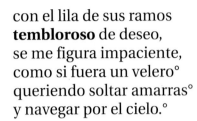

Después de leer... reflexiones

 A. Recitation Listen to "Jacarandá en California" being recited in your in-text audio. Then answer the following questions.

1. ¿Qué ve el poeta de lejos al regresar a su casa?
2. ¿De qué dice que está enamorado el árbol?
3. ¿Qué se le figura al poeta que es el árbol?
4. ¿Qué dice que quiere hacer el árbol?
5. ¿Qué admira el poeta?
6. ¿Qué hace el árbol para saludar al poeta?

 B. Expressing feelings With a partner, talk about how you feel when you are close to nature. (**Cuando estoy cerca de la naturaleza...**) Words you might include: **paz** (*peace*), **tranquilidad** (*tranquility*).

Sobre la libertad

¿De qué se hace un tirano?° De la vileza° de muchos y de la cobardía° de todos.

tyrant / vileness cowardice

    Enrique José Varona (Cuba: 1849–1933)

Mi único amor siempre ha sido el de la patria;° mi única ambición su libertad.

homeland

    Simón Bolívar (Venezuela: 1783–1830)

Libertad es el derecho° que todo hombre tiene a ser honrado° y a pensar y a hablar sin hipocresía.

right / honest, honorable

    José Martí (Cuba: 1853–1895)

La libertad no consiste en hacer lo que se quiere, sino° en hacer lo que se debe.

but

    Ramón de Campoamor (España: 1817–1901)

Comentarios...

A. With a partner, take turns reading the **Frases célebres,** and say which one appeals to you the most. Give reasons for your choice.

B. Can you think of any famous sayings in English about this topic?

Paraguay

- Paraguay es un país principalmente agrícola y su economía depende de sus bosques y sus fértiles tierras (*lands*). Sin embargo, desde la construcción de la planta hidroeléctrica de Itaipú, el país ha comenzado a industrializarse y empieza a convertirse en un centro de atracción turística. Itaipú, la mayor planta hidroeléctrica del mundo, obra del esfuerzo conjunto de Brasil y Paraguay, ha hecho de este país el mayor exportador de energía hidroeléctrica. Esta planta produce tanta energía como 10 plantas nucleares, y 6 veces más que la represa (*dam*) de Aswan en Egipto. Más importante aún, la planta evita la emisión de más de 67 millones de toneladas de dióxido de carbono al año.

- Al igual que Bolivia, Paraguay no tiene salida al mar, pero tiene más de 1.800 millas de ríos navegables, que son sus principales vías de transporte. En la frontera de Paraguay, Argentina y Brasil están las famosas cataratas de Iguazú, nombre guaraní que significa "agua grande".

- La mayor parte de los turistas que llegan a Paraguay, solamente van hasta el lado paraguayo de las cataratas y a la planta de Itaipú, pero los que visitan el resto del país, disfrutan de sus múltiples bellezas naturales y admiran su artesanía.

- Asunción, la capital de Paraguay, es también su principal puerto. Desde allí salen los barcos que, a través del río Paraná, transportan los productos del país hasta el río de la Plata. Asunción es una ciudad de más de 2 millones de habitantes en la que se mezclan los edificios coloniales con modernas construcciones.

◄ Cataratas de Iguazú, las más caudalosas del mundo, en la frontera (*border*) de Paraguay, Argentina y Brasil

Bolivia

- En realidad, La Paz es una de las dos capitales de Bolivia; la otra es Sucre. La Paz, situada a 12.000 pies de altura, es la capital administrativa, y Sucre, la capital política. El lago Titicaca está a 12.500 pies de altura y es, después del lago Maracaibo, el segundo más grande de América del Sur. El país es tan grande como los estados de California y Texas juntos, pero apenas puede explotar sus riquezas naturales porque no tiene salida al mar y su territorio es muy montañoso.

- Los indios quechua y aymará, que constituyen más de la mitad de su población, mantienen su cultura y sus lenguas tradicionales. El resto de la población lo constituyen las personas de ascendencia europea (un 15% de la población) y los mestizos producto de la integración de las razas indígenas y europeas. La mayor parte de los habitantes del país vive en el altiplano (*plateau*).

- Bolivia es uno de los más atractivos destinos turísticos por sus bellísimos paisajes andinos, que le han valido el nombre de "el Tibet de América", y por las ruinas doblemente milenarias de Tiahuanaco.

- Otras ciudades importantes, además de las capitales, son Santa Cruz de la Sierra, Oruro y Potosí.

◄ A 3.600 metros sobre (*above*) el nivel del mar, La Paz es la ciudad capital más alta del mundo y es la sede (*seat*) del gobierno y el centro administrativo, financiero y comercial del país.

Maravillas del ingenio[1] y del trabajo humanos

▲ Mineros de la plata (*silver*) de Potosí, Bolivia, nombre que dio origen a la palabra potosí, sinónimo poético de "gran riqueza" (*great wealth*).

▲ Represa (*Dam*) de Itaipú, la mayor planta hidroeléctrica del mundo (construida entre 1974 y 1991). En treinta años, la economía de la zona se ha transformado y la población ha aumentado considerablemente, debido a la represa.

Nuestro panorama cultural

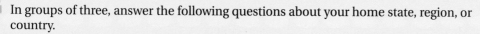

In groups of three, answer the following questions about your home state, region, or country.

1. ¿Hay grandes cataratas en su país? ¿Dónde están?
2. ¿Hay represas en su país? ¿Hay plantas que producen formas alternativas de energía en su región?
3. ¿Qué tipos de artesanía de su país o de su región se conocen en otros países?

For the next class: Go to the World Wide Web and find photos of your home-town, state, region, or country. Use the questions from **Nuestro panorama cultural** above as guidelines for choosing them. Be ready to present the photos to your classmates.

[1]**ingenio** = *creative powers*

Take this test. When you have finished, check your answers in the answer key provided in Appendix D. Then use a red pen to correct any mistakes you may have made. Are you ready?

Lección 13

A. Familiar commands (*tú*) Give the Spanish equivalent of the words in parentheses.

1. _____, Paco. ¿Pusiste el dinero en la billetera? (*Tell me*)
2. _____ el trabajo y luego _____ los baños, Ana. (*Do / clean*)
3. _____ de mi cuarto, Carlos. (*Leave*)
4. _____ con ella y _____ el vestido para Silvia, Pepe. (*Go / buy*)
5. ¿Los libros? _____ en la mesa, Dora. (*Put them*)
6. _____ conmigo. (*Come*)
7. _____ buena y _____ los aretes. (*Be / bring me*)
8. _____ paciencia. _____ unos minutos más. (*Have / Wait for me*)
9. _____ el camisón si no está en rebaja, Anita. (*Don't buy*)
10. ¿Los zapatos? _____ todavía (*yet*), Julio. (*Don't exchange them*)
11. _____, querido. (*Don't go away*)
12. _____ a las seis y _____ hasta las once. (*Get up / work*)

B. *Qué* and *cuál* used with *ser* Supply the questions that elicited the following responses. Begin each one with **qué** or **cuál,** as needed.

1. Mi número de teléfono es 862-4031.
2. El apellido de mi padre es Álvarez.
3. Una pulsera es una joya.
4. Las lecciones que necesitamos son la once y la doce.
5. Su dirección es calle Universidad, número treinta.
6. Una enchilada es un plato mexicano.

C. The subjunctive to express indefiniteness and nonexistence Complete the following sentences, using the present subjunctive or the present indicative of the verbs given.

1. ¿Hay alguien aquí que _____ (saber) hablar español?
2. Tengo unos zapatos que Uds. _____ (tener) que devolver.
3. No conozco a nadie que _____ (ser) chileno.
4. ¿Ud. quiere una blusa que _____ (tener) rayas?
5. Necesito una falda que _____ (hacer) juego con esta blusa.
6. Aquí hay una chica que _____ (hablar) francés, pero no hay nadie que _____ (hablar) italiano.

D. Just words . . . Complete the following sentences, using the vocabulary from Lección 13.

1. Voy a ir al centro _____ para comprar unos _____ de tenis. Hoy tienen una gran _____.

2. No tengo nada que _____; por eso voy a _____ de compras.

3. Estas botas no son estrechas; son muy _____.

4. ¿Qué número _____ Ud.?

5. La caja está al _____ del probador.

6. Voy a devolver este vestido porque me _____ grande. Yo uso _____ mediana.

7. Ernesto está en el _____ de caballeros porque necesita comprar _____ interior.

8. No me gustan las camisas de _____. Prefiero las de cuadros.

9. Voy a la _____ para comprar unos libros.

10. Tengo que comprar un _____ de zapatos negros.

11. ¿Qué les _____ si vamos de compras hoy?

12. Esta cartera cuesta solamente diez dólares; es una _____.

E. Culture Complete the following sentences, based on the **Panorama hispánico** section.

1. Chile es un país largo y _____.

2. Casi la _____ parte de los habitantes de Chile viven en la capital.

3. Viña del _____ es el balneario más conocido de Chile.

4. Chile es conocido como "la _____ del mundo".

Lección 14

A. The subjunctive or indicative after certain conjunctions Complete the following sentences with the present subjunctive or the present indicative of the verbs given.

1. Tan pronto como Marta _____ (llegar) a casa, le voy a dar el dinero.
2. Voy a esperarlos hasta que _____ (volver).
3. Cuando ellos _____ (ir) a la facultad, siempre salen temprano.
4. Cuando lo _____ (ver), dile que me llame.
5. Vamos a hablar con ellos antes de que _____ (tomar) una decisión.
6. Ella va a ir al laboratorio con tal que tú _____ (ir) con ella.
7. No puedo matricularme a menos que tú me _____ (dar) el dinero.
8. En caso de que ella _____ (necesitar) el horario, yo puedo traérselo.
9. Voy a llamar a Raúl para que nos _____ (llevar) a la universidad.

B. The past participle Give the past participle of the following verbs.

1. escribir
2. abrir
3. ver
4. hacer
5. romper
6. ir
7. hablar
8. comer
9. beber
10. recibir

C. Past participles used as adjectives Give the Spanish equivalent of the words in parentheses.

1. Los informes están _____ en español. (*written*)
2. ¿Están _____ las puertas del gimnasio? (*open*)
3. Ese escritor está _____. (*dead*)
4. El laboratorio está _____. (*closed*)
5. Los trabajos ya están _____. (*done*)

D. The present perfect Complete the sentences with the present perfect tense of the verbs given.

1. El arquitecto no _____ (venir) hoy.
2. Los abogados no me _____ (decir) nada.
3. ¿Tú _____ (escribir) el informe de biología?
4. Yo no _____ (hacer) el trabajo todavía.
5. ¿Uds. _____ (hablar) con la bibliotecaria?
6. Nosotros nunca _____ (enojarse) con ellos.

E. The past perfect (pluperfect) Complete the following sentences with the past perfect tense of the verbs given.

1. Cuando yo llegué, la clase ya _____ (terminar).
2. Elsa dijo que ellos _____ (ir) al laboratorio.
3. El carpintero me _____ (decir) que venía hoy.
4. Yo ya _____ (terminar) el trabajo.
5. Nosotros todavía no nos _____ (matricular).
6. ¿Tú le _____ (preguntar) cuál era su especialización?

F. Just words . . . Match the questions in column A with the answers in column B.

A	B
1. ¿Adónde vas?	a. Administración de empresas.
2. ¿Qué materias estás tomando? _____	b. El año próximo.
3. ¿Quién es tu consejero? _____	c. No, es plomero.
4. ¿Qué tal te va? _____	d. Al laboratorio.
5. ¿Qué tienes que escribir? _____	e. Sí, para pagar la matrícula.
6. ¿Qué nota sacaste? _____	f. Física, química y sociología.
7. ¿Estudia periodismo? _____	g. No, quedé suspendido.
8. ¿Necesitas dinero? _____	h. El Dr. Peña.
9. ¿Aprobaste el examen? _____	i. Un informe para mi clase de biología.
10. ¿Es carpintero? _____	j. No muy bien.
11. ¿Qué carrera estudia? _____	k. Una "B".
12. ¿Cuándo te gradúas? _____	l. Sí, quiere trabajar para el *Times*.

G. Culture Answer the following questions, based on the **Panorama hispánico** section.

1. ¿Cuál es la capital de Argentina?
2. ¿Cuál es la música típica de Argentina?
3. ¿Cómo ha sido llamada Buenos Aires?
4. ¿Qué cataratas famosas hay en Argentina?

Lección 15

A. The future Rewrite the following sentences using the future tense.

1. Le vamos a decir que necesita descansar.
2. ¿Qué van a hacer Uds.?
3. No van a querer ir.
4. Lo voy a saber mañana.
5. No van a poder venir.
6. ¿Adónde vamos a ir?
7. ¿Dónde lo vas a poner?
8. Nosotros vamos a venir con él.
9. Voy a tener que preguntárselo.
10. Vamos a salir mañana.

B. The conditional Rewrite the following sentences, using the conditional tense.

1. Yo voy a Paraguay.
2. Nosotros les recetamos antibióticos.
3. ¿Tú se lo dices?
4. Ellos hablan con Dora.
5. ¿Ud. lo pone en el consultorio?
6. ¿Uds. vienen el domingo?
7. Julio pide miel.
8. Nosotros lo hacemos hoy.
9. Tú no sales con ella.
10. Ella no va sola.

C. The future perfect Complete the following sentences, using the future perfect of the verbs given.

1. Para mañana, el médico me _____ (decir) qué medicina debo tomar.
2. Para las cuatro de la tarde, ellos _____ (volver) del consultorio.
3. Para el domingo, yo _____ (mejorar).
4. Para las cinco, nosotras ya _____ (merendar).
5. ¿Tú me _____ (traer) la silla de ruedas para el mediodía?

D. The conditional perfect
Complete the following sentences, using the conditional perfect of the verbs given.

1. Yo _____ (tomar) aspirinas.
2. Ellos _____ (venir) a eso de las tres.
3. La enfermera te _____ (poner) una inyección antitetánica.
4. De haber sabido que estabas enferma, nosotros _____ (ir) a verte.
5. ¿Qué _____ (hacer) tú?

E. Just words . . .
Choose the word or phrase in parentheses that best completes each sentence.

1. Ella es alérgica a la (radiografía, penicilina, clase).
2. Comemos con (los oídos, los dientes, el pecho).
3. Hablamos con (la espalda, los dedos, la lengua).
4. Vemos con (los ojos, la boca, las orejas).
5. Caminamos con (las manos, el cuello, los pies).
6. Tuvo un accidente. Lo llevaron al hospital en una (garganta, salud, ambulancia).
7. ¿Te (rompiste, atropellaste, evitaste) el brazo alguna vez?
8. Me dolía mucho (la pierna, el pelo, el consultorio).
9. Tenía ciento tres (fiebre, gripe, grados) de temperatura.
10. ¿Cuándo fue la última vez que le (cortaron, quebraron, pusieron) una inyección antitetánica?
11. ¿Por qué tomaste aspirina? ¿Tenías (dolor de cabeza, tos, frío)?
12. ¿Tienes Alka Seltzer? Es para (el pecho, el estómago, los dedos de los pies).
13. Va a tener un niño. Está (cansada, enferma, embarazada).
14. Raúl no se siente bien. El médico dice que tiene (pastillas, gripe, recetas).

F. Culture
Complete the following sentences, based on the **Panorama hispánico** section.

1. La mayoría de los paraguayos hablan dos idiomas, el español y el _____.
2. La represa de _____ es la mayor planta hidroeléctrica del mundo.
3. Paraguay y Bolivia no tienen salida al _____.
4. El _____ es el lago navegable más alto del mundo.
5. Bolivia tiene dos capitales: Sucre y _____.

Appendix A: Spanish Sounds

🎧 Vowels

There are five distinct vowels in Spanish: **a, e, i, o,** and **u.** Each vowel has only one basic, constant sound. The pronunciation of each vowel is constant, clear, and brief. The length of the sound is practically the same whether it is produced in a stressed or unstressed syllable.[1]

While producing the sounds of the English stressed vowels that most closely resemble the Spanish ones, the speaker changes the position of the tongue, lips, and lower jaw, so that the vowel actually starts as one sound and then glides into another. In Spanish, however, the tongue, lips, and jaw keep a constant position during the production of the sound.

> **English:** ban*a*na   **Spanish:** ban**a**na

The stress falls on the same vowel and syllable in both Spanish and English, but the English stressed *a* is longer than the Spanish stressed **a.**

> **English:** ban*a*na   **Spanish:** ban**a**na

Note also that the English stressed *a* has a sound different from the other *a*'s in the word, while the Spanish **a** sound remains constant.

a   The Spanish **a** sounds similar to the English *a* in the word *father.*

alta	casa	palma	Ana
cama	Panamá	alma	apagar

e   The Spanish **e** is pronounced like the English *e* in the word *eight.*

mes	entre	este	deje
ese	encender	teme	prender

i   The Spanish **i** has a sound similar to the English *ee* in the word *see.*

> fin   ir   sí   sin   dividir   Trini   difícil

o   The Spanish **o** is similar to the English *o* in the word *no,* but without the glide.

toco	como	poco	roto
corto	corro	solo	loco

u   The Spanish **u** is pronounced like the English *oo* sound in the word *shoot* or the *ue* sound in the word *Sue.*

su	Lulú	Úrsula	cultura
un	luna	sucursal	Uruguay

Diphthongs and Triphthongs

When unstressed **i** or **u** falls next to another vowel in a syllable, it unites with that vowel to form what is called a *diphthong.* Both vowels are pronounced as one syllable. Their sounds do not change; they are only pronounced more rapidly and with a glide. For example:

tra**i**ga	Lid**ia**	tre**i**nta	s**ie**te	**oi**go	ad**ió**s
Aurora	ag**ua**	b**ue**no	antig**uo**	c**iu**dad	L**ui**s

---

[1]In a stressed syllable, the prominence of the vowel is indicated by its loudness.

A triphthong is the union of three vowels: a stressed vowel between two unstressed ones (**i** or **u**) in the same syllable. For example: Para**guay,** estud**iéis**.

NOTE: Stressed **i** and **u** do not form diphthongs with other vowels, except in the combinations **iu** and **ui**. For example: **rí**-o, sa-**bí**-ais.

In syllabication, diphthongs and triphthongs are considered a single vowel; their components cannot be separated.

Consonants

p Spanish **p** is pronounced in a manner similar to the English *p* sound, but without the puff of air that follows after the English sound is produced.

pesca	pude	puedo	parte	papá
post	piña	puente	Paco	

k The Spanish **k** sound, represented by the letters **k, c** before **a, o, u** or a consonant, and **qu,** is similar to the English *k* sound, but without the puff of air.

casa	comer	cuna	clima	acción	que
quinto	queso	aunque	kiosko	kilómetro	

t Spanish **t** is produced by touching the back of the upper front teeth with the tip of the tongue. It has no puff of air as in the English *t*.

todo	antes	corto	Guatemala	diente
resto	tonto	roto	tanque

d The Spanish consonant **d** has two different sounds depending on its position. At the beginning of an utterance and after **n** or **l,** the tip of the tongue presses the back of the upper front teeth.

día	doma	dice	dolor	dar
anda	Aldo	caldo	el deseo	un domicilio

In all other positions the sound of **d** is similar to the *th* sound in the English word *they*, but softer.

medida	todo	nada	nadie	medio
puedo	moda	queda	nudo	

g The Spanish consonant **g** is similar to the English *g* sound in the word *guy* except before **e** or **i.**

goma	glotón	gallo	gloria	lago	alga
gorrión	garra	guerra	angustia	algo	Dagoberto

j The Spanish sound **j** (or **g** before **e** and **i**) is similar to a strongly exaggerated English *h* sound.

gemir	juez	jarro	gitano	agente
juego	giro	bajo	gente	

b, v There is no difference in sound between Spanish **b** and **v.** Both letters are pronounced alike. At the beginning of an utterance or after **m** or **n, b** and **v** have a sound identical to the English *b* sound in the word *boy.*

vivir	beber	vamos	barco	enviar
hambre	batea	bueno	vestido	

When pronounced between vowels, the Spanish **b** and **v** sound is produced by bringing the lips together but not closing them, so that some air may pass through.

sábado	autobús	yo voy	su barco

y, ll In most countries, Spanish **ll** and **y** have a sound similar to the English *y* sound in the word *yes.*

el llavero	trayecto	su yunta	milla
oye	el yeso	mayo	yema
un yelmo	trayectoria	llama	bella

NOTE: When it stands alone or is at the end of a word, Spanish **y** is pronounced like the vowel **i.**

rey	hoy	y	doy	buey
muy	voy	estoy	soy	

r The sound of Spanish **r** is similar to the English *dd* sound in the word *ladder.*

crema	aroma	cara	arena	aro
harina	toro	oro	eres	portero

rr Spanish **rr** and also **r** in an initial position and after **n, l,** or **s** are pronounced with a very strong trill. This trill is produced by bringing the tip of the tongue near the alveolar ridge and letting it vibrate freely while the air passes through the mouth.

rama	carro	Israel	cierra	roto
perro	alrededor	rizo	corre	Enrique

s Spanish **s** is represented in most of the Spanish world by the letters **s, z,** and **c** before **e** or **i.** The sound is very similar to the English sibilant *s* in the word *sink.*

sale	sitio	presidente	signo
salsa	seda	suma	vaso
sobrino	ciudad	cima	canción
zapato	zarza	cerveza	centro

h The letter **h** is silent in Spanish.

hoy	hora	hilo	ahora
humor	huevo	horror	almohada

ch Spanish **ch** is pronounced like the English *ch* in the word *chief.*

hecho	chico	coche	Chile
mucho	muchacho	salchicha	

f Spanish **f** is identical in sound to the English *f.*

difícil	feo	fuego	forma
fácil	fecha	foto	fueron

l Spanish **l** is similar to the English *l* in the word *let.*

dolor	lata	ángel	lago	sueldo
los	pelo	lana	general	fácil

m Spanish **m** is pronounced like the English *m* in the word *mother.*

mano	moda	mucho	muy
mismo	tampoco	multa	cómoda

n In most cases, Spanish **n** has a sound similar to the English *n.*

nada	nunca	ninguno	norte
entra	tiene	sienta	

The sound of Spanish **n** is often affected by the sounds that occur around it. When it appears before **b, v,** or **p,** it is pronounced like an **m.**

tan bueno	toman vino	sin poder
un pobre	comen peras	siguen bebiendo

ñ   Spanish **ñ** is similar to the English *ny* sound in the word *canyon.*

señor   otoño   ñoño   uña
leña   dueño   niños   años

x   Spanish **x** has two pronunciations depending on its position. Between vowels the sound is similar to English *ks.*

examen   exacto   boxeo   éxito
oxidar   oxígeno   existencia

When it occurs before a consonant, Spanish **x** sounds like *s.*

expresión   explicar   extraer   excusa
expreso   exquisito   extremo

NOTE: When **x** appears in **México** or in other words of Mexican origin, it is pronounced like the Spanish letter **j.**

Rhythm

Rhythm is the variation of sound intensity that we usually associate with music. Spanish and English each regulate these variations in speech differently, because they have different patterns of syllable length. In Spanish the length of the stressed and unstressed syllables remains almost the same, while the English stressed syllables are considerably longer than unstressed ones. Pronounce the following Spanish words, enunciating each syllable clearly.

es-tu-dian-te   bue-no   Úr-su-la
com-po-si-ción   di-fí-cil   ki-ló-me-tro
po-li-cí-a   Pa-ra-guay

Because the length of the Spanish syllables remains constant, the greater the number of syllables in a given word or phrase, the longer the phrase will be.

Linking

In spoken Spanish, the different words in a phrase or a sentence are not pronounced as isolated elements but are combined together. This is called *linking.*

Pepe come pan.   Pe-pe-co-me-pan
Tomás toma leche.   To-más-to-ma-le-che
Luis tiene la llave.   Luis-tie-ne-la-lla-ve
La mano de Roberto.   La-ma-no-de-Ro-ber-to

◆ The final consonant of a word is pronounced together with the initial vowel of the following word.

Carlos anda   Car-lo-san-da
un ángel   u-nán-gel
el otoño   e-lo-to-ño
unos estudios interesantes   u-no-ses-tu-dio-sin-te-re-san-tes

◆ A diphthong is formed between the final vowel of a word and the initial vowel of the following word. A triphthong is formed when there is a combination of three vowels (see rules for the formation of diphthongs and triphthongs on pages A-1–A-2).

su hermana   suher-ma-na
tu escopeta   tues-co-pe-ta
Roberto y Luis   Ro-ber-toy-Luis
negocio importante   ne-go-cioim-por-tan-te
lluvia y nieve   llu-viay-nie-ve
ardua empresa   ar-duaem-pre-sa

- When the final vowel of a word and the initial vowel of the following word are identical, they are pronounced slightly longer than one vowel.

Ana alcanza	A-n*a*l-can-za
lo olvido	l*o*l-vi-do
tiene eso	tie-n*e*-so
Ada atiende	Ad*a*-tien-de

The same rule applies when two identical vowels appear within a word.

crees	cr*e*s
Teherán	T*e*-rán
coordinación	c*o*r-di-na-ción

- When the final consonant of a word and the initial consonant of the following word are the same, they are pronounced as one consonant with slightly longer than normal duration.

el lado	e-*l*a-do
Carlos salta	Car-lo-*s*al-ta
tienes sed	tie-ne-*s*ed

Intonation

Intonation is the rise and fall of pitch in the delivery of a phrase or a sentence. In general, Spanish pitch tends to change less than English, giving the impression that the language is less emphatic.

As a rule, the intonation for normal statements in Spanish starts in a low tone, rises to a higher one on the first stressed syllable, maintains that tone until the last stressed syllable, and then goes back to the initial low tone, with still another drop at the very end.

Tu amigo viene mañana.	José come pan.
Ada está en casa.	Carlos toma café.

Syllable Formation in Spanish

General rules for dividing words into syllables:

Vowels

- A vowel or a vowel combination can constitute a syllable.

    a-lum-no   a-bue-la   Eu-ro-pa

- Diphthongs and triphthongs are considered single vowels and cannot be divided.

    bai-le   puen-te   Dia-na   es-tu-diáis   an-ti-guo

- Two strong vowels (**a**, **e**, **o**) do not form a diphthong and are separated into two syllables.

    em-ple-ar   vol-te-ar   lo-a

- A written accent on a weak vowel (**i** or **u**) breaks the diphthong, separating the vowels into two syllables.

    trí-o   dú-o   Ma-rí-a

Consonants

- A single consonant forms a syllable with the vowel that follows it.

    po-der   ma-no   mi-nu-to

NOTE: Spanish **ch, ll,** and **rr** are considered single consonants: **a-ma-ri-llo, co-che, pe-rro.**

◆ When two consonants appear between two vowels, they are separated into two syllables.

al-fa-be-to   cam-pe-ón   me-ter-se   mo-les-tia

EXCEPTION: When a consonant cluster composed of **b, c, d, f, g, p,** or **t** with **l** or **r** appears between two vowels, the cluster joins the following vowel: **so-bre, o-tros, ca-ble, te-lé-gra-fo.**

◆ When three consonants appear between two vowels, only the last one goes with the following vowel.

ins-pec-tor   trans-por-te   trans-for-mar

EXCEPTION: When there is a cluster of three consonants in the combinations described in rule 2, the first consonant joins the preceding vowel and the cluster joins the following vowel: **es-cri-bir, ex-tran-je-ro, im-plo-rar, es-tre-cho.**

Accentuation

In Spanish, all words are stressed according to specific rules. Words that do not follow the rules must have a written accent to indicate the change of stress. The basic rules for accentuation are as follows.

◆ Words ending in a vowel, **n,** or **s** are stressed on the next-to-last syllable.

hi-jo   **ca**-lle   **me**-sa   fa-**mo**-sos
flo-**re**-cen   **pla**-ya   **ve**-ces

◆ Words ending in a consonant, except **n** or **s,** are stressed on the last syllable.

ma-**yor**   a-**mor**   tro-pi-**cal**   na-**riz**   re-**loj**   co-rre-**dor**

◆ All words that do not follow these rules must have a written accent.

ca-**fé**   **lá**-piz   **mú**-si-ca   sa-**lón**
án-gel   **lí**-qui-do   fran-**cés**   **Víc**-tor
sim-**pá**-ti-co   rin-**cón**   a-**zú**-car   de-**mó**-cra-ta
sa-**lió**   **dé**-bil   e-**xá**-me-nes

◆ Pronouns and adverbs of interrogation and exclamation have a written accent to distinguish them from relative pronouns.

¿Qué comes?   *What are you eating?*
La pera que él no comió.   *The pear that he did not eat.*

¿Quién está ahí?   *Who is there?*
El hombre a quien tú llamaste.   *The man whom you called.*

¿Dónde está él?   *Where is he?*
En el lugar donde trabaja.   *At the place where he works.*

◆ Words that have the same spelling but different meanings take a written accent to differentiate one from the other.

el	*the*	él	*he, him*	te	*you*	té	*tea*
mi	*my*	mí	*me*	si	*if*	sí	*yes*
tu	*your*	tú	*you*	mas	*but*	más	*more*

Appendix B: Verbs

Regular Verbs

Model -ar, -er, -ir verbs

INFINITIVE

amar *(to love)*   **comer** *(to eat)*   **vivir** *(to live)*

PRESENT PARTICIPLE

amando *(loving)*   **comiendo** *(eating)*   **viviendo** *(living)*

PAST PARTICIPLE

amado *(loved)*   **comido** *(eaten)*   **vivido** *(lived)*

SIMPLE TENSES

Indicative Mood

Present

(I love)		*(I eat)*		*(I live)*	
amo	amamos	como	comemos	vivo	vivimos
amas	amáis	comes	coméis	vives	vivís
ama	aman	come	comen	vive	viven

Imperfect

(I used to love)		*(I used to eat)*		*(I used to live)*	
amaba	amábamos	comía	comíamos	vivía	vivíamos
amabas	amabais	comías	comíais	vivías	vivíais
amaba	amaban	comía	comían	vivía	vivían

Preterit

(I loved)		*(I ate)*		*(I lived)*	
amé	amamos	comí	comimos	viví	vivimos
amaste	amasteis	comiste	comisteis	viviste	vivisteis
amó	amaron	comió	comieron	vivió	vivieron

Future

(I will love)		*(I will eat)*		*(I will live)*	
amaré	amaremos	comeré	comeremos	viviré	viviremos
amarás	amaréis	comerás	comeréis	vivirás	viviréis
amará	amarán	comerá	comerán	vivirá	vivirán

Conditional

(I would love)		*(I would eat)*		*(I would live)*	
amaría	amaríamos	comería	comeríamos	viviría	viviríamos
amarías	amaríais	comerías	comeríais	vivirías	viviríais
amaría	amarían	comería	comerían	viviría	vivirían

Subjunctive Mood

Present

([that] I [may] love)		*([that] I [may] eat)*		*([that] I [may] live)*	
ame	amemos	coma	comamos	viva	vivamos
ames	améis	comas	comáis	vivas	viváis
ame	amen	coma	coman	viva	vivan

Imperfect (two forms: -ra, -se)

([that] I [might] love)	*([that] I [might] eat)*	*([that] I [might] live)*
amara(-ase)	comiera(-iese)	viviera(-iese)
amaras(-ases)	comieras(-ieses)	vivieras(-ieses)
amara(-ase)	comiera(-iese)	viviera(-iese)
amáramos(-ásemos)	comiéramos(-iésemos)	viviéramos(-iésemos)
amarais(-aseis)	comierais(-ieseis)	vivierais(-ieseis)
amaran(-asen)	comieran(-iesen)	vivieran(-iesen)

Imperative Mood

(love)	(eat)	(live)
am**a** (tú)	com**e** (tú)	viv**e** (tú)
am**e** (Ud.)	com**a** (Ud.)	viv**a** (Ud.)
am**emos** (nosotros)	com**amos** (nosotros)	viv**amos** (nosotros)
am**ad** (vosotros)	com**ed** (vosotros)	viv**id** (vosotros)
am**en** (Uds.)	com**an** (Uds.)	viv**an** (Uds.)

COMPOUND TENSES

Perfect Infinitive

haber amado	haber comido	haber vivido

Perfect Participle

habiendo amado	habiendo comido	habiendo vivido

Indicative Mood

Present Perfect

(I have loved)	(I have eaten)	(I have lived)
he amado	he comido	he vivido
has amado	has comido	has vivido
ha amado	ha comido	ha vivido
hemos amado	hemos comido	hemos vivido
habéis amado	habéis comido	habéis vivido
han amado	han comido	han vivido

Pluperfect

(I had loved)	(I had eaten)	(I had lived)
había amado	había comido	había vivido
habías amado	habías comido	habías vivido
había amado	había comido	había vivido
habíamos amado	habíamos comido	habíamos vivido
habíais amado	habíais comido	habíais vivido
habían amado	habían comido	habían vivido

Future Perfect

(I will have loved)	(I will have eaten)	(I will have lived)
habré amado	habré comido	habré vivido
habrás amado	habrás comido	habrás vivido
habrá amado	habrá comido	habrá vivido
habremos amado	habremos comido	habremos vivido
habréis amado	habréis comido	habréis vivido
habrán amado	habrán comido	habrán vivido

Conditional Perfect

(I would have loved)	(I would have eaten)	(I would have lived)
habría amado	habría comido	habría vivido
habrías amado	habrías comido	habrías vivido
habría amado	habría comido	habría vivido
habríamos amado	habríamos comido	habríamos vivido
habríais amado	habríais comido	habríais vivido
habrían amado	habrían comido	habrían vivido

Subjunctive Mood

Present Perfect

([that] I [may] have loved)	([that] I [may] have eaten)	([that] I [may] have lived)
haya amado	haya comido	haya vivido
hayas amado	hayas comido	hayas vivido
haya amado	haya comido	haya vivido
hayamos amado	hayamos comido	hayamos vivido
hayáis amado	hayáis comido	hayáis vivido
hayan amado	hayan comido	hayan vivido

([that] I [might] have loved)	Pluperfect (two forms: -ra, -se) ([that] I [might] have eaten)	([that] I [might] have lived)
hubiera(-iese) amado	hubiera(-iese) comido	hubiera(-iese) vivido
hubieras(-ieses) amado	hubieras(-ieses) comido	hubieras(-ieses) vivido
hubiera(-iese) amado	hubiera(-iese) comido	hubiera(-iese) vivido
hubiéramos(-iésemos) amado	hubiéramos(-iésemos) comido	hubiéramos(-iésemos) vivido
hubierais(-ieseis) amado	hubierais(-ieseis) comido	hubierais(-ieseis) vivido
hubieran(-iesen) amado	hubieran(-iesen) comido	hubieran(-iesen) vivido

Stem-changing verbs

The -ar and -er stem-changing verbs

Stem-changing verbs are those that have a spelling change in the root of the verb. Stem-changing verbs that end in **-ar** and **-er** change the stressed vowel **e** to **ie,** and the stressed **o** to **ue.** These changes occur in all persons, except the first- and second-persons plural, of the present indicative, present subjunctive, and imperative.

Infinitive	Indicative	Imperative	Subjunctive
cerrar (to close)	cierro	——	cierre
	cierras	cierra	cierres
	cierra	cierre	cierre
	cerramos	cerremos	cerremos
	cerráis	cerrad	cerréis
	cierran	cierren	cierren
perder (to lose)	pierdo	——	pierda
	pierdes	pierde	pierdas
	pierde	pierda	pierda
	perdemos	perdamos	perdamos
	perdéis	perded	perdáis
	pierden	pierdan	pierdan
contar (to count; to tell)	cuento	——	cuente
	cuentas	cuenta	cuentes
	cuenta	cuente	cuente
	contamos	contemos	contemos
	contáis	contad	contéis
	cuentan	cuenten	cuenten
volver (to return)	vuelvo	——	vuelva
	vuelves	vuelve	vuelvas
	vuelve	vuelva	vuelva
	volvemos	volvamos	volvamos
	volvéis	volved	volváis
	vuelven	vuelvan	vuelvan

Verbs that follow the same pattern:

acordarse	to remember	confesar	to confess
acostar(se)	to go to bed	costar	to cost
almorzar	to have lunch	demostrar	to demonstrate, show
atravesar	to go through		
cocer	to cook	despertar(se)	to wake up
colgar	to hang	empezar	to beg
comenzar	to begin	encender	to light; to turn on
		encontrar	to find

entender	*to understand*	pensar	*to think; to plan*
extender	*to stretch*	probar	*to prove; to taste*
llover	*to rain*	recordar	*to remember*
mover	*to move*	rogar	*to beg*
mostrar	*to show*	sentar(se)	*to sit down*
negar	*to deny*	soler	*to be in the habit of*
nevar	*to snow*	soñar	*to dream*
		torcer	*to twist*

The -ir stem-changing verbs

There are two types of stem-changing verbs that end in **-ir:** one type changes stressed **e** to **ie** in some tenses and to **i** in others, and stressed **o** to **ue** or **u;** the second type changes stressed **e** to **i** only in all the irregular tenses.

Type 1: -ir:e > ie or i / o > ue or u

These changes occur as follows.

Present Indicative: all persons except the first- and second-persons plural change **e** to **ie** and **o** to **ue.** *Preterit:* third person, singular and plural, changes **e** to **i** and **o** to **u.** *Present Subjunctive:* all persons change **e** to **ie** and **o** to **ue,** except the first- and second-persons plural, which change **e** to **i** and **o** to **u.** *Imperfect Subjunctive:* all persons change **e** to **i** and **o** to **u.** *Imperative:* all persons except the first- and second-persons plural change **e** to **ie** and **o** to **ue;** first-person plural changes **e** to **i** and **o** to **u.** *Present Participle:* changes **e** to **i** and **o** to **u.**

Infinitive	Indicative		Imperative	Subjunctive	
sentir *(to feel)*	PRESENT	PRETERIT		PRESENT	IMPERFECT
	siento	sentí		sienta	sintiera(-iese)
	sientes	sentiste	siente	sientas	sintieras
	siente	sintió	sienta	sienta	sintiera
PRESENT PARTICIPLE sintiendo	sentimos	sentimos	sintamos	sintamos	sintiéramos
	sentís	sentisteis	sentid	sintáis	sintierais
	sienten	sintieron	sientan	sientan	sintieran
dormir *(to sleep)*	duermo	dormí		duerma	durmiera(-iese)
	duermes	dormiste	duerme	duermas	durmieras
	duerme	durmió	duerma	duerma	durmiera
PRESENT PARTICIPLE durmiendo	dormimos	dormimos	durmamos	durmamos	durmiéramos
	dormís	dormisteis	dormid	durmáis	durmierais
	duermen	durmieron	duerman	duerman	durmieran

Other verbs that follow the same pattern:

advertir	*to warn*	herir	*to wound, hurt*
arrepentirse	*to repent*	mentir	*to lie*
consentir	*to consent; to pamper*	morir	*to die*
convertir(se)	*to turn into*	preferir	*to prefer*
discernir	*to discern*	referir	*to refer*
divertir(se)	*to amuse oneself*	sugerir	*to suggest*

The verbs in the second category are irregular in the same tenses as those of the first type. The only difference is that they have only one change: **e > i** in all irregular persons.

Infinitive	Indicative		Imperative	Subjunctive	
pedir *(to ask for, request)*	PRESENT	PRETERIT		PRESENT	IMPERFECT
PRESENT PARTICIPLE	pido pides pide	pedí pediste pidió	pide pida	pida pidas pida	pidiera(-iese) pidieras pidiera
pidiendo	pedimos pedís piden	pedimos pedisteis pidieron	pidamos pedid pidan	pidamos pidáis pidan	pidiéramos pidierais pidieran

Verbs that follow this pattern:

concebir	*to conceive*	repetir	*to repeat*
competir	*to compete*	reñir	*to fight*
despedir(se)	*to say good-bye*	seguir	*to follow*
elegir	*to choose*	servir	*to serve*
impedir	*to prevent*	vestir(se)	*to dress*
perseguir	*to pursue*		

Orthographic-Changing Verbs

Some verbs undergo a change in the spelling of the stem in some tenses in order to maintain the sound of the final consonant. The most common ones are those with the consonants **g** and **c**. Remember that **g** and **c** in front of **e** or **i** have a soft sound, and in front of **a, o,** or **u** have a hard sound. In order to keep the soft sound in front of **a, o,** or **u, g** and **c** change to **j** and **z,** respectively. In order to keep the hard sound of **g** or **c** in front of **e** and **i, u** is added to the **g** (**gu**) and the **c** changes to **qu.** The most important verbs that are regular in all the tenses but change in spelling are the following.

1. Verbs ending in **-gar** change **g** to **gu** before **e** in the first person of the preterit and in all persons of the present subjunctive.

   pagar   *to pay*
   Preterit: pa**gu**é, pagaste, pagó, etc.
   Pres. Subj.:   pa**gu**e, pa**gu**es, pa**gu**e, pa**gu**emos, pa**gu**éis, pa**gu**en

   Verbs that follow the same pattern: **colgar, llegar, navegar, negar, regar, rogar, jugar.**

2. Verbs ending in **-ger** or **-gir** change **g** to **j** before **o** and **a** in the first person of the present indicative and in all the persons of the present subjunctive.

   proteger   *to protect*
   Pres. Ind.:   prote**j**o, proteges, protege, etc.
   Pres. Subj.:   prote**j**a, prote**j**as, prote**j**a, prote**j**amos, prote**j**áis, prote**j**an

   Verbs that follow the same pattern: **coger, corregir, dirigir, elegir, escoger, exigir, recoger.**

3. Verbs ending in **-guar** change **gu** to **gü** before **e** in the first person of the preterit and in all persons of the present subjunctive.

   averiguar   *to find out*
   Preterit: averi**gü**é, averiguaste, averiguó, etc.
   Pres. Subj.:   averi**gü**e, averi**gü**es, averi**gü**e, averi**gü**emos, averi**gü**éis, averi**gü**en

   The verb **apaciguar** follows the same pattern.

4. Verbs ending in **-guir** change **gu** to **g** before **o** and **a** in the first person of the present indicative and in all persons of the present subjunctive.

   conseguir   *to get*
   Pres. Ind.:   consigo, consigues, consigue, etc.
   Pres. Subj.:   consiga, consigas, consiga, consigamos, consigáis, consigan

   Verbs that follow the same pattern: **distinguir, perseguir, proseguir, seguir.**

5. Verbs ending in **-car** change **c** to **qu** before **e** in the first person of the preterit and in all persons of the present subjunctive.

   tocar   *to touch; to play (a musical instrument)*
   Preterit: toqué, tocaste, tocó, etc.
   Pres. Subj.:   toque, toques, toque, toquemos, toquéis, toquen

   Verbs that follow the same pattern: **atacar, buscar, comunicar, explicar, indicar, pescar, sacar.**

6. Verbs ending in **-cer** or **-cir** preceded by a consonant change **c** to **z** before **o** and **a** in the first person of the present indicative and in all persons of the present subjunctive.

   torcer   *to twist*
   Pres. Ind.:   tuerzo, tuerces, tuerce, etc.
   Pres. Subj.:   tuerza, tuerzas, tuerza, torzamos, torzáis, tuerzan

   Verbs that follow the same pattern: **convencer, esparcir, vencer.**

7. Verbs ending in **-cer** or **-cir** preceded by a vowel change **c** to **zc** before **o** and **a** in the first person of the present indicative and in all persons of the present subjunctive.

   conocer   *to know, be acquainted with*
   Pres. Ind.:   conozco, conoces, conoce, etc.
   Pres. Subj.:   conozca, conozcas, conozca, conozcamos, conozcáis, conozcan
   Verbs that follow the same pattern: **agradecer, aparecer, carecer, entristecer** *(to sadden)*, **establecer, lucir, nacer, obedecer, ofrecer, padecer, parecer, pertenecer, reconocer, relucir.**

8. Verbs ending in **-zar** change **z** to **c** before **e** in the first person of the preterit and in all persons of the present subjunctive.

   rezar   *to pray*
   Preterit: recé, rezaste, rezó, etc.
   Pres. Subj.:   rece, reces, rece, recemos, recéis, recen

   Verbs that follow the same pattern: **abrazar, alcanzar, almorzar, comenzar, cruzar, empezar, forzar, gozar.**

9. Verbs ending in **-eer** change the unstressed **i** to **y** between vowels in the third-persons singular and plural of the preterit, in all persons of the imperfect subjunctive, and in the present participle.

   creer   *to believe*
   Pres. Part: creyendo
   Preterit: creí, creíste, creyó, creímos, creísteis, creyeron
   Imp. Subj.:   creyera(-ese), creyeras, creyera, creyéramos, creyerais, creyeran
   Past Part.:   creído

   Verbs that follow the same pattern: **leer, poseer.**

10. Verbs ending in **-uir** change the unstressed **i** to **y** between vowels (except **-quir,** which has the silent **u**) in the following tenses and persons.

    huir   *to escape, flee*
    Pres. Part.:   huyendo
    Pres. Ind.:   huyo, huyes, huye, huimos, huís, huyen
    Preterit: huí, huiste, huyó, huimos, huisteis, huyeron
    Imperative: huye, huya, huyamos, huid, huyan
    Pres. Subj.:   huya, huyas, huya, huyamos, huyáis, huyan
    Imp. Subj.:   huyera(-ese), huyeras, huyera, huyéramos, huyerais, huyeran

Verbs that follow the same pattern: **atribuir, concluir, constituir, construir, contribuir, destituir, destruir, disminuir, distribuir, excluir, incluir, influir, instruir, restituir, sustituir.**

11. Verbs ending in **-eír** lose the **e** in the third-person singular and plural of the preterit, in all persons of the imperfect subjunctive, and in the present participle.

reír   *to laugh*
Pres Ind.:   río, ríes, ríe, reímos, reís, ríen
Preterit: reí, reíste, rio, reímos, reísteis, rieron
Pres. Subj.:   ría, rías, ría, riamos, riáis, rían
Imp. Subj.:   riera(-ese), rieras, riera, riéramos, rierais, rieran
Pres. Part.:   riendo

Verbs that follow the same pattern: **freír, sonreír.**

12. Verbs ending in **-iar** add a written accent to the **i,** except in the first- and second-persons plural of the present indicative and subjunctive.

fiar(**se**)   *to trust*
Pres. Ind.:   (me) fío, (te) fías, (se) fía, (nos) fiamos, (os) fiáis, (se) fían
Pres. Subj.:   (me) fíe, (te) fíes, (se) fíe, (nos) fiemos, (os) fiéis, (se) fíen

Verbs that follow the same pattern: **ampliar, criar, desviar, enfriar, enviar, guiar, telegrafiar, vaciar, variar.**

13. Verbs ending in **-uar** (except **-guar**) add a written accent to the **u,** except in the first- and second-persons plural of the present indicative and subjunctive.

actuar   *to act*
Pres. Ind.:   actúo, actúas, actúa, actuamos, actuáis, actúan
Pres. Subj.:   actúe, actúes, actúe, actuemos, actuéis, actúen

Verbs that follow the same pattern: **acentuar, continuar, efectuar, exceptuar, graduar, habituar, insinuar, situar.**

14. Verbs ending in **-ñir** lose the **i** of the diphthongs **ie** and **ió** in the third-person singular and plural of the preterit and all persons of the imperfect subjunctive. They also change the **e** of the stem to **i** in the same persons in the present indicative and present subjunctive.

teñir   *to dye*
Pres. Ind.:   tiño, tiñes, tiñe, teñimos, teñís, tiñen
Preterit: teñí, teñiste, tiñó, teñimos, teñisteis, tiñeron
Pres. Subj.:   tiña, tiñas, tiña, tiñamos, tiñáis, tiñan
Imp. Subj.:   tiñera(-ese), tiñeras, tiñera, tiñéramos, tiñerais, tiñeran

Verbs that follow the same pattern: **ceñir, constreñir, desteñir, estreñir, reñir.**

Some Common Irregular Verbs

Only those tenses with irregular forms are given below.

adquirir   *to acquire*
Pres. Ind.:   adquiero, adquieres, adquiere, adquirimos, adquirís, adquieren
Pres. Subj.:   adquiera, adquieras, adquiera, adquiramos, adquiráis, adquieran
Imperative: adquiere, adquiera, adquiramos, adquirid, adquieran

andar   *to walk*
Preterit: anduve, anduviste, anduvo, anduvimos, anduvisteis, anduvieron
Imp. Subj.:   anduviera (anduviese), anduvieras, anduviera, anduviéramos, anduvierais, anduvieran

avergonzarse   *to be ashamed, to be embarrassed*
Pres. Ind.:   me avergüenzo, te avergüenzas, se avergüenza, nos avergonzamos, os avergonzáis, se avergüenzan
Pres. Subj: me avergüence, te avergüences, se avergüence, nos avergoncemos, os avergoncéis, se avergüencen
Imperative: avergüénzate, avergüéncese, avergoncémonos, avergonzaos, avergüéncense

caber   *to fit, to have enough room*

Pres. Ind.:	quepo, cabes, cabe cabemos, cabéis, caben
Preterit:	cupe, cupiste, cupo, cupimos, cupisteis, cupieron
Future:	cabré, cabrás, cabrá, cabremos, cabréis, cabrán
Conditional:	cabría, cabrías, cabría, cabríamos, cabríais, cabrían
Imperative:	cabe, quepa, quepamos, cabed, quepan
Pres. Subj.:	quepa, quepas, quepa, quepamos, quepáis, quepan
Imp. Subj.:	cupiera (cupiese), cupieras, cupiera, cupiéramos, cupierais, cupieran

caer   *to fall*

Pres. Ind.:	caigo, caes, cae, caemos, caéis, caen
Preterit:	caí, caíste, cayó, caímos, caísteis, cayeron
Imperative:	cae, caiga, caigamos, caed, caigan
Pres. Subj.:	caiga, caigas, caiga, caigamos, caigáis, caigan
Imp. Subj.:	cayera (cayese), cayeras, cayera, cayéramos, cayerais, cayeran
Past Part.:	caído

conducir   *to guide, to drive*

Pres. Ind.:	conduzco, conduces, conduce, conducimos, conducís, conducen
Preterit:	conduje, condujiste, condujo, condujimos, condujisteis, condujeron
Imperative:	conduce, conduzca, conduzcamos, conducid, conduzcan
Pres. Subj.:	conduzca, conduzcas, conduzca, conduzcamos, conduzcáis, conduzcan
Imp. Subj.:	condujera (condujese), condujeras, condujera, condujéramos, condujerais, condujeran

(All verbs ending in **-ducir** follow this pattern.)

convenir   *to agree (see **venir**)*

dar   *to give*

Pres. Ind.:	doy, das, da, damos, dais, dan
Preterit:	di, diste, dio, dimos, disteis, dieron
Imperative:	da, dé, demos, dad, den
Pres. Subj.:	dé, des, dé, demos, deis, den
Imp. Subj.:	diera (diese), dieras, diera, diéramos, dierais, dieran

decir   *to say, to tell*

Pres. Ind.:	digo, dices, dice, decimos, decís, dicen
Preterit:	dije, dijiste, dijo, dijimos, dijisteis, dijeron
Future:	diré, dirás, dirá, diremos, diréis, dirán
Conditional:	diría, dirías, diría, diríamos, diríais, dirían
Imperative:	di, diga, digamos, decid, digan
Pres. Subj.:	diga, digas, diga, digamos, digáis, digan
Imp. Subj.:	dijera (dijese), dijeras, dijera, dijéramos, dijerais, dijeran
Pres. Part.:	diciendo
Past Part.:	dicho

detener   *to stop; to hold; to arrest (see **tener**)*

entretener   *to entertain, amuse (see **tener**)*

errar   *to err; to miss*

Pres. Ind.:	yerro, yerras, yerra, erramos, erráis, yerran
Imperative:	yerra, yerre, erremos, errad, yerren
Pres. Subj.:	yerre, yerres, yerre, erremos, erréis, yerren

estar   *to be*

Pres. Ind.:	estoy, estás, está, estamos, estáis, están
Preterit:	estuve, estuviste, estuvo, estuvimos, estuvisteis, estuvieron
Imperative:	está, esté, estemos, estad, estén
Pres. Subj.:	esté, estés, esté, estemos, estéis, estén
Imp. Subj.:	estuviera (estuviese), estuvieras, estuviera, estuviéramos, estuvierais, estuvieran

haber   *to have*

Pres. Ind.:	he, has, ha, hemos, habéis, han
Preterit:	hube, hubiste, hubo, hubimos, hubisteis, hubieron
Future:	habré, habrás, habrá, habremos, habréis, habrán
Conditional:	habría, habrías, habría, habríamos, habríais, habrían
Pres. Subj.:	haya, hayas, haya, hayamos, hayáis, hayan
Imp. Subj.:	hubiera (hubiese), hubieras, hubiera, hubiéramos, hubierais, hubieran

hacer   *to do, to make*

Pres. Ind.:	hago, haces, hace, hacemos, hacéis, hacen
Preterit:	hice, hiciste, hizo, hicimos, hicisteis, hicieron

Future:	haré, harás, hará, haremos, haréis, harán
Imperative:	haz, haga, hagamos, haced, hagan
Pres. Subj.:	haga, hagas, haga, hagamos, hagáis, hagan
Imp. Subj.:	hiciera (hiciese), hicieras, hiciera, hiciéramos, hicierais, hicieran
Past Part.:	hecho

imponer   *to impose; to depose (see* **poner***)*

ir   *to go*

Pres. Ind.:	voy, vas, va, vamos, vais, van
Imp. Ind.:	iba, ibas, iba, íbamos, ibais, iban
Preterit:	fui, fuiste, fue, fuimos, fuisteis, fueron
Imperative:	ve, vaya, vayamos, id, vayan
Pres. Subj.:	vaya, vayas, vaya, vayamos, vayáis, vayan
Imp. Subj.:	fuera (fuese), fueras, fuera, fuéramos, fuerais, fueran

jugar   *to play*

Pres. Ind.:	juego, juegas, juega, jugamos, jugáis, juegan
Imperative:	juega, juegue, juguemos, jugad, jueguen
Pres. Subj.:	juegue, juegues, juegue, juguemos, juguéis, jueguen

obtener   *to obtain (see* **tener***)*

oír   *to hear*

Pres. Ind.:	oigo, oyes, oye, oímos, oís, oyen
Preterit:	oí, oíste, oyó, oímos, oísteis, oyeron
Imperative:	oye, oiga, oigamos, oíd, oigan
Pres. Subj.:	oiga, oigas, oiga, oigamos, oigáis, oigan
Imp. Subj.:	oyera (oyese), oyeras, oyera, oyéramos, oyerais, oyeran
Pres. Part.:	oyendo
Past Part.:	oído

oler   *to smell*

Pres. Ind.:	huelo, hueles, huele, olemos, oléis, huelen
Imperative:	huele, huela, olamos, oled, huelan
Pres. Subj.:	huela, huelas, huela, olamos, oláis, huelan

poder   *to be able to*

Preterit:	pude, pudiste, pudo, pudimos, pudisteis, pudieron
Future:	podré, podrás, podrá, podremos, podréis, podrán
Conditional:	podría, podrías, podría, podríamos, podríais, podrían
Imperative:	puede, pueda, podamos, poded, puedan
Pres. Subj.:	pueda, puedas, pueda, podamos, podáis, puedan
Imp. Subj.:	pudiera (pudiese), pudieras, pudiera, pudiéramos, pudierais, pudieran
Pres. Part.:	pudiendo

poner   *to place, to put*

Pres. Ind.:	pongo, pones, pone, ponemos, ponéis, ponen
Preterit:	puse, pusiste, puso, pusimos, pusisteis, pusieron
Future:	pondré, pondrás, pondrá, pondremos, pondréis, pondrán
Conditional:	pondría, pondrías, pondría, pondríamos, pondríais, pondrían
Imperative:	pon, ponga, pongamos, poned, pongan
Pres. Subj.:	ponga, pongas, ponga, pongamos, pongáis, pongan
Imp. Subj.:	pusiera (pusiese), pusieras, pusiera, pusiéramos, pusierais, pusieran
Past Part.:	puesto

querer   *to want, to wish; to like, to love*

Preterit:	quise, quisiste, quiso, quisimos, quisisteis, quisieron
Future:	querré, querrás, querrá, querremos, querréis, querrán
Conditional:	querría, querrías, querría, querríamos, querríais, querrían
Imp. Subj.:	quisiera (quisiese), quisieras, quisiera, quisiéramos, quisierais, quisieran

resolver   *to decide on, to solve*

Past Part.:	resuelto

saber   *to know*

Pres. Ind.:	sé, sabes, sabe, sabemos, sabéis, saben
Preterit:	supe, supiste, supo, supimos, supisteis, supieron
Future:	sabré, sabrás, sabrá, sabremos, sabréis, sabrán
Conditional:	sabría, sabrías, sabría, sabríamos, sabríais, sabrían

Imperative:	sabe, sepa, sepamos, sabed, sepan
Pres. Subj.:	sepa, sepas, sepa, sepamos, sepáis, sepan
Imp. Subj.:	supiera (supiese), supieras, supiera, supiéramos, supierais, supieran

salir *to leave; to go out*
Pres. Ind.:	salgo, sales, sale, salimos, salís, salen
Future:	saldré, saldrás, saldrá, saldremos, saldréis, saldrán
Conditional:	saldría, saldrías, saldría, saldríamos, saldríais, saldrían
Imperative:	sal, salga, salgamos, salid, salgan
Pres. Subj.:	salga, salgas, salga, salgamos, salgáis, salgan

ser *to be*
Pres. Ind.:	soy, eres, es, somos, sois, son
Imp. Ind.:	era, eras, era, éramos, erais, eran
Preterit:	fui, fuiste, fue, fuimos, fuisteis, fueron
Imperative:	sé, sea, seamos, sed, sean
Pres. Subj.:	sea, seas, sea, seamos, seáis, sean
Imp. Subj.:	fuera (fuese), fueras, fuera, fuéramos, fuerais, fueran

suponer *to assume, to suppose (see* **poner***)*

tener *to have*
Pres. Ind.:	tengo, tienes, tiene, tenemos, tenéis, tienen
Preterit:	tuve, tuviste, tuvo, tuvimos, tuvisteis, tuvieron
Future:	tendré, tendrás, tendrá, tendremos, tendréis, tendrán
Conditional:	tendría, tendrías, tendría, tendríamos, tendríais, tendrían
Imperative:	ten, tenga, tengamos, tened, tengan
Pres. Subj.:	tenga, tengas, tenga, tengamos, tengáis, tengan
Imp. Subj.:	tuviera (tuviese), tuvieras, tuviera, tuviéramos, tuvierais, tuvieran

traducir *to translate (see* **conducir***)*

traer *to bring*
Pres. Ind.:	traigo, traes, trae, traemos, traéis, traen
Preterit:	traje, trajiste, trajo, trajimos, trajisteis, trajeron
Imperative:	trae, traiga, traigamos, traed, traigan
Pres. Subj.:	traiga, traigas, traiga, traigamos, traigáis, traigan
Imp. Subj.:	trajera (trajese), trajeras, trajera, trajéramos, trajerais, trajeran
Pres. Part.:	trayendo
Past Part.:	traído

valer *to be worth*
Pres. Ind.:	valgo, vales, vale, valemos, valéis, valen
Future:	valdré, valdrás, valdrá, valdremos, valdréis, valdrán
Conditional:	valdría, valdrías, valdría, valdríamos, valdríais, valdrían
Imperative:	vale, valga, valgamos, valed, valgan
Pres. Subj.:	valga, valgas, valga, valgamos, valgáis, valgan

venir *to come*
Pres. Ind.:	vengo, vienes, viene, venimos, venís, vienen
Preterit:	vine, viniste, vino, vinimos, vinisteis, vinieron
Future:	vendré, vendrás, vendrá, vendremos, vendréis, vendrán
Conditional:	vendría, vendrías, vendría, vendríamos, vendríais, vendrían
Imperative:	ven, venga, vengamos, venid, vengan
Pres. Subj.:	venga, vengas, venga, vengamos, vengáis, vengan
Imp. Subj.:	viniera (viniese), vinieras, viniera, viniéramos, vinierais, vinieran
Pres. Part.:	viniendo

ver *to see*
Pres. Ind.:	veo, ves, ve, vemos, veis, ven
Imp. Ind.:	veía, veías, veía, veíamos, veíais, veían
Preterit:	vi, viste, vio, vimos, visteis, vieron
Imperative:	ve, vea, veamos, ved, vean
Pres. Subj.:	vea, veas, vea, veamos, veáis, vean
Imp. Subj.:	viera (viese), vieras, viera, viéramos, vierais, vieran
Past Part.:	visto

volver *to return*
| *Past Part.:* | vuelto |

Appendix C:
Glossary of Grammatical Terms

adjective: A word that is used to describe a noun: *tall* girl, *difficult* lesson.

adverb: A word that modifies a verb, an adjective, or another adverb. It answers the questions "How?" "When?" "Where?": She walked *slowly.* She'll be here *tomorrow.* She is *here.*

agreement: A term applied to changes in form that nouns cause in the words that surround them. In Spanish, verb forms agree with their subjects in person and number (**yo** habl**o, él** habl**a,** etc.). Spanish adjectives agree in gender and number with the noun they describe. Thus, a feminine plural noun requires a feminine plural ending in the adjective that describes it (cas**as** amarill**as**) and a masculine singular noun requires a masculine singular ending in the adjective (libr**o** negr**o**).

auxiliary verb: A verb that helps in the conjugation of another verb: I *have* finished. He *was* called. She *will* go. He *would* eat.

command form: The form of the verb used to give an order or a direction: *Go! Come* back! *Turn* to the right!

conjugation: The process by which the forms of the verb are presented in their different moods and tenses: I *am,* you *are,* he *is,* she *was,* we *were,* etc.

contraction: The combination of two or more words into one: *isn't, don't, can't.*

definite article: A word used before a noun indicating a definite person or thing: *the* woman, *the* money.

demonstrative: A word that refers to a definite person or object: *this, that, these, those.*

diphthong: A combination of two vowels forming one syllable. In Spanish, a diphthong is composed of one *strong* vowel (**a, e, o**) and one *weak* vowel (**u, i**) or two weak vowels: **ei, ua, ui.**

exclamation: A word used to express emotion: *How* strong! *What* beauty!

gender: A distinction of nouns, pronouns, and adjectives, based on whether they are masculine or feminine.

indefinite article: A word used before a noun that refers to an indefinite person or object: *a* child, *an* apple.

infinitive: The form of the verb generally preceded in English by the word *to* and showing no subject or number: *to do, to bring.*

interrogative: A word used in asking a question: *Who? What? Where?*

main clause: A group of words that includes a subject and a verb and by itself has complete meaning: *They saw me. I go now.*

noun: A word that names a person, place, or thing: *Ann, London, pencil.*

number: Refers to singular and plural: *chair, chairs.*

object: Generally a noun or a pronoun that is the receiver of the verb's action. A direct object answers the question *"What?"* or *"Whom?":* We know *her.* Take *it.* An indirect object answers the question *"To whom?"* or *"To what?":* Give *John* the money. Nouns and pronouns can also be objects of prepositions: The letter is *from Rick.* I'm thinking *about you.*

past participle: Past forms of a verb: *gone, worked, written.*

person: The form of the pronoun and of the verb that shows the person referred to: *I* (first-person singular), *you* (second-person singular), *she* (third-person singular), and so on.

possessive: A word that denotes ownership or possession: This is *our* house. The book isn't *mine.*

preposition: A word that introduces a noun or pronoun and indicates its function in the sentence: They were *with* us. She is *from* Nevada.

present participle: A verb form in English that ends in -*ing*: *eating, sleeping, working.* In Spanish, this form cannot be used as a noun or after a preposition.

pronoun: A word that is used to replace a noun: *she, them, us,* and so on. A **subject pronoun** refers to the person or thing spoken of: *They* work. An **object pronoun** receives the action of the verb: They arrested *us* (direct object pronoun). She spoke to *him* (indirect object pronoun). A pronoun can also be the object of a preposition: The children stayed with *us.*

reflexive pronoun: A pronoun that refers back to the subject: *myself, yourself, himself, herself, itself, ourselves,* and so on.

subject: The person, place, or thing spoken of: *Robert* works. *Our car* is new.

subordinate clause: A clause that has no complete meaning by itself but depends on a main clause: They knew *that I was here.*

tense: The group of forms in a verb that show the time in which the action of the verb takes place: *I go* (present indicative), *I'm going* (present progressive), *I went* (past), *I was going* (past progressive), *I will go* (future), *I would go* (conditional), *I have gone* (present perfect), *I had gone* (past perfect), *that I may go* (present subjunctive), and so on.

verb: A word that expresses an action or a state: We *sleep.* The baby *is* sick.

Appendix D:
Answer Key to the Self-Tests

Self-Test Lecciones 1–3

Lección 1

A. 1. ve-a-ere-ge-a-ese 2. eme-e-ene-a 3. be-o-te-e-ere-o 4. pe-e-eñe-a 5. jota-u-a-ere-e-zeta 6. ce-hache-a-ve-e-zeta 7. de-a-ve-i-ele-a 8. efe-e-ele-i-equis 9. cu-u-i-ere-o-zeta

B. 1. once 2. diecisiete 3. treinta 4. veinte 5. quince 6. trece 7. veintiocho 8. diecinueve 9. doce 10. catorce 11. dieciséis 12. veintidós

C. 1. verde 2. anaranjado 3. amarillo 4. rosado 5. negro 6. morado 7. marrón (café) 8. rojo, blanco y azul

D. 1. domingo 2. miércoles 3. viernes 4. martes 5. sábado 6. jueves 7. lunes

E. 1. noviembre 2. marzo 3. julio 4. enero 5. mayo 6. septiembre 7. otoño 8. primavera 9. diciembre

F. son / somos / eres / soy / es / es / son

G. 1. e 2. h 3. j 4. b 5. g 6. d 7. i 8. a 9. c 10. f

H. 1. María 2. Marité / Paco 3. unos cuarenta millones 4. una escritora mexicoamericana

Lección 2

A. 1. la 2. la 3. los 4. el 5. la 6. los 7. el 8. las 9. la 10. los 11. la 12. los

B. 1. unos 2. unos 3. una 4. unos 5. una 6. un 7. unos 8. un 9. una 10. una

C. 1. treinta y ocho 2. cien 3. noventa y uno 4. ochenta y cinco 5. setenta y dos 6. cincuenta y siete 7. cuarenta y seis 8. sesenta y tres 9. setenta y siete

D. 1. La clase de español es a las nueve y diez de la mañana. 2. La clase de inglés es a la una y cuarto de la tarde. 3. La clase de literatura es a las ocho y veinticinco de la noche.

E. 1. trabajas / trabajo / regresas 2. estudian / estudiamos / toman / tomo / toma 3. necesitan / necesita / necesita 4. deseas / deseo 5. hablan / hablamos

F. 1. Los estudiantes de la señorita son norteamericanos. 2. El profesor de Amanda es mexicano. 3. Los amigos de Paco son de California.

G. 1. biblioteca 2. dirección (domicilio) 3. dice 4. quiere 5. Cuándo 6. italiano / francés 7. idioma 8. todos 9. caso 10. poco

H. 1. las siete de la noche 2. uniforme 3. más de medio millón 4. un barrio cubano de Miami

Lección 3

A. 1. mi / mis 2. nuestra / su 3. tus 4. sus 5. nuestra / nuestros 6. su

B. 1. ciento noventa y cinco 2. doscientos ochenta y seis 3. trescientos setenta y uno 4. cuatrocientos sesenta 5. quinientos cincuenta y tres 6. seiscientos cuarenta y cuatro 7. setecientos treinta y dos 8. ochocientos veintisiete 9. novecientos dieciocho 10. mil quinientos trece

C. 1. La chica es alta. 2. Los escritorios son pequeños. 3. Las chicas son norteamericanas. 4. Es una mujer muy simpática. 5. Necesito las plumas rojas.

D. 1. aprendemos 2. comes 3. creo 4. leen 5. bebe 6. debe 7. venden 8. abro 9. reciben 10. escribimos

E. 1. vengo / tengo 2. tienes / viene 3. venimos / tenemos 4. viene / vienen 5. tienen

F. 1. Yo llamo a Rosa a las tres. 2. Nosotros llevamos los libros a la universidad. 3. Ellos llevan a Julio y a su novia a la biblioteca. 4. Nosotros tenemos muchos amigos.

G. 1. m 2. f 3. i 4. k 5. b 6. o 7. a 8. d 9. h 10. c 11. n 12. e 13. g 14. l 15. j

H. 1. Bueno. 2. castellano 3. Ni pasaporte ni visa. 4. Una famosa cantante colombiana.

Lección 4

A. 1. mí 2. ti 3. ellos 4. nosotros 5. conmigo 6. contigo

B. 1. al Sr. Estrada 2. del hospital 3. de la playa 4. a las chicas 5. del Sr. Soto

C. 1. voy 2. damos 3. está 4. está 5. van 6. dan 7. estoy 8. van 9. estás 10. doy

D. 1. Yo no voy a hablar con mi mamá hoy. 2. Mis hijos van a estudiar en Guadalajara. 3. Mi amiga va a leer un libro. 4. Uds. van a traer los discos compactos. 5. Tú vas a bailar en la fiesta. 6. Nosotros no vamos a brindar con vino.

E. 1. quiere 2. entendemos 3. pierde 4. cierras 5. empiezan (comienzan) 6. empezamos (comenzamos) 7. pienso (quiero) 8. preferimos (queremos)

F. 1. tienen prisa 2. no tengo hambre / tengo mucha sed 3. tenemos calor 4. tienen mucho sueño 5. tienes miedo 6. tiene razón / tiene diez años

G. 1. pasar 2. a la vez 3. empieza 4. agua 5. tía 6. sobrino 7. partido 8. invitados 9. ocupado 10. sacar

H. 1. no existe 2. santo 3. Guadalajara 4. pintor

Lección 5

A. 1. Mi hermano es el estudiante más inteligente de la clase. 2. La Lección 2 es menos interesante que la Lección 7. 3. Mi novia es más bonita que tu novia. 4. Mi primo es el más guapo de la familia. 5. El profesor Paz tiene menos de veinte estudiantes. 6. Mi sobrino es tan alto como yo.

B. 1. más grande 2. mejor 3. mejor / peor 4. mayor / menor 5. más pequeño

C. 1. cuesta 2. pueden 3. Recuerda 4. cuento 5. almorzamos 6. vuelves 7. llueve 8. Duerme

D. 1. Ella está diciendo que nosotros necesitamos más dinero. 2. Yo estoy hablando con mi abuela en español. 3. Nosotros estamos leyendo un libro muy bueno. 4. ¿Qué estás comiendo tú? ¿Biftec? 5. Luis está durmiendo en su cuarto. 6. Los chicos están pidiendo dinero.

E. 1. Elsa es la mamá de Marcela. 2. El restaurante Miramar está en la calle Siete. 3. ¡Mmmm! El pollo está delicioso. 4. Roberto es de México, pero ahora está en Guatemala. 5. El café está frío. 6. El escritorio es de metal. 7. Hoy es lunes. 8. Elvira es profesora de español. 9. La fiesta es en la casa de Armando. 10. Mariana es muy inteligente. 11. Ellos están cansados. 12. Mi suegra es guatemalteca.

F. 1. Está lloviendo 2. Hace frío 3. Hace calor 4. nieva 5. hace sol 6. lluvia

G. 1. de postre 2. lechón 3. pescado 4. primo 5. pollo 6. arroz 7. cuenta 8. mantel 9. hermoso 10. leche 11. platillo 12. camarero

H. 1. postre 2. propina 3. primavera 4. pequeño

Lección 6

A. 1. este / esta / esos 2. Aquel / aquellas / Eso

B. 1. sirven 2. pedimos / pides 3. consigo 4. siguen 5. digo / dice

C. 1. Ellos van a querer algo. 2. Hay alguien en la clase. 3. Tengo algunos amigos españoles. 4. Ellos siempre dicen algo. 5. Yo también ceno a las nueve. 6. Siempre tiene los libros que necesita. 7. Puedes ir o al cine o al teatro. 8. Ellos siempre quieren algo también.

D. 1. conduzco 2. sé 3. quepo 4. salgo 5. traduzco 6. veo 7. hago 8. pongo 9. conozco 10. traigo

E. 1. Nosotros sabemos que ella es su novia. 2. Yo conozco a Teresa, pero no sé dónde vive. 3. Peter conoce Madrid, pero no sabe hablar español. 4. Los chicos no saben los poemas de memoria.

F. 1. No, no quiero comprarlo (no lo quiero comprar). 2. No, no los llamo todos los días. 3. No, no la servimos a las siete. 4. No, no los tengo. 5. No, no va a llevarme (no me va a llevar) a la fiesta. 6. No, no podemos llevarte (no te podemos llevar). 7. No, no las conozco. 8. No, no las necesito. 9. No, no nos lleva. 10. No, no puedo llevarlos (no los puedo llevar).

G. 1. j 2. m 3. g 4. o 5. a 6. d 7. k 8. c 9. b 10. f 11. e 12. i 13. h 14. l 15. n

H. 1. Su apellido de soltera. 2. El imperio maya. 3. Porque las tierras volcánicas, por lo general, son buenas para la agricultura. 4. Tegucigalpa. 5. Copán.

Self-Test Lecciones 7–9

Lección 7

A. 1. Ella les trae las llaves.   2. Yo te voy a preparar (voy a prepararte) la cena.   3. El botones le trae el equipaje.   4. Ana me va a comprar (va a comprarme) las tarjetas.   5. Él nos trae el desayuno.   6. Les traen las maletas.

B. 1. (A nosotros) nos gusta más esta película.   2. A ellos les gusta mucho ese hotel.   3. (A ti) te gusta nadar.   4. (A mí) me gusta hacer ejercicio.   5. (A ella) no le gusta usar la escalera mecánica.

C. 1. Hace dos días que yo no duermo.   2. Hace un mes que tú no me llamas.   3. Hace media hora que nosotras estamos aquí.   4. Hace un año que ellos viven en Panamá.   5. Hace doce horas que Eva no come.

D. 1. Leo y yo compramos las valijas ayer.   2. La semana pasada yo viajé.   3. Ayer ella canceló la reservación.   4. ¿Confirmaron Uds. el viaje ayer?   5. Ellos hablaron con el empleado al mediodía.   6. Anoche les di las maletas.

E. 1. tercer   2. quinto   3. cuarto   4. décimo   5. octavo   6. primer

F. 1. aire   2. botones   3. elevador (ascensor)   4. desayuno / almuerzo   5. bañadera   6. doble   7. cámara   8. habitación (cuarto)   9. nadar   10. servirle   11. cambio   12. dejar

G. 1. ecoturismo   2. obligatoria   3. Atlántico / Pacífico   4. los Estados Unidos

Lección 8

A. 1. Se las van a mandar (Van a mandárselas) mañana.   2. Mi mamá me lo va a comprar (va a comprármelo).   3. Luis nos lo va a prestar (va a prestárnoslo).   4. Te la voy a traer (voy a traértela) esta tarde.   5. La profesora nos lo va a dar (va a dárnoslo).

B. 1. fuimos / dimos   2. fueron   3. diste   4. fui   5. dieron   6. fueron   7. fue   8. fui / di

C. 1. Durmieron   2. siguieron   3. servimos   4. mintió   5. consiguió   6. pidieron   7. murió   8. repitió

D. 1. por / para / para / por   2. para / por / por / para

E. 1. especialmente   2. frecuentemente   3. lenta / claramente   4. recientemente   5. Generalmente   6. Desafortunadamente

F. 1. tintorería   2. préstamo   3. robaron   4. una multa   5. gratis   6. violetas   7. fechar   8. regalo   9. encanta   10. prestar

G. 1. San Juan   2. Ponce   3. Antillas   4. béisbol

Lección 9

A. 1. Tú te vistes muy bien.   2. Ellos se afeitan todos los días.   3. Nosotros nos acostamos a las once.   4. ¿Uds. se preocupan por sus hijos?   5. Yo me pongo la camisa.   6. Juan se sienta aquí.   7. Ella se lava la cabeza todos los días.   8. Él se quita el suéter.   9. Yo no me acuerdo de eso.   10. Uds. se van.   11. ¿Cómo te llamas?   12. Daniel no se despierta hasta las diez.

B. 1. ¿Tú te quitas el abrigo?   2. Ellos están en la escuela.   3. Mi mamá me lava la cabeza.   4. Uds. no se lavan las manos.   5. Los padres se preocupan por sus hijos.   6. Nosotros preferimos el café.   7. La educación es lo más importante.

C. 1. El mío   2. las suyas   3. las nuestras   4. las tuyas   5. los nuestros   6. El suyo (El de él)

D. 1. tuve / estuvieron   2. trajeron / pusieron   3. vino / tradujo   4. pudo / tuvo   5. dijimos   6. supiste   7. vinieron / quisieron   8. condujeron   9. hizo

E. 1. Hace cuatro años que conocí a mi mejor amigo(-a).   2. Hace seis meses que mis amigos y yo fuimos de vacaciones.   3. Hace tres días que mi familia y yo fuimos a la playa.   4. Hace una semana que mis padres volvieron de Cuba.   5. Hace quince minutos que llegué a mi casa.

F. 1. h   2. j   3. a   4. e   5. c   6. i   7. b   8. g   9. d   10. f

G. 1. mayor   2. tabaco   3. merengue   4. primera

Self-Test Lecciones 10–12

Lección 10

A. 1. era / Eran   2. vivías / eras / vivía / íbamos / veías / vivían   3. era / quejaba   4. gustaba

B. 1. dijo / necesitaba / podía / tenía   2. compramos / éramos / llevábamos / íbamos   3. tenía / vinimos / hablábamos   4. fue / tuve / sentía   5. iba / vio / murieron

C. 1. La conoció en la universidad.   2. Sí, la conocía.   3. No, no quería venir.   4. No, no sabíamos que había examen hoy.   5. Lo supimos anoche.   6. No, él no quiso venir.

D. 1. Ésta es la señora que vino ayer.   2. Éstos son los niños de quienes te hablé.   3. Ésa es la profesora para quien compramos los libros.   4. Ésa es la chica que trajo la licuadora.

E. 1. mudar   2. incluye / electricidad   3. amueblado   4. lejos   5. amplio   6. edificio / desocupado   7. centro / mesita   8. calefacción   9. cortinas / espejo   10. secadora

F. 1. Caracas.   2. Significa "pequeña Venecia".   3. El petróleo.   4. El Salto Ángel.

Lección 11

A. 1. estemos 2. camines 3. saque 4. sugiera 5. den 6. sepa 7. vuelvas 8. me queje 9. sean 10. vaya 11. recoja 12. reciba

B. 1. ir / vayamos 2. venga / estés 3. ir / compre 4. hagan / visitar 5. viajes / viajar

C. 1. hagan una excursión. 2. vengan este verano. 3. sepas cuánto cuesta el vuelo. 4. esté enferma. 5. no podamos ir en ese viaje. 6. vayan a Colombia.

D. 1. g 2. j 3. h 4. e 5. c 6. i 7. b 8. f 9. d 10. a

E. 1. costas 2. café 3. esmeraldas 4. Shakira 5. Avianca

Lección 12

A. 1. Estén 2. Tráigamelo 3. Salgan 4. Désela 5. Vayan 6. Quédese 7. Mándenoslas 8. los ponga

B. 1. sea 2. esté 3. necesiten 4. está 5. se encuentran 6. necesito 7. cuesta 8. gusta

C. 1. ¿Qué idiomas se hablan en Perú? 2. ¿A qué hora se cierran las gasolineras? 3. ¿A qué hora se abre la peluquería? 4. ¿Dónde se vende gasolina? 5. ¿Por dónde se sale de aquí?

D. 1. peluquería 2. arranca 3. cambios mecánicos 4. costó 5. doblar 6. los frenos 7. chapa 8. la cajuela 9. vacío 10. valía

E. 1. nuevo sol 2. Cuzco / Machu Picchu 3. antigua 4. islas Galápagos

Self-Test Lecciones 13–15

Lección 13

A. 1. Dime 2. Haz / limpia 3. Vete 4. Ve / compra 5. Ponlos 6. Ven 7. Sé / tráeme 8. Ten / Espérame 9. No compres 10. No los cambies 11. No te vayas 12. Levántate / trabaja

B. 1. ¿Cuál es tu número de teléfono? 2. ¿Cuál es el apellido de tu padre? 3. ¿Qué es una pulsera? 4. ¿Cuáles son las lecciones que necesitan? 5. ¿Cuál es su dirección? 6. ¿Qué es una enchilada?

C. 1. sepa 2. tienen 3. sea 4. tenga 5. haga 6. habla / hable

D. 1. comercial / zapatos / liquidación (rebaja) 2. ponerme / ir 3. anchas 4. calza 5. lado 6. queda / talla 7. departamento / ropa 8. rayas 9. librería 10. par 11. parece 12. ganga

E. 1. estrecho 2. tercera 3. Mar 4. frutería

Lección 14

A. 1. llegue 2. vuelvan 3. van 4. veas 5. tomen 6. vayas 7. des 8. necesite 9. lleve

B. 1. escrito 2. abierto 3. visto 4. hecho 5. roto 6. ido 7. hablado 8. comido 9. bebido 10. recibido

C. 1. escritos 2. abiertas 3. muerto 4. cerrado 5. hechos

D. 1. ha venido 2. han dicho 3. has escrito 4. he hecho 5. han hablado 6. nos hemos enojado

E. 1. había terminado 2. habían ido 3. había dicho 4. había terminado 5. habíamos matriculado 6. habías preguntado

F. 1. d 2. f 3. h 4. j 5. i 6. k 7. l 8. e 9. g 10. c 11. a 12. b

G. 1. Buenos Aires. 2. El tango. 3. El París de Suramérica. 4. Las cataratas de Iguazú.

Lección 15

A. 1. Le diremos que necesita descansar. 2. ¿Qué harán Uds.? 3. No querrán ir. 4. Lo sabré mañana. 5. No podrán venir. 6. ¿Adónde iremos? 7. ¿Dónde lo pondrás? 8. Nosotros vendremos con él. 9. Tendré que preguntárselo. 10. Saldremos mañana.

B. 1. Yo iría a Paraguay. 2. Nosotros le recetaríamos antibióticos. 3. ¿Tú se lo dirías? 4. Ellos hablarían con Dora. 5. ¿Ud. lo pondría en el consultorio? 6. ¿Uds. vendrían el domingo? 7. Julio pediría miel. 8. Nosotros lo haríamos hoy. 9. Tú no saldrías con ella. 10. Ella no iría sola.

C. 1. habrá dicho 2. habrán vuelto 3. habré mejorado 4. habremos merendado 5. habrás traído

D. 1. habría tomado 2. habrían venido 3. habría puesto 4. habríamos ido 5. habrías hecho

E. 1. penicilina 2. los dientes 3. la lengua 4. los ojos 5. los pies 6. ambulancia 7. rompiste 8. la pierna 9. grados 10. pusieron 11. dolor de cabeza 12. el estómago 13. embarazada 14. gripe

F. 1. guaraní 2. Itaipú 3. mar 4. Titicaca 5. La Paz

Lección 16

A. 1. que fuera con ellos.   2. que no montaran a caballo hoy.   3. de que él fuera el campeón.   4. que se ahogaran.   5. a alguien que me enseñara a esquiar.   6. que él supiera armar la tienda de campaña.   7. alguien aquí que tuviera una caña de pescar?   8. que necesitáramos una raqueta.   9. que estuviera tomando el sol.   10. de que te sintieras bien.

B. 1. a / en / de / a / a   2. en / de / a / a / a   3. a / de / de   4. a / a   5. en / en

C. 1. hayan ido   2. hayas aprendido   3. haya leído   4. se haya aburrido   5. haya sabido   6. hayamos divertido

D. 1. i   2. e   3. j   4. a   5. g   6. c   7. d   8. f   9. b   10. h

E. 1. Montevideo.   2. El mate.   3. Un famoso centro turístico.   4. Se habla portugués.   5. Ipanema y Copacabana.

Lección 17

A. 1. hubiera visto   2. hubieran tenido   3. hubiéramos archivado   4. hubiera ofrecido   5. hubiera escrito

B. 1. tengo   2. pudiéramos   3. hubieran ido   4. necesitan   5. hubieras visto   6. supiera

C. 1. entrevistaran   2. puedas   3. avise   4. podamos / puede   5. haya   6. llegue   7. pudiera   8. paguemos

D. 1. aumento   2. departamento / público   3. equipos / procesador   4. impresionados / cartas   5. bienes   6. encargados   7. avisar   8. bajo / relaciones   9. mensajes   10. traductor

E. 1. Portugal   2. monarquía   3. euro   4. Madrid   5. Prado

Lección 18

A. 1. me olvido de   2. sueñan con   3. insiste en   4. venimos a   5. se comprometió con   6. me enamoré de

B. 1. Por desgracia   2. Para qué   3. sin qué ni para qué   4. por si acaso   5. por aquí cerca   6. para siempre   7. por eso   8. por suerte

C. 1. me dio las gracias   2. a principios de   3. sin falta   4. te hagas ilusiones   5. Dejó plantado   6. les importa   7. hoy en día   8. llevaba puesto

D. 1. director   2. boda / principios   3. película   4. toma   5. perillas   6. que esperen   7. cargo / grupo   8. A cuánto   9. bando   10. oeste

E. 1. Granada / Sevilla / Córdoba   2. Plaza de España   3. Jerez   4. "Huerta de España"   5. Miguel de Cervantes

Appendix E: Professions and Trades

accountant **contador(-a)**
actor **actor**
actress **actriz**
administrator **administrador(-a)**
agent **agente**
architect **arquitecto(-a)**
artisan **artesano(-a)**
artist **artista**
baker **panadero(-a)**
bank officer **empleado(-a) bancario(-a)**
bank teller **cajero(-a)**
banker **banquero(-a)**
barber **barbero(-a)**
bartender **barman, cantinero(-a)**
bill collector **cobrador(-a)**
bookkeeper **tenedor(-a) de libros**
brickmason (bricklayer) **albañil**
butcher **carnicero(-a)**
buyer **comprador(-a)**
camera operator **camarógrafo(-a)**
carpenter **carpintero(-a)**
cashier **cajero(-a)**
chiropractor **quiropráctico(-a)**
clerk **dependiente(-a)** *(store)*, **oficinista** *(office)*
computer operator **computista**
construction worker **obrero(-a) de la construcción**
constructor **constructor(-a)**
contractor **contratista**
cook **cocinero(-a)**
copilot **copiloto** *(masc., fem.)*
counselor **consejero(-a)**
dancer **bailarín(-ina)**
decorator **decorador(-a)**
dental hygienist **higienista dental**
dentist **dentista**
designer **diseñador(-a)**
detective **detective**
dietician **especialista en dietética**
diplomat **diplomático(-a)**
director **director(-a)**
dockworker **obrero(-a) portuario(-a)**
doctor **doctor(-a), médico(-a)**
draftsman **dibujante**
dressmaker **modista**
driver **conductor(-a)**
economist **economista**
editor **editor(-a)**
electrician **electricista**
engineer **ingeniero(-a)**
engineering technician **ingeniero(-a) técnico(-a)**

eye doctor **oculista**
farmer **agricultor(-a)**
fashion designer **diseñador(-a) de alta costura**
fire fighter **bombero(-a)**
fisherman **pescador(-a)**
flight attendant **auxiliar de vuelo**
foreman **capataz, encargado(-a)**
funeral director **empresario(-a) de pompas fúnebres**
garbage collector **basurero(-a)**
gardener **jardinero(-a)**
guard **guardia**
guide **guía**
hairdresser **peluquero(-a)**
home economist **economista doméstico(-a)**
housekeeper **mayordomo, ama de llaves**
inspector **inspector(-a)**
instructor **instructor(-a)**
insurance agent **agente de seguros**
interior designer **diseñador(-a) de interiores**
interpreter **intérprete**
investigator **investigador(-a)**
janitor **conserje**
jeweler **joyero(-a)**
journalist **periodista**
judge **juez(-a)**
lawyer **abogado(-a)**
librarian **bibliotecario(-a)**
machinist **maquinista**
maid **criada**
mail carrier **cartero(-a)**
manager **gerente**
mechanic **mecánico(-a)**
midwife **comadrona, partera**
miner **minero(-a)**
model **modelo**
musician **músico(-a)**
nurse **enfermero(-a)**
optician **óptico(-a)**
optometrist **optometrista**
painter **pintor(-a)**
paramedic **paramédico(-a)**
pharmacist **farmacéutico(-a)**
photographer **fotógrafo(-a)**
physical therapist **terapista físico(-a)**
physician **médico(-a)**
pilot **piloto** *(masc., fem.)*, **aviador(-a)**
plumber **plomero(-a)**

police officer **policía, agente de policía**
printer **impresor(-a)**
psychologist **psicólogo(-a)**
public relations agent **agente de relaciones públicas**
real estate agent **agente de bienes raíces**
receptionist **recepcionista**
reporter **reportero(-a), periodista**
sailor **marinero(-a)**
sales representative **vendedor(-a)**
scientist **científico(-a)**
secretary **secretario(-a)**
security guard **guardia**
social worker **trabajador(-a) social**
sociologist **sociólogo(-a)**
soldier **soldado, militar**
stenographer **estenógrafo(-a)**
stockbroker **bolsista**
student **estudiante**
supervisor **supervisor(-a)**
surgeon **cirujano(-a)**
systems analyst **analista de sistemas**
tailor **sastre**
taxi driver **chofer de taxi, taxista**
teacher **maestro(-a)** *(elem. school)*, **profesor(-a)** *(high school and college)*
technician **técnico(-a)**
telephone operator **telefonista**
television and radio announcer **locutor(-a)**
television and radio technician **técnico(-a) de radio y televisión**
teller **cajero(-a)**
therapist **terapista**
travel agent **agente de viajes**
truck driver **camionero(-a)**
typist **mecanógrafo(-a), dactilógrafo(-a)**
undertaker **director(-a) de pompas fúnebres**
veterinarian **veterinario(-a)**
waiter **mozo, camarero**
waitress **camarera**
watchmaker **relojero(-a)**
worker **obrero(-a)**
writer **escritor(-a)**

Vocabulary

The Spanish-English vocabulary contains all active and passive vocabulary that apears in the student text. Active vocabulary includes words and expressions that appear in the vocabulary lists that follow the dialogues and in charts and word lists that are part of the grammar explanations. Passive vocabulary consits of words and expressions that are given an English gloss in textual material throughout the book: readings, photo captions, exercises, activities, and authentic documents.

The English-Spanish Vocabulary contains both active and passive words and expressions.
The following abbreviations are used in the vocabularies:

abbr.	abbreviation	*indir. obj.*	indirect object	*poet.*	poetic
adj.	adjective	*inf.*	infinitive	*prep.*	preposition
adv.	adverb	*obj.*	object	*pron.*	pronoun
aux.	auxiliary	*lang.*	language	*p.p.*	past participle
dir. obj.	direct object	*m.*	masculine	*sing.*	singular
f.	feminine	*Mex.*	Mexico	*Sp.*	Spain
fam.	familiar	*obj.*	object	*Sp. Am.*	Spanish America
form.	formal	*pl.*	plural		

Spanish-English

A

a at, 2; to, 16; in, 16; —**casa** home; ¿ — **cómo está el cambio de moneda?** What is the exchange rate?, 6; ¿ — **cuánto estamos hoy?** What's the date today?, 18; — **deshoras** untimely; — **eso de** at about, 15; — **la derecha (izquierda)** to the right (left), 12; — **la parrilla** grilled, 5; — **la vez** at a time; — **lo mejor** maybe, 12; — **más tardar** at the latest, 18; — **menos que** unless, 14; — **menudo** often, 12; — **nuestra disposición** at our disposal, 16; — **pesar de (que)** in spite of, 9; — **pie** on foot, 12; — **plazos** in installments, 11; — **principios de** at the first part of, 18; ¿ — **qué hora?** At what time?, 2; — **(en) todas partes** everywhere, 12; — **todos lados** everywhere, 12; — **veces** sometimes, 6; — **ver** let's see, 3

abierto(-a) *(p.p. of* **abrir** *and adj.)* open(ed), 14

abogado(-a) *(m., f.)* lawyer, 14

abrazar to hug, 4

abrazo *(m.)* hug, 4

abrigo *(m.)* coat

abril April, 1

abrir to open, 3; — **una cuenta** to open an account, 8

abuela *(f.)* grandmother, 4

abuelo *(m.)* grandfather, 4

aburrido(-a) bored, 4

aburrirse (como una ostra) to be bored (to death), 16

acá here, 10

acabar de to have just, 4

acampar to camp, 16

accidente *(m.)* accident, 15

acción *(f.)* action, 18

accionista *(m., f.)* shareholder, 17

aceite *(m.)* oil, 9; — **de oliva** *(m.)* olive oil

aceituna *(f.)* olive

aceptar to accept, 3

acercarse to approach

aconsejar to advise, 11

acontecimiento *(m.)* event

acordarse (o:ue) (de) to remember, 9

acostar (o:ue) to put to bed, 9

acostarse to go to bed, 9

acostumbrarse (a) to get used to, 12

actividad *(f.)* activity, 16; — **al aire libre** *(f.)* outdoor activity, 16

actor *(m.)* actor, 18

actriz *(f.)* actress, 18

actualmente nowadays

actuación *(f.)* acting, 18

actuar to act

acumulador *(m.)* battery, 12

adelantado(-a) advanced

además besides, 5

adicional additional

adiós good-bye, 1

adjetivo *(m.)* adjective

administración de empresas *(f.)* business administration, 14

administrador(-a) administrator, 17

adolescente *(m., f.)* teenager, 7

¿adónde? where? (destination)

aduana *(f.)* customs, 7

advertencia *(f.)* warning

aerolínea *(f.)* airline, 11

aeropuerto *(m.)* airport, 4

afeitar(se) to shave, 9

agencia de viajes *(f.)* travel agency, 11

agente *(m., f.)* agent; — **de bienes raíces** *(m., f.)* real estate agent, 17 ; — **de policía** *(f.)* policewoman, 8; — **de relaciones públicas** *(m., f.)* public relations agent, 17; — **de seguros** *(m., f.)* insurance agent, 17; — **de viajes** *(m., f.)* travel agent, 11

agosto August, 1

agradecimiento *(m.)* gratefulness

agua *(f.)* water, 4; — **mineral** *(f.)* mineral water, 5

aguardar to wait

ahijado(-a) *(m., f.)* godson (daughter)

ahogarse to drown, 16

ahora now, 4

ahorrar to save, 8

ahorros *(m. pl.)* savings, 11

aire acondicionado *(m.)* air conditioning, 7

ajeno belonging to other people

al *(m. sing.)* *(contraction)* to the; — **aire libre** outdoor; — **contado** in cash, 8; — **fin y al cabo** after all, 18; — **horno** baked, cooked in the oven, 5; — **lado de** next to, 12; — **mes** a month, per month; — **teléfono** on the phone, 3

alacena (*f.*)   pantry
alba (*f.*)   dawn, daybreak
alberca (*f.*)   swimming pool (*Mex.*), 7
alegrarse (de)   to be glad, 11
alegre   merry
alérgico(-a)   allergic, 8
alfabetizar   to alphabetize
alfabeto (*m.*)   alphabet
alfombra (*f.*)   carpet, 10
alforja (*f.*)   saddlebag
algo   something, anything, 6
algodón (*m.*)   cotton, 13
alguien   someone, somebody, anyone, 6
alguno(-a), algún   any, some, 6
algunos(-as)   some, 6
allí   there
alma (*f.*)   soul
almacén (*m.*)   department store, 13
almohada (*f.*)   pillow, 10
almorzar (o:ue)   to have lunch, 5
almuerzo (*m.*)   lunch, 7
alojamiento (*m.*)   lodging
alquilar   to rent, 10
alquiler (*m.*)   rent, 10
altiplano (*m.*)   plateau
alto(-a)   tall, 3
alumno(-a) (*m., f.*)   student
amable   polite, courteous, 3; **Muy —.**   Very kind (of you)., 1
amante (*adj.*)   loving
amar   to love
amarillo(-a)   yellow, 1
ambos(-as)   both
ambulancia (*f.*)   ambulance, 15
americano(-a)   American, 2
amigo(-a) (*m., f.*)   friend, 1
amistad (*f.*)   friendship
amor (*m.*)   love
amplio(-a)   large, ample, 10
amueblado(-a)   furnished, 10
anaranjado(-a)   orange, 1
ancho(-a)   wide, 13
andén (*m.*)   platform
angosto(-a)   narrow, 13
anillo (*m.*)   ring, 13
anoche   last night, 7
anotar   to write down, 2
anteayer   the day before yesterday, 7
antes (de)   before, 7; **— de que** before, 14
antibiótico (*m.*)   antibiotic, 15
antiguo(-a)   former, 17
antipático(-a)   unpleasant, 3
antojársele a uno   to seem to one
anuncio (*m.*)   ad, 3
añadir   to add
año (*m.*)   year, 3; **— Nuevo** (*m.*)   New Year, 4
aparato electrodoméstico (*m.*)   home appliance, 10
aparcar   to park, 8
apariencia (*f.*)   appearance
apartamento (*m.*)   apartment, 3
apellido (*m.*)   last name, 3; **— de soltera** (*m.*)   maiden name

apio (*m.*)   celery, 9
aprender (**a**)   to learn, 3
apretar (e:ie)   to be tight, 15; to tie together
aprobar (o:ue)   to pass (*an exam or course*), 14
aprovechar   to take advantage of
aquel(los), aquella(s) (*adj.*)   that, those (*distant*), 6
aquél(los), aquélla(s) (*pron.*)   that one, those (*distant*), 6
aquello (*neuter pron.*)   that, 6
aquí   here, 3; **¡— va!**   Here it goes!
árbol (*m.*)   tree; **— de Navidad** Christmas tree, 4; **— frutal** (*m.*)   fruit tree, 15
archivar   to file, 17
arena (*f.*)   sand
arete (*m.*)   earring, 13
argentino(-a)   Argentinian, 11
armar   to pitch (*a tent*), 16
arquitecto(-a) (*m., f.*)   architect, 14
arrancar   to start (*car*), 12
arreglar   to tidy up, to fix, 6; to repair, 12
arreglo (*m.*)   repair, 12
arroz (*m.*)   rice, 5; **— con leche** (*m.*)   rice pudding, 5
arte (*f.*)   art
artículo (*m.*)   article, 16
asado (*m.*)   barbecue, 16
asado(-a)   roasted, barbecued, 9
ascendencia (*f.*)   ancestry, 14
ascensor (*m.*)   elevator, 7
Así es la vida.   Such is life.
así que   so, 18
asiento (*m.*)   seat; **— de pasillo** (*m.*)   aisle seat, 11; **— de ventanilla** (*m.*)   window seat, 11
asignatura (*f.*)   (school) subject, 14
asistente (*m., f.*)   assistant, 17
asistir (**a**)   to attend, 3
aspiradora (*f.*)   vacuum cleaner, 6
aspirina (*f.*)   aspirin, 15
ataque al corazón (*m.*)   heart attack, 15
atlético(-a)   athletic, 16
atónito(-a)   aghast
atravesar (e:ie)   to go through; **— con la mirada**   to look right through
aturdido(-a)   dazed, confused, 4
aumento (*m.*)   increase, 17
aunque   although, 9
auto (*m.*)   car, 10
autobús (*m.*)   bus, 6
automático(-a)   automatic, 12
automóvil (*m.*)   car, 10
autopista (*f.*)   freeway, highway, 12
auxiliar de vuelo (*m., f.*)   flight attendant, 11
avance (*m.*)   preview, 18
avenida (*f.*)   avenue, 12
avergonzado(-a)   ashamed
avión (*m.*)   plane, 11
avisar   to let know, to advise, 10

aviso (*m.*)   ad, 3; **— clasificado** (*m.*)   classified ad
ayer   yesterday, 7
ayudar (**a**)   to help, 6
azafata (*f.*)   female flight attendant, 11
azúcar (*m.*)   sugar, 9
azul   blue, 1
azulejo (*m.*)   tile

B

bailar   to dance, 4
bailarín(-ina) (*m., f.*)   dancer, 18
bajo(-a) (*adj.*)   short, 3; (*prep.*) under
balneario (*m.*)   resort
banana (*f.*)   banana, 9
banco (*m.*)   bank, 18
banda sonora (*f.*)   sound track, 18
bandera (*f.*)   flag
bañadera (*f.*)   bathtub, 7
bañar(se)   to bathe (oneself), 9
bañera (*f.*)   bathtub, 7
baño (*m.*)   bathroom, 6
barato(-a)   inexpensive, 13
¡Bárbaro!   Great!
barca (*f.*)   boat, 16
barco (*m.*)   ship, 11
barrer   to sweep, **6**
barrio (*m.*)   neighborhood, 10
bastante   quite, 14
batería (*f.*)   drums, 9; battery, 12; **— de cocina** (*f.*)   cookware, 10
batir   to beat
beber   to drink, 3; **— algo**   to have something to drink, 3
bebida (*f.*)   drink, 5
beca (*f.*)   scholarship, 14
belleza (*f.*)   beauty
besar   to kiss
beso (*m.*)   kiss
biblioteca (*f.*)   library, 2
bibliotecario(-a) (*m., f.*)   librarian, 14
bicicleta (*f.*)   bicycle, 12
bien   well, fine, 1; **— caliente**   nice and hot, 15
bienvenido(-a)   welcome, 4
biftec (*m.*)   steak, 5
billete (*m.*)   ticket, 11; **— de ida** (*m.*)   one-way ticket, 11; **— de ida y vuelta** (*m.*)   round-trip ticket, 11
billetera (*f.*)   wallet, 13
biología (*f.*)   biology, 14
bisabuela (*f.*)   great-grandmother
bisabuelo (*m.*)   great-grandfather
bistec (*m.*)   steak, 5
blanco(-a)   white, 1
blusa (*f.*)   blouse, 13
boca (*f.*)   mouth, 15; **— de incendios** (*f.*)   fire hydrant, 8
bocina (*f.*)   horn, 12
boda (*f.*)   wedding, 18
bolígrafo (*m.*)   pen, 2
bolsa de aire (*f.*)   air bag, 12
bolsa de dormir (*f.*)   sleeping bag, 10
bolso (*m.*)   purse, handbag, 9; **— de mano** (*m.*)   carry-on bag

bombilla (*f.*) straw (*for mate*)
bondad (*f.*) kindness
bonito(-a) pretty, 3
borrador (*m.*) first draft
bosque (*m.*) forest, 11
bosquejo (*m.*) outline
bota (*f.*) boot, 13
bote (*m.*) (*Mex.*) can, 9; boat, 16
botones (*m.*) bellhop, 7
brillante brilliant, 11
bromear to joke, to kid, 12
broncearse to get a tan, 16
bucear to scuba dive, 16
buenísimo(-a) extremely good, 11
bueno(-a), buen good, 1
  ¡Buen viaje! Have a nice trip!, 11
  buenas noches good evening, good night, 1
  buenas tardes good afternoon, 1
  bueno… well…, okay, 1
  buenos días good morning, 1
burlarse de to make fun of, 18
burro(-a) (*m., f.*) donkey
bus (*m.*) bus, 16
buscar to get, to pick up, 6; to look for; to find
búsqueda (*f.*) search
butaca (*f.*) armchair, 10

C

caballería (*f.*) chivalry
caballero (*m.*) knight
cabaña (*f.*) cabin, 16
cabello (*m.*) hair, 15
caber to fit, 6
cabeza (*f.*) head, 15
cacerola (*f.*) saucepan, 10
cada (*invariable adj.*) each, 13
caer(se) to fall, 16
café (*m.*) brown, 1; coffee, 3; café, 3
cafecito (*m.*) small (cup of) coffee, 15
cafetera (*f.*) coffee maker, 10
cafetería (*f.*) cafeteria, 1
caja (*f.*) cash register, 13
cajero automático (*m.*) automatic teller, 8
cajuela (*f.*) trunk (*car*), 12
calcetines (*m. pl.*) socks, 13
calculadora (*f.*) calculator
calefacción (*f.*) heating, 10
callar to be silent
calle (*f.*) street, 2
calor (*m.*) heat, 14
caloría (*f.*) calorie, 5
calzar to wear (a certain size in shoes), 13
cama (*f.*) bed, 16
cámara (fotográfica) (*f.*) camera, 7; **— de video** (*f.*) video camera, 7
camarero(-a) (*m., f.*) waiter, waitress, 5
camarones (*m. pl.*) shrimp, 5
cambiar to change, 6; to exchange, 13
cambio de moneda (*m.*) exchange rate

cambios mecánicos (*m. pl.*) standard shift, 12
camelia (*f.*) camellia, 8
caminar to walk, 12
camión (*m.*) truck, 13
camisa (*f.*) shirt, 6
camiseta (*f.*) T-shirt, 13
camisón (*m.*) nightgown, 13
campeón(-ona) (*m., f.*) champion, 16
campo (*m.*) country, 16
canal (*m.*) channel, 7
canario (*m.*) canary, 8
cancelar to cancel, 7
canción (*f.*) song, 9; **— infantil** (*f.*) children's song
candidato(-a) (*m., f.*) candidate, 17
canoa (*f.*) canoe, 16
cansado(-a) tired, 4
cantar to sing, 4
caña de azúcar (*f.*) sugar cane
caña de pescar (*f.*) fishing rod, 16
capital (*f.*) capital (city)
capó (*m.*) hood, 12
capullo (*m.*) bud
cara (*f.*) face, 15
¡caramba! gee!, 2
carbón (*m.*) coal
carburador (*m.*) carburetor, 12
cárcel (*f.*) jail
cargado(-a) (**de**) loaded with, 13
cargo (*m.*) position
cariño (*m.*) love
carnaval (*m.*) Mardi Gras
carne (*f.*) meat, 6; flesh; **— de res** (*f.*) beef
carnicería (*f.*) meat market, 9
caro(-a) expensive, 5
carpeta (*f.*) folder, 17
carpintero(-a) (*m., f.*) carpenter, 14
carrera (*f.*) career, 16
carro (*m.*) car, 10; carriage
carta (*f.*) letter, 17
cartelera (*f.*) movie (entertainment) section (of a newspaper), 18
cartera (*f.*) handbag, 9; wallet, 13
casa (*f.*) house, 2; home; **— de ancianos** (*f.*) nursing home
casado(-a) married, 3
casarse (con) to get married (to), 11
casi almost, 8
catarro (*m.*) cold, 15
cátedra (*f.*) faculty appointment
catorce fourteen, 1
cazar to hunt, 16
cebolla (*f.*) onion, 9
cédula (*f.*) document
celebrar to celebrate, 9
cena (*f.*) dinner, 7
cenar to have dinner, to dine, 7
censura (*f.*) censorship
centro (*m.*) downtown; **— commercial** (*m.*) shopping mall, 13
cerca close to, near, 10; around; **— de** near

cereza (*f.*) cherry
cero zero, 1
cerradura (*f.*) lock
cerrar (e:ie) to close, 4
cerveza (*f.*) beer, 5
cesto de papeles (*m.*) wastebasket, 2
champán (*m.*) champagne, 5
chapa (*f.*) license plate, 12
Chau. Good-bye., 1
cheque (*m.*) check, 8; **— de viajero** (*m.*) traveler's check, 8
chequeo (*m.*) checkup, 15
chequera (*f.*) checkbook, 8
¡Chévere! Great!
chica (*f.*) girl, young woman, 2
chico (*m.*) boy, young man, 2
chico(-a) small, 10
chino Chinese (*lang.*)
chocolate (*m.*) chocolate, 5; **— caliente** (*m.*) hot chocolate, 5
chorizo (*m.*) sausage
cielo (*m.*) sky, heaven
cien, ciento one hundred, 2
ciencia (*f.*) science, 14; **— ficción** (*f.*) science fiction, 18
cierto true
cinco five, 1
cincuenta fifty, 2
cine (*m.*) movie (theater), 4
cita (*f.*) appointment
ciudad (*f.*) city, 3
clarinete (*m.*) clarinet, 9
claro(-a) light; clear
clase (*f.*) class, 1; **— optativa** (*f.*) elective; **— turista** (*f.*) tourist class, 11
clasificado(-a) classified, 12
clavel (*m.*) carnation, 8
cliente (*m., f.*) customer
cobardía (*f.*) cowardice
cobrar un cheque to cash a check, 8
cobre (*m.*) copper
coche (*m.*) car, 10
cocina (*f.*) kitchen, 5
cocinar to cook, 6
cocinero(-a) (*m., f.*) cook, chef, 14
cognado (*m.*) cognate
col (*f.*) cabbage
cola (*f.*) tail
colchón (*m.*) mattress, 7
colega (*m., f.*) colleague
collar (*m.*) necklace, 13
colonial colonial, 15
color (*m.*) color, 1
colorado(-a) red
columna (*f.*) column, 18
combinar (con) to match, 13
comedia (*f.*) comedy, 7
comedor (*m.*) dining room, 6
comenzar (e:ie) (a) to begin, to start, 4
comer to eat, 3; **— algo** to have something to eat, 3
comida (*f.*) food, 4; meal, 5
como since, 7; about, 16; **— si** as if, 17

¿cómo? how?, 1; what?; **¿ — está usted?** How are you? (*form.*), 1; **¿ — estás?** How are you? (*fam.*); **¿ — están ustedes?** How are you?, 1; **¿ — le va?** How is it going (for you)? (*form.*), 1; **¿ — se dice...?** How do you say . . . ?, 2; **¿ — se escribe...?** How do you write . . .?; **¿ — se llama usted?** What's your name? (*form.*), 1; **¿ — te llamas tú?** What's your name? (*fam.*), 1; **¿ — te va?** How is it going (for you) (*fam.*)?

cómoda (*f.*) bureau, chest of drawers, 10

cómodo(-a) comfortable, 7

compacto(-a) compact, 12

compañero(-a) (*m., f.*) partner; **— de clase** (*m., f.*) classmate, 4; **— de cuarto** (*m., f.*) roommate, 3

compañía (*f.*) company, 3

comparar to compare, 14

comparativo(-a) comparative

compartir to share, 9

compensar to compensate, 17

complicado(-a) complicated, 12

compra (*f.*) purchase, 17

comprador(-a) (*m., f.*) buyer, 17

comprar to buy, 6

comprometerse con to get engaged to, 18

comprometido(-a) engaged, 18

computadora (*f.*) computer, 2 ; **— portátil** (*f.*) laptop computer, 17

con with, 1; **¿ — cuánta anticipación?** How far in advance?; **— él (ella) habla.** This is he (she) speaking., 3; **— permiso.** Excuse me., 1; **— razón** no wonder, 3; **— tal (de) que** provided that, as long as, 14; **— vista a** overlooking, 7

concierto (*m.*) concert, 4

concordancia (*f.*) agreement

condicional conditional

conducir to drive (*Sp.*), 6

conejillo de Indias (*m.*) Guinea pig, 8

conejo (*m.*) rabbit, 8

conferencia (*f.*) lecture

confiar to trust

confirmar to confirm, 7

conmigo with me, 2

conocer to know, to be acquainted, 6; to meet, 10

conocimiento (*m.*) knowledge, 3

conseguir (e:i) to get, to obtain, 6

consejero(-a) (*m., f.*) advisor, 14

consejo (*m.*) advice

consulado (*m.*) consulate, 7

consultorio (*m.*) doctor's office, 15

contabilidad (*f.*) accounting, 14

contado: al — in cash, 8

contador(-a) (*m., f.*) accountant, 5; **— público(-a)** (*m., f.*) certified public accountant, 17

contagioso(-a) contagious, 15

contaminación del aire (*f.*) smog

contar (o:ue) to count, 5; to tell, 18

contento(-a) happy, 4

contestar to answer, 3

contigo (*fam. sing.*) with you, 4

continente (*m.*) continent, 11

continuar to continue, 17

contra against

contrabajo (*m.*) bass, 9

contracción (*f.*) contraction

convencer to convince, 10

conversación (*f.*) conversation, 2

conversar to talk, to converse, 4

convivencia (*f.*) coexistence

copa (*f.*) glass, goblet, 5

corbata (*f.*) tie, 13

cordero (*m.*) lamb, 5

correo (*m.*) post office, 12; **— electrónico** (*m.*) e-mail, 17

correr to run, 3

corrida de toros (*f.*) bullfight

correspondencia (*f.*) correspondence, 17

corsario (*m.*) privateer

cortar(se) to cut (oneself), 9; **— el césped** to mow the lawn, 6

corte de pelo (*m.*) haircut, cut, 12

cortés polite, courteous, 3

cortina (*f.*) curtain, 10

cosa (*f.*) thing, 6

costar (o:ue) to cost, 5; **— un ojo de la cara** to cost an arm and a leg, 12

costumbre (*f.*) custom, 4

crear to create

crecer to grow, 9

creer to believe, to think, 3

creído (*p.p. of* **creer**) believed, 14

crema (*f.*) cream, 5

crepúsculo (*m.*) twilight

criada (*f.*) maid, 10

criticar to criticize, 18

crítico(-a) (*m., f.*) critic, 18

cuaderno (*m.*) notebook, 2

cuadro (*m.*) picture, painting, 10

de cuadros plaid, 13

¿cuál? what?, which?, 1; **¿ — es tu (su) número de teléfono?** What is your telephone number?, 1

cuando when, 14

¿cuándo? when?, 2

¿cuánto(-a)? how much?; **¿ — tiempo hace que...?** How long . . . ?, 7

¿cuántos(-as)? how many?

cuarenta forty, 2

cuarto (*m.*) room, 4; **— de baño** (*m.*) bathroom, 6; **menos —** quarter of/to (*time*), 2; **y —** quarter after/past (*time*), 2

cuarto(-a) fourth, 7

cuatro four, 1

cuatrocientos(-as) four hundred, 3

cubano(-a) Cuban, 2

cubierto(-a) (*p.p. of* **cubrir** *and adj.*) covered, 14

cubiertos (*m. pl.*) silverware, 5

cubrir to cover

cuchara (*f.*) spoon, 5

cucharada (*f.*) spoonful

cucharita (*f.*) teaspoon, 5

cuchillo (*m.*) knife, 5

cuello (*m.*) neck, 15; collar

cuenta (*f.*) bill, check, 5; account, 8; **— conjunta** (*f.*) joint account, 8; **— corriente** (*f.*) checking account, 8; **— de ahorros** (*f.*) savings account, 8

cuero (*m.*) leather, 13

cuerpo (*m.*) body, 15

cuidado (*m.*) care

cumbre (*f.*) pinnacle

cumpleaños (*m.*) birthday, 1

cumplir... años to turn . . . years old, 9

cuñada (*f.*) sister-in-law, 6

cuñado (*m.*) brother-in-law, 6

curandero(-a) (*m, f.*) healer

curarse to cure oneself, to get better, 15

currículum vitae (*m.*) curriculum vitae, 17

curtido(-a) weatherbeaten

D

dar to give, 4; **— alimento (a)** to feed; **— hacia** to overlook; **— la mano** to shake hands; **— las gracias** to express gratitude, 18; **— un beso** to kiss; **— una multa** to give a ticket (fine), 8; **— una película** to show a movie, 7; **— le rabia a uno** to be furious, 18; **—se cuenta (de)** to realize, 14

datos personales (*m. pl.*) personal data

de from, 1; of, 1; about, with, in, 16; **— acuerdo** in agreement, 13; **— acuerdo con** according to; **— cuadros** plaid, 13; **— estatura mediana** of medium height, 5; **— haber sabido** had I known, 15; **— la mañana** A.M., 2; **— la tarde** P.M., 2; **— lunares** polka-dotted, 13; **— manera que** so, 9; **— memoria** by heart; **— modo que** so, 9; **— nada.** You're welcome., 1; **— postre** for dessert, 5; **— pronto** suddenly, 18; **— rayas** striped, 13; **— repente** suddenly, 18; **— todos modos** anyway

debajo de under, 6

deber (+ *infinitive*) must, should, 3

deberse a to be due to

debidamente duly

decidir to decide, 3

décimo(-a) tenth, 7

decir (e:i) to say, to tell, 6

decisión (*f.*) decision, 17

dedo (*m.*) finger, 15; **— del pie** (*m.*) toe, 15

dejar to leave behind, 5; **— plantado(-a) a alguien** to stand somebody up, 18; **— tranquilo(-a)** to leave alone, 16

deletrear to spell
deletreo (*m.*) spelling
delgado(-a) thin, slender, 3
demás: los (las) — others
demasiado(-a)(s) too
demostrativo(-a) demonstrative
dentro inside
departamento (*m.*) department, section; **— de (ropa para) caballeros** (*m.*) men's department, 13; **— de (ropa para) damas** (*m.*) women's department, 13
depender to depend, 14
deporte (*m.*) sport, 16
depositar to deposit, 8
derecho (*m.*) right; **derecho(-a)** (*adj.*) right; **— ajeno** (*m.*) the other person's right; **a la derecha** to the right, 12
derretir (e:i) to melt
desafortunadamente unfortunately, 8
desafortunado(-a) unfortunate, 8
desagradecido(-a) (*adj.*) ungrateful
desamparo (*m.*) abandonment
desastre (*m.*) disaster, 8
desayuno (*m.*) breakfast, 7
descansar to rest, 15
descomponerse to break down, 12
descompuesto(-a) (*p.p. of* **descomponer** *and adj.*) out of order, not working, 12
desconcertado(-a) bewildered
describir to describe, 11
desde since, 6; from, 10
desear to want, to wish, 11
desempeñar to perform (a job), 17
desesperanza (*f.*) despair
desfallecer to faint
desocupado(-a) vacant, 10
desocupar el cuarto to vacate the room, 7
despacho (*m.*) office, 17
despacio slowly
despedazar to tear
despedida (*f.*) farewell, 1
despertarse (e:ie) to wake up, 9
desposar to marry, to betroth
despreciar to scorn
después afterwards, 3
desvestirse (e:i) to get undressed, 9
destacar to emphasize
destacarse to stand out
detener to stop (something); **—se** to stop
determinado(-a) definite
devolver (o:ue) algo to return (something), 13
devuelto(-a) (*p.p. of* **devolver** *and adj.*) returned, 14
día (*m.*) day, 1
diamante (*m.*) diamond
diariamente daily
diario (*m.*) newspaper, 3
dibujos animados (*m. pl.*) cartoons, 18

diccionario (*m.*) dictionary, 8
diciembre December, 1
dicho (*m.*) saying
dicho(-a) (*p.p. of* **decir** *and adj.*) said, told, 15
diecinueve nineteen, 1
dieciocho eighteen, 1
dieciséis sixteen, 1
diecisiete seventeen, 1
diente (*m.*) tooth, 15
dieta (*f.*) diet, 5
diez ten, 1
difícil difficult, 2
diligencia (*f.*) errand, 11
dinero (*m.*) money, 2
Dios God
dirección (*f.*) address, 2
directo(-a) direct, 11
director(-a) (*m., f.*) director, 18; **— de cine** (*m., f.*) movie director, 18
dirigir to direct, 18
disco compacto (*m.*) compact disc (CD), 4
discoteca (*f.*) discotheque, 4
diseño (*m.*) design, 13
disfrutar to enjoy
disquete (*m.*) diskette, 17
distinto(-a) different
distribución de papeles (*f.*) casting, 18
divertido(-a) fun, 16
divertirse (e:ie) to have a good time, to enjoy oneself, 6
divino(-a) divine, 16
divorciado(-a) divorced, 3
doblado(-a) dubbed
doblar to turn, 12; to dub; **— la ropa** to fold the clothes, 6
doble double, 7
doce twelve, 1
doctor(-a) (*m., f.*) doctor, 1
documental (*m.*) documentary, 18
doler (o:ue) to hurt, 15
dolor (*m.*) pain
domicilio (*m.*) address, 2
domingo (*m.*) Sunday, 1
don (*m.*) gift
¿dónde? where?, 1
dorado(-a) golden
dormir (o:ue) to sleep, 5
dormirse to fall asleep, 9
dormitorio (*m.*) bedroom, 6
dos two, 1
doscientos(-as) two hundred, 3
dramaturgo(-a) (*m., f.*) playwright
ducha (*f.*) shower, 7
dudar to doubt, 12
dulce fresh (*water*); sweet
dulces (*m. pl.*) sweets
durar to last, 13
durazno (*m.*) peach, 9

E

echar el bofe to be out of breath
económico(-a) financial, 3
edad (*f.*) age, 14
edificio (*m.*) building, 10

educación física (*f.*) physical education, 14
efectivo (*m.*) cash, 8
en — in cash, 8
efecto especial (*m.*) special effect, 18
ejecutivo(-a) (*m., f.*) executive, 14
ejército (*m.*) army
el the (*m. sing.*), 2; **— (la) que** he (she) who
él he, 1; him, 4
electricidad (*f.*) electricity, 10
electricista (*m., f.*) electrician, 14
elevador (*m.*) elevator, 7
ella she, 1; her, 4
ellas (*f. pl.*) they, 1; them, 4
ellos (*m. pl.*) they, 1; them, 4
embajada (*f.*) embassy, 7
embarazada pregnant, 15
embarcarse to get in a boat
emergencia (*f.*) emergency, 15
empanada (*f.*) meat turnover
empeorarse to get worse, 15
empezar (e:ie) (a) to begin, to start, 4
empleado(-a) (*m., f.*) clerk, 13; **— bancario** (*m., f.*) bank employee, 17
empleo (*m.*) job, 3
empresarial (*adj.*) business
en in, at, 1; on, inside, over, 16; **— casa** at home, 4; **— caso de que** in case, 14; **— cuanto** as soon as, 14; **— cuanto a** regarding; **— efectivo** in cash, 11; **— ese caso** in that case, 2; **— este momento** at this moment, 5; **— fin...** anyway . . ., 8; **— la actualidad** nowadays, 18; **— ningún lado** nowhere, 11; **— ninguna parte** nowhere, 11; **— parte** in part, 14; **¿— qué puedo servirle?** How can I help you?, 7; **— punto** on the dot; **— seguida** right away, 6; **— seguida vuelvo** I'll be right back, 6; **¿— serio?** seriously?, 2; **— vez de** instead of, 17
enamorado(-a) (de) in love (with), 16
enamorarse de to fall in love with, 18
encantado(-a) charmed
encantador(-a) charming, 3
encantarle a uno to love, 8
encargado(-a) (*m., f.*) super-(intendent), 10
encargado(-a) de in charge of, 17
enciclopedia (*f.*) encyclopedia, 8
encontrar (o:ue) to find, 5
encontrarse (con) to meet, 10
encuesta (*f.*) survey
enderezarse a to be for, to exist for
enero January, 1
enfriar to cool down
enojarse to get angry, 14
enorme enormous, 15
ensalada (*f.*) salad, 5
ensangrentado(-a) blood-stained
ensayar to rehearse, 18
ensayo (*m.*) essay

enseñar (a) to teach, 18
entablar to start
entender (e:ie) to understand, 4
enterrado(-a) buried
entonces then, in that case, 4
entrada (*f.*) entrance, 11; ticket (*to an event*), 16
entrante next, 18; **el mes —** (*m.*) next month, 18
entrar to enter, to come in, 12
entre among, between, 9
entregar to turn in, to deliver, 14
entrevista (*f.*) interview, 17
entrevistar to interview, 17
enviar to send, 7
envolver (o:ue) to wrap, 14
envuelto(-a) (*p.p. of* **envolver** *and adj.*) wrapped, 14
enyesar to put in a cast, 15
equipaje (*m.*) luggage, 7
equipo electrónico (*m.*) electronic equipment, 17
equipo estereofónico (*m.*) stereo system, 4
equivocado(-a) wrong, 4
errabundo wandering
es decir that is to say
es que... the fact is . . . , 13
escalar to climb, 16
escalera (*f.*) stairs, 7; **— mecánica** (*f.*) escalator, 7
escapar to escape, 14
esclavo(-a) (*m., f.*) slave
escoba (*f.*) broom, 6
escoger to choose
esconder to hide, 6
escopeta (*f.*) shotgun, 16
escribir to write, 3; **— a máquina** to type, 17
escrito(-a) (*p.p. of* **escribir** *and adj.*) written, 14
escritor(-a) (*m., f.*) writer, 14
escritorio (*m.*) desk, 2
escuchar to listen (to)
escuela (*f.*) school, 10; **— secundaria** (*f.*) high school, 18
ese(-os), esa(s) (*adj.*) that, those, (nearby), 6
ése(-os), ésa(s) (*pron.*) that one, those (*nearby*), 6
esfuerzo (*m.*) effort
eso (*neuter pron.*) that, 6
espada (*f.*) sword
espalda (*f.*) back, 15
España Spain
español (*m.*) Spanish (*lang.*), 2
especial special, 5
especialización (*f.*) major (*field of study*), 14
especializado(-a) specialized, 17
especialmente especially, 8
espectáculo (*m.*) show, 18
espejo (*m.*) mirror, 10
esperanza (*f.*) hope
esperar to wait (for), to expect, 6; to hope, 11

esposa (*f.*) wife, 5
esposo (*m.*) husband, 5
espuma (*f.*) foam
esquí acuático (*m.*) water ski, 16
esquiar to ski, 16
esquina (*f.*) corner
esta noche tonight, 2
estación (*f.*) season, 1; station, 12; **— de la seca** (*f.*) dry season; **— de servicio** (*f.*) gas (service) station, 12
estacionar to park, 8
estadio (*m.*) stadium, 16
estado (*m.*) state; **— civil** (*m.*) marital status, 3
Estados Unidos (*m. pl.*) United States
estampado(-a) print (fabric), 13
estar to be, 4; **— a cargo** to be in charge, 18; **— de acuerdo** to agree, 6; **— de vacaciones** to be on vacation, 7; **— equivocado(-a)** to be wrong, 4; **— loco(-a) por** to be crazy about, 18; **— muerto(-a) de hambre** to be starving, 15
¿Está... (name)? Is . . . (*name*) there?, 3
estatura (*f.*) height, 5
este east, 16
este(-os), esta(s) (*adj.*) this, 6; these, 6
este fin de semana (*m.*) this weekend, 4
éste(-os) ésta(s) (*pron.*) this one; these, 6
estimarse to have self-esteem
estirar to stretch
esto (*neuter pron.*) this, 6
estómago (*m.*) stomach, 15
estrechar to hold
estrecho(-a) narrow, 13
estrenar to show for the first time, 18
estreno (*m.*) première, 18
estribillo (*m.*) refrain
estrofa (*f.*) stanza
estudiante (*m., f.*) student, 1
estudiar to study, 2
etapa (*f.*) period
evaluación (*f.*) evaluation, 17
evitar to avoid, 17
exactamente exactly, 17
exactitud (*f.*) accuracy
examen (*m.*) exam, 3; checkup, 15; **— parcial (de mitad de curso)** (*m.*) midterm examination, 3
excelente excellent, 11
exceso de equipaje (*m.*) excess baggage, 11
excursión (*f.*) excursion, 11
exigir to demand
éxito (*m.*) success
experiencia (*f.*) experience, 3
experto(-a) (*m., f.*) expert, 14
expresión (*f.*) expression
extranjero(-a) foreign; **en el extranjero** abroad

extrañar to miss, 9
extraño(-a) (*m., f.*) stranger

F

fábrica (*f.*) factory, 5
fácil easy, 2
fácilmente easily
facsímile (*m.*) fax, 17
factoría (*f.*) factory, 5
facturar el equipaje to check luggage, 11
facultad (*f.*) college, school, 14
falda (*f.*) skirt, 13
fallecer to pass away, 9
falta (*f.*) lack
familia (*f.*) family, 4
fantasma (*m.*) ghost
farmacia (*f.*) pharmacy, 9
fastidiado(-a) annoyed
favorito(-a) favorite, 7
fax (*m.*) fax , 17
febrero February, 1
fecha de nacimiento (*f.*) date of birth, 3
fechar to date (*check or letter*), 8
feliz happy, 1
femenino(-a) feminine
feo(-a) ugly, 3
ferretería (*f.*) hardware store, 9
festejar to celebrate, 9
festival de cine (*m.*) film festival, 18
fiebre (*f.*) fever, 15
fiesta (*f.*) party, 1
fijarse en to notice, 18
filmar to film (make) a movie, 18
filosofía (*f.*) philosophy, 17
fin (*m.*) end; **— de semana** (*m.*) weekend, 4
fingir to pretend
firma (*f.*) signature, 8
firmar to sign, 8
física (*f.*) physics, 14
flan (*m.*) caramel custard, 5
flauta (*f.*) flute, 9
flor (*f.*) flower, 8
florería (*f.*) flower shop, 8
folleto (*m.*) brochure, 11
fortaleza (*f.*) fortress
foto (*f.*) photo, photograph, 4
fotocopiadora (*f.*) photocopy machine, 17
fotografía (*f.*) photo, photograph, 4
francamente frankly, 12
francés (*m.*) French (*lang.*), 2
frecuentar to visit frequently
frecuente frequent
frecuentemente frequently, 12
fregar (e:ie) los platos to wash the dishes, 6
freno (*m.*) brake, 12
frente a in front of, 8
fresa (*f.*) strawberry, 9
frijoles (*m. pl.*) beans, 5
frito(-a) fried, 5
frondoso(-a) leafy
fruta (*f.*) fruit, 9

fuego (*m.*) fire, 8
fuente (*f.*) source
fuera (*adv.*) outside
fumar to smoke
funcionar to work, to function, 12
funda (*f.*) pillowcase, 10
fundir to melt
fusilar to shoot
fútbol (*m.*) soccer, 16
futuro (*m.*) future, 14

G

ganadería (*f.*) livestock
ganar to earn, 3; to win, 16
ganga (*f.*) bargain, 13
garaje (*m.*) garage, 6
garganta (*f.*) throat, 15
gasolina (*f.*) gasoline, 12
gasolinera (*f.*) gas (service) station, 12
gato (*m.*) cat, 8; car jack, 12
general general, 8
generalmente generally, 8
género (*m.*) gender
gente de negocio (*f.*) businesspeople
geranio (*m.*) geranium, 8
gerente (*m., f.*) manager, 17
gimnasio (*m.*) gym, 14
goma de borrar (*f.*) eraser, 2
gordo(-a) fat, 3
grabar to tape, 18
gracias thank you, thanks, 1
grado (*m.*) degree, 15
graduarse to graduate, 14
grande big
gratis free (of charge), 8
gratuito(-a) free
gripe (*f.*) flu, 15
gris gray, 1
grúa (*f.*) tow truck, 12
grupo (*m.*) group, 18
guante (*m.*) glove, 13
guapo(-a) handsome, good-looking, 3
guatemalteco(-a) (*m., f.*) Guatemalan, 5
guerra (*f.*) war, 18
guía telefónica (*f.*) telephone book
guión (*m.*) script, screenplay, 18
guitarra (*f.*) guitar, 9
gustar to like, to be pleasing to, 7
gusto (*m.*) pleasure, joy; **El — es mío.** The pleasure is mine., 1

H

haber (*aux.*) to have
habitación (*f.*) room, 4; **— doble** (*f.*) double room, 7; **— sencilla** (*f.*) single room, 7
hablar to speak, 2
hace + *time* + **que** + *verb* (*present*) to have been doing something for a length of time, 7
hace + *time* + **que** + *verb* (*preterit/imperfect*) to have done something in the past (ago), 9

hacer to do, 4; to make, 6; **— buen tiempo** to be good weather, 5; **— calor** to be hot, 5; **— diligencias** to run errands, 8; **— ejercicio** to exercise, 7; **— escala** to make a stopover, 11; **— frío** to be cold, 5; **— juego (con)** to match, 13; **— las compras** to do the shopping, 6; **— las maletas** to pack; **— mal tiempo** to be bad weather, 5; **— sol** to be sunny, 5; **— surfing** to surf, 16; **— un crucero** to take a cruise, 11; **— un picnic** to have a picnic, 16; **— una radiografía** to take an X-ray, 15; **— viento** to be windy, 5; **—se cargo** to take charge; **—se ilusiones** to dream, to fool oneself, 18
hacia towards, 5
hambre (*f.*) hunger, 4; **tener —** to be hungry, 4
hamburguesa (f.) hamburger, 5
hasta until, 7; **— ahora** up to now, 14; **— la vista.** Good-bye., 1; **— mañana.** See you tomorrow., 1; **— que** until, 14
hay there is, there are, 1
hecho (*m.*) happening
hecho(-a) (*p.p. of* **hacer** *and adj.*) done, made, 14
helado (*m.*) ice cream, 5
herir (e:ie) to hurt
hermana (*f.*) sister, 4
hermanastra (*f.*) stepsister, 6
hermanastro (*m.*) stepbrother, 6
hermanita(-o) (*m., f.*) little sister (brother), 13
hermano (*m.*) brother, 4
hermoso(-a) beautiful, 5
hidrante (*m.*) fire hydrant, 8
hija (*f.*) daughter, 4
hijastra (*f.*) stepdaughter, 6
hijastro (*m.*) stepson, 6
hijito(-a) darling, 4
hijo (*m.*) son, 4
hijos (*m. pl.*) children
hilo (*m.*) linen, 13
historia (*f.*) history, 3
hogar (*m.*) home
hogareño(-a) family oriented
hoja (*f.*) leaf; **— de papel** (*f.*) sheet of paper, 2
hola hello, 1
hombre (*m.*) man; **— de negocios** (*m.*) businessman, 7
honrado(-a) honest, honorable
hora (*f.*) time (of day), 2; hour; **¿A qué —…?** (At) what time . . . ?, 2; **¿Qué — es?** What time is it?, 2
horario (*m.*) schedule, 14
horno (*m.*) oven, 10
hospedaje (*m.*) lodging, 11
hospedarse en to stay, to lodge (at a hotel), 11
hospital (*m.*) hospital, 2
hotel (*m.*) hotel, 7

hoy today, 1; **— en día** nowadays, 18

I

idea (*f.*) idea, 2
ideal (*adj.*) ideal, 11
idioma (*m.*) language, 2
iglesia (*f.*) church
igualmente likewise, 1
ilusión (*f.*) dream, 18
impaciencia (*f.*) lack of patience; **—s** (*f. pl.*) pressures
imperativo (*m.*) command
imperfecto (*m.*) imperfect
impermeable (*m.*) raincoat
importación (*f.*) import, 17
importarle a uno to matter, to concern
imposible impossible, 5
impresionado(-a) impressed, 17
impresora (*f.*) printer, 17
incendio (*m.*) fire, 8
incluir to include, 10
indeterminado(-a) indefinite
indicativo(-a) indicative
infancia (*f.*) childhood, 9
informe (*m.*) report, 3
ingeniero(-a) (*m., f.*) engineer, 14
inglés (*m.*) English (*lang.*), 2
ingreso(s) (*m.(pl.*)) income
insistir en to insist on, 14
instantáneo(-a) instant, 7
instrumento musical (*m.*) musical instrument, 9
inteligente intelligent, 3
interesante interesting, 11
interesar to interest, 18
Internet (*f.*) the World Wide Web, 7
intérprete (*m., f.*) interpreter, 17
interrogativo(-a) interrogative
investigación (*f.*) research, 14
invierno (*m.*) winter, 1
invitación (*f.*) invitation, 3
invitado(-a) (*m., f.*) guest, 10
invitado(-a) invited, 4
invitar (a) to invite, 18
inyección antitetánica (*f.*) tetanus shot, 15; **poner una —** to give a shot, 15
ir to go, 4; **ir a** + *infinitive* to be going (to) + *infinitive*, 4; **— a acampar** to go camping, 16; **— a pescar** to go fishing, 16; **— a pie** to go on foot, to walk, 12; **— caminando** to go on foot, to walk, 12; **— de pesca** to go fishing, 16
irse to go away, to leave, 9
isla (*f.*) island, 9
italiano (*m.*) Italian (*lang.*), 2
izquierdo(-a) left; **a la —** to (on, at) the left, 12

J

jabón (*m.*) soap, 7
jactarse (de) to brag (about)

jamás never, ever 6
jamón (*m.*) ham, 5
jardín (*m.*) garden, 13; **— de infantes (infancia)** (*m.*) kindergarten, 16
jefe(-a) (*m., f.*) boss, chief, 17; **— de compras** purchasing manager, 17
joven (*m., f.*) young man, young woman, 15; (*adj.*) young, 17
jóvenes (*m., f.*) young people
joyas (*f. pl.*) jewels, jewelry, 13
joyería (*f.*) jewelry store, 9
juego (*m.*) game, 4
jueves (*m.*) Thursday, 1
jugar (u:ue) to play (*game, sport*); **— al golf** to play golf, 16; **— al tenis** to play tennis, 16
jugo (*m.*) juice; **— de frutas** fruit juice, 5
julio July, 1
junio June, 1
juntos(-as) together, 7
justo(-a) fair
juventud (*f.*) youth, 9

L

la (*f. sing.*) the, 2; (*pron.*) her, it, you (*form.*), 6
labio (*m.*) lip
laboratorio (*m.*) laboratory, 14
labrador(-a) (*m., f.*) farmer
ladera (*f.*) hillside
lago (*m.*) lake
lámpara (*f.*) lamp, 10
lana (*f.*) wool, 13
langosta (*f.*) lobster, 5
lápiz (*m.*) pencil, 2
las (*f. pl.*) the, 2; (*pron.*) them, you (*form.*), 6
lástima (*f.*) pity, shame; **es una —** it's a pity, 11; **¡Qué —!** What a pity!, 15
lata (*f.*) can, 9
lavadora (*f.*) washing machine, 10
lavar(se) to wash (oneself), 9; **— la cabeza** to wash one's hair, 9; **— la ropa** to do the laundry, 6; **— los platos** to wash dishes, 6
le (to, for) her, (to, for) him, (to, for) you (*form.*), 7
leal loyal
leche (*f.*) milk, 5
lecho (*m.*) bed
lechón (*m.*) pork, 5
lechuga (*f.*) lettuce, 9
lector(-a) (*m., f.*) reader
leer to read, 3
legumbre (*f.*) vegetable, 5
leído (*p.p. of* **leer**) read, 14
lejano(-a) far away
lejos (*adv.*) far, 10
lengua (*f.*) language, 2; tongue, 15
lentamente slowly, 8
lento(-a) slow, 8
les (to, for) them, (to, for) you, (*form. pl.*), 7

levantar to lift, to raise, 9; **— se** to get up, 9
libertad (*f.*) liberty, freedom, 2
libra (*f.*) pound
libre vacant, 7; free, available, 13
librería (*f.*) bookstore, 13
libreta de ahorros (*f.*) savings passbook, 8
libreto (*m.*) script, screenplay, 18
libro (*m.*) book, 2
licencia para conducir (*f.*) driver's license, 12
licuadora (*f.*) blender, 10
liga (*f.*) league
ligero(-a) light
lila (*f.*) lilac, 8
limpiar el baño to clean the bathroom, 6
limpio(-a) clean
lino (*m.*) linen, 13
liquidación (*f.*) sale, 13
lista (*f.*) list; **— de espera** (*f.*) waiting list, 7
literatura (*f.*) literature, 3
llama (*f.*) flame
llamar to call, 3; **—se** to be called, 9; **¿Cómo se llama usted?** What is your name? (*form.*), 1; **¿Cómo te llamas?** What's your name? (*fam.*), 1; **Me llamo...** My name is . . . , 1
llano (*m.*) plain
llanta (*f.*) tire, 12; **— pinchada** (*f.*) flat tire, 12
llanura (*f.*) plain
llave (*f.*) key, 7
llegada (*f.*) arrival
llegar to arrive, 4
llenar to fill, to fill out, 3
lleno(-a) full, 12
llevar to take (*someone or something someplace*), 3; **— puesto(-a)** to have on, to be wearing (clothes), 18
llover (o:ue) to rain, 5
lluvia (*f.*) rain, 5
lo him, it, you (*form.*), 6; **— que** what, which, 6; **— siguiente** the following; **— soy.** Indeed I am.; **— + adj.** that which is + *adj.*
loco(-a) crazy, 16
logro (*m.*) achievement
loquito(-a) crazy
loro (*m.*) parrot, 8
los (*m. pl.*) the, 2; (*pron.*) them, you (*form.*), 6
luchar to fight
lugar (*m.*) place, 6; **— de nacimiento** (*m.*) place of birth, 3; **— donde trabaja** (*m.*) place of employment, 3
lujo (*m.*) luxury
luna (*f.*) moon, 11; **— de miel** (*f.*) honeymoon, 11
lunares: de — polka-dotted, 13

lunes (*m.*) Monday, 1
luz (*f.*) light, 2; headlight, 12

M

madera (*f.*) wood
madrastra (*f.*) stepmother, 6
madre (*f.*) mother, 1
madrina (*f.*) godmother
maestro(-a) (*m., f.*) teacher (elementary school), 7
magnífico(-a) excellent, 14; great, 4
mal bad, badly
maleta (*f.*) suitcase, 7
maletero (*m.*) (car) trunk, 12
maletín (*m.*) briefcase
maligno(-a) evil
malo(-a) bad
mamá mom, 1
mancha (*f.*) blemish, spot
mandar to send, 7; to order
manejar to drive
manga (*f.*) sleeve
mango (*m.*) mango, 9
mano (*f.*) hand, 15
mantel (*m.*) tablecloth, 5
mantener to maintain, 14; **— la conversación** to keep the conversation going
mantequilla (*f.*) butter, 9
manzana (*f.*) apple, 9; (*Sp.*) city block
mañana (*f.*) tomorrow; **— mismo** tomorrow and not a day later, 17
mapa (*m.*) map, 2
máquina contestadora (*f.*) answering machine, 17
máquina de afeitar (*f.*) razor
mar (*m.*) sea, 7
marca (*f.*) brand, 13
margarina (*f.*) margarine, 9
margarita (*f.*) daisy, 8
marido (*m.*) husband, 5
mariposa (*f.*) butterfly
mariscos (*m. pl.*) shellfish, 8
marrón brown, 1
martes (*m.*) Tuesday, 1
marzo March, 1
más more, 2; plus; **— allá** beyond; **— o menos** more or less, 3
mascota (*f.*) pet, 8
masculino male
matemáticas (*f. pl.*) math, mathematics, 14
materia (*f.*) (school) subject, 14
maternidad (*f.*) motherhood
matrícula (*f.*) registration, tuition, 14
matricularse to register, 14
matrimonio (*m.*) marriage
mayo May, 1
mayor older, 5; bigger, 5; **el (la) —** the oldest, 5
me me, 6; (to, for) me, 7; (to) myself, 9; **— llamo...** My name is . . . , 1
mecánico (*m.*) mechanic, 12
mecer to rock
mediano(-a) medium, 13
medicina (*f.*) medicine, 15

médico(-a) (*m., f.*) physician, doctor, 14

medida (*f.*) size, 13; measure

medio(-a) half; **medio** (*m.*) means; **media hermana** (*f.*) half sister, 6; **medio hermano** (*m.*) half brother, 6; **y media** half-past (*telling time*), 2

mejor best; better, 5; **el (la) —** the best, 5

mejorar to improve, 9; **—se** to get better, 15

melocotón (*m.*) peach, 9

menor younger, 5; **el (la) —** youngest, 5

menos to, till (*telling time*), 2; less, 5; minus; **— mal** it's a good thing, 15

mensaje electrónico (*m.*) e-mail, 3

menú (*m.*) menu, 5

mercadeo (*m.*) marketing, 17

mercado (*m.*) market, 6

merecer la pena to be worth it, 12

merendar (e:ie) to have an afternoon snack, 15

mes (*m.*) month, 1

mesa (*f.*) table, 4; **— de centro** (*f.*) coffee table, 10

mesita de noche (*f.*) night table, 10

meta (*f.*) goal

métrica (*f.*) meter (*poetry*)

metro (*m.*) subway, 10

mexicano(-a) Mexican, 1

mexicanoamericano(-a) Mexican American, 1

mezcla (*f.*) mixture

mezclar to mix

mi (*sing.*) my, 3; **— amor** my love, 3; **— vida** (*f.*) darling, (my life), 3

mí (*obj. of prep.*) me, 4

microcomputadora (*f.*) laptop computer, 17

microondas (*m.*) microwave, 10

miedo (*m.*) fear, 4

miel de abeja (*f.*) honey, 15

mientras while, 3

miércoles (*m.*) Wednesday, 1

mil one thousand, 3

milla (*f.*) mile, 12

millar (*m.*) thousand

millonario(-a) (*m., f.*) millionaire, 16

mío(s), mía(s) (*pron.*) mine, 9

mirar to look (at), 5; to watch (*i.e., TV*), 5; **— por la ventana** to look out the window, 6; **— vidrieras** to window shop, 13

mis (*pl.*) my, 3

misa (*f.*) mass (*Catholic service*), 16

mismo(-a) same, 10

misterio (*m.*) mystery

mitad (*f.*) half

mochila (*f.*) backpack, 2

moda (*f.*) fashion

moderno(-a) modern, 12

modista (*f.*) dressmaker

modo (*m.*) way

molestarse to bother (doing something), 15

momento (*m.*) moment, 3

moneda (*f.*) currency

mono (*m.*) monkey, 8

montaña (*f.*) mountain, 4

montar to ride, 16; **— a caballo** to ride a horse, 16; **— en bicicleta** to ride a bicycle, 16

monte (*m.*) mountain

montón (*m.*): **un montón de** a bunch of, 6

morado(-a) purple, 1

moreno(-a) dark, brunette, 3

morir (o:ue) to die, 5

mostrar (o:ue) to show

moto (*f.*) motorcycle, 8

motocicleta (*f.*) motorcycle, 8

mozo (*m.*) waiter, 5

muchacha (*f.*) girl, young woman, 2

muchacho (*m.*) boy, young man, 2

muchísimo a lot, 7

mucho(-a) much, 1

Mucho gusto. How do you do? Nice to meet you., 1

mucho tiempo a long time, 7

muchos(-as) many, 4

Muchas gracias. Thank you very much., 1

mudarse to move (from one house to another), 10

muebles (*m. pl.*) furniture, 10

muelle (*m.*) dock

muerte (*f.*) death

muerto(-a) (*p.p. of* **morir** *and adj.*) died, 14

mujer (*f.*) wife, 5; woman; **— de negocios** (*f.*) businesswoman, 7

multa (*f.*) fine, ticket, 8

mundo (*m.*) world, 17

museo (*m.*) museum, 4

música (*f.*) music

musical musical, 18

músico (*m.*) musician, 18

muy very, 1; **— bien** very well, 1

N

nacer to be born

nacido(-a) born

nacimiento (*m.*) birth

nacionalidad (*f.*) nationality

nada nothing, 1

nadar to swim, 7

nadie nobody, no one, not anyone, 6

naranja (*f.*) orange, 9

nariz (*f.*) nose, 15

Navidad (*f.*) Christmas, 4

necesario(-a) necessary, 3

necesitar to need, 2

negarse (e:ie) to refuse

negativo(-a) negative

negocio (*m.*) business, 17

negro(-a) black, 1

neumático (*m.*) tire, 12; **— pinchado** (*m.*) flat tire, 12

nevado(-a) snowed

nevar (e:ie) to snow, 5

ni nor, 6; **—... ni...** neither . . . nor . . . , 6

niebla (*f.*) fog, 5

nieta (*f.*) granddaughter, 6

nieto (*m.*) grandson, 6

nieve (*f.*) snow, 16

ninguno(-a), ningún no, none, not any, 6

niño(-a) (*m., f.*) child, 5

no no, not, 1; **—... más que** nothing but; **— muy bien** not very well, 1

noche (*f.*) evening, night, 3

nocturno (*m.*) nocturne

nombre (*m.*) (first) name, 1; noun; **— de pluma** (*m.*) pen name

norte north, 16

norteamericano(-a) North American, 2

nos us, 6; (to, for) us, 7; (to, for) ourselves, 9; **— vemos.** See you., 1

nosotros(-as) we, 1; us, 4

nota (*f.*) grade, 14

noticia(s) (*f. (pl.)*) (piece of) news, 7

novecientos(-as) nine hundred, 3

noveno(-a) ninth, 7

noventa ninety, 2

novia (*f.*) girlfriend, 3

noviembre November, 1

novio (*m.*) boyfriend, 3

nublado(-a) cloudy

nuera (*f.*) daughter-in-law, 5

nuestro(-a) our, 3; (*pron.*) ours, 9

nuestro(-as) our (*pl.*), 3

nueve nine, 1

nuevo(-a) new, 1

número (*m.*) number, 1; size (*of shoes*), 13; **— de identidad** (*m.*) I.D. number, 3; **— de la licencia de conducir** (*m.*) driver's license number, 3; **— de seguro social** (*m.*) social security number, 3; **— de teléfono** (*m.*) phone number, 1

nunca never, 6

nutrición (*f.*) nutrition, 14

O

o or, 6; **—... o...** either . . . or . . . , 6

objeto (*m.*) object

obligar to force, to make, 12

obra (*f.*) work (*of art*); **— teatral (de teatro)** (*f.*) play, 18

obrero(-a) (*adj.*) labor

ochenta eighty, 2

ocho eight, 1

ochocientos(-as) eight hundred, 3

octavo(-a) eighth, 7

octubre October, 1

ocultar to hide

ocupación (*f.*) occupation, 3

ocupado(-a) busy, 4

ocurrir to happen, 8

oeste west, 16

oficina (*f.*) office, 13; **— de correos** (*f.*) post office, 12

oficio (*m.*) trade, 14

ofrecer to offer, 17

oído (*m.*) (*p.p. of* **oír**) heard, 14; ear (inner), 17

oír to hear

ojalá I hope, God grant, 11

ojo (*m.*) eye, 15

ola (f.) wave

olvidar(se) (de) to forget, 9

ómnibus (*m.*) bus, 6

once eleven, 1

oportunidad (f.) opportunity, 13

oprimir to hold tightly

optativo(-a) elective

optimista (*invariable adj.*) optimistic, 3

opuesto(-a) opposite

oración (f.) sentence

orden (f.) order

ordenador (*m.*) computer (*Sp.*), 3

oreja (f.) ear, 15

orgulloso(-a) proud, 16; **no ser nada — ** not to be proud at all, 16

oro (*m.*) gold

orquesta (f.) orchestra, band, 18

orquídea (f.) orchid, 8

os you (*fam. pl.*), 6; (to, for) you, 7; (to) yourselves, 9

oscuro(-a) dark

ostra (f.) oyster, 16

otoño (*m.*) autumn, fall, 1

otro(-a) another, other, 2

otra vez again

oveja (f.) sheep

oye listen, 1

P

padrastro (*m.*) stepfather, 6

padre (*m.*) father, 1

padres (*m., pl.*) parents, 6

padrino (*m.*) godfather, 11

pagar to pay, 5

país (*m.*) country, 9

pájaro (*m.*) bird

palabra (f.) word, 17

palma (f.) palm, palm tree, 9

palo de golf (*m.*) golf club, 16

pan (*m.*) bread, 14

panadería (f.) bakery, 9

pantalla (f.) screen, 17; movie screen, 18

pantalones (*m. pl.*) pants, trousers, 8

pantimedias (f. pl.) pantyhose, 13

pañuelo (*m.*) handkerchief, 13

papa (f.) potato, 5

papá dad, 1

papel (*m.*) paper; role; **— higiénico** (*m.*) toilet paper, 9

paquete (*m.*) package, 11

par (*m.*) pair, 13

para in order, 2; for, 3; to, in order to, 8; by, 8; **— beber** to drink, 5; **— eso** for that, 18; **— peor** to make matters worse, 18; **— que** in order that, 14; ¿**— qué?** What for?;

— siempre forever, 18; **— ver** to see, 5

parabrisas (*m.*) windshield, 12

parada de autobuses (f.) bus stop, 6

paraguas (*m.*) umbrella

paraíso terrenal (*m.*) Garden of Eden

parecer to seem, 18

pared (f.) wall, 2

pareja (f.) couple

pariente (*m., f.*) relative, 6

parque (*m.*) park, 4; **— de diversiones** (*m.*) amusement park, 4

parquear to park, 8

partera (f.) midwife

partido (*m.*) game, 4

partir to leave

pasado(-a) last, 7

pasado mañana the day after tomorrow, 4

pasaje (*m.*) ticket, 11; **— de ida** (*m.*) one-way ticket, 11; **— de ida y vuelta** (*m.*) round-trip ticket, 11

pasaporte (*m.*) passport, 7

pasar to spend (*time*), 4; to happen, 8; **— la aspiradora** to vacuum, 6; **— por la aduana** to go through customs, 7; **— por las armas** to shoot; **— una película** to show a movie, 7

pasarlo bien to have a good time, 5

Pase. Come in., 1

pastel (*m.*) pie, 5

patinar to skate, 16

patio (*m.*) backyard, 15

patria (f.) homeland

pavo (*m.*) turkey, 8

paz (f.) peace

pecho (*m.*) chest, 15

pedazo (*m.*) piece, 5

pedido (*m.*) order, 5

pedir (e:i) to order, 5; to ask for, to request, 6; **— un préstamo** to apply for a loan, 8

película (f.) movie, 7; **— de misterio** (f.) mystery, murder mystery, 18; **— de suspenso** (f.) thriller, 18; **— de vaqueros** (f.) western, 18; **— del oeste** (f.) western, 18

peligroso(-a) dangerous

pelirrojo(-a) red-headed, 3

pelo (*m.*) hair, 15

peluquería (f.) beauty salon, 12

pena (f.) sorrow

pensamiento (*m.*) pansy, 8; thought

pensar (e:ie) to think, 4; (+ *inf.*) to plan (*to do something*), 4; **— en** to think about, 18

pensión (f.) boarding house, 10

peor worse, 5; **el (la) — ** the worst, 5

pepino (*m.*) cucumber, 9

pequeño(-a) small, little

perder (e:ie) to lose, 4; **— se (algo)** to miss (*out on something*), 18

Perdón. Pardon me., 1

perfectamente perfectly, 15

perfecto(-a) perfect, 2

periódico (*m.*) newspaper, 3

periodismo (*m.*) journalism, 14

pero but, 1

perro(-a) (*m., f.*) dog, 8; **— caliente** (*m.*) hot dog, 5

persona (f.) person, 4

personaje (*m.*) character, 18

personal (*m.*) personnel, 17

pertenecer to belong, 18

pesar to weigh

pescadería (f.) fish store, 9

pescado (*m.*) fish, 5

pescar to fish, to catch (*a fish*), 16

pesimista (*invariable adj.*) pessimistic, 3

pez (*m.*) fish; **— de color** (*m.*) goldfish, 8

piano (*m.*) piano, 9

pie (*m.*) foot, 15

piedra (f.) stone

pierna (f.) leg

pieza de repuesto (f.) spare part, 12

pimienta (f.) pepper, 5

pino (*m.*) pine tree, 16

pintor(-a) (*m., f.*) painter

piña (f.) pineapple, 9

piscina (f.) swimming pool, 7

piso (*m.*) floor, 6

placa (f.) license plate, 12

plancha (f.) iron, 10

planchar to iron, 6

planear to plan, 11

plástico (*m.*) plastic, 16

plata (f.) silver

plátano (*m.*) banana, 9

platicar to talk, to converse, 2

platillo (*m.*) saucer, 5

plato (*m.*) plate, 5; dish, 5

playa (f.) beach, 4

plomero(-a) (*m., f.*) plumber, 14

pluma (f.) pen, 2

pluscuamperfecto (*m.*) pluperfect

pobre poor (*unfortunate*), 4

pobrecito(-a) poor thing, 8

pobreza (f.) poverty

poder (o:ue) to be able to, can, 5; (*m.*) power

poema (*m.*) poem, 2

poesía (f.) poetry

policía (*m.*) policeman, 8

poliéster (*m.*) polyester, 13

pollo (*m.*) chicken, 5

ponche (*m.*) punch, 4

poner to put, to place, 6; **— una inyección** to give an injection, shot, 15; **— una multa** to give a ticket (*fine*), 8; **—se** to put on, 9; **—se en forma** to get into shape, 14; **no tener nada que — ** not to have anything to wear, 13

por along, 8; around, 8; because of, 8; by, 8; during, 8; for, 8; in, 8; in exchange for, 8; in search of, 8; on account of, 8; on behalf of, 8; per, 8; through, 8; **— aquí cerca** around here, 18; **— desgracia** unfortunately, 8; **— ejemplo** for example, 13; **— el contrario** on the contrary, 13; **— eso** that is why, 18; **— favor** please, 1; **— fin** finally, 18; **— la mañana** in the morning, 2; **— la noche** in the evening, at night, 2; **— la tarde** in the afternoon, 2; **— lo general** generally, 18; **— lo menos** at least, 13; **— mes** a month, per month, 12; **— primera vez** for the first time, 4; **¿ — qué?** why?; **— si acaso** just in case, 18; **— suerte** luckily, 18; **— supuesto** of course, 18; **— teléfono** on the phone, 3; **— un tiempo** for a while, 12

porque because
postre (*m.*) dessert, 5
porteño(-a) from Buenos Aires
portugués (*m.*) Portuguese (*lang.*), 2
practicar to practice, 2
precioso(-a) pretty, beautiful, 13
preferir (e:ie) to prefer, 4
pregunta (*f.*) question, 4
preguntar to ask (a question), 15
preocuparse (por) to worry (about), 9
preparar to prepare, 4
presentar to introduce, 18
presente present
presidente(-a) (*m., f.*) president, 17
préstamo (*m.*) loan, 8
prestar to lend, 8
presuroso(-a) in haste
prevalecer to prevail
primaria (*f.*) elementary school
primavera (*f.*) spring, 1
primera clase (*f.*) first class, 11
primero(-a), primer first, 2; **—** (*poet., pl.*) basic (i.e., elemental)
primo(-a) (*m., f.*) cousin, 4
principal main, 17
probable probable, 8
probablemente probably, 18
probador (*m.*) fitting room, 13
probar (o:ue) to try, 9; to taste, 9; **—se** to try on, 9
problema (*m.*) problem, 2
procesador de textos (*m.*) word processor, 17
productor(-a) (*m., f.*) producer, 18
profesión (*f.*) profession, 3
profesor(-a) (*m., f.*) professor, teacher, instructor, 1
profundidad (*f.*) depth
programa (*m.*) program, 2
programación (*f.*) programming, 18
programador(-a) (*m., f.*) programmer, 14
promedio (*m.*) grade point average, 14
prometer to promise, 7

prometido(-a) fiancé(e), 11
pronóstico del tiempo (*m.*) weather forecast
pronto soon, 14
propina (*f.*) tip, 5
propio(-a) own, 16; **propia página** (*f.*) home page
proponer to propose; **—se** to set out to
proporcionar to furnish
proseguir (e:i) to continue
protagonista (*m., f.*) protagonist, main character, 18
próximo(-a) next, 6
publicar to publish
pueblo (*m.*) town, 11; (*community, nation*) people
puente (*m.*) bridge
puerta (*f.*) door, 2; **— de calle** (*f.*) front door, 12; **— de salida** (*f.*) airline departure gate, 11
puertorriqueño(-a) (*m., f.*) Puerto Rican
pues… well . . ., 6
puesto(-a) (*p.p. of* **poner** *and adj.*) put, 14; (*m.*) position, job, 17
pulmonía (*f.*) pneumonia, 15
pulsera (*f.*) bracelet, 13
punto (*m.*) dot
puré de papas (*m.*) mashed potatoes, 5

Q

que (*rel. pron.*) that, who, 4; than, 5; which, 10; (*conj.*) than, 5; **— viene** coming, next, 11
¿qué? what?, 1; **¿A — hora?** (At) what time?, 2; **¡— Diablo!** What the heck!; **¡— esperen!** Let them wait!, 18; **¡ — gusto de verte!** How nice to see you!, 15; **¿ — hay (de nuevo)?** What's up (new)?, 1; **¿ — hora es?** What time is it?, 2; **¡— lástima!** What a pity!, 15; **¿ — les parece si…?** What do you think about . . .? 13; **¡— mala suerte!** Such bad luck!, 8; **¿ — quiere decir…?** What does . . . mean?; **¿ — tal?** How are you?, 1; **¿ — tal te va?** How's it going for you? (*fam.*), 14
quebrar(se) (e:ie) to break, 15
quedar to fit, to be; **— impresionado(-a)** to be impressed, 17; **—le grande (chico) a uno** to be too big (small) on someone, 13; **— suspendido(-a)** to fail (*an exam or a course*), 14; **—se** to stay, 11; **—se con** to keep; **—se sentado(-a)** to remain seated
quehaceres de la casa (*m. pl.*) housework, 6
quejarse to complain, 10
quemar to burn
querer (e:ie) to want, to wish, 4; **— decir** to mean; **no quise** I refused, 10

queso (*m.*) cheese, 5
quien(es) who, whom, that, 10
¿quién? who?; **¿de —?** whose?
química (*f.*) chemistry, 14
quince fifteen, 1
quinientos(-as) five hundred, 3
quinto(-a) fifth, 7
quitar to take away, 9; **—se** to take off, 9
quizás perhaps, 13

R

radiografía (*f.*) X-ray
raíz (*f.*) root
rama (*f.*) branch
ramo (*m.*) bouquet, 8
rápidamente rapidly, 8
rápido (*adv.*) quick, 6; rapid, 8
rápido(-a) fast, 13
raqueta (*f.*) racket, 16
rascacielos (*m. sing.*) skyscraper
rato (*m.*) while, 4
ratón (*m.*) mouse, 17
raya (*f.*) stripe, 13
rayón (*m.*) rayon, 13
razón (*f.*) reason; **tener —** to be right, 4
realista (*invariable adj.*) realistic, 3
realizar to make
rebaja (*f.*) sale, 13
rebajar to mark down, 13
recámara (*f.*) bedroom (*Mex.*), 6
recepción (*f.*) registration, 7
receta (*f.*) recipe, 9; prescription, 15
recetar to prescribe, 15
recibir to receive, 3
reciente recent, 8
recientemente recently, 8
recoger to pick up, 6
recomendación (*f.*) recommendation, 17
recomendar (e:ie) to recommend, 11
recompensa (*f.*) reward
recordar (o:ue) to remember, 5
recurrir a to turn to
Red (*f.*) the World Wide Web
refresco (*m.*) soft drink, soda pop, 5
refugiado(-a) (*m., f.*) refugee
regalar to give (*as a gift*), 8
regalo (*m.*) gift, 8
regatear to bargain
regla (*f.*) ruler
regresar to return, 2
reina (*f.*) queen
reírse (e:i) to laugh, 12
reloj (*m.*) clock, 2
remar to row, 16
remedio (*m.*) medicine, 15
remolcador (*m.*) tow truck, 12
renglón (*m.*) line
renunciar to resign
reparto de papeles (*m.*) casting, 18
repetir (e:i) to repeat
repollo (*m.*) cabbage, 9

represa (*f.*)   dam

reproductor de discos (*m.*)   CD player, 4

requisito (*m.*)   requirement, 14

reserva (*f.*)   reservation, 7

reservación (*f.*)   reservation, 7

resfriado (*m.*)   cold, 15

resfrío (*m.*)   cold, 15

resoplar   to blow

responsabilidad (*f.*)   responsibility, 17

respuesta (*f.*)   answer

restaurante (*m.*)   restaurant, 4

resto (*m.*)   the rest, 10

resumé (*m.*)   résumé, curriculum vitae, 17

resumen (*m.*)   summary

retrato (*m.*)   portrait

reunirse   to get together

revista (*f.*)   magazine, 6

revolución (*f.*)   revolution, 9

revolver (o:ue)   to stir

revuelo (*m.*)   fluttering

rey (*m.*)   king

rico(-a)   tasty, 5

risa (*f.*)   laughter

robar   to steal, 8

rodaja (*f.*)   slice

rodeado(-a)   surrounded

rodilla (*f.*)   knee, 15

rogar (o:ue)   to beg, to plead, 11

rojo(-a)   red, 1

romántico(-a)   romantic, 11

romper(se)   to break, 15

ropa (*f.*)   clothes, 6; clothing, 13; — **hecha** (*f.*)   ready-to-wear clothes; — **interior** (*f.*)   underwear, 13

rosa (*f.*)   rose, 8

rosado(-a)   pink, 1

rostro (*m.*)   face

roto(-a) (*p.p. of* **romper** *and adj.*) broken, 14

rubio(-a)   blond, 3

ruido (*m.*)   noise

S

sábado (*m.*)   Saturday, 1

sábana (*f.*)   sheet, 6

saber   to know, 6; to find out, 10

sabroso(-a)   tasty, 5

sacapuntas (*m.*)   pencil sharpener, 2

sacar   to get, to receive (*a grade*), 14; — **la basura**   to take out the garbage, 6; — **una foto**   to take a picture, 4

saco de dormir (*m.*)   sleeping bag, 10

sacudir los muebles   to dust the furniture, 6

sal (*f.*)   salt, 5

sala de estar (*f.*)   living room, 3

sala de rayos X (equis) (*f.*)   X-ray room, 15

salario (*m.*)   salary, 17

salida (*f.*)   exit, departure, 11

salir   to go out, 6; leave; — **de casa** to leave the house, 8

salón de belleza (*m.*)   beauty salon, 12

salsa (*f.*)   sauce, 9

salud (*f.*)   health, 15

¡Salud!   Cheers!

saludo (*m.*)   greeting, 1; —**s a...**   Say hello to . . . , 1

salvavidas (*m., f.*)   lifeguard, 16

sandía (*f.*)   watermelon, 9

sándwich (*m.*)   sandwich, 3

santo (*m.*)   saint's day

sartén (*f.*)   frying pan, skillet, 10

sastre (*m.*)   tailor

se   (to) himself, (to) herself, (to) yourself (*form.*), (to) yourselves, (to) themselves, 9; — **dice...**   You say . . . , One says . . . , 2

Sea.   So be it.

secadora (*f.*)   dryer, 10

secar   to dry, 6

sección de (no) fumar (*f.*)   (no) smoking section, 11

seco(-a)   dry

sed (*f.*)   thirst, 4; **tener** —   to be thirsty, 4

seda (*f.*)   silk, 13

seguir (e:i)   to follow, 6; to continue, 6; — **derecho**   to continue straight ahead, 12; — **los pasos**   to follow in the footsteps, 18

según   according to

segundo(-a)   second, 7; **Segunda Guerra Mundial** (*f.*)   Second World War; **segundo nombre** (*m.*)   middle name

seguro(-a)   sure, 8

seis   six, 1

seiscientos(-as)   six hundred, 3

selección (*f.*)   selection, 17

selva (tropical) (*f.*)   jungle, 11

semana (*f.*)   week, 4; **la semana que viene** (*f.*)   next week, 4; **la semana próxima** (*f.*)   next week, 4

sendero (*m.*)   path

sensibilidad (*f.*)   sensitivity

sentado(-a)   seated, sitting, 14

sentarse (e:ie)   to sit (down), 9

sentir(se) (e:ie)   to feel, 9; to be sorry, to regret

señal (*f.*)   sign

señor (Sr.)   mister, Mr., sir, gentleman, 1

señora (Sra.)   madam, Mrs., lady, 1

señorita (Srta.)   Miss, young lady, 1

septiembre   September, 1

séptimo(-a)   seventh, 7

sepulcro (*m.*)   tomb

ser   to be, 1

servicio (*m.*)   service, 7; — **de habitación (cuarto)** (*m.*)   room service, 7

servilleta (*f.*)   napkin, 5

servir (e:i)   to serve, 6; — **de**   to serve as, 17; **no** — **de mucho**   to not be much good, 14

sesenta   sixty, 2

setecientos(-as)   seven hundred, 3

setenta   seventy, 2

sexo (*m.*)   gender

sexto(-a)   sixth, 7

si   if, 14

sí   yes, 1

sicología (*f.*)   psychology, 14

siempre   always, 6

sierra (*f.*)   mountain

siete   seven, 1

siglo (*m.*)   century

signo (*m.*)   sign

siguiente   following

silla (*f.*)   chair, 2; — **de ruedas** (*f.*) wheelchair, 15

sillón (*m.*)   armchair, 10

simpatía (*f.*)   charm

simpático(-a)   nice, charming, 3

sin   without; — **embargo**   however, nevertheless, 13; — **falta**   without fail, 18; — **que**   without, 14; — **qué ni para qué**   without rhyme or reason, 18

sincero(-a)   sincere, 9

síntoma (*m.*)   symptom, 15

sistema (*m.*)   system. 2; — **de calificaciones** (*m.*)   grading system; — **de comunicación telefónica** (*m.*) telephone system, 17

sitio (*m.*)   room

sobre   about, 11; — **todo**   above all, especially, 17

sobrecama (*f.*)   bedspread, 10

sobrenombre (*m.*)   nickname

sobrina (*f.*)   niece, 4

sobrino (*m.*)   nephew, 4

sociología (*f.*)   sociology, 14

sofá (*m.*)   sofa, 6

sol (*m.*)   sun

solamente   only, 10

soledad (*f.*)   loneliness; solitude

solicitar un préstamo   to apply for a loan, 8

solicitud (*f.*)   application (form), 3; — **de empleo** (*f.*)   job application, 3

solo(-a)   alone, 5

sólo   only, 10

soltar (o:ue) amarras   to untie lines

soltero(-a)   single, 3

sombra (*f.*)   shadow

sombrero (*m.*)   hat

sonar (o:ue)   to ring, 15

sonido (*m.*)   sound

sonreír   to smile

soñar (o:ue) con   to dream about (of), 18

sopa (*f.*)   soup, 5; — **de fideos** (*f.*) noodle soup, 5

sorprender   to surprise, 11

sótano (*m.*)   basement, 6

su   his, her, its, your (*form.*), their, 3

subterráneo (*m.*)   subway, 10

subvencionado(-a)   subsidized

sucio(-a)   dirty

sucursal (*f.*)   branch (office)

suegra (*f.*)   mother-in-law, 6

suegro (*m.*)   father-in-law, 6

sueldo (*m.*)   salary, 17
sueño (*m.*)   dream; **tener —** to be sleepy, 4
suerte (*f.*)   luck, 8
suéter (*m.*)   sweater, 15
sugerir (e:ie)   to suggest, 11
supermercado (*m.*)   supermarket, 9
supersticioso(-a)   superstitious, 8
supervisión (*f.*)   supervision, 17
supervisor(-a) (*m., f.*)   supervisor, 17
sur   south, 16
sus   his, her, its, your (*form.*), their, 3
suspirar   to sigh, 6
sustantivo (*m.*)   noun
suyo(s), suya(s) (*pron.*)   his, hers, theirs, yours, 9

T

tabla de mar (*f.*)   surfboard, 16
tablilla de anuncios (*f.*)   bulletin board, 2
talla (*f.*)   size, 13
taller de mecánica (*m.*)   car repair shop, 12
talonario de cheques (*m.*) checkbook, 8
tamaño (*m.*)   size
también   also, too, 2
tampoco   neither, not either, 6
tan   as, 5; so, 17; **— pronto como**   as soon as, 14
tanque (*m.*)   tank, 12
tanto(-a)   as much, 5; so much, 11; **— como**   as much as, 5; **— en... como en...**   both in . . . and in . . .
tantos(-as)   as many, 5; **— como**   as many as, 5
tardar   to take (*time to do something*), 13
tarde (*f.*)   afternoon, 2; (*adv.*) late, 7; **— o temprano**   sooner or later, 18; **por la —**   in the afternoon, 2
tarjeta (*f.*)   card, 7; **— de crédito** (*f.*) credit card, 8; **— de embarque** (*f.*) boarding pass, 11; **— de turista** (*f.*) tourist card, 7; **— postal** (*f.*) postcard, 7
taxi (*m.*)   taxi, 6
taza (*f.*)   cup, 5
te (*pron.*)   you (*fam.*), 6; (to, for) you, 7; (to) yourself, 9
té (*m.*)   tea, 5; **— frío (helado)** (*m.*) iced tea, 5
teatro (*m.*)   theater, 4; **— de aficionados** (*m.*)   amateur theatre, 18
teclado (*m.*)   keyboard, 17
teja (*f.*)   tile
tela (*f.*)   material, 13
teléfono (*m.*)   telephone, 1; **— celular** (*m.*)   cellular phone, 12
telenovela (*f.*)   soap opera, 5
televisión (*f.*)   television, 2
televisor (*m.*)   TV, 7
tema (*m.*)   subject, theme, 2
temblar   to tremble
temer   to fear, to be afraid, 11

temperatura (*f.*)   temperature, 17
templado(-a)   mild
temprano   early, 9
tenedor (*m.*)   fork, 5
tener   to have, 3; **—... años (de edad)**   to be . . . years old, 4; **— calor**   to be hot, 4; **— cuidado**   to be careful, 4; **— ... de retraso (atraso)**   to be . . . behind schedule, 11; **— en cuenta**   to keep in mind; **— éxito**   to be successful, 18; **— frío**   to be cold, 4; **— hambre**   to be hungry, 4; **— lugar**   to take place; **— miedo**   to be afraid, 4; **— prisa**   to be in a hurry, 4; **— que** (+ *inf.*)   to have to (+ *inf.*), 3; **— razón**   to be right, 4; **— sed**   to be thirsty, 4; **— sueño**   to be sleepy, 4; **— un picnic**   to have a picnic, 16; **— un pinchazo**   to have a flat tire, 18; **no — razón**   to be wrong, 4
tenis (*m.*)   tennis, 16
tercero(-a), tercer   third, 7
terco(-a)   stubborn, 3
terminar   to finish, to end, 14
ternura (*f.*)   tenderness
terreno (*m.*)   land
ti   you (*obj. of prep.*), 4
tía (*f.*)   aunt, 4
tiburón (*m.*)   shark
tiempo (*m.*)   time, 2; weather, 5
tienda (*f.*)   store, 4; **— por departamentos** (*f.*)   department store, 13
tierra (*f.*)   land
timbre (*m.*)   doorbell, 15
tinto   red (wine), 5
tintorería (*f.*)   dry cleaner's, 8
tío (*m.*)   uncle, 4
tipo (*m.*)   type, 15
tirano(-a) (*m., f.*)   tyrant
tirar   to throw (away), to abandon ; **— basura**   to litter
título (*m.*)   degree, 14; title
toalla (*f.*)   towel, 7
tobillo (*m.*)   ankle, 15
tocador (*m.*)   dresser, 10
tocar   to play (*a musical instrument*), 9; **— a la puerta**   to knock on the door, 6
todo(-a)   all, 6
todo   all, everything, 8; **— el mundo**   everybody, 18
todos(-as)   everybody
todos los días   every day
tomar   to take, 2; to drink, 3; **— algo**   to have something to drink, 3; **— el sol**   to sunbathe, 16; **— una decisión**   to make a decision, 14; **— una foto**   to take a picture, 4
Tome asiento.   Have a seat., 1
tomate (*m.*)   tomato, 9
toque (*m.*)   touch
torpeza (*f.*)   stupidity
torre (*f.*)   tower
torta (*f.*)   cake, 5

tortuga (*f.*)   turtle, 8
tos (*f.*)   cough, 15
toser   to cough, 15
tostadora (*f.*)   toaster, 10
trabajar   to work, 2
trabajo (*m.*)   job, 3; work, 3; **— de la casa** (*m.*)   housework, 6
tradición (*f.*)   tradition, 4
traducir   to translate, 6
traductor(-a) (*m., f.*)   translator, 17
traer   to bring, 6
trágico(-a)   tragic
traído (*p.p. of* **traer**)   brought, 14
traje (*m.*)   suit, 13; **— de baño** (*m.*) bathing suit, 16
trama (*f.*)   plot, 18
tranquilidad (*f.*)   tranquility
trapear el piso   to mop the floor, 6
tratar de   to deal with
trece   thirteen, 1
treinta   thirty, 1
tren (*m.*)   train, 11
tres   three, 1
trescientos(-as)   three hundred, 3
trigo (*m.*)   wheat
trompeta (*f.*)   trumpet, 9
tropezar (e:ie)   to trip
trozo (*m.*)   piece, 5
tu   your (*fam. sing.*), 3
tú   you (*fam. sing.*), 1
tulipán (*m.*)   tulip, 8
turbio(-a)   muddy
turismo (*m.*)   tourism, 7
turista (*m., f.*)   tourist, 6
tus   your (*fam. pl.*), 3
tuyo(s), tuya(s) (*pron.*)   yours (*fam. sing.*), 9

U

ubicación (*f.*)   location
ubicar   to locate
último(-a)   last, 17
última vez   last time, 17
un   a, an, 1; **— poco +** *adj.*   a little + *adj.*, 4; **— poco (de)**   a little, 2; **— rato** (*m.*)   a while, 4
una   a, an 1; **— vez** (*f.*)   once, 16
único: lo —   the only thing, 14
universidad (*f.*)   university, 1
universitario(-a) (*adj.*)   university, 14
uno(-a)   one, 1
unos(-as)   a few, some, 2; about
usado(-a)   used, 12
usar   to use, 6; to wear
usted (Ud.)   you (*form., sing.*), 1; (*obj. of prep.*), 4
ustedes (Uds.)   you (*form. pl.*), 1; (*obj. of prep.*), 4
utilidad (*f.*)   usefulness
uva (*f.*)   grape, 9

V

vacaciones (*f. pl.*)   vacation, 7
vacío(-a)   empty, 12

valer to be worth; **(no) vale la pena** it's (not) worth the trouble, 12

valeroso(-a) brave

valija (*f.*) suitcase, 7

valor (*m.*) value

¡vamos! let's go!, 2; **— de compras** let's go shopping, 13

vaso (*m.*) glass, 4

vecindad (*f.*) neighborhood, 10

vecino(-a) (*m., f.*) neighbor, 4

veinte twenty, 1

veinticinco twenty-five, 1

veinticuatro twenty-four, 1

veintidós twenty-two, 1

veintinueve twenty-nine, 1

veintiocho twenty-eight, 1

veintiséis twenty-six, 1

veintisiete twenty-seven, 1

veintitrés twenty-three, 1

veintiuno twenty-one, 1

velero (*m.*) sailboat, 16

velocidad máxima (*f.*) speed limit, 12

vendedor(-a) (*m., f.*) salesperson, 14; merchant

vender to sell, 3

venir (a) to come, 3; **—le de perillas a uno** to suit one to perfection, 18

ventaja (*f.*) advantage

ventana (*f.*) window, 2

ventanilla (*f.*) window (of a vehicle or booth), 12

ventilador (*m.*) fan, 10

ver to see, 6

verano (*m.*) summer, 1

verbo (*m.*) verb

verdad (*f.*) truth; **¿verdad?** right?, 1

verdadero(-a) real, 18; true

verde green, 1

verdura (*f.*) vegetable, 5

versión (*f.*) draft

verso (*m.*) line (of poetry)

vestido (*m.*) dress, 13; **— de noche** (*m.*) evening gown, 13

vestido(-a) dressed; **— de gala** dressed up

vestirse (e:i) to get dressed, 9

vez (*f.*) time (*in a series*), 4; **a veces** at times, 6; **en — de** instead of, 17

viajar to travel, 7

viaje (*m.*) trip, 4

viajero(-a) (*m., f.*) traveler, 11

vida (*f.*) life

videograbadora (*f.*) VCR, 17

vidriera (*f.*) shop window, 18

viejo(-a) old

viento (*m.*) wind, 5; **hacer —** to be windy; **viernes** (*m.*) Friday, 1

vileza (*f.*) vileness

vinagre (*m.*) vinegar, 9

vino (*m.*) wine, 4; **— tinto** (*m.*) red wine, 8

violeta (*f.*) violet, 8

violín (*m.*) violin, 9

visitar to visit, 4

visto(-a) (*p.p. of* **ver** *and adj.*) seen, 14; **vista** (*f.*) eyes

viudo(-a) widowed, 3

vivir to live, 3

vocabulario (*m.*) vocabulary

volante (*m.*) steering wheel, 12

volar (o:ue) to fly, 5

vóleibol (*m.*) volleyball, 16

voltear to turn over

voluntad (*f.*) will power

volver (o:ue) to return, 5

vosotros(-as) (*subject pron.*) you (*fam. pl.*), 1; (*obj. of prep.*), you (*fam. pl.*), 4

vuelo (*m.*) flight, 11

vuelto(-a) (*p.p. of* **volver** *and adj.*) returned, 14

vuestro(-a) your (*fam. sing.*), 3; (*pron.*) yours (*fam. pl.*), 9

vuestros(-as) your (*fam. pl.*), 3

Y

y and, 1; past, after (time), 2

ya already, 2; now, 7; **— lo creo** I'll say, 13; **¡— verás!** You'll see!, 15

yerno (*m.*) son-in-law, 6

yo I, 1

Z

zanahoria (*f.*) carrot, 9

zapatería (*f.*) shoe store, 9

zapato (*m.*) shoe, 13; **— de tenis** (*m.*) tennis shoe, 13

zona postal (*f.*) zip code, 3

zoológico (*m.*) zoo, 4

English-Spanish

A

a, an un(a), 1

abandonment desamparo (*m.*)

about sobre, 11; de, 16; como, 16

above all sobre todo, 17

abroad en el extranjero

accept aceptar, 3

accident accidente (*m.*), 15

according to de acuerdo con; según

account cuenta (*f.*), 8

accountant contador(-a) (*m., f.*), 5

accounting contabilidad (*f.*), 14

accuracy exactitud (*f.*)

achievement logro (*m.*)

acorn bellota (*f.*)

act actuar

acting actuación (*f.*), 18

action acción (*f.*), 18

activity actividad (*f.*), 16

actor actor (*m.*), 18

actress actriz (*f.*), 18

ad anuncio (*m.*), aviso (*m.*), 3

add añadir

address dirección (*f.*), domicilio (*m.*), 2

adjective adjetivo (*m.*)

advanced adelantado(-a)

advice consejo (*m.*)

advise avisar, 10; aconsejar, 11

advisor consejero(-a) (*m., f.*), 14

afraid: to be — tener miedo, 4

after (*time*) y, 2; **— all** al fin y al cabo, 18

afternoon tarde (*f.*), 2

good — buenas tardes, 1

afterwards después, 3

again otra vez

against contra

age edad (*f.*), 14

agency agencia (*f.*), 11

aghast atónito(-a)

ago: … ago hace + *time*, 9

agree estar de acuerdo, 6

agreement concordancia (*f.*)

air aire (*m.*); **— bag** bolsa de aire (*f.*), 12; **— conditioner** aire acondicionado (*m.*), 7

airline aerolínea (*f.*), 11

airport aeropuerto (*m.*), 4

aisle seat asiento de pasillo (*m.*), 11

all todo(-a), 6; (*pron.*) todo, 8

allergic alérgico(-a), 8

almost casi, 8

alone solo(-a), 5

along por, 8

alphabet alfabeto (*m.*)

alphabetize alfabetizar

already ya, 7

also también, 2

always siempre, 6

A.M. de la mañana, 2

amateur theatre teatro de aficionados (*m.*), 18

ambulance ambulancia (*f.*), 15

American americano(-a), 2

among entre, 9

ample amplio(-a), 10

amusement park parque de diversiones (*m.*), 4

an un(a), 1

ancestry ascendencia (*f.*), 14

and y, 1

angry enfadado(-a), enojado(-a), 4

animated animado(-a), 4

ankle tobillo (*m.*), 15

annoyed fastidiado(-a)

another otro(-a), 2

answer contestar, 3; respuesta (f.)

answering machine máquina contestadora (f.), 17

antibiotic antibiótico (m.), 15

any alguno(-a), algún, 6; cualquier; **not —** ninguno(-a), ningún, 6

anyone alguien, 6; **not —** nadie, 6

anything algo, 6

anyway en fin..., 8; de todos modos

apartment apartamento (m.), 3

appearance apariencia (f.)

apple manzana (f.), 9

application (*form*) solicitud (f.), 3

apply for a loan pedir (e:i) un préstamo, 8

appointment cita (f.)

approach acercarse

April abril, 1

architect arquitecto(-a) (m., f.), 14

Argentinian argentino(-a), 11

armchair butaca (f.); sillón (m.), 10

army ejército (m.)

around por, 8; cerca de; **— here** por aquí cerca, 18

arrival llegada (f.), 4

arrive llegar, 4

art arte (f.)

article artículo (m.), 16

as tan, 5; **— ... —** tan... como, 5; **— if** como si, 17; **— long as** con tal de que, 14; **— many** tantos(-as), 5; **— many ... —** tantos(-as)... como, 5; **— much** tanto, 5; **— much —** tanto como, 5; **— soon —** en cuanto, tan pronto como, 14

ashamed avergonzado(-a)

ask (*a question*) preguntar, 15; **— (for)** pedir (e:i), 6

aspirin aspirina (f.), 15

assistant asistente (m., f.), 17

at en, 1; a, 2; **— a time** a la vez, 4; **— about** a eso de, 15; **— home** en casa, 4; **— least** por lo menos, 13; **— night** por la noche, 2; **— our disposal** a nuestra disposición, 16; **— the latest** a más tardar, 18; **— this moment** en este momento, 5; **at +** *time* a la (las) + *time*, 2

athletic atlético(-a), 16

attend asistir (a), 3

August agosto, 1

aunt tía (f.), 4

automatic automático(-a), 12; **— teller (ATM)** cajero automático (m.), 8

autumn otoño (m.), 1

available libre, 13

avenue avenida (f.), 12

avoid evitar

B

back espalda (f.), 15

backpack mochila (f.), 2

backyard patio (m.), 15

baked al horno, 5

bakery panadería (f.), 9

banana plátano (m.), 9

bank banco (m.), 8; **— employee** empleado(-a) bancario(-a) (m., f.), 17

banner divisa (f.)

bargain regatear

basement sótano (m.), 6

bass contrabajo (m.), 9

bathe (oneself) bañar(se), 9

bathing suit traje de baño (m.), 16

bathroom baño (m.), 6; cuarto de baño (m.), 6

bathtub bañadera (f.), 7

battery acumulador (m.), batería (f.), 12

be ser, 1; estar, 4; **— able to** poder (o:ue), 5; **— acquainted with** conocer, 6; **— afraid** tener miedo (de), 4; temer, 11; **— bad weather** hacer mal tiempo, 5; **— ... behind schedule** tener... de retraso (atraso), 11; **— bored (to death)** aburrirse (como una ostra), 16; **— called** llamarse, 9; **— careful** tener cuidado, 4; **— cold** tener frío, 4; (*weather*) hacer frío, 5; **— crazy about** estar loco(-a) por, 18; **— due to** debido a; **— for,** to exist for enderezarse a ; **— furious** darle rabia a uno, 18; **— glad** alegrarse (de), 11; **— going to +** *inf.* ir a + *inf.*, 4; **— good weather** hacer buen tiempo, 5; **— hot** tener calor, 4; (*weather*) hacer calor, 5; **— hungry** tener hambre, 4; **— impressed** quedar impresionado(-a), 17; **— in a hurry** tener prisa, 4; **— in agreement** estar de acuerdo, 6; **— in charge** estar encargado(-a), 18; **— named** llamarse, 9; **— not much good** no servir de mucho, 14; **— on vacation** estar de vacaciones, 7; **— pleasing to** gustar, 7; **— right** tener razón, 4; **— right back** volver en seguida, 6; **— scared** tener miedo, 4; **— silent** callar; **— sleepy** tener sueño, 4; **— sorry** sentir (e:ie), 11; **— successful** tener éxito, 18; **— sunny** hacer sol, 5; **— thirsty** tener sed, 4; **— too big (small) on someone** quedarle grande (chico) a uno, 13; **— wearing** llevar puesto(-a), 18; **— windy** hacer viento, 6; **— worth it** valer (merecer) la pena, 12; **— wrong** estar equivocado(-a), no tener razón, 4; **— ... years old** tener... años, 4

beach playa (f.), 4

beans frijoles (m. pl.), 5

beat batir

beautiful hermoso(-a), 5; precioso(-a), 13

beauty belleza (f.); **— salon** peluquería (f.), salón de belleza (m.), 12

because porque; **— of** por, 8

bed cama (f.), 6; lecho (m.); **to go to —** acostarse (o:ue), 9; **to put to —** acostar (o:ue), 9

bedroom dormitorio (m.); recámara (f.) (*Mex.*), 6

bedspread sobrecama (f.), 10

beef carne de res (f.)

beer cerveza (f.), 5

before antes (de), 7; antes de que, 14

beg rogar (o:ue), 11

begin comenzar (e:ie), empezar (e:ie) (a), 4

believe creer, 3

believed creído (*p.p. of* creer), 14

bellhop botones (m.), 7

belong pertenecer, 18; **—ing to other people** ajeno(-a)

besides además, 5

best el (la) mejor, 5

betroth desposar

better mejor, 5

beverage bebida (f.), 5

bewildered desconcertado(-a)

beyond más allá

bicycle bicicleta (f.), 12

big grande

bigger mayor, 5

bill cuenta (f.), 5

biology biología (f.), 14

bird pájaro (m.)

birth nacimiento (m.)

birthday cumpleaños (m.), 1

black negro(-a), 1

blemish mancha (f.)

blender licuadora (f.), 10

block (city) manzana (f.) (*Sp.*), cuadra (f.)

blond(e) rubio(-a), 3

blood-stained ensangrentado(-a)

blouse blusa (f.), 13

blow resoplar

blue azul, 1

boarding house pensión (f.), 10

boarding pass tarjeta de embarque (f.), 11

boat barca (f.), bote (m.), 16

body cuerpo (m.), 15

book libro (m.), 2

bookstore librería (f.), 13

boot bota (f.), 13

bored aburrido(-a), 4

born nacido(-a)

borrow pedir (e:i) prestado, 11

boss jefe(-a) (m., f.), 17

both ambos(-as); **— in ... and in ...** tanto en... como en...

bother (*doing something*) molestarse, 15

bouquet ramo (m.), 8

boy chico (m.), muchacho (m.), 2

boyfriend novio (m.), 3

bracelet pulsera (f.), 13

brake freno (*m.*), 12
branch rama (*f.*); (*office*) sucursal (*f.*)
brand marca (*f.*), 13
brave valeroso(-a)
bread pan (*m.*), 9
break romper(se), quebrar(se) (e:ie), 17; — **down** (*car*) descomponerse, 12
breakfast desayuno (*m.*), 7
bridge puente (*m.*)
brilliant brillante, 11
bring traer, 6
brochure folleto (*m.*), 11
broken roto(-a), 14
broom escoba (*f.*), 6
brother hermano (*m.*), 4
brother-in-law cuñado (*m.*), 6
brown marrón, café, 1
brought traído (*p.p. of* traer), 14
brunette moreno(-a), 3
bud capullo (*m.*)
building edificio (*m.*), 10
bulletin board tablilla de anuncios (*f.*), 2
bullfight corrida de toros (*f.*)
bunch: a —of un montón de (*m.*), 6
bureau cómoda (*f.*), 10
buried enterrado(-a)
burn quemar
bus autobús (*m.*), ómnibus (*m.*), bus (*m.*), 6; — **stop** parada de autobuses (*f.*), 6
business (*adj.*) empresarial; — **administration** administración de empresas (*f.*), 14
businessman (woman) hombre (mujer) de negocios (*m., f.*), 7
businesspeople gente de negocio (*f.*)
busy ocupado(-a), 4
but pero, 1; sino
butter mantequilla (*f.*), 9
butterfly mariposa (*f.*)
buy comprar, 6
buyer comprador(-a) (*m., f.*), 17
by para, 8; por, 8; — **heart** de memoria
bye chau, 1

C

cabbage repollo (*m.*), 9; col (*f.*)
cabin cabaña (*f.*), 16
cafe café (*m.*), 3
cafeteria cafetería (*f.*), 1
cake torta (*f.*), 5
calculator calculadora (*f.*), 2
call llamar, 3
calorie caloría (*f.*), 5
camellia camelia (*f.*), 8
camera cámara fotográfica (*f.*), 7
camp acampar, 16
can poder (o:ue), 5; bote (*m.*) (*Mex.*), lata (*f.*), 9
canary canario (*m.*), 8
cancel cancelar, 7
candidate candidato(-a) (*m., f.*), 17

canoe canoa (*f.*), 16
canyon desfiladero (*m.*)
capital (*city*) capital (*f.*)
car auto (*m.*), automóvil (*m.*), carro (*m.*), coche (*m.*), 10
caramel custard flan (*m.*), 5
carburetor carburador (*m.*), 12
card tarjeta (*f.*)
care cuidado (*m.*)
career carrera (*f.*), 14
carnation clavel (*m.*), 8
carpet alfombra (*f.*), 10
carpenter carpintero(-a), (*m., f.*), 14
carriage carro (*m.*)
carrot zanahoria (*f.*), 9
carry-on bag bolso de mano (*m.*)
cartoons dibujos animados (*m. pl.*), 18
carved tallado(-a)
case: in — en caso de que, 14
cash efectivo (*m.*), 8; — **a check** cobrar un cheque, 8; — **register** caja (*f.*), 13; **in —** al contado, en efectivo, 8
casting reparto de papeles (*m.*), distribución de papeles (*f.*), 18
cat gato (*m.*), 8
catch a fish pescar, 16
celebrate celebrar, 9
celery apio (*m.*), 9
cellular phone teléfono celular (*m.*), 12
censorship censura (*f.*)
ceramic tile azulejo (*m.*)
certified public accountant contador(-a) público(-a) certificado(-a), 17
chair silla (*f.*), 2
champagne champán (*m.*), 5
champion campeón(-ona) (*m., f.*), 16
change cambiar, 6
channel canal (*m.*), 7
character personaje (*m.*), 18
charge: in — encargado(-a), 17
charm simpatía (*f.*)
charmed encantado(-a)
charming simpático(-a), encantador(-a), 3
check cuenta (*f.*), 5; — **luggage** facturar el equipaje, 11
checkbook talonario de cheques (*m.*), chequera (*f.*), 8
checking account cuenta corriente (*f.*), 8
checkup examen (*m.*), chequeo (*m.*), 15
Cheers! ¡Salud!
cheese queso (*m.*), 5
chef cocinero(-a), (*m., f.*), 14
chemistry química (*f.*), 14
cherry cereza (*f.*)
chest pecho (*m.*), 15; — **of drawers** cómoda (*f.*), 10
chicken pollo (*m.*), 5
chief jefe(-a) (*m., f.*), 17

child niño(-a) (*m., f.*), 5; **only —** hijo(-a) único(-a), 11
childhood infancia (*f.*), 9
children hijos (*m. pl.*); —**'s** (*adj.*) infantil
Chinese (*lang.*) chino (*m.*), 2
chivalry caballería (*f.*)
chocolate chocolate (*m.*), 5
choose escoger
Christmas Navidad (*f.*), 4; — **tree** árbol de Navidad (*m.*), 4
church iglesia (*f.*)
city ciudad (*f.*), 3; — **block** manzana (*f.*) (*Sp.*), cuadra (*f.*)
class clase (*f.*), 1
classified clasificado(-a), 12; — **ad** aviso clasificado (*m.*), 3
classmate compañero(-a) de clase (*m., f.*), 4
clean limpio(-a); limpiar
clerk empleado(-a) (*m., f.*), 13
climb escalar, 16
clock reloj (*m.*), 2
close cerrar (e:ie), 4; (*adv.*) cerca, 10
clothes ropa (*f.*), 6
clothing ropa (*f.*), 13
cloudy nublado(-a)
coal carbón (*m.*)
coat abrigo (*m.*)
coffee café (*m.*), 3; (*small cup of*) cafecito (*m.*), 15; — **maker** cafetera (*f.*), 10
cognate cognado (*m.*)
cold catarro (*m.*), resfriado (*m.*), resfrío (*m.*), 15; **to be —** tener frío, 4; (*weather*) hacer frío, 5
collar cuello (*m.*)
colleague colega (*m., f.*)
college facultad (*f.*), 14; (*adj.*) universitario(-a), 14
colonial colonial, 15
color color (*m.*), 1
column columna (*f.*)
come venir (a), 3; — **in** entrar, 12; Pase., 1
comedy comedia (*f.*), 7
comfortable cómodo(-a), 7
compact compacto(-a); — **disc** disco compacto (*m.*), 4; — **disc player** reproductor de discos (*m.*), 4
company compañía (*f.*), 3
comparative comparativo(-a)
compare comparar, 14
compensate compensar, 17
complain quejarse, 10
computer computadora, (*f.*), 2; ordenador (*m.*) (*Sp.*), 3
concern importarle a uno, 18
concert concierto (*m.*), 4
conditional condicional (*m.*)
conduct conducir, 6
confirm confirmar, 7
confused aturdido(-a), 4
consulate consulado (*m.*), 6
continent continente (*m.*), 11
contagious contagioso(-a), 5

continue seguir (e:i), 6; continuar, 17; proseguir (e:i); **— straight ahead** seguir derecho, 12

contraction contracción (*f.*)

contrary: on the — por el contrario, 13

conversation conversación (*f.*), 2

converse conversar, platicar, 2

convince convencer, 10

cook cocinar, 6; cocinero(-a) (*m., f.*), 14

cookware batería de cocina (*f.*), 10

cool (down) enfriar

copper cobre (*m.*)

corner (*street*) esquina (*f.*)

correspondence correspondencia (*f.*), 17

cost costar (o:ue), 5; **— an arm and a leg** costar un ojo de la cara, 12

cotton algodón (*m.*), 13

cough tos (*f.*), 15; toser, 15

count contar (o:ue), 5

country país (*m.*), 9; campo (*m.*), 16

couple pareja (*f.*)

courteous amable, cortés, 3

cousin primo(-a) (*m., f.*), 4

covered cubierto(-a), 14

cowardice cobardía (*f.*)

crazy loco(-a), 16; loquito(-a)

cream crema (*f.*), 5

create crear

credit card tarjeta de crédito (*m.*), 8

critic crítico(-a) (*m., f.*), 18

criticize criticar, 18

cruise crucero (*m.*), 11

Cuban cubano(-a), 2

cucumber pepino (*m.*), 9

cup taza (*f.*), 5

cure oneself curarse, 15

currency moneda (*f.*)

curriculum vitae currículum vitae (*m.*), 17

curtain cortina (*f.*), 10

custom costumbre (*f.*), 4

customer cliente (*m., f.*)

customs aduana (*f.*), 7

D

dad papá (*m.*), 1

daily diariamente

daisy margarita (*f.*), 8

dam represa (*f.*)

dance bailar, 4

dancer bailarín(-ina) (*m., f.*), 18

dangerous peligroso(-a)

dark moreno(-a), 3; oscuro(-a)

darling mi amor (*m.*), mi vida, (*f.*), 3; hijito(-a) (*m., f.*), 4

date fechar, poner la fecha, 8; fecha; **— of birth** fecha de nacimiento (*f.*), 3

daughter hija (*f.*), 4; **— in-law** nuera (*f.*), 6

dawn alba (*f.*)

day día (*m.*), 1; **— after tomorrow,** pasado mañana, 4; **— before yesterday** anteayer, 8

dazed aturdido(-a), 4

deal with tratar de

death muerte (*f.*)

December diciembre, 1

decide decidir, 3

decision decisión (*f.*), 17

definite determinado(-a)

degree título (*m.*), 14; grado (*m.*), 15

deliver entregar, 14

demand exigir

demonstrative demostrativo(-a)

denial negación (*f.*)

deny negar (e:ie), 12

department store almacén (*m.*), tienda por departamentos (*f.*), 13

departure salida (*f.*), 11; **— gate** puerta de salida (*f.*), 11

depend depender, 14

deposit depositar, 8

depth profundidad (*f.*)

describe describir, 11

design diseño (*m.*), 13

desk escritorio (*m.*), 2

despair desesperanza (*f.*)

dessert postre (*m.*), 5; **for —** de postre, 5

diamond diamante (*m.*)

dictionary diccionario (*m.*), 8

die morir (o:ue), 5

died muerto(-a), 14

diet dieta (*f.*), 5

different distinto(-a)

difficult difícil, 2

dine cenar, 7

dining room comedor (*m.*), 6

dinner cena (*f.*), 7

to have — cenar, 7

direct directo(-a), 11; dirigir, 18

director director(-a) (*m., f.*), 18

dirty sucio(-a)

disaster desastre (*m.*), 8

discotheque discoteca (*f.*), 4

diskette disquete (*m.*), 17

divine divino(-a), 16

divorced divorciado(-a), 3

do hacer, 4; **— the laundry** lavar la ropa, 6; **— the shopping** hacer las compras, 6

dock muelle (*m.*)

doctor (Dr.) doctor(-a) (*m., f.*), 1; médico(-a) (*m., f.*), 14; **—'s office** consultorio (*m.*), 15

document documento (*m.*), 12; cédula (*f.*)

documentary documental (*m.*), 18

dog perro(-a) (*m., f.*), 8

done hecho (*p.p. of* hacer), 14

donkey burro(-a) (*m., f.*)

door puerta (*f.*), 2

doorbell timbre (*m.*), 15

dot punto (*m.*); **on the —** en punto

double doble, 7; **— room** habitación doble (*f.*), 7

doubt dudar, 12

draft borrador (*m.*), versión (*f.*)

dream ilusión (*f.*), 18; hacerse ilusiones, 18; **— about (of)** soñar (o:ue) con, 18

dress vestido (*m.*), 13

dressed: to get — vestirse (e:i), 9; **— up** vestido(-a) de gala

dresser tocador (*m.*), 10

dressmaker modista (*f.*)

drink beber, tomar, 3; bebida (*f.*), 5

drive conducir, manejar, 5

driver's license licencia para conducir (*f.*), 12; **— number** número de la licencia de conducir, 3

drown ahogarse, 16

drums batería (*f.*), 9

dry secar; seco(-a); **— cleaner's** tintorería (*f.*), 8; **— season** estación de la seca (*f.*)

dryer secadora (*f.*), 10

dubbed doblado(-a)

duly debidamente

during durante, 7; por, 8

E

each cada, 13

ear (*inner*) oído (*m.*), 17; (*external*) oreja (*f.*), 17

early temprano, 9

earn ganar, 3

earring arete (*m.*), 13

easily fácilmente

east este, 16

easy fácil, 2

eat comer, 3

effort esfuerzo (*m.*)

eight ocho, 1; **— hundred** ochocientos(-as), 3

eighteen dieciocho, 1

eighth octavo(-a), 7

eighty ochenta, 2

either . . . or o… o, 6; **not —** tampoco, 6

elective clase optativa (*f.*)

electrician electricista (*m., f.*), 14

electricity electricidad (*f.*), 10

electronic equipment equipo electrónico (*m.*), 17

elevator ascensor (*m.*), elevador (*m.*), 7

eleven once, 1

e-mail mensaje electrónico (*m.*), 3; correo electrónico (*m.*), 17

embassy embajada (*f.*), 7

emergency emergencia (*f.*), 17

emphasize destacar

empty vacío(-a), 12

encyclopedia enciclopedia (*f.*), 8

end terminar, 14; fin (*m.*)

engaged comprometido(-a), 18

engineer ingeniero(-a) (*m., f.*), 14

English (*lang.*) inglés (*m.*), 2

enjoy disfrutar; **— oneself** divertirse (e:ie), 16

enormous enorme, 15

enter entrar, 12

entertainment section (*of newspaper*) cartelera (*f.*), 18
enthused entusiasmado(-a), 4
entrance entrada (*f.*), 11
eraser goma de borrar (*f.*), 2
errand diligencia (*f.*), 8
to run —s hacer diligencias, 8
escalator escalera mecánica (*f.*), 7
escape escapar, 14
especially especialmente, 8; sobre todo, 17
essay ensayo (*m.*)
evaluation evaluación (*f.*), 17
evening noche (*f.*), 2; — **gown** vestido de noche (*m.*), 13
event acontecimiento (*m.*)
ever alguna vez
every day todos los días, 2
everybody todo el mundo, 18
everything todo, 8
everywhere a (de) todas partes, a todos lados, 12
evil maligno(-a)
exactly exactamente, 17
exaggerate exagerar, 13
exam examen (*m.*), 3
excellent excelente, 11; magnífico(-a), 14
exercise hacer ejercicio, 7
excess baggage exceso de equipaje (*m.*), 11
exchange cambiar, 13
excursion excursión (*f.*), 11
excuse: Excuse me. Con permiso., 1
executive ejecutivo(-a) (*m., f.*), 14
exit salida (*f.*), 11
expect esperar, 6
expensive caro(-a), 5
expert experto(-a) (*m., f.*), 14
experience experiencia (*f.*), 3
express gratitude dar las gracias, 18
expression expresión (*f.*)
extremely good buenísimo(-a), 11
eye ojo (*m.*), 15

F

face cara (*f.*), 15; rostro (*m.*)
fact: the — is … es que… , 13
factory fábrica (*f.*), factoría (*f.*), 5
faculty appointment cátedra (*f.*)
fail (*course or exam*) quedar suspendido(-a), 14
faint desfallecer
fair justo(-a)
fall otoño (*m.*), 1; caer, 16; — **asleep** dormirse (o:ue), 9; — **in love with** enamorarse de, 18
false falso(-a)
family familia (*f.*), 4; — **oriented** hogareño(-a); — **room** salón de estar (*m.*), 6
fan ventilador (*m.*), 10
far lejos, 10; — **away** lejano(-a)
farewell despedida (*f.*), 1
farmer labrador(-a) (*m., f.*)
fashion moda (*f.*)

fast rápido(-a), 13
fat gordo(-a), 3
father padre (*m.*), 1
father-in-law suegro (*m.*), 6
favorite favorito(-a), 7
fax fax (*m.*), facsímile (*m.*), 17
fear miedo (*m.*), 4; temer, 11
February febrero, 1
feed dar alimento (a), dar de comer
feel sentir(se) (e:ie), 9
fever fiebre (*f.*), 15
fiancé(e) prometido(-a) (*m., f.*), 11
fifteen quince, 1
fifth quinto(-a), 7
fifty cincuenta, 2
fight luchar
file archivar, 17
fill out llenar, 3
film película (*f.*), 7; filmar, 18; — **festival** festival de cine (*m.*), 18
finally por fin, 18
financial económico(-a), 3
find encontrar (o:ue), 5; — **out** saber, 10
fine (*adv.*), bien, 1; multa (*f.*), 8; (*verb*) dar (poner) una multa, 8
finger dedo (*m.*), 15
finish terminar, 14
fire hydrant boca de incendios (*f.*), hidrante (*m.*), 8
first primero(-a), primer, 2; — **class** primera clase, 11; — **name** nombre (*m.*), 3; — **part of** a principios de, 18
fish pescado (*m.*), 5; pez; pescar, 16; — **store** pescadería (*f.*), 9
fishing rod caña de pescar (*f.*), 16
fit caber, 6
five cinco, 1; — **hundred** quinientos(-as), 3
fix arreglar, 6
flame llama (*f.*)
flat tire llanta pinchada (*f.*), neumático pinchado (*m.*), 12
flesh carne (*f.*)
flight vuelo (*m.*), 11; — **attendant** auxiliar de vuelo (*m., f.*), 11; azafata (*f.*), 11
floor piso (*m.*), 7
flower flor (*f.*), 8; — **shop** florería (*f.*), 8
flu gripe (*f.*), 15
flute flauta (*f.*), 9
fly volar (o:ue), 5
foam espuma (*f.*)
fog niebla (*f.*), 5
fold the clothes doblar la ropa, 6
folder carpeta (*f.*), 17
follow seguir (e:i), 6; — **in the footsteps** seguir los pasos, 18
following siguiente
food comida (*f.*), 4
fool oneself hacerse ilusiones, 18
foot pie (*m.*), 15; **on —** a pie, 12
for para, 3; por, 8; — **example** por ejemplo, 13; — **that** para eso, 18

force obligar, 12
foreign extranjero(-a)
forest bosque (*m.*), 11
forever para siempre, 18
forget olvidar(se) (de), 9
fork tenedor (*m.*), 5
former antiguo(-a), 17
fortress fortaleza (*f.*)
forty cuarenta, 2
four cuatro, 1; — **hundred** cuatrocientos(-as), 3
fourteen catorce, 1
fourth cuarto(-a), 7
frankly francamente, 12
free (*of charge*) gratis, 8, gratuito(-a); libre, 13
freedom libertad (*f.*), 2
freeway autopista (*f.*), 12
French (*lang.*) francés (*m.*), 2
frequent frecuente
frequently a menudo, frecuentemente, 12
fresh (*water*) dulce
Friday viernes (*m.*), 1
fried frito(-a), 5
friend amigo(-a) (*m., f.*), 1
friendship amistad (*f.*)
from de, 1; desde, 10
front: in — of frente a, 8; — **door** puerta de calle (*f.*), 12
fruit juice jugo de frutas (*f.*), 5
fruit tree árbol frutal (*m.*), 15
frustrated frustrado(-a), 4
frying pan sartén (*f.*), 10
full lleno(-a), 12
fun (*adj.*) divertido(-a), 16
function funcionar, 12
furnish proporcionar
furnished amueblado(-a), 10
furniture muebles (*m. pl.*), 10
future futuro (*m.*), 14

G

game juego (*m.*), 4; partido (*m.*), 4
garage garaje (*m.*), 6
garden jardín (*m.*), 7; — **of Eden** paraíso terrenal (*m.*)
gas station gasolinera (*f.*), estación de servicio (*f.*), 12
gasoline gasolina (*f.*), 12
gee! ¡caramba!, 2
gender género (*m.*)
general general, 8
generally generalmente, 8; por lo general, 18
gentleman señor (*m.*), 1; caballero (*m.*)
geranium geranio (*m.*), 8
get buscar, 6; conseguir (e:i), 6; (*grade*) sacar, 14; — **a tan** broncearse, 16; — **angry** enojarse, 14; — **better** curarse, mejorarse, 15; — **dressed** vestirse (e:i), 9; — **engaged to** comprometerse con, 18; — **in shape** ponerse en forma, 14; — **married** casarse con, 11;

— **together** reunirse; — **undressed** desvestirse (e:i), 9; — **up** levantarse, 9; — **used to** acostumbrarse a, 12; — **worse** empeorarse, 15

ghost fantasma (*m.*)

gift regalo (*m.*), 8; don (*m.*)

girl chica (*f.*), muchacha (*f.*), 2

girlfriend novia (*f.*), 3

give dar, 4; (*as a gift*) regalar, 8; — **a shot** poner una inyección, 15

glass vaso (*m.*), 4; copa (*f.*), 5

glove guante (*m.*), 13

go ir (a), 4; — **away** irse, 9; — **camping** acampar, ir a acampar, 16; — **down** bajar, 12; — **fishing** ir de pesca, ir a pescar, 16; — **on foot** ir a pie, ir caminando, 12; — **out** salir, 6; — **through** atravesar (e:ie); — **through customs** pasar por la aduana, 7; — **to bed** acostarse (o:ue), 9; — **to be going (to)** + *infinitive* ir a + *infinitive*, 4

goal meta (*f.*)

goblet copa (*f.*), 5

God Dios; — **grant** ojalá, 11

goddaughter ahijada (*f.*)

godfather padrino (*m.*), 11

godmother madrina (*f.*)

godson ahijado (*m.*)

gold oro (*m.*)

golden dorado(-a)

goldfish pez de color (*m.*), 8

golf club palo de golf (*m.*), 16

good bueno(-a), buen, 1; — **afternoon** buenas tardes, 1; — **evening** buenas noches, 1; — **morning** buenos días, 1; — **night** buenas noches, 1

good-bye adiós, 1; Hasta la vista., 1

good-looking guapo(-a), 3

grade nota (*f.*), 14; — **point average** promedio (*m.*), 14

grading system sistema de calificaciones (*m.*)

graduate graduar(se), 14

granddaughter nieta (*f.*), 6

grandfather abuelo (*m.*), 4

grandmother abuela (*f.*), 4

grandson nieto (*m.*), 6

grape uva (*f.*), 9

gratefulness agradecimiento (*m.*)

gray gris, 1

great magnífico(-a), 14

Great! ¡Chévere!, ¡Bárbaro!

great-grandfather (mother) bisabuelo(-a) (*m., f.*)

green verde, 1

greeting saludo (*m.*), 1

grilled a la parrilla, 5

group grupo (*m.*), 18

grow crecer, 9

Guatemalan guatemalteco(-a) (*m., f.*), 10

guest invitado(-a) (*m., f.*), 10

guilty culpable

Guinea pig conejillo de Indias (*m.*), 8

guitar guitarra (*f.*), 9

gym gimnasio (*m.*), 14

H

hair pelo (*m.*), cabello (*m.*), 15

haircut corte (*m.*), 12

half medio(-a); mitad (*f.*); — **brother** medio hermano, 6; — **past** y media (*time*), 2; — **sister** media hermana, 6

ham jamón (*m.*), 5

hamburger hamburguesa (*f.*), 5

hand mano (*f.*), 15

handbag bolso (*m.*), cartera (*f.*), 10

handkerchief pañuelo (*m.*), 13

handsome guapo(-a), 3

happen pasar, ocurrir, 8

happening hecho (*m.*)

happy feliz, 1; contento(-a), 4

hardware store ferretería (*f.*), 9

hat sombrero (*m.*)

have tener, 3; haber (*aux.*); — **a good time** pasarlo bien, 5; divertirse (e:ie), 16; — **a nice trip** buen viaje, 11; — **a picnic** hacer un picnic, 16; — **a seat.** Tome asiento., 1; — **an afternoon snack** merendar (e:ie), 15; — **been doing something for a length of time** hace + *time* + que + *verb* (*present*), 7; — **dinner** cenar, 7; — **done something in the past** hace + *time* + que + *verb* (*preterit/ imperfect*), 9; — **just . . .** acabar de…, 4; — **lunch** almorzar (o:ue), 5; — **self-esteem** estimarse; — **something to drink (eat)** tomar (beber) algo, 3; — **to** tener que + *inf.*, 3

he él, 1; — **(she) who** el (la) que

head cabeza (*f.*), 15

headlight luz (*f.*), 12

healer curandero(-a) (*m., f.*)

health salud (*f.*), 15

hear oír

heard oído (*p.p. of* oír), 15

heart corazón (*m.*); — **attack** ataque al corazón (*m.*), 15

heat calor (*m.*), 14

heaven Cielo (*m.*)

hello hola, 1; **say — to . . .** saludos a…, 1

help ayudar (a), 6

her su(s), 3; ella, 4; la, 6; le, 7

here aquí, 3; acá, 10; — **it goes.** Aquí va.

hers suyo(-a)(s), 9

herself se, 9

hide esconder, 6; ocultar

high school escuela secundaria (*f.*), 18

highway autopista (*f.*), 12

hillside ladera (*f.*)

him él, 4; lo, 6; le, 7

himself se, 9

his su(s), 3; suyo(-a)(s), 9

history historia (*f.*), 3

hold estrechar; — **tightly** oprimir

home casa (*f.*), hogar (*m.*); — **appliance** aparato electro-doméstico (*m.*), 10; — **page** propia página (*f.*)

honest honrado(-a)

honey miel de abeja (*f.*), 15

honeymoon luna de miel (*f.*), 11

hood capó (*m.*), 12

hope esperar, 11; esperanza (*f.*); **I —** ojalá, 11

horn bocina (*f.*), 12

horse caballo (*m.*); — **rider** jinete (*m., f.*)

hospital hospital (*m.*), 2

hot caliente; — **chocolate** chocolate caliente (*m.*), 5; — **dog** perro caliente (*m.*), 5; **to be —** tener calor, 4; (*weather*) hacer calor, 5; **nice and —** bien caliente, 15

hotel hotel (*m.*), 7

hour hora (*f.*)

house casa (*f.*), 2

housework quehaceres (trabajo) de la casa, 6

how? ¿cómo?, 1; — **are you?** ¿Cómo está Ud.? (*form. sing.*),1; ¿Cómo están ustedes? (*form. pl.*), 1; ¿Cómo estás? (*fam.*), 1; ¿Qué tal?, 1; — **do you do?** Mucho gusto., 1; — **does one say . . . ?** ¿Cómo se dice…?, 2; — **far in advance?** ¿Con cuánta anticipación?; — **is it going (for you)?** ¿Qué tal te va?, 14; ¿Cómo le va? (*form.*), ¿Cómo te va? (*fam.*); — **long . . . ?** ¿Cuánto tiempo hace que…?; — **many?** ¿cuántos(-as)?; — **may I help you?** ¿En qué puedo servirle?, 7; — **much?** ¿cuánto(-a)?; — **nice to see you!** ¡Qué gusto de verte!, 15; — **that?** ¿Cómo?

however sin embargo, 13

hug abrazo (*m.*), 4; abrazar, 8

hundred cien, ciento, 2

hungry: to be — tener hambre, 4

hunt cazar, 16

hurt doler (o:ue), 15; herir (e:ie)

husband esposo (*m.*), marido (*m.*), 5

I

I yo, 1

ice cream helado (*m.*), 5

iced tea té helado, 5

I.D. number número de identidad (*m.*), 3

idea idea (*f.*), 2

ideal (*adj.*) ideal, 11

if si, 14

imperfect imperfecto(-a)

import importación (*f.*), 17

impossible imposible, 5

impressed impresionado(-a), 17

improve mejorar, 9

in en, 1; por, 8; de, 16; a, 16; — **case** en caso de que, 14; — **charge** encargado(-a), 17; — **exchange for** por, 8; — **front of** frente a, 8; — **haste** presuroso(-a); — **order** para, 2; — **order that** para que, 14; — **order to** a, 3; para, 8; — **part** en parte, 14; — **search of** en busca de, 8; — **spite of** a pesar de (que), 9; — **that case** en ese caso, 2; entonces, 4; — **the afternoon** de (por) la tarde, 2; — **the evening** de (por) la noche, 2; — **the morning** de (por) la mañana, 2

include incluir, 10
income ingreso (*m.*)
increase aumento (*m.*), 17
Indeed I am. Lo soy.
indefinite indeterminado(-a)
indicative indicativo(-a)
inexpensive barato(-a), 13
influenza gripe (*f.*), 15
injection inyección (*f.*), 15; **to give an** — poner una inyección, 15
inside en, 16; dentro
insist on insistir en, 14
installments plazos (*m. pl.*), 8; **in (on)** — a plazos, 8
instant instantáneo(-a), 7
instead of en vez de, 17
insurance agent agente de seguros (*m., f.*), 17
intelligent inteligente, 3
interest interesar, 18
interesting interesante, 11
interior interior, 6
interpreter intérprete (*m., f.*), 17
interrogative interrogativo(-a)
interview entrevista (*f.*), 17; entrevistar, 17
invitation invitación (*f.*), 3
invite invitar (a), 18
invited invitado(-a), 4
iron planchar, 6; plancha (*f.*), 10
Is. . . (*name*) there? ¿Está... (*name*)?, 3
island isla (*f.*), 9
it la, 6; lo, 6
Italian (*lang.*) italiano (*m.*), 2
its su(s), 3
itself se, 9

J

jack gato (*m.*), 12
jail cárcel (*f.*)
January enero, 1
jewelry joyas (*f. pl.*), 13; — **store** joyería (*f.*), 9
job empleo (*m.*), trabajo (*m.*), 3; puesto (*m.*), 17; — **application** solicitud de trabajo (*f.*), 3
joint account cuenta conjunta (*f.*), 8
joke bromear, 12
journalism periodismo (*m.*), 14
joy gusto (*m.*)
joyful alegre, 4
juice jugo (*m.*), 5

July julio, 1
June junio, 1
jungle selva (tropical) (*f.*), 11
just in case por si acaso, 18

K

keep quedarse con; (*something going*) mantener; — **in mind** tener en cuenta
key llave (*f.*), 6
keyboard teclado (*m.*), 17
kid: to — (*joke*) bromear, 12
kindergarten jardín de infantes (infancia) (*m.*), 16
kindness bondad (*f.*)
king rey (*m.*)
kiss beso (*m.*)
kitchen cocina (*f.*), 5
knee rodilla (*f.*), 15
knife cuchillo (*m.*), 5
knight caballero (*m.*)
knock on the door tocar a la puerta, 6
know conocer, 6; saber, 6
knowledge conocimiento (*m.*), 3

L

laboratory laboratorio (*m.*), 14
lack falta (*f.*); — **of patience** impaciencia (*f.*)
lady señora (*f.*), 1
lake lago (*m.*)
lamb cordero (*m.*), 5
lamp lámpara (*f.*), 10
land tierra (*f.*), terreno (*m.*)
language idioma (*m.*); lengua (*f.*), 2
laptop computer microcomputadora (*f.*), computadora portátil (*f.*), 17
large grande, amplio, 10
last pasado(-a), 7; último(-a), 17; durar, 13; — **name** apellido (*m.*), 3; — **night** anoche, 7; — **time** última vez (*f.*)
late tarde, 2
later después, 3
laugh reírse (e:i), 12
laughter risa (*f.*)
lawyer abogado(-a) (*m., f.*), 14
leaf hoja (*f.*)
leafy frondoso(-a)
league liga (*f.*)
learn aprender (a), 3
leather cuero (*m.*), 13
leave (behind) dejar, 5; salir, 6; irse, 9; partir; — **alone** dejar tranquilo(-a), 16; — **the house** salir de casa, 8
lecture conferencia (*f.*)
left izquierdo(-a); **to the** — a la izquierda, 12
leg pierna (*f.*)
lend prestar, 8
less menos, 5; — **. . . than** menos... que, 5; — **than** + *number* menos de + *number*, 5; **more or** — más o menos, 3

let know avisar, 10
Let them wait! ¡Que esperen!, 18
let's go vamos, 2; — **shopping** vamos de compras, 13
let's see a ver, 3
letter carta (*f.*), 17
lettuce lechuga (*f.*), 9
liberty libertad (*f.*), 2
librarian bibliotecario(-a) (*m., f.*), 16
library biblioteca (*f.*), 14
license licencia; — **plate** chapa (*f.*), placa (*f.*) (*Mex.*), 12
life vida (*f.*)
lifeguard salvavidas (*m., f.*), 16
lift levantar, 9
light luz (*f.*), 2; (*adj.*) claro(-a), ligero(-a)
like gustar, 7
likewise igualmente, 1
lilac lila (*f.*), 8
line renglón (*m.*); (*of poetry*) verso (*m.*)
linen hilo (*m.*), lino (*m.*), 13
lip labio (*m.*)
listen oye, 1; escuchar, 12
literature literatura (*f.*), 3
litter tirar basura
little pequeño(-a); — **sister (brother)** hermanita(-o) (*f., m.*), 13; **a** — un poco (de), 2; **a** — + *adjective* un poco + *adjective*, 4
live vivir, 3
livestock ganadería (*f.*)
living room sala (*f.*), 3
loaded (with) cargado(-a) (con), 13
loan préstamo (*m.*), 8
lobster langosta (*f.*), 5
locate ubicar
location ubicación (*f.*)
lock cerradura (*f.*)
lodging hospedaje (*m.*), 11; alojamiento (*m.*)
loneliness soledad (*f.*)
long time mucho tiempo, 7
look (at) mirar, 5; — **for** buscar, 6; — **out the window** mirar por la ventana, 6; — **right through** atravesar (e:ie) con la mirada
lose perder (e:ie), 4
lot: a — muchísimo(-a), 7
love encantarle a uno, 8; amar; cariño (*m.*), 8; **in** — **(with)** enamorado(-a) (de), 16
loving amante (*adj.*)
loyal leal
luck suerte (*f.*), 8
luckily por suerte, 18
luggage equipaje (*m.*), 7
lunch almuerzo (*m.*), 7; **to have** — almorzar (o:ue), 5
luxury lujo (*m.*)

M

madam señora (*f.*), 1
made hecho(-a) (*p.p. of* hacer), 14
magazine revista (*f.*), 6

maid criada (*f.*), 10
maiden name apellido de soltera (*m.*)
main principal, 17; — **character** protagonista (*m., f.*), 18
maintain mantener, 14
major especialización (*f.*), 14
make hacer, 6; obligar, 12; realizar; — **a decision** tomar una decisión, 14; — **a movie** filmar, 18; — **fun of** burlarse de, 18; — **matters worse** para peor, 18
man hombre (*m.*)
manager gerente (*m., f.*), 17
mango mango, 9
many muchos(-as), 4
map mapa (*m.*), 2
March marzo, 1
Mardi Gras carnaval (*m.*)
margarine margarina (*f.*), 9
marital status estado civil (*m.*), 3
mark down rebajar, 13
market mercado (*m.*), 6
marketing mercadeo (*m.*), 17
marriage matrimonio (*m.*)
married casado(-a), 3
marry casarse (con), 18
mashed potatoes puré de papas (*m.*), 5
mass (*Catholic service*) misa (*f.*), 16
match combinar, hacer juego, 13
material tela, 13
math(ematics) matemáticas (*f. pl.*), 14
matter importarle a uno, 18
mattress colchón (*m.*), 7
May mayo, 1
maybe a lo mejor, 12; tal vez
me mí, 4; me (*d.o.*), 6; me (*i.o.*), 7
meal comida (*f.*), 5
mean querer decir
means medio (*m.*)
measure medida (*f.*)
meat carne (*f.*), 6; — **market** carnicería (*f.*), 9; — **turnover** empanada (*f.*)
mechanic mecánico (*m.*), 12
medicine medicina (*f.*), remedio (*m.*), 15
medium mediano(-a), 13
meet conocer, 10; encontrarse (o:ue) (con), 10
melt fundir
men hombres (*m. pl.*); — **'s department** departamento de (ropa para) caballeros (*m.*), 13
menu menú (*m.*), 5
merchant vendedor(-a) (*m., f.*)
merry alegre
meter métrica (*f.*) (*poetry*)
Mexican mexicano(-a), 1; — **American** mexicanoamericano(-a), 1
microwave microondas (*m.*), 10
middle name segundo nombre (*m.*)
midterm exam examen parcial (*m.*), examen de mitad de curso (*m.*), 3

midwife partera (*f.*)
mild templado(-a)
mile milla (*f.*), 12
milk leche (*f.*), 5
millionaire millonario(-a) (*m., f.*), 16
mine mío(-a), míos(-as), 9
mineral water agua mineral (*f.*), 5
mirror espejo (*m.*), 10
miss extrañar, 9; (*out on something*) perderse (e:ie), 18
Miss señorita (Srta.) (*f.*), 1
mister señor (Sr.), 1
mix mezclar
mixture mezcla (*f.*)
modern moderno(-a), 12
mom mamá (*f.*), 1
moment momento (*m.*), 3
Monday lunes (*m.*), 1
money dinero (*m.*), 2
monkey mono (*m.*), 8
month mes (*m.*), 1; **a (per)** — al (por) mes, 12
moon luna (*f.*), 11
mop the floor trapear el piso, 6
more más, 2; — **or less** más o menos, 3
most el (la) más, 5
mother madre (*f.*), 1
motherhood maternidad
mother-in-law suegra (*f.*), 6
motorcycle motocicleta (*f.*), moto (*f.*), 8
mountain montaña (*f.*), 4; sierra (*f.*), monte (*m.*)
mouse ratón (*m.*), 17
mouth boca (*f.*), 15
move (*from one house to another*) mudarse, 10
movie película (*f.*), 7; — **director** director(-a) de cine (*m., f.*), 18; — **screen** pantalla (*f.*), 18; — **section** (*of newspaper*) cartelera (*f.*), 18; — **theater** cine (*m.*), 4
mow the lawn cortar el césped, 6
Mr. señor (*m.*), Sr., 1
Mrs. señora (*f.*), Sra., 1
much mucho(-a), 1
muddy turbio(-a)
murder mystery película de misterio (*f.*), 18
museum museo (*m.*), 4
music música (*f.*), 18
musical musical, 18; — **instrument** instrumento musical (*m.*), 9
musician músico (*m.*), 18
must deber, 3
my mi(s), 1; — **love** mi amor; — **name is . . .** Me llamo..., 1
myself me, 9
mystery (*movie*) película de misterio (*f.*), 18

N

name nombre (*m.*), 3; nombrar; **My — is . . .** Me llamo..., 1; **first —** nombre (*m.*), 3; **What's your —?**

¿Cómo se llama Ud.? (*form.*), 1; ¿Cómo te llamas? (*fam.*), 1
napkin servilleta (*f.*), 5
narrow estrecho(-a), 13
nation nación (*f.*); pueblo (*m.*)
nationality nacionalidad (*f.*), 3
natural ínsito(-a)
near (*adv.*) cerca, 10
necessary necesario(-a), 3
neck cuello (*m.*), 15
necklace collar (*m.*), 13
need necesitar, 2
negative negativo(-a)
neighbor vecino(-a) (*m., f.*), 4
neighborhood barrio (*m.*), vecindad (*f.*), 10
neither tampoco, 6; — **. . . nor** ni... ni, 6
nephew sobrino (*m.*), 4
nervous nervioso(-a), 4
never nunca, jamás, 6
new nuevo(-a), 1
New Year Año Nuevo (*m.*), 4
newspaper diario (*m.*), periódico (*m.*), 3
next próximo(-a), 6; que viene, 11; entrante, 18; — **to** al lado de, 13; — **month** el mes entrante (*m.*), 18; — **week** la semana que viene (*f.*), la semana próxima, 4
nice simpático(-a), 3; — **to meet you.** Mucho gusto., 1
niece sobrina (*f.*), 4
night noche (*f.*), 2; — **table** mesita de noche (*f.*), 10
nightgown camisón (*m.*), 13
nine nueve, 1; — **hundred** novecientos(-as), 3
nineteen diecinueve, 1
ninety noventa, 2
ninth noveno(-a), 7
no no, 1; ningún, ninguna, 6; — **one** nadie, 6; — **smoking section** sección de no fumar (*f.*), 11; — **wonder** con razón, 3
nobody nadie, 6
nocturne nocturno (*m.*)
noise ruido (*m.*)
none ninguno(-a), ningún, 6
noodle soup sopa de fideos (*f.*), 5
nor ni, 6
neither . . . — . . . ni... ni..., 6
north norte (*m.*), 16
North American norteamericano(-a), 2
nose nariz (*f.*), 15
not no, 1; — **any** ninguno(-a), 6; — **to be proud at all** no ser nada orgulloso(-a), 16; — **either** tampoco, 6; — **working** descompuesto(-a), 12
notebook cuaderno (*m.*), 2
nothing nada, 1; — **but** no... más que
notice fijarse en, 18
noun nombre (*m.*), sustantivo (*m.*)

November noviembre, 1
now ahora, 4
nowadays hoy en día, 18; actualmente
nowhere en ningún lado, en ninguna parte, 11
number número (*m.*), 1
nursing home casa de ancianos (*f.*)
nutrition nutrición (*f.*), 14

O

object objeto (*m.*)
obtain conseguir (e:i), 6
occupation ocupación (*f.*), 3
October octubre, 1
of de, 1; — **course** por supuesto, 7
offer ofrecer, 17
office oficina (*f.*), 13, despacho (*m.*), 17
often a menudo, frecuentemente, 12
oil aceite (*m.*), 9
old viejo(-a); **to be ... years —** tener... años, 4
older mayor, 5
oldest el (la) mayor, 5
olive aceituna (*f.*); — **oil** aceite de oliva (*m.*)
on en, 16; — **account of** por, 8; — **behalf of** por, 8; — **the other hand** por otro lado, 13; — **the phone** al (por) teléfono, 3
once una vez, 16
one uno, 1; — **says** se dice, 2; — **way (ticket)** de ida, 11
onion cebolla (*f.*), 9
only solamente, sólo, 10 ; — **thing** lo único, 14
open abrir, 3; abierto(-a), 12; — **an account** abrir una cuenta, 8
opened abierto (*p.p. of* abrir), 14
opportunity oportunidad (*f.*), 13
optimist(ic) optimista (*m., f.*), 3
or o, 6
orange anaranjado(-a), 1; naranja (*f.*), 9
orchestra orquesta (*f.*), 18
orchid orquídea (*f.*), 8
order pedir (e:i), 5; mandar, 11; pedido (*m.*), 5; orden (*f.*)
other otro(-a), 2; — **person's right** derecho ajeno (*m.*)
others los (las) demás
our nuestro(-a)(-os)(-as), 3
ours nuestro(-a)(s), 9
ourselves nos, 9
out of breath echando el bofe
out of order descompuesto(-a), 12
outdoor activity actividad al aire libre, 16
outline bosquejo (*m.*)
outside fuera
oven horno (*m.*), 10
over en, 16
overlook dar hacia
overlooking con vista a, 6

own propio(-a)
oyster ostra (*f.*), 16

P

pack hacer las maletas
package paquete (*m.*), 11
pain dolor (*m.*)
painting cuadro (*m.*), 10
pair par (*m.*), 13
palm (tree) palma (*f.*), 9
pansy pensamiento (*m.*), 8
pantry alacena (*f.*)
pants pantalones (*m. pl.*), 8
pantyhose pantimedias (*f. pl.*), 13
Pardon me. Perdón., 1
parents padres (*m. pl.*)
park parque (*m.*), 4; aparcar, estacionar, parquear, 8
parrot loro (*m.*), 8
partner compañero(-a) (*m., f.*)
party fiesta (*f.*), 1
pass (*an exam or course*) aprobar (o:ue), 14; — **away** fallecer, 9
passport pasaporte (*m.*), 7
past (*time*) y, 2
path sendero (*m.*)
pay pagar, 5
peace paz (*f.*)
peach durazno (*m.*), melocotón (*m.*), 9
pen pluma (*f.*), 2; bolígrafo (*m.*), 2; — **name** nombre de pluma (*m.*)
pencil lápiz (*m.*), 2
people (*nation*) pueblo (*m.*)
pepper pimienta (*f.*), 5
per por, 8
perfect perfecto(-a), 2
perfectly perfectamente, 15
perform (*a job*) desempeñar, 17
perhaps quizás, 13
period etapa (*f.*)
person persona (*f.*), 4
personnel personal, 17
pessimist(ic) pesimista (*m., f.*), 3
pet mascota (*f.*), 8
pharmacy farmacia (*f.*), 9
philosophy filosofía (*f.*), 17
phone book guía telefónica (*f.*)
phone number número de teléfono (*m.*), **photocopy machine** fotocopiadora (*f.*), 17
photo(graph) fotografía (*f.*), foto (*f.*), 4
physical education educación física (*f.*), 14
physician médico(-a) (*m., f.*), 15
physics física (*f.*), 14
piano piano (*m.*), 9
pick up recoger, 6; buscar, 6
picture cuadro (*m.*), 10
pie pastel (*m.*), 5
piece pedazo (*m.*), trozo (*m.*), 5; — **of news** noticia (*f.*), 7
pillow almohada (*f.*), 10
pillowcase funda (*f.*), 10
pine tree pino (*m.*), 16
pineapple piña (*f.*), 9

pink rosado(-a), 1
pinnacle cumbre (*f.*)
pitch (a tent) armar, 16
pity: it's a — es una lástima, 11
place lugar (*m.*), 6; poner, 6; — **of birth** lugar de nacimiento (*m.*), 3; — **of employment** lugar donde trabaja (*m.*), 3
plaid de cuadros, 13
plain llanura (*f.*), llano (*m.*)
plan pensar (e:ie) (+ *inf.*), 4; planear, 1
plane avión (*m.*), 11
plastic plástico (*m.*), 16
plateau altiplano (*m.*)
plate plato (*m.*), 5
platform andén (*m.*)
play (*instrument*) tocar, 9; jugar (u:ue), 16; obra teatral (de teatro) (*f.*), 18; — **golf** jugar (u:ue) al golf (*m.*), 16; — **tennis** jugar (u:ue) al tenis (*m.*), 16
playwright dramaturgo(-a) (*m., f.*)
plead rogar (o:ue), 11
please por favor, 1
pleasure: The — is mine. El gusto es mío., 1
plot trama (*f.*), 18
plumber plomero(-a) (*m., f.*), 14
pluperfect pluscuamperfecto
P.M. de la tarde, 2
pneumonia pulmonía (*f.*), 15
poem poema (*m.*), 2
poetry poesía (*f.*)
police policía (*f.*)
policeman policía (*m.*), 8
policewoman agente de policía (*f.*), 8
polite amable, cortés, 3
polka-dotted de lunares, 13
polyester poliéster (*m.*), 13
pool piscina (*f.*), 7
poor pobre (*unfortunate*), 4; — **thing** pobrecito(-a) (*m., f.*), 8
pork lechón (*m.*), 5
portrait retrato (*m.*)
Portuguese (*lang.*) portugués (*m.*), 2
position puesto (*m.*), 17; cargo (*m.*)
post office correo (*m.*), oficina de correos (*f.*), 12
postcard tarjeta postal (*f.*), 7
potato papa (*f.*), 5
pound libra (*f.*)
poverty pobreza (*f.*)
power poder (*m.*)
practice practicar, 2
prefer preferir (e:ie), 4
pregnant embarazada, 15
première estreno (*m.*), 18
prepare preparar, 4
prescribe recetar, 15
prescription receta (*f.*), 15
present regalo (*m.*), 8; presentar, 18
president presidente(-a) (*m., f.*), 17
pretend fingir
pretty bonito(-a), lindo(-a), 3; precioso(-a), 13

prevail prevalecer
preview avance (*m.*), 18
print (*fabric*) estampado(-a), 13
printer impresora (*f.*), 17
privateer corsario (*m.*)
probable probable, 8
probably probablemente, 8
problem problema (*m.*), 2
producer productor(-a) (*m., f.*), 18
profession profesión (*f.*), 3
professor profesor(-a) (*m., f.*), 1
program programa (*m.*), 2
programmer programador(-a), (*m., f.*), 14
programming programación (*f.*), 18
promise prometer, 7
propose proponer, 14
protagonist protagonista (*m., f.*), 18
proud orgulloso(-a), 16
provided that con tal (de) que, 14
psychology sicología (*f.*), 14
public relations agent agente de relaciones públicas (*m., f.*), 17
publish publicar
Puerto Rican puertorriqueño(-a) (*m., f.*), 3
pull someone's leg tomarle el pelo (a alguien), 18
punch ponche (*m.*), 4
purchase compra (*f.*), 17
purchasing department departmento de compras (*m.*), 17
purchasing manager jefe(-a) de compras (*m., f.*), 17
purple morado(-a), 1
purse bolso (*m.*), 9
put poner, 6; (*p.p. of* poner) puesto, 14; **— in a cast** enyesar, 15; **— on** ponerse, 9; **— to bed** acostar (o:ue), 9

Q

quarter after/past ...y cuarto (*time*), 2
quarter of/to ...menos cuarto (*time*), 2
queen reina (*f.*)
question pregunta (*f.*), 4
Quick! ¡Rápido!, 6
quite bastante, 14

R

rabbit conejo, 8
racket raqueta (*f.*), 16
rain lluvia (*f.*), 5; llover (o:ue), 5
raincoat impermeable (*m.*)
raise levantar, 9
rapid rápido(-a), 8
rapidly rápidamente, 8
rare raro(-a)
rate of exchange cambio de moneda (*m.*)
rayon rayón (*m.*), 13
razor máquina de afeitar (*f.*)
read leer, 3; (*p.p.*) leído, 14
reader lector(-a) (*m., f.*)

ready-to-wear clothes ropa hecha (*f.*)
real verdadero(-a), 18; **— estate agent** agente de bienes raíces (*m., f.*), 17
realist(ic) realista (*m., f.*), 3
realize darse cuenta (de), 14
reason razón (*f.*)
receive recibir, 3; (*grade*) sacar, 14
recent reciente, 8
recently recientemente, 8
recipe receta (*f.*), 9
recommend recomendar (e:ie), 11
recommendation recomendación (*f.*), 17
red rojo(-a), 1; (*wine*) tinto, 5; colorado(-a)
red-headed pelirrojo(-a), 3
refrain estribillo (*m.*)
refugee refugiado(-a) (*m., f.*)
refuse no querer (e:ie), 10
regarding en cuanto a
register matricularse, 14
registered matriculado(-a), 14
registration recepción (*desk*) (*f.*), 7; matrícula (*f.*), 14
regret sentir (e:ie), 11
rehearse ensayar, 18
relative pariente (*m., f.*), 6
remain seated quedar(-se) sentado (-a)
remember recordar (o:ue), 5; acordarse (o:ue) (de), 9
rent alquiler (*m.*), 10; alquilar, 10
repair arreglar, 12; arreglo (*m.*), 12; **— shop** taller de mecánica (*m.*), 12
report informe (*m.*), 3
request pedir (e:i), 6
requirement requisito (*m.*), 14
research investigación (*f.*), 14
reservation reserva (*f.*), reservación (*f.*), 7
resign renunciar
resort balneario
responsibility responsabilidad (*f.*), 17
rest el resto (*m.*), 10; descansar, 15
restaurant restaurante (*m.*), 4
résumé resumé (*m.*), 17
return regresar, 2; volver (o:ue), 5; (*some thing*) devolver (o:ue), 7
returned (*p.p.*) (de)vuelto(-a), 14
revolution revolución (*f.*), 9
reward recompensa (*f.*)
rice arroz (*m.*), 5; **— pudding** arroz con leche (*m.*), 5
ride (*a bicycle*) montar en bicicleta, 16; (*a horse*) montar a caballo, 16
right derecho (*m.*); (*adj.*) derecho (-a); **to the —** a la derecha, 12; **—?** ¿verdad?, 1; **— away** en seguida, 6
to be — tener razón, 4
ring anillo (*m.*), 13; (*phone*) sonar (o:ue), 15
roasted asado(-a), 9
rock mecer

role papel (*m.*)
romantic romántico(-a), 11
room cuarto (*m.*), habitación (*f.*), 4; sitio (*m.*); **— service** servicio de habitación (cuarto) (*m.*), 7
roommate compañero(-a) de cuarto (*m., f.*), 3
root raíz (*f.*)
rose rosa (*f.*), 8
round-trip de ida y vuelta, 11
row remar, 16
run correr, 3; **— errands** hacer diligencias, 8

S

sad triste, 4
saddlebag alforja (*f.*)
said (*p.p. of* decir) dicho, 14
sailboat velero (*m.*), 16
saint's day santo (*m.*)
salad ensalada (*f.*), 5
salary salario (*m.*), sueldo (*m.*), 17
sale liquidación (*f.*), rebaja (*f.*), 13
salesperson vendedor(-a) (*m., f.*), 1
salt sal (*f.*), 5
same mismo(-a), 10
sand arena (*f.*), 16
sandwich sándwich (*m.*), 3
Saturday sábado (*m.*), 1
sauce salsa (*f.*), 9
saucepan cacerola (*f.*), 10
saucer platillo (*m.*), 5
sausage chorizo (*m.*)
save ahorrar, 8
savings ahorros (*m. pl.*); **— account** cuenta de ahorros (*f.*), 8; **— passbook** libreta de ahorros (*f.*), 8
say decir (e:i), 6
schedule horario (*m.*), 14
scholarship beca (*f.*), 14
school escuela (*f.*), 10; facultad (*f.*), 14
science ciencia (*f.*), 14; **— fiction** ciencia ficción (*f.*), 18
scorn despreciar
screen pantalla (*f.*), 17; **—play** guión (*m.*), 18
script guión (*m.*), 18
scuba dive bucear, 16
sea mar (*m.*), 7
search búsqueda (*f.*)
season estación (*f.*), 1
seated sentado(-a), 14
second segundo(-a), 6; **—World War** Segunda Guerra Mundial (*f.*)
see ver, 6; **— you.** Nos vemos., 1
seem parecer, 13; antojársele (a uno)
seen (*p.p. of* ver) visto(-a), 14
selection selección (*f.*), 17
sell vender, 3
send enviar, mandar, 7
sensitivity sensibilidad (*f.*)
sentence oración (*f.*)
September septiembre, 1
seriously? ¿en serio?, 2
serve servir (e:i), 6

set out to proponerse

seven siete, 1; **— hundred** setecientos(-as), 3

seventeen diecisiete, 1

seventh séptimo(-a), 7

seventy setenta, 2

shadow sombra (f.)

shake hands darse la mano

shame: it's a — es una lástima, 11

share compartir, 9

shareholder accionista (m., f.), 17

shark tiburón (m.)

shave afeitar(se), 9

she ella, 1

sheep oveja (f.)

sheet sábana (f.), 6

ship barco (m.), 11

shirt camisa (f.), 6

shoe zapato (m.), 13; **— store** zapatería (f.), 9

shoot fusilar, pasar por las armas

shopping: to go — ir de compras, 13

shopping mall centro comercial (m.), 13

short bajo(-a), 3; corto(-a), 9

shot inyección (f.), 15; **to give a —** poner una inyección, 15

shotgun escopeta (f.), 16

should deber, 3

show mostrar (o:ue), 6; espectáculo (m.), 18; **— a movie** pasar (dar) una película, 7; **— for the first time** estrenar, 18

shower ducha (f.), 7

shrimp camarones (m. pl.), 5

sick enfermo(-a), 4

sigh suspirar, 6

sign firmar, 8; señal (f.); signo (m.)

signature firma (f.), 8

silently sin ruido

silk seda (f.), 13

silver plata (f.)

since desde, 6; como, 7

sincere sincero(-a), 9

sing cantar, 4

single soltero(-a), 3; **— room** habitación sencilla (f.), 7

sir señor, 1

sister hermana (f.), 4

sister-in-law cuñada (f.), 6

sit down sentarse (e:ie), 9

sitting sentado(-a), 14

six seis, 1; **— hundred** seiscientos(-as), 3

sixteen dieciséis, 1

sixth sexto(-a), 7

sixty sesenta, 2

size medida (f.), talla (f.), 13; (of shoes) número (m.), 13; tamaño (m.)

skate patinar, 16

ski esquiar, 16

skillet sartén (f.), 10

skirt falda (f.), 13

sky cielo (m.)

skyscraper rascacielos (m. sing.)

slave esclavo(-a) (m., f.)

sleep dormir (o:ue), 5

sleeping bag saco de dormir (m.), bolsa de dormir (f.), 10

sleepy: to be — tener sueño, 4

sleeve manga (f.)

slender delgado(-a), 3

slice rodaja (f.)

slippers zapatillas (f., pl.), 15

slow lento(-a), 8

slowly lentamente, 8; despacio

small chico(-a), 10; pequeño(-a); **to be too — (on someone)** quedar(le) chico(-a) (a uno), 13

smile sonreír

smog contaminación del aire (f.)

smoke fumar

smoking: (no) smoking section sección de (no) fumar (f.), 11

snow nevar (e:ie), 5; nieve (f.), 16

so de manera (modo) que, 9; tan, 17; así que, 18; **— be it.** Sea.; **— much** tanto, 11

soap jabón (m.), 7; **— opera** telenovela (f.), 5

soccer fútbol (m.), 16

social security number número de seguro social (m.), 3

sociology sociología (f.), 14

sock calcetín (m.), 13

soda pop refresco (m.), 5; soda (f.), 4

sofa sofá (m.), 6

some unos(-as), 2; algunos(-as), 6; alguno(-a), algún, 6

somebody alguien, 6

someone alguien, 6

something algo, 6

sometimes a veces

son hijo (m.), 4

son-in-law yerno (m.), 6

song canción (f.), 9

soon pronto, 16; **as — as** en cuanto, tan pronto como, 14; **—er or later** tarde o temprano, 18

sorrow pena (f.)

soul alma (f.)

sound sonido (m.)

sound track banda sonora (f.), 18

soup sopa (f.), 5

source fuente (f.)

south sur (m.), 16

Spanish (lang.) español (m.), 2

spare part pieza de repuesto (f.), 12

speak hablar, 2

special especial, 5; **— effect** efecto especial (m.), 18

specialized especializado(-a), 17

speed limit velocidad máxima (f.), 12

spell deletrear

spelling deletreo (m.)

spend (time) pasar, 4

spoon cuchara (f.), 5

spoonful cucharada (f.)

sport deporte (m.), 16

spring primavera (f.), 1

stadium estadio (m.), 16

stairs escalera (f.), 7

stand out destacarse

stand somebody up dejar plantado (-a) a alguien, 18

standard shift de cambios mecánicos, 12

stanza estrofa (f.)

start comenzar (e:ie), empezar (e:ie), 4; arrancar (car), 12; entablar

state estado (m.)

stay quedarse, 11; hospedarse (en) (at a hotel), 11

steak bistec (m.), biftec (m.), 5

steal robar, 8

steering wheel volante (m.), 12

stepbrother hermanastro (m.), 6

stepdaughter hijastra (f.), 6

stepfather padrastro (m.), 6

stepmother madrastra (f.), 6

stepsister hermanastra (f.), 6

stepson hijastro (m.), 6

stereo system equipo estereofónico (m.), 4

stir revolver (o:ue)

stockbroker bolsista (m., f.), 17

stomach estómago (m.), 15

stone piedra (f.)

stop detenerse; **— (something)** detener + d.o.

stopover: to make a — hacer escala, 11

store tienda (f.), 8

stranger extraño(-a) (m., f.)

straw (for mate) bombilla (f.)

strawberry fresa (f.), 9

street calle (f.), 2

stretch estirar

striped de rayas, 13

stubborn terco(-a), 3

student estudiante (m., f.), 1

study estudiar, 2

stupidity torpeza (f.)

subject tema (m.), 2; (course) asignatura, materia, 14

subsidized subvencionado(-a)

subway metro (m.), subterráneo (m.), 10

success éxito (m.)

Such bad luck! ¡Qué mala suerte!, 8

Such is life. Así es la vida.

suddenly de pronto, de repente, 18

sugar azúcar (m.), 9; **— cane** caña de azúcar (f.)

suggest sugerir (e:ie), 11

suit traje (m.), 13; **— one to perfection** venirle de perillas a uno, 18

suitcase maleta (f.); valija (f.), 7

summary resumen (m.)

summer verano (m.), 1

sun sol (m.)

sunbathe tomar el sol, 16

Sunday domingo (m.), 1

sunny: to be — hacer sol, 5
super (*of a building*) encargado(-a) (*m., f.*), 10
supermarket supermercado (*m.*), 9
supervision supervisión (*f.*), 17
supervisor supervisor(-a) (*m., f.*), 17
supper cena (*f.*), 7
sure seguro(-a), 8
surf hacer surfing, 16
surfboard tabla de mar (*f.*), 16
surprise sorpresa (*f.*), 8; sorprender, 11
surrounded rodeado(-a)
sweater suéter (*m.*)
sweep barrer, 6
sweet dulce
sweets dulces (*m. pl.*)
swim nadar, 7
swimming pool piscina (*f.*), alberca (*f.*) (*Mex.*), 7
sword espada (*f.*)
symptom síntoma (*m.*), 15
system sistema (*m.*)

T

T-shirt camiseta (*f.*), 13
table . mesa (*f.*), 4
tablecloth mantel (*m.*), 5
tail cola (*f.*)
tailor sastre (*m.*)
take tomar, 2; (*someone or something someplace*) llevar, 3; (*a taxi*), 6 ; **— a picture** sacar (tomar) una foto, 4; **— advantage of** aprovechar, 15; **— an X-ray** hacer una radiografía, 15; **— away** quitar, 9; llevarse, 11; **— charge** hacerse cargo; **— off** quitarse, 9; **— out the garbage** sacar la basura, 6; **— place** tener lugar
talk conversar, platicar, 2; hablar, 2
tall alto(-a), 3
tank tanque (*m.*), 12
tape grabar, 18
taste probar (o:ue), 9
tasty sabroso(-a), rico(-a), 5
taxi taxi (*m.*), 6
tea té (*m.*), 5
teach enseñar (a), 18
teacher (*elementary school*) maestro(-a) (*m., f.*), 7
tear despedazar
tease tomarle el pelo (a alguien), 18
teaspoon cucharita (*f.*), 5
teenager adolescente (*m., f.*), 7
teeth dientes (*m. pl.*), 15
telephone teléfono (*m.*), 1; **— system** sistema de comunicación telefónica (*m.*), 17
television televisión (*f.*), 2
tell decir (e:i), 6; contar (o:ue), 8
temperature temperatura (*f.*), 15
ten diez, 1
tenderness ternura (*f.*)
tennis tenis (*m.*), 16; **— shoes** zapatos de tenis (*m. pl.*), 13

tent tienda de campaña (*f.*), 16
tenth décimo(-a), 7
tetanus shot inyección antitetánica (*f.*), 15
than que, 5
thank you gracias, 1; **— very much.** Muchas gracias., 1
thanks gracias, 1
that (*adj.*) que, 4; aquel(la), 6; (*adj.*) ese, 6; (*adj.*) esa, 6; (*neuter pron.*) aquello, 6; (*neuter pron.*) eso, 6; **— is to say** es decir; **— one** aquél(la), 7; ése, 7; ésa, 7; **— which** lo que, 6; **— which is +** *adj.* lo + *adj.*; **—'s why** por eso, 18
the el, la, las, los, 2
theater teatro (*m.*), 4
their su(s), 3
theirs suyo(-a)(s), 9
them ellas, ellos, 4; las, 6; los, 6; les, 7
theme tema (*m.*), 2
themselves se, 9
then entonces (*in that case*), 4
there allí; **— are, is** hay, 1
these (*adj.*) estos(-as), 7; (*pron.*) éstos(-as), 7
they ellos 1; ellas, 1
thin delgado(-a), 3
thing cosa (*f.*), 6
think creer, 3; pensar (e:ie), 4; **— about** pensar en, 18
third tercero(-a), tercer, 7
thirsty: to be — tener sed, 4
thirteen trece, 1
thirty treinta, 1
this (*adj.*) este, esta, 6; (*neuter pron.*), esto, 6; **— is he (she) speaking.** Con él (ella) habla., 3
those (*adj.*) aquellos(-as), 6; (*pron.*) aquéllos(-as), 6; (*adj.*) esos(-as), 6; (*pron.*) ésos(-as), 6
thousand mil, 3; millar (*m.*)
three tres, 1; **— hundred** trescientos(-as), 3
thriller película de suspenso (*f.*), 18
throat garganta (*f.*), 15
through por, 8
Thursday jueves (*m.*), 1
ticket (*for plane, train, bus*) pasaje (*m.*), 11; (*to an event*) boleto (*m.*), entrada (*f.*), 16; (*fine*) multa (*f.*), 8; **one-way —** billete (pasaje) de ida (*m.*), 11; **round-trip —** billete (pasaje) de ida y vuelta (*m.*), 11
tidy up arreglar, 6
tie corbata (*f.*), 13; **— together** apretar (e:ie)
tile teja (*f.*); (*ceramic*) azulejo (*m.*)
till menos (*telling time*), 2
time hora (*f.*), 2; tiempo, 2; vez (*in a series*) (*f.*), 4; **for the first —** por primera vez, 4; **have a good —** divertirse (e:ie), 16; **What — is it?** ¿Qué hora es?, 2

tip propina (*f.*), 5
tire llanta (*f.*), neumático (*m.*), 12
tired cansado(-a), 4
to (*telling time*) menos, 2; a, 2; para, 3
toaster tostadora (*f.*), 10
today hoy, 1
toe dedo del pie (*m.*), 15
together juntos(-as), 13
toilet paper papel higiénico (*m.*), 9
tomato tomate (*m.*), 9
tomb sepulcro (*m.*)
tomorrow mañana, 3; **— and not a day later** mañana mismo, 17
tongue lengua (*f.*), 15
tonight esta noche, 2
too también, 2; demasiado(-a), 8
touch toque (*m.*)
tourism turismo (*m.*), 7
tourist turista (*m., f.*), 11; **— card** tarjeta de turista (*f.*), 7; **— class** clase turista (*f.*), 11
tow truck grúa (*f.*), remolcador (*m.*), 12
towards hacia, 5
towel toalla (*f.*), 7
tower torre (*f.*)
town pueblo (*m.*), 11
trade oficio (*m.*), 14
tradition tradición (*f.*), 4
tragic trágico(-a)
train tren (*m.*), 11
tranquility tranquilidad (*f.*)
translate traducir, 6
translator traductor(-a) (*m., f.*), 17
travel viajar, 7; **— agency** agencia de viajes (*f.*), 11; **— agent** agente de viajes (*m., f.*), 11
traveler viajero(-a) (*m., f.*), 11
traveler's check cheque de viajeros (*m.*), 6
traveling de viaje, 11
tremble temblar
trip viaje (*m.*), 4
trousers pantalón (*m.*), pantalones (*m. pl.*), 8
truck camión (*m.*), 13
true cierto
trumpet trompeta (*f.*), 9
true? ¿verdad?, 11
trunk (*car*) maletero (*m.*), cajuela (*f.*), 12
trust confiar
truth verdad (*f.*), 6
try probar (o:ue), 9; **— on** probarse (o:ue), 9
Tuesday martes (*m.*), 1
tuition matrícula (*f.*), 14
tulip tulipán (*m.*), 8
turkey pavo (*m.*), 5
turn doblar, 12; **— ... years old** cumplir ...años, 9; **— in** entregar, 14; **— over** voltear; **— to** recurrir a
turtle tortuga (*f.*), 8

TV set televisor (*m.*), 7
twelve doce, 1
twenty veinte, 1; — **-one** veintiuno, 1; — **-two** veintidós, 1; — **-three** veintitrés, 1; — **-four** veinticuatro, 1; — **-five** veinticinco, 1; — **-six** veintiséis, 1; — **-seven** veintisiete, 1; — **-eight** veintiocho, 1; — **-nine** veintinueve, 1
twilight crepúsculo (*m.*)
two dos, 1; — **hundred** doscientos(-as), 3
type tipo (*m.*), 15; escribir a máquina, 17
tyrant tirano(-a) (*m., f.*)

U

ugly feo(-a), 3
umbrella paraguas (*m. sing.*)
uncle tío (*m.*), 4
under debajo de, 6; bajo, 17
understand entender (e:ie), 4
underwear ropa interior (*f.*), 13
unfortunate desafortunado(-a), 8
unfortunately desgraciadamente, por desgracia, desafortunadamente, 8
ungrateful (*adj.*) desagradecido(-a)
United States Estados Unidos (*m. pl.*)
university universidad (*f.*), 1; (*adj.*) universitario(-a), 3
unless a menos que, 14
unpleasant antipático(-a), 3
untie lines soltar (o:ue) amarras
until hasta, 7; hasta que, 14
untimely a deshoras
up to now hasta ahora, 14
us (*obj. of prep.*) nosotros(-as), 4; nos, 6, 7
use usar, 6
used usado(-a), 12
usefulness utilidad (*f.*)

V

vacant libre, 7; desocupado(-a), 10
vacate the room desocupar el cuarto, 7
vacation vacaciones (*f. pl.*), 7
vacuum pasar la aspiradora, 6
value valor (*m.*)
VCR videograbadora (*f.*), 17
vegetable verdura (*f.*), vegetal (*m.*), 5
verb verbo (*m.*)
very muy, 1; (**not**) — **well** (no) muy bien, 1
video camera cámara de video (*f.*), 7
vinegar vinagre (*m.*), 9
violet violeta (*f.*), 8
violin violín (*m.*), 9
visit visitar, 4 ; — **frequently** frecuentar
vocabulary vocabulario (*m.*)
volleyball vóleibol (*m.*), 16

W

wait (for) esperar, 9; aguardar
waiter camarero (*m.*), mozo (*m.*), 5

waiting list lista de espera (*f.*), 7
waitress camarera (*f.*), 5
wake up despertarse (e:ie), 9
walk caminar, ir a pie, ir caminando, 12
wall pared (*f.*), 2
wallet billetera (*f.*), cartera (*f.*), 13
wandering errabundo
want querer (e:ie), 4; desear, 11
war guerra (*f.*), 18
warning advertencia (*f.*)
wash lavar(se), 9; — **dishes** lavar los platos, fregar (e:ie) los platos, 6; — **one's hair** lavarse la cabeza, 9
washing machine lavadora (*f.*), 10
wastebasket cesto de papeles (*m.*), 2
watch mirar, 5
water agua (*f.*), 4; — **ski** esquí acuático (*m.*), 16
watermelon sandía (*f.*), 9
wave ola (*f.*)
way modo (*m.*)
we nosotros(-as), 1
wear usar; — **a certain (shoe) size** calzar, 13; **not to have anything to** — no tener nada que ponerse, 13
weather tiempo (*m.*); — **forecast** pronóstico del tiempo; **to be good (bad)** — hacer buen (mal) tiempo, 6; **What's the weather like?** ¿Qué tiempo hace?, 6
weatherbeaten curtido(-a)
wedding boda (*f.*), 18
Wednesday miércoles (*m.*), 1
week semana (*f.*), 4
weekend fin de semana (*m.*), 4
weigh pesar
welcome bienvenido(-a), 4; **You're** —. De nada., 1
well bien, 1; pues, 6; —… **okay** bueno…, 1
west oeste (*m.*), 16
western (movie) película del oeste (de vaqueros) (*f.*), 18
what cuál, 1; qué, 2; lo que, 6; — **a pity!** ¡Qué lástima!, 15; — **do you think about** . . .? ¿Qué les parece si…?, 13; — **for?** ¿Para qué?, 18; — **is the rate of exchange?** ¿A cómo está el cambio de moneda?, 7; — **is your name?** ¿Cómo se llama Ud.? (*form.*), 1; ¿Cómo te llamas? (*fam.*), 1; — **is your phone number?** ¿Cuál es tu número de teléfono?, 1; — **the heck!** ¡Qué diablo!; — **time is it?** ¿Qué hora es?, 2; — **'s the date today?** ¿A cuánto estamos hoy?, 18; — **'s up (new)?** ¿Qué hay (de nuevo)?, 1
wheat trigo (*m.*)
wheelchair silla de ruedas (*f.*), 15
when? ¿cuándo?, 2; cuando, 14
where? ¿dónde?, 1; ¿adónde? (*destination*)
which? ¿cuál?, 1; (*rel. pron.*) que, 10

while mientras, 3; **a** — un rato, 4; **for a** — por un tiempo, 12
white blanco(-a), 1
who (*rel. pron.*) que, 4; quien(es), 10
whom quien, quienes, 10
whose de quién
why? ¿por qué?
wide ancho(-a), 13
widowed viudo(-a), 3
wife esposa (*f.*), mujer (*f.*), 5
will power voluntad (*f.*)
win ganar, 16
window ventana (*f.*), 2; (*of a vehicle or booth*) ventanilla (*f.*), 12; — **seat** asiento de ventanilla (*m.*), 11; **to** — **shop** mirar vidrieras, 13
windshield parabrisas (*m.*), 12
windy: to be — hacer viento, 6
wine vino (*m.*), 4
winter invierno (*m.*), 1
wish desear, 2; querer (e:ie), 4
with con, 1; de, 16; — **me** conmigo, 2; — **you** (*fam. sing.*) contigo, 4
without sin que, 14; sin; — **fail** sin falta, 18; — **rhyme or reason** sin qué ni para qué, 18
woman mujer (*f.*)
women's department departamento de (ropa para) damas, 13
wood madera (*f.*)
wool lana (*f.*), 13
word palabra (*f.*), 17; — **processor** procesador de textos (*m.*), 17
work trabajar, 2; trabajo (*m.*), 3; funcionar, 12; (*of art*) obra (*f.*)
world mundo (*m.*), 17; — **Wide Web** Internet (*f.*), Red (*f.*), 7
worried preocupado(-a), 4
worry (about) preocuparse (por), 9
worse peor, 5
worst el (la) peor, 5
worth: to be — **the trouble** valer la pena, 12
wrapped envuelto(-a), 14
write escribir, 3; — **down** anotar, 2
writer escritor(-a) (*m., f.*), 14
written escrito(-a), 14
wrong: to be — estar equivocado(-a), no tener razón, 4

X

X-ray radiografía (*f.*), 15; — **room** sala de rayos X (*f.*), 15

Y

year año (*m.*), 3; **to be** . . . —**s old** tener… años, 4
yellow amarillo(-a), 1
yes sí, 2
yesterday ayer, 7
you (*subj.*) tú (*fam.*), usted (Ud.) (*form.*); ustedes, vosotros(-as), 1; (*d.o. pron.*) la(s), lo(s), os, te, 6; (*i.o. pron.*) le(s), os, te, 7; (*obj. of prep.*) ti, usted(es), vosotros(-as), 4

young joven (*m.*, *f.*), 17; **— man** chico (*m.*), muchacho (*m.*), 2; joven (*m.*), 15; **— lady** señorita (*f.*), 1; **— people** jóvenes (*m.*, *f.*); **— woman** chica (*f.*), muchacha (*f.*), 2; joven (*f.*), 15

younger menor, 5

youngest el (la) menor, 5

your su(s), tu(s), vuestro(-a)(-os)(-as), 3

yours suyo(-a)(s), tuyo(-a)(s), vuestro(-a)(s), 9

yourself se, te, 9

yourselves os, se, 9

youth juventud (*f.*), 9

Z

zero cero, 1

zip code zona postal (*f.*), 3

zoo zoológico (*m.*), 4

Index

Contents

STUDENT ACTIVITIES MANUAL

¿Cómo se dice...?

Lección **1**

Workbook Activities

Estructuras

A. The alphabet Spell the names of the following persons.

1.

Sandra Cisneros

2.

Antonio Villarraigosa

3.

Bill Richardson

1.   Este (*This*) nombre se escribe así:

_____

2.   Este nombre se escribe así:

_____

3.   Este nombre se escribe así:

_____

B. Cardinal numbers 0–30 Write, in Spanish, the number of students that each of the professors has in his/her class.

1.   Luis Acosta: 15   (_____) estudiantes

2.   Marta Vega: 24   (_____) estudiantes

3.   Ana Ruiz: 30   (_____) estudiantes

4.   Oscar Paz: 14   (_____) estudiantes

5.   Raúl Montes: 19   (_____) estudiantes

6.   Olga Vera: 13   (_____) estudiantes

7.   Rafael Soto: 17   (_____) estudiantes

8.   Nora Vargas: 12   (_____) estudiantes

C. Colors You are teaching some Spanish-speaking children to paint. Tell them what colors will result by mixing the following colors.

1. azul y amarillo: _____

2. blanco y rojo: _____

3. blanco y negro: _____

4. amarillo y rojo: _____

5. azul y rojo: _____

D. Days of the week You are in charge of making a calendar for your Spanish class. Write the days of the week below. Remember that in Spanish-speaking countries the week starts on Monday.

SEPTIEMBRE						
		1	2	3	4	5
6	7	8	9	10	11	12
13	14	15	16	17	18	19
20	21	22	23	24	25	26
27	28	29	30			

E. Months and seasons of the year Keeping in mind that the seasons are reversed in the Southern Hemisphere, write the months that correspond to the following seasons in Argentina.

1. invierno: _____, _____, _____

2. primavera: _____, _____, _____

3. otoño: _____, _____, _____

4. verano: _____, _____, _____

F. Subject pronouns How do you and your friends refer to yourselves and others? Complete the following sentences, using Spanish subject pronouns.

MODELO: You refer to your teachers as . . .
          You refer to your teachers as *ellos*.

1. You speak to your best friend and call him _____.

2. You refer to María as _____.

3. You address your teacher as _____.

4. You refer to your parents and yourself as _____.

5. Nora and Marisol refer to themselves as _____.

6. You refer to your friends as _____.

7. You refer to Mr. Hidalgo as _____.

8. You speak to your classmates as a group and call them _____.

9. You talk about yourself and say _____.

G. Present indicative of *ser* You work for the school paper and are interviewing a Mexican American student about herself and her friends. Complete the interview, using the correct forms of the verb **ser**.

—¿De dónde _____ tú?

—Yo _____ de Arizona.

—¿Y Fernando Monteros?

—Él _____ de Arizona también (*also*).

—¿Ustedes _____ de Phoenix?

—No, nosotros _____ de Tucson.

—¿Y Anabel y Sara?

—Ellas _____ de California.

H. Situaciones You find yourself in the following situations. What do you say?

1. You thank someone for a favor and then say good-bye.

   _____

2. You greet Miss Rojas in the afternoon and ask how it's going for her.

   _____

3. You are saying good-bye to your friend, whom you will see tomorrow. You ask him to say hello to Gustavo.

   _____

4. You ask a girl you just met where she is from.

   _____

5. You tell a classmate you'll see each other on Monday.

   _____

6. You say that nothing has happened to someone who wants to know what's new with you.

   _____

I. Crucigrama

Horizontal

2. sobrenombre de **José**
4. viernes, sábado, _____
5. ¡_____ cumpleaños!
6. signo del zodíaco
8. septiembre, octubre, _____
9. ¿Cuál es tu _____ de teléfono?
11. martes, miércoles, _____
14. dieciséis más catorce
15. ella y él
16. los colores de la bandera (*flag*) americana: rojo, blanco y _____
18. tú y yo
20. mamá
21. diminutivo de **Carlos**
22. papá
24. saludos y _____

Vertical

1. rojo y amarillo
3. otoño, invierno, _____
7. trece más dos
10. Ella es _____; es de Guadalajara.
12. usted y él
13. j
17. Harvard o Yale
19. Marta y yo _____ de México.
23. nueve más once

J. ¿Qué pasa aquí? (*What's happening here?*) Look at the illustrations and answer the following questions about them.

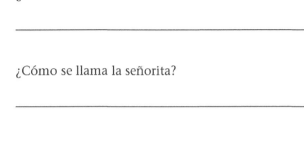

1. ¿Cómo se llama el señor?

   _____

2. ¿Cómo se llama la señorita?

   _____

3. ¿Julián es estudiante?

   _____

4. ¿El profesor Nieto es mexicano o colombiano?

   _____

5. ¿Hay una fiesta hoy?

   _____

6. ¿.Qué fecha es hoy?

   _____

7. ¿Graciela Calderón es profesora o estudiante?

   _____

8. ¿De qué parte de California es la doctora Calderón?

   _____

Panorama hispánico

Complete the following chart.

Los mexicoamericanos

Campos en los que se destacan muchos mexicoamericanos: ______________________________,

______________________________, ______________________________ y ______________________________

Nombre de una famosa escritora mexicoamericana: ______________________________

Mural de Diego Rivera: ______________________________

Mural de Leo Tanguma: ______________________________

Lección 1

Laboratory Activities

Diálogos

Un día con María Inés Listen to the dialogues twice, paying close attention to the speakers' intonation and pronunciation patterns. First, listen to the entire dialogue; then, as you listen for a second time, pause the recording after each sentence and repeat after the speaker.

En la clase

MARÍA INÉS	Buenos días. Usted es el Dr. Trujillo, ¿verdad?
DR. TRUJILLO	Sí, señorita. Y usted, ¿cómo se llama?
MARÍA INÉS	Me llamo María Inés Hidalgo.
DR. TRUJILLO	Mucho gusto, señorita Hidalgo.
MARÍA INÉS	El gusto es mío, profesor.
DR. TRUJILLO	Tome asiento, por favor.
MARÍA INÉS	Gracias.

En la cafetería

MARÍA INÉS	Buenas tardes, señora. ¿Cómo está usted?
SEÑORA	Muy bien, gracias. ¿Y tú, María Inés?
MARÍA INÉS	Bien, gracias. Bueno, hasta mañana.
SEÑORA	Hasta mañana. Saludos a Teresa.
MARÍA INÉS	Gracias.

MARÍA INÉS	Hola. ¿Cómo están?
RODOLFO	Bien. ¿Qué hay de nuevo?
MARÍA INÉS	Nada. Bueno... no mucho...
RODOLFO	María Inés: mi amigo Sergio.
MARÍA INÉS	Encantada, Sergio.
SERGIO	Igualmente. ¿De dónde eres, María Inés?
MARÍA INÉS	Yo soy de Los Ángeles, pero mi mamá es mexicana y mi papá es de Tejas. Oye, Rodolfo, ¿cuál es tu número de teléfono?
RODOLFO	Tres-ocho-seis-nueve-cuatro-siete-dos.
MARÍA INÉS	Gracias. Bueno, nos vemos el lunes, Rodolfo. Adiós, Sergio.
RODOLFO Y SERGIO	Adiós.

En el parque

MARÍA INÉS	¡Hola! ¿Cómo te llamas?
CARLITOS	Carlitos
MARÍA INÉS	Yo me llamo María Inés. Oye... ¿hay una fiesta hoy?
CARLITOS	Sí... es mi cumpleaños...
MARÍA INÉS	¡Feliz cumpleaños, Carlitos!
CARLITOS	Gracias.

En una fiesta

MARÍA INÉS   Buenas noches, señor Paz. ¿Cómo le va?
SR. PAZ   Muy bien, gracias. Señorita, ¿de dónde es usted?
MARÍA INÉS   Yo soy de Los Ángeles. Y ustedes, ¿de dónde son?
SR. PAZ   Nosotros somos de Arizona. Usted es estudiante, ¿verdad?
MARÍA INÉS   Sí, soy estudiante de la Universidad de California.

A. Preguntas y respuestas (*Questions and answers*) You will now hear questions about the dialogues. Answer each one, omitting the subject. The speaker will confirm your response. Repeat the correct response.

B. Situaciones (*Situations*) The speaker will present several situations based on the dialogues. Respond appropriately in Spanish to each situation. The speaker will confirm your response. Repeat the correct response. Follow the model.

> MODELO: You ask your professor where he or she is from.
> **¿De dónde es usted?**

Pronunciación (*Pronunciation*)

A. *The sound of the Spanish* ***a***

- Repeat the words in each pair after the speakers, imitating their pronunciation.

English	Spanish
alpaca	alpaca
banana	banana
cargo	cargo
canal	canal

- Repeat each word, imitating the speaker's pronunciation.

Ana	Ágata
Marta	sábado
llamas	mayo
analista	hasta mañana

- When you hear the number, read the corresponding sentence aloud. Then listen to the speaker and repeat the sentence.
  1. Hasta mañana, Ana.
  2. La mamá trabaja.
  3. Panamá gana fama.

B. *The sound of the Spanish* ***e***

- Repeat the words in each pair after the speakers, imitating their pronunciation.

English	Spanish
mesa	mesa
preposition	preposición
adobe	adobe
Los Angeles	Los Ángeles

- Repeat each word, imitating the speaker's pronunciation.

qué	usted
enero	Pepe
Ester	teléfono
secretaria	Teresa

- When you hear the number, read the corresponding sentence aloud. Then listen to the speaker and repeat the sentence.
  1. /Te besé y te dejé./
  2. /Mereces que te peguen./

Estructuras

A. The alphabet First, read the name and then spell it. The speaker will confirm your response. Repeat the correct response.

> MODELO: Olga
> **o-ele-ge-a**

1. Elena
2. Úrsula
3. Beatriz
4. Gustavo
5. Camila

B. Colors The speaker will name several familiar objects. State the color or colors of each object in Spanish. The speaker will confirm your response. Repeat the correct response. Follow the model.

> MODELO: a violet
> **morado**

C. Days of the week The speaker will name days of the week. State the day that precedes each day given. The speaker will confirm your response. Repeat the correct response. Follow the model.

> MODELO: martes
> **lunes**

D. Months of the year The speaker will name a month. Give the month that follows. The speaker will confirm your response. Repeat the correct response. Follow the model.

> MODELO: noviembre
> **diciembre**

E. Present indicative of *ser* You will hear some questions. Answer them, using the cues provided and omitting the subject. The speaker will confirm your response. Repeat the correct response. Follow the model.

> MODELO: ¿De dónde es Carlos? (Arizona)
> **Es de Arizona.**

A. Dibujos (*Drawings*) You will hear three statements about each drawing. Choose the letter of the statement that best corresponds to the drawing. The speaker will verify your response.

1.

a   b   c

2.

a   b   c

3.

a   b   c

4.

a   b   c

5.

a   b   c

B. Un diálogo breve (*A short dialogue*) Before listening to the dialogue in this section, study the comprehension questions below. Reviewing the questions ahead of time will help you to remember key information as you listen. Then listen carefully to the dialogue and answer each question, omitting the subject. The speaker will confirm your response. Repeat the correct answer.

1. ¿La señorita Acosta se llama Isabel o Inés?
2. ¿La señorita Acosta es de Colorado o de México?
3. ¿El Sr. Gómez es de Tejas o de California?
4. ¿La señorita Acosta es profesora o estudiante?
5. ¿La señorita Acosta es estudiante de la Universidad de Arizona o de la Universidad de California?

C. Para contestar (*To answer*) Answer the speaker's questions, using the cues provided. The speaker will confirm your answers. Repeat the correct response.

1. (California)
2. (San Diego)
3. (San Francisco)
4. (Santa Bárbara)
5. (sí)

6. (martes)
7. (el 2 de mayo)
8. (sí)
9. (el 12 de julio)
10. (Cáncer)

D. Tome nota (*Take note*) You will hear someone interviewing a woman. First listen carefully for general comprehension. Then, as you listen for a second time, fill in the information requested.

ENTREVISTA

Nombre: _____

Ciudad: _____ País:° _____   *country*

Profesión: _____

E. Dictado (*Dictation*): **Números cardinales 0–30** The speaker will say some numbers. Write each one in words in the space provided. Each number will be read twice.

1. _____
2. _____
3. _____
4. _____
5. _____

6. _____
7. _____
8. _____
9. _____
10. _____

F. Dictado: Oraciones (*Sentences*) The speaker will read six sentences. Each sentence will be read twice. After the first reading, write what you heard. After the second reading, check your work and fill in what you missed.

1. _____
2. _____
3. _____
4. _____
5. _____
6. _____

Lección 2

Workbook Activities

Estructuras

A. Indefinite articles These are the things that the professor needs for his class. Write the corresponding indefinite article before each noun.

1. _____ borrador

2. _____ reloj

3. _____ libro

4. _____ marcadores

5. _____ mapa

6. _____ papeles

7. _____ pupitres

8. _____ pizarra

9. _____ plumas rojas

10. _____ mochila

B. Definite articles I These are some things that you might see in an office. Write the corresponding definite article before each noun.

1. _____ ventanas

2. _____ puerta

3. _____ luz

4. _____ reloj

5. _____ mujeres

6. _____ paredes

7. _____ sillas

8. _____ escritorio

9. _____ hombres

10. _____ libros

C. Definite articles II These are statements heard in a Social Studies class. Place **el**, **la**, **los**, or **las** before each noun.

1. Necesitamos hablar de _____ problemas de _____ ciudades

   norteamericanas. ¿Cuáles son _____ soluciones?

2. _____ sistema de gobierno de _____ Estados Unidos es una democracia.

   _____ libertad es muy importante en este país.

3. Muchas personas critican _____ programas de _____ televisión

   norteamericana.

4. _____ idioma español es muy importante en California y en Tejas.

D. Cardinal numbers 31–100 It's inventory time. In Spanish, write how many there are of each item using **hay**.

1. 44 erasers: _____

2. 98 pencils: _____

3. 75 notebooks: _____

4. 100 pens: _____

5. 53 maps: _____

6. 82 chairs: _____

7. 66 books: _____

8. 43 blackboards: _____

9. 38 clocks: _____

10. 96 student desks: _____

E. Telling time In a bilingual program, children are learning to tell time. Complete the following chart to express the times given.

English	es/son	la/las	hora	y/menos	minutos
It is one o'clock.	Es	la	una.		
It is a quarter after four.	Son	las	cuatro	y	cuarto.
1. It is ten to seven.				menos	diez.
2. It is twenty after six.		las			
3. It is one-thirty.					media.
4. It is five to ten.			diez		
5. It is a quarter to two.				menos	
6. It is twenty-five to eight.			ocho		
7. It is nine o'clock.	Son				

14 Lección 2, Workbook Activities

F. Telling time / Days of the week Look at this class schedule and write the time and days of the week each class is held. Follow the model.

MODELO: educación física
La clase de educación física es los martes y jueves a las cinco.

HORA	LUNES	MARTES	MIÉRCOLES	JUEVES	VIERNES	SÁBADO
8:00–9:00	Psicología		Psicología		Psicología	
9:00–10:00	Biología		Biología		Biología	Tenis
10:00–11:30		Historia		Historia		
12:15–1:00			ALMUERZO			
1:00–2:00	Literatura		Literatura		Literatura	Laboratorio de biología
5:00–6:30		Educación física		Educación física		
7:00–8:30	Danza aeróbica		Danza aeróbica			

1. psicología _____

   _____

2. biología _____

   _____

3. historia _____

   _____

4. literatura _____

   _____

5. educación física _____

   _____

6. danza aeróbica _____

   _____

G. Present indicative of regular -*ar* verbs I Match each verb with its corresponding subject pronoun.

1. yo _____   a. estudiamos

2. ustedes _____   b. llama

3. nosotros _____   c. trabajan

4. ella _____   d. hablas

5. tú _____   e. regreso

H. Present indicative of regular -*ar* verbs II The students are talking while waiting for the instructor. What are they saying? Complete the following exchanges, using the verbs in the list. The numbers in parentheses indicate how many times each verb should be used.

estudiar (1)   necesitar (2)   tomar (2)
regresar (3)   desear (2)   trabajar (2)

1. MARISOL —¿Cuántas clases _____ tú, Pablo?

   PABLO   —Yo _____ cinco clases.

   MARISOL —¿Tú _____ en el hospital San Marcos?

   PABLO   —Sí, _____ por la noche y por la tarde

   _____ .

2. RAQUEL —¿A qué hora _____ ustedes a casa (*home*)?

   JULIO   —Nosotros _____ a las dos y media. ¿A qué hora

   _____ Jaime?

   RAQUEL —A la una.

3. ANA   —¿Qué _____ usted, señora?

   SEÑORA —Yo _____ un bolígrafo.

4. ROBERTO —¿Tú _____ hablar con el profesor?

   DANIEL —No, yo _____ hablar con la secretaria.

I. Possession with *de* What do we know about these people? Practice possession with **de** by forming sentences with the elements given. Follow the model.

    MODELO: Mario / maestra / ser / Colombia
             La maestra de Mario es de Colombia.

   1.   la Sra. Gómez / necesitar / dirección / Marta

       _____

   2.   Ana / trabajar / con profesora / Julio

       _____

   3.   la Dra. Soto / estudiantes / regresar / a las cuatro

       _____

   4.   la Sra. Juárez / secretaria / no trabajar / hoy

       _____

   5.   yo / necesitar / Sergio / número de teléfono

       _____

J. Situaciones You find yourself in the following situations. What do you say?

   1.   You tell a friend what time your Spanish class is. Then ask him or her what time it is.

       _____

       _____

   2.   You want to know whether your friend studies in the morning or in the afternoon.

       _____

   3.   You ask a friend if he or she wants to study with you, and suggest a day and time and the place.

       _____

   4.   Your friend Carlos is taking English. You ask him whether English is easy or difficult and give him advice on what he must do to learn.

       _____

K. Crucigrama

Horizontal

2. dirección
3. opuesto (*opposite*) de **fácil**
4. tipo de pluma
6. ¿Qué _____ es? ¿la una?
7. chica
10. Ella es _____; es de California.
13. platicar
14. ¿Cómo se dice *backpack*?

16. ¿Es una puerta o una _____?
18. Ana _____ cuatro clases.
19. idioma que hablan en México
20. Yo trabajo _____ los días.
21. ¿Cómo se dice *clock*?
23. cuarenta más sesenta
24. cincuenta más veinte

Vertical

1. Estudiamos aquí.
5. idioma que hablan en París
8. hombre de La Habana
9. idioma que hablan en Brasil
11. lengua

12. Necesito una _____ de anuncios.
15. Necesitamos un cesto de _____.
17. idioma que hablan en Roma
22. ¿Cómo se dice *lights*?

L. ¿Qué pasa aquí? Look at the illustration and choose **V** for **verdadero** (*true*) or **F** for **falso** (*false*) in response to the following statements.

1.	Es una clase de matemáticas.	V	F
2.	El profesor Dumont es profesor de historia.	V	F
3.	Hay quince estudiantes en la clase.	V	F
4.	Hay 30 pupitres.	V	F
5.	Hay un reloj en la pared.	V	F
6.	La clase de francés es a las dos.	V	F
7.	Son las doce y cinco.	V	F
8.	Hay una ventana en la clase.	V	F
9.	Hay una puerta en la clase.	V	F
10.	Hay un mapa de México en la clase.	V	F
11.	Hay un libro en el escritorio.	V	F
12.	Hay cuatro lápices en el escritorio.	V	F

Panorama hispánico

Complete the following chart.

Los cubanoamericanos

Número de cubanos que viven en Miami: ______________________________

Porcentaje de hispanos de origen cubano: ______________________________

Nombres de dos políticos importantes de origen cubano: ______________ y ______________

Nombres de dos cubanos famosos en la música: ______________ y ______________

Artistas de origen cubano que se destacan en el cine: ______________, ______________ y

____

Famoso barrio cubano en Miami: ______________________________

Lección 2

Laboratory Activities

Diálogos

El primer día de clases Listen to the dialogues twice, paying close attention to the speakers' intonation and pronunciation patterns. First, listen to the entire dialogue; then, as you listen for a second time, pause the recording after each sentence and repeat after the speaker.

Gloria, una chica cubanoamericana, habla con un muchacho de El Salvador.

GLORIA ¿Qué hora es?
JULIO Son las diez y cuarto. ¿A qué hora es la clase de inglés?
GLORIA A las diez y media. ¡Caramba! ¡Es tarde! Oye, Julio, ¿Olga y tú estudian en la biblioteca esta noche?
JULIO No, yo trabajo en el hospital por la noche. Olga estudia con José Luis.
GLORIA ¡Pero chico! Tú trabajas por la tarde también. ¡Y tomas cinco clases! ¿Cuándo estudias?
JULIO Los sábados y los domingos.
GLORIA ¡Necesitas más tiempo para estudiar!
JULIO Sí, y también necesito más dinero. Oye, ¿deseas estudiar conmigo el sábado por la mañana?
GLORIA ¡Sí! ¿Estudiamos en mi casa? Y por la tarde vamos a la Calle Ocho.
JULIO Buena idea. ¿Cuál es tu dirección?
GLORIA Calle Quinta, número 120. Y mi número de teléfono es 3-54-67-98.
JULIO (*Anota la dirección y el número de teléfono de Gloria*) ¡Perfecto! Nos vemos el sábado.

Por la tarde, Gloria conversa con una chica norteamericana.

SANDRA Oye, Gloria, ¿cómo se dice "backpack" en español?
GLORIA Se dice "mochila".
SANDRA Gracias. El español es un idioma difícil.
GLORIA No, Sandra. ¡Es fácil! Pero necesitas practicar todos los días.
SANDRA ¿Tú hablas otros idiomas?
GLORIA Sí, hablo francés y un poco de portugués. ¿Y tú?
SANDRA Yo hablo italiano.
GLORIA ¿En serio?
SANDRA ¡Sí! Pizza... ravioles.
GLORIA ¡Ay, chica! ¡En ese caso yo hablo chino!

A. **Preguntas y respuestas** You will now hear questions about the dialogues. Answer each one, omitting the subject. The speaker will confirm your response. Repeat the correct response.

B. **Situaciones** The speaker will present several situations based on the dialogues. Respond appropriately in Spanish to each situation. The speaker will confirm your response. Repeat the correct response. Follow the model.

MODELO: You ask how to say "chair" in Spanish.
¿Cómo se dice "*chair*" en español?

Pronunciación

A. *The sound of the Spanish* **i**

- Repeat the words in each pair, imitating the speaker's pronunciation.

English	*Spanish*
director	director
diversion	diversión
Lidia	Lidia
inspector	inspector
tropical	tropical

- Repeat each word, imitating the speaker's pronunciation.

sí	días	necesitar
dice	cinco	hospital
inglés	dirección	domicilio

- When you hear the number, read the corresponding sentence aloud. Then listen to the speaker and repeat the sentence.
  1. Fifí mira a Rin-Tin-Tín.
  2. Mimí dice que es difícil vivir aquí.

B. *The sound of the Spanish* **o**

- Repeat the words in each pair, imitating the speaker's pronunciation.

English	*Spanish*
noble	noble
no	no
opinion	opinión
Colorado	Colorado

- Repeat each word, imitating the speaker's pronunciation.

no	Mario	noche
como	once	ocho
poco	número	teléfono

- When you hear the number, read the corresponding sentence aloud. Then listen to the speaker and repeat the sentence.
  1. Yo como pollo con Rodolfo.
  2. Lolo compró los loros.

C. *The sound of the Spanish* **u**

- Repeat the words in each pair, imitating the speaker's pronunciation.

English	*Spanish*
universal	universal
club	club
Hugo	Hugo
humor	humor
Uruguay	Uruguay

Name _____ Section _____ Date _____

- Repeat each word, imitating the speaker's pronunciation.

estudiar	puerta
usted	luz
Susana	universidad
mucho	gusto

- When you hear the number, read the corresponding sentence aloud. Then listen to the speaker and repeat the sentence.
    1. Las universidades uruguayas están en las urbes.
    2. Úrsula usa uniforme únicamente en el club.

Estructuras

A. Definite and indefinite articles You will hear several singular nouns, each preceded by a definite or an indefinite article. Make the nouns and the articles plural. The speaker will confirm your response. Repeat the correct response. Follow the model.

> MODELO: el alumno
> **los alumnos**

B. Telling time Your friend's watch is always running ten minutes behind. Correct him when he says what time it is. The speaker will confirm your response. Repeat the correct response. Follow the model.

> MODELO: Son las seis.
> **No, son las seis y diez.**

C. Negative sentences Give a negative response to each question you hear. Include the subject in your answer. The speaker will confirm your response. Repeat the correct response. Follow the model.

> MODELO: ¿Uds. trabajan en el hospital?
> **No, nosotros no trabajamos en el hospital.**

D. Possession with *de* Answer the following questions to indicate ownership, using the cues. The speaker will confirm your response. Repeat the correct response. Follow the model.

> MODELO: ¿Es el lápiz de Rosa? (María)
> **No, es el lápiz de María.**

1. (Carlos)
2. (la profesora)
3. (Elisa)
4. (Irene)
5. (Rodolfo)

Copyright © Cengage Learning. All rights reserved.   Lección 2, Laboratory Activities   **23**

A. Dibujos (*Drawings*) You will hear three statements about each drawing. Choose the letter of the statement that best corresponds to the drawing. The speaker will verify your response.

1.

SOFÍA

a b c

2.

a b c

3.

FERNANDO

a b c

4.

a b c

5.

a b c

B. Una narración breve Before listening to the narration in this section, study the comprehension questions below. Reviewing the questions ahead of time will help you to remember key information as you listen. Then listen carefully to the narration and answer each question, omitting the subject. The speaker will confirm your response. Repeat the correct answer.

1. ¿Daniel es cubanoamericano o mexicoamericano?
2. ¿Daniel estudia en una universidad de Los Ángeles o estudia en una universidad de Miami?
3. ¿Daniel toma clases por la mañana o por la noche?
4. ¿Daniel trabaja en un hospital o en la biblioteca?
5. ¿Daniel estudia por la tarde o por la noche?
6. ¿Daniel habla un idioma o tres idiomas?

C. Para contestar Answer the speaker's questions, using the cues provided. The speaker will confirm your answers. Repeat the correct response.

1. (las ocho)
2. (la mañana)
3. (la biblioteca)
4. (no)
5. (cinco)
6. (el sábado)
7. (difícil)
8. (no)
9. (sí)
10. (una computadora)

D. Tome nota You will hear two people talking. First listen carefully for general comprehension. Then, as you listen for a second time, fill in the information requested.

Nombre del profesor: _____

Nombre de la estudiante: _____

Día: _____

Hora: _____

Número de estudiantes: _____

E. Dictado: Números cardinales 31–100 The speaker will read some numbers. Write each one in the space provided. Each number will be read twice.

1. _____
2. _____
3. _____
4. _____
5. _____

6. _____
7. _____
8. _____
9. _____
10. _____

F. Dictado: Oraciones The speaker will read six sentences or phrases. Each sentence will be read twice. After the first reading, write what you heard. After the second reading, check your work and fill in what you missed.

1. _____

2. _____

3. _____

4. _____

5. _____

6. _____

Hasta ahora... Una prueba (*So far. . . A quiz*)

You have finished **Lecciones 1** and **2**. How much have you learned so far about structure and vocabulary?

A. Complete the following exchanges, using the present indicative of the verbs given.

1. —¿De dónde _____ ustedes? (ser)

   —Nosotros _____ de California, pero _____ español.

   (ser / hablar)

2. —¿El doctor Fuentes _____ profesor de español? (ser)

   —Sí, _____ en la Universidad de California. También

   _____ francés. (trabajar / hablar)

3. —¿Tú _____ estudiante? (ser)

   —Sí, _____ en la Universidad de Arizona. (estudiar)

4. —¿A qué hora _____ ustedes? (regresar)

   —Yo _____ a la una y Rosa _____ a las dos.

   (regresar / regresar)

5. —¿De dónde _____ usted, señorita? (ser)

   —Yo _____ de Tejas. (ser)

6. —¿Cuántas clases _____ tú? (tomar)

   —Dos, pero _____ tomar dos más (*more*). (desear)

B. How much does everybody need? Indicate this, by using the verb **necesitar** appropriately and writing the numbers in Spanish. (Hint: dollars: **dólares**)

1. Fernando / 15

   _____

2. yo / 98

   _____

3. Eva y Mario / 79

   _____

4. tú / 45

_____

5. Sergio y yo / 64

_____

6. ustedes / 53

_____

7. Marisol / 100

_____

8. usted / 32

_____

9. las chicas / 86

_____

10. nosotras / 27

_____

C. Arrange the following words and phrases in groups of three, according to categories. Examples of categories: greeting questions, courtesy phrases, writing instruments, etc.

Mucho gusto.	platicar	dirección	Hasta mañana	amarillo
tablilla de anuncios	día	lengua	bolígrafo	negro
muchacho	pizarra	¿Qué tal?	blanco	martes
Muchas gracias.	Nos vemos.	hablar	domicilio	gris
El gusto es mío.	francés	jueves	calle	lápiz
¿Cómo estás?	Encantada	despedida	azul	chico
Muy amable.	conversar	pluma	idioma	amigo
¿Cómo te va?	De nada.	mapa	verde	

1. _____ _____ _____

2. _____ _____ _____

3. _____ _____ _____

4. _____ _____ _____

5. _____ _____ _____

6. _____ _____ _____

28   Hasta ahora… Una prueba (Lecciones 1 y 2)

7. _____   _____   _____

8. _____   _____   _____

9. _____   _____   _____

10. _____   _____   _____

11. _____   _____   _____

12. _____   _____   _____

13. _____   _____   _____

Hasta ahora... Una prueba (Lecciones 1 y 2)   **29**

Un paso más (*A step further*)

A. Taking into account this student's class schedule, answer the questions that follow.

Horario de clases

Nombre del estudiante _____Marcel Dubois_____

hora	lunes	martes	miércoles	jueves	viernes	sábado	aula[1]
7 – 8							
8 – 9	Español	Español	Español	Español			115
9 – 10	Física		Física		Física	Tenis	223
10 – 11	Sociología		Sociología		Sociología		180
11 – 12	Geología		Geología		Geología		210
1 – 2							
2 – 3							

Consejero[2] _____David Saldívar_____

[1]*classroom*   [2]*adviser*

1. ¿De dónde es Marcel probablemente (*probably*): de París o de Madrid?

_____

2. ¿Marcel toma clases de siete a ocho?

_____

3. ¿Qué idioma estudia Marcel?

_____

4. De nueve a diez, ¿Marcel habla de Isaac Newton o de Freud en su (*his*) clase?

_____

5. ¿Qué clase toma Marcel los lunes, miércoles y viernes de diez a once?

_____

6. ¿Hasta (*Until*) qué hora toma clases Marcel?

_____

7. ¿Cuántas clases toma Marcel los martes y jueves?

_____

8. ¿Qué días juega (*plays*) Marcel al tenis?

_____

9. ¿Marcel toma clases por la tarde?

_____

10. ¿En qué aula es la clase de español?

_____

11. ¿La clase de sociología es en el aula 190?

_____

12. ¿Quién es David Saldívar?

_____

B. Combine the vocabulary and the structure learned in **Lecciones 1** and **2** to give information about yourself. Include name, origin, address and phone number, classes, schedule, work, study habits, things needed, etc. Write at least ten statements.

Lección 3

Workbook Activities

Estructuras

A. Possessive adjectives I We all need something. Indicate this by adding the corresponding possessive adjectives, according to each subject.

1. Yo necesito _____ computadora y _____ cuadernos. Carlos necesita _____ libro

   de francés y _____ bolígrafos. Tú necesitas _____ reloj y _____ lápices.

2. Elsa y yo necesitamos _____ mapas y _____ tablilla de anuncios.

   Ester y Aurora necesitan _____ escritorio y _____ mochilas.

B. Possessive adjectives II Answer the following questions with complete sentences, using the cues provided and the appropriate possessive adjectives. Follow the model.

MODELO: ¿Dónde trabaja la amiga de Alicia? (en el hospital)
Su amiga trabaja en el hospital.

1. ¿De dónde son tus amigos? (de Nueva York)

   _____

2. ¿De dónde es la profesora de ustedes? (de Puerto Rico)

   _____

3. ¿Dónde trabaja tu amiga? (en la universidad)

   _____

4. ¿Los amigos de ustedes son de México? (sí)

   _____

5. ¿Tú necesitas hablar con mi profesora? (no) (Use **Ud.** form for the possesive.)

   _____

6. ¿Elsa necesita mis libros? (sí) (Use **tú** form for the possesive)

   _____

C. Cardinal numbers 101–1,000 You are using checks to pay bills for the amounts shown below. Write each amount in Spanish.

1. 110 _____

2. 840 _____

3. 514 _____

4. 760 _____

5. 1.280 _____

6. 4.672 _____

7. 20.950 _____

D. Descriptive adjectives You are describing your classmates. Use the adjectives given appropriately and add the corresponding definite or indefinite articles.

rubia   guapo   cubanos
puertorriqueñas   simpáticas   alto
bonitas   encantadores   delgada

1. _____ chicas _____ son _____ y muy _____.

2. Héctor es _____ muchacho _____ y _____.

3. _____ muchachos _____ son _____.

4. _____ novia de Ernesto es _____ chica _____ y _____.

E. Present indicative of regular -er and -ir verbs I Complete the following chart with the corresponding present indicative forms.

Infinitive	yo	tú	Ud., él, ella	nosotros	Uds., ellos, ellas
leer	**leo**	**lees**	**lee**	**leemos**	**leen**
1. comer	como			comemos	
2. creer		crees			creen
3. beber					
4. escribir		escribes		escribimos	
5. recibir	recibo		recibe		reciben
6. decidir					

F. Present indicative of regular -er and -ir verbs II These people are conversing in the cafeteria. What are they saying? Complete the following dialogues, using the verbs listed.

escribir   comer   vivir   aprender   leer

1. —¿Dónde _____ Uds.?

    —Nosotros _____ en la cafetería. ¿Y tú?

    —Yo _____ en mi casa.

2. —¿Ud. _____ libros en español?

    —No, yo _____ libros en inglés.

3. —¿En qué calle _____ Uds.?

    —Nosotros _____ en la calle Lima. ¿Dónde _____ tú?

    —Yo _____ en la avenida Juárez.

    —¿Y Teresa?

    —Ella _____ en la calle Colombia.

4. —¿En qué idioma _____ Uds.?

    —Yo _____ en español y John _____ en inglés.

5. —¿Tú _____ mucho en la clase?

    —No, yo no _____ mucho porque no estudio.

G. Present indicative of the irregular verbs _tener_ and _venir_ Use the correct forms of **tener** or **venir** to report about these students' activities.

1. Teresa no _____ los viernes porque no _____ clases.

2. Ana y yo _____ con César porque no _____ coche (_car_).

3. Yo _____ a las ocho menos cuarto porque _____ una clase a las ocho.

4. Los estudiantes _____ a las siete cuando _____ exámenes.

5. ¿Tú _____ clases los martes o _____ a la universidad solamente los lunes?

H. *Tener que* + **infinitive** Indicate what everybody has to do by using the present indicative of **tener** + **que** to complete the following sentences.

1. Yo _____ estudiar y mis amigos _____ trabajar.

2. Estela y yo _____ escribir un informe y Gustavo _____

   regresar a la biblioteca.

3. ¿Tú _____ venir a clase?

I. **Situaciones** You find yourself in the following situations. What do you say?

1. You answer the phone and the caller asks to speak with you. Respond.

   _____

2. You tell someone that you have to work because you need money.

   _____

3. Ask your friend if he/she wants something to drink.

   _____

4. You are giving directions to Adela's house and to Julio's house. Tell your friends that her house is located (*queda*) on Magnolia Street and his house is located on Washington Street.

   _____

   _____

5. You ask a friend if he wants to take Raquel and Olga to the party.

   _____

J. **Crucigrama**

Horizontal

1. Hoy es lunes; _____ es martes
6. Recibo mensajes _____.
9. linda
10. opuesto de **gordo**
12. Tengo mi _____ de conducir.
13. ocupación
14. ¿Vives en una casa o en un _____?
17. Mi _____ es García.
18. que acepta la realidad
21. anuncio
23. de Puerto Rico
25. Necesito su número de _____ social.
26. tomamos
27. Tengo un _____ parcial.

Vertical

2. opuesto de **bajo**
3. cortés
4. diario
5. No es morena; es _____.
7. Estudiamos a Shakespeare en la clase de _____.
8. opuesto de **feo**
11. opuesto de **pesimista**
15. opuesto de **simpático**
16. computadora
19. trabajo
20. Ella es mi _____ de cuarto.
22. ¿Es soltera o _____?
24. ¿Cuál es su _____ civil?

K. ¿Qué pasa aquí? Look at the illustrations and answer the following questions.

A.
B.
C.

A.   1.   ¿Dónde conversan Oscar y Elba?

_____

2.   ¿Qué beben Oscar y Elba?

_____

3.   ¿Qué tiene que escribir Elba?

_____

4.   ¿Quién es la novia de Oscar?

_____

B.   1.   ¿Qué tiene Jorge en su escritorio?

_____

2.   ¿Qué recibe Jorge?

_____

3.   ¿De dónde viene el mensaje?

_____

4.   ¿Jorge tiene que estudiar literatura?

_____

5.   ¿Qué tiene que estudiar Jorge?

_____

C. 1. ¿A quiénes (*Whom*) lleva la Sra. Vega a su casa?

_____

2. ¿Cuál es la dirección de la Sra. Vega?

_____

3. ¿Luz es rubia o morena?

_____

Para leer

La familia de Hilda López

La Sra. Hilda López Ramírez es de San Juan, pero ahora° vive en Nueva York. *now*
Es enfermera° y trabaja en un hospital de Nueva Jersey. Sus padres son *nurse*
médicos° y viven en Ponce, una ciudad de Puerto Rico. *physicians*
 Julio, el esposo° de la Sra. López, es profesor. Ellos tienen tres hijos:° *husband / children*
Eduardo, Irene y Teresa. Eduardo es rubio y muy alto. Las chicas son morenas
y muy bonitas. Los tres son muy inteligentes y muy simpáticos. Hablan inglés
y español. En la escuela,° leen y escriben en inglés. *school*
 La familia vive en la ciudad de Nueva York, en la calle Quinta, número
quinientos treinta.

¡Conteste! Answer the following questions based on the reading.

1. ¿Hilda López es norteamericana?

_____

2. ¿De qué país (*country*) es ella?

_____

3. ¿Dónde vive ahora?

_____

4. ¿Cuál es la profesión de Hilda? ¿Cuál es la profesión de su esposo?

_____

5. ¿Dónde trabaja Hilda?

_____

6. ¿Cuál es la profesión de los padres de Hilda?

_____

7. ¿Los padres de Hilda viven en San Juan?

_____

8. ¿Cuántos hijos tienen Hilda y Julio? ¿Cómo son?

_____

9. ¿Qué idiomas hablan los niños? ¿En qué idioma leen y escriben en la escuela?

_____

10. ¿En qué ciudad vive la familia?

_____

11. ¿Cuál es la dirección de la familia Ramírez?

_____

Panorama hispánico

Complete the following chart.

Los puertorriqueños en los Estados Unidos

Número de personas de origen puertorriqueño en los Estados Unidos:

_____

Porcentaje de puertorriqueños que vive en Nueva York y Nueva Jersey: _____

Capital de Puerto Rico: _____

Congresistas de origen puertorriqueño: _____ y _____

Cantantes puertorriqueños: _____, _____ y _____

Dos actores puertorriqueños: _____ y _____

Famoso campeón de boxeo: _____

Lección 3

Laboratory Activities

Diálogos

Dos puertorriqueñas en Nueva York Listen to the dialogues twice, paying close attention to the speakers' intonation and pronunciation patterns. First, listen to the entire dialogue; then, as you listen for a second time, pause the recording after each sentence and repeat after the speaker.

Olga Carrera y su compañera de cuarto, Mariana Zayas, conversan en la sala de su apartamento mientras comen sándwiches y beben café. Las chicas viven en Nueva York, donde trabajan y asisten a la universidad de CUNY. Olga es morena, alta, bonita y muy inteligente. Mariana es baja, rubia y muy simpática.

MARIANA Tengo que llenar la solicitud de empleo de la compañía Sandoval. Necesito ganar más dinero.

OLGA Pero tú no tienes conocimiento de computadoras... y no tienes la experiencia necesaria...

MARIANA ¡Pero tengo problemas económicos! A ver... (*Lee el anuncio en el periódico.*) Debe hablar, leer y escribir portugués...

OLGA Tú no hablas portugués.

MARIANA Pero recibo mensajes electrónicos de mi amiga de Brasil... y no son en castellano.

OLGA Oye, el teléfono...

Mariana contesta el teléfono. Es Rafael.

MARIANA Hola.

RAFAEL Hola. ¿Está Mariana?

MARIANA Sí, con ella habla. ¿Rafael?

RAFAEL Sí. ¿Cómo estás, Mariana?

MARIANA Más o menos. ¿Qué hay de nuevo?

RAFAEL No mucho. Oye, mañana tenemos el examen parcial en la clase de historia. Estudiamos esta noche?

MARIANA Sí. ¿Por qué no vienes aquí, a mi apartamento?

RAFAEL Buena idea. Nos vemos a las seis. Oye... ¿está Olga?

MARIANA Sí, un momento. (*Llama a Olga.*) ¡Olga! ¡Tu novio!

OLGA ¿Qué tal, mi amor?

RAFAEL Bien. Oye, mi vida... Mariana y yo tenemos que estudiar, pero después... ¿deseas beber algo en el café París?

OLGA Bueno... tengo que escribir un informe para mi clase de literatura, pero... ¡acepto tu invitación! ¡Chau!

MARIANA ¡Ajá! ¡Con razón Rafael viene a estudiar conmigo!

Después de estudiar, Rafael lleva a Olga y a Mariana a tomar algo.

A. Preguntas y respuestas You will now hear questions about the dialogues. Answer each one, omitting the subject. The speaker will confirm your response. Repeat the correct response.

B. Situaciones The speaker will present several situations based on the dialogues. Respond appropriately in Spanish to each situation. The speaker will confirm your response. Repeat the correct response. Follow the model.

> MODELO: You ask if Carlos is at home.
> **¿Está Carlos?**

Pronunciación

Linking When you hear the number, read the corresponding sentence aloud. Then listen to the speaker and repeat the sentence.

1. Trabajan y asisten a la universidad.
2. Lee el anuncio en el periódico.
3. Tenemos el examen en la clase de historia.
4. Tengo que escribir un informe.
5. Lleva a Olga y a Mariana a tomar algo.

Estructuras

A. Possessive adjectives Answer each question you hear in the affirmative, using the appropriate possessive adjectives. The speaker will confirm your response. Repeat the correct response. Follow the model.

> MODELO: ¿Es tu amigo?
> **Sí, es mi amigo.**

B. Descriptive adjectives The speaker will read several phrases. Repeat each phrase, and then change each adjective according to the new cue. Make sure the adjectives agree with the nouns in gender and number. The speaker will confirm your response. Repeat the correct response. Follow the model.

> MODELO: el profesor español
> la profesora
> **la profesora española**
> los profesores
> **los profesores españoles**
> las profesoras
> **las profesoras españolas**

C. Present indicative of regular -er and -ir verbs Answer each question you hear in the negative, using the subject in your answer. The speaker will confirm your response. Repeat the correct response. Follow the model.

> MODELO: ¿Abres la puerta?
> **No, yo no abro la puerta.**

D. Present indicative of the irregular verbs *tener* and *venir* Answer each question you hear, using the cue provided. The speaker will confirm your response. Repeat the correct response. Follow the model.

> MODELO: ¿Quién viene hoy? (Carlos)
> **Carlos viene hoy.**

1. más tarde
2. Teresa
3. a las seis
4. sí

5. no
6. sí
7. Marisa
8. no

E. *Tener que* + infinitive Certain people are not doing what they are supposed to do. Say what they have to do. The speaker will confirm your response. Repeat the correct response. Follow the model.

> MODELO: Tú no estudias.
> **Tú tienes que estudiar.**

Más práctica

A. Dibujos (*Drawings*) You will hear three statements about each drawing. Choose the letter of the statement that best corresponds to the drawing. The speaker will verify your response.

1.
   a   b   c

2.
   a   b   c

3.
   a   b   c

4.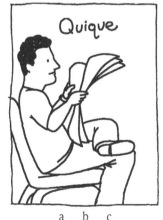
   a   b   c

5.
   a   b   c

B. Unos diálogos breves Before listening to the dialogues in this section, study the comprehension questions below. Reviewing the questions ahead of time will help you to remember key information as you listen. Then listen carefully to the dialogues and answer each question, omitting the subject. The speaker will confirm your response. Repeat the correct answer.

1. ¿Dónde come Rosa mañana?
2. ¿Tiene que estudiar?
3. ¿Está Carmen?
4. ¿A qué hora regresa?
5. ¿Alicia tiene conocimiento de computadoras?
6. ¿Alicia tiene experiencia?
7. ¿Alicia habla portugués?
8. ¿Qué no debe llenar Alicia?

C. Para contestar The speaker will ask you some questions. Answer each question, using the cue provided. The speaker will confirm your response. Repeat the correct response.

1. (sí)
2. (no, simpáticos)
3. (no, parcial)
4. (sí, todos los días)
5. (no)
6. (sí)
7. (realista)
8. (sí)
9. (soltero)
10. (Roberto)

D. Tome nota You will hear a brief telephone conversation. First listen carefully for general comprehension. Then, as you listen for a second time, fill in the information requested.

Compañía: _____

Mensaje telefónico para: _____

De parte de: _____

Hora: _____

Mensaje: _____

_____

E. **Dictado: Números cardinales 101–1,000** The speaker will say some numbers. Write each one in the space provided. Each number will be read twice.

1. _____

2. _____

3. _____

4. _____

5. _____

6. _____

F. **Dictado: Oraciones** The speaker will read six sentences. Each sentence will be read twice. After the first reading, write what you heard. After the second reading, check your work and fill in what you missed.

1. _____

2. _____

3. _____

4. _____

5. _____

6. _____

Lección 3, Laboratory Activities   **45**

Lección **4**

Workbook Activities

Estructuras

A. Contractions Say what these people are doing by supplying *the definite article*, **de** + *the definite article*, or **a** + *the definite article*, as required.

1. Marta viene   _____ universidad.

    _____ parque

    _____ hospital.

    _____ Ciudad de México.

2. Rodolfo lleva   _____ señora.

    _____ primo de Mario.

    _____ profesor Soto.

    _____ novia de Pedro.

    _____ chicas.

    _____ Sr. Vargas.

    _____ muchachos.

3. Eva llama   _____ Sr. Ortega.

    _____ Srta. Rojas.

    _____ muchachas.

    _____ profesor.

B. Present indicative of the irregular verbs *ir*, *dar*, and *estar* You and a friend are talking about Nora's party. Complete the dialogue, using the present indicative of **dar**, **estar**, and **ir** as appropriate.

1. —Nora _____ una fiesta en su casa hoy. ¿Tú _____?

    —Sí, _____ con Fernando.

    —¿Arturo y Sandra _____ también?

    —No, ellos _____ en Acapulco.

    —¿Tu hermano _____?

—No, él _____ muy cansado.

—Yo también _____ muy cansada.

—Ah, ¿tú _____ dinero para la fiesta?

—Sí, yo _____ cien dólares.

C. *Ir a* + infinitive We need to decide what we are going to do according to each circumstance. Using the verbs on the list, say what's going to happen.

ir　　　bailar　　　llevar　　　dar　　　invitar

1. Mañana es mi cumpleaños.

   Yo _____.

2. Los chicos están en una fiesta.

   Ellos _____.

3. Nuestros amigos desean venir a la fiesta.

   Nosotros _____.

4. Tú deseas escuchar (*listen*) música de Beethoven.

   Tú _____.

5. El hermano de Elsa desea ver (*to see*) animales.

   Elsa _____.

D. Present indicative of *e:ie* stem-changing verbs I Complete the following chart.

	Subject	Infinitive	Present Indicative
1.	Las chicas	preferir	
2.			entiendo
3.	Uds.	querer	
4.			cerramos
5.	Fernando	perder	
6.			empiezas
7.	Ud.	pensar	
8.			comenzamos

E. Present indicative of *e:ie* stem-changing verbs II Complete the following paragraph about Elena and her friends, using the verbs listed. Use each verb once.

entender　　　cerrar　　　querer　　　pensar　　　preferir　　　empezar

Elena no (1.) _____ ir a la fiesta de Teresa mañana;

(2.) _____ ir al club. Nosotros (3.) _____

ir a la fiesta con José Luis. La fiesta (4.) _____ a las nueve de

la noche.

Elena tiene una amiga que es de París y se llama Michèle. Las amigas de Elena no

(5.) _____ a Michèle porque ella no habla español. Esta noche

Elena y Michèle van a estudiar en la biblioteca hasta (*until*) las ocho y media. La biblioteca

(6.) _____ a las nueve.

F. Expressions with *tener* Two roommates are talking about how they and other people feel. Complete the following exchanges, using expressions with **tener**.

1. —¿Deseas comer un sándwich?

   —No, gracias, _____.

2. —¿_____, Aurora?

   —Sí, ¿hay refrescos en el refrigerador?

   —Sí, hay Coca-Cola.

3. —¿Tienes _____, Alicia?

   —Sí, necesito dormir (*to sleep*).

4. —¿Necesitas un suéter?

   —No, no _____.

5. —¿Por qué abre Elba la ventana?

   —Porque _____.

6. —¿_____, Teresa?

   —Sí, son las dos y veinte y yo tengo que estar en la universidad a las dos y media.

G. Situaciones You find yourself in the following situations. What do you say?

1. You ask a friend if he/she wants to go to a party with you. You tell him/her that you want to dance with him/her.

   _____

   _____

2. There's going to be a party. You are going to do the following:

   a. Prepare a lot of food.

   b. Take pictures.

   _____

   _____

3. There is a glass of water on the table. You ask a friend whether it's for you or for him or her.

   _____

4. You ask a little girl what her name is and how old she is.

   _____

5. You propose a toast and say "cheers".

   _____

   _____

H. Crucigrama

Horizontal

1. Hoy es sábado; _____ mañana es lunes.
4. cuarto
5. Voy a _____ muchas fotos.
8. En un baile nosotros _____.
10. El 25 de diciembre celebramos la _____.
12. Tomo agua porque tengo _____.
13. empezamos
16. Deseo un _____ de agua.
18. No voy al cine; _____ ir al teatro.
19. Tiene siete días.
21. Muchas personas están _____ a la fiesta.
23. El papá de mi mamá es mi _____.
24. Disneylandia es un parque de _____.

Vertical

2. Elsa _____ de llegar.
3. En el _____ hay muchos animales.
4. La hija de mi mamá es mi _____.
6. Hoy celebramos el año _____.
7. Raúl no quiere bailar porque está _____.
9. alegre
11. Ellos van a un _____ de fútbol.
14. enfadado
15. Elsa trabaja mucho. Está muy _____.
17. Ella tiene muchos problemas. Está muy _____.
19. El hijo de mi hermana es mi _____.
20. Van a comer porque tienen _____.
22. No es mi cumpleaños. Es mi _____.

Lección 4, Workbook Activities   **51**

I. ¿Qué pasa aquí? Look at the illustration and answer the following questions.

1. ¿Es una fiesta de Navidad?

   _____

2. ¿Es el cumpleaños de Pablo?

   _____

3. ¿Cuántos años tiene Armando?

   _____

4. ¿Quién da la fiesta?

   _____

5. ¿Carmen es la novia de Armando?

   _____

6. ¿Por qué no baila Hernán?

   _____

7. ¿Qué va a comer Hernán?

   _____

8. ¿Con quién baila Gabriela?

   _____

9. ¿Con quién está Elsa?

   _____

10. ¿Con qué brindan Elsa y Fernando?

    _____

11. ¿Marcos tiene hambre o tiene sed?

    _____

12. ¿Ud. cree que Ana y José son novios o que son hermanos?

    _____

Panorama hispánico

Complete the following chart.

México
Población: _____
Área: _____
Capital: _____
Población de la capital: _____
Playas famosas: _____, _____ y _____
Ruinas arquitectónicas: _____, _____ y _____
Ciudad fundada por los aztecas en 1328: _____
La segunda ciudad más grande del país: _____
Otras ciudades importantes: _____ y _____
Pintores famosos: _____, _____, _____ y _____

Lección 4

Laboratory Activities

Diálogos

Julia visita la Ciudad de México Listen to the dialogues twice, paying close attention to the speakers' intonation and pronunciation patterns. First, listen to the entire dialogue; then, as you listen for a second time, pause the recording after each sentence and repeat after the speaker.

Julia Lara, una chica mexicoamericana que vive en Colorado con su familia, visita México por primera vez. Acaba de llegar del aeropuerto con sus primos y ahora está en la casa de sus tíos, que están muy contentos con la llegada de la muchacha. Julia va a pasar la Navidad y el Año Nuevo con ellos.

Doña Luz	¡Bienvenida, hijita! ¡Ay! ¡Dame un abrazo! ¿Cómo estás? ¿Y cómo está mi hermano... tu papá...? ¿Tienes hambre?
Lupita	¡Mamá! ¡Una pregunta a la vez! ¡La pobre Julia está aturdida!
Julia	(*Abraza a su tía.*) Estoy bien, gracias, tía. Y su hermano... está bien, también. Y no tengo hambre, pero tengo mucha sed...
Doña Luz	(*A su hijo Mario*) Mario, una soda para tu prima.
Julia	Prefiero un vaso de agua, tía.
Don Rodolfo	¿Cómo estás, sobrina? ¿Qué tal el viaje?
Julia	Muy bien, tío. Estoy un poco cansada, pero estoy muy contenta de estar aquí con ustedes.

Por la noche, Julia está en el cuarto de Lupita. Las dos primas conversan.

Lupita	Mañana vamos a ir al parque de Chapultepec y por la noche vamos a ir al cine con unos amigos.
Julia	¡Perfecto! También quiero ir a una tienda por la tarde. Oye, ¿qué vamos a hacer pasado mañana?
Lupita	Pasado mañana damos una fiesta aquí, en casa. Es el santo de mi abuelo.
Julia	Ah, sí don Gustavo.
Lupita	Sí, él vive con nosotros. Mamá va a preparar mucha comida y vamos a tener mariachis...
Julia	¡Entonces quiero sacar muchas fotos! ¿Vamos a bailar?
Lupita	Sí. Muchos de nuestros amigos van a venir a la fiesta y van a querer bailar contigo.
Julia	¿Cuántas personas están invitadas?
Lupita	Unas cincuenta... O más, porque muchos vecinos van a venir también.
Julia	¿Y cuándo empiezan las posadas?
Lupita	La semana que viene. Este fin de semana pensamos ir a una discoteca de la Zona Rosa. Oye... es tarde.
Julia	Tienes razón. ¡Son las once! ¡Pero no tengo sueño! Quiero platicar un rato más.

A. Preguntas y respuestas You will now hear questions about the dialogue. Answer each one, omitting the subject. The speaker will confirm your response. Repeat the correct response.

B. Situaciones The speaker will present several situations based on the dialogue. Respond appropriately in Spanish to each situation. The speaker will confirm your response. Repeat the correct response. Follow the model.

> MODELO: You ask a child if he is hot.
> **¿Tienes calor?**

Pronunciación

A. *The sound of the Spanish **b** and **v***

- Repeat each word, imitating the speaker's pronunciation.

veinte	bien
venir	baile
Viviana	bebida
Víctor	sobrina

- When you hear the number, read the corresponding sentence aloud. Then listen to the speaker and repeat the sentence.
  1. ¿Vas a Burgos para buscar a Viviana?
  2. Victoria baila con Vicente Barrios.
  3. En el verano, Bárbara va a Varsovia con Basilio.

B. *The sound of the Spanish **d***

- Repeat each word, imitating the speaker's pronunciation.

delgado	universidad
de	sábado
debe	bebida
dos	adiós

- When you hear the number, read the corresponding sentence aloud. Then listen to the speaker and repeat the sentence.
  1. Dorotea mide dos yardas de seda.
  2. ¿Cuándo es la boda de Diana y Dionisio?
  3. ¿Por dónde anda Delia, doña Dora?

C. *The sound of the Spanish **g** (before **a**, **o**, or **u**)*

- Repeat each word, imitating the speaker's pronunciation.

delgado	Durango
guapo	gusto
gordo	Gabriel

- Repeat the following words.

amigo	hago
pregunta	llega
uruguaya	Hugo

- Repeat the following words.

Guevara	guitarra
Guillermo	guerra
alguien	

- When you hear the number, read the corresponding sentence aloud. Then listen to the speaker and repeat the sentence.
  1. Gustavo Guerrero ganó la guerra.
  2. El águila lanzó la daga en el agua.
  3. El gordo guardó la guitarra en el gabinete.

Estructuras

A. Pronouns as objects of prepositions Answer each of the following questions, using the second alternative given. The speaker will confirm your response. Repeat the correct response. Follow the model.

> MODELO: ¿Vas a ir con ellas o con nosotros?
> **Voy a ir con ustedes.**

1. (Luis)
2. (primas)
3. (amiga)

4. (profesora)
5. (cuadernos)

B. Contractions Answer each question you hear, using the cue provided. The speaker will confirm your response. Repeat the correct response. Follow the model.

> MODELO: ¿A quién llamas? (profesor Vega)
> **Llamo al profesor Vega.**

1. (doctor)
2. (club)
3. (señor López)

4. (novia de Luis)
5. (profesora)
6. (amigo de Juan)

C. Present indicative of the irregular verbs *ir*, *dar*, and *estar* You will hear several statements, each followed by a question. Answer each question, using the cue provided. The speaker will confirm your response. Repeat the correct response. Follow the model.

> MODELO: Luis va a la fiesta. ¿Y tú? (al baile)
> **Yo voy al baile.**

1. (con Raúl)
2. (con Carmen)
3. (el domingo)

4. (en Colorado)
5. (no)
6. (el domingo)

D. *Ir a* + infinitive You will hear some statements about what people do on different occasions. Using the cues provided, respond by saying what the new subjects are *going* to do. The speaker will confirm your response. Repeat the correct response. Follow the model.

> MODELO: Ana trabaja los lunes. (yo / los sábados)
> **Yo voy a trabajar los sábados.**

1. (nosotros / por la mañana)
2. (tú / los martes)
3. (Anita / el viernes)

4. (yo / a las seis)
5. (ellos / entremeses)

E. Present indicative of *e:ie* stem-changing verbs The speaker will ask several questions. Answer each one, using the cue provided. The speaker will confirm your response. Repeat the correct response. Follow the model.

> MODELO: ¿Adónde quieren ir ustedes? (a la universidad)
> **Queremos ir a la universidad.**

1. (a las siete)
2. (a las ocho)
3. (no, con Antonio)
4. (no, esta tarde)

5. (sí)
6. (a las diez)
7. (sí)

F. Expressions with *tener* Use expressions with **tener** to say how the people described in each statement feel, according to the situation. The speaker will confirm your response. Repeat the correct response. Follow the model.

> MODELO: I am in Alaska in January.
> **Yo tengo mucho frío.**

Más práctica

A. Dibujos (*Drawings*) You will hear three statements about each drawing. Choose the letter of the statement that best corresponds to the drawing. The speaker will verify your response.

1.

   a b c

2.

   a b c

3.

   a b c

4.

   a b c

5.

   a b c

B. Unos diálogos breves Before listening to the dialogues in this section, study the comprehension questions below. Reviewing the questions ahead of time will help you to remember key information as you listen. Then listen carefully to the dialogues and answer each question, omitting the subject. The speaker will confirm your response. Repeat the correct answer.

1. ¿Por qué no quiere comer Estela?
2. ¿Estela tiene sed?
3. ¿Qué prefiere tomar?
4. ¿Cuántos años tiene Marta?
5. ¿Qué celebra Marta hoy?
6. ¿Dónde va a dar Marta la fiesta?
7. ¿A qué hora empieza la fiesta?
8. ¿Jorge está invitado a la fiesta?
9. ¿Por qué quiere bailar Silvia?
10. ¿Qué va a abrir Silvia?

C. Para contestar Answer the questions you hear, using the cues provided. The speaker will confirm your answers. Repeat the correct answer.

1. (cine)
2. (la casa de mi familia)
3. (parque de diversiones)
4. (mi mamá)
5. (museo)
6. (mi vecino)
7. (ir a una discoteca)
8. (mi tía)
9. (sí, un rato)
10. (sí)

D. Tome nota You will hear a young man describe his birthday party. First listen carefully for general comprehension. Then, as you listen for a second time, fill in the information requested.

¡Es una fiesta de _____!

Para _____

Día _____

Hora _____

Lugar _____

E. Dictado The speaker will read six sentences. Each sentence will be read twice. After the first reading, write what you heard. After the second reading, check your work and fill in what you missed.

1. _____

2. _____

3. _____

4. _____

5. _____

6. _____

Hasta ahora... Una prueba

You have finished **Lecciones 3** and **4**. How much have you learned about structure and vocabulary?

A. Complete the following exchanges, using the present indicative of the verbs given.

1. —¿Dónde _____ (estar) tú ahora?

   —_____ (Estar) en la casa de mi tía.

   —¿Tus padres _____ (venir) hoy?

   —No, porque no _____ (tener) tiempo.

   —¿Tú _____ (querer) ir a la fiesta de Ada?

   —Sí, (yo) _____ (ir) con Antonio. ¿Y tú?

   —Yo _____ (preferir) ir al cine.

2. —¿Dónde _____ (comer) ustedes?

   —Nosotros _____ (comer) en la cafetería y después

   _____ (ir) a la biblioteca.

   —¿A qué hora _____ (cerrar) ellos la biblioteca hoy?

   —A las diez. ¿Tú _____ (ir) esta noche?

   —Sí, _____ (ir) a las siete.

3. —¿Tú _____ (dar) fiestas los sábados?

   —No, yo _____ (dar) fiestas los viernes.

   —¿Dónde _____ (vivir) tú?

   —Yo _____ (vivir) en la calle Ocho.

   —¿Adónde _____ (pensar) ir tú y Carlos mañana?

   —_____ (Pensar) ir a la fiesta del club.

   —¿A qué hora _____ (empezar) la fiesta?

   —A las ocho.

B. Solve these arithmetic problems.

1. siete mil + cuatro mil + cien + cuatrocientos = _____

2. cuatrocientos mil + trescientos mil = _____

3. doscientos ochenta + trescientos veinte = _____

4. cuatrocientos cincuenta + cuatrocientos noventa = _____

5. setenta mil + treinta mil + ochocientos = _____

C. Complete the following exchanges, using the Spanish equivalent of the words in parentheses.

1. —Estela es _____. (*a very pretty girl*)

    Ella vive en _____. (*our house*)

    —¿Cuántos años tiene ella?

    —_____ años. (*She's nineteen*)

2. —¿Jorge está _____, Anita? (*with you*)

    —Sí, está _____. (*with me*)

    —¿Uds. _____ hoy? (*are going to study*)

    —Sí, con _____. (*Mr. Soto's son*)

3. —¿Tú visitas _____ los domingos?

    (*your parents*)

    —Sí, pero mañana ellos _____. (*are*

    going to be busy)

4. —¿_____ un vaso de agua, señorita?

    (*Do you want*)

    —Sí, por favor. _____. (*I'm very thirsty*)

    —¿Desea _____? (*to have something*

    to eat)

    —No, gracias. _____. (*I'm not hungry*)

D. Arrange these words and phrases in groups of three, according to categories.

tener sed	hija	nervioso	abuela	alegre	periódico	habitación
tener hambre	querer	primo	concierto	tomar	brindis	amable
comer algo	cine	empleo	animado	diario	mi amor	asistir
encantador	venir	bonita	salud	preferir	solicitud	enojado
pasado mañana	vino	frustrado	morena	en casa	pelirroja	mi vida
la semana que viene	leer	linda	trabajo	cortés	beber	abrazar
entusiasmado	ir	comida	desear	simpática	hermana	
este fin de semana	tío	rubia	sobrino	teatro	cuarto	

1. _____   _____   _____

2. _____   _____   _____

3. _____   _____   _____

4. _____   _____   _____

5. _____   _____   _____

6. _____   _____   _____

7. _____   _____   _____

8. _____   _____   _____

9. _____   _____   _____

10. _____   _____   _____

11. _____   _____   _____

12. _____   _____   _____

13. _____   _____   _____

14. _____   _____   _____

15. _____   _____   _____

16. _____   _____   _____

17. _____   _____   _____

18. _____   _____   _____

Hasta ahora... Una prueba (Lecciones 3 y 4)

Un paso más

					●	
					Octubre	
lunes	martes	miércoles	jueves	viernes	sábado	domingo
	1	Conferencia Dra. Nieto 2	3	Discoteca 11:00 4	Concierto 8:30 5	6
7	Examen de francés 8	9	Informe de sociología 10	11	Tenis Sergio 9:00 12	13
Examen de matemáticas 14	15	Tía Marta viene de Guanajuato 16	17	18	Fiesta de cumpleaños (Eva) 19	20
Llevar a Nora al aeropuerto 21	22	Examen de física 23	24	25	Picnic— Playa Preparar sándwiches 26	27
Examen de biología 28	29	Dentista 2:00 30	31			

A. El mes de octubre en el calendario de Verónica Answer the questions below, according to what Verónica's calendar reflects.

1. ¿Cuántos exámenes tiene Verónica en octubre?

_____

2 ¿En qué fecha da la Dra. Nieto una conferencia?

_____

3. ¿Dónde va a ser el picnic?

_____

4. ¿Qué tiene que preparar Verónica para el picnic?

_____

5. ¿De dónde viene la tía de Verónica?

_____

6. ¿Quién celebra su cumpleaños este mes?

_____

7. ¿Da una fiesta?

_____

8. ¿A qué hora es el concierto?

_____

9. ¿Para qué clase tiene que escribir Verónica un informe?

_____

10. ¿Verónica piensa ir a la discoteca el sábado?

_____

11. ¿Con quién va a jugar (*play*) al tenis?

_____

12. ¿Qué idioma estudia Verónica?

_____

13. ¿Adónde tiene que ir Verónica el 30 de octubre?

_____

14. ¿A qué hora tiene que estar en el consultorio (*office*) del dentista?

_____

15. ¿A quién tiene que llevar Verónica al aeropuerto?

_____

B. Two Mexican students are coming to your city and are staying for a week. On a separate sheet of paper, prepare a list of all the places they are going to see, the people they are going to meet (**conocer**), and the activities you will organize for them. Make sure they have a wonderful time. Give details!

Workbook Activities

Estructuras

A. Comparative forms Imagine that this picture is a photo taken at a party that you attended. Look at the picture and complete the following sentences, relating what the people are doing and establishing comparisons among them.

1. Alberto _____ _____ con Rita. Rita es _____ _____

    _____ que Alberto. Él es _____ _____ que ella.

2. Julio y Elisa _____. Julio es mucho _____ _____ que ella. Elisa

    es la _____ _____ de la fiesta.

3. Luis es _____ _____ que Mario. Mario es el _____

    _____ de la fiesta.

4. Pedro es _____ _____ que Alberto.

5. Estela y Dora _____ _____ café. Estela es _____ _____ que Dora.

6. Rita es bonita, pero no es _____ _____ _____ Estela.

B. Irregular comparative forms Compare the following people, places, and things to each other.

1. Anabel: 5'11" / Alina: 5'11"

_____

2. Beto: veinticinco años / Tito: catorce años

_____

3. el restaurante Don Pepe: bueno / el restaurante Miramar: excelente

_____

4. el hotel Siesta: malo / el hotel Costa: muy, muy malo

_____

5. yo: veinte años / mi primo: veintidós años

_____

C. Present indicative of *o:ue* stem-changing verbs I Complete the chart below.

Subject	Infinitive	Present Indicative
1. yo	poder	
2.		volvemos
3. Uds.	almorzar	
4.		encuentras
5. Luis	dormir	
6.		vuelo
7. los chicos	recordar	
8.		podemos
9. el cuadro	costar	

D. Present indicative of *o:ue* stem-changing verbs II Somebody wants to know about your plans. Answer his questions, using the cues provided.

1. ¿Puede Ud. viajar a México este verano? (sí)

   _____

2. ¿Cuánto cuesta viajar a México? (quinientos dólares)

   _____

3. ¿Ud. y su familia vuelan a México? (sí)

   _____

4. ¿A qué hora vuelve Ud. a su casa hoy? (a las cinco)

   _____

5. Ud. y sus amigos, ¿almuerzan en la cafetería o en su casa? (en la cafetería)

   _____

6. Ud. necesita hablar con su profesor hoy. ¿Recuerda su número de teléfono? (no)

   _____

E. Present progressive You are reporting on what everybody is doing. Use the present progressive tense to describe everyone's actions as completely as possible.

1. Ella _____

   _____

   _____

2. Tú _____

   _____

   _____

3. Ellos _____

   _____

   _____

4. El camarero _____

_____ la cena.

5. Yo _____

_____

una carta (*letter*).

6. Nosotros _____

_____.

F. Uses of *ser* and *estar* Complete each of the following sentences with either **ser** or **estar**, as appropriate. Indicate the reason for your choice by placing the corresponding number in the blank provided before the sentence.

Uses of **ser**

1. characteristic / expressions of age
2. material that something is made of
3. nationality / origin / profession
4. time and dates
5. event that is taking place
6. possession / relationship

Uses of **estar**

7. condition
8. location
9. reaction / sensory perception

_____ 1. ¡La ensalada _____ deliciosa!

_____ 2. Ellos _____ enfermos.

_____ 3. Miguel Ángel _____ mi hermano.

_____ 4. La fiesta _____ en el Club Tropicana.

_____ 5. Nosotros _____ norteamericanos: yo _____ de Arizona y ella

_____ de Utah.

_____ 6. El hospital _____ en la calle Cuarta.

_____ 7. Ana _____ muy bonita.

_____ 8. Los cuadernos _____ de Irene.

_____ 9. El café _____ frío.

_____ 10. ¿Dónde _____ tu hermana?

_____ 11. Rogelio _____ muy inteligente.

_____ 12. Yo _____ profesor.

_____ 13. _____ las dos y media.

_____ 14. La mesa _____ de metal.

G. Weather expressions Say what the weather is like in different parts of the country.

| Chicago | Miami | Alaska | Oregón |

1. En Chicago _____ y _____.

2. En Miami _____ y _____.

3. En Alaska _____ y _____.

4. En Oregón _____.

Lección 5, Workbook Activities   **71**

H. Situaciones You find yourself in the following situations. What do you say?

1. You are trying to convince your friend Amalia to go on a blind date with Hugo. Tell her he's tall, dark, and handsome, and that he is a little older than she (is).

   _____

   _____

2. You call a friend on the phone and ask him what he's doing. Tell him that you are reading a book and writing a report.

   _____

   _____

3. You are at a restaurant. Tell the waiter to bring you steak with French fries and vegetable soup.

   _____

   _____

4. You are telling on your brother and sister. You tell your mother that she is watching T.V. and he is sleeping.

   _____

   _____

5. You e-mail a friend who lives in Guatemala. Ask her what the weather is like there and tell her it's cold and it's raining in . . . (your city).

   _____

   _____

I. Crucigrama

Horizontal

5. Quiero _____ de papas.
6. salmón, por ejemplo
9. Trabaja en un restaurante.
12. hombre de Guatemala
16. Necesito sal y _____.
19. rico
21. ¿Es alto, bajo o de _____ mediana?
22. Provolone, por ejemplo
23. Necesito el mantel y las _____.
24. Necesito uno para cortar (*cut*) un biftec.
25. Comemos _____ en McDonald's.

4. regresar
6. trozo
7. ¿Quieres _____ de manzana?
8. esposo
10. factoría
11. muy, muy bonito
13. comer al mediodía
14. ¿Quieres vino blanco o vino _____?
15. De postre quiero arroz con _____.
17. ¿Quieres una _____ de café?
18. Necesito una para el café.
20. La Coca-Cola es uno.

Vertical

1. Quiero _____ de fideos.
2. ¿Quieres _____ de naranja?
3. legumbre

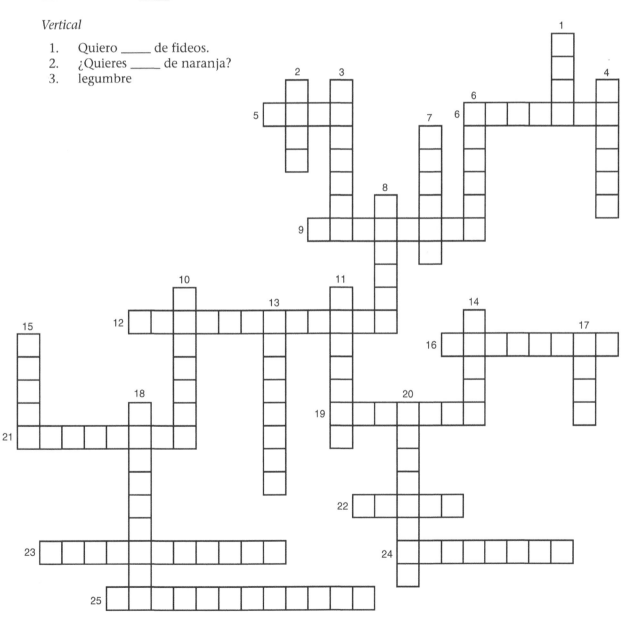

J. ¿Qué pasa aquí? Look at the illustration and answer the following questions.

1. ¿En qué restaurante están estas personas?

   _____

2. ¿Qué celebran Héctor y Viviana?

   _____

3. ¿Es su segundo (*second*) aniversario?

   _____

4. ¿Cuánto deja Alfredo para el mozo?

   _____

5. ¿Adónde quiere ir Alfredo ahora?

   _____

6. ¿Con quién quiere ir?

   _____

7. ¿Con quién cena Marcelo?

_____

8. ¿Qué recomienda el mozo?

_____

9. ¿Qué pide (*orders*) Marcelo para tomar?

_____

10. ¿Qué va a pedir Delia?

_____

11. ¿Con quiénes cena Carlos?

_____

12. ¿Qué va a pedir Carlos de postre?

_____

13. ¿Qué va a pedir Ana?

_____

14. Mientras Ana y Carlos comen el postre, ¿qué va a hacer Beto?

_____

La carta de Cristina

Querida Esmeralda:

 ¿Cómo estás? Nosotros estamos bien, pero estamos trabajando mucho, especialmente Fernando, que siempre está muy ocupado.

 Esta noche vienen unos amigos a cenar° con nosotros, y voy a servir pescado a la parrilla, papas al horno y vegetales. De postre, arroz con leche y, para beber, un buen vino blanco.

 Esmeralda, si vienes en octubre, podemos ir a Antigua, una de las ciudades más interesantes de Centroamérica. Si tenemos tiempo, también podemos ir a Tikal, las famosas ruinas mayas.

 ¿Hace mucho calor en México ahora? Aquí, como siempre, hace buen tiempo.

 Bueno, tengo que empezar a cocinar. Saludos a tu familia.

 Un abrazo,

    Cristina

to have dinner

¡Conteste! Answer the following questions based on the reading.

1. ¿Qué está escribiendo Cristina?

_____

2. ¿Quién está muy ocupado siempre?

_____

3. ¿Quiénes vienen a cenar esta noche?

_____

4. ¿Qué va a servir Cristina para comer?

_____

5. ¿Qué va a preparar de postre?

_____

6. ¿Van a beber vino tinto?

_____

7. ¿Cuándo piensa venir Esmeralda a Guatemala?

_____

8. ¿Cómo es Antigua?

_____

9.   ¿Qué otro lugar (*place*) pueden visitar?

_____

10.   ¿Qué tiempo hace ahora en Guatemala?

_____

Panorama hispánico

Complete the following charts.

Guatemala

Capital: _____

Idioma oficial: _____

Clima: _____

Famosa ciudad maya: _____

Base de la economía del país: _____

Principales productos de importación: _____, _____,

_____ y _____

Moneda del país: _____

Famoso escritor guatemalteco: _____

El Salvador

Capital: _____

Población: _____

Número de volcanes: _____

Deporte más popular en las playas: _____

Clima: _____

Productos agrícolas de exportación: _____ y _____

Lección 5

Laboratory Activities

Diálogos

En un restaurante Listen to the dialogues twice, paying close attention to the speakers' intonation and pronunciation patterns. First, listen to the entire dialogue; then, as you listen for a second time, pause the recording after each sentence and repeat after the speaker.

Fernando Madera es de El Salvador, pero vive en la ciudad de Guatemala. Es contador y trabaja en una fábrica. Fernando es casado y su esposa Cristina es guatemalteca, de la ciudad de Antigua. Él es delgado y de estatura mediana. No es muy guapo, pero es inteligente y simpático. Cristina es un poco más baja que él, y es muy hermosa.

En este momento están en un restaurante. Cristina está leyendo el menú.

CRISTINA   Arroz con pollo... biftec con papas al horno o puré de papas, ensalada...pescado frito...

FERNANDO   Yo a veces almuerzo aquí. Preparan una ensalada de camarones muy rica. También tienen langosta...

CRISTINA   La langosta cuesta 80 quetzales. Es un poco cara...

El camarero viene a la mesa.

CAMARERO   ¿Qué desean comer?

CRISTINA   Pollo a la parrilla con ensalada y una papa al horno. Para beber, agua mineral. (*A Fernando*) Tengo que contar calorías.

CAMARERO   (*Anota el pedido.*) Muy bien, señora. ¿Y usted, señor?

FERNANDO   Tráigame biftec con papas fritas y sopa de verduras. Para beber, vino tinto. (*A Cristina*) Las papas fritas son más sabrosas que la papa al horno.

El mozo va hacia la cocina.

CRISTINA   Voy a llamar a mamá para ver qué están haciendo los niños. Estoy un poco preocupada...

FERNANDO   ¡Cristina! ¡Están en su casa, con su abuela! ¡Están bien! ¡Eres imposible!

Cristina habla por teléfono y después vuelve a la mesa.

CRISTINA   Amanda está estudiando, Fernandito está durmiendo y mamá está mirando su telenovela. Hay un mensaje electrónico de tu hermano. Lo están pasando muy bien en Cancún. Hace sol, pero no hace calor...

FERNANDO   ¡Perfecto! Oye, voy a pedir flan con crema de postre.

CRISTINA   Y yo voy a pedir helado de chocolate...

FERNANDO   ¿No estás contando calorías?

CRISTINA   Sí, pero el helado no tiene muchas calorías. Además... hoy es un día especial.

FERNANDO   ¿Un día especial...?

CRISTINA   ¡Sí! Estamos solos... podemos conversar... Creo que voy a pedir un pedazo de torta y después, café. Mañana vuelvo a mi dieta...

Fernando paga la cuenta y deja una buena propina.

A. Preguntas y respuestas You will now hear questions about the dialogue. Answer each one, omitting the subject. The speaker will confirm your response. Repeat the correct response.

B. Situaciones The speaker will present several situations based on the dialogue. Respond appropriately in Spanish to each situation. The speaker will confirm your response. Repeat the correct response. Follow the model.

> MODELO: You ask the waiter to bring you the menu.
> **Tráigame el menú.**

Pronunciación

A. *The sound of the Spanish* **p**

- Repeat each word, imitating the speaker's pronunciation.

perfectamente	tiempo	oportunidad
propina	papá	septiembre
pescado	primo	poder

- When you hear the number, read the corresponding sentence aloud. Then listen to the speaker and repeat the sentence.
  1. Para practicar, preciso tiempo y plata.
  2. Pablo puede pedirle la carpeta.
  3. El pintor pinta un poco para pasar el tiempo.

B. *The sound of the Spanish* **t**

- Repeat each word, imitating the speaker's pronunciation.

nieta	restaurante	practicar
tío	torta	tinto
otro	este	foto

- When you hear the number, read the corresponding sentence aloud. Then listen to the speaker and repeat the sentence.
  1. ¿Todavía tengo tiempo o es tarde?
  2. Tito trae tomates para ti también.
  3. Teresa tiene tres teléfonos en total.

C. *The sound of the Spanish* **c**

- Repeat each word, imitating the speaker's pronunciation.

café	contar	cuñado
nunca	copas	cuánto
calle	simpático	cuándo

- When you hear the number, read the corresponding sentence aloud. Then listen to the speaker and repeat the sentence.
  1. Carmen Cortés compró un coche.
  2. Cándido conoció a Paco en Colombia.
  3. Coco canta canciones cubanas.

D. *The sound of the Spanish* **q**

- Repeat each word, imitating the speaker's pronunciation.

  Quintana   aquí
  Roque   quiere
  queso   Quique

- When you hear the number, read the corresponding sentence aloud. Then listen to the speaker and repeat the sentence.

  1. ¿Qué quiere Roque Quintana?
  2. ¿Quieres quedarte en la quinta?
  3. El pequeño Quique quiere queso.

Estructuras

A. Comparisons of inequality Respond to each statement you hear, using the comparative form. The speaker will confirm your response. Repeat the correct response. Follow the model.

> MODELO: Yo soy alto.
> **Yo soy más alto que tú.**

B. Comparisons of equality Establish comparisons of equality between the people described in each pair of statements you hear. The speaker will confirm your response. Repeat the correct response. Follow the model.

> MODELO: Jorge es bajo. Pedro es bajo.
> **Jorge es tan bajo como Pedro.**

C. The superlative You will hear several statements describing people or places. Using the cues provided, express the superlative. The speaker will confirm your response. Repeat the correct response. Follow the model.

> MODELO: Tomás es muy guapo. (de la clase).
> **Sí, es el más guapo de la clase.**

1. (de California)   3. (de la familia)
2. (de la clase)   4. (de la ciudad)

D. Present indicative of *o:ue* stem-changing verbs Answer each question you hear, using the cue provided. The speaker will confirm your response. Repeat the correct response. Follow the model.

> MODELO: ¿Marcos puede venir hoy? (no)
> **No, no puede venir.**

1. (en la cafetería)   4. (sí)
2. (dos dólares)   5. (no)
3. (en enero)   6. (no)

E. Present progressive Rephrase each of the following statements, using the present progressive tense. The speaker will confirm your response. Repeat the correct response. Follow the model.

> MODELO: Jorge come ensalada.
> **Jorge está comiendo ensalada.**

F. Uses of *ser* and *estar* Combine the phrases given to form sentences, using the appropriate form of **ser** or **estar**. The speaker will confirm your response. Repeat the correct response. Follow the model.

> MODELO: mis padres / de Guatemala
> **Mis padres son de Guatemala.**

G. Weather expressions Using the cues provided, say what the weather is like in each place. The speaker will confirm your response. Repeat the correct response. Follow the model.

> MODELO: ¿Qué tiempo hace en Phoenix? (calor)
> **Hace calor.**

1. (mucho frío)
2. (llover mucho)
3. (viento)

4. (nevar)
5. (haber niebla)

Más práctica

A. Dibujos (*Drawings*) You will hear three statements about each drawing. Choose the letter of the statement that best corresponds to the drawing. The speaker will verify your response.

1.

a   b   c

2.

a   b   c

3.

a   b   c

4.

a   b   c

5.

a   b   c

B. Unos diálogos breves Before listening to the dialogues in this section, study the comprehension questions below. Reviewing the questions ahead of time will help you to remember key information as you listen. Then listen carefully to the dialogues and answer each question, omitting the subject. The speaker will confirm your response. Repeat the correct answer.

1. ¿Rosa y Carlos almuerzan en la cafetería?
2. ¿Dónde almuerzan?
3. ¿Por qué no almuerzan en la cafetería?
4. ¿Por qué no va a almorzar Luis con Rosa y con Carlos?
5. ¿Qué no recuerda Oscar?
6. ¿Cuándo vuela Rita a México?
7. ¿Cuándo vuelve?
8. ¿Anita es mayor o menor que Carlos?
9. ¿Quién es más alto?
10. ¿Anita es la hermana de Carlos?

C. Para contestar Answer the questions, using the cues provided. The speaker will confirm your response. Repeat the correct response.

1. (baja)
2. (menor)
3. (a la parrilla)
4. (en un restaurante)
5. (no)
6. (el mantel y las servilletas)
7. (sol)
8. (té frío)
9. (jugo de frutas)
10. (perro caliente)

D. Tome nota You will hear a couple ordering food in a restaurant. First listen carefully for general comprehension. Then, as you listen for a second time, fill in the information requested.

	Señora	Señor
Comida	_____	_____
	_____	_____
Bebida	_____	_____
	_____	_____
Postre	_____	_____
	_____	_____

E. Dictado The speaker will read six sentences. Each sentence will be read twice. After the first reading, write what you heard. After the second reading, check your work and fill in what you missed.

1. _____

2. _____

3. _____

4. _____

5. _____

6. _____

Lección **6**

Workbook Activities

Estructuras

A. Demonstrative adjectives We are pointing to these objects and people. Write the names of the items illustrated, using the Spanish equivalent of the demonstrative adjectives given.

1. this, these

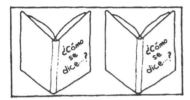

a. _____

b. _____

c. _____

d. _____

2. that, those

a. _____

Lección 6, Workbook Activities   **85**

b. _____

c. _____

d. _____

3. that (over there), those (over there)

a. _____

b. _____

c. _____

d. _____

B. Present indicative of *e:i* stem-changing verbs I Complete the chart below.

Infinitive	yo	tú	Ud., él, ella	nosotros	Uds., ellos, ellas
1. servir					
2.	pido				
3.		dices			
4.			sigue		
5.					consiguen

C. Present indicative of *e:i* stem-changing verbs II Complete the following paragraphs to explain what you and your friends do when you eat out and shop. Use the verbs listed. The numbers in parentheses indicate how many times each verb should be used.

pedir (3)   conseguir (1)   decir (2)   servir (1)

En el restaurante El Azteca _____ los mejores tamales y las mejores

enchiladas. Roberto y yo siempre _____ tamales y Jorge

_____ enchiladas. Nora _____ que nosotros siempre

_____ lo mismo (*the same thing*).

    Mañana, Jorge va a ir a una tienda donde él siempre _____ discos

compactos de música mexicana. Él _____ que la música de México es

la mejor.

D. Stem-changing verbs: Review Someone is always asking questions. Complete the following dialogues, using stem-changing verbs **(e:ie, o:ue, and e:i)**. This will give you a chance to review them.

1. —Carla, ¿tú _____ ir a la fiesta de Juan?

    —Yo no _____ ir porque tengo que trabajar. ¿Tú vas?

    —No, yo _____ ir al club a bailar.

2. —¿A qué hora _____ a servir el desayuno en el hotel?

—A las siete. _____ desayuno continental y desayuno americano.

—¿Cuánto _____ el desayuno continental?

—_____ cinco dólares, pero yo siempre

_____ el desayuno americano.

3. —¿Cuándo _____ Uds. de sus vacaciones?

—_____ en agosto, porque las clases

_____ en septiembre.

—Cuando Uds. van a Chile, ¿_____ o van en coche?

—_____, porque es más rápido (*faster*).

4. —¿Tú _____ en la cafetería?

—No, porque la cafetería _____ a las dos y yo trabajo hasta las tres.

5. —(Yo) no _____ mis llaves. ¿Dónde están?

—Tú siempre _____ tus llaves.

6. —Cuando tus abuelos hablan en italiano, ¿tú _____ lo que (*what*)

_____?

—No, no _____ nada.

E. Affirmative and negative expressions Someone is quite wrong about Elena and her husband. Set him straight. Rewrite the following story, making all sentences negative.

Elena siempre va a San Francisco y su esposo también va. Siempre compran algo porque tienen mucho dinero. Algunos de sus amigos vienen a su casa los domingos, y Elena sirve vino o refrescos. Elena es muy simpática y su esposo también es muy simpático.

_____

_____

_____

_____

_____

_____

F. Verbs with irregular first-person forms Tell about yourself by answering the following questions. Use the cues provided.

1. ¿A qué hora sales de tu casa? (siete)

   _____

2. ¿Qué coche conduces? (Ford)

   _____

3. ¿Traes los libros a la universidad? (sí)

   _____

4. ¿Conoces a muchos de los estudiantes de la universidad? (sí)

   _____

5. ¿Sabes el número de teléfono de tu profesor? (no)

   _____

6. En la clase, ¿traduces del inglés al español? (sí)

   _____

7. ¿Haces los quehaceres por la mañana o por la tarde? (la mañana)

   _____

8. ¿Dónde pones tus libros cuando llegas a tu casa? (en mi escritorio)

   _____

9. ¿Qué días ves a tus amigos? (los domingos)

   _____

G. *Saber* vs. *conocer* What does everybody "know"? Write sentences using **saber** or **conocer** and the elements given.

1. nosotros / Teresa

   _____

2. yo / el poema / de memoria

   _____

3. Elsa / no / California

   _____

Lección 6, Workbook Activities **89**

4. ellos / cocinar

_____

5. tú / novelas de Cervantes

_____

6. Armando / no bailar

_____

H. Direct object pronouns I Complete the following dialogues, using direct object pronouns.

MODELO: ¿Ella llama _a Teresa_?
Sí, ella _____ llama.
Sí, ella la llama.

1. ¿Ellos _te_ visitan?

Sí, ellos _____ visitan.

2. ¿Tú llamas _a Jorge_?

Sí, yo _____ llamo.

3. ¿Tú vas a comprar _las revistas_?

Sí, yo voy a comprar_____.

4. ¿Uds. _nos_ llaman (a nosotras)?

Sí, nosotros _____ llamamos.

5. ¿Jorge va a llevar a _los chicos_?

Sí, Jorge va a llevar_____.

6. ¿Anita limpia el baño?

Sí, Anita _____ limpia.

7. ¿Tú _me_ llamas mañana? (_Use_ **tú** _form_)

Sí, yo _____ llamo mañana.

8. ¿Ellos _las_ llevan (_a Uds._) a la fiesta?

Sí, ellos _____ llevan a la fiesta.

9. ¿Ellos _las_ llevan (_a ellas_) a la fiesta?

Sí, ellos _____ llevan a la fiesta.

10. ¿Tú puedes traer _la camisa de Jorge_?

Sí, yo puedo traer_____.

I. Direct object pronouns II Your friend is asking you many questions about your plans. Answer them, using the cues provided and the appropriate direct object pronouns.

1. ¿Cuándo puedes traer *las maletas*? (mañana)

    _____

2. ¿Puedes llamar*me* esta noche? (sí) (***tú** form*)

    _____

3. ¿Tú tienes *las sábanas*? (no)

    _____

4. ¿Tú aceptas todas *las invitaciones* que recibes? (sí)

    _____

5. ¿Quién *te* lleva a la parada de autobuses? (mi tío)

    _____

6. ¿Tú vas cortar *el césped* hoy? (sí)

    _____

7. ¿Vas a visitar *a tus amigos* esta noche? (sí)

    _____

8. ¿Quién *los* va a llevar *a Uds.* al aeropuerto? (mi prima)

    _____

J. Situaciones You find yourself in the following situations. What do you say?

1. You ask a friend what he serves at his parties, and ask him where he gets a good red wine.

    _____

2. Describe to a friend all the chores you are going to do next Saturday: wash and fold clothes, iron some shirts, make the beds, and cook.

    Voy a _____

    _____

3. Complain to your roommate. Tell him/her that he/she never helps you with the housework.

    _____

4. Tell a friend that you and your brother are going to be at the bus stop and ask him if he can go pick you up.

    _____

K. Crucigrama

Horizontal

3. Olga me va a _____ a limpiar la casa.
6. opuesto de **nada**
7. Uso Tide para _____.
8. opuesto de **vender**
9. Nosotros no _____ dónde viven.
12. Lo voy a poner _____ de la cama.
15. El papá de mi esposo es mi _____.
16. Allí ponemos el coche.
17. La uso para barrer.
18. No voy a barrer. Voy a pasar la _____.
22. lo opuesto de **nunca**
23. Voy al mercado para hacer las _____.
25. Yo pongo la _____ en la cama.
26. habitación

Vertical

1. Ana _____ el piso.
2. La esposa de mi hermano es mi _____.
4. conocer: yo
5. Ellos van a _____ en autobús.
10. autobús
11. ahora mismo; en _____
13. Rita hace los _____ de la casa.
14. Ellos _____ la basura.
19. *People* es una _____.
20. Hoy voy a cortar el _____.
21. El esposo de mi hija es mi _____.
23. Se usa con un pantalón.
24. Tenemos que _____ los muebles.

L. ¿Qué pasa aquí? Look at the illustration and answer the following questions about what is going on in each apartment on a Saturday morning.

1. ¿Quién está pasando la aspiradora?

    _____

2. ¿Qué va a hacer Eva?

    _____

3. ¿Qué está limpiando Rita?

   _____

4. ¿Qué está haciendo la Sra. Miño?

   _____

5. ¿Qué está haciendo Lisa?

   _____

6. ¿Qué tiene que hacer José?

   _____

7. ¿Qué va a necesitar José para hacerlo?

   _____

8. ¿José está mirando una telenovela o está mirando un partido de fútbol?

   _____

9. ¿Qué está haciendo Adolfo?

   _____

10. ¿Quién está haciendo la cama?

   _____

Panorama hispánico

Complete the following charts.

Honduras
Capital: _____
Población: _____
Base de la economía del país: _____
Porcentaje de la población que trabaja en la agricultura: _____
Mayor atracción turística del país: _____

Nicaragua

Capital: _____

Lagos importantes: _____ y _____

Ciudades más importantes: _____, _____ y

_____

Base de la economía del país: _____

Principales productos de exportación: _____, _____ y

_____

Gran poeta nicaragüense: _____

Lección 6

Laboratory Activities

Diálogo

Hoy llega tía Nora Listen to the dialogue twice, paying close attention to the speakers' intonation and pronunciation patterns. First, listen to the entire dialogue; then, as you listen for a second time, pause the recording after each sentence and repeat after the speaker.

La familia Núñez Arzuaga, de Tegucigalpa, Honduras, está esperando la llegada de doña Nora, la hermana mayor del señor Núñez. Ella vive en Managua y siempre viene a visitarlos en el verano. Hoy, Ester y sus hijos están haciendo los trabajos de la casa.

ESTER	¡Amalia! Yo estoy cocinando. Tú tienes que lavar los platos y barrer la cocina. ¿Dónde está la escoba?
AMALIA	¿Y qué va a hacer Celia mientras yo hago todo el trabajo? ¡Ella nunca hace nada!
CELIA	¡Ja! ¡Eso no es verdad! Yo estoy planchando las camisas de papá...
ESTER	Sí, y después va a hacer las camas y va a cambiar las sábanas.
AMALIA	¿Y Daniel? ¿Está haciendo algo? Él nunca nos ayuda.
ESTER	Él está arreglando su cuarto...
CELIA	¡Ay, mamá! ¿Desde cuándo? Para él, arreglar su cuarto es esconderlo todo debajo de la cama.
ESTER	Pues esta vez tiene que poner las cosas en su lugar, porque tu tía Nora va a usar ese cuarto y Daniel va a dormir en el sofá de la sala.
AMALIA	¿Quién va a hacer las compras en el mercado?
ESTER	Tu papá. (*Llama a su esposo.*) ¡Pedro! Tienes que ir al Mercado Municipal. Y a ver si esta vez consigues carne buena... Aquí tengo la lista...
PEDRO	¡No la necesito! Yo sé lo que tengo que comprar. En seguida vuelvo. (*Sale del cuarto.*)
ESTER	¡Quién sabe lo que va a traer! (*Suspira.*) ¡Qué trabajo tenemos cuando mi cuñada viene a visitarnos...!
AMALIA	¡El año próximo nosotros podemos visitarla a ella! Yo quiero conocer Managua.
CELIA	¡Estoy de acuerdo! Yo también quiero ir a Managua.
AMALIA	¿Papá va a ir a buscar a tía Nora a la parada de autobuses?
ESTER	No, ella dice que es mejor tomar un taxi...
CELIA	¡Tocan a la puerta! (*Mira por la ventana.*) ¡Es tía Nora! ¡Daniel! ¡Rápido! ¡Todo esto va debajo de la cama!

A. Preguntas y respuestas You will now hear questions about the dialogue. Answer each one, omitting the subject. The speaker will confirm your response. Repeat the correct response.

B. Situaciones The speaker will present several situations based on the dialogue. Respond appropriately in Spanish to each situation. The speaker will confirm your response. Repeat the correct response. Follow the model.

> MODELO: You ask a friend if he knows Rafael's address.
> **¿Tú sabes la dirección de Rafael?**

Pronunciación

A. *The sound of the Spanish* ***g***

- Repeat each word, imitating the speaker's pronunciation.

Gerardo	Argentina	recoger
agencia	general	agente
Ginés	inteligente	Genaro

- When you hear the number, read the corresponding sentence aloud. Then listen to the speaker and repeat the sentence.
  1. Gerardo le da el registro al agente.
  2. El general y el ingeniero recogieron los giros.
  3. Ginés gestionó la gira a Argentina.

B. *The sound of the Spanish* ***j***

- Repeat each word, imitating the speaker's pronunciation.

Julia	dejar	garaje
jota	hijo	debajo
jugo	viajar	jueves

- When you hear the number, read the corresponding sentence aloud. Then listen to the speaker and repeat the sentence.
  1. Julia juega con Josefina en junio.
  2. Juan Juárez trajo los juguetes de Jaime.
  3. Esos jugadores jamás jugaron en Jalisco.

C. *The sound of the Spanish* ***h***

- Repeat each word, imitating the speaker's pronunciation.

hay	Hilda	habitación
Honduras	hermano	hasta
ahora	hotel	hija

- When you hear the number, read the corresponding sentence aloud. Then listen to the speaker and repeat the sentence.
  1. Hay habitaciones hasta en los hoteles.
  2. Hernando Hurtado habla con su hermano.
  3. Hortensia habla con Hugo en el hospital.

Estructuras

A. Demonstrative adjectives and pronous Answer each of the following questions by saying that you prefer the object that is farthest from you and the speaker, using the verb **preferir** and the equivalent of *that one over there* or *those over there*. The speaker will confirm your response. Repeat the correct response. Follow the model.

> MODELO: ¿Quieres esta lista o ésa?
> **Prefiero aquélla.**

B. Present indicative of *e:i* stem-changing verbs Answer each question you hear, using the cue provided. The speaker will confirm your response. Repeat the correct response. Follow the model.

> MODELO: ¿Qué piden Uds.? (agua mineral)
> **Pedimos agua mineral.**

1. (pollo y ensalada)
2. (a las doce)
3. (sí)
4. (sí)
5. (no)

C. Affirmative and negative expressions Give a negative response to each question you hear. The speaker will confirm your response. Repeat the correct response. Follow the model.

> MODELO: ¿Quieres comprar algunas revistas?
> **No, no quiero comprar ninguna revista.**

D. Verbs with irregular first-person forms Answer the following questions in the affirmative. The speaker will confirm your response. Repeat the correct response. Follow the model.

> MODELO: ¿Traes a tu amiga a la fiesta?
> **Sí, traigo a mi amiga a la fiesta.**

E. *Saber* vs. *conocer* Say what or whom the following people know, using **saber** or **conocer** and the cues provided. The speaker will confirm your response. Repeat the correct response. Follow the model.

> MODELO: Sergio (a María)
> **Sergio conoce a María.**

1. (hablar español)
2. (Nicaragua)
3. (dónde viven)
4. (las novelas de Cervantes)
5. (a sus padres)

F. Direct object pronouns Say that Luis will be able to take the following people to a party in his car. The speaker will confirm your response. Repeat the correct response. Follow the model.

> MODELO: Yo no tengo coche.
> **Luis puede llevarme.**

A. Dibujos (*Drawings*) You will hear three statements about each drawing. Choose the letter of the statement that best corresponds to the drawing. The speaker will verify your response.

1.

Maria

a   b   c

2.

ENRIQUE

a   b   c

3.

Irene

a   b   c

4.

ENRIQUE

a   b   c

5.

CLORO   la señora Díaz

a   b   c

B. Unos diálogos breves Before listening to the dialogues in this section, study the comprehension questions below. Reviewing the questions ahead of time will help you to remember key information as you listen. Then listen carefully to the dialogues and answer each question, omitting the subject. The speaker will confirm your response. Repeat the correct answer.

1. ¿A qué hora llama Sergio a Gloria?
2. ¿Por qué no puede llamarla a las siete?
3. ¿Quién tiene los libros de Gloria?
4. ¿Cuándo piensa visitar Ana a Olga?
5. ¿Va a invitar a Daniel?
6. ¿A qué hora sirven la comida en la casa de Amalia?
7. ¿Quién está sirviendo la comida ahora?

C. Para contestar The speaker will ask you some questions. Answer each question, using the cues provided. The speaker will confirm your response. Repeat the correct response.

1. (mi mamá)
2. (los sábados)
3. (sí)
4. (los viernes)
5. (París)

6. (sí)
7. (no, nunca)
8. (no)
9. (no)
10. (tres)

D. Tome nota You will hear a dialogue in which Delia and her husband, Mario, discuss household chores. First listen carefully for general comprehension. Then, as you listen for a second time, list the chores that each one is going to do.

Delia	Mario
1. _____	1. _____
_____	_____
2. _____	2. _____
_____	_____
3. _____	3. _____
_____	_____
4. _____	4. _____
_____	_____

E. Dictado The speaker will read six sentences. Each sentence will be read twice. After the first reading, write what you heard. After the second reading, check your work and fill in what you missed.

1. _____
2. _____
3. _____
4. _____
5. _____
6. _____

Hasta ahora... Una prueba

Let's combine the structure and the vocabulary from **Lecciones 5** and **6**. How much can you remember?

A. Complete the following exchanges, using the present indicative of the verbs given.

1. —¿Tú _____ (poder) estudiar conmigo y con Saúl el sábado?

    —Yo no _____ (conocer) a Saúl... y los sábados, _____

    (salir) con Roberto.

2. —¿(Ellos) _____ (servir) comida mexicana en ese restaurante?

    —No necesitamos ir a un restaurante. Yo _____ (hacer) tamales muy

    buenos...

    —Yo no _____ (saber) hacer tamales, pero _____

    (conseguir) tacos muy sabrosos en una taquería.

3. —¿Dónde _____ (almorzar) ustedes?

    —_____ (Almorzar) en el restaurante Miramar. Yo siempre

    _____ (pedir) langosta o camarones.

    —Yo siempre _____ (decir) que ese restaurante es excelente.

4. —¿A qué hora _____ (volver) tú a tu casa?

    —Si tomo el ómnibus, _____ (volver) a las seis, pero si

    _____ (conducir) mi coche, estoy en mi casa a las cinco.

B. Complete the following exchanges, using the Spanish equivalent of the words in parentheses.

1. —¿Necesita _____? (*anything*)

    —Sí, quiero leer _____. (*these magazines*)

2. —¿Quién _____ la comida? (*is serving*)

    —Mi mamá. Ana _____ y Teresa

    _____ en su cuarto. (*is studying* / *is sleeping*)

    —Y tú?

    —Yo _____ (*am not doing anything*)

3. —¿Tú vas a fregar los platos?

   —Sí. ¿Tú puedes _____? (*dry them*)

   —No, no puedo _____, Anita. Estoy ocupado. (*help you*)

4. —¿Ustedes van a ir a la casa de Marta?

   —Sí, ella _____. (*needs us*)

   —¿Hay _____ en su casa en _____

   momento? (*anybody / this*)

   —No, _____. (*there's nobody*)

5. —¿Dónde _____ la fiesta de Silvia? (*is*)

   —En el hotel Azteca, _____ la ciudad. (*the best in*)

6. —¿Dices que _____? (*it's raining*)

   —Sí, y _____. (*it's very cold*)

7. —¿Ana _____ Pablo? (*is older than*)

   —Sí, pero él _____ ella. (*is much taller than*)

8. —Esteban _____ muy inteligente. (*is*)

   —¡Tú _____ inteligente _____ él! (*are as / as*)

9. —¡El pollo _____ muy sabroso! ¿Quieres un pedazo? (*is*)

   —No, gracias. No tengo mucha hambre. Voy a comer _____

   ensalada. (*that*)

C. Arrange this vocabulary in groups of three, according to the different categories.

a la parrilla	helado	pagar	dormitorio	padrastro
jugo de frutas	frito	cuñada	barrer	cuchillo
lavar la ropa	vino tinto	té frío	comedor	taxi
sala de estar	cuenta	taza	autobús	al horno
pasar la aspiradora	refresco	legumbre	ómnibus	verdura
madrastra	cuchara	camarones	propina	champán
doblar la ropa	suegra	torta	hijastra	langosta
trapear el piso	vaso	pescado	nuera	cerveza
planchar	ensalada	copa	flan	tenedor

1. _____ _____ _____

2. _____ _____ _____

3. _____ _____ _____

4. _____   _____   _____

5. _____   _____   _____

6. _____   _____   _____

7. _____   _____   _____

8. _____   _____   _____

9. _____   _____   _____

10. _____   _____   _____

11. _____   _____   _____

12. _____   _____   _____

13. _____   _____   _____

14. _____   _____   _____

15. _____   _____   _____

Un paso más

A. Look at this ad for a restaurant, and answer the questions that follow.

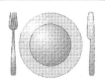

Restaurante
El favorito

Especialidad de la casa: Pescados y mariscos
Menú Internacional

Ambiente familiar
Vista panorámica
Música y baile los
sábados y domigos
Almuerzo y cena

Postres caseros
Vinos importados
Salones privados
para grupos de 12
a 20 personas

Desde el año 1975... ¡Y continuamos sirviendo la comida más fabulosa de Managua!

Para hacer reservaciones, llame al teléfono 63-48-90

Aceptamos tarjetas de crédito°   *credit cards*

Abierto de martes a domingo desde las 11 hasta las 23 horas

Calle Central, número 550

1.   ¿Cuál es la dirección del restaurante El favorito?

     _____

2.   ¿Cómo puedo hacer reservaciones?

     _____

3.   ¿Puedo comer en el restaurante un lunes?

     _____

4.   ¿Qué podemos usar para pagar la cuenta?

     _____

5.   ¿Sirven desayuno (*breakfast*) en el restaurante El favorito?

     _____

6. ¿Podemos pedir langosta y camarones en el restaurante?

_____

7. ¿Sirven solamente comida típica de Nicaragua?

_____

8. ¿Cree usted que los postres son buenos? ¿Por qué?

_____

9. Si yo voy con siete amigos, ¿podemos tener un salón privado?

_____

10. ¿El restaurante El favorito es nuevo?

_____

11. ¿Es un restaurante adecuado para familias?

_____

12. ¿Qué podemos hacer los sábados y los domingos?

_____

B. You are taking the weekend off, so you must do all your household chores during the week. Make a to-do list, indicating what chores you are going to do every day. Include what you are going to prepare for meals. Name at least twelve chores.

Lección **7**

Workbook Activities

Estructuras

A. Indirect object pronouns I Carlos is very helpful. Write what he brings to the following people, using indirect object pronouns. Follow the model.

MODELO: Adela pide una toalla.
Carlos le trae una toalla.

1. Yo pido jabón.

   _____

2. Uds. piden una cámara fotográfica.

   _____

3. Nosotros pedimos las maletas.

   _____

4. Ud. pide la llave.

   _____

5. Tú pides una cámara de video.

   _____

6. Ernesto pide el almuerzo.

   _____

7. María y Jorge piden la cena.

   _____

8. Estela pide el desayuno.

   _____

B. Indirect object pronouns II Someone wants to know what is being done for everybody. Tell him, by answering the following questions, using the cues provided.

1. ¿A quién le vas a dar el dinero? (a Raúl)

   _____

2. ¿Me vas a comprar algo a mí? (no, nada)

_____

3. ¿Qué te va a traer el botones? (el equipaje)

_____

4. ¿Qué nos vas a comprar tú? (un reloj)

_____

5. ¿Qué les sirve a ustedes su mamá? (pollo y ensalada)

_____

6. ¿Cuánto dinero le vas a dar a tu hermana? (cien dólares)

_____

C. Constructions with _gustar_ I Complete the following chart, using the verb **gustar**.

	English	Indirect object	Verb _gustar_	Person(s) or thing(s) liked
1.	I like John.	**Me**	**gusta**	**Juan.**
2.	I like these suitcases.	**Me**	**gustan**	**estas maletas.**
3.	You (_fam._) like the book.	Te		
4.	He likes the pens.			
5.	She likes her job.	Le		
6.	We like this restaurant.	Nos		
7.	You (_pl._) like this city.	Les		
8.	They like to work.			
9.	I like to dance.			
10.	You (_fam._) like this hotel.			
11.	He likes to travel.			
12.	We like this class.			
13.	They like their professors.			

D. Constructions with *gustar* II A group of people is going to travel. Say what they like better by rewriting each sentence. Substitute the expression **gustar más** for **preferir**.

MODELO: Ana prefiere viajar con su familia.
A Ana le gusta más viajar con su familia.

1. Yo prefiero viajar en el verano.

_____

2. Ella prefiere el hotel Hilton.

_____

3. Nosotros preferimos este restaurante.

_____

4. Ellos prefieren ir a Panamá.

_____

5. Tú prefieres las maletas azules.

_____

6. Ustedes prefieren salir por la mañana.

_____

E. Time expressions with *hacer* I Complete the following chart, using the Spanish construction for length of time.

English	**Hace**	Length of time	que	Subject	Verbs in the present tense
1. I have been studying for three years.	**Hace**	**tres años**	**que**	**(yo)**	**estudio.**
2. You have been working for two days.				(tú)	
3. You have been traveling for a month.				(Ud.)	
4. She has been reading for four hours.					
5. He has been sleeping for six hours.					
6. You have been dancing for two hours.				(Uds.)	
7. They have been writing for two hours.					

F. Time expressions with *hacer* II Say how long each action has been going on. Follow the model.

MODELO: Son las siete. Trabajo desde (*since*) las tres.
Hace cuatro horas que trabajo.

1. Estamos en diciembre. Vivo aquí desde febrero.

   _____

2. Son las ocho. Estoy aquí desde las ocho menos veinte.

   _____

3. Estamos en el año 2009. Estudio en esta universidad desde el año 2007.

   _____

4. Estamos en noviembre. No veo a mis padres desde julio.

   _____

5. Son las cuatro de la tarde. No como desde las diez de la mañana.

   _____

Name ______________________ Section ____________ Date ____________

G. Preterit of regular verbs I Complete the following chart with the corresponding preterit forms.

Infinitive	***yo***	***tú***	***Ud., él, ella***	***nosotros***	***Uds., ellos, ellas***
1. hablar	hablé	hablaste	habló	hablamos	hablaron
2. trabajar	trabajé			trabajamos	
3. cerrar			cerró		
4. empezar		empezaste			
5. llegar				llegamos	
6. buscar					buscaron
7. comer	comí	comiste	comió	comimos	comieron
8. beber			bebió		
9. volver	volví				
10. leer			leyó		
11. creer	creí				
12. vivir	viví	viviste	vivió	vivimos	vivieron
13. escribir		escribiste			
14. recibir				recibimos	
15. abrir			abrió		

H. Preterit of regular verbs II Miguel has a daily routine. Rewrite the paragraph, changing the verbs to the preterit to say what happened yesterday.

Yo salgo de mi casa a las diez y llego a la universidad a las once. Ada y yo estudiamos en la biblioteca y después comemos en la cafetería. Después de las clases trabajo en la oficina. Vuelvo a mi casa a las seis, leo un rato y ceno. Mis padres me llaman a las siete.

_____

_____

_____

_____

_____

_____

_____

_____

_____

I. Ordinal numbers These people are attending a convention in Panama. According to their room number, say which floor they are on.

MODELO:　Carlos Reyes: 597
Carlos Reyes está en el quinto piso.

1.　Miguel Fuentes: 245

_____

2.　Ángel Batista: 750

_____

3.　Silvia Larra: 386

_____

4.　Arturo Gálvez: 960

_____

5.　Ester Vázquez: 437

_____

6.　Nora Ballesteros: 124

_____

7. Rubén Acosta: 689

_____

8. Alberto Cortés: 817

_____

9. Caridad Basulto: 1045

_____

J. Situaciones You find yourself in the following situations. What do you say?

1. At a hotel, you ask if they have vacant rooms. You tell them that you don't have a reservation, but your name (*nombre*) is on the waiting list.

_____

_____

2. You ask if the bellhop can take your suitcases to the room. Ask also where the elevator is.

_____

_____

3. You ask a friend if he likes a room with an ocean view or a room with a view of the mountain better.

_____

_____

4. At a hotel, you ask what time you have to vacate the room. You also ask what the rate of exchange is.

_____

_____

5. Back from a trip, you tell your parents that you sent them a postcard and ask if they got it.

_____

_____

　　　　　　　　　Lección 7, Workbook Activities　**115**

K. Crucigrama

Horizontal

2. comida de la mañana
4. Pasan una buena ____ en el cine Rex.
5. ¿A cómo está el cambio de ____?
7. valija
9. opuesto de **drama**
11. ascensor
12. hacer una promesa
14. En un hotel, lleva las maletas al cuarto.
17. ¿Puede poner mi nombre en la lista de ____?
18. Está en mi cama.
20. Tengo muchas flores en mi ____.
22. Está en el baño.
23. Nadamos en una ____.
24. opuesto de **confirmar**
25. Viene después del cuarto.

Vertical

1. Le mandé una ____ postal.
2. Hay ____ y bañadera.
3. ¿Es una habitación doble o ____?
4. documento que necesitamos para viajar
6. primero, segundo, ____
8. La necesito para abrir la puerta.
10. chico de catorce años
13. Hay una ____ y un consulado.
15. Hay un ascensor y una escalera ____.
16. ¿Tienen servicio de ____?
19. Es un hombre de ____.
21. Hoy es martes; ____ fue (*was*) domingo.

L. **¿Qué pasa aquí?** Look at the illustration and answer the following questions.

1. ¿A qué hora es el desayuno?

   _____

2. ¿A qué hora es el almuerzo?

   _____

3. ¿A qué hora es la cena?

   _____

4. ¿El cuarto es interior?

   _____

5. ¿Es una habitación sencilla o doble?

   _____

6. ¿Tiene el cuarto baño privado?

   _____

7. ¿Cuántas maletas tienen Magali y Javier?

_____

8. ¿Qué no tiene Magali?

_____

9. ¿Qué quiere comprar Magali? ¿Cuánto cuesta?

_____

10. ¿Dónde está Javier?

_____

11. ¿Qué va a pedir Javier?

_____

12. ¿Cuántas toallas hay en el baño?

_____

Para leer

De vacaciones

Marta y su esposo Rubén están de vacaciones, viajando por Costa Rica.
Antes de salir de su casa, llamaron por teléfono al hotel Herradura, en San
José, para reservar una habitación doble con vista a la calle y con aire
acondicionado.

Cuando llegaron al hotel, hablaron con un empleado y recogieron° la   *picked up*
llave de la habitación. El botones llevó las maletas al cuarto y Rubén le dio°   *gave*
una buena propina. A Marta le gustó mucho la habitación, y después de
descansar° un rato decidieron comer en el restaurante del hotel antes de   *rest*
salir a pasear° por la ciudad para visitar algunos lugares de interés.   *walk around*

¡Conteste! Answer the following questions based on the reading.

1. ¿Qué están haciendo Marta y Rubén en Costa Rica?

_____

2. ¿Para qué llamaron al hotel Herradura?

_____

3. ¿En qué ciudad está el hotel?

_____

118 Lección 7, Workbook Activities

4. ¿La habitación es con vista a la calle o interior?

_____

5. Marta y Rubén no van a tener calor en su cuarto. ¿Por qué?

_____

6. ¿Quién llevó las maletas al cuarto?

_____

7. ¿Qué recibió el botones?

_____

8. ¿Le gustó la habitación a Marta?

_____

9. ¿Dónde comieron Marta y Rubén?

_____

10. ¿Qué visitaron en San José?

_____

Panorama hispánico

Complete the following charts.

Costa Rica
Capital: _____
Principales productos de exportación: _____, _____,
_____ y _____
Segunda fuente de ingreso: _____
Número de parques nacionales: _____
Porcentaje de personas que saben leer y escribir: _____
Instrumentos musicales más populares: _____, _____ y
_____

Panamá

Capital: _____

Principal fuente de ingreso: _____

Ciudades más importantes: _____ y _____

Fecha en que el canal pasó a poder de Panamá: _____

Océanos que une el canal: _____ y _____

Deporte más popular: _____

Lección 7

Laboratory Activities

Diálogo

Una familia panameña en Costa Rica Listen to the dialogues twice, paying close attention to the speakers' intonation and pronunciation patterns. First, listen to the entire dialogue; then, as you listen for a second time, pause the recording after each sentence and repeat after the speaker.

Rubén Saldaña, su esposa Beatriz y sus hijas Paola y Ariana están en un hotel de San José, la capital de Costa Rica. El Sr. Saldaña es un hombre de negocios y su esposa es maestra. Paola y Ariana son adolescentes.

EMPLEADO	¿En qué puedo servirle, señor?
RUBÉN	Me llamo Rubén Saldaña. Mi familia y yo necesitamos una habitación para cuatro personas, con dos camas dobles. Tenemos reservación. Yo llamé anteayer para confirmarla.
EMPLEADO	A ver... Rubén Saldaña... Sí, señor. Su habitación está en el tercer piso.
ARIANA	¿Los cuartos tienen televisor? Yo quiero ver mi programa favorito.
PAOLA	¿Tienen servicio de Internet? Yo necesito mandarle un mensaje instantáneo a Carolina. Hace mucho tiempo que no hablamos.
BEATRIZ	Hablaste con ella ayer. ¡Y anoche le mandaste una tarjeta postal! Ahora tenemos que llevar el equipaje al cuarto.
EMPLEADO	Tiene que dejarnos el número de su tarjeta, señor. El botones puede llevar las maletas a su cuarto. (*Le da la llave.*) Aquí tiene la llave. Debe dejarla con nosotros, en la recepción, si sale del hotel.
RUBÉN	¿El hotel tiene servicio de habitación?
EMPLEADO	Sí, señor. Sirven la cena hasta las once de la noche.
BEATRIZ	Rubén... ya cenamos... ¡Y tú comiste muchísimo!
RUBÉN	Sí, pero me gusta comer algo antes de dormir...
BEATRIZ	Vamos a nuestro cuarto. ¿Dónde está el ascensor? Estoy cansada.
ARIANA	Yo voy a usar la escalera. Necesito hacer ejercicio.
PAOLA	¿El hotel tiene piscina? Yo quiero nadar un rato.

En el cuarto

ARIANA	Mamá, ¿el cuarto tiene aire acondicionado? Tengo calor.
PAOLA	No me gusta la cama. El colchón no es muy cómodo...
RUBÉN	Es tarde. Vamos a dormir. Mañana vamos a ir al jardín Lankester y al parque Braulio Carrillo.
ARIANA	¡Pero, papá! ¡Estamos de vacaciones! Yo quiero mirar televisión hasta tarde...
BEATRIZ	Ariana tiene razón. A ver, Rubén... ¿Qué programas te gustan?
RUBÉN	Bueno...
ARIANA	A Paola y a mí nos gusta la película que pasan en el canal 4.
RUBÉN	Bueno... a mí me gusta más mirar las noticias...
BEATRIZ	A las chicas les gusta la película... ¡Y a mí también! Yo la vi el mes pasado.
RUBÉN	Buenas noches...
BEATRIZ	¿Por qué no miras la película con nosotras? Te prometo que te va a gustar. Es una comedia romántica...
RUBÉN	Hasta mañana...

A. Preguntas y respuestas You will now hear questions about the dialogues. Answer each one, omitting the subject. The speaker will confirm your response. Repeat the correct response.

B. Situaciones The speaker will present several situations based on the dialogue. Respond appropriately in Spanish to each situation. The speaker will confirm your response. Repeat the correct response. Follow the model.

> MODELO: You ask a friend if he likes to travel.
> **¿Te gusta viajar?**

Pronunciación

A. *The sound of the Spanish* **ll**

- Repeat each word, imitating the speaker's pronunciation.

calle	llegar	botella
llevar	llave	platillo
cuchillo	pollo	

- When you hear the number, read the corresponding sentence aloud. Then listen to the speaker and repeat the sentence.
  1. Allende lleva la silla amarilla.
  2. Las huellas de las llamas llegan a la calle.
  3. Lleva la llave, los cigarrillos y las botellas.

B. *The sound of the Spanish* **ñ**

- Repeat each word, imitating the speaker's pronunciation.

español	señorita	España
señor	mañana	año
niño	otoño	

- When you hear the number, read the corresponding sentence aloud. Then listen to the speaker and repeat the sentence.
  1. La señorita Muñoz le da una muñeca a la niña.
  2. La señora española añade vino añejo.
  3. Toño tiñe el pañuelo del niño.

Estructuras

A. Indirect object pronouns Respond to the following questions with complete sentences, using the cues provided. The speaker will confirm your response. Repeat the correct response. Follow the model.

> MODELO: ¿Qué me traes?
> **Te traigo un libro.**

1. (una cámara de video)
2. (la hora)
3. (dinero)
4. (el desayuno)
5. (las maletas)

B. Constructions with *gustar* Answer the following questions, using expressions with **gustar** and the cues provided. The speaker will confirm your response. Repeat the correct response. Follow the model.

> MODELO: ¿Prefieres Costa Rica o Panamá? (Costa Rica)
> **Me gusta más Costa Rica.**

1. (playa)
2. (película)
3. (escalera)
4. (el canal dos)
5. (con vista al mar)
6. (otoño)

C. Time expressions with *hacer* Answer the following questions, using the cues provided. The speaker will verify your response. Repeat the correct response. Follow the model.

> MODELO: ¿Cuánto tiempo hace que trabajas en este hotel? (dos meses)
> **Hace dos meses que trabajo en este hotel.**

1. (un año)
2. (diez años)
3. (una hora)
4. (veinte minutos)
5. (dos semanas)

D. Preterit of regular verbs Answer the following questions, changing the verbs to the preterit. The speaker will confirm your response. Repeat the correct response. Follow the model.

> MODELO: ¿No vas a estudiar?
> **Ya estudié.**

E. Ordinal numbers You will hear nine cardinal numbers. After each one, give the corresponding ordinal number. The speaker will confirm your response. Repeat the correct response. Follow the model.

> MODELO: cinco
> **quinto**

A. Dibujos (*Drawings*) You will hear three statements about each drawing. Choose the letter of the statement that best corresponds to each drawing. The speaker will verify your response.

1.

a   b   c

2.

a   b   c

3.

a   b   c

4.

a   b   c

5.

a   b   c

B. Unos diálogos breves Before listening to the dialogues in this section, study the comprehension questions below. Reviewing the questions ahead of time will help you to remember key information as you listen. Then listen carefully to the dialogues and answer each question, omitting the subject. The speaker will confirm your response. Repeat the correct answer.

1. ¿Qué le gustó más a Amelia de su viaje ?
2. ¿Les mandó tarjetas postales a sus amigos?
3. ¿Le escribió a su mamá?
4. ¿En qué piso está la habitación de Teresa?
5. ¿Teresa va a usar el ascensor?
6. ¿Qué va a usar?
7. ¿Por qué va a usar la escalera?
8. ¿Cuánto tiempo hace que Ana conoce a Guillermo?
9. ¿Dónde lo conoció?
10. ¿Le gustó Panamá a Ana?

C. Para contestar Answer the questions you hear, using the cues provided. The speaker will confirm your answers. Repeat the correct answer.

1. (de vacaciones)
2. (la piscina)
3. (las seis)
4. (mucho tiempo)
5. (sí, mucho)
6. (no)
7. (no)
8. (la escalera mecánica)
9. (a las doce)
10. (el botones)

D. Tome nota You will hear a radio ad for a hotel in Costa Rica. First listen carefully for general comprehension. Then, as you listen for a second time, fill in the information requested.

— HOTEL SAN JOSÉ —

Dirección: _____

Teléfono: _____

Lista de precios

Habitaciones exteriores   Habitaciones interiores

    Dobles: $_____   Dobles: $_____

    Sencillas: $_____   Sencillas: $_____

Servicio de restaurante

Desayuno: De _____ a _____

Almuerzo: De _____ a _____

Cena: De _____ a _____

E. Dictado The speaker will read six sentences. Each sentence will be read twice. After the first reading, write what you heard. After the second reading, check your work and fill in what you missed.

1. _____

2. _____

3. _____

4. _____

5. _____

6. _____

Lección 8

Workbook Activities

Estructuras

A. Direct and indirect object pronouns used together I Complete the following chart.

English	Subject	pronoun	Indirect object pronoun	Direct object Verb
1. I give it to you.	**Yo**	**te**	**lo / la**	**doy.**
2. You give it to me.	Tú			
3. I give it to him.		se		
4. We give it to her.				damos.
5. They give it to us.				
6. I give it to you. (**Ud.**)				
7. You give it to them.	Tú			

B. Direct and indirect object pronouns used together II We all help each other! Who's going to do what? Complete the following sentences, using the appropriate direct and indirect object pronouns.

1. Yo necesito los diccionarios. ¿Tú _____ _____ puedes traer esta tarde?

2. A Teresa le gusta esta orquídea. Yo _____ _____ voy a comprar.

3. Nosotros no tenemos las enciclopedias. Sergio _____ _____ va a conseguir.

4. Tú no tienes el regalo para Raquel. Yo _____ _____ puedo llevar a tu

   casa hoy.

5. Carlos no sabe dónde está el talonario de cheques. ¿Tú _____ _____

   puedes decir?

6. Si tú necesitas estas copas, ellos _____ _____ pueden prestar.

C. Direct and indirect object pronouns used together III We are going on a trip. Who is sending, buying, or lending necessary items? Answer the following questions, using the cues provided and substituting direct object pronouns for the direct objects.

MODELO: ¿Cuándo me traes el equipaje? (esta tarde)
Te lo traigo esta tarde.

1. ¿Quién te compra los pasajes (*tickets*)? (mi hermano)

    _____

2. ¿A quién le prestas las maletas? (a Carmen)

    _____

3. ¿Quién te va a prestar el dinero? (mi prima) (*two ways*)

    _____

    _____

4. ¿Quién les manda a ellos las tarjetas postales? (sus amigos)

    _____

5. ¿Quién les compra a Uds. la ropa? (mi tía)

    _____

6. ¿Tú puedes traerme los pasaportes? (sí) (*two ways*)

    _____

    _____

D. Preterit of *ser*, *ir*, and *dar* What happened yesterday? Complete the following paragraph, using the preterit of **ser**, **ir**, and **dar**.

Ayer José Enrique y yo _____ a un restaurante a almorzar para

celebrar su cumpleaños. José Enrique _____ mi compañero de clase

el semestre pasado. Yo le compré un regalo y se lo _____ en el

restaurante. Por la noche sus padres le _____ una fiesta en el Club

Náutico y todos sus amigos _____. _____

una fiesta magnífica.

E. Preterit of *e:i* and *o:u* stem-changing verbs These people are talking about what took place yesterday. Complete the following exchanges, using the preterit of the verbs given.

1. **servir / pedir**

   —¿A qué hora _____ ellos el almuerzo?

   —A las doce.

   —¿Qué _____ Uds.?

   —Yo _____ langosta y Aurora _____

   camarones.

2. **dormir**

   —¿Cómo _____ Uds.?

   —Yo _____ muy bien, pero Ana y Eva

   _____ muy mal.

3. **conseguir**

   —¿Dónde _____ ellos esas copas?

   —En Puerto Rico.

4. **morir**

   —¿Cuántas personas _____ en el accidente?

   —No _____ nadie.

5. **repetir / mentir**

   —Beto dice que el profesor no _____ las preguntas.

   —Beto te _____.

F. Uses of *por* and *para* I Look at the pictures below and describe what is happening, using **por** or **para**.

1. _____ pasa

_____ el banco.

2. El _____ es

_____ María.

3. Viajamos _____

_____.

4. Hay vuelos _____

_____.

5. Necesito el vestido (*dress*)

_____.

6. Pagó diez _____

_____.

7. Vengo _____

_____

_____.

8. Me dio _____

_____ comprar

el _____.

G. Uses of *por* and *para* II To talk about what is going on, complete each sentence with either **por** or **para**, as appropriate. Indicate the reason for your choice by placing the corresponding number in the blank provided before the sentence.

*Uses of **por***

1. motion, *along*
2. cause or motive of an action
3. means, manner, unit of measure
4. *in exchange for*
5. period of time during which an action takes place
6. *in search of*

*Uses of **para***

7. destination
8. goal for a point in the future
9. whom or what something is for
10. *in order to*
11. objective or goal

_____   1. Tenemos una sorpresa _____ Elena.

_____   2. Pagamos cuatro dólares _____ la pluma.

_____   3. Las chicas caminan _____ la plaza.

_____   4. Mañana _____ la noche vamos al teatro.

_____   5. El mozo fue a la cocina _____ el pavo y el lechón.

_____   6. Mañana te llamo _____ teléfono.

_____   7. Necesitamos los cubiertos _____ el sábado.

_____   8. Tengo que traer el mantel _____ poner la mesa.

_____   9. Esa maleta es _____ mi sobrina.

_____   10. Carlos estudia _____ profesor.

_____   11. No podemos dormir afuera (*outside*) _____ la lluvia.

H. Formation of adverbs Roberto is talking about his grandparents. Form adverbs from the adjectives below, and then use them to complete what he is saying.

lento y claro	raro	especial
desgraciado	probable	general

_____ voy al banco los lunes, pero el próximo lunes _____ voy a ir a

casa de mis abuelos. Yo los veo muy _____, porque _____ ellos viven

muy lejos. Voy a tomar dos días de vacaciones _____ para ir a visitarlos.

   Mi abuela es francesa y a veces no me entiende cuando le hablo en español; siempre

tengo que hablarle _____ y _____.

I. Situaciones You find yourself in the following situations. What do you say?

1. You ask Mr. Barrios if he slept well last night, and whether they served him breakfast.

   _____

   _____

2. You ask Miss Fuentes whether they gave her the loan she asked for.

   _____

   _____

3. You tell a friend that, unfortunately, the goldfish that you bought for your niece died yesterday.

   _____

   _____

4. You mention that you saved money in order to buy a motorcycle and they stole it from you.

   _____

   _____

J. Crucigrama

Horizontal

5. Siempre lee el horóscopo; es muy _____.
8. Voy a llevar los pantalones a la _____.
9. boca de incendios
10. aparcar
13. Pagó con cheques de _____.
14. Snoopy es un _____.
17. Saqué dinero del _____ automático.
18. Luis tiene _____ suerte.
20. José me dio un _____ de rosas.
22. Le compramos un _____ para su cumpleaños.
23. No tenemos tarjetas de _____.
25. animal muy lento (*slow*)
27. ¿Dónde está mi _____ de ahorros?
28. poner la fecha
29. No tengo cheques. Voy a pagar en _____.
32. fuego
34. Vamos a _____ cien dólares en la cuenta.
35. Elsa pidió un _____ en el banco.
36. Rita va a _____ una cuenta.

Vertical

1. Tengo dos _____ de colores.
2. Me gusta mucho; me _____.
3. El policía me puso una _____.
4. moto
6. opuesto de **gastar**
7. Morris es uno de ellos.
11. pasar
12. Necesito el _____ para buscar una palabra.
14. Raúl necesita dinero. ¿Uds. se lo pueden _____?
15. opuesto de **al contado**; a _____.
16. por desgracia
19. animal que habla
21. flor muy cara
24. No tienen que pagar. Es _____.
26. Tiene alergias. Es _____.
30. lugar donde venden flores
31. Hoy tengo que hacer muchas _____.
33. Mi esposa y yo tenemos una cuenta _____.

K. ¿Qué pasa aquí? Look at the illustration and answer the following questions.

1. ¿Dónde estaciona Mario su motocicleta?

   _____

2. Si un policía ve la moto, ¿qué le va a poner a Mario?

   _____

3. ¿Adónde va Mario?

   _____

4. ¿Qué tipo de cuenta tiene Mario en el banco?

   _____

5. ¿Qué tipo de cuenta no tiene?

   _____

6. ¿Qué solicita Olga?

   _____

7. ¿Cuánto dinero necesita?

_____

8. ¿Para qué quiere el dinero?

_____

9. ¿Le van a dar el préstamo?

_____

10. ¿Qué piensa solicitar Juan?

_____

Panorama hispánico

Complete the following chart.

Puerto Rico
Capital: _____
Archipiélago al cual pertenece: _____
Área: _____
Parte antigua de la capital: _____
Famosas fortalezas: _____ y _____
Segunda ciudad en importancia: _____
Influencias en su cultura: _____, _____ y _____
Deporte más popular: _____
Poetisa de fama internacional: _____

Laboratory Activities

Diálogo

Un martes 13 Listen to the dialogue twice, paying close attention to the speakers' intonation and pronunciation patterns. First, listen to the entire dialogue; then, as you listen for a second time, pause the recording after each sentence and repeat after the speaker.

En una casa de la avenida Ponce de León, en San Juan, Puerto Rico, vive la familia Burgos Trinidad: Sara y Luis Burgos y su hijo Edwin. Edwin tiene mucho sueño hoy porque anoche no durmió muy bien. Ahora está desayunando y hablando con su mamá. Le está contando todo lo que le pasó ayer.

MAMÁ ¿Fuiste a la tintorería a recoger tus pantalones?

EDWIN Sí... Ése fue mi primer problema... Estacioné la motocicleta frente a una boca de incendios y un policía me dio una multa.

MAMÁ ¡Pobrecito! Y después... ¿fuiste al banco?

EDWIN Sí, deposité dinero en mi cuenta de ahorros y en mi cuenta corriente. Después pedí un préstamo, pero no me lo dieron.

MAMÁ Tu papá tampoco consiguió el préstamo que pidió... ¡Qué mala suerte!

EDWIN Después compré dos peces de colores para Martita pero... murieron... Creo que les di demasiada comida.

MAMÁ Probablemente. ¿Compraste el regalo para tu novia?

EDWIN Sí, pero no se lo di.

MAMÁ ¿Por qué no? Le compraste un diccionario, ¿no? Un buen regalo para una chica que estudia para maestra...

EDWIN Sí, pero su ex novio le regaló una enciclopedia. En fin... fui a la florería y le compré un ramo de rosas.

MAMÁ ¡Perfecto! Estoy segura de que le encantaron.

EDWIN Bueno... desgraciadamente es alérgica a las flores...

MAMÁ ¡Ay, Edwin! ¡Qué desastre!

EDWIN ¡Eso no es todo! Ahora tengo que ahorrar dinero para comprar una motocicleta.

MAMÁ Pero tú tienes una moto casi nueva...

EDWIN ¡Se la presté a Raúl y se la robaron!

MAMÁ ¡Ay, bendito! ¡Ya sé por qué ocurrió todo eso! ¡Ayer fue martes 13!

EDWIN Ay, mamá... yo no soy supersticioso... ¡Pero el próximo martes 13 no salgo de casa!

A. Preguntas y respuestas You will now hear questions about the dialogue. Answer each one, omitting the subject. The speaker will confirm your response. Repeat the correct response.

B. Situaciones The speaker will present several situations based on the dialogue. Respond appropriately in Spanish to each situation. The speaker will confirm your response. Repeat the correct response. Follow the model.

MODELO: You tell your friend that he shouldn't park his motorcycle in front of a fire hydrant.
No debes estacionar tu motocicleta delante de una boca de incendios.

Pronunciación

A. *The sound of the Spanish* **l**

- Repeat each word, imitating the speaker's pronunciation.

Emilio	Silvia	sólo
mala	helado	regalo
capital	él	flores

- When you hear the number, read the corresponding sentence aloud. Then listen to the speaker and repeat the sentence.
    1. Aníbal habla español con Isabel.
    2. El coronel Maldonado asaltó con mil soldados.
    3. El libro de Ángel está en el laboratorio.

B. *The sound of the Spanish* **r**

- Repeat each word, imitating the speaker's pronunciation.

loro	ahora	tarde
dejar	Teresa	canario
fechar	Ariel	gratis

- When you hear the number, read the corresponding sentence aloud. Then listen to the speaker and repeat the sentence.
    1. Es preferible esperar hasta enero.
    2. Carolina quiere estudiar con Darío ahora.
    3. Aurora y Mirta son extranjeras.

C. *The sound of the Spanish* **rr**

- Repeat each word, imitating the speaker's pronunciation.

regalo	rosa	Reyes
rico	Rita	Roberto
ramo	Raúl	robar

- When you hear the number, read the corresponding sentence aloud. Then listen to the speaker and repeat the sentence.
    1. El perro corrió en el barro.
    2. Los carros del ferrocarril parecen cigarros.
    3. Roberto y Rita recogen rosas rojas.

D. *The sound of the Spanish* **z**

- Repeat each word, imitating the speaker's pronunciation.

pizarra	vez	Pérez
Zulema	zoológico	taza
lápiz	mozo	azul

- When you hear the number, read the corresponding sentence aloud. Then listen to the speaker and repeat the sentence.
    1. Zulema y el Zorro me dieron una paliza.
    2. ¡Zas! El zonzo Pérez fue al zoológico.
    3. La tiza y la taza están en el zapato.

Estructuras

A. Direct and indirect object pronouns used together I Rephrase each sentence you hear by replacing the direct object with the corresponding direct object pronoun. Be sure to make any other necessary changes. The speaker will confirm your response. Repeat the correct response. Follow the model.

> MODELO: Le traen la libreta de ahorros.
> **Se la traen.**

B. Direct and indirect object pronouns used together II Answer each question you hear, using direct and indirect object pronouns and the cue provided. The speaker will confirm your response. Repeat the correct response. Follow the model.

> MODELO: ¿Quién te manda el periódico? (mi hijo)
> **Me lo manda mi hijo.**

1. (mi abuela)	4. (a mí)	
2. (el profesor)	5. (a ti)	
3. (a mi prima)	6. (a los muchachos)	

C. Preterit of *ser*, *ir*, and *dar* Rephrase each sentence you hear, changing the verb to the preterit. The speaker will confirm your response. Repeat the correct response. Follow the model.

> MODELO: Yo voy al banco.
> **Yo fui al banco.**

D. Preterit of *e:i* and *o:u* stem-changing verbs Answer each question your hear in the negative, and then state that your friend did the things you are being asked about. The speaker will confirm your response. Repeat the correct response. Follow the model.

> MODELO: Tú lo pediste, ¿no?
> **No, yo no lo pedí. Lo pidió ella.**

1. Tú lo conseguiste, ¿no?	3. Tú lo repetiste, ¿no?	
2. Tú la serviste, ¿no?	4. Tú me seguiste, ¿no?	

Now listen to the new model.

> MODELO: Uds. pidieron el café, ¿no?
> **No, nosotros no lo pedimos. Lo pidieron ellos.**

5. Uds. sirvieron la cena, ¿no?	7. Uds. siguieron a José, ¿no?	
6. Uds. repitieron la lección, ¿no?	8. Uds. consiguieron los peces, ¿no?	

E. Uses of *por* and *para* Answer each question you hear, using the cue provided. Pay special attention to the use of **por** or **para** in each question. The speaker will confirm your response. Repeat the correct response. Follow the model.

> MODELO: ¿Para quién es el dinero? (Rita)
> **El dinero es para Rita.**

1. (el lunes)
2. (sí)
3. (quince días)
4. (quinientos dólares)

5. (sí)
6. (dinero)
7. (mañana por la mañana)
8. (un reloj)

Más práctica

A. Dibujos (*Drawings*) You will hear three statements about each drawing. Choose the letter of the statement that best corresponds to the drawing. The speaker will verify your response.

1.
$100
EVA
DORA
a   b   c

2.

$100 $50 $20
ADA
a   b   c

3.

Irma
a   b   c

4.

GERARDO
a   b   c

5.

Paco
a   b   c

B. Unos diálogos breves Before listening to the dialogues in this section, study the comprehension questions below. Reviewing the questions ahead of time will help you to remember key information as you listen. Then listen carefully to the dialogues and answer each question, omitting the subject. The speaker will confirm your response. Repeat the correct answer.

1. ¿Qué les pasó a los peces de colores?
2. ¿Anita les dio mucha comida?
3. ¿Qué les dio Anita?
4. ¿Qué le compró Dora a Paco?
5. ¿Qué quiere Paco?
6. ¿Qué dice Dora de los monos?
7. ¿Por qué no le puede comprar un gato?

C. Para contestar Answer the questions you hear, using the cues provided. The speaker will confirm your answers. Repeat the correct answer.

1. (banco)
2. (muchas diligencias)
3. (a las diez)
4. (sí)
5. (no, a plazos)
6. (sí, con Ana)
7. (no / gratis)
8. (no / tarjeta de crédito)
9. (los pantalones)
10. (no)

D. Tome nota You will hear two friends talking. First listen carefully for general comprehension. Then, as you listen for a second time, fill in the information requested.

Nombre de la florería: _____

Para la mamá:

Flores: _____

Ocasión: _____

Para su esposa:

Flores: _____

Ocasión: _____

Para Julia:

Flores: _____

Ocasión: _____

E. Dictado The speaker will read six sentences. Each sentence will be read twice. After the first reading, write what you heard. After the second reading, check your work and fill in what you missed.

1. _____

2. _____

3. _____

4. _____

5. _____

6. _____

Hasta ahora... Una prueba

Let's combine the structure and the vocabulary learned in **Lecciones 7** and **8**. How much can you remember?

A. Complete the following exchanges, using the preterit of the verbs given.

1. —¿Adónde _____ (ir) ustedes ayer?

   —_____ (Ir) al cine. Después, Carlos _____ (llevar) a José al

   parque. ¿Y tú? ¿_____ (Almorzar) con tu mamá?

   —Sí, _____ (almorzar) con ella.

   —¿Qué _____ (comer) (ustedes)?

   —Yo _____ (pedir) biftec y ella _____ (pedir) pescado.

2. —¿Tú _____ (ser) estudiante de la Dra. Peña?

   —Sí, ella _____ (ser) mi profesora el año pasado. Me _____ (dar)

   una "A". Yo _____ (aprender) mucho en su clase.

   —¿Tú _____ (escribir) el informe para la clase de francés?

   —No, desgraciadamente mi hermano no me _____ (conseguir) el libro que (yo)

   le _____ (pedir).

3. —¿Cómo _____ (dormir) usted anoche, señora?

   —No muy bien. (Yo) _____ (trabajar) hasta muy tarde y _____

   (llegar) a mi casa a las diez. Esta mañana, mi hija me _____ (servir) el

   desayuno en la cama. ¡Yo le _____ (dar) un abrazo!

B. Answer the following questions, using the cues provided. Whenever possible, substitute direct object pronouns for the direct objects.

1. ¿Qué les gusta hacer a ustedes los sábados? (ir a bailar)

   _____

2. En un hotel, ¿te gusta más estar en el primer piso o en el décimo piso? (en el décimo piso)

   _____

3. ¿Qué les vas a mandar a tus amigos? (una tarjeta postal)

   _____

4. ¿Cuánto tiempo hace que conoces a tu mejor amigo? (cuatro años)

   _____

5. ¿Cuándo puedes traerme el libro que te pedí? (mañana)

   _____

6. ¿Tú puedes darle las flores a tu abuela? (sí)

   _____

7. ¿Tú le diste el diccionario a tu amigo? (no)

   _____

8. ¿Cuándo te pidió tu amigo la motocicleta? (anteayer)

   _____

9. ¿Qué nos vas a traer de la florería? (un ramo de rosas)

   _____

10. ¿Qué le dieron ustedes a su padre? (una maleta)

    _____

C. Arrange this vocabulary in groups of three, according to categories.

cuenta corriente	desayuno	maleta	contador	piscina
con tarjeta de crédito	pensamiento	televisor	escalera	cena
desgraciadamente	confirmar	estacionar	lavabo	conejo
desafortunadamente	ducha	maestro	elevador	bañadera
hacer reservación	por desgracia	viajar	clavel	
pasar una película	en efectivo	almuerzo	ayer	
estar de vacaciones	tortuga	alberca	nadar	
con cheque de viajero	equipaje	aparcar	banco	
hombre de negocios	valija	anteayer	anoche	
tarjeta de turista	margarita	cancelar	canal	
cuenta de ahorros	parquear	ascensor	mono	

1. _____ _____ _____

2. _____ _____ _____

3. _____ _____ _____

4. _____ _____ _____

5. _____ _____ _____

6. _____ _____ _____

7. _____ _____ _____

8. _____ _____ _____

9. _____ _____ _____

10. _____ _____ _____

11. _____ _____ _____

12. _____ _____ _____

13. _____ _____ _____

14. _____ _____ _____

15. _____ _____ _____

16. _____ _____ _____

Un paso más

A. Read the ad for the Hotel La Torre, and then answer the questions that follow.

HOTEL LA TORRE

¡Para gozar de unas vacaciones fabulosas en la playa!

Servicio de transporte desde el aeropuerto

Dos restaurantes

Servicio de fax

Salones para reuniones

Gimnasio

Dos piscinas

Tienda de regalos

Actividades especiales para niños

Servicio de habitación

Para alquilar: tablas de mar, parasoles y bicicletas

Todos los cuartos tienen:
Baño privado con ducha y bañadera · Televisor y videocasetera
Microondas y refrigerador · Teléfono · Balcón con mesa y sillas
Aire acondicionado

Llame hoy mismo para hacer reservaciones
al número 465-39-27

1.   ¿Dónde está el hotel La Torre?

_____

2.   ¿Por qué no necesitamos tener coche (*car*) para ir desde el aeropuerto al hotel?

_____

3.   ¿A qué número tenemos que llamar para hacer reservaciones?

_____

4. ¿Podemos mirar la tele en nuestro cuarto?

    _____

5. ¿Puedo llamar a alguien desde mi cuarto?

    _____

6. ¿Voy a tener calor en el cuarto?

    _____

7. ¿Qué podemos alquilar (*rent*) en el hotel?

    _____

8. ¿Podemos comer en nuestro cuarto si no queremos ir a un restaurante?

    _____

9. ¿Puedo hacer ejercicio en el hotel?

    _____

10. Si quiero comprar recuerdos (*souvenirs*), ¿dónde puedo hacerlo?

    _____

11. Si no quiero ir a la playa, ¿dónde puedo nadar?

    _____

12. Si traigo algunos refrescos a mi cuarto, ¿dónde puedo ponerlos?

    _____

B. Write a memo to your assistant. Tell him or her what has to be done: reserve a room at a hotel and run some errands. Tell him or her what accommodations you want (*e.g.*, **un cuarto con**..., **un hotel con**...) and how long you're going to be there. Tell him/her also what errands he/she has to run.

Workbook Activities

Lección 9

Estructuras

A. Reflexive constructions This is my daily routine. Rewrite it twice, changing the subject **yo** first to **tú** and then to **él**.

Yo me despierto a las seis de la mañana y me levanto a las seis y cuarto. Me baño, me lavo la cabeza, me afeito y me visto. A las siete y media me voy a trabajar. Trabajo hasta las cinco y luego vuelvo a casa. No me preocupo si llego tarde. Leo un rato y luego como con mi familia. Siempre me acuesto a las diez pero no me duermo hasta las once porque miro las noticias (*news*).

Tú _____

_____

_____

_____

_____

_____

_____

_____

_____

_____

Él _____

_____

_____

_____

_____

_____

_____

_____

_____

_____

B. Review of personal pronouns Complete the following dialogues, using the appropriate subject and object pronouns.

1. —Alicia, ¿_____ quieres ir al banco hoy?

   —No, _____ estoy muy ocupada hoy. Teresa puede ir con_____.

   —_____ voy a llamar por teléfono y _____ voy a decir que tiene que ir

   con_____.

2. —¿A qué hora _____ levantaron Uds. hoy?

   —_____ levantamos a las seis. ¿Y tú?

   —_____ _____ levanté a las ocho.

   —¿_____ escribiste a tus padres hoy?

   —No, pero _____ llamé por teléfono.

3. —¿Para quién es el regalo? ¿Es para mí?

   —Sí, es para _____. ¿_____ gusta?

   —Sí, _____ gusta mucho. Gracias. Oye, ¿a quién _____ vas a dar el reloj?

   —_____ _____ voy a dar a mi hermano.

   —_____ va a gustar mucho.

4. —¿A Ud. _____ gusta esta mesa, señora?

   —Sí, pero no _____ voy a comprar, porque es muy cara. Yo _____ tengo

   que mandar dinero a mi hijo.

   —¿Dondé está _____?

   —En Santo Domingo.

5. —¿Quién _____ va a llevar a Uds. a la fiesta?

   —_____ va a llevar Carmen. Oye, ¿Hugo _____ llamó hoy? Quiere

   hablar contigo.

   —Sí, _____ llamó esta mañana. _____ voy a ver esta noche.

C. Some uses of the definite article These are comments that people make. Complete them, using the Spanish equivalent of the words in parentheses.

1. Anita, tienes que _____. (*wash your hands*)

2. _____ es más importante que _____. (*Liberty / money*)

3. Ella dice que _____ son más inteligentes que _____. (*women / men*)

4. Ellos se van a poner _____. (*their white shirts*)

5. Tienes que lavarte _____. (*your hair*)

6. No me gusta _____; prefiero _____. (*wine / soft drinks*)

7. _____ va a _____ con nosotros. (*Mr. Mena /*

    church)

8. Nosotros tenemos clases _____ a _____. (*on Mondays / nine*)

D. Possessive pronouns I Everyone went shopping and Nora wants to know to whom things belong. Answer her questions, using the appropriate possessive pronouns.

> MODELO: ¿Teresa compró este libro?
> **Sí, es suyo.**

1. ¿Tú compraste estas camisas?

    _____

2. ¿Yo compré esta revista? (*Use* **tú** *form*)

    _____

3. ¿Roberto compró estos diccionarios?

    _____

4. ¿Tú y yo compramos este reloj?

    _____

5. ¿Amalia compró esta mochila?

    _____

E. Possessive pronouns II To make comparisons, complete the following with the Spanish equivalent of the words in parentheses.

1. Mi novio es muy guapo. ¿Cómo es _____, Anita? (*yours*)

2. La casa de Olga queda lejos, pero _____ queda muy cerca. (*his*) (*Clarify!*)

3. Los hermanos de Graciela viven en Santo Domingo. _____ viven en

    La Habana. (*Mine*)

4. La profesora de ellos es de Chile. _____ es de Cuba. (*Ours*)

5. Las maletas de Jorge son azules. _____ son verdes. (*Mine*)

6. Mi hermano vive en Venezuela. ¿Dónde vive _____, Sr. Mendoza? (*yours*)

F. Irregular preterits Indicate what everybody did last week by using the preterit of the verbs in parentheses.

1. —¿Ustedes _____ (traer) la cama?

   —Sí, la _____ (traer) y la _____ (poner) en tu cuarto.

2. —¿Qué _____ (hacer) tú el sábado pasado?

   —(Yo) _____ (estar) en casa de Luis toda la tarde.

3. —¿Tú _____ (poder) ir a la tintorería?

   —No, porque no _____ (tener) tiempo.

4. —¿Roberto _____ (venir) a verte?

   —Sí, y yo no _____ (saber) qué decirle.

5. —¿Sergio _____ (pedir) un préstamo en el banco?

   —No, no _____ (querer) pedirlo.

6. —¿Qué _____ (decir) ustedes cuando llegó tu tío?

   —No _____ (decir) nada.

7. —¿Qué auto _____ (conducir) tú?

   —Yo _____ (conducir) el auto de Tito.

8. —¿Uds. _____ (traducir) los documentos?

   —No, nosotros no los _____ (traducir).

G. *Hace...* meaning *ago* How long ago did all this happen? Use the information given to indicate it.

   MODELO: Estamos en marzo. Yo vine a esta ciudad en septiembre.
   Hace seis meses que yo vine a esta ciudad.

1. Son las cinco. Ellos llegaron a la una.

   _____

2. Estamos en el año 2009. Jorge empezó a trabajar en el año 2004.

   _____

3. Hoy es sábado. Mis hijos vinieron el martes.

   _____

4. Es la una. Teresa me llamó a la una menos cuarto.

_____

5. Estamos en octubre. Nosotros volvimos de Lima en septiembre.

_____

H. Situaciones You find yourself in the following situations. What do you say?

1. You ask a friend what time he generally gets up and what time he went to bed last night.

_____

2. You ask Mrs. López how long ago her husband passed away and when she came to live with her children.

_____

3. You ask your roommate if he/she brought the fish and whether he/she put it in the refrigerator.

_____

4. You tell someone where your father spent his childhood.

_____

5. You are picking up a friend to go out. Ask her if she can bathe and get dressed in twenty minutes.

_____

Lección 9, Workbook Activities **153**

I. Crucigrama

Horizontal

3. fruta cítrica
5. celebrar
8. opuesto de **olvidarse**
11. Necesitamos papel _____ para el baño.
13. lugar donde compramos carne
14. Cuba, por ejemplo
16. banana
17. de modo que: de _____ que

Vertical

1. opuesto de **tarde**
2. ¿Quieres _____ o margarina?
4. Necesitamos _____ y vinagre.
6. lugar donde compramos pan
7. durazno
9. opuesto de **levantarse**
10. instrumento musical
12. lugar donde compramos medicinas
14. lugar donde compramos pescado
15. lugar donde compramos zapatos

J. **¿Qué pasa aquí?** Look at the illustrations and answer the following questions.

1. ¿Nora se levantó tarde o temprano?

   _____

2. ¿A Nora le gusta levantarse temprano?

   _____

3. ¿Con qué champú se lavó Nora la cabeza?

   _____

4. ¿A qué tienda fue Nora?

   _____

5. ¿Qué le compró Nora a su tía?

   _____

6. ¿A qué hora volvió Nora a su casa?

   _____

7. ¿Qué compró Nora además del regalo?

   _____

8. ¿Con quién almorzó Nora?

_____

9. ¿Nora barrió la sala?

_____

10. ¿Cómo se llama el perro de Nora?

_____

11. ¿Para qué fue Nora a la casa de su tía Rosa?

_____

12. ¿A qué hora se acostó Nora?

_____

Para leer

Todos los días...

Yo siempre me levanto temprano porque tengo que estar en la universidad
a las ocho de la mañana. Me despierto a las seis y media y, después de
bañarme, afeitarme y vestirme, desayuno. Me siento en la cocina y estudio;
salgo para la universidad a las siete y media. No llego tarde porque mi
profesor de matemáticas es muy estricto.

Tengo clase por la mañana, y por la tarde voy a la biblioteca a estudiar.
A veces° me duermo leyendo algunos de mis libros.   *At times*

Vuelvo a casa a las cinco. Me desvisto, me quito los zapatos° y duermo   *shoes*
un rato. Cocino algo para la cena, estudio y después miro las noticias. Me
acuesto a las once y media.

Los fines de semana, mis amigos y yo generalmente vamos a una
discoteca porque nos gusta mucho bailar.

¡Conteste! Answer the following questions based on the reading.

1. ¿Por qué me levanto siempre temprano? (**tú** *form*)

_____

2. ¿A qué hora me despierto?

_____

3. ¿Qué hago después de bañarme, afeitarme y vestirme?

_____

156 Lección 9, Workbook Activities

4. ¿Qué hago en la cocina?

_____

5. ¿A qué hora salgo para la universidad?

_____

6. ¿Por qué no llego tarde?

_____

7. ¿Cuándo tengo clases?

_____

8. ¿Qué hago por la tarde?

_____

9. ¿Qué pasa a veces en la biblioteca?

_____

10. ¿A qué hora vuelvo a casa?

_____

11. ¿Qué hago cuando vuelvo a casa?

_____

12. ¿Qué hago después de dormir un rato?

_____

13. ¿A qué hora me acuesto?

_____

14. ¿Adónde voy generalmente los fines de semana?

_____

Complete the following charts.

Cuba

Capital: _____

Productos de exportación: _____, _____,

_____ y _____

Principales fuentes de ingreso: _____ y _____

Fortalezas importantes: _____ y _____

Famosos cantantes cubanos: _____, _____ y

_____

Deporte más popular: _____

Famosos "peloteros" cubanos: _____ y _____

Escritores de fama internacional: _____, _____ y

_____

República Dominicana

Capital: _____

País que ocupa parte de la isla: _____

Base de la economía: _____

Principales centros turísticos: _____ y _____

Música típica del país: _____

Deporte más popular: _____

Famoso jugador dominicano: _____

Catedral más antigua del continente americano: _____

Laboratory Activities

Diálogo

"Guantanamera" Listen to the dialogue twice, paying close attention to the speakers' intonation and pronunciation patterns. First, listen to the entire dialogue; then, as you listen for a second time, pause the recording after each sentence and repeat after the speaker.

En el mar Caribe hay una isla que comparten dos países: Haití y la República Dominicana. La capital de la República Dominicana es Santo Domingo. A esta ciudad llegaron muchos cubanos hace muchos años, después de la revolución castrista. Entre ellos, vinieron Rogelio Peña, su esposa Isabel y sus hijos, César y Graciela.

La esposa de don Rogelio falleció hace tres años, de modo que él vive con su hija, su yerno, y sus nietos, Mario y Magali. Hoy don Rogelio cumple setenta años y su familia está preparando una cena para festejar su cumpleaños.

GRACIELA	Magali, ¿trajiste el arroz y los frijoles para preparar el congrí? Tu tío César va a hacer el lechón asado.
MAGALI	Sí, y traje lechuga, tomates, cebollas, pepinos y zanahorias para la ensalada. Lo puse todo en el refrigerador.
GRACIELA	¿Y tú, Mario? ¿Qué hiciste?
MARIO	Yo tuve que levantarme muy temprano para ir a la pescadería para comprar un pargo, el pescado que le gusta a abuelo.
MAGALI	¡Ay, pobrecito! Yo me levanté a las cinco, a pesar de que anoche no me acosté hasta las once.
MARIO	Porque estuviste hablando con Ramón hasta muy tarde... ¡Ah! ¿Te acordaste de comprar las frutas para la ensalada? Necesito naranjas, mangos, plátanos, manzanas y uvas. Es mi receta especial.
MAGALI	Es la receta de la señora Torales...
MARIO	¡Pero yo la mejoré! Yo le pongo azúcar, y la sirvo con crema...
MAGALI	¡Ay, caramba! Me olvidé de comprar café, dulce de leche, pan y mantequilla, y leche para el flan.
GRACIELA	Y dos latas de salsa de tomate... Aquí tengo mi lista.
MAGALI	Yo dejé la mía en el supermercado. Mamá, ¿a qué hora es la cena?
GRACIELA	A las ocho. ¡Ay! Todavía tengo que bañarme, lavarme la cabeza y vestirme.
MAGALI	Yo también. Oye... ¿dónde está abuelo? Voy a ver si está en su cuarto.

En el cuarto de don Rogelio

MAGALI	¿Qué estás haciendo, abuelo?
DON ROGELIO	Estoy leyendo unos poemas de José Martí.
MAGALI	Extrañas Cuba, ¿verdad?
DON ROGELIO	Mucho... Extraño los lugares donde pasé mi infancia y mi juventud. La Habana, Camagüey... Pinar del Río...
MAGALI	Abuelo, ¿por qué no tocas la guitarra y cantamos nuestra canción favorita?

Don Rogelio toma su guitarra y los dos cantan.

> Yo soy un hombre sincero,
> de donde crece la palma...

A. Preguntas y respuestas You will now hear questions about the dialogue. Answer each one, omitting the subject. The speaker will confirm your response. Repeat the correct response.

B. Situaciones The speaker will present several situations based on the dialogue. Respond appropriately in Spanish to each situation. The speaker will confirm your response. Repeat the correct response. Follow the model.

> MODELO: You ask a little girl what her father's name is.
> **¿Cómo se llama tu papá?**

Pronunciación

A. *Declarative statements*

- Repeat each sentence, imitating the speaker's intonation.

  1. Yo compré el regalo para Elena.

  2. Mario tiene listo el equipaje.

  3. Yo tengo turno en la barbería.

  4. Necesitamos el dinero para el pasaje.

  5. Yo pienso aprender japonés este verano.

B. *Information questions*

- Repeat each sentence, imitating the speaker's intonation.

  1. ¿Cómo está tu hermano?

  2. ¿Por qué no fuiste con nosotros?

  3. ¿Cuánto tiempo hace que no comes?

  4. ¿Dónde pasaron el verano?

  5. ¿Cuántos años hace que estudias?

C. *Yes/no questions*

- Repeat each sentence, imitating the speaker's intonation.

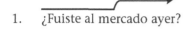

1. ¿Fuiste al mercado ayer?

2. ¿Tienes listo el equipaje?

3. ¿Le diste el regalo a Elena?

4. ¿Tienes turno para la peluquería?

5. ¿Necesitas dinero para el pasaje?

D. *Exclamations*

- Repeat each sentence, imitating the speaker's intonation.

1. ¡Qué bonita es esa alfombra!

2. ¡No compré el regalo para Elena!

3. ¡Qué bueno es este champú!

4. ¡Cuánto te quiero!

Estructuras

A. Reflexive constructions Answer the following questions, using the cues provided. The speaker will confirm your response. Repeat the correct response. Follow the model.

MODELO: ¿A qué hora te levantas tú generalmente? (a las seis)
Generalmente me levanto a las seis.

1. (a las ocho)
2. (a las once)
3. (por la mañana)
4. (sí)
5. (por la mañana)
6. (con el champú Prell)
7. (no)

B. Some uses of the definite article Answer each question you hear in the affirmative, paying special attention to the use of the definite article. The speaker will confirm your response. Repeat the correct response. Follow the model.

MODELO: ¿Te vas a lavar la cabeza?
Sí, me voy a lavar la cabeza.

C. Possessive pronouns Answer each question you hear in the negative, using the appropriate possessive pronoun. The speaker will confirm your response. Repeat the correct response. Follow the model.

> MODELO: ¿Este libro es tuyo?
> **No, no es mío.**

D. Irregular preterits Answer the following questions, using the cues provided. Substitute direct objects with direct object pronouns when possible. The speaker will confirm your response. Repeat the correct response. Follow the model.

> MODELO: ¿Quién tradujo la lección? (Isabel y Eva)
> **Isabel y Eva la tradujeron.**

1. (yo)
2. (en el refrigerador)
3. (conmigo)
4. (nosotros)
5. (no)

6. (en el banco)
7. (sí)
8. (Estela)
9. (nada)
10. (en la farmacia)

E. *Hace* meaning *ago* Answer each question you hear, using the cues provided. The speaker will confirm your response. Repeat the correct response. Follow the model.

> MODELO: ¿Cuánto tiempo hace que empezaste a estudiar español?
> **Hace seis meses que empecé a estudiar español.**

1. (veinte minutos)
2. (tres semanas)
3. (un mes)

4. (un año)
5. (una hora)

Más práctica

A. Dibujos (*Drawings*) You will now hear three statements about each drawing. Choose the letter of the statement that best corresponds to the drawing. The speaker will verify your response.

1.

a   b   c

2.

a   b   c

3.

a   b   c

4.

Elba

a b c

5.

Mario

a b c

B. Unos diálogos breves Before listening to the dialogues in this section, study the comprehension questions below. Reviewing the questions ahead of time will help you to remember key information as you listen. Then listen carefully to the dialogues and answer each question, omitting the subject. The speaker will confirm your response. Repeat the correct answer.

1. ¿A qué hora se levantó Celia hoy?
2. ¿Por qué se levantó tan tarde?
3. ¿Adónde fue?
4. ¿Qué trajo?
5. ¿Adónde fue Amalia?
6. ¿Qué frutas trajo?
7. ¿Trajo melocotones?
8. ¿Por qué no trajo melocotones?
9. ¿Cuándo es el cumpleaños de Oscar?
10. ¿Lucía le trajo el regalo?
11. ¿Lucía pudo comprar el regalo?
12. ¿Qué tuvo que hacer Lucía ayer?

C. Para contestar Answer the questions you hear, using the cues provided. The speaker will confirm your answers. Repeat the correct answer.

1. (veinte)
2. (no)
3. (lechuga y tomate)
4. (ir a la panadería)
5. (cebolla)
6. (sí)
7. (sí)
8. (crema y azúcar)
9. (sí)
10. (no)

D. Tome nota You will hear a conversation between two roommates as they discuss what they are going to buy at the supermarket. First listen carefully for general comprehension. Then, as you listen for a second time, fill in the shopping list.

Frutas	Verduras	Carnes	Otros
1. _____	1. _____	1. _____	1. _____
2. _____	2. _____	2. _____	2. _____
3. _____	3. _____	3. _____	3. _____
4. _____	4. _____		4. _____
5. _____	5. _____		5. _____

E. Dictado The speaker will read six sentences. Each sentence will be read twice. After the first reading, write what you heard. After the second reading, check your work and fill in what you missed.

1. _____

2. _____

3. _____

4. _____

5. _____

6. _____

Workbook Activities

Lección 10

Estructuras

A. The imperfect I Complete the following chart with the corresponding forms of the imperfect.

Infinitive	yo	tú	Ud., él, ella	nosotros	Uds., ellos, ellas
1. prestar					
2.	terminaba				
3.		devolvías			
4.			nadaba		
5.				leíamos	
6.					salían

B. The imperfect: Irregular verbs What did these people do as children? Complete the following sentences according to each new subject.

Cuando yo era niño, iba a la playa y veía a mis amigos.

1. Cuando tú _____ niño, _____ a la montaña y _____ a tus

   abuelos.

2. Cuando Luis _____ niño, _____ al campo y _____ a sus tíos.

3. Cuando él y yo _____ niños, _____ al zoológico y _____ los

   elefantes.

4. Cuando ellos _____ niños, _____ a Caracas y _____ a sus

   primos.

C. The imperfect II Sandra is describing her childhood. Use the imperfect of the verbs in parentheses to complete her story.

Cuando mi hermano y yo _____ (ser) niños,

_____ (vivir) cerca de la playa y todos los fines de semana

_____ (ir) a nadar. Nos _____ (gustar)

mucho ir a los partidos de fútbol y siempre lo _____ (pasar) muy

bien. Nuestros abuelos _____ (vivir) lejos y nosotros no los

_____ (ver) frecuentemente, pero los _____ (visitar)

todos los veranos. Siempre _____ (comer) mucho porque mi abuela

_____ (cocinar) muy bien. Nuestro padre _____ (viajar)

mucho y siempre nos _____ (traer) regalos cuando

_____ (volver) de sus viajes.

D. The preterit contrasted with the imperfect I How do you view these actions or events? Complete each sentence with the preterit or the imperfect of the verbs in parentheses.

1. Yo _____ (ir) a la piscina anoche. (*reporting an act viewed as completed*)

2. Yo _____ (ir) a la piscina cuando _____ (ver) a José. (**ir**: *describing an action in progress in the past;* **ver**: *reporting an action viewed as completed*)

3. Ayer ella _____ (estar) muy enferma todo el día. (*summing up a condition viewed as a whole*)

4. Ella _____ (estar) muy cansada. (*describing a condition in the past*)

5. Yo _____ (ir) a la tienda el sábado pasado. (*reporting an act viewed as completed*)

6. Yo _____ (ir) a la tienda todos los sábados. (*indicating a habitual action*)

7. Susana _____ (decir) que _____ (necesitar) un coche. (**decir**: *reporting an act viewed as completed;* **necesitar**: *indirect discourse*)

8. _____ (Ser) las nueve de la noche cuando él _____ (llegar) anoche.

   (**ser**: *time in the past;* **llegar**: *reporting an act viewed as completed*)

E. The preterit contrasted with the imperfect II Complete the following paragraph about Eva and her family. Use the preterit or the imperfect of the verbs in parentheses.

Cuando Eva _____ (ser) niña _____ (vivir) en

Caracas. Todos los fines de semana _____ (ir) al cine o al parque de

diversiones con sus amigos. Cuando Eva _____ (tener) doce años, sus

padres _____ (decidir) ir de vacaciones a la isla Margarita. Ella no

_____ (saber) nadar, pero su papá le _____

(decir) que _____ (ser) fácil aprender. En dos días, Eva

_____ (aprender) a nadar y lo _____ (pasar) muy

bien. Eva y su familia _____ (estar) en la isla Margarita por dos semanas.

F. Preguntas: Eva y su familia Write eight questions about what you read in Exercise E.

1. _____

2. _____

3. _____

4. _____

5. _____

6. _____

7. _____

8. _____

G. Verbs that change meaning in the preterit Juan and Diego are talking about Rafael's girlfriend and a party that Diego attended. Complete the conversations, using the verbs **querer**, **conocer**, and **saber** in the preterit or the imperfect as needed.

JUAN ¿Tú _____ a la novia de Rafael?

DIEGO No, la _____ anoche en la fiesta.

JUAN ¿Tú _____ que ella era venezolana?

DIEGO No, lo _____ cuando hablé con ella y me lo dijo. Oye, ¿por qué

no fuiste a la fiesta?

JUAN Porque mi novia no _____ ir. Prefirió ir al cine.

DIEGO Yo tampoco _____ ir porque estaba cansado, pero fui y lo pasé

muy bien.

H. The relative pronouns *que* and *quien* Sara and her husband are going to rent an apartment and are now discussing details. Complete the conversation, using **que**, **quien**, or **quienes** as needed.

SARA Ayer hablé con la señora _____ vende los muebles _____

necesitamos para la sala.

HÉCTOR Y yo hablé con los hombres _____ nos van a ayudar a mudarnos.

Sara Ah, ¿ésos son los hombres de _____ te habló papá?

Héctor Sí. Oye, una chica con _____ yo trabajo quiere vender un ventilador. Yo creo que debemos comprarlo.

Sara Sí, porque el ventilador _____ nosotros tenemos no funciona.

I. Situaciones You find yourself in the following situations. What do you say?

1. You ask Mr. Mendoza where he lived when he was a child and what he liked to do with his friends.

   _____

   _____

2. You ask a classmate what time it was when he got home yesterday.

   _____

3. You ask an apartment manager whether the rent includes (the) electricity, (the) water and (the) phone. Ask also if there is a vacant apartment on the third floor.

   _____

   _____

4. You tell someone that you need a dresser, a night table, and a coffee table because the apartment is not furnished.

   _____

   _____

J. Crucigrama

Horizontal

4. Tiene muebles. Está _____.
5. opuesto de **lejos**
6. Compré una funda para mi _____.
7. No es un hotel; es una _____.
11. coche
12. Tiene invitación. Está _____.
13. Yo tengo que limpiar porque no tengo _____.
14. Necesito una mesa de _____.
15. No tengo _____ de dormir para ir a acampar.
16. cambiar de casa
19. metro
20. Pongo la _____ cuando tengo frío.
21. La casa tiene _____ de estar.
25. El Empire State es uno de ellos.
27. Tengo lavadora, pero no tengo _____.
28. barrio
29. silla, mesas, cama, etc.

Vertical

1. bolso
2. No tengo aire acondicionado. Tengo un _____.
3. No voy a comprar la casa; la voy a _____.
8. ¿El alquiler incluye la _____?
9. ¿Dónde está la _____? Voy a planchar.
10. Estas _____ son para mi ventana.
17. sólo
18. sillón
22. dar aviso
23. Puse el pan en el _____.
24. dar quejas
26. Necesito la _____ para hacer el café.

K. ¿Qué pasa aquí? Look at the illustration and answer the following questions.

1. ¿En qué parte de la casa están las chicas?

    _____

2. ¿Qué muebles hay allí?

    _____

3. ¿La casa tiene calefacción o aire acondicionado?

    _____

4. ¿Las chicas necesitan un ventilador en la sala? ¿Por qué?

    _____

5. ¿Qué hay en la ventana?

    _____

6. ¿El apartamento tiene alfombra?

    _____

7. Beatriz y Lucía quieren mudarse. ¿Qué tipo de barrio busca Beatriz?

    _____

8. ¿Cuántos dormitorios quiere Beatriz?

_____

9. ¿Por qué no quiere Lucia vivir lejos de la universidad?

_____

10. ¿Qué tenía la familia de Julia cuando ella era chica?

_____

Panorama hispánico

Complete the following chart.

Venezuela
Capital: _____
Otras ciudades importantes: _____, _____ y _____
Área de Venezuela: _____
Población: _____
Principal producto de exportación: _____
El lago más grande del país : _____
Principal atracción turística: _____
Nombre del Libertador de América: _____
Famoso novelista venezolano: _____
Música típica de Venezuela: _____

Lección 10

Laboratory Activities

Diálogos

Marisol se queja de todo Listen to the dialogues twice, paying close attention to the speakers' intonation and pronunciation patterns. First, listen to the entire dialogue; then, as you listen for a second time, pause the recording after each sentence and repeat after the speaker.

Silvia, Marisol y Cristina son tres chicas de Mérida, Venezuela, que vinieron a Caracas el mes pasado para asistir a la universidad. Silvia y Marisol son primas, pero ellas conocieron a Cristina cuando estaban en la escuela. Ahora están en una pensión, pero quieren mudarse a un apartamento.

SILVIA	¿Llamó Cristina?
MARISOL	Sí, y me dijo que podía encontrarse con nosotras a las tres para ver el apartamento.
SILVIA	¿Te dio la dirección?
MARISOL	Sí, aquí la tengo. Nosotras podemos ir en el metro y Hugo dijo que él iba a llevar a Cristina en su coche.
SILVIA	El apartamento tiene que estar amueblado porque no tenemos muebles.
MARISOL	Bueno... tenemos bolsas de dormir.
SILVIA	Vamos, que es tarde. ¿Dónde pusiste la llave?
MARISOL	Te la di esta mañana... ¡Ah, no! Está en mi bolso.

En el apartamento

ENCARGADO	Ésta es la sala comedor. Como ven, es muy amplia. Tiene un sofá, una mesa y cuatro sillas.
MARISOL	(*A Cristina*) Podemos tener solamente un invitado a la vez.
CRISTINA	¡Shh! Vamos a ver el resto del apartamento.
SILVIA	(*Al encargado*) ¿El alquiler incluye la electricidad, el agua y el teléfono?
ENCARGADO	No, el teléfono, no. ¿Quiere ver el cuarto de baño?
SILVIA	Sí, (*Desde el baño*)... Es muy chico...
MARISOL	¿Te acuerdas de la criada que tenían mis padres cuando nosotras éramos chicas? Su cuarto era más grande que este apartamento.
CRISTINA	Yo sé que a ti te gustó el apartamento que vimos anteayer...
MARISOL	Sí... yo no quería ver éste porque tampoco me gusta el barrio donde está y el otro estaba más cerca de la universidad. Éste está muy lejos.

Silvia viene adonde están las chicas.

SILVIA	¿No hay una cómoda en el dormitorio? Y hay solamente una mesita de noche.
MARISOL	Cuando veníamos para acá vi un edificio de apartamentos mucho mejor que éste. Y había algunos desocupados...
CRISTINA	¡Ay... Marisol! Siempre la misma. Cuando eras chica también te quejabas de todo.
SILVIA	¡Yo estoy de acuerdo con Marisol! Ahora mismo voy a escribirle a papá para tratar de convencerlo de que necesitamos más dinero.
MARISOL	¡Chévere!
ENCARGADO	Entonces, ¿no piensan alquilar el apartamento?
MARISOL	¡Le vamos a avisar...!

A. Preguntas y respuestas You will now hear questions about the dialogues. Answer each one, omitting the subject. The speaker will confirm your response. Repeat the correct response.

B. Situaciones The speaker will present several situations based on the dialogue. Respond appropriately in Spanish to each situation. The speaker will confirm your response. Repeat the correct response. Follow the model.

> MODELO: You tell your parents that you want to move to an apartment.
> **Quiero mudarme a un apartamento.**

Pronunciación

When you hear the number, read the corresponding sentence aloud. Then listen to the speaker and repeat the sentence.

1. Podemos tener solamente un invitado a la vez.
2. ¿El alquiler incluye la electricidad?
3. Tampoco me gusta el barrio donde está.
4. ¿No hay una cómoda en este dormitorio?
5. Vi un edificio de apartamentos.
6. Cuando eras chica también te quejabas.

Estructuras

A. The imperfect Repeat each sentence you hear, changing the verb to the imperfect tense. The speaker will confirm your response. Repeat the correct response. Follow the model.

> MODELO: ¿Tú trabajas?
> **¿Tú trabajabas?**

B. The preterit contrasted with the imperfect The speaker will ask several questions. Pay close attention to the use of the preterit or the imperfect in each question and respond in the appropriate tense, using the cue provided. The speaker will confirm your response. Repeat the correct response. Follow the model.

> MODELO: ¿Qué hora era? (las ocho)
> **Eran las ocho.**

1. (a las doce)
2. (estudiar)
3. (Venezuela)
4. (a las cuatro)
5. (sí)
6. (una butaca)
7. (a la tienda)
8. (ocho años)
9. (a la playa)

C. **Verbs that change meaning in the preterit** Answer each question you hear, using the model as a guide. The speaker will confirm your response. Repeat the correct response.

> MODELO: 1. ¿No conocías al doctor Rodríguez?
> **No, lo conocí esta mañana.**
>
> 2. ¿Sabían Uds. que él era casado?
> **Lo supimos anoche.**
>
> 3. ¿No dijiste que podías venir?
> **Sí, pero no quise.**

D. **The relative pronouns *que* and *quien*** Answer each question you hear, using the cue provided. The speaker will confirm your response. Repeat the correct response. Follow the model.

> MODELO: ¿Quién es María? (chica / trajo las sillas)
> **Es la chica que trajo las sillas.**

1. (muchacho / vino ayer)
2. (profesor / te hablé)
3. (muchacha / mandó el sillón)
4. (señora / llamó por teléfono)
5. (señor / vimos ayer)

Más práctica

A. **Dibujos** (*Drawing*) You will hear three statements about each drawing. Choose the letter of the statement that best corresponds to the drawing. The speaker will verify your response.

1.

   a   b   c

2.

   a   b   c

3.

   a   b   c

4.

a   b   c

5.

a   b   c

B. Unos diálogos breves Before listening to the dialogues in this section, study the comprehension questions below. Reviewing the questions ahead of time will help you to remember key information as you listen. Then listen carefully to the dialogues and answer each question, omitting the subject. The speaker will confirm your response. Repeat the correct answer.

1. ¿Qué dice Alina que tienen que hacer ella y Marcos?
2. ¿Necesitan un apartamento más pequeño?
3. ¿Qué está leyendo Marcos?
4. ¿En qué calle está el apartamento?
5. ¿Cuántos dormitorios tiene?
6. ¿Qué más tiene?
7. ¿Cuándo pueden ir a verlo?
8. ¿A qué hora va a estar Marcos en su casa?
9. ¿Le gusta mucho el apartamento a Teresa?
10. ¿Está amueblado el apartamento?
11. ¿Qué les va a regalar la mamá de Teresa?
12. ¿Para qué cuarto necesitan muebles?
13. ¿Qué muebles tienen para el dormitorio?
14. ¿Tienen colchón?
15. ¿Qué necesitan hacer para poder mudarse?

C. Para contestar Answer the questions you hear, using the cues provided. The speaker will confirm your answers. Repeat the correct answer.

1. (en la escuela)
2. (sí)
3. (cine)
4. (sí)
5. (un sofá y una butaca)
6. (una cómoda y un tocador)
7. (no)
8. (muy amplia)
9. (tres)
10. (dos)

D. Tome nota You will hear a conversation between a real estate agent and a client. First listen carefully for general comprehension. Then, as you listen for a second time, fill in the agent's form.

Agencia La Cubana
Calle 8, número 325
Miami, Florida
Tel. (305) 428-6345

❏ Se vende   ❏ Casa   ❏ Amueblado(a)
❏ Se alquila   ❏ Apartamento   ❏ Sin muebles

Dirección: _____

Número de dormitorios: _____

Número de cuartos de baño: _____

❏ Sala   ❏ Calefacción
❏ Comedor   ❏ Aire acondicionado
❏ Salón de estar   ❏ Lavaplatos
❏ Jardín   ❏ Refrigerador
❏ Piscina
❏ Garaje (_____ coches)

Precio: _____

Puede verse: Días _____

                            Horas _____

     Lección 10, Laboratory Activities

E. Dictado The speaker will read six sentences. Each sentence will be read twice. After the first reading, write what you heard. After the second reading, check your work and fill in what you missed.

1. _____

2. _____

3. _____

4. _____

5. _____

6. _____

Hasta ahora... Una prueba

Let's combine the structure and the vocabulary from **Lecciones 9** and **10**. How much can you remember?

A. Complete the following exchanges, using the preterit or the imperfect of the verbs given.

1. —¿Qué hora _____ (ser) cuando tú _____ (llegar) a

   casa ayer?

   —_____ (Ser) las seis. (Yo) _____ (traer) la carne y la

   _____ (poner) en el refrigerador.

   —¿Teresa _____ (venir) contigo?

   —No, (ella) no _____ (querer) venir.

   —¿Y Carlos?

   —Él no _____ (poder) venir porque _____ (tener) que

   trabajar.

2. —¿Dónde _____ (vivir) ustedes cuando _____ (ser)

   niños?

   —En Lima, y siempre _____ (ir) de vacaciones a Buenos Aires. Allí

   _____ (ver) a nuestros amigos argentinos y lo _____

   (pasar) muy bien.

   —¿Dónde _____ (conocer) (tú) a tu esposo?

   —En la universidad; él _____ (ser) muy guapo, pero muy tímido.

3. —Anoche Tito me _____ (decir) que _____ (necesitar)

   dinero.

   —¿Dónde _____ (ver) tú a Tito?

   —En el parque, cuando _____ (venir) para casa.

   —Yo no _____ (saber) que tú _____ (conocer) a Tito...

   —¿Y tú? ¿Qué _____ (hacer) anoche?

   —Nada... _____ (acostarse) temprano porque _____

   (estar) muy cansada.

B. Complete the following, using the Spanish equivalent of the words in parentheses.

1. ¿Viste a la señora _____ estaba en la sala? (*who*)

2. Carlos tiene sus libros y yo tengo _____. ¿Tú tienes

   _____? (*mine / yours*)

3. Nosotros _____ en clase. (*fall asleep*)

4. Tú siempre _____ cuando ella _____

   _____. (*worry / doesn't feel well*)

5. ¿Tú _____ antes de comer? (*washed your hands*)

6. Las chicas _____ en mi cuarto. (*took off their coats*)

7. Yo voy a _____ con Adela _____.

   (*church / on Sundays*)

8. _____ conducen mejor que _____.

   (*Women / men*)

9. Eva llegó a California _____. (*four years ago*)

10. Alberto es el muchacho _____ yo bailé anoche. (*with whom*)

C. Arrange the following vocabulary in groups of three, according to categories.

manzanas	mueble	mar	carro	almohada	violín
carnicería	mudarse	bañarse	quitarse	apio	repollo
infancia	pescadería	joyería	juventud	fiesta	coche
secadora	ventilador	levantarse	ponerse	adolescente	isla
uvas	licuadora	celebrar	lavarse la cabeza	vecindad	sábana
contrabajo	lechuga	probarse	barrio	plancha	palma
despertarse	cómoda	festejar	vestirse	panadería	clarinete
naranjas	lavadora	cafetera	tocador	tostadora	funda
acostarse	automóvil	calefacción	aire acondicionado	zapatería	ferretería

1. _____ _____ _____

2. _____ _____ _____

3. _____ _____ _____

4. _____ _____ _____

5. _____ _____ _____

6. _____ _____ _____

7. _____ _____ _____

8. _____ _____ _____

9. _____   _____   _____

10. _____   _____   _____

11. _____   _____   _____

12. _____   _____   _____

13. _____   _____   _____

14. _____   _____   _____

15. _____   _____   _____

16. _____   _____   _____

17. _____   _____   _____

18. _____   _____   _____

Hasta ahora… Una prueba (Lecciones 9 y 10)   **181**

Un paso más

A. Read the ad below, and then answer the questions that follow.

ANUNCIOS CLASIFICADOS

SE ALQUILA

VIVA EN EL CENTRO DE CARACAS

cerca de la estación del metro

Apartamentos sin amueblar
Una o dos habitaciones,
sala-comedor,
cocina totalmente equipada,
baño completo,
lavadora y secadora,
aire acondicionado

Para más información llamar al teléfono
456-7843 de 9 a 5, de lunes a viernes y, de 10 a 2 los sábados

APARTAMENTOS DE LUJO EN BARRIO ELEGANTE
Apartamentos amueblados con vista a la piscina o al jardín

Sala y comedor amplios,
tres dormitorios,
dos baños,
cocina equipada con horno
microondas y
aparatos electrodomésticos.

Lugar para estacionamiento.
El alquiler incluye
el servicio de agua,
pero no la electricidad
ni el teléfono.

Pueden verse de lunes a viernes, de 2 a 5.
Avenida Simón Bolívar, 327

1. Si alquilo el apartamento que anuncian en el centro de Caracas, ¿necesito tener auto o no? ¿Por qué?

_____

2. ¿Por qué necesito tener muebles para vivir en ese apartamento?

_____

3. ¿Es necesario comprar algunos aparatos para la cocina? ¿Por qué?

_____

4. ¿Por qué puedo lavar mi ropa en el apartamento?

   _____

5. ¿Necesito usar un ventilador en el verano o no? ¿Por qué?

   _____

6. ¿Qué puedo hacer para recibir más información sobre los apartamentos?

   _____

7. ¿Cómo son los apartamentos que se anuncian en la Avenida Simón Bolívar?

   _____

8. ¿En qué tipo de vecindario están?

   _____

9. ¿Todos los apartamentos tienen vista al jardín?

   _____

10. Para mudarme a estos apartamentos, ¿necesito tener muebles? ¿Por qué?

    _____

11. ¿Por qué puedo ir a nadar si vivo en estos apartamentos?

    _____

12. ¿Voy a necesitar comprar algo para la cocina?

    _____

13. ¿Por qué no voy a tener problemas para parquear mi coche?

    _____

14. ¿Qué no está incluido en el alquiler?

    _____

B. Your best friend is celebrating her 20th birthday and you are going to have a party for her and some 15 friends. Prepare a list of all the things that you are going to need for the party. Also state what activities you are planning to have and the things that you will need for the activities. Be sure the party will be a success.

Workbook Activities

Estructuras

A. The subjunctive mood Complete the following chart with the corresponding present subjunctive forms.

Infinitive	yo	tú	Ud., él, ella	nosotros	Uds., ellos, ellas
1. cobr**ar**	cob**re**	cob**res**	cob**re**	cob**remos**	cob**ren**
2. estudi**ar**					
3. deb**er**	deb**a**	deb**as**	deb**a**	deb**amos**	deb**an**
4. beb**er**					
5. abr**ir**	abr**a**	abr**as**	abr**a**	abr**amos**	abr**an**
6. recib**ir**					
7. hacer	haga				
8. decir		digas			
9. entender			entienda		
10. volver				volvamos	
11. sugerir					sugieran
12. dormir				durmamos	
13. mentir					mientan
14. buscar	busque				
15. pescar					
16. dar		des			
17. estar			esté		
18. ir				vayamos	
19. ser					sean
20. saber	sepa				

B. The subjunctive with verbs of volition I Everybody wants everybody else to do something. Indicate this by completing the chart below.

	English	Subject	Verb	que	Subject of subordinate clause	Verbs in the subjunctive
1.	He wants me to speak.	Él	quiere	que	yo	hable.
2.	I want you to learn.				tú	
3.	You want him to go out.	Tú				
4.	She wants us to drink.					bebamos.
5.	We want her to come.				ella	
6.	You want them to understand.	Uds.				
7.	They want us to remember.				nosotros	
8.	You want us to study.	Uds.				
9.	They want us to write.					escribamos.
10.	He wants us to lie.	Él				
11.	I want you to walk.				tú	
12.	They want you to wait.				Uds.	
13.	She wants him to work.					
14.	We want them to go.					

C. The subjunctive with verbs of volition II My mother wants my brothers and me to do many things today. Indicate what they are, using the present subjunctive.

Mi mamá quiere que...

1. ...yo _____ (ir) a la agencia de viajes y _____ (comprar) dos pasajes.

2. ...Julio _____ (llevar) la ropa a la tintorería y _____ (recoger) los

   pantalones que ella dejó ayer.

3. ...Raúl y yo _____ (sacar) dinero de nuestra cuenta de ahorros y _____

   (pagar) la cuenta del gas.

4. ...Tito y Paco _____ (pedir) unos folletos sobre Bogotá y se los _____ (traer).

5. ...Mario _____ (comprar) dos maletas y _____ (dárselas) a papá.

6. ...nosotros _____ (hacer) todas estas diligencias por la mañana.

D. The subjunctive with verbs of emotion These conversations can be heard in the college cafeteria. Complete each one, using the infinitve or the present subjunctive, as appropriate.

1. —Yo te sugiero que _____ (pedir) un préstamo en el banco para comprar el coche.

   —Voy a pedirlo, pero temo que (ellos) no me lo _____ (dar).

2. —Mañana es sábado. Espero _____ (poder) quedarme en casa.

   —Yo te aconsejo que _____ (ir) a la aerolínea y _____ (reservar) el pasaje.

   —Ojalá que no _____ (ser) muy caro.

3. —¿Es necesario _____ (llenar) la tarjeta?

   —Sí, tienes que llenarla.

4. —Es una lástima que nosotros no _____ (tener) la tarde libre hoy, pero me alegro

   de no _____ (tener) que venir a la universidad mañana.

   —Sí, pero yo necesito que mañana tú _____ (ir) a mi casa y me _____

   (ayudar) a escribir el informe de literatura.

5. —¿Tú quieres _____ (ir) a Canadá con nosotros?

   —Sí, pero mi hermana me sugiere que _____ (ir) a Colombia.

   —Espero que (tú) _____ (poder) ir con nosotros el próximo año.

6. —Necesito _____ (lavar) estos pantalones.

   —Yo te aconsejo que no los _____ (lavar). Te sugiero que los _____

   (llevar) a la tintorería.

   —Temo no _____ (poder) ir hoy.

7. —¿Qué nos sugiere que _____ (hacer) en el verano?

   —Les sugiero que _____ (hacer) un crucero por el Caribe.

8. —Me alegro de que mi padrino _____ (estar) aquí hoy.

   —Sí, siento no _____ (tener) tiempo para conversar con él.

9. —¿En qué hotel me aconsejas que me _____ (hospedar)?

   —Te aconsejo que no _____ (ir) a un hotel.

10. —Yo quiero que ustedes _____ (venir) a verme.

   —Ojalá que (nosotros) _____ (poder) ir a verte el mes que viene.

E. Situaciones You find yourself in the following situations. What do you say?

1. You tell a travel agent that you want a round-trip ticket to Bogotá.

   _____

   _____

2. You ask a traveling companion if he wants a window seat or an aisle seat.

   _____

   _____

3. You tell a travel agent that you want a direct flight to Bogotá.

   _____

   _____

4. You tell your friend that you checked your luggage and that you had to pay excess luggage.

   _____

   _____

5. You suggest to a friend that he travel by train or by boat.

   _____

   _____

F. Crucigrama

Horizontal

2. pasaje
4. Trabaja en una _____ de viajes.
6. no irse
7. Hicimos un _____ por el Mediterráneo.
9. Europa, por ejemplo
10. ¿A quién le doy la tarjeta de _____?
11. hombre que viaja
12. femenino de **padrino**
14. hacer planes
15. opuesto de **entrada**
16. a ningún lado: a ninguna _____
18. quedarse cuando uno viaja
20. TWA o United
21. El avión tiene dos horas de _____.

Vertical

1. Quiero un pasaje de ida y _____.
3. ¿Adónde van de _____ de miel?
5. buenísimo

8. mujer con quien uno se va a casar
13. Sirve comida y bebidas en el avión.
14. ¿Es un asiento de ventanilla o de _____?
17. No es un vuelo directo; hace _____.
19. Tengo que pagar _____ de equipaje.

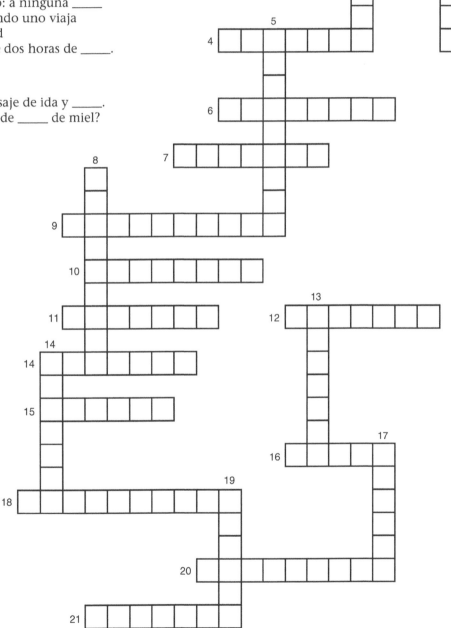

G. ¿Qué pasa aquí? Look at the illustration and answer the following questions.

1. ¿En qué agencia de viajes están estas personas?

    _____

2. ¿Cuántos agentes de viaje trabajan en la agencia?

    _____

3. ¿Adónde quiere viajar Silvia?

    _____

4. ¿Cómo va a viajar?

    _____

5. ¿En qué fecha puede viajar?

    _____

6. ¿Cuánto cuesta el viaje a Lima (en dólares)?

    _____

7. ¿Qué días hay vuelos a Lima?

    _____

8. ¿A la capital de qué país quiere viajar Daniel?

    _____

9. ¿Cómo quiere viajar Daniel?

_____

10. ¿Cuándo hay tren para Asunción?

_____

11. ¿A qué ciudad de Argentina quiere viajar Olivia?

_____

12. ¿Ella va con alguien? ¿Cómo lo sabe Ud.?

_____

13. ¿Olivia va a comprar un pasaje de ida?

_____

14. ¿Qué tipo (*type*) de asiento reserva Norberto? ¿En qué sección lo reserva?

_____

Para leer

A planear las vacaciones

Rubén y Marisol planean ir de vacaciones en agosto y no pueden decidir adónde ir. Rubén quiere ir a España porque sus padres viven en Sevilla y hace tres años que él no los ve. Marisol prefiere ir a Canadá y pasar dos semanas viajando por Montreal, Toronto y Quebec.

Rubén convence a Marisol y deciden viajar a España. Van a la agencia de viajes, compran dos billetes de ida y vuelta en primera clase y reservan un asiento de ventanilla y un asiento de pasillo.

Cuando vuelven a su casa, Rubén les escribe una carta a sus padres, diciéndoles que llegan a Sevilla el trece de agosto.

¡Conteste! Answer the following questions based on the reading.

1. ¿En qué mes planean ir de vacaciones Marisol y Rubén?

_____

2. ¿A qué país quiere viajar Rubén?

_____

3. ¿En qué ciudad española viven los padres de Rubén?

_____

4. ¿Cuánto tiempo hace que él no los ve?

_____

5. ¿Marisol quiere ir a España también?

   _____

6. ¿Qué lugares quiere visitar Marisol?

   _____

7. ¿Cuánto tiempo quiere pasar Marisol en Canadá?

   _____

8. ¿Quién convence a quién?

   _____

9. ¿Marisol y Rubén van a viajar en clase turista?

   _____

10. ¿Qué asientos reservan?

    _____

11. ¿Qué hace Rubén cuando vuelve a su casa?

    _____

12. ¿En qué fecha van a llegar a Sevilla Marisol y Rubén?

    _____

Panorama hispánico

Complete the following chart.

Colombia
Capital: _____
Principales productos de exportación: _____, _____,
_____ y _____
Porcentaje de esmeraldas que provienen de Colombia: _____
Música típica colombiana: _____ y _____
Deporte más popular: _____
Escritores famosos: _____ y _____
Famoso pintor y escultor colombiano: _____
Primera línea aérea de América: _____
Museo más famoso: _____

Lección 11

Laboratory Activities

Diálogos

¿Dónde pasamos la luna de miel? Listen to the dialogues twice, paying close attention to the speakers' intonation and pronunciation patterns. First, listen to the entire dialogue; then, as you listen for a second time, pause the recording after each sentence and repeat after the speaker.

Gustavo Cisneros y Victora Villarreal son de Chía, un pueblo que está cerca de Bogotá. Hoy están en una agencia de viajes de la capital. Planean casarse el mes que viene y quieren decidir dónde van a pasar la luna de miel. La mamá de Gustavo, que es argentina, espera que vayan a Buenos Aires. Los padrinos de Victoria les sugieren que viajen a Costa Rica, porque a ellos les encanta ese país.

VICTORIA Mi amor, si tú quieres ir a Buenos Aires, no hay problema. A mí me encantan las ciudades grandes.

GUSTAVO Bueno... la verdad es que yo quiero conocer los bosques de Costa Rica... Estos folletos describen unos paquetes buenísimos, que incluyen los pasajes, el hospedaje y algunas excursiones.

VICTORIA Sí, pero éstos que yo tengo también describen viajes muy interesantes que incluyen Río de Janeiro... ¡Ah! El agente nos está llamando. Ojalá que podamos reservar los pasajes hoy.

Con el agente de viajes

GUSTAVO Vamos a necesitar que usted nos aconseje sobre cuál es el lugar ideal para pasar la luna de miel. Espero que nos dé buenas ideas.

AGENTE Yo les recomiendo que hagan un crucero por el Mediterráneo. ¡Viajar en barco es muy romántico! Y después, una semana en Italia.

GUSTAVO Bueno... temo que eso sea un poco caro. Mi prometida y yo preferimos quedarnos en este continente...

AGENTE ¡Tengo una idea brillante! Les sugiero que visiten Canadá. Pueden ir en avión hasta Toronto y después viajar en tren hasta Vancouver...

VICTORIA Sí, todo eso es muy bonito, ¡pero no tenemos tanto dinero! Queremos dos pasajes de ida y vuelta a San José, en clase turista. ¿Tienen vuelos directos? Preferimos no hacer escala en ninguna parte...

AGENTE Sí, señorita. ¡Excelente idea!

GUSTAVO ¿Estás segura, mi amor?

VICTORIA Sí, estoy segura, pero el año próximo... ¡me llevas a Buenos Aires!

A. **Preguntas y respuestas** You will now hear questions about the dialogues. Answer each one, omitting the subject. The speaker will confirm your response. Repeat the correct response.

B. **Situaciones** The speaker will present several situations based on the dialogues. Respond appropriately in Spanish to each situation. The speaker will confirm your response. Repeat the correct response. Follow the model.

MODELO: You tell your teacher that you hope he'll give you an "A."
Espero que me dé una "A".

Pronunciación

When you hear the number, read the corresponding sentence aloud. Then listen to the speaker and repeat the sentence.

1. Tengo una idea brillante.
2. Yo quiero conocer los bosques de Costa Rica.
3. Preferimos quedarnos en este continente.
4. Describen viajes que incluyen Río de Janeiro.
5. Yo les recomiendo que hagan un crucero por el Mediterráneo.
6. Gustavo Cisneros y Victoria Villarreal están en una agencia de viajes.

Estructuras

A. The subjunctive with verbs of volition I Answer each question you hear, using the cue provided. The speaker will confirm your response. Repeat the correct response. Follow the model.

> MODELO: ¿Qué quieres que yo haga? (comprar los billetes)
> **Quiero que compres los billetes.**

1. (traer los folletos)
2. (venir mañana)
3. (ir a la agencia de viajes)
4. (estar aquí a las cinco)
5. (volver temprano)
6. (dar una fiesta)
7. (pagar los pasajes)
8. (quedarse aquí)
9. (facturar el equipaje)
10. (traer las maletas)

B. The subjunctive with verbs of volition II The speaker will say what different people want to do. Say that you don't want them to do these things. Always use direct object pronouns in your answers. The speaker will confirm your response. Repeat the correct response. Follow the model.

> MODELO: Nosotros queremos invitar a las chicas.
> **Yo no quiero que las inviten.**

C. The subjunctive with verbs of emotion I Respond to each statement you hear, using the cue provided. The speaker will confirm your response. Repeat the correct response. Follow the model.

> MODELO: Yo me alegro de estar aquí. (de que tú)
> **Yo me alegro de que tú estés aquí.**

1. (que Carlos)
2. (que ustedes)
3. (de que mi hijo)
4. (que tú)
5. (que nosotros)

D. The subjunctive with verbs of emotion II Respond to each statement you hear, using the cue provided. The speaker will confirm your response. Repeat the correct response. Follow the model.

> MODELO: Ana va con Teresa. (Espero)
> **Espero que Ana vaya con Teresa.**

1. (Siento)
2. (Me alegro)
3. (Es una lástima)
4. (Temo)
5. (Espero)
6. (Ojalá)

Más práctica

A. Dibujos (*Drawing*) You will hear three statements about each drawing. Choose the letter of the statement that best corresponds to the drawing. The speaker will verify your response.

1.

2.

3.

      a   b   c   a   b   c   a   b   c

4.

5.

     a   b   c   a   b   c

B. Unos diálogos breves Before listening to the dialogues in this section, study the comprehension questions below. Reviewing the questions ahead of time will help you to remember key information as you listen. Then listen carefully to the dialogues and answer each question, omitting the subject. The speaker will confirm your response. Repeat the correct answer.

1. ¿El avión hace escala en alguna parte?
2. ¿El Sr. Acosta quiere un pasaje en clase turista?
3. ¿Cuándo va a viajar el Sr. Acosta?
4. ¿El Sr. Acosta quiere un asiento de ventanilla o de pasillo?
5. ¿En qué sección quiere viajar el Sr. Acosta?
6. ¿Qué tiene Silvia?
7. ¿Qué le sugiere Héctor que le pida a la azafata?
8. ¿Qué quiere tomar Silvia?
9. ¿Qué le dice Héctor que necesita tomar?
10. ¿Por qué quiere Silvia que sirvan la comida?
11. ¿A qué hora sale el avión?
12. ¿Cuántas horas de atraso tiene?
13. ¿Cuál es la puerta de salida?
14. ¿Dónde puso Sara las tarjetas de embarque?
15. ¿Qué quiere comprar Sara para leer?
16. ¿Qué dice Andrés de la idea?

C. Para contestar Answer the questions you hear, using the cues provided. The speaker will confirm your answers. Repeat the correct answer.

1. (no)
2. (Colombia)
3. (avión)
4. (sí)
5. (Hawai)

6. (American)
7. (buen viaje)
8. (en el verano)
9. (en el Hilton)
10. (no, nunca)

D. Tome nota You will hear three flight announcements at the airport in Bogotá. First listen carefully for general comprehension. Then, as you listen for a second time, fill in the information requested.

AEROPUERTO INTERNACIONAL DE BOGOTÁ

LLEGADAS

Aerolínea: _____

_____

Vuelo: _____

Procedente de: _____

_____

Hora: _____

Puerta de salida: _____

SALIDAS

Aerolínea: _____

Vuelo: _____

Con destino a: _____

Puerta de salida: _____

Aerolínea: _____

Vuelo: _____

Con destino a: _____

Hora: _____

Puerta de salida: _____

E. Dictado The speaker will read six sentences. Each sentence will be read twice. After the first reading, write what you heard. After the second reading, check your work and fill in what you missed.

1. _____

2. _____

3. _____

4. _____

5. _____

6. _____

Workbook Activities

Estructuras

A. The *Ud.* and *Uds.* commands I Complete the chart below, with **Ud.** and **Uds.** command forms.

	Command	
Infinitive	**Ud.**	**Uds.**
1. preparar	prepare	preparen
2. caminar		
3. aprender	aprenda	aprendan
4. beber		
5. abrir	abra	abran
6. salir		
7. venir	venga	vengan
8. hacer		
9. dar	dé	den
10. estar		
11. empezar	empiece	empiecen
12. comenzar		
13. pedir		
14. contar		
15. ir	vaya	
16. ser		sean

B. The *Ud.* and *Uds.* commands II You will be out of the office tomorrow. Tell Miss Montalván, your assistant, to do the following.

1. estar en la oficina a las siete

   _____

2. traducir las cartas y llevarlas al correo

   _____

3. ir al banco y depositar los cheques

   _____

4. decirle al Sr. Díaz que el lunes hay una reunión (*meeting*)

   _____

5. poner los documentos en mi escritorio / no dárselos a la Srta. Valdés

   _____

   _____

6. mandarle un fax al Sr. Uribe o llamarlo por teléfono para que venga el lunes

   _____

   _____

7. quedarse en la oficina hasta las cinco

   _____

C. The *Ud.* and *Uds.* commands III You and your brother are asking your father what to do. Write his answers to your questions, using commands and the cues provided.

1. ¿A qué hora tenemos que salir? (ahora)

   _____

2. ¿Qué autobús tomamos? (el # 40)

   _____

3. Para ir a la parada de autobuses, ¿seguimos derecho o doblamos? (seguir derecho)

   _____

4. ¿A qué hora tenemos que estar en el correo? (a las cuatro)

   _____

5. ¿A quién tenemos que llamar esta noche? (al Sr. Paz)

   _____

6. ¿Qué tenemos que decirle? (que lo necesito)

_____

7. Jorge necesita el coche; ¿se lo prestamos? (no)

_____

8. Paquito quiere un teléfono celular, ¿se lo compramos? (no)

_____

D. The subjunctive to express doubt, disbelief, and denial These people are discussing cars. Complete their conversations by writing the verbs given in the present subjunctive or the present indicative.

1. —Aníbal quiere vender su coche. Yo creo que nosotros _____ (poder) comprarlo.

    —No, no creo que eso _____ (ser) una buena idea porque su coche funciona un día

    sí y otro no.

    —Estoy seguro de que el mecánico _____ (poder) arreglarlo.

    —Dudo que _____ (valer) la pena arreglarlo.

2. —Yo creo que tú _____ (tener) que llevar el coche al taller de mecánica.

    —Yo dudo que _____ (estar) abierto hoy porque es sábado.

    —No es verdad que ellos _____ (cerrar) los sábados. Yo creo que sólo _____

    (cerrar) los domingos.

3. —Este taller de mecánica es el mejor de la ciudad.

    —Es verdad que _____ (ser) bueno, pero no es cierto que _____ (ser) el

    mejor.

4. —El coche que tú quieres cuesta un ojo de la cara.

    —Yo no niego que _____ (ser) caro, pero no dudo que _____ (valer) la

    pena comprarlo.

E. Constructions with *se* You are talking to a student from Ecuador, who has many questions about your town. Answer his questions, using the cues provided.

1. ¿A qué hora se abren los bancos? (a las diez)

_____

2. ¿A qué hora se cierra el correo? (a las seis)

_____

Lección 12, Workbook Activities **199**

3. ¿Cómo se dice **grúa** en inglés? (*tow truck*)

_____

4. ¿Qué se come aquí? (pollo)

_____

5. ¿Dónde se venden coches usados? (en la calle Quinta)

_____

F. Situaciones You find yourself in the following situations. What do you say?

1. You are going to rent a car. Tell the agent you want a two-door compact car with standard shift.

_____

_____

2. You tell a friend that your car won't start and that you need to call a tow truck. Tell him/ her also that you need a new battery.

_____

_____

3. You are complaining about your car. Say that it costs you an arm and a leg because it breaks down often.

_____

4. You ask your roommate what time the beauty salon opens and you add that you need a haircut.

_____

5. Your son is driving too fast. Tell him that the speed limit on the freeway is sixty-five miles per hour.

_____

G. Crucigrama

Horizontal

5. Mi coche no funciona; está _____.
7. ir a pie
10. a menudo
11. Necesito el _____ para cambiar la llanta.
13. Tengo un teléfono _____ en el coche.
15. opuesto de **lleno**
17. No es una calle; es una _____.
19. La necesito para poder conducir: _____ para conducir.
21. No está a la derecha. Está a la _____.
22. No siga derecho. Debe _____ aquí.
24. No es un coche grande. Es un coche _____.

26. persona que arregla coches
27. Necesitan piezas de _____.
29. El coche tiene dos _____ de aire.
30. _____ la pena comprarlo.

Vertical

1. oficina de correos
2. salón de belleza
3. Me costó un _____ de la cara.
4. Mi coche es de cambios _____.
6. Ana necesita un _____ de pelo.
8. Me gusta más un coche _____.
9. La _____ máxima es de 65 millas.
12. tener dudas

200   Lección 12, Workbook Activities

14. estación de servicios
16. batería
18. grúa
20. Los necesito para parar el coche.

23. opuesto de **cerrado**.
25. en todos lados: en todos _____
28. Mi coche tiene problemas. Lo voy a llevar al _____ de mecánica

H. ¿Qué pasa aquí? Look at the illustrations and answer the following questions.

A. 1. ¿Dónde está Carlos en este momento? _____

2. ¿Cómo se llama el taller? _____

3. ¿Qué levantó el mecánico? _____

4. ¿Qué cree el mecánico que necesita para arreglar el coche?

_____

5. ¿Él cree que las tiene en el taller?

_____

6. ¿Cuándo cree él que puede recibir las piezas de repuesto?

_____

7. ¿Ud. cree que Carlos piensa que el arreglo le va a costar un ojo de la cara?

_____

B. 1. ¿Qué necesita Ana?

_____

2. ¿Por qué no puede Ana manejar hasta la gasolinera?

_____

3. ¿Cuánto cuesta la gasolina?

_____

4. ¿Qué otra cosa necesita Ana?

_____

5. ¿Qué no tiene Ana en el maletero?

_____

Panorama hispánico

Complete the following charts.

Perú

Capital: _____

Población: _____

Moneda del país: _____

Principal fuente de riqueza: _____

Otras industrias importantes: _____ y _____

Animales típicos de la fauna peruana: _____, _____

y _____

Principales atracciones turísticas: _____ y _____

Universidad más antigua de Suramérica: _____

Ecuador

Capital: _____

Islas pertenecientes a Ecuador: _____

Población: _____

Base de la economía: _____, _____ y

_____

Moneda oficial: _____

Monumento importante: _____

Famoso mercado de artesanías: _____

Lección 12

Laboratory Activities

Diálogos

Se venden coches usados Listen to the dialogues twice, paying close attention to the speakers' intonation and pronunciation patterns. First, listen to the entire dialogue; then, as you listen for a second time, pause the recording after each sentence and repeat after the speaker.

En el Distrito de Miraflores de Lima, Perú, vive la familia Ugarte, de Guayaquil, Ecuador. Liliana, una sobrina de la Sra. Ugarte, y su esposo Ramiro están viviendo con ellos por un tiempo. Ramiro trabaja y va a asistir a la Universidad de San Marcos. Ahora están en el comedor, bebiendo café, leyendo el diario y hablando.

RAMIRO Creo que voy a necesitar un carro si tengo que ir al trabajo después de mi última clase...

LILIANA Bueno... aquí dice que se venden coches usados, pero dudo que podamos comprar uno con el dinero que tenemos.

RAMIRO A ver... (*Mira el anuncio.*) Coche compacto de dos puertas, de cambios mecánicos... Mm... Me gustan más los carros automáticos.

Don José Ugarte entra en el comedor, se sirve una taza de café y se sienta a hablar con Liliana y Ramiro.

DON JOSÉ Buenos días. ¿Están leyendo los avisos clasificados?

RAMIRO Sí. Dígame, don José, ¿usted cree que necesitamos comprar un carro?

DON JOSÉ Francamente, no creo que valga la pena. Escuchen lo que me pasó la semana pasada: El lunes por la mañana, mi auto no arrancó.

LILIANA Porque necesitaba un acumulador nuevo, ¿no?

DON JOSÉ No... Llamé una grúa, que llevó el coche al taller de mecánica. El arreglo me costó un ojo de la cara...

ILIANA Pero tía Marta dice que usted sabe arreglar carros.

DON JOSÉ No, no es verdad que yo sepa arreglar nada. Los coches modernos son muy complicados.

RAMIRO ¿Cuántas veces al mes va a una gasolinera para comprar gasolina, don José?

DON JOSÉ Tres veces... cuatro... Eso es porque Marta me obliga a ir a pie a todas partes...

RAMIRO (*Se ríe.*) En serio... ¿su carro se descompone a menudo?

DON JOSÉ ¡Sí! Funciona un día sí y otro no.

LILIANA ¡Ay! Tengo que ir al correo y después a la peluquería. Necesito un corte de pelo. ¿A qué hora se cierra el correo?, ¿a las seis?

DON JOSÉ Dudo que esté abierto hasta las seis, pero váyanse ahora. Si toman el ómnibus, a lo mejor pueden llegar. Sigan derecho por la calle Esperanza hasta llegar a la avenida José Larco. Doblen a la izquierda y ahí pueden tomar el ómnibus.

LILIANA Vamos, Ramiro. Tenemos que acostumbrarnos a usar colectivos...

DON JOSÉ (*Bromeando*) Si quieren, les vendo mi coche...

RAMIRO No, gracias. ¡Prefiero una bicicleta!

A. Preguntas y respuestas You will now hear questions about the dialogues. Answer each one, omitting the subject. The speaker will confirm your response. Repeat the correct response.

B. Situaciones The speaker will present several situations based on the dialogue. Respond appropriately in Spanish to each situation. The speaker will confirm your response. Repeat the correct response. Follow the model.

> MODELO: You tell a friend modern cars are very complicated.
> **Los coches modernos son muy complicados.**

Pronunciación

When you hear the number, read the corresponding sentence aloud. Then listen to the speaker and repeat the sentences.

1.   La familia Ugarte es de Guayaquil.
2.   Aquí dice que se venden coches usados.
3.   Se sirve una taza de café.
4.   Están leyendo los avisos clasificados.
5.   Marta me obliga a ir a pie a todas partes.
6.   Doblen a la izquierda y ahí pueden tomar el ómnibus.

Estructuras

A. *Ud.* and *Uds.* commands You will hear a series of indirect commands with the construction **tener que** + *infinitive*. Change each one to a direct **Ud.** or **Uds.** command. The speaker will confirm your response. Repeat the correct response. Follow the model.

> MODELO: Ud. tiene que estudiar la lección.
> **Estudie la lección.**

B. Position of object pronouns with commands Answer each question you hear in the affirmative or in the negative, according to the cue provided. The speaker will confirm your response. Repeat the correct response. Follow the model.

> MODELO: ¿Compro la bicicleta? (sí)
> **Sí, cómprela.**
>
> ¿Compro el acumulador? (no)
> **No, no lo compre.**

1.   no
2.   sí
3.   sí
4.   no
5.   no

6.   no
7.   sí
8.   no
9.   sí
10.   sí

C. The subjunctive to express doubt, disbelief, and denial Respond to each statement you hear by expressing doubt, disbelief, or denial. The speaker will confirm your response. Repeat the correct response. Follow the model.

> MODELO: Creo que Ana tiene el libro.
> **No creo que Ana tenga el libro.**

D. Constructions with *se* Answer the following questions, using the cues provided. The speaker will confirm your response. Repeat the correct response. Follow the model.

> MODELO: ¿A qué hora se abre el zoológico? (a las siete)
> **Se abre a las siete.**

1. (español)
2. (a las nueve)
3. (lleno)
4. (taller)

5. (en California)
6. (español)
7. (inglés y francés)
8. (a las seis)

Más práctica

A. Dibujos (*Drawing*) You will hear three statements about each drawing. Choose the letter of the statement that best corresponds to the drawing. The speaker will verify your response.

1.

Ana

a   b   c

2.

Eva

a   b   c

3.

a   b   c

4.

a   b   c

5.

a   b   c

B. Unos diálogos breves Before listening to the dialogues in this section, study the comprehension questions below. Reviewing the questions ahead of time will help you to remember key information as you listen. Then listen carefully to the dialogues and answer each question, omitting the subject. The speaker will confirm your response. Repeat the correct answer.

1. ¿Por qué volvió Fernando en ómnibus a su casa?
2. ¿Qué tuvo que llamar Fernando?
3. ¿Dónde dejó el coche?
4. ¿Qué dijo el mecánico que necesitaba el coche?
5. ¿Tiene el coche otros problemas?
6. ¿Cuándo va a ir Fernando al taller?
7. ¿Qué dice Adela que tiene que hacer?
8. ¿Cómo va a ir Fernando a la oficina?
9. ¿Qué está leyendo Blanca?
10. ¿Qué necesita comprar Blanca?
11. ¿Dónde se venden coches usados?
12. ¿Adónde tiene que ir Gerardo?
13. ¿Qué necesita Gerardo?
14. ¿Cuándo puede ir Gerardo con Blanca?

C. Para contestar Answer the questions you hear, using the cues provided. The speaker will confirm your answers. Repeat the correct answer.

1. (sí)
2. (sí)
3. (no)
4. (popular)
5. (dos)

6. (no)
7. (sí)
8. (no)
9. (sí)
10. (sí)

D. Tome nota You will hear some excuses that four brothers and sisters give their Mom so they don't have to visit some boring relatives. First, listen carefully for general comprehension. Then as you listen a second time, fill in the information requested.

EXCUSA

Graciela: Lugares: 1. _____

                                  2. _____

Irene: Lugar: _____

        Para comprar: _____

Fernando: Lugar: _____

        Razón: _____

Ángel: Lugar: _____

        Va a comprar: 1. _____

                                2. _____

E. Dictado The speaker will read six sentences. Each sentence will be read twice. After the first reading, write what you heard. After the second reading, check your work and fill in what you missed.

1. _____

2. _____

3. _____

4. _____

5. _____

6. _____

Hasta ahora... Una prueba

Let's combine the structure and the vocabulary from **Lecciones 11** and **12**. How much can you remember?

A. Complete the following exchanges, using the infinitive, the present indicative, or the present subjunctive of the verbs given.

1. —¿Qué van a hacer tus padres este verano?

   —Ellos quieren _____ (viajar) a Colombia, pero no quieren _____

   (gastar) mucho dinero.

   —¿Qué les sugieres tú?

   —Yo les sugiero que _____ (viajar) entre semana y que no _____ (ir)

   en primera clase, pero ellos temen que no _____ (ser) muy cómodo viajar en

   clase turista.

2. —¿Tú necesitas que yo _____ (ir) a la agencia de viajes hoy?

   —Sí, y quiero que le _____ (pedir) al agente folletos sobre Perú y Ecuador.

   —Dudo que yo _____ (poder) ir hoy porque voy a terminar tarde en la oficina.

3. —¿Tú quieres que Carlos _____ (comprar) un coche nuevo?

   —Sí, y deseo que _____ (ser) un coche automático, pero creo que él

   _____ (preferir) uno de cambios mecánicos, porque él espera que

   _____ (costar) menos y que _____ (gastar) menos gasolina.

   —Ojalá que ustedes _____ (poder) estar de acuerdo cuando compren el coche.

4. —¿A qué taller me aconsejas que _____ (llevar) el coche?

   —Te aconsejo que lo _____ (llevar) al Taller Salgado. Es el mejor.

   —Es verdad que es bueno, pero no creo que _____ (ser) el mejor. Además, creo

   que _____ (cobrar) mucho.

   —No te niego que _____ (cobrar) mucho, pero hacen un buen trabajo.

B. Complete the following exchanges, using the Spanish equivalent of the words in parentheses.

1. —¿Adónde quiere Ud. que yo _____? (*go*)

   —_____ Ud. a la estación de servicio y _____ una

   batería nueva. (*Go / buy*)

2. —¿A qué hora quiere Ud. que nosotros _____? (*come*)

   —_____ aquí a las ocho y, por favor, _____ Uds.

   puntuales. (*Be / be*)

3. —¿Le damos los folletos a Teresa?

   —No, _____ Teresa. _____ Carmen. (*don't give

   them to / Give them to*)

4. —Tú siempre gastas mucho dinero.

   —_____ que, a veces, _____ mucho,

   _____ que _____ siempre. (*I don't deny /

   I spend / but it's not true / I do it*)

5. —Marta, ¿_____ a las nueve? (*the banks open*)

   —No, _____ a las diez. (*they open*)

   —¿Y el correo? ¿_____? (*What time does it open*)

   —_____ a las nueve. (*It opens*)

C. Arrange the following vocabulary in groups of three, according to categories.

excelente	avión	hotel	padrino	pasaje	acumulador
corte de pelo	turista	peluquería	automóvil	avenida	gasolina
taller de mecánica	grúa	caminar	billete	magnífico	arrancar
estación de servicio	arreglo	correr	tren	neumático	boleto
de cambios mecánicos	gato	hospedaje	autopista	descomponerse	gasolinera
salón de belleza	vuelo	remolcador	automático	mecánico	madrina
buenísimo	viajero	llanta	batería	calle	ahijado
ir a pie	barcos	pensión			

1. _____   _____   _____

2. _____   _____   _____

3. _____   _____   _____

4. _____   _____   _____

5. _____   _____   _____

6.   _____   _____   _____

7.   _____   _____   _____

8.   _____   _____   _____

9.   _____   _____   _____

10.   _____   _____   _____

11.   _____   _____   _____

12.   _____   _____   _____

13.   _____   _____   _____

14.   _____   _____   _____

15.   _____   _____   _____

Un paso más

A. Read the ad for Renta Autos Perú, and then answer the questions that follow.

Renta Autos Perú

¿Necesita alquilar un coche? ¡Visítenos!

Tenemos coches completamente nuevos, grandes, medianos y compactos, automáticos o de cambios mecánicos. Todos con dos bolsas de aire.

Le ofrecemos:

- Los precios más bajos sin límite de kilómetros
- Entrega y recogida en cualquier lugar sin costo adicional
- Oficinas en todos los aeropuertos del país

Nota: Los coches se deben entregar con el tanque lleno.

Haga su reservación por teléfono o visite cualquiera de nuestras agencias.

Oficina Central ☎ 453-4532

1. ¿Cómo se llama la compañía que se anuncia?

   _____

2. Si quiero alquilar un auto que no gaste mucha gasolina, ¿cuál es mi mejor opción?

   _____

3. En mi familia somos seis personas, ¿debo alquilar un coche compacto o no? ¿Por qué?

   _____

4. ¿Cómo son los precios de la compañía?

   _____

5. Si llego a Perú en avión, ¿va a ser fácil alquilar un coche de Renta Auto Perú? ¿Por qué?

   _____

6. ¿Por qué son seguros (*safe*) los autos de esta compañía?

_____

7. Si alquilo con esta compañía, ¿debo pagar por los kilómetros?

_____

8. Si alquilo el coche en el aeropuerto, ¿puedo dejarlo en una agencia en la ciudad?

_____

9. ¿Debo pagar extra por este servicio?

_____

10. ¿Qué debo hacer antes de devolver (*to return*) el coche?

_____

11. ¿Qué puedo hacer si quiero reservar un auto con esta compañía?

_____

12. ¿A qué número de teléfono debo llamar?

_____

_____

B. Your best friend is going to be married in a month and you are helping her and her future husband to plan their honeymoon trip. Give them some ideas of places to visit. Tell them about different things they can do and see in those places, and also give them some ideas about how much the trips will cost. Suggest at least two or three different places.

Workbook Activities

Estructuras

A. The familiar commands (*tú*) I Fill in the chart with the appropriate **tú** command forms.

	Affirmative Command	Negative Command
1. hablar		
2. comer		
3. escribir		
4. hacerlo		
5. venir		
6. bañarse		
7. afeitarse		
8. dormirse		
9. ponérselo		
10. ir		
11. ser		
12. vendérmelo		
13. levantarse		
14. tener		
15. salir		
16. decírselo		

B. The familiar commands (*tú*) II Someone is asking you for instructions. Tell this person what to do, using **tú** commands and the cues provided. Follow the model.

MODELO: Aquí esta el vestido. ¿Dónde lo pongo? (en mi cuarto)
Ponlo en mi cuarto.

1. ¿Con quién voy a la tienda? (con Aurora)

_____

2. ¿Qué les compro a los chicos? (calcetines)

_____

3. ¿Qué te traigo a ti? (una billetera)

_____

4. Aquí están las pantimedias. ¿A quién se las doy? (a Nora)

_____

5. ¿Qué hago con los zapatos? ¿Se los doy a José? (no)

_____

6. ¿Qué vestido me pruebo? (el vestido amarillo)

_____

7. ¿Qué abrigo me pongo? (el abrigo verde)

_____

8. ¿Voy a la tienda ahora? (no)

_____

9. Ana trajo las camisetas. ¿Las pongo en la cama? (no)

_____

10. Hoy tenemos la fiesta. ¿Se lo digo a Rita? (no)

_____

11. ¿Qué hago para la cena? (pollo a la parrilla)

_____

12. ¿A qué hora vengo mañana? (a las siete)

_____

C. The familiar commands (*tú*) III According to each person's situation, tell him/her what to do. Use **tú** commands. Follow the model.

MODELO: Tengo mucha sed y aquí hay refrescos.
           Bebe un refresco.

1. Tengo mucha hambre y hay sándwiches en la cocina.

    _____

2. Tengo un examen difícil mañana.

    _____

3. Yo necesito leer el periódico y mi hermano quiere que se lo dé.

    _____

4. Estoy cansada y aquí hay una silla.

    _____

5. Necesito aretes y allí hay una joyería muy buena.

    _____

6. No puedo venir esta tarde, pero puedo venir esta noche.

    _____

7. No puedo llamar a Eva hoy, pero puedo llamarla mañana.

    _____

8. No puedo ponerme este vestido, pero puedo ponerme el vestido negro.

    _____

9. Necesito los guantes de Nora y quiero pedírselos.

    _____

10. Es tarde y quiero acostarme porque tengo sueño.

    _____

D. ¿Qué? and ¿cuál? used with _ser_ These are answers that David Torales gave. Write the questions that elicited each statement given as a response, using **qué** or **cuál** as appropriate.

1. _____

   Mi apellido es Torales.

2. _____

   Mi número de teléfono es 8–75–43–30.

3. _____

   Un pasaporte es un documento que se necesita para viajar.

4. _____

   Mi dirección es avenida Olmos, número 436, Lima.

5. _____

   Mi número de seguro social es 756–89–6523.

6. _____

   El polo es un deporte (_sport_) que se juega a caballo.

E. The subjunctive to express indefiniteness or nonexistence I Look at the pictures below, and then complete each sentence with either the indicative or the subjunctive.

1. Vamos a un _____

   _____ donde

   _____ .

2. ¿Hay algún _____

   donde _____

   _____ ?

3. Tengo una empleada _____

_____

_____ .

4. Necesito una _____

_____

_____ .

5. Tengo una amiga que _____

_____

_____ .

6. No conozco a nadie que _____

_____

_____ .

7. Hay un señor que _____

_____

_____ .

8. No hay nadie que _____

_____

_____ .

F. The subjunctive to express indefiniteness or nonexistence II Alicia just got home and found many messages waiting for her. Complete each one, using the present subjunctive or the present indicative.

1. ¿Tienes una cartera que _____ (hacer) juego con mis zapatos rojos?

   ¡La necesito para el sábado! Yo tengo tres carteras que no _____ (hacer)

   juego con nada.   Mabel

2. ¿Conoces a algún muchacho que _____ (poder) ir a una fiesta con mi

   hermanita el sábado? Yo no conozco a nadie que _____ (ser) de la edad de

   ella y los muchachos que ella conoce _____ (tener) novia.   Isabel

3. No vamos a ir al centro comercial porque no hay ninguna tienda que _____

   (tener) liquidación este sábado. Hay una zapatería que _____ (tener) las

   botas de cuero que a ti te gustan, pero no están en rebaja.   Rosario

4. Mi papá busca una secretaria que _____ (saber) francés y alemán. Yo conozco a

   dos chicas que _____ (hablar) los dos idiomas, pero ninguna quiere trabajar los

   fines de semana. ¿Tú conoces a alguien que _____ (necesitar) trabajo?   Raúl

G. Situaciones You find yourself in the following situations. What do you say?

1. You tell your roommate that you don't have anything to wear and ask him/her if he/she wants to go shopping with you.

   _____

   _____

2. At a store, you ask the clerk where the fitting room is. Ask also if they have blue pants in size medium.

   _____

   _____

3. You ask your sister to go to the store and return the shirt that she gave you because it's too small for you.

   _____

   _____

4. You ask someone if there is a bookstore that sells books in Spanish.

   _____

   _____

5. Your friend always worries about everything. Tell him/her not to worry.

   _____

H. Crucigrama

Horizontal

2. Vamos al centro _____.
6. No tengo nada que _____.
7. Fuimos a mirar _____.
8. hermana pequeña
9. tienda donde compramos libros
12. Los hombres usan calcetines y las mujeres usan _____.
16. estrecho
17. talla
19. Los hombres la usan.
21. Luis compra su ropa en el departamento de _____.
23. Necesito por lo _____ cien dólares.
25. lino
26. rebaja

Vertical

1. cuarto de una tienda donde nos probamos ropa
2. Los zapatos son de _____.
3. Necesito ropa _____.
4. Es una tienda por _____.
5. muy bonita

10. Se usa con una falda.
11. Necesito _____ de tenis.
13. ni grande ni pequeña
14. hace juego
15. lo usan las mujeres
18. *Nike*, por ejemplo
20. Ponemos el dinero en la _____.
22. tipo de tela
24. *truck*, en español

I. ¿Qué pasa aquí? Look at the illustration and answer the following questions.

1. ¿Qué se va a probar Carmen?

   _____

2. ¿El vestido está en liquidación?

   _____

3. ¿Qué descuento[1] da la tienda hoy?

   _____

4. ¿Qué le quiere comprar Carmen a Pablo?

   _____

5. ¿Qué quiere comprar Rosa?

   _____

6. ¿Qué lleva Rosa en la mano?

   _____

---

[1]discount *Hint:* % por ciento

7. ¿Qué número calza Adela?

_____

8. ¿Le van a quedar bien los zapatos a Adela?

_____

9. ¿Le van a quedar grandes o chicos?

_____

10. ¿Cree Ud. que las botas son de buena calidad? (*quality*)

_____

11. ¿Adela piensa comprar las botas?

_____

12. ¿Cómo se llama la tienda?

_____

Para leer

El mensaje de José Luis Éste es un mensaje electrónico que José Luis les mandó a sus padres.

¡Hola! ¿Cómo están todos? Yo estoy bien, pero muy cansado porque
Carlos y yo estuvimos trabajando mucho para limpiar y arreglar nuestro
apartamento.

Ayer fui de compras porque tenían una gran liquidación en mi tienda
favorita. Ya compré casi todos los regalos de Navidad. A abuelo le compré
unos pañuelos y una corbata y a abuela un camisón. Para Anita compré una
blusa rosada y para Jorge una billetera. No les digo lo que compré para
ustedes porque quiero que sea una sorpresa.

Yo invité a Carlos a pasar la Navidad con nosotros, pero él va a pasar
las vacaciones en la casa de los padres de su novia.

¡Ah! Todavía estoy buscando a alguien que me lleve en coche a Viña
del Mar en diciembre. Si no encuentro a nadie, voy a alquilar un coche.

Mamá, hazme un favor: dile a Silvia que me escriba o me llame por
teléfono. ¡La extraño mucho!

Bueno, denle cariños° a toda la familia. Los veo en diciembre.   *love*
Besos.

José Luis

¡Conteste! Answer the following questions based on the reading.

1. ¿Qué les mandó José Luis a sus padres?

   _____

2. ¿Qué estuvieron limpiando y arreglando él y Carlos?

   _____

3. ¿Qué hizo José Luis ayer?

   _____

4. ¿Qué tenían en su tienda favorita?

   _____

5. ¿Qué le compró a su abuelo?

   _____

6. ¿Qué compró para Anita?

   _____

7. ¿Le compró algo a Jorge?

   _____

8. ¿Por qué no les dice a sus padres lo que les compró?

   _____

9. ¿Dónde va a pasar Carlos las vacaciones?

   _____

10. ¿Qué está buscando José Luis?

    _____

11. ¿Qué quiere que su mamá le diga a Silvia?

    _____

12. ¿En qué mes va a ver José Luis a toda la familia?

    _____

Name ______________________ Section ____________ Date ____________

Panorama hispánico

Complete the following chart.

Chile

Capital: ______________________

Población: ______________________

Nombre que se le da a Chile: ______________________

Porcentaje de personas que saben leer y escribir: ______________________

Productos de exportación: ____________, ____________,

____________ y ____________.

Balneario muy famoso: ______________________

Dos grandes poetas chilenos: ____________ y ____________

Famosa novelista chilena: ______________________

Lección **13**

Laboratory Activities

Diálogos

Vamos de compras Listen to the dialogues twice, paying close attention to the speakers' intonation and pronunciation patterns. First, listen to the entire dialogue; then, as you listen for a second time, pause the recording after each sentence and repeat after the speaker.

Ángela y Rebeca Montoya son dos hermanas que viven con sus padres en Santiago, Chile. Asisten a la misma universidad, trabajan en la misma oficina y muchas veces salen juntas. Hoy, por ejemplo, van de compras con Fernando, el novio de Ángela, y con Gonzalo, el novio de Rebeca. Primero, los cuatro van a almorzar.

En un restaurante de comida rápida

ÁNGELA	Fernando, ¿qué te parece si Rebeca y yo vamos a los Almacenes París y Gonzalo y tú van a la zapatería?
FERNANDO	Buena idea. Yo quiero cambiar un par de botas que me quedan chicas y Gonzalo necesita zapatos.
GONZALO	También quiero ir a la librería y después voy a tratar de encontrar algún disco compacto que le guste a mi hermanita.
REBECA	Oye, ¿no dijiste que necesitabas calcetines y zapatos de tenis? Cómpralos hoy que tienes la oportunidad.
FERNANDO	Sí... y yo necesito una camiseta... Dime, Ángela, ¿cuánto tiempo crees tú que van a tardar en hacer sus compras?
ÁNGELA	Por lo menos dos horas, quizás tres... Yo tengo mi teléfono celular. Llámame para saber a qué hora nos encontramos.
FERNANDO	A ver... ¿cuál es tu número de teléfono...?
ÁNGELA	¡¿Qué?!
REBECA	(*Se ríe.*) No te preocupes. Él sabe tu número mejor que el suyo. ¡Vamos!

En la tienda

ÁNGELA	Ven acá, Rebeca. Mira esta falda. Hace juego con la blusa que compré ayer. Y este vestido... ¿no es precioso?
REBECA	¡Pruébatelo! Pero la falda te va a quedar grande. Busca una en talla mediana.
ÁNGELA	Aquí hay una. ¿Dónde está el probador?
REBECA	Allí, al lado de la caja. Yo tengo algunas cosas también... ¡Es que no tengo nada que ponerme!

En la zapatería

FERNANDO	(*Al empleado*) ¿Tienen botas como éstas que sean más anchas? Éstas son un poco estrechas... Yo calzo el número cuarenta.
GONZALO	(*Al empleado que le está probando unos zapatos de tenis*) Éstos me quedan bien.
EMPLEADO	Y le van a durar, porque son de una marca muy buena.

A las cuatro, todos se encuentran a la salida del centro comercial. Ángela y Rebeca están cargadas de paquetes, pero Fernando y Gonzalo sólo tienen uno cada uno.

FERNANDO	(*A su novia*) No hay nadie que pueda comprar tanto como ustedes dos en un par de horas...
ÁNGELA	Hazme un favor... ¡Llama un taxi!
GONZALO	(*Bromeando*) ¡Necesitamos un camión!
REBECA	No exageres y ayúdame...
FERNANDO	¡Ahí viene uno libre! ¡Taxi!

A. Preguntas y respuestas You will now hear questions about the dialogues. Answer each one, omitting the subject. The speaker will confirm your response. Repeat the correct response.

B. Situaciones The speaker will present several situations based on the dialogue. Respond appropriately in Spanish to each situation. The speaker will confirm your response. Repeat the correct response. Follow the model.

MODELO: You ask your friend what size shoe she takes.
¿Qué número calzas?

Pronunciación

When you hear the number, read the corresponding sentence aloud. Then listen to the speaker and repeat the sentence.

1. Fernando y Gonzalo van a la zapatería.
2. ¿No dijiste que necesitabas calcetines y zapatos de tenis?
3. ¿Cuánto tiempo van a tardar en hacer sus compras?
4. Él sabe tu número mejor que el suyo.
5. Hace juego con la blusa que compré.
6. Se encuentran a la salida del centro comercial.

Estructuras

A. The familiar commands (*tú*) Answer each question you hear with the familiar **tú** command of the corresponding verb. The speaker will confirm your response. Repeat the correct response. Follow the model.

MODELO: ¿No vas a ir al baile?
No, ve tú.

B. *Tú* commands: Negative forms Answer each question you hear in the negative, using the familiar **tú** command and the corresponding object pronoun. Remember that the negative **tú** command forms are the same as **tú** forms of the present subjunctive. The speaker will confirm your response. Repeat the correct response. Follow the model.

MODELO: ¿Abro la puerta?
No, no la abras.

C. ¿Qué? and ¿cuál? used with *ser* Respond to each statement you hear by using **qué** or **cuál** to formulate the question that would elicit the statement as an answer. The speaker will confirm your response. Repeat the correct response. Follow the model.

> MODELO: Mi dirección es calle Libertad, número 120.
> **¿Cuál es su dirección?**

D. The present subjunctive to express indefiniteness and nonexistence I Answer the following questions, using the present subjunctive and the cues provided. The speaker will confirm your response. Repeat the correct response. Follow the model.

> MODELO: ¿Qué necesita? (casa / ser cómoda)
> **Necesito una casa que sea cómoda.**

1. (casa / tener garaje)
2. (secretaria / hablar español)
3. (empleado / saber francés)
4. (empleo / pagar bien)
5. (a alguien / poder trabajar los sábados)
6. (alquilar apartamento / ser grande)
7. (coche / no costar mucho)
8. (apartamento / estar amueblado)

E. The present subjunctive to express indefiniteness and nonexistence II Answer the following questions, using the present indicative and the cues provided. The speaker will confirm your response. Repeat the correct response. Follow the model.

> MODELO: ¿No hay nadie que sepa hablar inglés? (chica)
> **Sí, hay una chica que sabe hablarlo.**

1. (alguien)
2. (tres muchachos)
3. (muchas personas)
4. (una empleada)
5. (chica)

Más práctica

A. Dibujos (*Drawings*) You will hear three statements about each drawing. Choose the letter of the statement that best corresponds to the drawing. The speaker will verify your response.

1.
ISABEL

a   b   c

2.
CARLOS

a   b   c

3.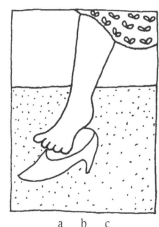

a   b   c

4.

a   b   c

5.

a   b   c

B. Unos diálogos breves Before listening to the dialogues in this section, study the comprehension questions below. Reviewing the questions ahead of time will help you to remember key information as you listen. Then listen carefully to the dialogues and answer each question, omitting the subject. The speaker will confirm your response. Repeat the correct answer.

1. ¿Cuándo es la fiesta de Carmen?
2. ¿Por qué no va a poder ir Alicia a la fiesta?
3. ¿Qué hay en la tienda La Francia?
4. ¿Por qué no puede ir de compras Alicia?
5. ¿Qué puede prestarle Marta a Alicia?
6. ¿Qué talla usan Marta y Alicia?
7. ¿Qué desea el señor?
8. ¿Qué talla usa?
9. ¿Cómo le queda el traje?
10. ¿Qué más va a probarse el señor?
11. ¿Dónde está el probador?
12. ¿Qué más necesita el señor?
13. ¿Qué quiere probarse la señorita?
14. ¿Qué número calza ella?
15. ¿Le quedan bien los zapatos?
16. ¿Tienen zapatos más grandes?
17. ¿Tienen una rebaja en la zapatería hoy?
18. ¿La señorita quiere comprar algo más?

C. Para contestar Answer the questions you hear, using the cues provided. The speaker will confirm your answers. Repeat the correct answer.

1. (oficina)
2. (tres horas)
3. (sí)
4. (no)
5. (mediana)
6. (departamento de ropa para damas)
7. (de algodón)
8. (de cuadros)
9. (un reloj)
10. (un collar y un par de aretes)

D. Tome nota You will hear a conversation in which Eva and José discuss their plans to go shopping. First listen carefully for general comprehension. Then, as you listen for the second time, fill in each person's shopping list.

La lista de Eva	La lista de José
1. _____ _____	1. _____ _____
2. _____ _____	2. _____ _____
3. _____ _____	3. _____ _____
4. _____ _____	4. _____ _____
5. _____ _____	5. _____ _____

E. Dictado The speaker will read six sentences. Each sentence will be read twice. After the first reading, write what you heard. After the second reading, check your work and fill in what you missed.

1. _____

2. _____

3. _____

4. _____

5. _____

6. _____

Lección 13, Laboratory Activities   **233**

Workbook Activities

Estructuras

A. Conjunctions that are always followed by the subjunctive Nora is trying to do many things. Say what they are by completing the following sentences with the verbs given in parentheses.

1. Voy a ayudar a Eva para que (ella) _____ (poder) terminar su informe.

2. No puedo ir a la biblioteca a menos que Uds. _____ (llevarme) ni

   tampoco puedo matricularme sin que papá _____ (darme) el dinero.

3. Voy a limpiar el apartamento en caso de que mis compañeros _____

   (venir) a visitarme y voy a preparar una ensalada de pollo para que ellos

   _____ (poder) comer algo cuando lleguen. Quiero hacer todo esto antes

   de que mi compañera de cuarto _____ (venir) de la universidad.

4. Quiero llamar a Ernesto para que me _____ (traer) los libros, pero no

   puedo hacerlo a menos que tú _____ (darme) el número de su celular.

5. Yo voy a tomar física con tal de que tú la _____ (tomar) también.

B. Conjunctions that are followed by the subjunctive or indicative Some students are talking about their plans and daily activities. Complete these exchanges, using the present subjunctive or the present indicative.

1. —¿Qué vas a hacer tú en cuanto _____ (graduarte)?

   —Voy a tratar de conseguir un puesto. Y tú, ¿qué vas a hacer el próximo semestre?

   —No puedo tomar una decisión hasta que (ellos) me _____ (decir)

   si me van a dar la beca o no.

2. —¿Qué van a hacer Uds. cuando _____ (llegar) a su casa?

   —Vamos a cenar. Nosotros siempre cenamos en cuanto _____

   (llegar) porque tenemos hambre. ¿Qué vas a hacer tú?

   —Voy a estudiar. Yo nunca puedo cenar hasta que mi padre _____

   (volver) de la oficina.

3. —Mis padres siempre se enojan cuando yo _____ (olvidarme)

   de llamarlos.

   —Pues llámalos tan pronto como (nosotros) _____ (conseguir)

   un teléfono.

4. —Cuando tú _____ (ver) a Rogelio, dile que se matricule para

   el próximo semestre.

   —Él siempre se matricula tan pronto como sus padres le _____

   (mandar) el dinero.

Name ______________________ Section ______________ Date ____________

C. Forms of the past participle Complete the following chart, providing past participles.

	Participios pasados	
	Español	*Inglés*
1.	hablado	
2.		used
3.	aprendido	
4.		written
5.	recibido	
6.		died
7.	comparado	
8.		returned
9.	insistido	
10.		seen
11.	propuesto	
12.		broken
13.	terminado	
14.		done
15.	matriculado	
16.		said
17.	entregado	
18.		opened
19.	mantenido	
20.		put
21.	sido	
22.		covered

D. Past participles used as adjectives Complete each sentence so that it describes the corresponding illustration.

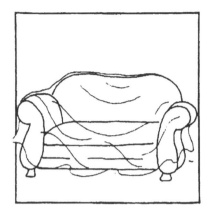

1. El sofá está _____

_____

2. Los niños _____

_____

3. La _____

_____

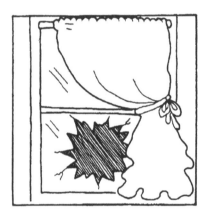

4. Los _____

_____

5. La carta _____

_____

6. La _____

_____

7. Los hombres _____

_____

8. La mujer _____

_____

9. El baño _____

_____

238 Lección 14, Workbook Activities

E. The present perfect Mariana's parents have been away. Tell them what has happened during their absence, using the present perfect of the verbs given.

1. Rosalía / graduarse

_____

2. Carlos y Amalia / decidir mudarse

_____

3. Graciela / no hacer nada

_____

4. yo / escribir un informe

_____

5. Ernesto / volver de su viaje a Argentina

_____

6. Gerardo / romper con su novia

_____

7. Ada y yo / ver varios apartamentos

_____

8. Olga y Luis / hablar con su consejero

_____

9. Gustavo / leer dos novelas

_____

10. el Sr. Paz / abrir un restaurante

_____

F. The past perfect You and I and some of our friends traveled last summer, and we did things that we had never done before. Use the past perfect to indicate what everybody had never done, according to the information provided. Follow the model.

> MODELO: Los Suárez viajaron a Canadá.
> **Los Suárez nunca habían viajado a Canadá.**

1. Yo hice un crucero.

   _____

2. Fernando y Esperanza fueron a México.

   _____

3. Tú viste las pirámides de Egipto.

   _____

4. Amalia y yo comimos comida griega (*Greek*).

   _____

5. Alberto escaló (*climbed*) montañas.

   _____

6. Tú y Elba viajaron por el Nilo.

   _____

7. Claudia se hospedó en un castillo (*castle*).

   _____

8. Mirta y Susana estuvieron en Buenos Aires.

   _____

G. Situaciones You find yourself in the following situations. What do you say?

1. You ask a friend if he/she has taken all the requirements.

   _____

2. You ask your roommate what you have to tell the plumber when he comes this afternoon.

   _____

3. You tell your roommate to leave the door open so the electrician can come in.

   _____

4. You ask a classmate whether he/she has decided what his/her major is going to be.

   _____

5. You tell your friend that you are going to study for your physics class in case your professor gives a test tomorrow. Add that you don't want to fail.

   _____

   _____

6. Ask a classmate if he/she had taken accounting and business administration before he/she came to this college.

   _____

   _____

H. Crucigrama

Horizontal

4. opuesto de **empezar**
6. opuesto de **pasado**
7. Estudio _____ de empresas.
9. lo que nos da el profesor después de un examen
10. Tenemos que _____ una decisión.
11. opuesto de **parado**
13. muy bueno
15. Necesito el _____ de clases.
16. persona que cocina en un restaurante
18. Estudia en la universidad. Es estudiante _____.
20. lo que recibimos cuando terminamos en la universidad
22. terminar la carrera
23. Voy a ir con _____ que tú vayas también.
24. ¿Mi _____? Veinte años.
25. persona que escribe libros

Vertical

1. dinero que recibe un estudiante para estudiar
2. lugar donde hacemos ejercicio
3. Mi especialización es _____ física.
5. persona que trabaja en una biblioteca
8. Sacó una "F". Él quedo _____.
12. Tiene una "A" y una "C". Su _____ es "B".
14. materia
17. materia que todos los estudiantes tienen que tomar
19. ciencia que estudia los problemas sociales
21. persona que vende

I. ¿Qué pasa aquí? Look at the illustration and answer the following questions.

1. ¿Qué nota teme recibir Andrés en el examen de química?

   _____

2. ¿Cree Julio que Andrés va a quedar suspendido?

   _____

3. ¿Qué espera el papá de Julia que estudie su hija?

   _____

4. ¿Qué quiere estudiar Julia?

   _____

5. ¿Qué cree el papá de Lola que va a pasar en el año 2008?

   _____

6. ¿Qué va a hacer Lola cuando termine el semestre?

   _____

7. ¿Qué nota cree Jorge que él va a sacar en matemáticas?

_____

8. ¿Cree Ud. que a Jorge le gusta la literatura?

_____

9. ¿Cree Ud. que Jorge estudia mucho para su clase de literatura?

_____

10. ¿Qué promedio tiene que mantener Adela para que le den la beca?

_____

11. ¿Qué cree Ud. que va a hacer Adela para que le den la beca?

_____

Panorama hispánico

Complete the following chart.

Argentina

Capital: _____

Lugar que ocupa en el mundo por su extensión: _____

Población: _____

Origen étnico de sus habitantes: _____, _____,

_____ y _____

Base de la economía tradicional: _____ y _____

Base de la economía actual: _____ y _____

Música típica: _____

Nombre que se le ha dado a Buenos Aires: _____

Una de las avenidas más anchas del mundo: _____

Atracciones turísticas del país: _____, _____,

_____ y _____

Laboratory Activities

Lección 14

Diálogo

Comparando notas Listen to the dialogue twice, paying close attention to the speakers' intonation and pronunciation patterns. First, listen to the entire dialogue; then, as you listen for a second time, pause the recording after each sentence and repeat after the speaker.

Mónica Valenzuela, una chica norteamericana de ascendencia mexicana, se graduó de la escuela secundaria en mayo y decidió escapar del calor de Arizona y volar a Buenos Aires. Allí visita a su amiga porteña, Norma Benedetti, que había pasado un año con ella y su familia. Mónica tuvo que llevar suéteres y un abrigo porque el 21 de junio empieza el invierno en Argentina. Hoy las dos muchachas están sentadas en un café de la avenida de Mayo, mirando pasar a la gente y hablando de sus planes para el futuro.

MÓNICA Tú empezaste a asistir a la Facultad de Medicina en marzo, ¿no? ¿Qué tal te va?

NORMA Me va bastante bien. Las clases son interesantísimas y pronto vamos a comenzar a trabajar en el hospital.

MÓNICA Yo empiezo las clases en septiembre. Ya estoy matriculada en inglés, matemáticas, química, psicología y sociología. ¡Cinco requisitos!

NORMA ¿Qué otras materias son requisito?

MÓNICA Física, biología, comunicación pública... Depende en parte de la especialización del estudiante... Oye, ¿no vamos a encontrarnos con tu hermano?

NORMA Más tarde. Cuando él termine su última clase, me va a llamar.

MÓNICA ¡Ay! Tengo que llamar a mi mamá en cuanto lleguemos a tu casa esta noche, para que me diga si puede comprarme los libros que voy a necesitar.

NORMA ¿Ya has decidido cuál va a ser tu especialización?

MÓNICA Bueno... todavía no he tomado ninguna decisión... Mi padre se enoja conmigo porque cuando él tenía mi edad, ya había decidido ser médico. Me gusta el periodismo, pero a veces quiero ser abogada... o arquitecta, o escritora...

NORMA Bueno, cuando empieces a tomar clases, vas a darte cuenta de cuáles te gustan.

MÓNICA Hasta ahora, lo único que me ha gustado siempre ha sido ir al gimnasio.

NORMA Bueno... eso no te va a servir de mucho, ¡a menos que quieras ser profesora de educación física!

MÓNICA ¡Me has dado una magnífica idea! ¡Profesora de educación física! ¡Y quizás experta en nutrición! ¿Por qué no corremos en Palermo mañana, en caso de que tenga que ponerme en forma?

NORMA ¡No, no, no! Ya te he dicho que el único ejercicio que yo hago es ir de la sala de estar a mi cuarto... ¿Por qué no invitas a mi hermano? A él le encanta correr.

MÓNICA ¡Perfecto! Se lo voy a proponer en cuanto lo vea.

NORMA ¡Bárbaro! Con tal de que no insistas en que yo corra...

A. Preguntas y respuestas You will now hear questions about the dialogues. Answer each one, omitting the subject. The speaker will confirm your response. Repeat the correct response.

B. Situaciones The speaker will present several situations based on the dialogue. Respond appropriately in Spanish to each situation. The speaker will confirm your response. Repeat the correct response. Follow the model.

> MODELO: You ask a classmate what subjects he/she has taken.
> **¿Qué asignaturas has tomado?**

Pronunciación

When you hear the number, read the corresponding sentence aloud. Then listen to the speaker and repeat the sentences.

1. Mónica tuvo que llevar suéteres y un abrigo.
2. El 21 de junio empieza el invierno.
3. Vamos a comenzar a trabajar en el hospital.
4. Depende en parte de la especialización.
5. Todavía no he tomado ninguna decisión.
6. Me has dado una magnífica idea.

Estructuras

A. Conjunctions that are followed by the subjunctive or indicative Rephrase each statement you hear, using the cue provided. The speaker will confirm your response. Repeat the correct response. Follow the model.

> MODELO: Me escribió cuando llegó. (Me va a escribir)
> **Me va a escribir cuando llegue.**

1. (Me voy a matricular)
2. (Va a terminar)
3. (Van a esperar)
4. (Voy a salir)

B. Conjunctions that are always followed by the subjunctive Answer the following questions in the affirmative, using the cues provided. The speaker will confirm your response. Repeat the correct response. Follow the model.

> MODELO: ¿Me vas a llevar a la playa? (no llover)
> **Sí, te voy a llevar con tal que no llueva.**

1. (tener tiempo)
2. (tú / darme dinero)

Now answer the questions in the negative, using the cues provided. Follow the model.

> MODELO: ¿Van a escribir Uds. el informe? (Uds. / traernos los libros)
> **No podemos escribirlo sin que Uds. nos traigan los libros.**

3. (Uds. / darnos el número)
4. (Uds. / prestarnos el coche)

Now answer the following questions, using the cues provided. Follow the model.

> MODELO: ¿Piensas ir al laboratorio? (tener que trabajar)
> **Pienso ir a menos que tenga que trabajar.**

5. (hacer frío) 6. (ser muy difícil)

C. The past participle You will hear a series of verbs in the infinitive. Give the past participle of each verb. The speaker will confirm your response. Repeat the correct response. Follow the model.

> MODELO: hablar
> **hablado**

D. Past participles used as adjectives Answer each question you hear by saying that the action described has already been completed. The speaker will confirm your response. Repeat the correct response. Follow the model.

> MODELO: ¿No van a abrir los libros?
> **Están abiertos.**

E. The present perfect Change the verb in each sentence you hear to the present perfect tense. The speaker will confirm your response. Repeat the correct response. Follow the model.

> MODELO: Yo hablo con mi consejero.
> **Yo he hablado con mi consejero.**

F. The past perfect (pluperfect) Change the verb in each sentence you hear to the past perfect tense. The speaker will confirm your response. Repeat the correct response. Follow the model.

> MODELO: Ella no se fue.
> **Ella no se había ido.**

Más práctica

A. Dibujos (*Drawings*) You will hear three statements about each drawing. Choose the letter of the statement that best corresponds to the drawing. The speaker will verify your response.

1.

    a b c

2.

    a b c

3.

    a b c

Lección 14, Laboratory Activities **247**

4.

5.

a   b   c

a   b   c

B. Unos diálogos breves Before listening to the dialogues in this section, study the comprehension questions below. Reviewing the questions ahead of time will help you to remember key information as you listen. Then listen carefully to the dialogues and answer each question, omitting the subject. The speaker will confirm your response. Repeat the correct answer.

1. ¿Con quién habló Susana?
2. ¿Cuándo habló con él?
3. ¿Qué quiere el consejero que tome?
4. ¿Qué clases va a tomar Susana?
5. ¿Qué le gustaría ser a Susana?
6. ¿Dónde estudia Carlos?
7. ¿Qué quería ser el papá de Anita cuando era chico?
8. ¿El papá de Anita pudo ser abogado?
9. ¿Cuándo decidió ser profesor de francés?
10. ¿Cuándo fue a París?
11. ¿Dónde había estudiado francés antes?
12. ¿Qué otra asignatura le gustaba cuando estaba en la escuela secundaria?
13. ¿Qué quería escribir cuando estaba en la escuela secundaria?
14. ¿Cuándo piensa escribir un libro?

C. Para contestar Answer the questions you hear, using the cues provided. The speaker will confirm your answers. Repeat the correct answer.

1. (2003)
2. (no)
3. (el español)
4. (sí)
5. (no, nunca)
6. (cinco)
7. (sí)
8. (sí)
9. (sí)
10. (ir de vacaciones)

D. Tome nota You will hear a conversation between a student and her academic advisor. First listen carefully for general comprehension. Then, as you listen for a second time, fill in the student's name and class schedule.

Horario de clases		Sr. Sra. _____ Srta.				
Hora	_lunes_	_martes_	_miércoles_	_jueves_	_viernes_	_sábado_
8:00						
9:00						
10:00						
11:00						
12:00						
1:00						
2:00						
3:00						
4:00						
5:00						

E. Dictado The speaker will read six sentences. Each sentence will be read twice. After the first reading, write what you heard. After the second reading, check your work and fill in what you missed.

1. _____

2. _____

3. _____

4. _____

5. _____

6. _____

Hasta ahora... Una prueba

Let's combine the structure and the vocabulary from **Lecciones 13** and **14**. How much can you remember?

A. Complete the following exchanges, using the present indicative or the present subjunctive of the verbs given.

1. —¿Qué buscas?

    —Busco una bolsa que _____ (hacer) juego con mis zapatos.

    —Yo tengo una que _____ (hacer) juego con esos zapatos. Te la puedo prestar.

2. —¿Hay alguna tienda por aquí cerca que _____ (vender) artículos de cuero?

    —No, no hay ninguna tienda por aquí cerca, pero en el centro comercial hay dos tiendas que

    los _____ (vender).

3. —¿Qué vas a hacer cuando _____ (llegar) a tu casa?

    —Tan pronto como _____ (llegar) voy a empezar a estudiar, y después voy a

    cenar. ¿Y tú?

    —Yo siempre empiezo a estudiar en cuanto _____ (llegar), pero nunca ceno

    hasta que _____ (venir) mis padres.

4. —¿Vas a ir hoy al gimnasio?

    —¡Sí, con tal que mis hijos _____ (ir) conmigo!

    —En caso de que ellos no _____ (querer) ir, yo puedo acompañarte (*go with you*).

5. —¿Te vas a matricular mañana?

    —No, no puedo hacerlo sin que mis padres _____ (mandarme) dinero.

    —Yo puedo prestártelo hasta que tú lo _____ (recibir).

6. —¿Vas a hablar hoy con tu consejero?

    —Sí, voy a hablar con él en cuanto lo _____ (ver).

    —¿Qué le vas a decir cuando _____ (hablar) con él?

    —Que necesito que me dé el horario antes de que _____ (empezar) las clases.

B. Complete the following exchanges, using the Spanish equivalent of the words in parentheses.

1. —¿Tú sabes si la biblioteca _____ los domingos? (*is open*)

    —No, los domingos _____. (*is closed*)

2. —¿La tarjeta que recibiste _____ en inglés o en español? (*was written*)

    —_____ en inglés. (*was written*)

3. —Eva ¿_____ a Raúl? (*have you seen*)

    —No, no _____ esta semana. Sus amigos _____ que

    está de vacaciones. (*I haven't seen him / have told me*)

4. —¿Tú _____ en Chile antes? (*had been*)

    —Sí, yo _____ allí dos veces. (*had been*)

5. —Mamá, ¿me llamaste?

    —Sí, Paquito, _____ aquí, _____ un favor

    _____ los libros en la mesa. (*come / do me / put*)

    —¿Después puedo ir al jardín?

    —Sí, pero antes _____ a casa de Marta y _____ que

    venga a las cinco. (*go / tell her*)

6. —Marisol, ¿_____ el número de teléfono de Mario? (*what is*)

    —No sé el número de teléfono, pero sé _____ su dirección. (*what is*)

7. —Ernesto, ¿tú sabes _____ el mate? (*what is*)

    —Sí, es una bebida argentina.

C. Arrange the following vocabulary in groups of three, according to categories.

liquidación	botas	almacén	librería	grande	ancho
electricista	biología	hermoso	de rayas	nota	rayón
arquitecto	precioso	aretes	algodón	plomero	libro
centro comercial	rebaja	collar	pequeño	zapatos	estrecho
quedar suspendido	ingeniero	leer	vestido	anillo	bonito
carpintero	química	seda	ganga	física	promedio
de lunares	tienda	angosto	calzar	falda	abogado
de cuadros	blusa	mediano			

1. _____   _____   _____

2. _____   _____   _____

3. _____   _____   _____

4. _____   _____   _____

5. _____   _____   _____

6. _____   _____   _____

7. _____   _____   _____

8. _____   _____   _____

9. _____   _____   _____

10. _____   _____   _____

11. _____   _____   _____

12. _____   _____   _____

13. _____   _____   _____

14. _____   _____   _____

15. _____   _____   _____

Hasta ahora… Una prueba (Lecciones 13 y 14)

Un paso más

A. Read the ad below, and then answer the questions that follow.

CURSOS DE VERANO
UNIVERSIDAD CENTRAL

Ofrecemos clases en las siguientes materias:

Periodismo

Física

Biología

Sociología

Idiomas

Química

Matrícula abierta de lunes a jueves, de 8:00 a 12:00 y de 2:00 a 5:00

Tenemos becas disponibles para estudiantes con un promedio de "B" o más.

Nota: Para poder graduarse necesita haber aprobado todas las asignaturas correspondientes a su carrera en cursos regulares y haber llenado todos los requisitos.

Para más información visite nuestras oficinas en avenida 9 de Julio No. 564, o llame a nuestros teléfonos 4381-6758 y 4381-9742

1. ¿Cómo se llama la universidad?

_____

2. ¿Dónde tiene sus oficinas?

_____

3. ¿En qué estación del año se ofrecen las clases?

_____

4. ¿Cuándo está abierta la matrícula?

_____

5.   ¿A qué hora puedo ir a matricularme?

_____

6.   ¿Puedo ir los sábados? ¿Por qué?

_____

7.   ¿Qué materias de ciencias puedo tomar?

_____

8.   ¿Qué otros cursos se ofrecen?

_____

9.   ¿Qué promedio necesito tener para solicitar una beca?

_____

10.   Para graduarme, ¿puedo haber quedado suspendido en alguno de mis cursos regulares?

_____

B. You are going on a vacation trip, and you will be on a very elegant beach resort for a week. Make a list of all the clothes that you will need to take with you. When you select your clothes, keep in mind the activities that you plan to do during your vacation. Explain why you are taking the different types of clothes.

Lección 15

Workbook Activities

Estructuras

A. The future I Complete the chart with the corresponding forms of the future tense.

Infinitive	yo	tú	Ud., él, ella	nosotros	Uds., ellos, ellas
1. sacar					
2. decir	diré				
3. hacer		harás			
4. querer			querrá		
5. saber				sabremos	
6. poder					podrán
7. caber	cabré				
8. poner		pondrás			
9. venir			vendrá		
10. tener				tendremos	
11. salir					saldrán
12. valer	valdré				
13. ir		irás			
14. ser			será		

B. The future II What will these people do? Answer the questions, using the cues provided and substituting direct objects for direct object pronouns when appropriate. Follow the model.

MODELO: ¿Cuándo visitarán ustedes a la Sra. Fuentes? (el viernes)
La visitaremos el viernes.

1. ¿Cuándo hablarás tú con el médico? (mañana)

   _____

2. ¿Cuándo irán ustedes al consultorio del doctor Mena? (la semana próxima)

   _____

3. ¿Cuándo sabrás tú el resultado del examen? (esta tarde)

   _____

4. ¿Cuándo podrá venir la enfermera? (esta noche)

   _____

5. ¿Dónde pondrás las aspirinas? (en tu cuarto)

   _____

6. ¿Con quién vendrás al hospital? (con David)

   _____

7. ¿Traerán Uds. los antibióticos? (sí)

   _____

8. ¿Qué tendremos que hacer él y yo? (comprar el remedio)

   _____

9. ¿Dónde pondrás la silla de ruedas? (en el coche)

   _____

10. ¿A qué hora saldrán ustedes mañana? (a las seis)

   _____

C. The conditional I You are giving information about what everyone, including yourself, intended to do. Follow the model.

MODELO: ¿Qué dijo él? (venir)
Dijo que vendría.

1. ¿Qué dijo usted? (ir a la sala de emergencia)

   _____

2. ¿Qué dijo Magali? (descansar mañana)

   _____

3. ¿Qué dijeron ustedes? (salir temprano)

   _____

4. ¿Qué dije yo? (traerme un cafecito) (*Use* **tú** *form*)

   _____

5. ¿Qué dijeron tus padres? (prestarme dinero)

   _____

6. ¿Qué dijo la enfermera? (ponerle una inyección al niño)

   _____

7. ¿Qué dijimos Rafael y yo? (ir a Asunción)

   _____

8. ¿Qué dijiste? (tener que llamar una ambulancia)

   _____

9. ¿Qué dijeron ellos? (ustedes no saber el resultado del análisis)

   _____

10. ¿Qué dijo el médico? (no poder vernos hoy)

    _____

D. The conditional II Complete the following sentences, using the conditional tense.

En un mundo perfecto, …

1. … yo _____ (levantarse) más temprano y

   _____ (acostarse) más tarde. _____ (Ir)

   a la biblioteca los sábados y _____ (estudiar) hasta las cinco.

   _____ (Salir) de mi casa a las siete y

   _____ (pasar) una hora en la biblioteca, estudiando.

2. … mis padres _____ (trabajar) menos y

   _____ (divertirse) más. _____ (Tener)

   más tiempo libre y _____ (hacer) muchas cosas que siempre han

   querido hacer.

3. … todos nosotros _____ (ahorrar) más dinero y

   _____ (poder) comprar el coche que queremos.

4. … tú _____ (mantener) un promedio de "A",

   _____ (conseguir) una beca y _____

   (graduarse) con honores.

E. The future perfect The following is what will have happened at our house by 11 o'clock. Complete each statement, using the future perfect of the verbs given.

1. Mi hermano y yo _____ (limpiar) el garaje.

2. Mi mamá _____ (ir) al hospital a visitar a mi tía.

3. Yo _____ (volver) de la oficina.

4. Los chicos _____ (hacer) la tarea (*homework*).

5. Tú _____ (hablar) con el médico.

6. Ustedes _____ (preparar) la cena.

7. Todos nosotros _____ (cenar).

8. Mis padres _____ (acostarse).

F. The conditional perfect I Complete the chart with the corresponding forms of the conditional perfect tense.

English	Subject	Conditional **haber**	Past participle
1. I would have gone.	**Yo**	**habría**	**ido.**
2. You would have walked.	Tú		
3. He would have come.			venido.
4. She would have worked.	Ella		
5. We would have finished.		habríamos	
6. I would have helped.			ayudado.
7. They would have had lunch.			almorzado.
8. I would have danced.		habría	
9. You would have called.	Tú		
10. He would have written.		habría	
11. She would have driven.	Ella		
12. We would have eaten.		habríamos	
13. They would have returned.			vuelto.

G. The conditional perfect II Complete the following sentences to say what everyone would have done before graduating from college, using the conditional perfect tense.

Antes de graduarnos, ...

1. ... yo _____ (tomar) los requisitos antes (*sooner*).

2. ... tú _____ (solicitar) una beca.

3. ... mi hermano _____ (jugar) al fútbol americano.

4. ... mi hermana _____ (aprender) otros idiomas.

5. ... mi compañera de cuarto _____ (estudiar) más.

6. ... mi novio y yo _____ (ir) a todos los partidos.

7. ... Uds. _____ (gastar) menos dinero.

8. ... yo _____ (mantener) un promedio de "A".

H. Review of the tenses of the indicative Complete the following dialogues, using the verbs given in parentheses and the tenses indicated.

1. *Presente*

   —¿Dónde _____ (estar) mi libro? No lo _____

   (encontrar).

   —Yo no _____ (saber). Tú nunca lo _____

   (poner) en tu escritorio.

   —¿Tú _____ (poder) prestarme el tuyo?

   —No, no lo _____ (tener) aquí.

2. *Pretérito*

   —¿Tú _____ (ir) al cine anoche?

   —No, no _____ (poder) ir porque _____

   (tener) que estudiar. ¿Qué _____ (hacer) tú?

   —Yo _____ (trabajar) hasta las nueve y

   _____ (volver) a casa a las diez.

3. *Imperfecto*

   —¿Uds. _____ (ir) a todos los partidos de fútbol cuando

   _____ (estar) en la universidad?

   —Sí, _____ (ser) fanáticos de los deportes (*sports*). También

   _____ (ver) todos los partidos en la televisión, ¿y tú?

   —Yo _____ (preferir) ir a fiestas.

4. *Futuro*

   —¿Qué _____ (hacer) tú mañana? ¿_____

   (Ir) al club?

   —No, no _____ (poder) ir porque _____

   (tener) que estudiar para el examen parcial.

5. *Conditional*

—Voy a tomar química.

—Yo no la _____ (tomar) este semestre. _____

(Esperar) hasta el próximo semestre.

—En ese caso _____ (tener) que tomar biología y eso

_____ (ser) más difícil.

6. *Pretérito perfecto*

—¿Dónde _____ (estar) tú hoy?

—_____ (Estar) en la universidad, hablando con unos jóvenes que

_____ (venir) de Cuba. ¿Y qué _____

(hacer) Uds.?

—No _____ (hacer) nada.

7. *Pluscuamperfecto*

—Cuando tú llegaste a casa, ¿ya _____ (venir) los carpinteros?

—No, porque Olga no los _____ (llamar).

8. *Futuro perfecto*

—Yo ya _____ (graduarme) para el año 2012. Y Uds.,

¿_____ (terminar) su carrera?

—Sí, y _____ (empezar) a trabajar.

9. *Condicional perfecto*

—De haber sabido que esta asignatura era tan difícil, yo no la _____

(tomar).

—Eva y yo no la _____ (tomar) tampoco.

—¿Qué _____ (hacer) Uds.?

—_____ (tomar) literatura.

I. Las partes del cuerpo Write the parts of the body that correspond to the numbers in the illustrations.

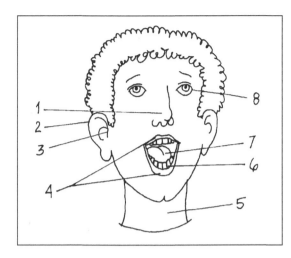 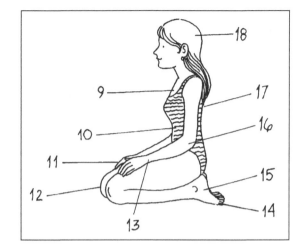

1. _____

2. _____

3. _____

4. _____

5. _____

6. _____

7. _____

8. _____

9. _____

10. _____

11. _____

12. _____

13. _____

14. _____

15. _____

16. _____

17. _____

18. _____

J. El mundo de la medicina Supply the missing words. The letters in the center column will form a Spanish proverb. Write the proverb on the line provided below.

1. Trabaja con un médico; es _____.

2. Soy _____ a la penicilina.

3. Tiene una _____ de 39 grados.

4. Cuando me duele la cabeza tomo _____.

5. El médico me _____ una medicina ayer.

6. Lo llevaron al hospital en una _____.

7. Es un antibiótico.

8. Está en el consultorio del _____.

9. Tuvo un _____; lo llevaron al hospital.

10. Está en la _____ de emergencia.

11. Veo con los _____.

12. _____ X

13. Tengo _____ de cabeza.

    Proverbio: _____

K. Situaciones You find yourself in the following situations. What do you say?

1. You ask a friend if she would like to live in a colonial house with fruit trees and an enormous garden.

    _____

    _____

2. You ask a classmate what he will have to do tomorrow. You tell him that you will have to go to the doctor because you don't feel well.

    _____

    _____

3. You are talking to your doctor and describing your symptoms: your throat hurts, your head hurts, and you are coughing a lot.

_____

_____

4. You want to visit a friend tomorrow night. Ask her if she will have gone to bed by ten.

_____

_____

5. A friend of yours and his family went to Nebraska on vacation. You tell him where you and your family would have gone.

_____

_____

6. Your friend is sick. You tell her that you hope she gets better soon.

_____

_____

L. Crucigrama

Horizontal

3. Es rubia, de _____ azules.
6. ¿Quieres miel de _____?
9. Hubo un accidente. Llame una _____.
10. medicina
12. penicilina, por ejemplo
14. Le pusieron una inyección _____.
16. muy, muy grande
18. Tengo árboles _____ en mi patio.
20. El médico está en su _____.
21. Elsa está _____. Va a tener el bebé en julio.
22. comer algo por la tarde
23. Necesita una silla de _____.
24. Si tiene una temperatura de 103 grados, tiene _____.

Vertical

1. La necesitamos para hablar.
2. Es parte de la pierna.
4. examen
5. resfriado
7. Está en la sala de rayos X. Le van a hacer una _____.
8. ¿No puedes ir? ¡Qué _____!
11. Son parte de la mano.
12. Las tomo cuando me duele la cabeza.
13. romperse
15. a la perfección
17. opuesto de **empeorarse**
19. Los necesitamos para comer.

M. ¿Qué pasa aquí? Look at the illustration and answer the following questions.

1. ¿Qué le duele a Alberto?

_____

2. ¿Cuántas aspirinas tomó?

_____

3. ¿Se siente mejor ahora?

_____

4. ¿Qué le pasó a Rita?

_____

5. ¿Qué le van a tener que poner a Rita?

_____

6. ¿Cuándo fue la última vez que le pusieron una inyección antitetánica?

_____

7. ¿Cómo trajeron a Luis al hospital?

_____

8.   ¿Adónde lo llevan?

_____

9.   ¿Se siente bien Isabel?

_____

10.   ¿Está embarazada Isabel?

_____

11.   ¿A qué medicina es alérgica Rosa?

_____

Para leer

Del diario de Ana Luisa

Jueves, 15 de febrero

Querido diario:

    ¡Ayer fue un desastre! Cuando me levanté no me sentía bien y me dolía la garganta. Llamé al Dr. Medina, pero él no estaba. Tuve que ir a ver a otro médico. Llegué a su consultorio a eso de las nueve y estuve allí hasta las once. Me recetó un antibiótico y me dijo que tenía gripe y que tenía que descansar. No pude ir a mi clase de química y el profesor dio un examen.

    Anoche fue la fiesta de Juliana y yo no pude ir. Mamá me hizo té con miel de abeja y me acosté. A las nueve, Juliana me llamó para decirme que Carlos estaba en la fiesta con Marisol. De haber sabido que él iba a ir con ella, habría ido a la fiesta.

    Bueno... creo que lo que tengo es contagioso porque tengo una temperatura de 39 grados.

    Mañana tendré que llamar a Carlos y decirle que estoy enferma. Además, lo voy a invitar a ir a la discoteca con todos nuestros amigos porque para entonces ya me habré curado. Yo creo que a él le gustaría ir a bailar. ¡Pero no pienso decirle nada a Marisol!

    Bueno, espero sentirme mejor mañana. Voy a tomar dos aspirinas porque todavía me duele la cabeza. ¡Hasta mañana! ¡El sábado estaré bailando con Carlos!

¡Conteste! Answer the following questions based on the reading.

1.   ¿Ayer fue un buen día para Ana Luisa?

_____

2.   ¿Cómo se sentía cuando se levantó?

_____

3.   ¿Quién es el médico de Ana Luisa?

_____

4. ¿Por qué tuvo que ver a otro médico?

_____

5. ¿A qué hora llegó a su consultorio?

_____

6. ¿Hasta qué hora estuvo allí?

_____

7. ¿Qué le recetó el médico?

_____

8. ¿Qué le dijo?

_____

9. ¿Qué dio el profesor de química?

_____

10. ¿A dónde no pudo ir Ana Luisa anoche?

_____

11. ¿Qué tomó Ana Luisa antes de acostarse?

_____

12. ¿Para qué llamó Juliana a Ana Luisa?

_____

13. ¿Qué habría hecho Ana Luisa de haber sabido que Carlos iba a ir a la fiesta con Marisol?

_____

14. ¿Por qué cree Ana Luisa que lo que tiene es contagioso?

_____

15. ¿Para qué tendrá que llamar mañana a Carlos?

_____

16. ¿Por qué cree Ana Luisa que podrá ir a la discoteca el sábado?

_____

17. ¿Ana Luisa piensa invitar a Marisol?

_____

18. ¿Por qué va a tomar dos aspirinas Ana Luisa?

_____

Panorama hispánico

Complete the following charts.

<table>
<tr><td colspan="2" align="center">Paraguay</td></tr>
<tr><td>Capital: _____</td></tr>
<tr><td>Población _____</td></tr>
<tr><td>Idiomas oficiales: _____ y _____</td></tr>
<tr><td>Planta hidroeléctrica importante: _____</td></tr>
<tr><td>Principales vías de transporte: _____</td></tr>
<tr><td>Significado (Meaning) de la palabra guaraní "Iguazú": _____</td></tr>
</table>

<table>
<tr><td align="center">Bolivia</td></tr>
<tr><td>Capitales: _____ y _____</td></tr>
<tr><td>Otras ciudades importantes: _____,</td></tr>
<tr><td>_____ y _____</td></tr>
<tr><td>Lago navegable más alto del mundo: _____</td></tr>
<tr><td>Grupos indígenas más importantes: _____ y</td></tr>
<tr><td>_____.</td></tr>
<tr><td>Nombre que se le ha dado: _____</td></tr>
<tr><td>Ruinas milenarias: _____</td></tr>
</table>

Laboratory Activities

Lección 15

Diálogos

¿Qué síntomas tiene Adriana? Listen to the dialogues twice, paying close attention to the speakers' intonation and pronunciation patterns. First, listen to the entire dialogue; then, as you listen for a second time, pause the recording after each sentence and repeat after the speaker.

La familia Vargas, de Villarrica, Paraguay, vive ahora en Asunción, en una casa de tipo colonial, con árboles frutales en el patio y un jardín enorme. Adriana, la hija menor, está en la sala, hablando por teléfono con una compañera de la universidad.

ADRIANA ¿Anabel? Habla Adriana. Hoy no quiero ir a la facultad, de modo que le voy a decir a mi mamá que no me siento bien. ¿Te gustaría venir a visitarme esta tarde? Podríamos mirar la tele y comer algo. Bueno... ¡te espero a eso de las cuatro! ¡Chau!

Adriana se acuesta en el sofá de la sala y llama a su mamá.

ADRIANA Mamá... Tendré que quedarme en casa hoy. Creo que tengo catarro... o gripe... o pulmonía... Me duele la cabeza, me duele la garganta y ¡tengo fiebre! (*Tose.*)

DOÑA EVA ¡Tienes tos! Sería una buena idea llevarte al médico. El doctor Viñas está en su consultorio...

ADRIANA No, no será necesario que me vea. Me quedaré en casa, tomaré dos aspirinas y mañana estaré perfectamente bien. ¡Ya verás!

DOÑA EVA Bueno, mi hija, pero tendrás que acostarte y tomar una taza de té bien caliente, con miel de abeja. Voy a llamar al médico para que te recete algún antibiótico.

Más tarde suena el timbre. La criada abre la puerta.

CRIADA Señora, aquí hay un joven que quiere hablar con la señorita Adriana.

DOÑA EVA ¡Ignacio! ¡Qué gusto de verte! De haber sabido que venías, habría preparado algo para merendar. ¿Un cafecito?

IGNACIO No, gracias, señora. ¡No se moleste! Vine a preguntarle a Adriana si le gustaría ir a una fiesta en la embajada de Bolivia esta noche.

DOÑA EVA ¡Ay, qué lástima! Adriana está enferma. Tiene una temperatura de 39 grados, creo... Supongo que lo que tiene es contagioso... ¡Menos mal que hoy es viernes! Para el lunes ya se habrá curado y podrá volver a la universidad.

ADRIANA ¡No, mamá! Para esta noche ya habré tomado un montón de remedios, y me sentiré mejor...

IGNACIO No, Adriana... podrías empeorarte. Necesitas descansar... Voy a llamar a Carolina, a ver si ella puede ir conmigo. ¡Ojalá que te mejores pronto!

A. Preguntas y respuestas You will now hear questions about the dialogues. Answer each one, omitting the subject. The speaker will confirm your response. Repeat the correct response.

B. Situaciones The speaker will present several situations based on the dialogue. Respond appropriately in Spanish to each situation. The speaker will confirm your response. Repeat the correct response. Follow the model.

> MODELO: You tell a friend that you don't feel well.
> **No me siento bien.**

Pronunciación

When you hear the number, read the corresponding sentence aloud. Then listen to the speaker and repeat the sentence.

1. ¿Te gustaría venir a visitarme esta tarde?
2. Creo que tengo catarro o gripe.
3. Sería una buena idea llevarte al médico.
4. Voy a llamar al médico para que te recete algún antibiótico.
5. Tiene una temperatura de treinta y nueve grados.
6. Supongo que lo que tiene es contagioso.

Estructuras

A. The future Answer each question in the affirmative, using the future tense. The speaker will confirm your response. Repeat the correct response. Follow the model.

> MODELO: ¿Tú vas a ir a Asunción?
> **Sí, iré a Asunción.**

B. The conditional You will hear some statements about what people are going to do. Using the cues provided, say what others would do. The speaker will confirm your response. Repeat the correct response. Follow the model.

> MODELO: Carlos va al hospital hoy. (yo / mañana)
> **Yo iría mañana.**

1. nosotros / por la noche
2. ustedes / un libro
3. yo / en un restaurante
4. ella / mañana
5. tú / café

6. nosotros / a las diez
7. yo / el domingo
8. Nora / a las siete
9. él / en su cuarto
10. yo / más tarde

C. The future perfect Respond to the following questions, using the cues provided and the future perfect tense. The speaker will confirm your response. Repeat the correct response. Follow the model.

> MODELO: ¿Qué habrá hecho Jorge para las ocho? (cenar)
> **Para las ocho habrá cenado.**

1. (empezar a trabajar)
2. (levantarme)
3. (terminar el trabajo)

4. (hablar con el médico)
5. (ir al hospital)

D. The conditional perfect Respond to each statement you hear, using the cue provided and the conditional perfect tense. The speaker will confirm your response. Repeat the correct response. Follow the model.

MODELO: Luis no entendió nada. (tú)
Tú tampoco habrías entendido nada.

1. (yo)
2. (tú)
3. (ella)

4. (ustedes)
5. (usted)
6. (nosotros)

Más práctica

A. Dibujos (*Drawings*) You will hear three statements about each drawing. Choose the letter of the statement that best corresponds to the drawing. The speaker will verify your response.

1.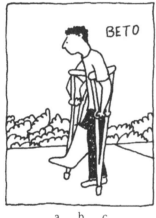

   a   b   c

2.

   a   b   c

3.

   a   b   c

4.

   a   b   c

5.

   a   b   c

B. Unos diálogos breves Before listening to the dialogues in this section, study the comprehension questions below. Reviewing the questions ahead of time will help you to remember key information as you listen. Then listen carefully to the dialogues and answer each question, omitting the subject. The speaker will confirm your response. Repeat the correct answer.

1. ¿Qué hora era cuando Pablo llegó?
2. ¿Por qué no pudo venir más temprano?
3. ¿A qué hora se acostó Dora?
4. ¿Por qué se acostó tan temprano?
5. ¿Qué tomó?
6. ¿Cómo se siente ahora?
7. ¿Cuánto tiempo hace que la señora tiene dolor de estómago?
8. ¿Qué medicina toma cuando le duele mucho el estómago?
9. ¿Qué le va a dar el médico?
10. ¿Qué van a hacerle a la señora si no se siente mejor?
11. ¿Qué le pasó a Roberto?
12. ¿Lo atropelló un coche?
13. ¿Adónde lo llevaron?
14. ¿Le hicieron radiografías de la pierna?
15. ¿Qué se cortó Roberto?
16. ¿Por qué no le pusieron una inyección antitetánica?
17. ¿Por qué va a tomar dos aspirinas?

C. Para contestar Answer the questions you hear, using the cues provided. The speaker will confirm your answers. Repeat the correct answer.

1. (no)
2. (al cine)
3. (aspirinas)
4. (sí)
5. (Nyquil)
6. (la semana próxima)
7. (Pepto Bismol)
8. (no)
9. (sí)
10. (sí)

D. Tome nota You will hear a conversation between a doctor and a patient. First listen carefully for general comprehension. Then, as you listen for a second time, fill in the information requested.

Hoja Clínica

Nombre del paciente: _____

Síntomas: _____

_____

Medicinas que está tomando: _____

_____

Alergias: _____

_____

Radiografías de: _____

_____

Próxima visita: _____

_____

E. Dictado The speaker will read six sentences. Each sentence will be read twice. After the first reading, write what you heard. After the second reading, check your work and fill in what you missed.

1. _____

2. _____

3. _____

4. _____

5. _____

6. _____

Mar Caribe

Barranquilla
Cartagena
Maracaibo
Caracas
TRINIDAD Y
TOBAGO
Puerto España
San Carlos
La Guaira
Ciudad Bolívar
VENEZUELA
OCÉANO
ATLÁNTICO
Medellín
Zipaquirá
Salto Ángel
Río Orinoco
Georgetown
Paramaribo
GUYANA
Cayena
Cali
Bogotá
SURINAM
**GUAYANA
FRANCESA**
COLOMBIA
Popayán
San Agustín
Ecuador
Otavalo
Santo Domingo
de los Colorados
Pichincha
Quito
Río Negro
Río Amazonas
Belén
ECUADOR
Chimborazo
Manaos
Guayaquil
Iquitos
Río Madeira
B R A S I L
Recife
Sipán
Trujillo
PERÚ
Callao
Lima
Machu Picchu
Cuzco
Lago
Titicaca
Puno
La Paz
Cochabamba
Salvador
Río Paraguay
Arequipa
Tiahuanaco
Brasilia
Arica
Sucre
BOLIVIA
Bello
Horizonte
Potosí
Iquique
Filadelfia
PARAGUAY
Asunción
San Pablo
Río de Janeiro
Trópico de Capricornio
Antofagasta
Salta
Río Paraná
Santos
San Miguel
de Tucumán
Puerto Iguazú
Resistencia
Río Uruguay
Puerto Alegre
CHILE
OCÉANO
PACÍFICO
Córdoba
Aconcagua
Mendoza
Rosario
URUGUAY
Montevideo
Viña del Mar
Valparaíso
Santiago
Buenos Aires
La Plata
Punta del Este
Río de la Plata
ARGENTINA
Concepción
Mar del Plata
Bahía Blanca
CORDILLERA DE LOS ANDES
Río Colorado
Bariloche
Puerto Montt

ISLAS GALÁPAGOS
San
Salvador
Ecuador
Santa Cruz
San Cristóbal
Isabela
ECUADOR
Quito
Guayaquil

PATAGONIA

América del Sur

0   250   500 Km.

0   250   500 Mi.

Estrecho de
Magallanes
**TIERRA
DEL FUEGO**
Islas
Malvinas
Punta Arenas
Cabo de Hornos